American National Government

AMERICAN NATIONAL GOVERNMENT

Stephen T. Early, Jr.
DE PAUW UNIVERSITY

BLAISDELL PUBLISHING COMPANY
A Division of Ginn and Company
NEW YORK TORONTO LONDON

First Edition, 1964
SECOND PRINTING, 1965
© Copyright 1964, by Blaisdell Publishing Company,
a Division of Ginn and Company.

Preface

The following pages present the subject matter of American national government in a traditional and introductory manner to form the body of a one semester course. The intention has been to make this commentary as academically solid as possible, to expose the beginning student to as thorough a knowledge of his governmental and political heritage and the system that is based upon it as could be accomplished within the compass of the allotted number of pages. Every effort has been made, particularly in the first half-dozen chapters, to establish the theoretical background and the primary values upon which the national government is built and by virtue of which it is presumed to operate. However, it has been felt that while a knowledge of institutional form and process is essential to informed membership in the body politic, as well as to the curious student in college, it needs to be reinforced by the value judgments that make the particular system what it is. Because our system is predicated upon the Constitution and the Constitution is law, the basic principles of the political order have received their most authoritative interpretation at the hands of the Supreme Court. Accordingly, those chapters which set out the fundamental myths and doctrines incorporate many quotations from the opinions of the highest court. As a result, the portions so treated have a strong legalistic flavor, but this method has been employed so that the student can read in the original words of the interpreting authority what it had to say, rather than what the author of the book interpreted it to have said. Those chapters or portions of chapters which cover the various phases of the political process have been treated in a manner akin to that of the current behavioral approach to the study of political science. In several controversial areas questions have been posed in a more or less rhetorical fashion for consideration by students, in the hope that the guiding principles for analysis will afford an adequate basis for independent thinking. As much information as could be included, much of it elementary fact, has been incorporated into this treatment on the theory that students in basic courses must learn to walk before they can run. But facts without ordering principles become random and uncorrelated. Hence, an effort has also been made to provide a conceptual framework within which the facts can be systematized. Because of limitations of space, some subjects or phases of subjects have been completely omitted or only slightly touched upon; but the instructor can supplement by lecture or by the use of books of readings and by short special studies, of which there are an increasingly large number available in inexpensive paperback form. All of us are captives of our biases and predilections, and a conscious effort has been made in the preparation of these pages to prevent their reflection herein. It is hoped that they mirror no particular orientation; but if they do, that fault as well as any others of omission or commission can be attributed only to the author.

S. E.

Credits

Contents

American National Government

CHAPTER I

The Constitution of the United States

GENERAL CONSIDERATIONS

The starting point of any examination of the American National Government is logically the Constitution of the United States. No other document is as important to the American political system as this is, for every valid aspect of that system must directly or indirectly be based upon the fundamental law. But from the beginning the student is admonished to keep constantly in mind that theory and practice, ideals and reality, are seldom identical. The document known as the Constitution embodies the grand design and implies, without specifying them, the values of the political order in America. But what men do to those values by way of violating or fulfilling them, and how they use the institutions and authority of the system, may, in general or particular, differ widely from the first impressions left by a study of the basic charter. Congress *is not* ideally representative, political parties *do* buy votes, stuff ballot boxes, and make questionable "deals," public office *is* abused, private rights *are* violated, contrary to the niceties of constitutional theory and institutional practice. Yet, the fact that all is not as it might ideally be is not an adequate reason

3

for failing to ascertain and gain some appreciation of what *ought* to be. The national government operates within a framework of law, and the Constitution is the source of that framework. In spite of its importance, too few citizens are familiar with its character, understand its provisions, or appreciate its significance.

An American uses the word "constitution" in a very specific sense. When he refers to "The Constitution," he has in mind a definite, written collection of rules, having the force of law, which provide for the structure and functioning of the political system. He thinks of the Constitution as a "written" or "assembled" plan of government. He is prone to ignore those determinants of the structure and functioning of the American political system which are not written in the Constitution and which do not possess the character of law. Non-legal factors such as customs, conventions, and usages, play a significant part in making the political system what it is. They are as important as are the written parts which everyone agrees shall be called "The Constitution of the United States." Consequently, although the Constitution was one of the first modern *written* constitutions, its non-legal *unwritten* portions should not be neglected. In its broadest sense the Constitution includes all the principles which determine the structure and functioning of the national government, whether they are written or unwritten, assembled or unassembled, legal or non-legal.

The Constitution of the United States is said to be a "rigid" one, which means that it can be amended only by a special procedure which is different from that employed to enact ordinary laws. A rigid constitution, with its difficult and often complex and cumbersome amending process, gives protection to the fundamental principles of the governmental system, principles which ought to be protected from ill-considered actions of transitory majorities or from encroachments by the governors of the day. The amending process forms a barrier against the assaults of popular passion and provides a slower, more deliberate method of making alterations in the basic law than is used to enact statutory law. It permits change, yet it ensures a large degree of stability and continuity with the past. There is a danger that the method of amendment may prove inadequate in times of emergency because it will not permit essential major modifications in the structure and functioning of government to be made with sufficient speed and ease. Yet, it is precisely during periods of emergency that barriers against excessive exercise of governmental power prove most valuable; moreover, over time the "rigid" Constitution of the United States has not proved to be an insurmountable obstacle to the exercise of governmental power during emergencies. In the final analysis, the degree of ease with which change is achieved in the constitutional system of the United States is determined by whether opinion favors or opposes the established condition of things, and not by the *formal* rigidity of the Constitution.

Furthermore, the Constitution of the United States provides for a federal system of government and may be classified, therefore, as a "federal" constitution. Such a system, as will be examined at greater length below, is one which divides the powers of government between a general government and two or more component units which are independent of and equal to the general government when acting within their proper sphere of authority.

The Constitution establishes a "presidential" system of national government characterized by a *separation* of the legislative and executive powers. Not only are the powers of each authority distinct from those of the other, but the legislators may not, while they are legislators, hold office in the executive. The system also vests authority and responsibility in the citizenry as voters to choose from among their own number individuals who will be their representatives for the purpose of carrying on the government. Hence, the system is "republican" in character, and the Constitution may appropriately be called "republican." Thus, helpful initial insight can be gained into the American national government by ascertaining that it is established by a written, rigid, federal, republican, presidential, and supreme constitution. However, the fact that these traits can be gleaned from an examination of the fundamental law does not mean that there is nothing more of value to be learned.

The Synoptic Nature of the Constitution. The American Constitution provides only for a framework, a skeleton, around which the particular agencies of government are built and operated. This framework of government must be supplemented and implemented, for since it is merely an outline it is largely devoid of details. These must be supplied before the system can come to "life." Its provisions were left general so that they might be as flexible and adaptable as possible. And those that were included were restricted to aspects of the political system which were of a fundamental and an essential nature. All else was left to regulation by statute, since no constitution by itself can create a government: its provisions must be implemented by men. The agencies of government that it authorizes must be established and manned. Within the limits of constitutional authorization, therefore, legislative and executive interpretations, customs, judicial decisions, and statutes inevitably provide specificity to the general principles, and authorize the detailed machinery of government which is necessary to make the system operational.

A Constitution, to contain an accurate detail of all the subdivisions of which its great powers will admit, and of all the means by which they may be carried into execution, would partake of the prolixity of a legal code, and could scarcely be embraced by the human mind. Its nature, therefore, requires that only its great outlines should be marked, its important objects designated, and the minor ingredients which compose those objects be deduced from the nature of the objects themselves.[1]

[1] *McCulloch* v. *Maryland* (1819), 4 Wheaton 316.

The documentary Constitution of the United States has three major purposes which it accomplishes in only seven relatively brief articles. To them have been added twenty-three amendments, but of these only the Fourteenth, Sixteenth and Nineteenth can be said to have significant operative force. The seven original articles provide for the existence of the major organs of the national government, authorize the creation of less important ones, and determine the relationships between them. They distribute the powers of government by providing for a division of power between the national and state governments, and for a separation of power between the legislative, executive, and judicial branches of the national government. They impose limitations upon the exercise of power by both the general and state governments, and thereby establish, to a considerable extent, the relationship of the individual to governmental power in the United States.

The general character of these provisions, their concern with only the most fundamental aspects of the political system, has been largely responsible for the fact that the Constitution of the United States has endured longer than any other similar document in modern history. Within its provisions, as originally written, have been accommodated all of the changes that have been made in the structure and functioning of the national government since 1789. The population of the nation has grown from a few million to its present size. The geographical extent of the United States has expanded from ocean to ocean. The United States has been transformed from a puny member of the community of nations to one of the most powerful. Its population has shifted from the country to the cities, has abandoned agriculture for industry, and has created a highly complex social and economic society. Each change has produced problems undreamed of by the men who framed the Constitution at Philadelphia; and in many instances the national government has been called upon to solve them. Throughout the entire process of growth and transformation the Constitution has endured without any major change. Practical necessity has been the mother of constitutional adaptation in the United States.

There is virtually nothing in the Constitution that is designed to meet the day to day exigencies of government. Problems of detail were left to statute, custom, and practice for their regulation or solution. Thus:

The Constitution unavoidably deals in general language. It did not suit the purposes of the people, in framing this great charter of our liberties, to provide for minute specifications of its powers or to declare the means by which those powers should be carried into execution. It was foreseen that this would be a perilous and difficult, if not an impracticable, task. The instrument was not intended to provide merely for the exigencies of a few years, but was to endure through a long lapse of ages, the events of which were locked up in the inscrutable purposes of Providence. It could not be foreseen what new changes and modifications of power might be indispensable to effectuate the general objects of the charter; and restrictions and specifications, which, at present, might seem salutary, might, in the end, prove the overthrow of the system itself. Hence, its powers are expressed in general terms, leaving to the legislature, from time to time, to adopt its own means to effectuate legitimate objects, and to mould and model the exercise of its powers, as its own wisdom, and the public interest, should require.[2]

The men who drafted the Constitution recognized not only the need for generality but also for compromise. The finished document completely satisfied no one; but neither did it incur the enmity of very many. Most of the personages who at first strongly opposed its ratification ultimately became its supporters. There was little that was entirely new and still less that was extreme among the provisions of the document. Moderation typifies its clauses.

Brevity, clarity, and conciseness are concomitants of the generality of the Constitution. The document, including the articles of amendment, is approximately 7,000 words in length. It can be reproduced on about twenty pages of average size, and read in less than thirty minutes. Compared to the constitutions of the states of California and Louisiana, which are respectively 150 and 300 pages in length, that of the United States is a very brief foundation for a system as large and complex as is that of the national government.

The Constitution both grants power and imposes limitations upon its exercise. On its face it appears to be more concerned with limiting than with granting power. But that is probably because the framers thought of "liberty" primarily in terms of *freedom from* governmental authority. It restricts power in a number of ways, both direct and indirect. It imposes specific limitations upon the national government and upon the governments of the states. It also incorporates numerous indirect limitations such as federalism, the separation of powers, bicameralism, and judicial review. The direct, specific limitations are mainly designed to protect the rights of individuals against the encroaching authority of government. The indirect limitations are mostly concerned with curtailing the potentials of power that are inimical to democratic government.

Plan of the Document. At the beginning of the Constitution is a short preamble; it has no legal force. As can be understood from the text, it serves only as a statement of ideals and purpose:

We, the People of the United States, in Order to form a more perfect Union, establish Justice, insure domestic Tranquility, provide for the common defence, promote the general Welfare, and secure the Blessings of Liberty to ourselves and our Posterity, do ordain and establish this Constitution for the United States of America.

[2] *Martin* v. *Hunter's Lesee* (1816), 1 Wheaton 304.

The preamble is followed by seven articles which, with the preamble, constituted the original body of the Constitution. The first three of these articles provide for the establishment of, and for the powers, qualifications, and modes of choice of the national legislature, the executive, and the judiciary. Article Four establishes the position of the states in the Union, provides for the admission of new states into it, and vests in Congress control over the territory and other property of the United States. Article Five defines the process by which amendments are to be made; and Article Six obligates state officers to swear to uphold the Constitution, and guarantees that the United States will pay all debts incurred by the government under the Articles of Confederation. Most important, however, is the "supremacy clause." This declares that the Constitution, the laws made in pursuance of it, and all treaties made or to be made under authority of the United States, are to be the "supreme law of the land." Moreover, this clause obligates the judges of every state to apply these as supreme law, in spite of anything in the laws or constitutions of their respective states which contradicts them. This is doubtless the most important clause in the Constitution, for it underlies the entire pattern of legal relationships between the national government and the states. The last, Article Seven, defines the method by which the Constitution was to be adopted. After it come the Articles of Amendment in the order in which they have been added to the Constitution.

INFORMAL METHODS
OF CHANGING THE CONSTITUTION

Preliminary Considerations. The Constitution of the United States reflects the ideals and institutions which its framers felt to be important and which they desired to make permanent. It indicates that strong support existed at Philadelphia for the institution of private property, for the theory of natural law and natural rights, and for such concessions to popular democracy as were necessary to obtain ratification. However, ideals and institutions are never static. Therefore, great importance attaches to an understanding of how the Constitution can be changed; if it had not been adaptable it would soon have ceased to be adequate, because it would have embodied ideals and institutions which were no longer in keeping with the needs and ideals of the American people.

Informal changes and formal amendments have both contributed to the enduring quality of the fundamental law. Although the Constitution is classified as "rigid," it is flexible in a very real way. Its flexibility results from the scope and opportunity for adaptation that its written words afford. As exigencies arise that demand the assumption of new functions or the creation of new political institutions by the national government, authorization for such changes can, with only rare exceptions, be found within its provisions. Ours is an adaptable constitution that has been expanded by interpretation, and by the growth of customs, to a degree far beyond that attained by the formal process of amendment. Wars, economic emergencies, and the results of technology have required the exercise of national powers which have been of a magnitude and of a kind not previously thought to exist. Even though the language of the Constitution has not been significantly altered to augment national power, the impact of these factors upon the governmental system has brought about two major changes in the original pattern of authority. The power of the national government has been expanded through the cooperation of Congress and the Supreme Court, but almost wholly within the literal provisions of the Constitution; and the power and influence of the President have undergone a similar expansion at the expense of the power and influence of Congress and of the judiciary.

Change by Statute. Social, political, and economic circumstances leave the language of the Constitution unchanged, but they occasionally produce a need for a major shift of political power within the governmental system, or lead to the adoption of new institutional forms and practices which have a profound effect upon it. They thus provide a major cause of informal changes in the Constitution. Congress enacts laws in response to the changing circumstances of the body politic, but it cannot legislate responsibly without paying some heed to the Constitution, unless it is willing to enact laws which it knows will violate the fundamental law. It must interpret the meaning of the written document. Moreover, as has been noted above, all statutes which affect the structure and functioning of the government are a part of the Constitution. They augment its skeletal and synoptic provisions by supplying the details necessary to make the government operable. Examples are many: the statutes regulating succession to the Presidency after the Vice President, establishing the departments and other agencies of the executive branch, and creating the judicial system, all "add" to the Constitution. As change becomes necessary it can be made through new statutes rather than through formal constitutional amendment.

Change by Executive Action. The President himself is also called upon to interpret and expand the written Constitution. The instances of executive amplification of the Constitution are probably not as numerous or as far reaching as are those of Congress, but some important ones can be found. Presidential use of personal diplomatic representatives, appointed without senatorial confirmation, and of executive agreements which have the force of treaties but which do not require approval by two-thirds of the Senate, have long been common. Presidents have purchased territory without any clear grant of constitutional power to do so. On these and other occasions precedents have been established which have had a direct effect upon the functioning of the government under the Constitution.

Change by Judicial Interpretation. By far the most important informal method by which the meaning of the Constitution is changed is by judicial interpretation. Its significance cannot be overestimated; its effects will readily become apparent from much of the material that is included in the following chapters, and one example will suffice here to illustrate its importance. The Constitution states that

A Person charged in any State with Treason, Felony, or other Crime, who shall flee from Justice, and be found in another State, shall on Demand of the executive Authority of the State from which he fled, be delivered up, to be removed to the State having Jurisdiction of the Crime.

That language seemingly imposes a legal obligation which has to be performed by any governor of a state upon whom it falls. It is true that Congress may authorize a state officer to perform a particular duty, but if he declines to do so, it does not follow that he may be coerced or punished for his refusal. When the Constitution was framed it was confidently believed that a sense of justice and of mutual interest would ensure a faithful execution of this provision by the executive of every state, for every state has an equal interest in the effective execution of a process so highly beneficial to its peace and well-being as a member of the Union. Hence, the Supreme Court has rejected the mandatory meaning and interpreted the words to impose a moral obligation, which any governor of a state may disregard when he sees fit.[3]

Change by the Growth of Custom. Some changes in the constitutional system have been achieved without the aid of legislative, executive, or judicial action, but by means of slow growth and development. Numerous reasons can be suggested for their evolution. In some instances the subjects involved have been too unimportant and too non-controversial to warrant attention; others have been beyond the scope of judicial power. Formal action on some has been made difficult or impossible by political factors. Others have met dimly-felt needs of the political system which by their nature could not be dealt with by statute. Whatever the efficient causes of their origin, there are now many significant customs attaching to the American Constitution. The emergence of the President's Cabinet, and of the political parties, are but two of them.

None of the customs attaching to the Constitution have been established by amendment, or by any other means possessing legal authority, but this is not to say that they are unknown to law. Political parties were not brought into being by law, statutory or constitutional; but the statutes that impose controls upon their activities clearly assume that they exist, and by not forbidding them imply that they are valid.[4]

[3] See *Kentucky* v. *Dennison* (1861), 24 Howard 66.
[4] See also "An Act to Establish Eligibility for Burial in National Cemeteries, and for Other Purposes," 62 *Statutes* 234, taking note of the Cabinet's existence.

THE FORMAL METHOD
OF AMENDING THE CONSTITUTION

Preliminary Considerations. The Constitution is the foundation of the governmental system of the United States. It establishes the relationship between the governments of the states and of the nation. Although it is the supreme law and serves as a standard by which to determine the validity of other laws, there is another source of law that has authority over it. This is the power to amend the Constitution, the power to make of the governmental system anything that is thought to be desirable. It can be employed to modify, in any way and to any extent, the distribution of governmental authority which is the essence of federalism. It can, therefore, be employed to destroy federalism and to substitute a confederated or unitary government in its stead. In other words, the amending power can be utilized to change the fundamental character of the constitutional system.

This explains why a federal constitution probably must be rigid in type. It is rigid so that neither the states, nor the national government in our federal system, can alone alter the relationship of the one to the other. As will be seen, the amending process prescribed by Article Five of the Constitution divides the power to change the written word of the document between the national government and the states, so that neither can make a change without the consent of the other.

The Amending Process. Informal methods for constitutional change cannot make alterations in the literal content of the document. Whenever, for any reason, it is desired to change the language of the Constitution resort must be had to the formal method of amendment. The Constitution prescribes the method to be employed:

> The Congress, whenever two thirds of both Houses shall deem it necessary, shall propose Amendments to this Constitution, or, on the Application of the Legislatures of two thirds of the several States, shall call a Convention for proposing Amendments, which, in either Case, shall be valid to all Intents and Purposes, as Part of this Constitution, when ratified by the Legislatures of three fourths of the several States, or by Conventions in three fourths thereof, as the one or the other Mode of Ratification may be proposed by the Congress. . . .

Close examination of this provision will reveal that there are four possible combinations of means, by any one of which an amendment can be brought into being. The entire process is divisible into two parts, that of proposal and that of ratification. Two methods are provided by which each can be accomplished, making a total of four combinations; but no matter which method is used Congress decides upon the proposal of amendments. Of the twenty-three amendments thus far added to the Constitution all have been proposed by the houses of Congress.

Any method of amendment that is employed leaves the final decision concerning adoption or rejection to the states. They alone are able to determine whether the distribution of governmental power in the federal system is to be altered.

Process of Amendment—Brief Description. No formal amendment can become a part of the Constitution unless it is proposed and ratified by one of the four available combinations of procedures. When an amendment is proposed the resolution containing it is transmitted to the head of the General Services Administration, who distributes copies to the governors of the several states. Each transmits the proposal to the ratifying authority of his state. When action has been taken, the head of the General Services Administration is notified. A record is maintained of those states which ratify and those which reject each amendment currently before the states. Then, when the necessary ratifications have been received, the amendment to which they relate is proclaimed a part of the Constitution. The proclamation may emanate from Congress, but usually stems from the executive branch. However, the process is completed by the final act of ratification by the last necessary state, and not by the proclamation which follows it.

Survey of the Amendments. How important has the amending process been in keeping the Constitution up to date? The answer to this query must be: not very! Only two of the amendments, the Fourteenth and the Sixteenth, have changed the constitutional system in such a way as to add to the actual powers of the national government. The Fourteenth Amendment forbids the states to deprive any person of life, liberty, or property without due process of law, or to deny to any person the equal protection of the laws, or to abridge the privileges and immunities of United States citizens. These phrases, and the clause granting Congress power to enact implementing legislation, have generated a power of superintendence that in appropriate instances may be used by national courts to control the substance of state laws and the procedures of state actions.

The Sixteenth Amendment freed the national power to tax incomes from previously imposed restraints, and thereby greatly increased its utility as a means of raising revenue and of accomplishing social and economic objectives not ordinarily and immediately associated with taxation. All of these implications for national power will be made more clear in subsequent chapters.

The effect of the amendments has been as follows: the first eight, the Thirteenth, Fifteenth, and Nineteenth imposed limitations upon the exercise of governmental authority in the interest of protecting individual rights; and the Eleventh reduced the power of United States courts. Hence, all curtailed the authority of the national government. The Ninth Amendment confirmed that certain rights unenumerated in the Bill of Rights had not been given up to government by the people, and the Tenth

Amendment affirmed that powers not denied the states or delegated to the national government by the Constitution were reserved to the states or to the people. The Twelfth, Seventeenth, Twentieth, Twenty-Second, and parts of the Fourteenth and Sixteenth, altered the operation of specific processes. Although the Eighteenth Amendment temporarily conveyed additional power to the national government, that amendment was repealed by the Twenty-First; and the Twenty-Third extended limited voting rights to citizens of the national capital.

In spite of the limited significance of the changes made by amendment to the Constitution, the outstanding feature of the American federal system is the tremendous growth of national power which has come about since 1789. The Constitution has been transformed. The original emphasis was upon the limiting of governmental power; the modern emphasis is on the Constitution as a grant of authority to govern. The old negative attitude, that regarded governmental power as inimical to individual freedom, has given way to a positive attitude that regards it as the means by which individual freedom is to be attained.

The Meaning of the Fifth Article.

Preliminary Considerations. Because of the importance that attaches to the amending power, numerous questions have been raised about aspects of its exercise. These questions are divisible into three categories: those which involve the substance, the proposal, and the ratification of amendments. Hence, the validity of an amendment may be attacked either because of its substance or because of the procedure of its proposal or ratification.

Questions of Substance. An attack upon the validity of an amendment, based on its substance, is in effect an assertion that there is a limit to the amending power. However, such a position immediately raises both logical and legal difficulties.

The power to alter the Constitution is by definition the sovereign *legal* power, that is, the power to make law of such superior force that no other law can transcend it. Thus, it is the source of law above which there is none higher, none that can limit it. If there is a subject to which this supreme lawmaking power cannot be extended, the logical implication is that there is a source of law which limits the amending power by withdrawing from its scope the protected subject. If that is the situation, then the amending power is not the legal sovereign, but, instead, whatever limits it is the legal sovereign. Therefore, from the viewpoint of logic, it seems impossible to admit that there is any matter which cannot be made the subject of a constitutional amendment.

The same conclusion results from an attempt to obtain a judicial ruling upon the applicability of the amending power to particular subjects. When judges declare that an act is "unconstitutional" they use that word in one of two ways. They may mean that the act was done without authority and that its commission violated the Constitution, or they may mean that the power to act was granted by the Constitution but was used in an illegal manner. In either instance they declare it void, and the Constitution has supplied them with a standard by which to determine its validity.

However, suppose a court is asked to consider the validity of making a particular item the substance of an amendment to the Constitution. What can be used as a standard of validity in this situation? Not the Constitution, because the amending power can make or unmake constitutional provisions. Moreover, the challenged amendment is a part of the Constitution. If its validity is determined by using the Constitution as a standard of measurement, one part of the document is being used to test the legality of another part, in spite of the fact that both possess equal force as law. In other words, there seems to be no legal "ruler" with which to measure the validity of an amendment that has been challenged as being beyond the scope of the amending power.

Nevertheless, Article Five did purport to limit the substance of amendments by withdrawing from the power proposals to abolish the importation of slaves prior to 1808 and to deprive the states of equal representation in the Senate. Time has made the first limitation obsolete, but the second theoretically remains in force.

It is possible to argue that if an amendment to end equal representation of the states in the Senate were proposed, the process of its ratification would differ from that prescribed in the Constitution. *No* state can be deprived of its equal representation without its consent. If one of several equal things is made unequal in respect to the others, they are made unequal in regard to it, though not to each other. Hence, if the representation of a state is increased or diminished, all other states are deprived of their equality. Consequently, an amendment to attain that end might have to be ratified by every state in order to become a part of the Constitution.

However, the best answer is probably that these limitations never did possess any legal force. That is to say, they cannot be applied to the amending process by any court, because they possess only moral force. They are the equivalent of an assertion that the amending process *ought not* to be used to attain the ends prohibited; the same power that put the prohibitions into the Constitution could be invoked to take them out, after which it would be possible to do what they had forbidden.

At most, these are interesting speculative questions. Given the constitutional equality of the states, state pride, and mutual interest in maintaining the status quo, it is almost inconceivable that the Senate would support an amendment to destroy the equality of representation of the states in that body.[5]

Withal, there has never been any authoritative denial of limitations upon the subject matter of an amendment.

Aspects of Proposal. The process for proposing amendments is a simple one. It can be accomplished by a vote of *two-thirds* of a quorum of the membership of both houses of Congress.[6] Joint resolutions are used for this purpose, but they are not submitted to the President for his approval or veto although the Constitution declares that this is necessary for "Every Order, Resolution, or Vote to which the Concurrence of the Senate and the House of Representatives may be necessary. . . ." The President has nothing to do with the proposal or adoption of amendments, for the Constitution differentiates between the ordinary legislative process, in which the President may participate through the exercise of his veto power, and the special constitutional function of proposing amendments. A joint resolution proposing an amendment does not take effect and constitute an action of the national government, as a statute does; it must be submitted to, and approved by the states before it acquires any force or effect.[7]

The intention of the framers of the Constitution to provide a safe and orderly method for amending the document has been realized. Fundamental principles of government ought not to be subjected to flights of

---

[5] On at least two occasions the Supreme Court has been asked to declare an amendment unconstitutional because of its subject matter. See *National Prohibition Cases* (1920), 253 U.S. 350, and *Lesser v. Garnett* (1922), 258 U.S. 130.

[6] See *National Prohibition Cases, supra.*

[7] See *Hollingsworth v. Virginia* (1798), 3 Dallas 378.

popular passion or whim. Approximately three thousand amendments have been suggested to Congress, but fewer than thirty have received the two-thirds vote necessary to secure their formal proposal and submission to the states.

Congress is authorized to call a national convention to propose amendments whenever two-thirds of the state legislatures petition it to do so. If used this power would enable the states to propose amendments which their experiences suggest are desirable, or by which a general revision of the Constitution could be undertaken.

This method of proposal has never been employed, so that nothing authoritative can be said about it. It seems clear, however, that Congress cannot call the convention on its own initiative, but must await requests from two-thirds of the state legislatures. The initiative resides with the states, and congressional participation is limited to calling the convention and to requesting the states to select delegates who are to attend it. However, it may pass a resolution asking the states to petition for a convention. Thereby, it can regain part of the initiative; but if the states fail to comply, there is nothing that Congress can do to compel them. Presumably a simple majority vote would be sufficient to request the states to submit petitions and to call a convention after the necessary two-thirds had been received. It may also be presumed that presidential approval would be unnecessary in either case.

What is meant by "two-thirds" is not at all clear. If the provision refers to an aggregate of petitions from the state legislatures, counted regardless of when they were received or to what they referred, the requisite number has been received, and Congress is now obligated, if, indeed, the language is mandatory, to call a convention. If "two-thirds" relates to petitions received within a reasonably short period of time and referring to the same subject of amendment the necessary conditions for a convention have not been fulfilled and Congress is not yet obligated to call one.

Other questions abound. It is not known whether the petitions must relate to one or more definite proposals of amendment or whether they can propose a general revision of the Constitution. Will the authority of the convention to propose be limited or unlimited? Can Congress prescribe how delegates to the convention shall be chosen, how many should attend, and whether they will represent the states or the people?

These, and many other questions which relate to the calling of a national convention for the purpose of proposing amendments to the Constitution, must remain unanswered until a convention is held. When that occurs some precedents will be set and some questions will be answered by them. Moreover, these may give rise to legal disputes which will demand settlement by the courts. From the decisions of these disputes will come other answers, until, at length, the meaning of this alternate method of proposal is made known. Until that time uncertainty will surround it.

Aspects of Ratification.

The 5th article is a grant of authority by the people to Congress. The determination of the method of ratification is the exercise of a national power specifically granted by the Constitution; that power is conferred upon Congress, and is limited to two methods; by action of the legislatures of three-fourths of the states, or conventions in a like number of states. . . . The framers of the Constitution might have adopted a different method. Ratification might have been left to a vote of the people, or to some authority of government other than that selected. The language of the article is plain, and admits of no doubt in its interpretation. It is not the function of courts or legislative bodies, national or state, to alter the method which the Constitution has fixed. . . .[8]

The function of a state in ratifying an amendment, like that of Congress in proposing it, is a special constitutional function. It does not partake of the legislative power of a state, which can be controlled as each state desires, but transcends all limitations, qualifications, or conditions which a state might try to impose upon it.[9]

Can Congress specify that ratification must take place within a *reasonable* period of time? Is seven years, as stipulated in the Eighteenth, Twentieth, and later amendments a reasonable limitation?

Although Article Five says nothing about the time within which ratification must take place, neither by way of limiting it nor by way of authorizing Congress to do so, there is nothing in that article which suggests that an amendment, once proposed, shall be open for ratification for all time. Neither is there anything to support the contention that ratification in some states may be separated from that in others and yet be effective. There is much, in fact, to suggest the contrary:

First, proposal and ratification are not treated as unrelated acts, but as succeeding steps in a single endeavor, the natural inference being that they are not to be widely separated in time. Secondly, it is only when there is deemed to be a necessity therefor that amendments are to be proposed, the reasonable implication being that when proposed they are to be considered and disposed of presently. Thirdly, as ratification is but the expression of the approbation of the people and is to be effective when had in three-fourths of the states, there is a fair implication that it must be sufficiently contemporaneous in that number of states to reflect the will of the people in all sections at relatively the same period, which, of course, ratification scattered through a long series of years would not do. . . .[10]

Hence the logic of the amending process infers that ratification must take place within a reasonable period after proposal, and it is firmly established that seven years is a reasonable period.

[8] *Hawke* v. *Smith* (1920), 253 U.S. 221.
[9] For example, see *Hawke* v. *Smith, supra, Lesser* v. *Garnett, supra,* and *United States* v. *Sprague* (1922), 282 U.S. 716.
[10] *Dillon* v. *Gloss* (1921), 256 U.S. 368.

Congress can set a reasonable period within which ratification must occur; but if it fails to do so, how long do the states have to act? No fixed answer suffices. The reasonableness of the period between proposal and ratification varies with the nature of amendments. Its determination in a given instance requires

. . . an appraisal of a great variety of relevant conditions, political, social and economic, which can hardly be said to be within the appropriate range of evidence receivable in a court of justice. . . . On the other hand, these conditions are appropriate for the consideration of the political departments of the Government. The questions they involve are essentially political and not justiciable. They can be decided by the Congress with the full knowledge and appreciation ascribed to the national legislature of the political, social and economic conditions which have prevailed during the period since the submission of the amendment.

Our decision that the Congress has the power under Article V to fix a reasonable limit of time for ratification in proposing an amendment proceeds upon the assumption that the question, what is a reasonable time, lies within the congressional province. If it be deemed that such a question is an open one when the limit has not been fixed in advance, we think it should also be regarded as an open one for the consideration of the Congress when, in the presence of certified ratifications by three-fourths of the states, the time arrives for the promulgation of the adoption of the amendment.[11]

Congress also has authority to decide what actions of the states shall be counted toward ratification. It determines the effect of a rejection followed by ratification, or of an attempt to withdraw a ratification. Neither is a question to be decided by a court. Precedent indicates that only ratification is a final action. It will overcome a prior rejection but cannot be overcome by a later one.[12]

The Amending Process and Constitutional Government. The United States is said to possess "constitutional government." Constitutional government is government which rests on, and maintains, an adjustment of individual freedom and governmental authority through known law. In the United States it is felt that this adjustment can best be accomplished by setting forth the most important features of it in a written constitution. But not even the written constitution purports to state in rigid terms what the exact balance between individual liberty and governmental authority shall be. The formal amending processes, supplemented by those of informal change, give recognition to the ideal that each generation of individuals should be free to determine which values it will consider important and which it will assert against the government.

Thus, constitutional government does not attempt to prescribe for all men of all times who are subject to its authority what rights they shall

[11] *Coleman* v. *Miller* (1939), 307 U.S. 433.
[12] *Ibid.*, pp. 448-449.

have; instead, it leaves men free to adjust their relations to government so that they can realize what they believe to be their best needs and interests. The substance of liberty is left free to change from time to time as the conditions change within which that liberty is to be exercised. Only the ideal of liberty remains permanent. Therefore, constitutional government may be seen as an effort to find the best adjustment between individual liberty and governmental power. It is a method for securing liberty whereby the governors who operate the agencies of coercive control reflect the thought and needs of the governed. Its purpose is to bring the two into agreement, to provide machinery of government that is both responsive and responsible. When changes must be made in the language of the Constitution in order to attain more effectively the ideal of constitutional government, the formal method of amendment must be relied upon. This it is that gives rise to the importance of the processes which have been discussed above.

CHAPTER II

Some Principles of the Constitution

THE TIMES; & POLITICAL PORTRAIT.

Triumph Government: perish all its enemies.—
Traitors be warned—justice though slow is sure

GENERAL CONSIDERATIONS

The framers of the Constitution assumed that the authority of government ought to be limited in nature and scope, that governors and governed should be answerable to the law, that the law should be known to all and be interpreted by impartial courts, that the people should be the source of all governmental powers, that the powers of government should be organized to secure the people against arbitrary rule, and that the state governments should be preserved to function concurrently with the national government. These ideas became the principles of the fundamental law and by implication became incorporated into the new plan of government. None was specifically stated to be a fundamental principle of the new system, but the fact that they were reflected in public opinion was an assurance that the new system of government would contain little or nothing to contradict them.

The roots of these principles penetrated deeply into American experience. They were accepted because they answered the practical and philosophical needs of the times. Accordingly, whatever the content of a

21

particular principle might be, all had a common purpose. This was to guarantee, so far as written law and institutional arrangements could do so, that government should exist as a means to an end but never as an end in itself. Thus, it will be found that each idea here called a "principle of the Constitution" in fact limits the authority of government.

However, the idea that governmental authority must be limited may be said to embody *the* fundamental principle of the Constitution. Other principles stand in subordination to it, since their reflection in institutions merely provides particular arrangements by which the primary objective of limited government is achieved in practice.

FEDERALISM

A federal system is one in which the powers of government are divided vertically between a central authority and one or more component authorities. The division of power is fixed so that neither jurisdiction can alter the arrangement against the will of the other.

No statement of federalism can be found in the Constitution, but it is embedded in all of the provisions which determine the relationship of the national power to that of the states. The closest approximation to a statement of federalism is found in the Tenth Article of Amendment which declares:

The powers not delegated to the United States by the Constitution, nor prohibited by it to the States, are reserved to the States respectively, or to the people.

This article was added to the original text of the Constitution to pacify critics of the plan. The federal nature of the new system could easily have been deduced from the Constitution as it was written, but the Tenth Amendment was added to verify that the states possessed powers of government independently of the national authority. The statement added nothing to the Constitution as it was originally ratified. It did nothing to add to, or detract from, the powers of either the national or the state governments.

Not only are the states retained as primary units of government but they are also coordinate and equal in status to the central government when they act within the proper sphere of their authority.

"Both the States and the United States existed before the Constitution. The people, through that instrument, established a more perfect union, by substituting a national government, acting with ample powers directly upon the citizens, instead of the confederate government, which acted with powers greatly restricted, only upon the states. But in many of the articles of the Constitution, the necessary existence of the states, and within their proper spheres, the independent authority of the states, are distinctly recognized. To them nearly the whole charge of interior regulation is committed or left; to them, and to the people, all powers, not expressly delegated to the national government, are reserved." Upon looking into the Constitution, it will be found that but few of the articles of that instrument could be carried into practical effect without the existence of the states.[1]

The existence of both jurisdictions is essential to the preservation of the federal relationship.

It seems to be often overlooked that a National Constitution has been adopted in this country, establishing a real government therein, operating upon persons and territory and things; and which, moreover, is, or should be, as dear to every American citizen as his State Government is. Whenever the true conception of the nature of his Government is once conceded, no real difficulty will arise in the just interpretation of its powers. But if we allow ourselves to regard it as a hostile organization, opposed to the proper sovereignty and dignity of the State Governments, we shall continue to be vexed with difficulties as to its jurisdiction and authority. No greater jealousy is required to be exercised towards this government in reference to the preservation of our liberties, than is proper to be exercised towards the State Governments. Its powers are limited in number, and clearly defined; and its action within the scope of those powers is restrained by a sufficiently rigid bill of rights for the protection of its citizens from oppression. The true interest of the people of this country requires that both the National and State Governments should be allowed, without jealous interference on either side, to exercise all the powers which respectively belong to them according to a fair and practical construction of the Constitution. State rights and the rights of the United States should be equally respected. . . .

We hold it to be an incontrovertible principle, that the Government of the United States may, by means of physical force, exercised through its official agents, execute on every foot of American soil the powers and functions that belong to it. This necessarily involves the power to command obedience to its laws, and hence the power to keep the peace to that extent.[2]

The jurisdictions of the federal system are intended to be complementary, to work together to pursue and attain the public good. They are but different agents and trustees of the people, constituted with different powers and designed for different purposes. They are not mutual rivals and enemies; both are controlled by the ultimate authority of a common superior, the people.[3]

[1] *Collector* v. *Day* (1871), 11 Wallace 113.
[2] *Ex parte Siebold* (1880), 100 U.S. 371.
[3] James Madison's analysis of the relationship between state and national governments, and the dependence of the latter upon the former, can be found in Numbers 45 and 46 of the *Federalist Papers*. Easily obtainable is the Modern Library edition (New York: Random House, 1937), hereafter cited as *Federalist Papers*. Events have not proven the writer to be accurate, but interesting comparisons can be made between his statements and modern conditions.

Federal Distribution of Powers.

General Considerations. The Constitution distributes the powers of government in the United States between the national and state jurisdictions. Therefore, federalism denotes a *vertical* division of authority between jurisdictions or "levels" of government. It might have been accomplished by granting specific powers to the states, with the residue remaining in the general government. However, the framers of the Constitution, keeping in mind the theory that the powers of the national government should be delegated to it out of those possessed by the states, adopted the solution incorporated in the fundamental law.

Residual (Reserved) Powers of the States. Hence, the national government possesses only the authority delegated to it by the Constitution. What was neither delegated to it by the Constitution, nor prohibited to the states, belongs to the states. It is known as "residual" or "reserved" power, since it is the residue of power left to the states after some has been delegated to the national government. It is "reserved" in the sense that it consists of power reserved to them, as distinguished from that which was taken from them.

The Tenth Amendment does not limit national power. The fact that states possess residual power does not stop the national government from exercising its delegated authority, although the latter may interfere with the former. Hence, the states have only the power which remains after the scope of national power has been determined.

The residual power of the states is vast and undefined; the Constitution imposes on it a few limitations of importance to the federal system. But the delegated power of the national government is reasonably well defined and limited. Accordingly, the Constitution serves as the measure of both national and state power. It grants no authority to the states, but the limitations on state power serve to curb or clarify its scope. A power must be presumed to belong to the state that exercises it until the Constitution can be shown to *deny* it. However, the Constitution *does grant* power to the national government; so that any power that it exercises must be shown to have been delegated. In short, the Constitution serves as a measure of state power through the *limitations* that it *imposes;* as a measure of national power through the *powers* that it *grants.*

Types of Delegated Power—Enumerated. The national government is one of delegated powers; it possesses only those granted to it by the Constitution, and those not granted to it are reserved to the states or to the people. Some of its powers are said to be "enumerated" or "expressed" and are held by it in accord with the "doctrine of delegated powers." These powers are set forth specifically in the Constitution. However, the authority of the national government is not limited to the powers of Congress, but includes those vested in the executive and judicial branches.

Types of Delegated Power—Implied. One of the expressly delegated powers of Congress declares that

The Congress shall have Power . . . To make all Laws which shall be necessary and proper for carrying into Execution the foregoing Powers, and all other Powers vested by this Constitution in the Government of the United States, or in any Department or Officer thereof.

This is the "necessary and proper" or "elastic" clause of the Constitution, which grants to Congress authority to enact laws "necessary and proper" to the execution not only of its own enumerated powers but also to those of the other branches of the national government. It was placed in the Constitution to remove all doubt about the power of Congress to legislate upon the great mass of incidental matters necessary to make the enumerated powers effective.

Scope of the Implied Powers. The power that Congress would derive from the "elastic" clause depended upon what the word "necessary" meant. If it meant *indispensable,* then Congress would be able to use only those means of carrying out the enumerated powers of the national government without which they would be rendered nugatory. The scope of the implied power would then be very narrow. If, however, "necessary" meant *useful, incidental, convenient, needful* or *conducive* to, Congress would be able to employ any reasonable means to carry the enumerated powers into effect. The scope of its implied power would then be very broad.[4]

In 1819 the scope of the implied powers was authoritatively determined by the Supreme Court according to the following reasoning:

It is not denied, that the powers given to the government imply the ordinary means of execution. . . . The government which has a right to do an act, and has imposed on it, the duty of performing that act, must, according to the dictates of reason, be allowed to select the means. . . .

Does [the word "necessary"] always import an absolute physical necessity, so strong, that one thing, to which another may be termed necessary, cannot exist without that other? We think it does not. If reference be had to its use, in the common affairs of the world, or in approved authors, we find that it frequently imports no more than that one thing is convenient, or useful, or essential to another. To employ the means necessary to an end, is generally understood as employing any means calculated to produce the end, and not as being confined to those single means, without which the end would be entirely un-

[4] For the arguments of Jefferson and Hamilton in support of these respective interpretations, see the report of each to President Washington on the power of Congress to incorporate a bank of the United States incidental to the discharge of its coinage, taxing, and other enumerated powers. They may be conveniently found in Henry Steele Commager, editor, *Documents of American History* (New York: Appleton-Century-Crofts, 5th edition, 1947), Nos. 93 and 94.

attainable. Such is the character of human language, that no word conveys to the mind, in all situations, one single definite idea. . . . The word "necessary" is of this description. It has not a fixed character, peculiar to itself. It admits of all degrees of comparison. A thing may be necessary, very necessary, absolutely or indispensably necessary. . . . This word, then, like others, is used in various senses; and, in its construction, the subject, the context, the intention of the person using them, are all to be taken into view. . . .

We admit, as all must admit, that the powers of the government are limited, and that its limits are not to be transcended. But we think the sound construction of the constitution must allow to the national legislature that discretion, with respect to the means by which the powers it confers are to be carried into execution, which will enable that body to perform the high duties assigned to it, in the manner most beneficial to the people. Let the end be legitimate, let it be within the scope of the constitution, and all means which are appropriate, which are plainly adapted to that end, which are not prohibited, but which consist with the letter and spirit of the constitution, are constitutional.[5]

Thus the national government derived by implication from the Constitution a vast area of authority which the view of the "strict constructionists" would have denied it. The doctrine of delegated power contains its corollary the doctrine of implied power. Implied power may be derived from the enumerated power of any branch of the national government, from a single enumerated power, or from any combination of two or more of them. Thus, the national government, though a limited government of delegated power, possesses a great undefined power derived by implication from those which are enumerated.

Inherent Powers. If the above statements are valid, can the national government possess inherent power, that is, power which is not given to it from any source but which inheres in it merely because it is the government of a nation? It may well be asked: can a limited government of delegated power at the same time possess authority that is inherent and, therefore, not dependent for its existence upon a delegation? It cannot. The concepts of delegated and inherent power are wholly incompatible. The possession of inherent power would nullify the limitation on national authority which was imposed and made effective by the doctrine of delegated powers.[6]

However, there is one very important area of concern to the national government in which it does possess inherent power. That is the vital area of foreign affairs. The distinction between the power of the general government in regard to internal and external affairs is based on the fact

That there are differences between them, and that these differences are fundamental, may not be doubted.

[5] *McCulloch* v. *Maryland* (1819), 4 Wheaton 316.
[6] A claim was once unsuccessfully made that the national government possessed inherent powers. See *Kansas* v. *Colorado* (1907), 206 U.S. 46.

The two classes of powers are different, both in respect of their origin and their nature. The broad statement that the federal government can exercise no powers except those specifically enumerated in the Constitution, and such implied powers as are necessary and proper to carry into effect the enumerated powers, is categorically true only in respect of our internal affairs. In that field, the primary purpose of the Constitution was to carve from the general mass of legislative powers *then possessed by the states* such portions as it was thought desirable to vest in the federal government, leaving those not included in the enumeration still in the states. . . . That this doctrine applies only to the powers which the states had is self-evident. And since the states severally never possessed international powers, such powers could not have been carved from the mass of state powers but obviously were transmitted to the United States from some other source. . . .

As a result of the separation from Great Britain by the colonies, acting as a unit, the powers of external sovereignty passed from the Crown not to the colonies severally, but to the colonies in their collective and corporate capacity as the United States of America. . . . Rulers come and go; governments end and forms of government change; but sovereignty survives. A political society cannot endure without a supreme will somewhere. Sovereignty is never held in suspense. When, therefore, the external sovereignty of Great Britain in respect of the colonies ceased, it immediately passed to the Union. . . .

It results that the investment of the federal government with the powers of external sovereignty did not depend upon the affirmative grants of the Constitution. The powers to declare and wage war, to conclude peace, to maintain diplomatic relations with other sovereignties, if they had never been mentioned in the Constitution, would have been vested in the federal government as necessary concomitants of nationality. . . . As a member of the family of nations, the right and power of the United States in that field are equal to the right and power of the other members of the international family. Otherwise, the United States is not completely sovereign. . . . The power to acquire territory by discovery and occupation . . . , the power to expel undesirable aliens . . . , the power to make such international agreements as do not constitute treaties in the constitutional sense . . . , none of which is expressly affirmed by the Constitution, nevertheless exist as inherently inseparable from the concept of nationality. . . .[7]

Concurrent and Exclusive Powers. Some powers of government are possessed and exercised by both national and state jurisdictions. Both, for example, must be able to make and administer laws, collect taxes, spend public monies, preserve the peace, and administer justice. Such shared authority is known as concurrent power.

There are also powers possessed exclusively by the national government. They are few in number and cannot be exercised by the states without either destroying the efficacy of national power or creating great confusion within the federal system. They are called "exclusive" powers.

[7] *United States* v. *Curtiss-Wright Export Corporation* (1936), 299 U.S. 304.

What is the relationship between concurrent and exclusive powers?

The constitution containing a grant of powers in many instances similar to those already existing in the state governments, and some of these being of vital importance also to State authority and state legislation, it is not to be admitted that a mere grant of such powers in affirmative terms to Congress, does, per se, transfer an exclusive sovereignty on such matters to the latter. On the contrary, a reasonable interpretation of that instrument necessarily leads to the conclusion, that the powers so granted are never exclusive of similar powers existing in the States, unless where the constitution has expressly in terms given an exclusive power to Congress, or the exercise of a like power is prohibited to the States, or there is a direct repugnancy or incompatibility in the exercise of it by the States. The example of the first class is to be found in the *exclusive* legislation delegated to Congress over places purchased by consent of the legislature of the State in which the same shall be, for forts, arsenals, dock-yards, etc.; of the second class, the prohibition of a State to coin money or emit bills of credit; of the third class, as this Court have already held, the power to establish an uniform rule of naturalization, and the delegation of admiralty and maritime jurisdiction. In all other cases not falling within the classes already mentioned, it seems unquestionably that the States retain concurrent authority with Congress. . . .[8]

Doctrine of National Supremacy. It is inevitable that when coordinate jurisdictions of government exist within the same system the exercise of their powers will conflict. This contingency was provided for by the "supremacy" clause of the Constitution which declares that

This Constitution, and the Laws of the United States which shall be made in Pursuance thereof; and all Treaties made, or which shall be made, under the Authority of the United States, shall be the supreme Law of the Land; and the Judges in every State shall be bound thereby, any Thing in the Constitution or Laws of any State to the Contrary notwithstanding.

It follows, therefore,

. . . that the government of the Union, though limited in its powers, is supreme within its sphere of action. This would seem to result, necessarily, from its nature. It is the government of all; its powers are delegated by all; it represents all, and acts for all. . . . The nation, on those subjects on which it can act, must necessarily bind its component parts. . . .[9]

When the national government acts within the sphere of its authority its actions have superior force over those of any state which conflict with them. This supremacy of national authority is necessary to the operation of a federal system so that doubt about the relative standing of the two spheres of power can be eliminated. If there were no "supremacy" clause

---

[8] *Houston* v. *Moore* (1820), 5 Wheaton 1.
[9] *McCulloch* v. *Maryland, supra.*

its absence would imply that each of the two spheres of power was the absolute legal equal of the other, and that in cases of conflict neither would take precedence over the other. However, its effect is to ensure that national power supersedes the exercise of any conflicting concurrent or non-concurrent state power.

The United States is a government with authority extending over the whole territory of the Union, acting upon the States and upon the people of the States. While it is limited in the number of its powers, so far as its sovereignty extends it is supreme. No state government can exclude it from the exercise of any authority conferred upon it by the Constitution, obstruct its authorized officers against its will, or withhold from it, for a moment, the cognizance of any subject which that instrument has committed to it.[10]

Moreover, the supremacy of national power protects its officers and agents, for state statutes which conflict with the performance of their official functions must give way to national authority, but

. . . no one will contend that when a man becomes an officer or employee of the National Government he ceases to be subject to the laws of the State. The principle we are discussing has its limitations. . . . The limitation is, that the agencies of the Federal Government are only exempted from state legislation, so far as that legislation may interfere with, or impair their efficiency in performing the functions by which they are designed to serve that government. Any other rule would convert a principle founded alone in the necessity of securing to the Government of the United States the means of exercising its legitimate powers, into an unauthorized and unjustifiable invasion of the rights of the States. . . . A federal officer . . . may be exempted from any personal service which interferes with the discharge of his official duties, because those exemptions are essential to enable him to perform those duties. But he is subject to all the laws of the State which affect his family or social relations, or his property, and he is liable to punishment for crime, though that punishment be imprisonment or death.[11]

If the Union is to be preserved it is essential that neither of the two jurisdictions composing it should be able to destroy the other. It is also essential that neither should be able substantially to burden, impede, or control the performance of governmental functions by the other. If either jurisdiction could do so, the other would exist at its suffrance. Accordingly, an implied limitation upon the exercise of governmental power arises from the federal system; it prevents each jurisdiction from destroying or interfering with the other. Nevertheless, under the doctrine of national supremacy, it must be remembered that Congress can exercise its delegated powers even when its acts conflict with the laws or constitutions of the states.

[10] *Tennessee* v. *Davis* (1880), 100 U.S. 257.
[11] *First National Bank* v. *Kentucky* (1870), 9 Wallace 353.

DOCTRINE OF THE SEPARATION OF POWERS

Not only is governmental power in the United States limited by the vertical division inherent in federalism, but also

The Federal Constitution and State Constitutions of this country divide the governmental power into three branches. The first is the legislative, the second is the executive, and the third is the judicial, and the rule is that in the actual administration of the government Congress or the legislature should exercise the legislative power, the President or the State executive, the Governor, the executive power, and the courts or the judiciary the judicial power, and in carrying out that constitutional division into three branches it is a breach of the National fundamental law if Congress gives up its legislative power and transfers it to the President, or to the Judicial branch, or if by law it attempts to invest itself or its members with either executive power or judicial power. This is not to say that the three branches are not coordinate parts of one government and that each in the field of its duties may not invoke the action of the other two branches in so far as the action invoked shall not be an assumption of the constitutional field of action of another branch. In determining what it may do in seeking assistance from another branch, the extent and character of that assistance must be fixed according to common sense and the inherent necessities of the governmental co-ordination.[12]

Although federalism and the separation of powers are incorporated into the Constitution, neither bears any relation to the other, and each may exist in a political system without the other. Each denotes a different principle of governmental organization, but both are designed to limit the exercise of governmental power and to protect liberty.

Origin of the Doctrine of the Separation of Powers. The ancient idea of separating the powers of government has been given many different forms, but the one best known to the framers of the Constitution was that of Baron Charles Louis Secondat de Montesquieu, who wrote:

Political liberty is to be found only in moderate governments; and even in these it is not always found. It is there only when there is no abuse of power. . . .

To prevent this abuse, it is necessary from the very nature of things that power should be a check to power. A government may be so constituted as no man shall be compelled to do things to which the law does not oblige him, nor forced to abstain from things which the law permits. . . .

In every government there are three sorts of power: the legislative; the executive in respect to things dependent on the law of nations; and the executive in regard to matters that depend on the civil law.

By virtue of the first, the prince or magistrate enacts temporary or perpetual laws, and amends or abrogates those that have been already enacted. By the

[12] *Hampton and Company* v. *United States* (1928), 276 U.S. 394.

second, he makes peace or war, sends or receives embassies, establishes the public security, and provides against invasions. By the third, he punishes criminals, or determines the disputes that arise between individuals. The latter we shall call the judiciary power, and the other simply the executive power of the state.

The political liberty of the subject is a tranquility of mind arising from the opinion each person has of his safety. In order to have this liberty, it is requisite the government be so constituted as one man need not be afraid of another.

When the legislative and executive powers are united in the same person, or in the same body of magistrates, there can be no liberty; because apprehensions may arise, lest the same monarch or senate should enact tyrannical laws, to execute them in a tyrannical manner.

Again there is no liberty if the judicial power be not separated from the legislative and executive. Were it joined with the legislative, the life and liberty of the subject would be exposed to arbitrary control; for the judge would then be the legislator. Were it joined to the executive power, the judge might behave with violence and oppression.

There would be an end of everything, were the same man or the same body, whether of the nobles or of the people, to exercise those three powers, that of enacting laws, that of executing the public resolutions, and of trying the causes of individuals.[13]

Of more immediate influence upon the framers of the Constitution were factors of a practical nature. The royal governors had exercised the three types of governmental power in combination. American colonial experiences under their rule led to the conclusion that such a combination was the essence of tyranny. By 1787, this object lesson had been given explicit recognition in the constitutions of half the states. All operated under some form of separated powers. The doctrine had been an accepted axiom of American state political systems for a decade when the Constitution was drafted, and in Convention Madison referred to it as a "fundamental principle of free government."

Separation of Powers in the Constitution. The Constitution states none of Montesquieu's assumptions in explicit language, but a statement of the doctrine may be extracted from the document by combining the three "distributive" clauses thus:

All legislative Powers . . . shall be vested in a Congress of the United States. . . . The executive Power shall be vested in a President of the United States. . . . The judicial Power of the United States shall be vested in one supreme Court, and in such inferior Courts as the Congress may from time to time ordain and establish.

[13] Baron Charles Louis Secondat de Montesquieu, *The Spirit of the Laws*, translated by Thomas Nugent (New York: "Hafner Library of Classics," Hafner Publishing Company, 1949) Bk. XI, chap. 6.

This derived statement takes note of the three types of power, assigns each to a distinct branch of the governmental structure, and implies that each branch shall be equal to and independent of the others.[14]

Checks and Balances. The doctrine of the separation of powers does not require that each branch of government should be *isolated* from the others. Such isolation would compel each branch to perform its functions independently of the other two. Under such conditions government could not be carried on. The doctrine states only that where the *whole* power of one branch is exercised by the same person, or persons, who exercises the whole power of another branch, the fundamental principles of a free constitution are lost. No branch ought to possess, directly or indirectly, an overruling influence over the others in the administration of their respective powers. However, the doctrine of the separation of powers assumes that some of each type of power will be possessed by each branch, so that any may check the others to prevent a concentration in any one. Each branch ought to have a *partial agency* in, and control over, the acts of the others, so that "power should be a check to power." In this way are given to those

. . . who administer each department the necessary constitutional means and personal motives to resist the encroachments of the others. The provision for defense must in this, as in all other cases, be made commensurate to the danger of attack. Ambition must be made to counteract ambition. . . . It may be a reflection on human nature, that such devices should be necessary to control the abuses of government. But what is government itself, but the greatest of all reflections on human nature. If men were angels, no government would be necessary. If Angels were to govern men, neither external nor internal controls on government would be necessary. In framing a government which is to be administered by men over men, the great difficulty lies in this: you must first enable the government to control the governed; and in the next place oblige it to control itself. A dependence on the people is, no doubt, the primary control on the government; but experience has taught mankind the necessity of auxiliary precautions. . . .[15]

By this partition of power, known as the system of checks and balances, the interior structure of the government is so contrived that its several parts, through their mutual relations, are the means of keeping each other in their proper places. Hence, checks and balances are an outgrowth of the doctrine of the separation of powers, but the two in unmixed forms are mutually exclusive. The one anticipates independence;

[14] Because the Constitution does not define the doctrine of the separation of powers in precise language, its opponents during the struggle for ratification asserted that it did not embody this indispensable safeguard of liberty. Their charges against the new plan of government called forth several numbers of the *Federalist* in which their criticisms were refuted and the doctrine elaborated. See *Federalist Papers*, Nos. 47, 48, and 51.

[15] *Federalist Papers*, No. 51.

the other requires interdependence and cooperation. Neither can exist in the presence of the other, for if there is a complete separation, there can be no checks and balances. Conversely, to the extent that there is a system of checks and balances there can be no pure separation of powers. However, their complementary nature greatly exceeds their conflicting characteristics.

Checks and Balances in the National Government. A brief examination of the Constitution will reveal the extent to which the system of checks and balances has been implemented. The examination is illustrative only, for the separation affects every practical relationship which develops between the three branches of the national government. To consider all of them here is impossible.

The more important ways in which the three powers have been mingled include the following: The legislative power is vested in Congress, but the President may veto bills, recommend legislation, issue rules, orders, and regulations which make law, and call special sessions. The executive thus possesses a portion of the *legislative power*. The President nominates, but the Senate must "advise and consent" before he can appoint. The President negotiates treaties, but he may ratify them only if the Senate gives its approval. The Senate thus shares in the exercise of these two important *executive powers* of the President. The power of the President to appoint implies the power to remove his appointees from office, but the removal power can be restricted by Congress in certain instances. Congress controls the purse strings, and by denying or otherwise controlling funds can do much to regulate the activities, even the existence, of the other two branches. It has created most of the administrative agencies, controls their authority, and can abolish them as it desires. It created the judicial system, and controls its existence and jurisdiction subject to a few constitutional limitations. The courts exercise the power of judicial review, but the President can influence their attitudes by carefully selecting their judges. Behind the President and the judges, moreover, lurks the power of impeachment, which is vested in the two houses of Congress. Many agents and organs of the executive branch formulate policy, a legislative function, and determine and enforce rights, a judicial function. Congress enacts laws, but the executive determines the manner of their administration. Thus the Constitution blends and connects the three powers of government, so that each is given a limited control over the others. Each may exert a limited influence over the others, but none is at the mercy of any other in fulfilling its essential function.

The Separation of Powers in Modern Times. The doctrine of the separation of powers retains a high degree of its value in contemporary government; for modern government in the United States is "big" government, and "big" government can easily escape the controls of a democratic political system. In response to pressures brought to bear upon it, the national government today is undertaking functions, providing services, and regulating social conflict to a greater extent than ever before. The expansion of its activities has produced a corresponding expansion in the number of its functionaries. Its laws and regulations are no longer few and easily understood. Its activities can no longer be administered by a few agencies operating under the guidance of competent laymen. These agencies have multiplied until they constitute a bewildering array of departments, boards, services, commissions, offices, authorities, corporations, and other types. Civil servants of general ability recruited from the public at large can no longer handle unaided the problems of administration. The technical character of modern government has tended to produce a new class of civil servant, the expert. He is no longer merely the advisor of the general administrator, but controls functions of government in many important areas. The expert makes decisions that often affect important individual and property rights, which the man in the street can seldom judge wisely, although they may affect him directly. The latter cannot overcome the prestige and authority of the scientist, diplomat, general, and administrator. He lacks the time and knowledge necessary to do so. The issues for his decision come in too rapid succession. Information is often withheld from him. The ordinary citizen upon whose common sense democratic government traditionally has depended is seemingly threatened with obsolescence and the loss of his former ability to control government.

These and other factors make it more and more difficult for the processes of political democracy to control government; yet, such control is indispensable if responsive and responsible government is to endure.

The value of separated powers endures because government today is not as dependent upon "the people," but they are more dependent upon it than was formerly the case. It is thought in many quarters that they are now less prone to challenge and scrutinize the policies and acts of government. To the extent, therefore, that the partition of power continues to fulfill its original purpose it remains a valuable adjunct of the system of American national government.

However, a price must be paid for the security gained. The value of separated powers is dependent in part upon the existence of jealousies, frictions, and suspicions which cause each branch of government to watch cautiously the acts of the others. But "big" government demands smoothness and harmony of operation. Cooperation, not friction, is required between them. Will this eighteenth century device permit these attributes to develop adequately? Only during times of emergency do the three branches of government seem to function with the unity which ought uniformly to prevail, and even that is attained more in spite of the separation of powers, than because of it.

The exigencies of modern government have produced several modifications of relationship which testify to the doubtful suitability of separated powers. The lines of demarcation between the legislative, executive, and judicial powers have been much obscured by the evolution of new administrative forms and procedures. The legislative branch has been compelled by the changing circumstances of government to give the executive a growing share of its power over the formulation of national policy. A number of reasons may be cited in explanation of this development. First, Congress lacks any marked capacity to provide the nation with leadership of other than a temporary and a personal nature. Strong guidance can come only from the executive branch. Second, as the problems of society have increased, and become more complex and technical, Congress has been forced to rely upon the executive for programs of integrated policy. Third, the nature and pressure of issues has compelled Congress to enact laws that establish general policies. It cannot prescribe in detail how its acts should be applied to every set of conditions which come within the scope of their control. An attempt to do so would only produce injustice to those to whom the laws were applied, hamper the application of the laws by destroying administrative discretion, and create a great degree of rigidity in the law. For these reasons the influence and prestige of the executive power have increased at the expense of the legislative.

Constitutional Problem—The Delegation of Legislative Power. A question of constitutional propriety arises from this necessity of modern government. Can Congress delegate its legislative power, or any share of it, to the executive branch without violating the doctrine of the separation of powers?

The Constitution provides that "All legislative powers herein granted shall be vested in a Congress of the United States, which shall consist of a Senate and House of Representatives." . . . The Congress manifestly is not permitted to abdicate, or to transfer to others, the essential legislative functions with which it is vested. Undoubtedly legislation must often be adapted to complex conditions involving a host of details with which the national legislature cannot deal directly. The Constitution has never been regarded as denying to Congress the necessary resources of flexibility and practicality, which will enable it to perform its function in laying down policies and establishing standards, while leaving to selected instrumentalities the making of subordinate rules within prescribed limits and the determination of facts to which the policy as declared by the legislature is to apply. Without capacity to give authorization of that sort we should have the anomaly of a legislative power which in many circumstances calling for its exertion would be but a futility. . . . Applying that principle, authorizations given by Congress to select instrumentalities for the purpose of ascertaining the existence of facts to which legislation is directed, have constantly been sustained. Moreover, the Congress may . . . establish primary standards, devolving upon others the duty to carry out the declared legislative policy, that is . . . "to fill up the details" under the general provisions made by the legislature. . . .[16]

[16] *Panama Refining Co.* v. *Ryan* (1935), 293 U.S. 388.

Congress may not constitutionally abdicate legislative power to the President. It may, however, grant the executive, its officers or agencies, power "to fill up the details" of broad policies laid down by Congress, and to carry out such policies whenever the executive finds that their implementation will attain the ends that the legislature desires to achieve. When Congress sets a policy, prescribes standards to be followed by the executive, and in other ways limits the exercise of executive discretion, it may grant authority to the executive to determine when and in what manner the prescribed policy shall be carried out. To that extent only may the executive exercise legislative power without violating the doctrine of the separation of powers. But when an administrative officer or agency is authorized to make and enforce rules and regulations, having the force of law, that result can only be achieved by combining, in violation of the doctrine of the separation of powers, legislative, executive, and judicial authority in the same official or unit of government. This development is a major characteristic of modern government in the United States, as well as in virtually all other industrialized nations. More law is made by administrative regulations and orders than is made by Congress; more disputes are settled by units of the executive branch than are settled by courts of law.

The Delegation of Legislative Power in Regard to External Affairs. It has been noted above that the authority of the general government to control its external affairs is inherent, that this power is different in origin and nature from that over internal affairs, and that it is not limited to the specific grants made by the Constitution. Therefore, in the handling of matters within the realm of foreign affairs, the freedom allowed the legislative branch to make delegations of power to the executive is theoretically greater than that permitted in connection with internal affairs.

The validity of legislative grants of power to the President in the area of foreign affairs must be determined in the light of the very delicate, plenary and exclusive power of the President as the sole organ of the federal government in the field of international relations—a power which does not require as a basis for its exercise an act of Congress, but which, of course, like every other governmental power, must be exercised in subordination to the applicable provisions of the Constitution. It is quite apparent that if, in the maintenance of our international relations, embarrassment—perhaps serious embarrassment—is to be avoided and success for our aim achieved, congressional legislation which is to be made effective through negotiation and inquiry within the international field must often accord to the President a degree of discretion and freedom from statutory restrictions which would not be admissible were domestic affairs alone involved. . . .[17]

[17] *United States* v. *Curtiss-Wright Export Corporation, supra.*

However, the power of Congress to make delegations of authority to the executive in domestic matters is actually as free of limitations as it is in the area of foreign affairs. The Supreme Court has permitted Congress to give authority to the executive in a host of recent statutes pertaining to internal affairs under conditions so permissive that they have all but eliminated the theoretical, constitutional standards of validity. There are no discernible effective restraints now in force, but at any time that a challenge is brought the old ones may be reinvigorated.

CHAPTER III

Further Principles of the Constitution

THE RULE OF LAW

The Constitution incorporates a principle which exerts tremendous influence upon the organization and operation of the national government. The expressions "equality before the law," "a government of laws but not of men," "supremacy of law," and "the rule of law" are often heard. Each is employed to express the idea that "absolutely arbitrary power, or governing without settled standing laws, can neither of them consist with the ends of society and government."[1]

According to the rule of law persons who hold and exercise the coercive powers of government may employ them only according to laws, which bestow authority and impose limitations upon its use. The law, not the arbitrary whim of the agents of government, shall control what is done and the manner in which it is accomplished. The law must be known or knowable to all, must be understandable, and must be applied without favoritism or discrimination to all who fall within the scope of its

[1] John Locke, *Second Treatise on Civil Government* (New York: Hafner Publishing Company, 1947), Chap. XI, sec. 137, pp. 190-191.

application. Decency, liberty and security demand that officers and agents of government should be subjected to the same rules of conduct that are addressed to the citizens. In a government of laws, the existence of the government will be endangered if it fails scrupulously to observe the laws. Thus it is that

No man in this country is so high that he is above the law. No officer of the law may set that law at defiance with impunity. All the officers of the Government, from the highest to the lowest, are creatures of the law and are bound to obey it.

It is the only supreme power in our system of government, and every man who, by accepting office, participates in its functions, is only the more strongly bound to submit to that supremacy, and to observe the limitations it imposes upon the exercise of the authority which it gives.

Courts of justice are established not only to decide upon the controverted rights of the citizens as against each other, but also upon rights in controversy between them and the Government. . . .[2]

The laws may be "good" or "bad," "wise" or "unwise," but everyone should be subject to their command, and should be entitled to their fair and impartial administration.

The rule of law is nowhere stated in the Constitution, but virtually every limitation, device, arrangement, and procedural requirement is intended to prevent the development of personal government. Federalism, the doctrine of the separation of powers, and constitutionalism, contribute to its realization.

The essence of free government is "leave to live by no man's leave, underneath the law." The ideal is government by impersonal law. The greatest dangers to free government and liberty come from the insidious encroachments of well-meaning but misguided men of zeal. The constitutional system is designed to fulfill the ideal as far as it is humanly possible by precluding acts which originate in whim and caprice; for official actions which lack the authority of law obscure both the limits of official power and the extent of private rights.

The rule of law has its defects, delays, and inconveniences, but men have discovered no technique for preserving free government except through law—and through law that is made by open legislative processes. For free government under the rule of law to exist there must be some way by which persons who are subject to the exercise of official power can hold their governors accountable. Claims to power, as well as the manner of its exercise, must be subject to challenge if the agents and organs of government are to be kept responsible and the supremacy of law is to be assured. Democratic political processes play their role, but challenges to the legitimacy of power are usually brought, and injuries caused by its

[2] *United States* v. *Lee* (1882), 106 U.S. 196.

wrongful exercise are usually redressed, through the courts, which must, therefore, be as independent of control by both the citizenry and the governmental officials as it is possible to make them.

This is not to say that officers of government never act illegally, never violate statutory or constitutional provisions, never infringe rights of person or property. The important consideration is not that occasionally authority is used or force exerted wrongly, but that the aggrieved parties can secure rectification of the wrongs done. By seeking the protection of known rules of law which can be enforced administratively or judicially against the wrongdoers, citizens can hold their governors to account. Not only can they do so, but it is an obligation of responsible citizenship to do so, and one that should not be neglected.

Men born to freedom are naturally alert to repel invasion of their liberty by evil-minded rulers. The greatest dangers to liberty lurk in insidious encroachments by men of zeal, well-meaning, but without understanding.

Decency, security, and liberty alike demand that government officials shall be subjected to the same rules of conduct that are commands to the citizen. In a government of laws, existence of the government will be imperiled if it fails to observe the law scrupulously. . . .[3]

However, no officer or agent of government is compelled to take every action that is authorized. Some actions are made mandatory and *must* be performed when the occasion arises. They are known as ministerial duties and nonperformance can be enforced; but the vast majority of actions authorized by law are not of that type, and are discretionary in nature. When the exercise of discretionary authority is involved a public official is free to take no action, or any action that is permissible within the scope of his valid authority. Thus, the rule of law does not compel the taking of a discretionary act. The official may determine, for reasons known only to himself, that the time is not right to act, that the action is administratively impracticable, or that it is impolitic. Hence, legal considerations alone do not determine what government officers and employees do; the rule of law only determines *what* may be done, or the *manner* of doing it, but politics frequently governs *whether* and *when* it shall be done.

Administration and the Rule of Law. Much of modern "big" government consists of administrative action which is taken to regulate or settle disputes in society. Formerly the function was performed by the courts of law when parties in conflict invoked the aid of judicial power. While courts continue to perform this traditional function, the well-ordered condition of society is probably due more to administrative processes and actions than to judicial ones. Similarly, administrative agencies today make policy in the form of rules and orders, which are promulgated and

[3] Justice Brandeis dissenting in *Olmstead* v. *United States* (1928), 277 U.S. 438.

enforced through their own, and not judicial, action. Modern government, then, is mainly administrative government which combines definite characteristics of legislative, executive and judicial power, and does this in violation of the doctrine that these three powers must be kept separate if liberty is to exist. Moreover, most administrative authority is of the discretionary type. The combination of powers, coupled with broad discretion in the hands of political appointees and routine civil servants, is regarded by many persons as a threat to the ideal that the governed should be free from arbitrary rule by their governors. Extensive authority, backed by broad discretion, is regarded as an invitation to government by *will* instead of by law. Administrators make law, enforce it upon all who come within its scope, and determine important rights of person and property which involve significant private and public interests. The traditional concept of the rule of law posited as its primary tenets that

. . . every citizen is entitled, first, to have his rights adjudicated in a regular common law court, and secondly, to call into question in such a court the legality of any act done by an administrative official.[4]

Administrative lawmaking and determination of private rights have tended to weaken the first element in this traditional definition of the rule of law. But as long as courts of law retain authority to review the validity of administrative actions, the principle of the rule of law will remain unendangered. Administrative lawmaking exists contrary to the rule of law only in so far as administrative determinations are not subject to correction by a court of law.

The role of the courts has changed; because of the inadequacies of the judicial process, problems of modern society and government which were formerly under the control of the judiciary have been shifted to administrative agencies where speed, initiative, and expert knowledge can be brought to bear upon them. This does not mean, however, that rights safeguarded by the rule of law are soon to become things of the past. It only suggests that the rule of law should be flexible enough to accommodate the practical exigencies of modern government. If a partial combination of legislative, executive, and judicial authority in administrative agencies and tribunals is the most effective way for government to meet the demands made on it, then the problem is that of devising guarantees to ensure that abuse of authority and the use of unfair methods do not occur. In fact, these guarantees have to a considerable extent been worked out and implemented, and the rule of law has been adjusted to the extensive use of administrative action in modern "big" government.

Judicial Supremacy. If it is understood that all agents and organs of the national government are limited in their official acts to those au-

[4] John Dickinson, *Administrative Justice and the Supremacy of Law* (Cambridge, Mass.: Harvard University Press, 1927), p. 35.

thorized by law, and that none are valid unless so authorized, we are left with the necessity of determining whom individuals can appeal to when they wish to challenge an act which is alleged to violate law. Where in the governmental system is the power lodged to declare that what purports to be a valid action of government is really within the authority of the doer, and is not actually one of arbitrariness and caprice?

This function is one which is peculiarly dependent upon the interpretation of law; hence, it has traditionally been performed by the courts in democratic political systems. The novel feature of its incorporation in the American system of national government is that for the first time it has been made to cover acts of the political branches. Thus, although each of the three branches of the national government is theoretically independent of and equal to each of the others, the judiciary can in practice determine the validity of the acts of the other two branches. It is not at the same time subject to the exercise by them of any similar control over the use of its powers.

This is what is meant by "judicial supremacy." The situation has been candidly described by Justice Stone:

> The power of courts to declare a statute unconstitutional is subject to two guiding principles of decision which ought never to be absent from judicial consciousness. One is that courts are concerned only with the power to enact statutes, not with their wisdom. The other is that while unconstitutional exercise of power by the executive and legislative branches of the government is subject to judicial restraint, the only check upon our own exercise of power is our own sense of self-restraint. For the removal of *unwise* laws from the statute books appeal lies not to the courts but to the ballot and to the democratic processes of government.[5]

Judicial supremacy, therefore, is a significant feature of the constitutional system for enforcing the rule of law upon the political branches of the government. However, the practical supremacy of the courts results from the exercise of judicial review.

Judicial Review. Judicial review is a function performed by a national or state court which is incidental to its decisions on cases and controversies that are brought before it. It consists in determining the constitutionality of a law which a court is asked to recognize and enforce but which it may declare void, and refuse to apply. The significance of its exercise by the Supreme Court of the United States is particularly great, because that court has the last word in deciding all questions of constitutional interpretation. Its decisions cannot be appealed to any higher legal authority, for there is none; and they may be overturned, with very few exceptions, only by amending the Constitution.

[5] Justice Stone dissenting in *United States* v. *Butler* (1936), 297 U.S. 1. Italics added.

Source of the Power of Judicial Review. The function of judicial review is nowhere provided for specifically in the Constitution. From whence does it come? Established principle and long practice affirm that it is an implied power derived from two provisions of the Constitution. These are, first, the clause of Article Three which establishes the authority of national courts to exercise the judicial power of the United States, which is declared to extend

. . . to all Cases, in Law and Equity, arising under this Constitution, the Laws of the United States, and Treaties made, or which shall be made, under their Authority. . . .

Second, is the "supremacy clause" of the Constitution, which, it will be recalled, declares that the Constitution is "the supreme law of the land." The power of judicial review, therefore, is implied from the authority of courts to decide cases and controversies arising from the supreme law of the land.

The following analysis by Alexander Hamilton sets forth the generally accepted explanation of the origin of, and necessity for, judicial review:

. . . No legislative act . . . contrary to the Constitution can be valid. To deny this, would be to affirm . . . that the representatives of the people are superior to the people themselves; that men acting by virtue of powers, may do not only what their powers do not authorize, but what they forbid.

If it is said that the legislative body are themselves the constitutional judges of their own powers, and that the construction that they put upon them is too conclusive upon the other departments, it may be answered, that this cannot be the natural presumption, where it is not to be collected from any particular provisions of the Constitution. It is not otherwise to be supposed, that the Constitution could intend to enable the representatives of the people to substitute their *will* for that of their constituents. It is far more rational to suppose, that the courts were designed to be an intermediate body between the people and the legislature, in order, among other things, to keep the latter within the limits assigned to their authority. The interpretation of the laws is the proper and peculiar province of the courts. A constitution is in fact, and must be regarded by the judges, as a fundamental law. It therefore belongs to them to ascertain its meaning, as well as the meaning of any particular act proceeding from the legislative body. If there should happen to be an irreconcilable variance between the two, that which has the superior obligation and validity ought, of course, to be preferred; or, in other words, the Constitution ought to be preferred to the statute, the intention of the people to the intention of their agents.

Nor does this conclusion by any means suppose a superiority of the judicial to the legislative power. It only supposes that the power of the people is superior to both; and that where the will of the legislature declared in its statutes, stands in opposition to that of the people, declared in the Constitution, the judges ought to be governed by the latter rather than the former. They ought to regulate their decisions by the fundamental laws, rather than by those that are not fundamental.[6]

In spite of the fact that it has been firmly established and practiced for over 150 years, the power of judicial review has never met with complete approval. Periodic attacks upon its possession and use, based on allegations of usurpation by the Supreme Court, have been raised whenever a significant decision has disturbed the *status quo*.

The Significance of Judicial Review. The exercise of judicial review by the Supreme Court has important results. In the first place, it makes the Supreme Court arbiter of the federal system, resolving conflicts of power between the national government and the states. Its decisions afford the chief means by which the states are prevented from encroaching upon, or interfering with, the powers of the national government. Therefore national supremacy, established in theory by the Constitution, is given practical application by the Supreme Court, in spite of the fact that the Supreme Court is part of the governmental structure of the very jurisdiction whose authority it protects. In so far as the Court functions to protect national power from diminution at the hands of the states, it cannot be regarded as a wholly impartial arbiter. In the second place, the function of judicial review is one of the most important means by which rights of persons and property are protected against abridgement or denial by agents of government. The Supreme Court is, of course, the highest source from which determinations of rights can be obtained. In the third place, the Supreme Court, through its power of judicial review, acts to maintain the separation of powers within the national government. The doctrine of the separation of powers would probably have little meaning or effect if there were not in the governmental structure a final arbiter to decide on the authority of each branch. Through its authoritative decisions on questions of conflict between the branches of the national government, the Supreme Court confines each within its proper sphere of constitutional power and prevents unrestrained rivalry between them.[7]

INDIVIDUAL RIGHTS

The theories of John Locke furnished a philosophical justification for the American Revolution. They taught that every person, because he was a human being, had been given certain rights by nature which could neither be voluntarily relinquished nor legitimately taken away. These

---

[6] *Federalist Papers*, No. 78.

[7] More extensive consideration of judicial review will be reserved for the last chapter of this text.

"natural rights" were inherent in each individual, existed before government was created, and continued to endure after it came into being. Their preservation was the great end for which government was established. Their existence and possession by men, in other words, were in no way dependent upon organized political authority.

Although the theory of inherent natural rights once received wide acceptance, it has now lost much of its former appeal. Nevertheless, one still finds references to "natural rights" in columns dedicated to "Letters to the Editor." Few Fourth of July orators fail to mention them, and almost every schoolchild becomes familiar with them in the language of the Declaration of Independence.

The creation of conditions that will promote a maximum of individual freedom for the exercise of those rights is still regarded by the democratic tradition to be the only legitimate end of government; for freedom, and the conditions that foster it, are thought to be essential to the full realization of each individual's nature as a rational moral being. However, in spite of the support still given to the concept of natural rights, Locke's theory has now been replaced by another.

The Modern Theory of Rights. Rights of the individual are no longer thought to have come from "nature" or "natural law." Instead the rights that men possess are regarded as having been created, defined, and granted by law, and their enjoyment is assured by the "rule of law." It is through rights created by law that the freedom of the individual is guaranteed, made safe, and given specific content.

A state of liberty is still thought to be the most desirable condition for man; by means of his liberty he can formulate his own idea of what will constitute the "good life" for him, and seek to attain it by his own choice of means. However, a condition of complete freedom, characterized by the absence of all restraint and constraint, has probably never existed except in the realm of speculation. It does not exist in politically organized society, for every law restrains one person and constrains another. Obviously, then, law does not increase freedom. Yet, in the absence of law there could be no liberty and no rights. If there were no law, regulating the efforts of different individuals to attain their respective goals by whatever means they chose, chaos would prevail, and the weak would be at the mercy of the strong. Hence, laws which grant rights, and regulate the conduct of those who enjoy them, are essential if everyone is to be secure in the possession of his person and his property, and have any freedom at all.

The liberty which men who live in a free society possess is liberty under law. It is a conditioned liberty under which no claim of absolute right can be made; for a law which grants a right to one man imposes on other men a duty to observe that right, and upon its recipient the duty to respect the rights of others. Rights and duties, therefore, are reciprocal: one person cannot possess a right unless other persons possess a correlative duty against which the right can be enforced. A right without a correlative duty is meaningless. Since each person living under government possesses rights extended to him by law, each incurs the duty to respect the rights of others, and to that extent his freedom to act without restraint or compulsion is limited. Individual freedom on any other basis would probably produce only an absence of rights, a condition of lawlessness; for in the absence of a rule of law when the interests of two or more persons conflicted each would be required to use self-help against the others. The strong would dominate, and the only "right" would be that established by the rule of force. Whoever was strongest would automatically have right on his side and could claim whatever he wished; but whoever could overthrow him would immediately succeed to his right. The concept of right would be reduced to the level of nonsense and obedience would be dictated by prudence rather than by duty.[8]

Such vestiges of "natural rights" as remain today take the form of value judgments which have become incorporated into the law of the Constitution by judicial interpretation. They reflect the efforts of the Supreme Court to extend the protection of the Constitution to rights which *ought* to prevail in society, and to make them part of those that do. The attitudes of the justices suggest that they have conceived of rights, existing apart from the Constitution, which are so inherently fundamental and essential to a free society that they have had to be given special protection by its provisions. Although they are of special value to free men, they are nevertheless legal rights granted and protected by the Constitution. At one time not more than a decade ago these rights were accorded a special, highly preferred position because they were avowed to be "essential to the existence of a scheme of ordered liberty." They included the rights to freedom of speech and of the press, to peaceable assembly, and to freedom of religion, the rights to petition the government for redress of grievances, and to be free from unreasonable searches and seizures. Although they are guaranteed in the Bill of Rights, this does not expressly indicate that they are more important to personal freedom than are other "non-fundamental" rights; but they have been accepted as if they were.[9]

Nevertheless, it is possible to draw an analogy between Locke's "natural rights" and the "fundamental rights"; both groups have been singled out for special attention because they were felt to be necessary to the dignity and freedom of men. Yet, there is a real difference in the attitudes with

[8] The difference between the original and modern view of rights can be excellently illustrated by comparing the letter of Thomas Jefferson to Colonel W. S. Smith, November 13, 1787, with the comments of the Supreme Court in *United States* v. *Dennis* (1951), 341 U.S. 494, 501. Both concern the "right of revolution." See H. A. Washington, editor, *The Writings of Thomas Jefferson* (Washington, D.C.: Taylor and Maury, 1854), Vol. II, p. 317.

[9] This doctrine of preference, however, has been strongly challenged in recent years, and although never repudiated has been weakened to the point that there is doubt about its general acceptance today.

which the two groups have been regarded. Locke's were accepted as existing anterior to man and apart from him. That is to say, man had no part in creating them. He found them, like the air, already existing in the world into which he was born. When, through the exercise of his reason, he had ascertained what they were, he created government to make their enjoyment more secure; and he reserved to himself the power to replace the government if it failed to fulfill its mission. The modern conception of fundamental rights regards them as the creation of enacted laws which give them reality. It is now said that government, in order to permit maximum freedom to the individual, especially in matters of conscience and belief, *ought* to be restrained as far as possible from destroying the enjoyment of these rights by the governed. To the extent that they have received special protection against governmental abridgement, they have been shifted from the realm of the desirable potential to that of established freedom guaranteed by the supreme law of the land. They may be called "natural" rights in the sense that their possession and enjoyment is natural, that is, compatible, harmonious, reasonable, amiable, and proper to the full development of man's individual capabilities in a political community.

POPULAR SOVEREIGNTY

The ideal of popular sovereignty is synonymous with that of democracy, if by the latter is meant a form of political organization in which ultimate control of the governmental processes is vested in the bulk of the people to whom the governors are responsible. It refers to a government which is responsible and responsive to the will of the people in some meaningful sense.

The Constitution provided for the establishment of a representative system of democracy resting upon the consent of the governed. Although the framers of the Constitution distrusted democracy, government in post-Revolutionary America rested upon a broader foundation of popular participation than did any other contemporary political system. The Revolutionary War was in part fought to bring about democratic government, but the framers of the Constitution looked askance at democracy defined as full popular participation in, and actual, as well as theoretical, control over the political processes. They were willing to accept as ideals the Revolutionary assertions that all men were morally equal, that they possessed rights equally from nature, that they had an equal right to demand the benefit and protection of government, that legitimate government had to be limited in its power and based on the consent of the governed. However, these were ideals of an earlier and more dynamic time; they were excellent for a repudiation of British rule and for an assertion of the right to colonial self-government; but the sentiment of the framers was not that of 1776. The problem which faced them was to put together a permanent and operable system of government. They were willing to accept the theory of the Revolution, but they were unwilling to provide for much more than the appearance that they were implementing it in the new constitutional system. Government proceeding directly from "the people" was made the base of the constitutional system in the United States, but the Constitution also assured that the powers of government should be exercised by elected officers and representatives, not by "the people" directly. This attitude accounted for the inclusion in the Constitution of the devices and arrangements to guard against the excesses of popular democracy, and for the absence therein of the obvious manifestations of democracy, such as direct popular election of the President and senators, popular control of the amending process, and universal manhood suffrage.

Nevertheless, the framers of the Constitution did accept the ideal of popular sovereignty. They included in the Preamble the statement that "We, the People of the United States . . . do ordain and establish this Constitution for the United States of America." Their acceptance of this ideal was also revealed in their decision to submit the Constitution for approval by popularly chosen ratifying conventions in the several states. By that means it was given the direct approval and consent of the people. Both the Preamble and the method of ratification testify to an acceptance of the prevailing belief that all legitimate political power comes from the people, and that it is given by them to government to be exercised with their consent and for their benefit.

Representative Government. The national government is also a representative government. The framers of the Constitution did not provide for a system of direct democracy in which all eligible citizens could come together periodically to decide matters of policy and administration. Instead, the voters of the United States elect agents, legislative and executive, in whom they vest the power to make such decisions, and who they believe will exercise the powers of government in the general interest. The people delegate to their chosen officers the authority to act in their name.

Such an arrangement has obvious advantages. Historically, it afforded an arrangement of institutions which satisfied those persons who distrusted the ability of the ordinary man to govern himself intelligently by providing for the selection of individuals in whom confidence could be reposed. It also satisfied the mass of men who demanded at least the appearance of self-government. From a practical point of view, it made possible the extension of political democracy over greater areas and larger numbers of people than could ever have been possible under direct democracy.

CHAPTER IV

The Position of the States in the Union

PATIENT WAITERS ARE NO LOSERS.

*Uncle Sam—I ain't in a hurry;—it'll drop
into my basket when it gets ripe!*

ADMISSION OF NEW STATES

The United States began with thirteen members. That it would grow was anticipated by the Articles of Confederation, which authorized the admission of new states with the consent of nine of the existing ones. The Northwest Ordinance of 1787 established the basic national policy toward new states. Thus:

There shall be formed in the said territory not less than three nor more than five states. . . . And whenever any of the said States shall have sixty thousand free inhabitants therein, such State shall be admitted, by its delegates, into the Congress of the United States, on an equal footing with the original States, in all respects whatever; and shall be at liberty to form a permanent constitution and State government: *Provided,* The constitution and government, so to be formed, shall be republican, and in conformity to the principles contained in these articles, and, so far as it can be consistent with the general interest of the confederacy, such admission shall be allowed at an earlier period, and when there may be a less number of free inhabitants in the State than sixty thousand.[1]

[1] Commager, *op. cit.,* No. 82.

With these expectations and precedents before them, the framers of the Constitution provided:

New States may be admitted by the Congress into this Union; but no new State shall be formed or erected within the Jurisdiction of any other State; nor any State be formed by the Junction of two or more States, or Parts of States, without the Consent of the Legislatures of the States concerned as well as of the Congress.

By virtue of this authority the number of states has been increased from thirteen to fifty. Of those admitted since 1789, thirty-one were organized territories of the United States; one, Texas, was first an independent republic; five were composed of territory separated from various of the original states, for instance Maine which was formerly eastern Massachusetts. Thirteen states created the Union, but the Union created the other thirty-seven.

Procedure of Admission. Congress has never established a uniform procedure for creating new states. The effort to gain admission into the Union is usually begun by the people of the territory concerned, who petition Congress to pass an "enabling act." The "enabling" legislation gives congressional consent to the holding of a territorial convention, the purpose of which is to draft a tentative constitution for the prospective state. When ratified by a majority of the voters of the territory and approved by Congress, this goes into effect upon the proclamation by the President of the new state's admission into the Union.

Departures from this usual procedure are common, as in the admission of Alaska and Hawaii. In these cases the territorial legislatures many times unsuccessfully requested Congress to pass enabling legislation.[2] When Congress failed to respond to their petitions for enabling acts, Hawaii and Alaska moved ahead with their plans to gain admission to the Union. The procedure followed by Alaska was typical of the action taken in advance of congressional permission. Thus:

November, 1955. 55 delegates previously chosen by popular vote met for 75 days to prepare a draft constitution which was agreed to February 5, 1956.

April 24, 1956. Draft constitution for proposed State of Alaska was approved by the voters of the Territory. In the same election, two senators-designate and one representative-designate were selected to go to Washington to work on behalf of statehood. This procedure was followed by Tennessee, Michigan, Iowa, California, Minnesota, Oregon, and Kansas.

[2] The history of the Alaskan statehood movement, and the final petition by the territorial legislature for enabling legislation, are in *Hearings Before the Committee on Interior and Insular Affairs, U.S. Senate on S. 49 and S. 35, March 25 and 26, 1957*, 85th Congress, 1st session, *passim;* the Alaska Territorial Admission Act, July 7, 1958, is in 72 *Statutes* 339; Proclamation 3269, Admission of the State of Alaska into the Union, is in *Federal Register*, Vol. 24, No. 3 (January 6, 1959).

January, 1957. The Alaskan territorial legislature petitioned Congress for final time to pass legislation admitting Alaska as a state of the Union and seating the duly elected representatives.

June, 1958. Congress passed Alaska Territorial Admission Bill.

July 7, 1958. Bill signed by President. This act was the "enabling" legislation for Alaska. It provided, *inter alia,* for steps toward admission like those already taken. It thereby regularized them.

It required a referendum on and approval of the question: "Shall Alaska immediately be admitted into the Union as a State?" and of two propositions dealing with land and boundary provisions.

It further authorized the election of 2 senators and 1 representative in Congress to represent the new state if admitted. They were to displace those previously selected.

August 26, 1958. Referendum held as required. Admission approved by ratio of 7 votes to 1.

Nominations also were made for candidates for 2 senators, 1 representative, a governor, a secretary of state, 20 members of the state Senate and 40 of the state House of Representatives.

November 25, 1958. General election held. Results certified to President of the United States.

January 6, 1959. The President proclaimed Alaska to be a state of the Union.

January 6, 1959. The senators-elect tossed a coin to determine who should draw first to fix the length of terms.

They tossed a second time to determine who should be "senior" senator from Alaska.

January 7, 1959. The final steps anticipated by the first toss of the coin were completed as follows.

On January 7, 1959, Senators Gruening and Bartlett drew numbered slips of paper from a box, to ascertain the classes to which their positions should be assigned, according to the system begun in 1789. Senator Gruening, having won the toss of the coin, drew first and chose the paper numbered *three.* Accordingly, his term before having to stand for re-election was set at four years, to expire on January 2, 1963. In his turn Senator Bartlett drew the paper numbered *two,* with the result that his term before re-election was set at two years. Had either senator drawn a slip numbered *one,* he would have joined the class of senators whose terms will expire on January 2, 1964 and, therefore, would have served a full term of six years before having to seek re-election.[3] Hence, all departures from the usual procedure of admission were regularized when Alaska was admitted into the Union and its congressmen were seated.

Power of Congress. The authority of Congress over the admission of new states is limited only by the conditions imposed by Article Four of the Constitution. No territory has a *right* to be admitted into the Union,

[3] The complete account of this episode can be found in *Congressional Record,* 86th Congress, 1st session, pp. 6-8.

and Congress enjoys complete discretion over the process. If in its judgment a territory is qualified to become a state it will normally be admitted when it indicates a desire for statehood.

Many factors, however, influence the congressional determination. Legitimate ones include such considerations as the ability of a prospective state to maintain itself, and to meet the needs of its people and its obligations to the Union. The size of its population, its financial status, its geographical position, the advantages to it of statehood, and the effect of statehood upon the Union, are all proper subjects for evaluation. Others which are less easily justified may also be important. A desire to maintain a balance between free and slave states made the admission of one without the other virtually impossible. The relative strength of the political parties in Hawaii and Alaska was an important cause of their failure to gain admission. Yet, whatever may influence its judgment, Congress alone decides whether to admit a prospective state.

Congress uses its plenary power, when passing an enabling act or when approving the draft constitution of a future state, to impose conditions that must be met before statehood will be granted. The President may also make suggestions. If statehood is desired, the prospective state has no alternative except to comply with them or to wait passively in the hope that congressional opinion will change. For there is no way that it can compel Congress either to admit it or to withdraw the conditions.

Status of the States in the Union. This practice of imposing conditions has caused difficulties, for the principle governing the existence of the states in the Union is that each shall stand on an equal footing with every other. The basic question is: which, if any, of the conditions imposed upon a prospective state remain binding upon it after it has been admitted into the Union?

The question, then, comes to this: Can a state be placed upon a plane of inequality with its sister states in the Union if the Congress chooses to impose conditions which so operate, at the time of its admission?

The power of Congress in respect to the admission of new states . . . is not the power to admit political organizations which are less or greater, or different in dignity or power, from those political entities which constitute the Union. It is a power . . . "to admit new states."

The power is to admit "new states into *this* Union."

"This Union" was and is a union of states equal in power, dignity, and authority. . . . To maintain otherwise would be to say that the Union, through the power of Congress to admit new states, might come to be a union of states unequal in power, as including states whose powers were restricted only by the Constitution, with others whose powers had been further restricted by an act of Congress accepted as a condition of admission.

The plain deduction from this . . . is that when a new state is admitted into the Union, it is admitted with all of the powers . . . and jurisdiction which pertain to the original states, and that such powers may not be constitutionally

diminished, impaired, or shorn away by any conditions, compacts, or stipula-
tions embraced in the act under which the new state came into the Union,
which would not be valid and effectual if [made] the subject of congressional
legislation after admission. . . . But [in the latter] case such legislation would
derive its force not from any agreement or compact with the proposed new
state, nor by reason of its acceptance of such enactment as a term of admission,
but solely because the power of Congress extended to the subject, and therefore would not operate to restrict the state's legislative power in respect of any
matter which was not plainly within the regulating power of Congress. . . .

To this we may add that the constitutional equality of the states is essential
to the harmonious operation of the scheme upon which the Republic was organized. When that equality disappears we may remain a free people, but the
Union will not be the Union of the Constitution.[4]

Congress may impose any condition it desires upon a prospective state,
but there is a distinction between those which remain binding after the
state has assumed its place in the Union and those which do not. The test
of the enduring nature of a condition seems to be whether Congress,
through the exercise of its ordinary powers, can impose a similar limitation upon a state already in the Union. If it cannot, then one of that same
kind imposed as a condition of admission loses its binding force immediately after admission is completed. If Congress insists upon imposing a
non-enduring limitation upon a prospective state, the state becomes free
to ignore it as soon as it gains its full power and status as a state. Because the process of admission is irrevocable, neither Congress, nor
the President, nor the judiciary can do anything about the situation. Thus,
the states of the Union differ when compared in terms of the size of their
populations, their geographical extent, their per capita wealth, or any
other characteristic. Yet, from a constitutional point of view they all
possess equal rights and obligations as members of the Union.

THE NATURE OF THE UNION

Consolidated or Confederated? One of the major forces that determined the nature of the constitutional system was the emphasis placed,
in 1789, upon the rights and powers of the states. That emphasis clouded
understanding of the nature of the Union that had been established by
the Constitution, and long thereafter much respectable opinion held to
the view that in the American constitutional system sovereignty was
divided between the nation and the states.[5]

[4] *Coyle* v. *Smith* (1911), 221 U.S. 559.
[5] See *Chisholm* v. *Georgia* (1793), 2 Dallas 419; the Virginia and Kentucky
Resolutions; the Resolution of the Hartford Convention of 1815; the South
Carolina Nullification Ordinance of November 24, 1832; and the South Caro-
lina statute of March 18, 1833, nullifying the Force Bill. All may be found in
H. S. Commager, *op. cit.*, Nos. 95, 102, 115, 143, and 146.

With two sovereignties present in the system, conflict between them was inevitable, but the Constitution failed to state how clashes between them should be resolved. Some of the states undertook to exercise that authority for themselves. The most extreme view of the Union regarded it as founded on a compact between the states and the Union. Each party to the compact, therefore, could determine for itself whether an act of the other sovereignty violated its terms and, if so, what the proper remedy might be. John C. Calhoun insisted upon the right of any state to refuse obedience to an act of Congress whenever the act was thought by it to violate the Constitution. In his opinion the states were independent units which were in no way irrevocably bound to the Union, but as sovereign political units could withdraw from it if they so desired.

The alleged right of a state to withdraw from the Union was destroyed on the battlefields of the Civil War, for that conflict established beyond question that the Union is a consolidated, national union, and that sovereignty resides in it, and not in the states. The states are not free, sovereign political units able to withdraw from the Union.

It is needless to discuss, at length, the question whether the right of a State to withdraw from the Union for any cause, regarded by herself as sufficient, is consistent with the Constitution of the United States.

The Union of the States never was a purely artificial and arbitrary relation. It began among the colonies and grew out of common origin, mutual sympathies, kindred principles, similar interests and geographical relations. It was confirmed and strengthened by the necessities of war, and received definite form, and character, and sanction from the Articles of Confederation. By these the Union was solemnly declared to "be perpetual." And when these Articles were found to be inadequate to the exigencies of the country, the Constitution was ordained "to form a more perfect Union." It is difficult to convey the idea of indissoluble unity more clearly than by these words. What can be indissoluble if a perpetual Union, made more perfect, is not?

But the perpetuity and indissolubility of the Union, by no means implies the loss of distinct and individual existence, or the right of self government by the States. . . . And we have already had occasion to remark . . . that "without the States in union, there could be no such political body as the United States." . . . Not only, therefore, can there be no loss of separate and independent autonomy to the States, through their union under the Constitution, but it may be not unreasonably said that the preservation of the States, and the maintenance of their governments, are as much within the design and care of the Constitution as the preservation of the Union and the maintenance of the National Government. The Constitution in all its provisions looks to an indestructible Union, composed of indestructible States.[6]

Obligations of the National Government to the States. The Union is composed of states which owe it obligations under the Constitution. In return, the Constitution makes certain guarantees to the states on behalf of the Union. Hence,

The United States shall guarantee to every State in this Union a Republican Form of Government, and shall protect each of them against Invasion; and on Application of the Legislature, or of the Executive (when the Legislature cannot be convened) against domestic Violence.

Republican Form of Government. What is a "republican form of government?" The Constitution does not explain, or designate a particular form to be republican. The phrase clearly was used to differentiate republican forms from non-republican forms; but there is no indication that the framers of the Constitution had in mind any particular type to which all state governments had to conform. Madison, in *Federalist Paper* number 39, gave attention to the phrase:

If we resort for a criterion to the different principles on which different forms of government are established, we may define a republic to be, or at least may bestow that name on, a government which derives all its powers directly or indirectly from the great body of the people, and is administered by persons holding their offices during pleasure for a limited period, or during good behavior. It is *essential* to such a government that it be derived from the great body of the society, not from an inconsiderable proportion, or a favored class of it. . . . It is *sufficient* for such a government that the persons administering it be appointed, either directly or indirectly, by the people; and that they hold their appointments by either of the tenures just specified; otherwise every government in the United States, as well as every other popular government that has been or can be well organized or well executed, would be degraded from the republican character.

[6] *Texas* v. *White* (1869), 7 Wallace 700.

Moreover,

All the States had governments when the Constitution was adopted. In all, the people participated to some extent through their representatives elected in the manner specially provided. These governments the Constitution did not change. They were accepted precisely as they were, and it is, therefore, to be presumed that they were such as it was the duty of the States to provide. Thus we have unmistakable evidence of what was republican in form, within the meaning of that term as employed in the Constitution.[7]

The Constitution originally obligated the national government to help any state to throw off a form of government that *it* did not wish to retain; but the meaning has altered. It is now a requirement that each state *must* maintain a republican form of government. Whether it is doing so is not a question to be answered by the people of the state; the *national government* decides.

Which part of the national government is to decide? The Constitution gives no answer, but

. . . it rests with Congress to . . . determine whether it is republican or not. And when the senators and representatives of a state are admitted into the councils of the Union, the authority of the government under which they are appointed, as well as its republican character, is recognized by the proper constitutional authority. And its decision is binding on every other department of the government, and could not be questioned in a judicial tribunal.[8]

Protection from Invasion. The national government is obligated to protect the states from invasion. The phrase imposing this duty does not qualify its execution by requiring that national action must await an invitation from the state to render it assistance. The invasion of a state is at the same time an invasion of the United States, and there is no legal or moral reason why the national strength ought not to be brought immediately to the defense of the Union.

Protection from Domestic Violence. The Constitution also obligates the national government to protect the states against domestic violence, but recognizes that the states should maintain their own internal peace. Thus, primary responsibility for curbing riots, insurrections, and other forms of domestic disorder rests upon the states; but when a state is unable to cope with a situation the Constitution anticipates that the national government will become involved with it. The decision whether this should happen is left to the state authorities, for national intervention is dependent upon "application of the legislature, or of the executive (when the legislature cannot be convened)" of the state. Nevertheless, the President may decline to provide national assistance if, in his opinion, the state can and ought to restore order by its own effort.

[7] *Minor* v. *Happersett* (1875), 21 Wallace 162.
[8] *Luther* v. *Borden* (1849), 7 Howard 1.

However, the situations of domestic disorder which arise in the states do not always permit the easy application of a nice balance between national and state power. Must the national government remain inactive until requested by a state to take action when domestic violence has destroyed national property and disrupted national functions?

The entire strength of the nation may be used to enforce in any part of the land the full and free exercise of all national powers and the security of all rights entrusted by the Constitution to its care. The strong arm of the national government may be put forth to brush away all obstructions to the freedom of interstate commerce or the transportation of the mails. If the emergency arises, the army of the nation, and all its militia, are at the service of the nation to compel obedience to its laws.[9]

Obligations of the States to the Union.
Maintenance of Republican Government and Domestic Order. The states by virtue of their membership in the Union incur obligations to it, which are in part the guarantees to them viewed in a different light. They are obligated to establish and preserve a republican form of government; and the primary responsibility for preserving internal peace and order, and for protecting the lives and property of all persons within their jurisdictions, rests upon them.

Conduct of National Elections. It is their obligation to conduct elections to choose members of Congress and of the Electoral College. The states play such an important part in the regulation and administration of elections in the United States, by virtue of power which they alone possess under the Constitution, that if they refused to fulfill these obligations it would be impossible to select a President or a Congress. The national government could not function under the present arrangement without the cooperation of the states.

Participation in the Amending Process. The duty of the states to participate in the amending process, and all the authority necessary to its performance, are derived from the Constitution. The process, therefore, cannot be undertaken unless the states fulfill their responsibility to participate in it. Moreover, the participation of the states in the amending process is an essential part of federalism, and for that reason also the states are morally bound to act when necessary.

Obligations of the States to One Another.
General Considerations. Each of the states in the Union in some respects bears to the others a relationship which is similar to that found between the sovereign international states. They are legal equals and exercise their powers without being subordinated to a common superior. Each state in the Union exercises its own authority over a definite geographical area and population. In these particulars every state is inde-

[9] *In re Debs* (1895), 158 U.S. 564.

pendent of the others. Nevertheless, the states must have contact with one another, so that it becomes a matter of necessity for each to accept obligations toward the others. Hence, the Constitution provides for the regulation of several aspects of interstate relations.

Full Faith and Credit. The Constitution states that

Full Faith and Credit shall be given in each State to the public Acts, Records, and judicial Proceedings of every other State. And the Congress may by general Laws prescribe the Manner in which such Acts, Records, and Proceedings shall be proved, and the Effect thereof.

This section of the Constitution applies only to civil matters, and in regard to them it guarantees that the duly authenticated statutes and the "records and judicial proceedings" of one state will be given the same effect in the courts of another state as they receive in those of the state of origin. Thus, a will made under the laws of Michigan may be probated in the courts of Tennessee; a judgment awarded by the courts of Ohio may be executed in the courts of Maine.

The Congress by law has fixed the manner in which the public acts, records, and judicial proceedings shall be authenticated as follows:

The acts of the legislature of any State or Territory, or of any country subject to the jurisdiction of the United States, shall be authenticated by having the seals of such State, Territory, or country affixed thereto. The records and judicial proceedings of any State or Territory, or of any such country, shall be proved or admitted in any other court within the United States, by the attestation of the clerk, and the seal of the court annexed, if there be a seal, together with a certificate of the judge, chief justice, or presiding magistrate, that the said attestation is in due form. And the said records and judicial proceedings, so authenticated shall have such faith and credit given to them in every court within the United States as they have by law or usage in the courts of the State from which they are taken.[10]

The intent of the "full faith and credit" clause was to make the judgment of any state court in a civil action uniformly effective throughout the Union, and thereby to facilitate the conduct of business and social activities extending across state boundaries. On the whole, the clause has been of great benefit to the states, and a major factor in coordinating the separate state legal systems. It has made it virtually impossible for persons who flee across state lines to escape from their legal obligations. However, the states have shown considerable reluctance to recognize within their jurisdictions rights granted by other states to their citizens but not by themselves to their own citizens. Licenses and permits are not included within the obligation of the clause.

Brief special notice must be taken of the problem of the "full faith and

[10] *U.S. Code*, Title 28, sec. 687.

credit" clause as it relates to matters of marriage and divorce. The binding force of the clause has been considerably impaired, because the state of domicile of divorced, and divorced and remarried, persons is not required to give "full faith and credit" to "quickie" divorces awarded to them by the courts of states having "easy" divorce procedures. The state of domicile is entitled to determine to its satisfaction that the court of the state in which the divorce was obtained had bona fide jurisdiction over the action. Should it find to the contrary, it need not recognize the divorce. Of course, any subsequent remarriage would be invalid. The situation of doubt thus clouding many divorces and marriages has caused considerable hardship to individuals; but most states do not press the issue.

In general, however, the principle holds true that when a person acquires rights under the public acts, records, or judicial decisions of a state he may expect and obtain recognition of them by other states.

Privileges and Immunities of State Citizenship. The Constitution guarantees that

The Citizens of each State shall be entitled to all Privileges and Immunities of Citizens in the several States.

Note, however, that the clause applies only to citizens. Its purpose has been succinctly stated to be:

. . . to declare to the several States, that whatever those rights, as you grant or establish them to your own citizens, or as you limit or qualify, or impose restrictions on their exercise, the same, neither more nor less, shall be the measure of the rights of citizens of other States within your jurisdiction.[11]

It was undoubtedly the object of the clause

. . . to place the citizens of each State upon the same footing with citizens of other States, so far as the advantages resulting from citizenship in those States are concerned. It relieves them from the disability of alienage in other States; it inhibits discriminating legislation against them by other States; it gives them the right of free ingress into other States, and egress from them; it insures to them in other States the same freedom possessed by the citizens of those States in the acquisition and enjoyment of property and in the pursuit of happiness; and it secures to them in other States the equal protection of their laws. It has been justly said that no provision of the Constitution has tended so strongly to constitute the citizens of the United States one people as this.

Indeed, without some provision of the kind removing from the citizens of each State the disabilities of alienage in the other States, and giving them equality of privilege with citizens of those States, the Republic would have constituted little more than a league of States; it would not have constituted the Union which now exists.[12]

[11] *Slaughter-House Cases* (1873), 16 Wallace 36.
[12] *Paul* v. *Virginia* (1868), 8 Wallace 168.

What are the privileges and immunities of the citizens in the several states that are protected by this clause?

We feel no hesitation in confining these expressions to those privileges and immunities which are, in their nature, fundamental; which belong, of right, to the citizens of all free governments; and which have, at all times, been enjoyed by the citizens of the several states. . . . What these fundamental principles are, it would perhaps be more tedious than difficult to enumerate. They may, however, be all comprehended under the following general heads: protection of the government; the enjoyment of life and liberty, with the right to acquire and possess property of every kind, and to pursue and obtain happiness and safety; subject nevertheless to such restraints as the government may justly prescribe for the general good of the whole. The right of a citizen to pass through, or to reside in any other state, for purposes of trade, agriculture, professional pursuits, or otherwise; to claim the benefit of the writ of habeas corpus; to institute and maintain actions of any kind in the courts of the state; to take, hold, and dispose of property, either real or personal; and an exemption from higher taxes or impositions than are paid by the other citizens of the state. . . . These and many others which might be mentioned, are, strictly speaking, privileges and immunities, and the enjoyment of them by the citizens of each state, was manifestly calculated . . . "the better to secure and perpetuate mutual friendship and intercourse among the people of the different states of the Union."[13]

However,

Special privileges enjoyed by citizens in their own States are not secured in other States by this provision. It was not intended by the provision to give to the laws of one State any operation in other States. They can have no such operation, except by the permission, express or implied, of those States. The special privileges which they confer must, therefore, be enjoyed at home, unless the assent of other states to their enjoyment therein be given.[14]

By this exception to the general requirement of interstate "comity" there is no right of citizenship to participate in, or conduct, a licensed business or profession in another state. Accordingly, the operation of motor vehicles, the practice of law, medicine, nursing, dentistry, or any of the other licensed professions, or the holding of public office, are not covered by the "comity" clause. These are privileges granted by each state subject to its obligation to protect the health, safety, and welfare of its citizens, so that it may restrict the enjoyment of them although this involves discriminating against citizens of other states.

Second, every state holds certain forms of property in common for its own citizens. This property includes such things as bodies of water, fish, shell fish, wild animals and birds, and public educational facilities.

[13] *Corfield* v. *Coryell* (1825), 4 Wash. C.C. 371, Fed. Case 3230.
[14] *Paul* v. *Virginia, supra.*

It is the property of all; to be enjoyed by them in subordination to the laws which regulate its use. They may be considered as tenants in common of this property; and they are so exclusively entitled to the use of it, that it cannot be enjoyed by others without the tacit consent, or the express permission of the sovereign who has the power to regulate its use.[15]

Third, corporations created by a state are not entitled to the benefit of the "comity" clause when seeking to do business in other states. The clause does not diminish the power of the states to control corporations which do business within their respective jurisdictions.

Now a grant of corporate existence is a grant of special privileges to the corporators, enabling them to act for certain designated purposes as a single individual, and exempting them (unless otherwise specially provided) from individual liability. The corporation being the mere creation of local law, can have no legal existence beyond the limits of the sovereignty where created. . . . The recognition of its existence even by other States . . . depends purely upon the comity of those States—a comity which is never extended where the existence of the corporation or the exercise of its powers are prejudicial to their interests or repugnant to their policy. Having no absolute right of recognition in other States, but depending for such recognition . . . upon their assent, it follows, as a matter of course, that such assent may be granted upon such terms and conditions as those States may think proper to impose. They may exclude the foreign corporation entirely; they may restrict its business to particular localities, or they may exact such security for the performance of its contracts with their citizens as in their judgment will best promote the public interest. The whole matter rests in their discretion.[16]

But, foreign corporations engaged in interstate commerce may not be excluded from a state, or discriminated against, solely because of their interstate character.

Interstate Rendition. The Constitution also declares:

A person charged in any State with Treason, Felony, or other Crime, who shall flee from Justice, and be found in another State, shall on Demand of the executive Authority of the State from which he fled, be delivered up, to be removed to the State having Jurisdiction of the Crime.

The clause imposes a clear duty on the executive authority of each state. In 1793 Congress, without apparent authority to do so, enacted the procedure to be followed in performing the duty, but this act of Congress did

. . . not provide any means to compel the execution of this duty, nor inflict any punishment for neglect or refusal on the part of the executive of the state; nor is there any clause or provision in the Constitution which arms the Government of the United States with this power. Indeed, such a power would place

[15] *Corfield* v. *Coryell, supra.*
[16] *Paul* v. *Virginia, supra.*

every state under the control and dominion of the general government, even in the administration of its internal concerns and reserved rights. And we think it clear, that the Federal government, under the Constitution, has no power to impose on a state officer, as such, any duty whatever, and compel him to perform it; for if it possessed this power, it might overload the officer with duties which would fill up all his time, and disable him from performing his obligations to the state, and might impose on him duties of a character incompatible with the rank and dignity to which he was elevated by the state. . . .

And it would seem that when the Constitution was framed, and when this law was passed, it was confidently believed that a sense of justice and of mutual interest would insure a faithful execution of the constitutional provision by the executive of every state, for every state had an equal interest in the execution of a compact absolutely essential for their peace and well-being in their internal concerns, as well as members of the Union. Hence, the use of words ordinarily employed when an undoubted obligation is required to be performed, "It shall be his duty."

But if the governor . . . refuses to discharge this duty, there is no power delegated to the general government, either through the judicial department or any other department, to use any coercive means to compel him.[17]

Therefore, governors possess, and frequently exercise, discretion in responding to a request for rendition made by the executive of another state. Normally, requests are complied with, but refusals have been made because there has been a long delay between the discovery of a crime and receipt of the request for rendition; because the fugitive has lived an exemplary life as a respected member of his adopted community; or because there was reason to believe that the fugitive would not receive a fair trial if he were returned to the requisitioning state.

A "fugitive" is any person who flees the legal processes of a state whether or not he has been charged with, or convicted of, a crime. It applies to accessories, suspects, witnesses, and other persons who might flee from one state to another to escape the law. A person seized for extradition is entitled to no relief from the process, and once in the state from which he fled, may be tried for any crime, whether or not it was the one for which he was rendered up. Interstate "fugitives" often waive rendition and voluntarily return.

Because of the occasional failure of the interstate rendition process to function as it was intended to, attempts have been sought to make it more effective. A uniform interstate rendition statute has been available for adoption by the states for a number of years. It will, if adopted, establish a clear-cut legal obligation upon every state to honor rendition requests. In 1935, Congress attempted to lend its authority to the effort to prevent fugitives from avoiding justice. Relying on its power to regulate commerce among the states, it enacted the Fugitive Felon Law by which it

[17] *Kentucky* v. *Dennison* (1881), 24 Howard 66.

made the crossing of a state line in order to escape justice a federal crime. However, governors in the various states, jealous of their discretion and the independence of their political units, have shown little inclination to seek the aid of the national government to secure the return of fugitives under this law. Consequently, the purpose of the Fugitive Felon Act has been largely unrealized, and the effect of the interstate rendition clause remains only as great as the governors are willing for it to be.

METHODS OF INTERSTATE COOPERATION

Formal Methods of Interstate Cooperation.

Interstate Compacts. "No State shall, without the Consent of Congress, . . . enter into any Agreement or Compact with another State. . . ." Although this provision is phrased as a limitation, it is construed as a grant of power. In other words, the states may enter into compacts among themselves with the consent of Congress.

A compact is a contract between states which can be enforced in the courts; for although

. . . the circumstances of its drafting are likely to assure great care and deliberation, all avoidance of disputes as to scope and meaning is not within human gift. Just as this Court has power to settle disputes between States where there is no compact, it must have final power to pass upon the meaning and validity of compacts. It requires no elaborate argument to reject the suggestion that an agreement solemnly entered into between States by those who alone have political authority to speak for a State can be unilaterally nullified, or given final meaning by an organ of one of the contracting States. A State cannot be its own ultimate judge in a controversy with a sister State. To determine the nature and scope of obligations as between States . . . is the function and duty of the Supreme Court of the Nation.[18]

Uses of Compacts. Interstate compacts have two important uses. They are an important means for settling amicably disputes among the states, and they are of utmost importance as a means by which the states can cooperate to solve problems which are regional in extent. They provide a means by which the states can reconcile diverse interests, solve common problems, or settle disputes without invoking the intervention of the national government. However, they may not be used to deprive Congress of its constitutional powers.

The compact clause adjusts the treaty-making process employed between international states to the needs of the states in the Union. Thus,

If the Congress consented [to a compact], then the States were in this respect restored to their original inherent sovereignty; such consent, being the sole limitation imposed by the Constitution, when given, left the States as they

[18] *Dyer* v. *Sims* (1951), 341 U.S. 22.

were before . . . whereby their compacts became of binding force . . . operating with the same effect as a treaty between sovereign powers.[19]

The subjects to which compacts have been applied are varied and numerous. Boundary adjustments, determinations of water rights, flood control, interstate crime control, harbor improvement, stream pollution control, taxation, minimum wages, maximum hours, regional educational arrangements, conservation, and elimination of child labor have each been made, *inter alia,* the subject of compacts between states.

Consent of Congress. The requirement of congressional consent is not as inflexible as the language of the Constitution suggests. Consent may be expressed or implied, may be given to specific compacts or on a blanket basis, and may be granted before or after the compact is concluded. Implied consent may be derived from legislation subsequent to a compact to which Congress had not expressed its consent; it may also be implied from the failure of Congress over a period of time to disapprove a compact.

Do all compacts entered into by states require the consent of Congress? The "compact" clause employs general language to prohibit all compacts or agreements "without the consent of Congress." However,

There are many matters upon which different states may agree that can in no respect concern the United States. If, for instance, Virginia should come into possession and ownership of a small parcel of land in New York which the latter state might desire to acquire as a site for a public building, it would hardly be deemed essential for the latter state to obtain the consent of Congress before it could make a valid agreement with Virginia for the purchase of the land. . . . If, then, the terms "compact" or "agreement" in the constitution do not apply to every possible compact or agreement between one state and another, for the validity of which the consent of Congress must be obtained, to what compacts or agreements does the constitution apply?[20]

The requirement of congressional consent is a safeguard for federalism which is designed to protect the powers granted to Congress from encroachment by combinations of states. Therefore, any compact, which increases the political power or influence of the states affected, poses a threat to the full and free exercise of the delegated authority of Congress and must be consented to by it.

Evaluation of the Compact. The full advantage to be gained through use of the interstate compact has not yet been realized. The number of compacts entered into by the states during our history under the Constitution approximates about one hundred and ten, but only one of these has been accepted by every state. Prior to 1930 the device was used for rela-

---

[19] *Rhode Island* v. *Massachusetts* (1838), 12 Peters 657.
[20] *Virginia* v. *Tennessee* (1893), 148 U.S. 503.

tively unimportant matters such as boundary settlements, interstate bridges, and the determination of jurisdiction over interstate bodies of water. In the 1930's, however, interest in the interstate compact as a means for settling broader problems was revived. Since then, efforts have been made to regulate the production of oil, to facilitate interstate crime control, and to establish a uniform minimum wage among the states.

Refusal by Congress to give its consent has not been an obstacle to the more extensive use of interstate compacts, for it has been withheld on rare occasions only. Other difficulties stand in the way of achieving greater use of the device. The important interstate problems to which it might be applied are either controversial, or involve important economic interests of the states. In both instances, experience has demonstrated the difficulty, even the impossibility, of finding a common basis for agreement. The refusal of states to yield competitive advantages that they enjoy has destroyed the effort to establish uniform minimum wages, maximum hours and other conditions of labor by compact. The modification of existing compacts to meet changed conditions often proves to be as difficult as the process of negotiation to obtain initial agreement, for the legislature of each participating state must usually consent to the changes. Machinery for administering the compacts is difficult to create, and equally difficult to maintain. Although compacts are contracts that cannot be terminated at will by a contracting state, the problem of enforcement is a serious one. States that subscribe to agreements in good faith fail to fulfill their obligations. The aid of courts may be invoked to secure fulfillment of a reluctant state's obligations, but in the last analysis obedience rests upon the willingness of the state to comply.

For these and other reasons the interstate compact has not served, to the full extent of its potential, as a means of enabling the states to curb the growing concentration of power in the national government. It works well when relatively unimportant subjects are involved, or when no elaborate and permanent administrative machinery is necessary to implement the compact. However, until the states learn to overcome their jealousies and to subordinate their particular interests to the advantages of cooperative action, the device will continue to possess only potential importance for the relationship of the states to the national government.

Judicial Determination of Differences Between States. The Constitution provides a second method for promoting harmony among the states. By this method differences are settled by litigation before the Supreme Court of the United States. Accordingly, both Congress and the Supreme Court can act to facilitate the maintenance of good relations among the states, but the compact device has more utility for positive action than does resort to the Court. The compact is preventive; adjudication is remedial. In this sense, the settlement of interstate disputes by judicial action may be regarded as supplementary to settlement by compact.

The Supreme Court has indicated its preference for settlement by compact rather than by litigation:

> Control of pollution in interstate streams might, on occasion, be an appropriate subject for national legislation. . . . But with prescience, the Framers left the States to settle regional controversies in diverse ways. Solution of the problem . . . may be attempted directly by the affected States through contentious litigation before this Court. . . . This Court decides such controversies according to "principles it must have power to declare." . . . But the delicacy of interstate relationships and the inherent limitations on this Court's ability to deal with multifarious local problems have naturally led to exacting standards of judicial intervention. . . .

> Indeed, so awkward and unsatisfactory is the available litigious solution for the problems that this Court deemed it appropriate to emphasize the practical constitutional alternative provided by the Compact Clause. Experience led us to suggest that a problem such as [stream pollution] is "more likely to be wisely solved by cooperative study and by conference and mutual concessions on the part of representatives of the States so vitally interested in it than by proceedings in any court however constituted." . . . The suggestion has had fruitful response.[21]

Informal Methods of Cooperation Among the States. A number of informal methods of obtaining cooperation among the states have come into existence, a fact suggesting that the formal ones have not proved adequate to the task of establishing and maintaining harmonious interstate relations.

A major problem of the American Union is the multiplicity, diversity, and complexity of state laws. Each state enacts its own laws, but the Constitution provides no way to obtain desirable uniformity among them. Through the use of their powers over taxation, business, banking, commerce, and the health, safety, morals, and welfare of their citizens, the states have created among themselves a condition of rivalry and competition not unlike that which existed under the Articles of Confederation.

This lack of uniformity, the discrimination, and competition for advantage embedded in state laws affects many of the most important subjects of legislation and virtually every citizen who has occasion to engage in interstate activities. The diversity that exists in the laws of the states on the subject of marriage and divorce is well known, but similar diversity also exists in laws regulating such varied subjects as school attendance, insurance, banking, use of highways, quarantines, liquor, trucking, corporations, and factory safety, to mention only a few.

Appeal to the courts does not provide an adequate answer to the problem. When laws discriminate against interstate commerce or impinge upon a national power they violate the Constitution, but their validity

---

[21] *Dyer* v. *Sims, supra.*

must first be attacked in a court. The laws are numerous, litigation is slow and expensive, and diversity, *per se,* does not violate any constitutional provision.

Congress can enact uniform laws on subjects within its authority, but this remedy has two defects. It drains initiative and self-reliance from the states, and tends toward a further concentration of responsibility and influence in the national government. More significant is the fact that many subjects on which the states legislate are beyond the power of Congress to control.

This situation has produced a tendency among the states to devise means for promoting cooperation and statutory uniformity that are unknown to the Constitution. Several of these informal methods deserve mention.

Governors' Conference. The annual conference of governors is an assembly of the governors of the several states held for the purpose of discussing common problems, exchanging views and experiences, and promoting interstate cooperation. The Conference has no authority to take action. Its meetings are usually poorly attended and controversial problems are more often ignored than considered. The conferences have produced little increased cooperation among the states, but they have heightened gubernatorial concern that the states are losing too much power to the national government.

Sectional and regional meetings of governors are also held annually or occasionally. They have been more successful than their national counterparts, perhaps because the identity of interests is more obvious, the need for agreement is usually greater, the agenda is more concisely related, and the participants are more often personally acquainted. In this group are the New England, the Southeastern, and the Western governors' conferences. Others meet as the need arises to discuss the solution of some crisis.

Associations of State Officials. Numerous professional organizations of various types have come into being for the purpose of bringing together state officials who are involved in the same type of work. Their meetings provide opportunities for exchanging information and experiences, for finding ways to cooperate. Most of the organizations publish periodicals of professional interest and serve as research agencies. Uniform practices and the development of cooperation and of reciprocal relations are their ultimate aims. They include such familiar names as the National Association of State Purchasing Officials, the Conference of Chief Justices, the National Association of State Budget Officers, a similar one for attorneys general, and still another for secretaries of state.

American Legislators' Association. The American Legislators' Association has especial importance for the effort to secure cooperation and uniform legislation among the states. It is composed of participating members of state legislatures, and a number of administrators, who meet in convention each two years. Its purpose is to give attention to problems of interstate concern. To this end it has established the permanent Interstate Commission on Conflicting Taxation which maintains an expert research staff to study interstate and national-state tax policies and laws. All levels of government are represented on the tax revision council. Interstate bus and trucking regulation, crime control, and public welfare regulation have occupied the Association's attention. However, the Association and its assisting units are research, advisory, and study organizations. They cannot act to implement the results of their efforts, but must work through the law-making authorities of the states. They provide expert knowledge on technical questions which are likely to be the subject of state legislation, they seek to raise the standard of legislation, to provide forums for the discussion of regional, state, or national legislative problems, and through all of these seek to promote uniformity and cooperation.

National Conference of Commissioners on Uniform State Laws. The need for greater legislative uniformity has resulted in the establishment of the National Conference of Commissioners on Uniform State Laws. Each state, territory, and the District of Columbia, is represented by a team of three legal experts. The Conference is financed partly by appropriations from the states and partly by the American Bar Association. It operates through committees of experts who draft model state laws—which are approved by the general conference and then submitted to the state legislatures for adoption. More than one hundred such laws have been prepared, but very few have been accepted by every state.

The idea and advantages of uniform laws are attractive, but reality fails to conform to hope. Legislatures often destroy uniformity by insisting upon alterations as the price of adoption. State courts invariably create diversity out of uniformity whenever they interpret the various model laws which have been accepted.

A number of specialized organizations also work on behalf of uniform laws relating to their particular interests. The American Law Institute has published approximately twenty volumes of American law in an effort to instill order and clarity into the common law rules and doctrines applied by state courts. These digests should provide a firm foundation for uniformity of application and interpretation by the judicial systems of the states. A number of model codes have also been published to aid in bringing about greater uniformity in criminal procedure, evidence, and other phases of criminal law. Other organizations which seek the same end but which have met with less success include the National Association of State Aviation Officials, the National Conference on Street and Highway Safety, the Mortgage Bankers' Association, and others.

The Council of State Governments. The Council of State Governments is something of a parent organization to these groups discussed above. A board of managers includes a delegate from each state, ten elected members, and a number of *ex officio* members who include presidents of the national organizations of attorneys general, secretaries of state, state budget directors, state purchasing officials, chief justices, and the executive organ of the Governors' Conference. The executive director of the Council is also the director of the American Legislators' Association and the secretary-treasurer of the Governors' Conference. It is thus tied to these groups. The Council also provides services for them and numerous other organizations not directly related to it.

The Council of State Governments engages in research and consultations, studies problems of interest to the states, promotes regional and national conferences of legislators and administrators, and issues the periodical *State Government* bulletins, and the biennial *Book of the States*. The Council has taken over many of the functions of the older American Legislators' Association. However, neither the Council, nor the affiliated groups, possess any power to dictate policy to any state legislature or to any executive officer or agency. They give advice and make recommendations, the influence of which depends solely upon the integrity, expertness, and impartiality of those who make them.

Commissions on Interstate Cooperation. Within each state is a commission on interstate cooperation, usually composed of five members from each house of the legislature and five administrators appointed by the governor. The legislative members generally compose the standing committee on interstate cooperation of their respective chambers. Each commission works constantly on behalf of interstate cooperation to anticipate and solve interstate problems. The Council of State Governments exerts its influence and works with individual state governments through the commissions. Because of the composition of each commission, the Council can usually count on having important supporters in each political branch of each state government. Most commissions are active, well financed, and expertly staffed, but some exist in name only.

Withal, it must be admitted that the elaborate informal machinery for promoting interstate cooperation, and for strengthening the position of the states in the Union, has not yet produced the results which ought to flow from it. The states are just beginning to awaken to the need for cooperation and uniform legislation. Much of the machinery is less than twenty-five years old and has scarcely had an opportunity to be perfected or to make its influence felt. Much has been accomplished, but a greater amount remains to be done. However, the greatest obstacle to reform is often the difficulty of gaining recognition of the need. Once the need is admitted, results often flow rapidly. So it may yet be in the case of interstate cooperation and statutory uniformity.

THE CHANGING RELATIONSHIP
OF THE STATES TO THE UNION

Grants-in-Aid to the States. To a considerable extent the position of the states in the Union has been determined not by formal legal provisions in the Constitution but by a practice that has developed within the federal system. Theoretically the states have their proper sphere of power which may not be taken from them except by amending the Constitution. The national government theoretically may not use its powers to encroach upon and reduce the powers of the states. The powers of the states would seem to be firmly established. However, during much of our history under the Constitution, the national government has followed the practice of granting various types of subventions to the states; and out of this practice has developed what many persons feel is a threat to the continued existence of the states.

The aid thus provided has been in the form either of aids-in-kind or of cash payments. The use of money grants has increased to the point where it has virtually displaced aids-in-kind. In 1960 Congress, under the "elastic" clause, extended to the states over seven billion dollars to help finance about sixty programs. That sum represents over one-fifth of the total expenditures made annually by the states.

RECENT TRENDS IN GRANTS-IN-AID*
(By fiscal years, in millions of dollars)

	1955	1956	1957	1958	1959	1960
Total Grants	$4,595	$5,152	$6,468	$7,421	$9,590	$9,175
To state and local units only	3,149	3,463	4,064	4,932	6,457	7,011
To individuals only	1,446	1,689	2,404	2,488	3,134	2,163
INCREASE OR DE-CREASE—ANNUAL						
Total Grants	+7%	+12%	+25%	+15%	+29%	−4%
To state and local units only	+5%	+10%	+17%	+21%	+31%	+9%
To individuals only	+13%	+17%	+42%	+3%	+26%	−31%
Federal tax collections	$66,289	$75,113	$80,172	$79,978	$79,798	$91,775
Percent returned to states as grants	10%	7%	7%	8%	9%	12%

* Includes shared revenues and loans.
Adapted from *Congressional Quarterly Weekly Report*, Vol. 18, No. 16, p. 637; *Congressional Quarterly Weekly Report*, Vol. 19, No. 14, p. 615.

The Characteristics and Foundation of Grants-in-Aid. Money grants to the states are usually characterized by three features, although one or more of them may be omitted from a particular measure. First is that of apportionment. Grants may be made on an equal basis to the states, but they are usually apportioned according to a formula which is designed to take into account the differences of need existing among the recipients. Thus, grants may be apportioned on a per capita basis, or according to area, or the number to be aided, or some combination of these and other factors.

The second feature is that of a matching requirement. Congress frequently requires that the states put up funds to match all or some part of those provided by the national government. The ratio may be on a one-for-one basis, whereby the state supplies one dollar for each one received, or it may be higher or lower.

The third feature is the imposition by the national government of conditions which the states must meet in order to obtain subventions. The matching requirement is one form of condition; but the one which many persons regard as objectionable, and as a threat to the autonomy of the states, requires that they submit to administrative controls. Congress often stipulates that funds can be obtained only if the receiving states administer their expenditures subject to conditions and standards imposed by it. It has on many occasions stipulated the specific purposes for which funds could be spent; it has required that funds must be administered by personnel protected by a civil service merit system that meets national approval; it has prescribed that funds must be invested, and how that must be done; it has required that states must obtain advance approval of their plans for expending the funds granted, and submit to inspection and audit of their administration. The conditions imposed vary considerably from one program to the next. When conditions are imposed, however, the national government reserves the right to withdraw or deny aid to any state which fails to fulfill them.

Congress derives constitutional power for providing subventions to the states from a number of sources. It is authorized to tax and spend to promote the general welfare; hence, it can aid the construction of hospitals, provide aid for maternal care, and for assistance to the blind and to dependent children. It can regulate interstate commerce; hence, it can help with forest-fire prevention, reforestation, and work to control erosion in the watershed areas which provide water that fills interstate streams and makes them usable as instruments of commerce. It can finance the building of highways under either its power to regulate interstate commerce or to establish post offices and post roads.

Pros and Cons of the Grant-in-Aid. The grant-in-aid has provided the means by which more extensive and often greatly improved services can be made available to the people of the states. It makes possible the financing of programs on a nation-wide basis, and the transfer of funds from wealthy states to those that lack revenue and cannot provide adequate or sufficiently numerous services for their people. Moreover, the device offers

RANK OF THE STATES BY GRANTS-IN-AID RECEIVED
AND BY TAXES PAID
(Fiscal 1960)

States	Grants Received	Taxes Paid	States	Grants Received	Taxes Paid
Alabama	15	24	Montana	37	39
Alaska	42	45	Nebraska	33	30
Arizona	32	31	Nevada	47	43
Arkansas	27	35	New Hampshire	45	39
California	1	2	New Jersey	21	7
Colorado	26	26	New Mexico	31	37
Connecticut	30	12	New York	2	1
Delaware	48	32	North Carolina	14	18
District of Columbia	34	29	North Dakota	31	42
Florida	12	9	Ohio	6	4
Georgia	11	19	Oklahoma	17	25
Hawaii	44	40	Oregon	26	27
Idaho	39	41	Pennsylvania	5	3
Illinois	4	3	Rhode Island	43	33
Indiana	19	10	South Carolina	27	30
Iowa	22	22	South Dakota	36	42
Kansas	24	25	Tennessee	13	21
Kentucky	18	23	Texas	3	6
Louisiana	9	20	Utah	35	38
Maine	41	36	Vermont	46	44
Maryland	29	14	Virginia	23	15
Massachusetts	10	8	Washington	38	17
Michigan	7	5	West Virginia	28	28
Minnesota	16	16	Wisconsin	20	13
Mississippi	25	34	Wyoming	40	44
Missouri	8	11			

Adapted from *Congressional Quarterly Weekly Report*, Vol. 19, No. 14, p. 617.

a compromise between national assumption of functions and the continued failure of states to provide them at all or to provide them adequately. By bringing the states and the national government into contact, the device has done much to replace a federal relationship characterized by rivalry and jealousy with one characterized by cooperation. It places the superior administrative, technical, and financial resources of the national government at the disposal of the states.

Nevertheless, use of the grant-in-aid device has been subjected to strong criticism. Its opponents assert that it is only a means of enabling the national government to invade the powers of the states, in violation of the Tenth Amendment, because it induces them through bribery to give up authority over local matters that is theirs under the Constitution. The argument is that the subventions are so attractive that the states cannot afford to pass them by. Therefore, they accept the conditions imposed by the national government and subject themselves to its control over

RANK OF THE STATES BY PERCENT OF TAXES PAID
AND GRANT-IN-AID FUNDS RECEIVED
(Fiscal 1960)

State	% of Taxes Paid	% of Receipts	State	% of Taxes Paid	% of Receipts
Alabama	1.03	2.16	Montana	0.32	0.75
Alaska	0.12	0.60	Nebraska	0.64	0.91
Arizona	0.57	0.92	Nevada	0.20	0.25
Arkansas	0.48	1.31	New Hampshire	0.32	0.44
California	10.48	7.38	New Jersey	4.20	1.73
Colorado	0.92	1.49	New Mexico	0.39	0.94
Connecticut	2.11	0.98	New York	13.22	7.15
Delaware	0.55	0.22	North Carolina	1.46	2.17
District of			North Dakota	0.23	0.94
Columbia	0.69	0.88	Ohio	5.82	4.04
Florida	2.46	2.31	Oklahoma	1.02	2.07
Georgia	1.37	2.50	Oregon	0.89	1.49
Hawaii	0.30	0.45	Pennsylvania	7.08	4.36
Idaho	0.27	0.67	Rhode Island	0.52	0.46
Illinois	7.08	4.77	South Carolina	0.64	1.31
Indiana	2.38	1.87	South Dakota	0.23	0.81
Iowa	1.19	1.69	Tennessee	1.20	2.21
Kansas	1.02	1.53	Texas	4.43	5.82
Kentucky	1.12	1.97	Utah	0.38	0.85
Louisiana	1.23	2.75	Vermont	0.18	0.37
Maine	0.44	0.61	Virginia	1.75	1.65
Maryland	1.90	1.16	Washington	1.57	0.73
Massachusetts	3.40	2.67	West Virginia	0.77	1.24
Michigan	4.66	3.03	Wisconsin	2.07	1.76
Minnesota	1.68	2.13	Wyoming	0.18	0.62
Mississippi	0.50	1.50			
Missouri	2.34	2.84			

Adapted from *Congressional Quarterly Weekly Report*, Vol. 19, No. 14, p. 617.

matters beyond its legitimate authority. It is insisted that the constitutional position of the states will eventually be destroyed, and they will exist only as administrative areas of the national government. Moreover, the device forces wealthy states to support the poorer ones. It weakens the initiative of the states and makes them financially dependent on the national government. It encourages reckless and extravagant spending by both jurisdictions. It tempts the states into slighting services which are not aided in order to obtain funds to match grants for those that are.

Validity of the Grant-in-Aid Device. Withal, the use of grants-in-aid is a long and well-established factor affecting the position of the states in the Union. The constitutional status of the grant-in-aid is a political question, but the gratuitously expressed views of the Supreme Court can be easily summarized. The grant-in-aid imposes no obligation upon a state, but merely extends an option which it is free to accept or reject. Nothing is done or can be done under a grant-in-aid without the consent of the states. If the states suspect that the motive of Congress is the ulterior one of tempting them to consent to an invasion of their powers, they need only withhold their consent in order to escape the trap. States which elect to participate in grant-in-aid programs are not unconstitutionally coerced; they make the option freely. They suffer no invasion of their reserved powers in violation of the Tenth Amendment by accepting the conditions that Congress attaches to the grants. Moreover, it must be implied from its extensive use by Congress that it regards the grant-in-aid as valid under the Constitution.

Use of the grant-in-aid device does enable the national government to influence the conduct and content of state activities. It has produced attendant growth in the size of the national government. However, it also enables the states to undertake more extensive functions than they otherwise would be able to; and it leaves under their control the administration of aided programs subject only to supervision and assistance from the national government. It brings superior financial and administrative resources to the aid of the states. The device thus involves something of a paradox; it produces a tendency toward centralization of government, but it also serves to keep administration under the control of state and local governments. It prevents the further centralization that could be brought about by the states' failure or inability to respond to the demands of their citizenry.

Use of the grant-in-aid recognizes that many of the problems of present-day government are produced by forces nation-wide in extent, although their manifestations appear at the state and local levels. Illiteracy, lack of purchasing power, and poor public health are matters of concern to the states, but they are also matters of grave concern to the national welfare. Their causes and effects transcend the geographical limits and the constitutional authority of the individual states. Long experience has demonstrated that they cannot successfully be dealt with by the states separately; and the unwillingness and inability of states to cooperate leaves no alternative but cooperative national-state action. There is recognition of the need to preserve the identity of the states. The grant-in-aid device is far more valuable as a means of accomplishing that end than it is dangerous as a means of centralizing political power in the national government at the expense of the states.

The Changed Concept of National-State Relations. Two different views may be taken of the proper relationship between the national and state governments. The first sees them existing in a condition of mutual jealousy and rivalry, and places primary emphasis upon state power and autonomy. That view prevailed throughout more than one-half of our history under the Constitution, and has not yet lost all of its attractiveness. The national government was seen as a threat to the state governments, and its powers were limited by those that the states originally possessed. In consequence, problems of national scope and significance remained unsolved or were inadequately dealt with by the states acting individually.

The second view of the proper federal relationship is more aptly characterized as one of cooperation. It regards the states as parts of a political system in which the governmental machinery of the nation and the states complement one another. It recognizes that the tasks of modern government vary in nature and scope, but insists that the governmental system is competent to meet the demands. The task at hand may involve the authority of the states alone, of the national government alone, or of both working together. This is the concept which underlies the use of grants-in-aid. It also supplies Congress with the impetus to use its powers over taxation, commerce, the postal system, and other subjects, to make acts crimes against the United States which would otherwise be crimes only against those states that forbade them. It underlies the use by Congress of its powers to prevent persons from escaping the application of valid state laws by taking advantage of some technicality arising out of the federal relationship. It prompts state and national officers to work in close cooperation in many areas of mutual concern, such as law enforcement, agricultural development, conservation, and the protection and preservation of game. By these and other means the national government demonstrates its desire to cooperate with the states, and reveals that it has no desire to swallow them up in the exercise of its authority. Cooperative federalism has replaced the older federalism of suspicion, jealousy, and rivalry.

Growth of National Power. The American federal system has retained its form, but since its creation in 1789 the internal distribution of authority has undergone a quiet but steady transformation. There has occurred a persistent growth of the influence and authority of the national government vis-à-vis the states. Several factors account for this change, but it is not one that has taken place dramatically or at any one time. These factors include the following:

1. The emergence of an integrated national economic system transcending state boundaries and the scope of state authority. The number of interstate industries, commercial and financial enterprises, transportation and communications facilities, has increased to the point where none but the most localized endeavor is of solely state interest. In the last half century these economic activities have escaped the abilities of the states to cope with them; for economic areas of the United States today are not measured in terms of states but of regions, yet the power of a state to regulate extends only to the limits of its territory. "Big business," "big labor," "big agriculture," and "big finance" have brought within the ambit of national authority transactions and things that only a few decades ago were thought to be well beyond its most extended range.

2. The use of the amending power. Although only slight additional expressed authority has been granted to the national government by amendment of the Constitution, much additional implied power has been gained by interpretation and application of some of these amendments. The Fourteenth Amendment by itself and in conjunction with the First Amendment has been a great source of national supervisory authority over state activities. The Sixteenth Amendment, by freeing the income tax from the requirement of apportionment among the states, has made it available for regulatory purposes as well as for raising revenue. Their net effect has been to impose restrictions upon the states at the same time that it has broadened the base of the democratic process, and has thus increased the relative authority of the national government and has made it easier for the force of political democracy to be brought to bear upon Washington.

3. The superior resources of the general government. Whereas the capacity of a state to raise revenue and to incur debts is limited, the superior financial base of the national government enables it to call upon an almost limitless supply of income, and to borrow as the need arises. Its administrative machinery is, or can be, made adequate for almost any task. It employs the most up-to-date techniques in matters of personnel management, production control, organization, budgeting, and so on. Among its employees are experts knowledgeable and experienced in virtually every subject of concern to modern men and their society. In combination these factors enable it to respond to the demands of voters that the states themselves cannot possibly meet.

4. The grant-in-aid. The centralizing effect of this device, now commonly used to aid local as well as state governments, has been explored elsewhere and is therefore merely noted here.

5. The changed popular attitude toward government. Since the end of the last century the people of the United States have come to look with favor upon positive, active government. No longer, for most Americans, is that government best which governs least. They expect government to do things, not drift and flounder tossed about by the events of the time. An administration is judged by its program, and by its success in bringing about its enactment and implementation. Federalism is now viewed as cooperative, not competitive, and the Constitution has come to be regarded as a *grant* of authority, not a statement of limitations on power.

6. The impact of emergency. Two world wars, several recessions, one "Great Depression," and a continuing "cold war" have combined, over the years, to create situations calling for the exercise of extraordinary powers under conditions that have not admitted of the luxury of constitutional niceties. Each has required the doing of things, and the use of techniques and procedures, unknown to more orderly periods. Each has carried the authority of the national government into new areas, and has accustomed

the people of the country to the new experiences. Each period of expansion has been followed by a period of contraction; but the latter has never quite curtailed the new authority, reduced the expanded administration, or cut back the numbers of employees to the pre-expansion levels.

7. The broadened interpretation of the powers of Congress. Most important, perhaps, is the broadened construction of the powers of Congress by the Supreme Court. This amounts to a return to the doctrines of national authority which were developed by the Court under John Marshall between 1800 and 1835. A permissive attitude by the judiciary toward the programs of an activist Congress can easily result in the resolution in its favor of any vagaries or doubts about the scope of national power. The doctrine of implied power has given new meaning to interstate commerce and the power to regulate it, and to the taxing, spending, war, and postal powers.

By virtue of this expansion of national power it has become next to impossible in many areas of public policy to distinguish sharply between national and state spheres. Lottery tickets, disease-infected cattle, business, transportation, communications, insurance, finance, agricultural and industrial production, firearms, narcotics, slot machines and parts, kidnapped persons, civil defense, highways, hospitals, airports, water systems, sewage disposal, blind, aged, and handicapped persons, standards of quality of motion pictures and paperback books, working conditions of labor, employment of women and children, and regulation of wages and hours, to mention but a few, are subjects which, not long ago, were thought to be exclusively the concern of the states. But under the conditions of modern life they have acquired a relationship to the national well-being and interest that does not recognize state boundaries. The states remain the theoretical equals of the national government in the federal system, but their equality in fact has been greatly diminished.

CHAPTER V

Constitutional Limitations upon the States

'Well, of Course, It's Our Right to be Wrong.'

GENERAL CONSIDERATIONS

The Constitution establishes a distribution of powers between the national and the state governments that is precise to the extent that it specifies both powers and prohibitions, but general to the extent that neither is stated in detail. The extent and the meaning of the relative powers, therefore, must await application to particular situations before they can be ascertained, and in many instances they only become known after successive interpretations by the courts. In most instances their meaning never becomes fully established, for the circumstances to which they are applied, and which give rise to interpretation, constantly differ. Yet, some limitations on the states are intended to give greater precision to the powers of the general government or to confirm that they belong exclusively to it. Others protect individual or property rights. Some are found in the original body of the Constitution; others are found in the Articles of Amendment. Regardless of their purpose, or place in the Constitution, they go far to determine the position of the states in the Union.

Implied Limitations. Implied limitations upon the exercise of state power are derived from federalism, which assumes the existence of both national and state governments. Hence, the states may not act to usurp the authority of the national government, endanger its existence in any other way, or prevent the exercise of its authority by its lawful agents. If the states could do any or all of these things, they would be able to destroy the federal system.

LIMITATIONS OF THE ORIGINAL CONSTITUTION

The framers of the Constitution incorporated in the new plan of government several specific limitations on state power, declaring that

No State shall enter into any Treaty, Alliance, or Confederation; grant Letters of Marque and Reprisal; coin Money; emit Bills of Credit; make any Thing but gold and silver Coin a Tender in Payment of Debts; pass any Bill of Attainder, ex post facto Law, or Law impairing the Obligation of Contracts, or grant any Title of Nobility. . . .

No State shall, without the Consent of Congress, lay any Duty of Tonnage, keep Troops, or Ships of War in time of Peace, enter into any Agreement or Compact with another State, or with a foreign Power, or engage in War, unless actually invaded, or in such imminent Danger as will not admit of delay.

In general, these limitations upon the states reflect unhappy experiences under the Articles of Confederation (1781-1789), or during the colonial period. The Constitution's framers wanted to make certain that the new general government would be supreme beyond challenge in matters relating to foreign and military affairs, the internal monetary system, and foreign commerce. The stated limitations restrain state legislation on subjects entrusted to the government of the Union. They are subjects of common concern to citizens of all the states. Hence, the authority of the states to deal with them was expressly withdrawn or made conditional upon the consent of Congress. Other denials of authority set out in this clause were made effective against the states in order to protect individual equality and liberty, as will be examined immediately below. Care should be taken to distinguish between those powers that are absolutely denied to the states and those that may be employed with the consent of Congress.

Treaties, Alliances and Confederations. One of the main purposes of the framers was to concentrate in the national government all powers pertaining to the conduct of foreign relations. Therefore, many of the prohibitions cited here were intended to protect that authority in its plenary control of external affairs from usurpation and infringement by action of the states. The states were flatly forbidden to enter into any treaty, alliance, or confederation, for if these compacts were with foreign nations they would interfere with the treaty-making power that was conferred entirely on the national government.

Ex Post Facto Laws and Bills of Attainder. The states *and* the national government are unqualifiedly forbidden to enact ex post facto laws or bills of attainder, or to grant titles of nobility.

What is an ex post facto law?

I will state what laws I consider *ex post facto* laws, within the words and the intent of the prohibition. 1st. Every law that makes an action done before the passing of the law; and which was innocent when done, criminal; and punishes such action. 2nd. Every law that aggravates a crime, or makes it greater than it was, when committed. 3rd. Every law that changes the punishment, and inflicts a greater punishment than the law annexed to the crime, when committed. . . . All these, and similar laws, are manifestly unjust and oppressive. . . . Every *ex post facto* law must necessarily be retrospective, but every retrospective law is not an *ex post facto* law; the former only are prohibited. Every law that takes away or impairs, rights vested, agreeably to existing laws, is retrospective, and is generally unjust, and may be oppressive; and it is a good general rule, that a law should have no retrospect. . . . But I do not consider any law *ex post facto*, within the prohibition, that mollifies the rigor of the criminal law; but only those that create, or aggravate, the crime; or increase the punishment. . . .[1]

What is a bill of attainder?

A bill of attainder is a legislative act, which inflicts punishment without a judicial trial.

If the punishment be less than death, the act is termed a bill of pains and penalties. Within the meaning of the Constitution, bills of attainder include bills of pains and penalties. In these cases the legislative body, in addition to its legitimate functions, exercises the powers and office of judge; it assumes, in the language of the textbooks, judicial magistracy; it pronounces upon the guilt of the party, without any of the forms or safeguards of trial; it determines the sufficiency of the proofs produced, whether conformable to the rules of evidence or otherwise; and it fixes the degree of punishment in accordance with its own notions of the enormity of the offense.[2]

Those who wrote our Constitution well knew the danger inherent in special legislative acts which take away the life, liberty, or property of particular named persons because the legislature thinks them guilty of conduct which deserves punishment. They intended to safeguard the people of this country from punishment without trial by duly constituted courts. . . . When our Constitution and Bill of Rights were written, our ancestors had ample reason to know that legislative trials and punishments were too dangerous to liberty to exist in the nation of free men they envisioned. And so they proscribed bills of attainder.[3]

[1] *Calder* v. *Bull* (1798), 3 Dallas 386.
[2] *Cummings* v. *Missouri* (1866), 4 Wallace 277.
[3] *United States* v. *Lovett* (1946), 328 U.S. 303.

Titles of Nobility and Related Honors. The Constitution also limits the state and national governments by prohibiting the granting by either of titles of nobility.

To quote Alexander Hamilton:

Nothing need be said to illustrate the importance of the prohibitions of titles of nobility. This may truly be denominated the cornerstone of republican government; for so long as they are excluded, there can never be serious danger that the government will be any other than that of the people.[4]

No State Shall Coin Money, Emit Bills of Credit, or Make Anything but Gold and Silver Coin a Tender in Payment of Debts.

These prohibitions, associated with the powers granted to Congress "to coin money, and to regulate the value thereof, and of foreign coin," most obviously constitute members of the same family, being upon the same subject, and governed by the same policy.

This policy was to provide a fixed and uniform standard of value throughout the United States, by which the commercial and other dealings between the citizens thereof, or between them and foreigners, as well as the moneyed transactions of the government, should be regulated. For it might well be asked, why vest in Congress the power to establish a uniform standard of value by the means pointed out, if the states might use the same means, and thus defeat the uniformity of the standard, and, consequently, the standard itself. And why establish a standard at all, for the government of the various contracts which might be entered into, if those contracts might afterwards be discharged by a different standard, or by that which is not money, under the authority of state tender laws? It is obvious, therefore, that these prohibitions . . . are entirely homogeneous, and are essential to the establishment of a uniform standard of value in the formation and discharge of contracts.[5]

States may not issue coins or paper currency to circulate for ordinary purposes as money, for money so issued and circulated would compete with that issued by or under the authority of the national government. However, the states may issue certificates of indebtedness, such as warrants amounting to obligations against their treasuries, to pay their debts to persons or corporations when funds are lacking. They may issue coupons to their creditors which may be returned to the state in payment of future taxes. When returned to the state that has issued them the warrants or coupons are cancelled, so that they do not circulate as money in any normal sense. Hence, their use does not violate the Constitution, for the monetary powers of Congress are not endangered.

Obligation of Contracts. Until the Fourteenth Amendment became a part of the Constitution, the clause forbidding the states to pass any "law impairing the obligation of contracts" was the most important limitation

[4] *Federalist Papers*, No. 84.
[5] Justice Washington in *Ogden* v. *Saunders* (1827), 12 Wheaton 213.

on the exercise of state power that was contained in the Constitution. The "obligation of a contract" is that which binds the parties to the contract. Behind its force is the idea that state power should not be used to help or hinder lawful private interests. Neither party should be given an advantage over the other by a state's action. If a state violates that obligation the effect is to permit one or more parties to the agreement to escape without fulfilling its duty to the others, and this will inflict injury upon the latter. The state's power ought not to be used to destroy the relationship between contracting parties who have entered into it in good faith.

There is ample reason to believe that this prohibition was originally meant to protect only private contracts from abridgement by state action; but its scope was soon extended to include those to which a state was a party, such as a grant of land or the grant of a charter of incorporation to a business. However, the prohibition against state laws that violate the obligation of a contract is not an absolute one which is to be read with literal exactness. All the laws of a state relating to its subject, and existing when a contract is made, are part of that contract. Moreover, no contract can deprive a state of any essential governmental power, such as its power to protect the health, safety, morals and welfare of its people or its power of eminent domain. They must possess without major impairment authority to protect the vital interests of their people, even though laws to that end have the effect of modifying or abrogating contracts already in existence. Hence, the states can enact general laws to protect the public interests with the assurance that all contracts entered into thereafter will be subject to those laws. They can also reserve the right to alter any contract subsequently made by themselves, for the reservation is part of the contract and its alteration does not violate the Constitution.

Effect of the "Contracts" Clause on State Power Today. Although this clause has lost much of its restrictive force and is no longer the major limitation on state power that it once was, it still protects contracts from arbitrary impairment. However, what constitutes forbidden impairment has been narrowed to permit increased state authority. The authority of a state cannot be so restricted that it is rendered impotent, for the peace and order of society depend upon the existence of effective government. Therefore, the immunity of contracts from state power must be tempered by the presence of a government competent to make the existence of contracts meaningful and worthwhile.

Imposts or Duties on Imports or Exports. The Constitution states:

No State shall, without the Consent of Congress, lay any Imposts or Duties on Imports or Exports, except what may be absolutely necessary for executing its inspection Laws: and the net Produce of all Duties and Imposts, laid by any State on Imports or Exports, shall be for the Use of the Treasury of the United States; and all such Laws shall be subject to the Revision and Controul of the Congress.

Regulation of foreign trade presented great difficulties under the Articles of Confederation, for the Congress lacked adequate power to control it. As a consequence,

From the vast inequality between the different states of the confederacy, as to commercial advantage, few subjects were viewed with deeper interest, or excited more irritation, than the manner in which the several states exercised, or seemed disposed to exercise, the power of paying duties on imports. From motives that were deemed sufficient by the statesmen of that day, the general power of taxation, indispensably necessary as it was, and jealous as the states were of any encroachment on it, was so far abridged as to forbid them to touch imports or exports, with the single exception which has been noted. Why are they restrained from imposing these duties? Plainly because, in the general opinion the interest of all would be best promoted by placing the whole subject under the control of Congress. . . .[6]

If the states were permitted to tax imports and exports, they might be free to impose taxes so burdensome as to destroy the thing taxed. In turn this would destroy the revenue of the United States that was derived from duties on imports. Hence, this limitation realistically anticipated the fact

. . . that every state would, in legislation on this subject, provide judiciously for its own interests, [for] it cannot be conceded, that each would respect the interests of others. A duty on imports is a tax on the article, which is paid by the consumer. The great importing states would thus levy a tax on the non-importing states, which would not be less a tax because their interest would afford ample security against its ever being so heavy as to expel commerce from their ports.

This would necessarily produce countervailing measures on the part of those states whose situation was less favorable to importation. For this, among other reasons, the whole power of paying duties on imports was, with a single and slight exception, taken from the states.[7]

The "single and slight exception" recognizes that the states might desire to inspect imports and exports to ascertain and improve the quality of articles produced domestically to fit them for export, and to protect the people from injury and fraud by determining the fitness for use of imports. The states may impose and collect fees to defray the costs of conducting the inspections; but any surplus fees must be paid to the United States. State inspection laws are carefully examined by Congress to determine that they really are inspection laws and not schemes designed to raise revenue, or to discriminate against foreign trade in favor of local business and industry.

This prohibition applies only to foreign commerce. Its purpose is to make the authority of Congress complete in that sphere. It does not

[6] *Brown* v. *Maryland* (1827), 12 Wheaton 419.
[7] *Ibid.*

prevent the states from using their police powers to control the size, weight, purity, quality, capacity, packing, marking, labeling, or other characteristics of goods and commodities moving in interstate commerce. Other provisions of the Constitution protect interstate commerce from discriminatory and burdensome state actions.

Duty of Tonnage. A duty of tonnage is a charge assessed against a vessel according to its cubic capacity for the privilege of entering, lying in, or trading at a port.

If the states had been left free to tax the privilege of access by vessels to their harbors, the prohibition against duties on imports and exports could have been nullified by taxing the vessels transporting the merchandise. At the time of the adoption of the Constitution "tonnage" was a well understood commercial term. . . . And duties of tonnage and duties on imports were known to commerce as levies upon the privilege of access by vessels or goods to the ports or to the territorial limits of a state and were distinct from fees or charges by authority of a state for services facilitating commerce, such as pilotage, towage, charges for loading and unloading cargoes, wharfage, storage, and the like.[8]

The prohibition against duties of tonnage, then, is intended to strengthen the security of interstate and foreign commerce from obstructions and burdens imposed by discriminatory state action. Tonnage duties may be assessed *with* the consent of Congress; further, the limitation does not prevent the states from assessing charges, although measured by the tonnage of a vessel, which are collected as fees for services rendered.

LIMITATIONS ON THE STATES FOUND IN THE AMENDMENTS

Three amendments to the Constitution limit the powers of the states. Two of these pertain to qualifications for voting, and will be considered elsewhere in relation to that subject. The third is the Fourteenth Amendment, which states in part:

Section 1. . . . No State shall make or enforce any law which shall abridge the privileges or immunities of citizens of the United States; nor shall any State deprive any person of life, liberty, or property, without due process of law; nor deny to any person within its jurisdiction the equal protection of the laws.

This amendment was added to the Constitution in 1868 to protect the newly freed Negro in the enjoyment of rights which the abolition of slavery and the acquisition of citizenship had bestowed upon him; but its application has been extended far beyond the scope of its original purpose. Its meaning has been successively broadened by judicial inter-

[8] *Clyde Mallory Lines* v. *Alabama* (1935), 296 U.S. 261.

pretation until it has become the most important constitutional standard by which the validity of state statutes and actions is determined. These provisions of the Fourteenth Amendment give rise to more cases before the Supreme Court than does any other portion of the Constitution.

The quoted portion of the Fourteenth Amendment contains three distinct but not unrelated clauses. They are known as the "privileges or immunities," "due process," and "equal protection of the laws" clauses. Each has its particular part to play in limiting the activities of the states, but the "privileges and immunities" clause has been so narrowly construed by the Supreme Court that it has now virtually no practical significance. The "due process" and "equal protection" clauses remain the chief constitutional bulwarks against the abusive exercise of power by the states.

In this connection it is proper to state that civil rights, such as are guaranteed by the Constitution against State aggression, cannot be impaired by the wrongful acts of individuals *unsupported by State authority* in the shape of laws, customs or judicial or executive proceedings. The wrongful act of an individual, unsupported by any such authority is simply a private wrong, or a crime of that individual; an invasion of the rights of the injured party, it is true, whether they affect his person, his property or his reputation; but if not sanctioned in some way by the State, or not done under State authority, his rights remain in full force, and may presumably be vindicated by resort to the laws of the State for redress. An individual cannot deprive a man of his right to vote, to hold property, to buy and sell, to sue in the courts or to be a witness or a juror; he may, by force or fraud, interfere with the enjoyment of the right in a particular case; he may commit an assault against the person, or commit murder, or use ruffian violence at the polls, or slander the good name of a fellow citizen; but unless protected in these acts by some shield of State law or State authority, he cannot destroy or injure the right; he will only render himself amenable to satisfaction or punishment; and amenable therefor to the laws of the State where the wrongful acts are committed. Hence, in all those cases where the Constitution seeks to protect the rights of the citizen against discriminative and unjust laws of the State prohibiting such laws, it is not individual offenses, but abrogation and denial of rights, which it denounces. . . .[9]

Due Process of Law. The Fifth Amendment to the Constitution also contains a "due process" clause, identical in phraseology and similar in meaning and application to that of the Fourteenth Amendment, but one that restricts only the national government. Together the due process clauses protect all *"persons"* against state and national action in the enjoyment of their "life, liberty, and property;" and since corporations are recognized to be "persons" they too may claim the protection afforded against the actions of both jurisdictions.

Therefore, in the United States one's life, liberty, or property may not be taken away except when, and as, law permits. The complete meaning

[9] *Civil Rights Cases* (1883), 109 U.S. 3. Italics added.

of "due process of law," and the full extent of the protection that it affords, are unknown. It is often equated with the phrase "according to the law of the land;" but no one knows what that embraces, for due process has never been defined. However, it is not merely a summary statement of the Bill of Rights, although the conception of "due process of law" does assume that there are certain immutable principles of justice inherent in the idea of free government which no state can abridge. The scope of its protection is determined by the fact that the rights protected by it are of such a nature that neither liberty nor justice could exist if they were sacrificed. Whether a particular deprivation of right denies due process can be determined by weighing all the attendant circumstances in the light of their impact upon the values of the political system and the standards of decency and fairness which comprise our national standards of justice. Essential to these standards are freedom of speech, freedom of religion, freedom of the press, freedom of peaceable assembly and of petition, and freedom of the mind, for it is doubtful that liberal democracy could exist without them. Of a different order are: the right not to be tried without the aid of counsel; the right to be judged guilty only after a trial amounting to a real hearing, not one that is a sham or pretense; the right to be tried only on the charge for which one is charged; the right to be punished only as prescribed by law; and the right not to be subjected to physical or mental torture while in the hands of a public officer. These are rights the violation of which it is too shocking to our sense of decency and justice to permit. However, denial of trial by jury, of indictment by grand jury, of immunity from compulsory self-incrimination and from being twice placed in jeopardy for the same offense, are not violations of due process that are forbidden to the states because they are inherently fundamental to our notions of fairness and decency. Justice *can* result, although it may not always, in spite of their absence.

At the same time, *all* of these guarantees have been classified as privileges and immunities of citizens. The protection of the first group by the "due process" clause has done much to compensate for loss of the "privileges and immunities" clause of the Fourteenth Amendment as a safeguard against arbitrary acts of state governments. Not everything authorized by law conforms to "due process of law." That alone is "due process" of law which is suitable and proper to a situation and approved by the courts. Thus a statute which proclaimed that the property of X should be forfeited to Y would presumptively be part of the law, but no right-thinking man would argue that it was fair and reasonable and therefore consonant with the essence of "due process of law." Therefore, legislatures are not free to approve whatever they may desire, and by their fiat to declare it compatible with the "requirements of due process of law."

Types of "Due Process of Law." There are two types of "due process of law." The oldest and original guarantees that the procedures employed by agents of government shall be fair. It is known as "procedural due process" and controls *how* things are done. The second is concerned with *what* is done, with the substance, or subject of governmental activity; it is known as "substantive due process" and is employed to test whether authority exists to do whatever is undertaken. Often, however, it is extremely difficult to distinguish between the two types. The difference between the unreasonable and arbitrary enforcement of a law, and an unreasonable and arbitrary law, is not always obvious even to a court.

"Procedural Due Process"—Illustration. As a restriction upon the procedures that agents of government may use, the "due process clause" limits judicial and executive officers. Its most obvious application is its use to obtain fairness in the methods of police officers and courts. The following account needs no clarifying comment.

"The crime with which these defendants, all ignorant negroes, are charged, was discovered about 1 o'clock p.m. on Friday, March 30, 1934. On that night one Dial, a deputy sheriff, accompanied by others, came to the house of Ellington, one of the defendants, and requested him to accompany them to the house of the deceased, and there a number of white men were gathered, who began to accuse the defendant of the crime. Upon his denial they seized him, and with the participation of the deputy they hanged him by a rope to the limb of a tree, and, having let him down, they hung him again, and when he was let down the second time, and he still protested his innocence, he was tied to a tree and whipped, and, still declining to accede to the demands that he confess, he was finally released, and he returned with some difficulty to his home, suffering intense pain and agony. The record of the testimony shows that the signs of the rope on his neck were plainly visible during the so-called trial. A day or two thereafter the same deputy, accompanied by another, returned to the home of the said defendant and arrested him, and departed with the prisoner towards the jail in an adjoining county, but went by a route which led into the state of Alabama; and while on the way, in that state, the deputy stopped and again severely whipped the defendant declaring that he would continue the whipping until he confessed, and the defendant then agreed to confess to such a statement as the deputy would dictate, and he did so, after which he was delivered to jail.

"The other two defendants, Ed Brown and Henry Shields, were also arrested and taken to the same jail. On Sunday night, April 1, 1934, the same deputy, accompanied by a number of white men, one of whom was also an officer, and by the jailer, came to the jail, and the two last named defendants were made to strip and they were laid over chairs and their backs were cut to pieces with a leather strap with buckles on it, and they were likewise made by the said deputy definitely to understand that the whipping would continue unless and until they confessed, and not only confessed, but confessed in every matter of detail as demanded by those present; and in this matter the defendants confessed the crime, and, as the whippings progressed and were repeated, they changed or adjusted their confession in all particulars of detail so as to conform to the demands of their torturers. When the confessions had been obtained in the exact form and contents as desired by the mob, they left with the parting admonition and warning that, if the defendants changed their story at any time in any respect from that last stated, the perpetrators of the outrage would administer the same or equally effective treatment. . . .

"All this having been accomplished, on the next day, that is, on Monday, April 2, when the defendants had been given time to recuperate somewhat from the tortures to which they had been subjected, the two sheriffs, one of the county where the crime was committed, and the other of the county of the jail in which the prisoners were confined, came to the jail, accompanied by eight other persons, some of them deputies, there to hear the free and voluntary confessions of these miserable and abject defendants. The sheriff of the county of the crime admitted that he had heard of the whipping, but averred that he had no personal knowledge of it. He admitted that one of the defendants, when brought before him to confess, was limping and did not sit down, and that this particular defendant then and there stated that he had been strapped so severely that he could not sit down, and, as already stated, the signs of the rope on the neck of another of the defendants were plainly visible to all. Nevertheless the solemn farce of hearing the free and voluntary confessions was gone through with, and these two sheriffs and one other person then present were the three witnesses used in court to establish the so-called confessions, which were received by the court and admitted in evidence over the objections of the defendants duly entered. . . .

"The spurious confessions having been obtained—and the farce last mentioned having been gone through with on Monday, April 2d—the court, then in session, on the following day, Tuesday, April 3, 1934, ordered the grand jury to reassemble on the succeeding day, April 4, 1934, at 9 o'clock, and on the morning of the day last mentioned the grand jury returned an indictment against the defendants for murder. Late that afternoon the defendants were brought from the jail in the adjoining county and arraigned, when one or more of them offered to plead guilty, which the court declined to accept, and, upon inquiry whether they desired counsel, they stated that they had none, and did not suppose that counsel could be of any assistance to them. The court thereupon appointed counsel, and set the case for trial for the following morning at 9 o'clock and the defendants were returned to the jail in the adjoining county about thirty miles away.

"The defendants were brought to the courthouse of the county on the following morning, April 5th, and the so-called trial was opened, and was concluded on the next day, April 6, 1934, and resulted in a pretended conviction with death sentences. The evidence upon which the conviction was obtained was the so-called confessions. . . . The facts are not only undisputed, they are admitted, and admitted to have been done by officers of the state, in conjunction with other participants, and all this is definitely well known to everybody connected with the trial, and during the trial, including the state's prosecuting attorney and the trial judge presiding."

The state is free to regulate the procedure of its courts in accordance with its own conception of policy, unless in so doing it "offends some principle of justice so rooted in the traditions and conscience of our people as to be ranked as fundamental." . . . A state may abolish trial by jury. It may dispense with indictment by a grand jury and substitute complaint or information. . . . But the freedom of the state in establishing its policy is the freedom of constitutional government and is limited by the requirement of due process of law. Because a state may dispense with jury trial, it does not follow that it may substitute trial by ordeal. The rack and torture chamber may not be substituted for the witness stand. The state may not permit an accused to be hurried to conviction under mob domination—where the whole proceeding is but a mask —without supplying corrective process. . . . The state may not deny to the accused the aid of counsel. . . . Nor may a state, through the action of its officers, contrive a conviction through the pretense of a trial which in truth is "but used as a means of depriving a defendant of liberty through a deliberate deception of court and jury by the presentation of testimony known to be perjured." . . . And the trial equally is a mere pretense where the state authorities have contrived a conviction resting solely upon confessions obtained by violence. The due process clause requires "that state action, whether through one agency or another, shall be consistent with the fundamental principles of liberty and justice which lie at the base of all our civil and political institutions." . . . It would be difficult to conceive of methods more revolting to the sense of justice than those taken to procure the confessions of these petitioners, and the use of the confessions thus obtained as the basis for conviction and sentence was a clear denial of due process.[10]

The fairness demanded by "procedural due process" does not impose upon the states an obligation to establish and maintain *ideal* systems of police and judicial administration. It is not an inflexible test of fairness. It permits the adoption of new methods of police and judicial procedure as long as they do not deprive the individual of his life, liberty, or property without "due process of law."

"Substantive Due Process" of Law. The use of the "due process" clause as a test of *what* government can do has had a long and varied history. From 1875 to 1937 it provided a powerful and comprehensive weapon to be used against social and economic legislation, although there is little in their origin to suggest that either of the "due process" clauses was intended to apply to other than questions of procedure. During that period the courts placed serious obstacles in the path of legislative efforts to cope with new social and economic problems demanding attention by government, and "substantive due process" served as one of the chief sources of protection for rights of property at the expense of individual and general welfare. In the mid-1930's, however, the courts began to withdraw this protection and to uphold state and national regulatory and remedial legislation of the types that for many years had been declared unconstitutional.

[10] *Brown* v. *Mississippi* (1936), 297 U.S. 278.

Today, government is free to control virtually any aspect of economic activity the regulation of which is necessary in the public interest. Under our form of government the use of property and the making of contracts are normally matters of private concern which are free of governmental interference, yet:

. . . neither property rights nor contract rights are absolute; for government cannot exist if the citizen may at will use his property to the detriment of his fellows, or exercise his freedom of contract to work them harm. Equally fundamental with the private right is that of the public to regulate it in the common interest. . . . These correlative rights, that of the citizen to exercise exclusive dominion over property and freely to contract about his affairs, and that of the state to regulate the use of property and the conduct of business, are always in collision. No exercise of the private right can be imagined which will not in some respect, however slight, affect the public; no exercise of the legislative prerogative to regulate the conduct of the citizen which will not to some extent abridge his liberty or affect his property. But subject only to constitutional restraint the private right must yield to the public need.

The Fifth Amendment, in the field of federal activity, and the Fourteenth, as respects state action, do not prohibit governmental regulation for the public welfare. They merely condition the exertion of the admitted power, by securing that the end shall be accomplished by methods consistent with due process. And *the guaranty of due process demands . . . only that the law shall not be unreasonable, arbitrary, or capricious, and that the means selected shall have a real and substantial relation to the end to be attained.*

The Constitution does not guarantee the unrestricted privilege to engage in a business or to conduct it as one pleases . . . and the function of courts . . . is to determine in each case whether circumstances vindicate the challenged regulation as a reasonable exertion of governmental authority or condemn it as arbitrary or discriminating. . . . There can be no doubt that upon proper occasion and by appropriate measures the state may regulate a business in any of its aspects. . . . So far as the requirements of due process is concerned, and in the absence of other constitutional restriction, a state is free to adopt whatever economic policy may reasonably be deemed to promote public welfare, and to enforce that policy by legislation adapted to its purpose.[11]

Withal, the "due process" clause of the Fourteenth Amendment endures as a limitation upon the exercise of state power, but "substantive due process of law" is today primarily important as a restraint upon legislation and activities which impinge upon civil liberties.

Due Process of Law and Civil Liberties. The major protection afforded by the Constitution of the United States to civil liberties is that provided by the Bill of Rights, but the Bill of Rights restricts only the national government and has no *direct* effect upon the states. Therefore, prior to 1868, when individuals sought to prevent a state from interfering with

[11] *Nebbia* v. *New York* (1934), 291 U.S. 502. Italics added.

their civil liberties they were required to rely upon prohibitions in the state constitutions, or upon some relevant section of the national Constitution which was applicable to the states. If those sources gave no relief the states were free to impose censorship, to control religion, forbid public gatherings, suppress newspapers or other publications, shut off freedom of discussion, or to take any other prohibited action which the Bill of Rights prevents the national government from taking. In such circumstances aggrieved individuals could have no recourse to the courts, for no limitation on state power had been violated.

The "Nationalization" of Civil Liberties. The Fourteenth Amendment was added to the Constitution in 1868. Some people thought that the "due process of law" clause was intended to restrict state power in the same way that the Bill of Rights limited national power. This interpretation received no support; but the idea gained acceptance that *some* provisions of the first eight amendments were included in the concept of "liberty" that was protected by the Fourteenth Amendment. Those which have been "read into" the Fourteenth Amendment by judicial interpretation have been "nationalized." They are now protected against unconstitutional impairment by both national and state governments.

However, the Fourteenth Amendment has not been made to guarantee against the states every right set out in the Bill of Rights. Which ones have, and which ones have not, been "read into" that amendment? What is the criterion of selection by which it is decided which shall, and which shall not, be included?

There emerges the perception of a rationalizing principle which gives to discrete instances a proper order and coherence. The right to trial by jury and the immunity from prosecution except as the result of an indictment may have value and importance. Even so, they are not of the very essence of a scheme of ordered liberty. To abolish them is not to violate a "principle of justice so rooted in the traditions and conscience of our people as to be ranked as fundamental." . . . Few would be so narrow or provincial as to maintain that a fair and enlightened system of justice would be impossible without them. . . . The exclusion of these immunities and privileges from the privileges and immunities protected against the action of the states has not been arbitrary or casual. It has been dictated by a study and appreciation of the meaning, the essential implications, of liberty itself.

We reach a different plane of social and moral values when we pass to the privileges and immunities that have been taken over from the earlier articles of the federal Bill of Rights and brought within the Fourteenth Amendment by a process of absorption. These in their origin were effective against the federal government alone. If the Fourteenth Amendment has absorbed them, the process of absorption has had its source in the belief that neither liberty nor justice would exist if they were sacrificed. . . . This is true, for illustration, of freedom of thought and speech. Of that freedom one may say that it is the matrix, the indispensable condition, of nearly every other form of freedom.

With rare aberrations a pervasive recognition of that truth can be traced in our history, political and legal. So it has come about that the domain of liberty, withdrawn by the Fourteenth Amendment from encroachment by the States, has been enlarged by latter-day judgments to include liberty of the mind as well as liberty of action. . . .[12]

Limitation of Rights by Government. All rights of the individual, non-fundamental as well as fundamental, are subject to some valid control by government. Liberty is not license to do just as one chooses. One's right to freedom of speech does not justify slander or make invalid the laws providing for its punishment. Although the enjoyment of constitutionally guaranteed rights ought to be surrounded by stringent safeguards, the problem is one of balancing individual freedom and governmental power. The public interest can normally be presumed to be superior to a conflicting claim of individual right; but, to what extent can the overriding of individual interests be permitted in the name of the general welfare? If rights of the individual are uniformly sacrificed to what is felt to be the overwhelming common good, how long can the process be allowed to endure before the common good itself begins to suffer? Is the general welfare superior to, and different from, the sum of particular interests? When uniformity of belief is compelled in the name of patriotism, does a coerced expression of allegiance really increase the dedication of the conforming speaker? At what point does majority control of standards of public morality and decency cross the line between permissible regulation and censorship? To what extent should individualism, creativeness, and idiosyncracy be denied expression in the name of uniformity, orthodoxy, and public peace and order? Differences are always unsettling to some segments of society; if a majority is aroused should its members be allowed to suppress what is to them distasteful? Should "due process" incorporate *all* the guarantees of the Bill of Rights and make them effective against the states? What, if any, is the difference between the impermissible use of public resources to aid an establishment of religion and their permissible use to aid private citizens, as pupils at a parochial school? Where is the line to be drawn? On what basis? Does the First Amendment's declaration that Congress "shall make no law respecting an establishment of religion or the free exercise thereof" mean literally *no law* or merely no law except one that is felt to be justified by the public interest? Is the highest value of the constitutional system, with which no other can successfully contend, that of national self-preservation?

Use of Substantive Due Process of Law—An Example. May children whose religious belief forbids them to salute the flag of the United States be compelled by a state government to do so on the theory that national unity and their love of country will be enhanced thereby? Or does the

[12] *Palko* v. *Connecticut* (1937), 302 U.S. 319.

Fourteenth Amendment forbid it, because "compulsory unification of opinion achieves only the unanimity of the graveyard," if allowed to progress to its logical conclusion?

The sole conflict is between authority and rights of the individual. The State asserts power to condition access to public education on making a prescribed sign and profession and at the same time to coerce attendance by punishing both parent and child. . . . To sustain the compulsory flag salute we are required to say that a Bill of Rights which guards the individual's right to speak his own mind, left it open to public authorities to compel him to utter what is not in his own mind. . . .

The question which underlies the flag salute controversy is whether such a ceremony so touching matters of opinion and political attitude may be imposed upon the individual by official authority under powers committed to any political organization under our Constitution. . . .

The very purpose of a Bill of Rights was to withdraw certain subjects from the vicissitudes of political controversy, to place them beyond the reach of majorities and officials and to establish them as legal principles to be applied by the courts. One's right to life, liberty, and property, to free speech, a free press, freedom of worship and assembly, and other fundamental rights may not be submitted to vote; they depend upon the outcome of no elections. . . .

It seems trite but necessary to say that the First Amendment to our Constitution was designed to avoid these ends by avoiding these beginnings. . . . We set up government by consent of the governed, and the Bill of Rights denies those in power any legal opportunity to coerce that consent. Authority here is to be controlled by public opinion, not public opinion by authority. . . .

We can have intellectual individualism and the rich cultural diversities that we owe to exceptional minds only at the price of occasional eccentricity and abnormal attitudes. When they are so harmless to others or to the state as those we deal with here, the price is not too great. But freedom to differ is not limited to things that do not matter much. That would be a mere shadow of freedom. The test of its substance is the right to differ as to things that touch the heart of the existing order.

If there is any fixed star in our constitutional constellation, it is that no official, high or petty, can prescribe what shall be orthodox in politics, nationalism, religion, or other matters of opinion or force citizens to confess by word or act their faith therein.

We think the action of the local authorities in compelling the flag salute and pledge transcends constitutional limitations on their power.[13]

Clearly the enjoyment of individual freedom can produce consequences detrimental, even intolerable, to the common good. The line between private right and public interest *can* be crossed: a free press does not sanction criminal libel, nor does free speech sanction incitement to riot, obscenity, indecency, or immorality; *actions* which are offensive to public morality, such as the practice of polygamy, or detrimental to public

---

[13] *West Virginia State Board of Education* v. *Barnette* (1943), 319 U.S. 624.

safety or health, such as the handling of poisonous snakes to demonstrate religious faith, cannot be justified by a claim to enjoyment of religious freedom. The list of examples is endless, but the question remains: what standard, if any, can be formulated and applied with reasonable certainty to protect both the public and private interests?

Should those guaranteed by the First Amendment be given a preferred position at the top of a hierarchy of rights because they really are indispensable to democratic government?[14] Should a statute that is alleged to violate a claim of constitutional right be presumed to be void, so that the government must prove that it is valid? From 1938 to 1952 both principles were employed as guides to determine, under the Fourteenth Amendment, whether challenged statutes did deprive persons of their constitutionally protected liberties. Since 1952, however, both principles have lost much of their force, although neither has been formally repudiated—it is even held in some quarters that they are dead. If a state legislature anticipates the growth of a public evil or danger and acts to forestall it, to what extent can it, constitutionally, restrict rights of person or property? Must it wait until the evil is fully developed, the danger "clear and present," "substantial and imminent," or is it enough that the legislature should now recognize it as "grave," although its realization is only "probable" at some future time? Or, is it enough to sustain acts which restrict rights because their enjoyment will have merely a "tendency" to produce evils inimical to orderly government? By that standard a right might be constitutionally limited from evidence that its exercise would have a "natural tendency and probable effect" at some indefinite future time to produce harm to the public. Perhaps it should only be necessary that a reasonable relationship should exist between the legislative means adopted and the end to be attained. Then any state statute which was alleged to abridge a guaranteed right, however basic it might be to democratic government or to individual freedom, could be sustained if it was found to have a "rational basis." Or, perhaps the value of the public interest to be protected should be "balanced" against that of the affected right to determine on which side of the scale the weight of the Constitution rests.

The choice of private right versus public interest will always be delicate, for the questions raised are not capable of easy solution; and at the time of this writing the members of the Supreme Court are divided over the issue. Generalizations of this type are always apt to be unreliable to a degree, but it seems safe to say that one group holds to the balancing test—by which the value to the public of the ends that a regulation might

---

[14] *Beauharnais* v. *Illinois* (1952), 343 U.S. 250 was the first case to challenge the preferred status of First Amendment rights previously created by *U.S.* v *Carolene Products Co.* (1938), 304 U.S. 144; *Schneider* v. *State* (1939), 308 U.S. 147; and *Thomas* v. *Collins* (1945), 323 U.S. 516.

achieve must be weighed (balanced) against the loss caused by the regulation to the *entire freedom of individual action* within the body politic. If the former outweighs the latter, the challenged statute will stand; if the loss of individual freedom is greater than the public gain derived, it will fall. Obviously, then, the justices must decide in each case which shall prevail. The second bloc of justices, headed by Justice Black, holds that the First Amendment establishes absolute rights that neither Congress nor the states can limit. It generally reflects the belief that rights of the individual are superior to powers of government, and therefore tends to side with the former in cases involving political rights, First Amendment freedoms, and criminal law procedures. It is much less concerned with precedents and with limitations on the judicial function than is the first group, and believes the Court should use its power to protect individuals whenever necessary.

Equal Protection of the Laws. The Fourteenth Amendment, as previously noted, declares that "no state shall deny to any person within its jurisdiction the equal protection of the laws." This prohibition and its relationship to the "due process of law" has been clearly set forth, as follows:

> The clause is associated in the amendment with the due process clause, and it is customary to consider them together. It may be that they overlap, that a violation of one may involve at times the violation of the other, but the spheres of the protection they offer are not coterminus. The due process clause . . . was found in the 5th Amendment to the Federal Constitution as a limitation upon the executive, legislative, and judicial powers of the Federal government, while the equality clause does not appear in the 5th Amendment, and so does not apply to congressional legislation. The due process clause requires that every man shall have the protection of his day in court, and the benefit of the general law,—a law which hears before it condemns, which proceeds not arbitrarily or capriciously, but upon inquiry, and renders judgment only after trial, so that every citizen shall hold his life, liberty, property and immunities under the protection of the general rules which govern society.
>
> It, of course, tends to secure equality of law in the sense that it makes a required minimum of protection for every man's right to life, liberty, and property, which . . . the Legislature may not withhold. Our whole system of law is predicated on the general fundamental principle of equality of application of the law. "All men are equal before the law;" "This is a government of law and not of men;" "No man is above the law,"—are all maxims showing the spirit in which legislatures, executives, and courts are expected to make, execute, and apply laws. But the framers and adopters of [the Fourteenth] Amendment were not content to depend on a mere minimum secured by the due process clause, or upon the spirit of equality which might not be insisted upon by local public opinion. They therefore embodied that spirit in a specific guaranty.
>
> The guaranty was aimed at undue favor and individual or class privilege, on the one hand, and at hostile discrimination or the oppression of inequality, on

the other. It sought an equality of treatment of all persons, even though all enjoyed the protection of due process.[15]

The Problem of Statutory Classification and Equal Protection. The ideal of equality before the law does not mean that everyone must be treated exactly alike by the law. The classification of persons and things for different treatment by law is the essence of modern legislation. Different regulations control the insurance business than control the production, distribution, and sale of milk. Within the milk industry different regulations apply to the wholesale and the retail sale of the commodity. Equal protection of the law means only that differences of treatment must be reasonable, and not arbitrary, and must be pertinent to the attainment of a permitted end.

The application of the "equal protection of the laws" clause is sufficiently broad to make it a ready source of protection against state action. It may be claimed by "any person," citizen or alien, natural or corporate. It extends to the acts of all agents of state power and protects rights of property as well as of the individual. Moreover:

Though the law itself be fair on its face and impartial in appearance, yet, if it is applied and administered by public authority with an evil eye and an unequal hand, so as practically to make unjust and illegal discriminations between persons in similar circumstances, material to their rights, the denial of equal justice is still within the prohibition of the Constitution.[16]

Recent Use of the Clause. The "equal protection of the laws" clause has become one of the main constitutional limitations on state authority that has been invoked by persons subjected to the burdens of state discrimination. Its most dramatic use has been by opponents of racial segregation in public education. They have argued that segregated public schools are not equal and cannot be made equal. It is now firmly established that persons required to attend segregated schools are denied the "equal protection of the laws" to which the Constitution entitles them, because,

Today, education is perhaps the most important function of state and local governments. Compulsory school attendance laws and the great expenditures for education both demonstrate our recognition of the importance of education to our democratic society. . . . Such an opportunity, where the state has undertaken to provide it, is a right which must be made available to all on equal terms.

We come then to the question presented: Does segregation of children in public schools solely on the basis of race, even though the physical facilities and other "tangible" factors may be equal, deprive the children of the minority group of equal educational opportunities? We believe that it does.

[15] *Truax* v. *Corrigan* (1921), 257 U.S. 312.
[16] *Yick Wo* v. *Hopkins* (1886), 118 U.S. 356.

. . . To separate them from others of similar age and qualifications solely because of their race generates a feeling of inferiority as to their status in the community that may affect their hearts and minds in a way unlikely ever to be undone. . . .

"Segregation of white and colored children in public schools has a detrimental effect upon the colored children. The impact is greater when it has the sanction of the law; for the policy of separating the races is usually interpreted as denoting the inferiority of the Negro group. A sense of inferiority affects the motivation of a child to learn. Segregation with the sanction of law, therefore, has a tendency to retard the educational and mental development of Negro children and to deprive them of some of the benefits they would receive in a racially integrated school system." . . .

We conclude that in the field of public education the doctrine of "separate but equal" has no place. Separate educational facilities are inherently unequal. Therefore, we hold that the plaintiffs and others similarly situated for whom the actions have been brought are, by reason of the segregation complained of, deprived of the equal protection of the laws guaranteed by the Fourteenth Amendment.[17]

The "equal protection of the laws" clause has also done yeoman service in the struggle to end discrimination against Negroes in voting, to abolish restrictive covenants directed against racial and religious groups, to invalidate state statutes designed to discriminate against aliens, and to end the exclusion of Negroes from grand and petit juries. It has emerged after an inauspicious beginning, and the passage of many years, as one of the most important constitutional limitations applicable to state authority.

IN CONCLUSION

Several points deserve a few words of comment in conclusion of this subject. First, the constitutional limitations on state power have been successfully used to instill a reasonable degree of uniformity of principle, respecting rights of persons and property, into the laws of the several states. The process of developing and refining these principles never ends. Withal, the attribute of flexibility remains. The meaning and content of liberty are seldom the same for very long. The ideals of "fairness," "reasonableness," "equality," continue from decade to decade, but the specific content of each ideal varies as the values which men accept, and for which they demand protection, change.

Second, the extent of the uniformity thus developed must not be exaggerated. State courts, legislatures, and executive agents are not required to follow the decisions of national courts, even those of the Supreme Court. Many state courts do; some do not. Legislatures normally exercise

[17] *Brown* v. *Board of Education of Topeka* (1954), 347 U.S. 483.

reasonable care to avoid enacting statutes which conflict with the national Constitution; yet, such laws are continually passed. No one knows how many unconstitutional ones escape detection because their validity is never challenged in a court. Executive agents observe, for the most part, the constitutional rules of the process of governing; yet, many of their actions have violated some limitation on state power, and there is no reason to suppose that every instance of invalid executive action is detected. These are weaknesses in the protection of personal and property rights which are inherent in the fallibility of human nature and the complexities and divided responsibilities of federalism. They go far to counteract the uniformity of state action taken in accord with agreed-upon fundamental principles.

Third, the protection of rights of person and property depends in the last analysis more upon public opinion than upon legal guarantees. Legal limitations reflect the force of public opinion. They are part of the "law of the land" because they embrace values which are thought to be worthy of protection, because most men comprehend the correctness of their commands, and render obedience out of a sense of duty. Should their claim to obedience lose popular acceptance, the fact that they are formally part of the "law of the land" will not save them from extensive disregard and violation. The judiciary does much to determine the position and power of the states in the Union, but behind the decisions of every court stands the consent of the people and the force of public opinion. This gives value and reality to the existing system of rights in the United States. Without its support constitutional safeguards would be little more than paper limitations.

CHAPTER VI

Constitutional Limitations on the
Powers of the National Government

IT IS THE
RIGHT
OF EVERY MAN
TO BE TRIED
BY A JURY
OF HIS
PEERS.
BLACKSTONE

The intelligent jury

GENERAL CONSIDERATIONS

The original Constitution contained no bill of rights, and the omission nearly caused its rejection by the state ratifying conventions. Insistence upon a bill of rights guaranteed against the national government reflected the fear that a strong central government would revive the grievances that had been suffered at the hands of the British rulers, and also reflected a realization that an overpowering legislature was no better than an over-powering executive. The demand for greater security for individual rights was rooted in theories of social contract, natural law, natural rights, individual equality, popular sovereignty, and limited government, in state bills or declarations of rights, and in the idea of a written constitution for a national government, that granted powers to it but imposed limitations upon their exercise.

Thus, a primary consideration was the belief that liberty consisted of freedom *from* government. To the minds of many men that government was best which interfered least with freedom of individual action. This attitude is far from extinct today, but the general tendency of the American people in recent years has been to look to government for aid in securing the "good life." Today most men accept the idea of freedom *under* government. The important thing, however, is that the value of liberty as a foundation of the political system should be left undiminished, not that the specific content of liberty should be left unaltered in the face of a dynamic society. A static liberty in a changing society would be almost as bad as no liberty at all.

In recent decades there has occurred in the United States a heartening revival of interest in the subject of individual freedom. Certain highly questionable practices and conditions at home, and the object lessons of modern totalitarianism, have done much to induce the public conscience to re-evaluate the *status quo.* Government is increasingly accepted as the guardian of individual and group freedom, especially that of minority groups, from inroads made in the guise of majority rule. Majority rule and minority rights are frequently at war. The public in general has become aware that the realities of American government fall short of the ideals which are presumed to lie at its foundation.

The national government is limited to the exercise of its delegated powers, but it is also restricted by other limitations, some expressed in, and others implied from, the Constitution of the United States. The limitations imposed upon the national government by the Constitution are either (a) derived from the federal nature of the political system or (b) stated expressly in the fundamental law in the form of particular prohibitions.

Limitations Arising From the Federal Nature of the American Political System. The only *inherent* limitation upon the power of the national government arises from the fact that all the powers held by government are divided in keeping with federalism. Therefore, it is limited to the exercise of those powers which are delegated to it. However, it should be emphasized that the exercise of national power is not limited by the exercise of a state power with which it comes into conflict. An *implied* limitation arises from federalism: the national government may not exercise its powers in a manner that either destroys the states as political units or impairs the performance by them of essential governmental functions. The national government may not employ its powers to destroy the federal nature of the governmental system.

Particular Limitations of the Constitution. There are numerous particular limitations upon national power written into the Constitution of the United States. They reflect value judgments made about powers which the people feel that the national government should not exercise. They either withdraw a stipulated power from national authority or resist its exercise in a particular manner. Except in the cases relating to "due process of law," ex post facto laws and bills of attainder, and titles of nobility, which were considered in the previous chapter, they do not apply to the states. Thus, the power of the national government is both limited and defined by the principles (1) that it may exercise only that authority which is delegated to it by the Constitution and (2) that its exercise may not violate a constitutional limitation either expressed or implied.

LIMITATIONS IN THE BODY OF THE CONSTITUTION

Habeas Corpus.

The Privilege of the Writ of Habeas Corpus shall not be suspended, unless when in Cases of Rebellion or Invasion the public Safety may require it.

What is the writ of habeas corpus, and of what value is it? This writ is an order issued by a court and directed to a police or other officer of government who has taken a person into custody and detained him. The order directs the detaining officer to bring the detained person before the court at a stipulated time, and to demonstrate to its satisfaction that there is legal justification for the detention. If the arresting officer cannot do so, the Court will order his immediate release. However, if the detaining officer can justify his action, the court will permit continued custody.

The ability of an individual, who suddenly finds himself taken into custody by an agent of government, to invoke the privilege of the writ is an important means of safeguarding his personal liberty. He may obtain a writ himself, if he is permitted to do so by his captors, or, if not, it may be obtained on his behalf by a friend, relative, or lawyer. If the spirit of the law-enforcement process is not violated by police-state methods on the part of the detaining officers, the privilege of the writ of habeas corpus remains as one of the most important safeguards against arbitrary, and illegal, invasions of personal freedom. Resort to the privilege gives a prisoner the right to have a judicial inquiry made by a court of the United States into the truth and substance of the causes of his imprisonment.

Suspension of the Privilege. The clause limits the power of the national government to suspend the privilege in question, although it authorizes suspension under specified circumstances. However, it fails to state what authority shall exercise this power to suspend the privilege. Nevertheless, the principle seems firmly established that only Congress can suspend, or authorize suspension of, the privilege of the writ of habeas corpus.[1]

[1] *Ex parte Bollman* and *Ex parte Swarthout* (1807), 4 Cranch 75.

Treason. Treason is the only crime defined in the Constitution.[2]

The idea that loyalty will ultimately be given to a government only so long as it deserves loyalty and that opposition to its abuses is not treason has made our government tolerant of opposition based on differences of opinion that in some parts of the world would have kept the hangman busy. But the basic law of treason in this country was framed by men who . . . were taught by experience and by history to fear abuse of the treason charge almost as much as they feared treason itself.

Historical materials . . . show two kinds of dangers against which the framers were concerned to guard the treason offense: (1) perversion by established authority to repress peaceful political opposition; and (2) conviction of the innocent as a result of perjury, passion, or inadequate evidence. The first danger could be diminished by closely circumscribing the kind of conduct which should be treason—making the constitutional definition exclusive, making it clear, and making the offense one not susceptible of being inferred from all sorts of insubordinations. The second danger lay in the manner of trial and was one which would be diminished mainly by procedural requirements. . . . The words of the Constitution were chosen . . . to make the proof of acts that convict of treason as sure as trial processes may be.[3]

Definition of Treason. To guard against the possibility that charges of treason would be wrongfully employed, the framers of the Constitution defined the crime of treason in narrow and specific language. Thus:

Treason against the United States shall consist only in levying War against them, or in adhering to their Enemies, giving them Aid and Comfort. . . .

To constitute the specific crime of treason by making war it must be actually levied against the United States. However reprehensible may be the crime of conspiring to subvert by force the government of our country, such a conspiracy is not treason. To conspire to levy war, and actually to levy war, are distinct offenses. The first must be brought into open action by the assemblage of men for a purpose treasonable in itself, or the fact of levying cannot have been committed.[4]

Treason may also consist in adhering to the enemy, "giving them Aid and Comfort." This does not constitute a waging of war but it does amount to a betrayal of allegiance to one's country. This type of treason

. . . consists of two elements: adherence to the enemy; and rendering him aid and comfort. A citizen intellectually or emotionally may favor the enemy and harbor sympathies or convictions disloyal to this country's policy or interest, but so long as he commits no act of aid and comfort to the enemy, there is no treason. On the other hand, a citizen may take actions which do aid and comfort the

[2] Treason can also be committed by an alien against the country of his domicile.
[3] *United States* v. *Cramer* (1945), 325 U.S. 1.
[4] See *Ex parte Bollman* (1807), *supra.*

enemy—making a speech critical of the government or opposing its measures, profiteering, striking in defense plants or essential work, and the hundred other things which impair our cohesion and diminish our strength—but, if there is no adherence to the enemy in this, if there is no intent to betray, there is no treason.[5]

Trial of Treason.

Having thus by definition made treason consist of something outward and visible and capable of direct proof, the framers turned to safeguarding procedures of trial and ordained that "No person shall be convicted of Treason unless on the Testimony of two witnesses to the same overt Act, or on Confession in open Court." This repeats in procedural terms the concept that thoughts and attitudes alone cannot make a treason. . . .

While to prove giving of aid and comfort would require the prosecution to show actions and deeds, if the Constitution stopped there, such acts could be inferred from circumstantial evidence. This the framers thought would not do. So they added what in effect is a command that the overt acts must be established by direct evidence, and the direct testimony must be that of two witnesses instead of one. . . . Of course, the overt acts of aid and comfort must be intentional as distinguished from merely negligent or undesigned ones. . . . But to make treason the defendant not only must intend the act, but he must intend to betray his country by means of the act. . . . Every act, movement, deed, and word of the defendant charged to constitute treason must be supported by the testimony of two witnesses.[6]

Corruption of the Blood. The treason clause not only deprives Congress of the power to define treason, but also restricts its authority to provide punishment for that crime. Thus:

The Congress shall have Power to declare the Punishment of Treason, but no Attainder of Treason shall work Corruption of Blood, or Forfeiture except during the Life of the Person attainted.

In explanation of this provision it may be said that

In England, attainders of treason worked corruption of blood and perpetual forfeiture of the estate of the person attainted, to the disinherison of his heirs, or of those who would otherwise be his heirs. Thus innocent children were made to suffer because of the offense of their ancestor. When the Federal Constitution was framed, this was felt to be a great hardship, and even rank injustice. For this reason it was ordained that no attainder of treason should work corruption of blood or forfeiture, except during the life of the person attainted. No one ever doubted that it was a provision introduced for the benefit of the children and heirs alone; a declaration that the children should not bear the iniquity of the fathers.[7]

[5] *United States* v. *Cramer, supra.*
[6] *Ibid.*
[7] *Wallach* v. *Van Riswick* (1876), 92 U.S. 202.

Other Acts Against the United States not Treason.

Crimes so atrocious as those which have for their object the subversion by violence of those laws and those institutions which have been ordained in order to secure the peace and happiness of society, are not to escape punishment because they have not ripened into treason. The wisdom of the legislature is competent to provide for the case; and the framers of our constitution . . . must have conceived it more safe that punishment in such cases should be ordained by general laws, formed upon deliberation, under the influence of no resentments, and without knowing on whom they were to operate, than that passion which the occasion seldom fails to excite, and which a flexible definition of the crime, or a construction which would render it flexible, might bring into operation. It is, therefore, more safe as well as more consonant to the principles of our constitution . . . that crimes not clearly within the constitutional definition of treason should receive such punishment as the legislature in its wisdom may provide.[8]

Accordingly, Congress has provided severe penalties for non-treasonous acts against the United States such as sabotage, failure to disclose knowledge of treason, rebellion, insurrection, sedition, or advocacy of the overthrow of government by force or violence.[9]

LIMITATIONS IN THE AMENDMENTS TO THE CONSTITUTION—THE BILL OF RIGHTS

It will be recalled that during the struggle for ratification of the Constitution promises were made by its proponents that a bill of rights would be added to it. These promises were made necessary by the absence of specific guarantees to safeguard, from the powers of the central government, many rights of the individual and of property which were thought to be essential to liberty and democratic government.[10] During the course of ratification the states proposed 124 amendments to the Constitution, and from these grew the Bill of Rights.

Against whom do these amendments apply? Do they restrict governments or private individuals; if governments, the national government only, the state governments only, or both?

The Bill of Rights protects only against invasions of personal freedom and rights of property by agents of government. It affords no protection against abuse, discrimination, coercion, oppression, or any other form of persecution by private persons or groups against other private persons or groups. Such acts may be made illegal by statutes, but they do not violate the Bill of Rights.

[8] *Ex parte Bollman, supra,* pp. 126-127.
[9] See *U.S. Code,* Title 18, secs. 2381-2385 for definitions of and punishments prescribed by Congress for conviction of these crimes.
[10] See Hamilton's ingenious argument in opposition to a bill of rights in *Federalist Papers,* No. 84.

If, then, the Bill of Rights restricts only agents of Government, which government does its limitations affect? It was insisted

. . . that the Constitution was intended to secure the people of the several states against the undue exercise of power by their respective state governments; as well as that which might be attempted by their general government. . . .

Had the people of the several States, or any of them, required changes in their constitutions; had they required additional safeguards to liberty from the apprehended encroachments of their particular governments, the remedy was in their own hands, and would have been applied by themselves. A convention would have been assembled by the discontented State, and the required improvements would have been made by itself. . . . Had the framers of these amendments intended them to be limitations on the powers of the State governments, they would have . . . expressed that intention. . . . These amendments contain no expression indicating an intention to apply them to the state governments. This Court cannot so apply them.[11]

This principle continues to be valid today, but it must be remembered that some freedoms guaranteed by the Bill of Rights have been made parts of the "liberty" which is protected against state action by the Fourteenth Amendment. It should also be remembered that every state constitution contains a bill or declaration of rights, and many of these are similar in all important respects to that of the national Constitution. Accordingly, apart from implied restraints arising from federalism, state action cannot violate the national Constitution unless a limiting clause of that document specifically applies to it.[12]

Application of the Bill of Rights to the Territories. To what extent do the limitations of the Bill of Rights protect the inhabitants of territories of the United States from misrule by the authorities governing them? This is an important question. On the one hand, if all applied without distinction of any kind, serious problems of practical administration might easily arise. On the other hand, if none of them applied to any of the territories, their populations would be at the mercy of whatever whimsical or arbitrary legislation Congress might enact for them.

The Constitution states that

The Congress shall have Power to dispose of and make all needful Rules and Regulations respecting the Territory or other Property belonging to the United States; . . .

By use of this power Congress may expressly, or by implication, classify a territory of the United States as "incorporated" or "unincorporated." The first is regarded as part of the United States; the second is merely an appurtenance to, a dependency or possession of, the United States. With

---

[11] *Barron* v. *Baltimore* (1833), 7 Peters 243.
[12] This statement ignores the significant extensions made through interpretation of the due process clause of the Fourteenth Amendment.

the admission of Alaska and Hawaii into the Union, the last of the "in-corporated" territories disappeared; but Congress may still make an "incorporated" territory out of any of the remaining unincorporated ones should it so desire.

The applicability of constitutional limitations to a territory is directly related to its classification. All provisions of the document which are not clearly inapplicable apply through their inherent force to "incorporated" territories. But with the "unincorporated" group only limitations which guarantee fundamental rights automatically restrict Congress and such territorial governments as it may authorize. Of course, Congress can, if it wishes, extend by law any or all relevant constitutional limitations to "unincorporated" territories.

The First Amendment. The primary limitations on national power essential to free government are found in the First Amendment. This states:

> Congress shall make no law respecting an establishment of religion, or prohibiting the free exercise thereof; or abridging the freedom of speech, or of the press; or the right of the people peaceably to assemble, and to petition the Government for a redress of grievances.

Their incorporation in the "due process" clause of the Fourteenth Amendment has made possible their more uniform interpretation and application throughout the United States. Their application to the national government has seldom been required, for most infringements of these rights result from state action.

Freedom of Religion. Democracy depends in part upon the denial to government of complete power over the citizenry. The Constitution from beginning to end is a secular document that contains no reference to God.[13] Most important is its denial of authority to control matters of belief and conscience, for these are among the most fundamental deter-minants of individual personality. What a man believes largely determines what he is, and what the people believe will go far to determine what a government will be. Freedom of conscience, guided by religious belief, is commonly accepted as the primary source of individual and public morality.

The constitutional inhibition of legislation on the subject of religion has a dual aspect. On the one hand, the "establishment" clause forestalls the compulsory acceptance of any creed by law, or the compulsory practice of any prescribed form of religion. It protects *institutions of religion* from interference or domination by the state. Accordingly,

> The "establishment of religion" clause of the First Amendment means at least this: Neither a state nor the Federal Government can set up a church. Neither

---

[13] It does mention religious oaths when it prohibits them as a qualification for office under the United States.

can pass laws which aid one religion, aid all religions, or prefer one religion over another. Neither can force nor influence a person to go to or remain away from church against his will or force him to profess a belief or disbelief in any religion. No person can be punished for entertaining or professing religious beliefs or disbeliefs, for church attendance or nonattendance. No tax in any amount, large or small, can be levied to support any religious activities or institutions, whatever they may be called, or whatever form they may adopt to teach or practice religion. Neither a state nor the Federal Government can, openly or secretly, participate in the affairs of any religious organizations or groups. . . . In the words of Thomas Jefferson, the clause against establishment of religion by law was intended to erect a "wall of separation between church and State."[14]

The meaning of the "establishment" clause is probably overstated as it is set forth above. Jefferson asserted that this clause erected a "wall of separation between church and state," but the amendment does not say so, nor does any other part of the Constitution or comparable authority. Historical evidence is vague at best. Does separation of church and state mean literally that? The construction attributed to Jefferson could be a misinterpretation of history, a distortion of the intent of the amendment. Does the "establishment" clause as Jefferson construed it necessitate a complete divorce of government from religious establishments or does it only mean that government should be neutral toward all, forbidden to favor one, or some over others? Can government aid religion if it grants aid equally among all with scrupulous impartiality, avoiding all preference and discrimination?

Is it desirable, even if possible, to separate religion and politics in a democracy? Ought the moral teachings of religion to be available to influence politics and the conduct of public affairs? Can the church be kept out of politics? Politics out of the church?

Organized religions have long used governmental processes and politics for their own purposes when possible. They have sought the enactment of laws supporting their doctrinal positions, aiding their disciplinary functions, and for other of their ends relating to subjects like birth control, dancing, smoking, gambling, released-time for religious instruction, aid to parochial education, motion picture and book censorship, all in the name of religious freedom. Church organizations lobby, and their spokesmen influence public opinion and foster favorable or adverse pressure on public issues depending on their substance or their effect upon religion. Organized religions do endeavor to gain the aid and comfort of temporal power. But, although such activities may conjure up visions of

[14] *Everson* v. *Board of Education* (1947), 330 U.S. 1. This point was reaffirmed in *McGowan* v. *Maryland* (1961), 366 U.S. 420; *Torcaso* v. *Watkins* (1961), 367 U.S. 488; and *McCollum* v. *Board of Education* (1948), 333 U.S. 203. *Everson* contains an account of the historical origins of this protection now dimmed by the passage of time.

a state-dominated church or a church-dominated state, it should also raise the query: Are all questions, in which organized religions take an interest, religious questions? Are there not secular issues with strong moral or religious overtones upon which warnings from the pulpit are not only constitutionally correct but desirable? Does the "establishment" clause mean, for example, that the churches of America should have no legitimate interest in ending discrimination based on race? Conversely, who would argue that government ought to be concerned with internal church organization or administration, or with defining heresy and enforcing orthodoxy? Separation of church and state is only one of several possible arrangements—religion could be elevated above the temporal power, or made subject to its control. The dangers inherent in both are obvious. The policy of separation is thought safer for both parties to the relationship, and for the individual who might be subjected to tyranny of belief and conscience, as well as of the body, should the spiritual and temporal powers be joined. But, these are value judgments at the base of the "separation" as they are presumed to be established by the First Amendment, and not truths of a revealed origin.

Religion and government in the United States are linked at many points. "In God We Trust" is imprinted on our money; we are "One nation under God"; God is mentioned in many state constitutions and in the Declaration of Independence; the national government employs clerics in all military forces; church attendance is compulsory at the service academies; the House and Senate have chaplains who open each days' sitting with prayer; corporal oaths are administered in all national courts; the property and income of religious organizations are exempt from paying tribute to Caesar; police, fire, water, sewage disposal and other governmental services are supplied religious establishments; public regulations controlling teacher certification, school attendance, and accreditation, apply to church schools; public funds may pay for parochial school pupil transportation and school books; church-related schools are not disqualified from the school lunch, the surplus property disposal, or the borrowing programs administered and financed by the national government. In practice, then, "separation of church and state" does not literally mean that.

On the other hand, the "free exercise" clause was probably intended to protect the *individual*, as opposed to the *establishment* protected by the other, by safeguarding his freedom of conscience and by placing the free exercise of his chosen form of belief, if any, beyond the pale of governmental power. But, "free exercise" involves two sides, freedom to believe the substance of doctrine held inwardly, and freedom to act by participating in external forms, in ceremonials. Are they treated the same way? Freedom to believe is absolute, but can the second also be, given the nature of things?[15] In spite of the "free exercise" clause,

Conduct remains subject to regulation for the protection of society. The freedom to act must have appropriate definition to preserve the enforcement of that protection. In every case the power to regulate must be so exercised as not, in attaining a permitted end, unduly to infringe the protected freedom. No one would contest the proposition that a State may not, by statute, wholly deny the right to preach or to disseminate religious views. Plainly such a previous and absolute restraint would violate the terms of the guarantee. It is equally clear that a State may by general and non-discriminatory legislation regulate the times, the places, and the manner of soliciting upon its streets, and of holding meetings thereon; and may in other respects safeguard the peace, good order and comfort of the community. . . .[16]

All agree, probably, that the clause guaranteeing freedom of religion forbids restraint or constraint in matters of religious belief by the states or the national government; but does it really place beyond the reach of governmental power all constraint in matters of religious belief? Cadets and midshipmen *must* attend religious services of their choice. Does that compulsion violate the religious freedom not to go? What is the constitutional right of an appointee to be admitted to a service academy in spite of his atheism or agnosticism? Would his exclusion deny him religious liberty? A few years ago Congress added to the pledge of allegiance the

---

[15] *Cantwell* v. *Connecticut* (1940), 310 U.S. 296.
[16] *Ibid.*

phrase "under God." School children in great numbers are required by law to repeat the pledge daily. Does that compulsion violate the religious freedom of a non-believer, either atheist or agnostic? Under what God? Doubtless the Christian God is meant, but not all citizens of the United States believe in Him. To them another deity is the supreme being. Are they to be excluded from participation in the pledge or are they to be forced to utter words devoid of meaning and conviction? Does the action of Congress amount to a compulsory avowal of a tenet of the dominant Christian religion, which is thus unconstitutional even though not objectionable to the majority of people and churches?

Further, the "free exercise" clause forbids only laws that "prohibit" the free exercise of religion. Does that fact leave open the enactment of laws that aid religious freedom? Is there a middle position between good and evil? Can governmental power be neutral toward religion without being irreligious? If government does not aid religion does its inactivity amount to opposition or to indifference? If to the latter, is it not then hindering religion in violation of the "free exercise," if not of the "establishment," clause as well. Many persons today, especially proponents of federal aid to parochial schools, insist that it is. Can government leave to the family, and to organized religion, the conflict between religion and irreligion and remain true to the idea that Americans are a religious people whose institutions presuppose a Supreme Being? Does the "free exercise" clause require that temporal power shall be neutral or wholly inert?

Interplay Between the "Free Exercise" and "Establishment" Clauses. Proponents of aid to parochial education emphasize the neutrality aspect and the negative connotation of the clause. Aid, they insist, would benefit, not hinder, freedom of religion. Their opponents, however, emphasize the "establishment" clause and the "wall" separating church and state. The interplay between contentions opens up for inquiry the relationship between the clauses. Does the "establishment" clause have independent force equal to that of the "free exercise" clause? Are they two statements of the same idea? Or, is the "free exercise" clause primary, so that the other gives expression to the supporting principle that state interference with religious establishments is a threat to the free exercise of religion? Do the clauses together embody a principle of cooperation between church and state, or of secularization? How are they related to the guarantees of freedom of speech, of the press, and of peaceable assembly? It would seem that they provide all the protection necessary for religion if they are construed and applied broadly. But surely, the "free exercise" and the "establishment" clauses are not superfluous. Is the "establishment" clause essential to religious freedom? Could not an established church exist in an atmosphere of toleration side-by-side with non-conformist churches, atheism, and agnosticism? Perhaps the "establishment" clause was meant to do nothing more than prevent the new general government from meddling with, or seeking to destroy, the several state establishments of religion then extant. Hence, the "establishment" clause can be interpreted to forbid, and the "free exercise" clause to permit, federal aid to parochial schools. Suppose these schools were omitted and aid were extended to public schools only, would the disadvantage thereby incurred by the former amount to an interference with their religious freedom? Can it plausibly be argued that tax support of public education by parents of parochial school children violates the religious freedom of the taxpayers? Can it be argued that because the states support public education the "free exercise" clause requires that they pay also for parochial education? If the "establishment" clause merely supplements the "free exercise" provision and helps attain its fulfillment, must it yield to the former whenever its effect, if rigidly adhered to, would defeat or hinder religious freedom? Is an act of government void if it violates either but not both clauses? Can either be violated without violating the other?

These are but a few of the queries which are generated by the religion clauses of the First Amendment. Some have been answered for the moment; but a thoughtful examination of the first quotation above should reveal that several statements contained in it cannot be reconciled with present practice. The meaning of the guarantees is not yet resolved, and considerable soul searching by all three branches of government will be necessary before final answers can be shaped.

Freedom of Speech and of the Press. These freedoms go hand in hand. They comprehend every medium and publication for disseminating information and opinion. Both are probably essential to democratic government, which assumes that men in the mass can determine their own best interests better than one or a few men can do it for them. But realization of this ideal requires freedom to disseminate information on public questions in order to inform the people, so that they may make their opinions known and influence the government. They must be free to criticize, analyze, speak, think, and publish their views, without arbitrary interference by government but subject to the consequences of their expressions. Freedom of expression does not guarantee democracy, but without it democracy probably cannot result. If men are to be guided by the truth, they must have an opportunity and a desire to learn it. Popular as well as unpopular ideas must be permitted to compete for acceptance. All men and groups must be permitted to urge acceptance of their views if the right of others to do so is respected, and the views are lawful and compatible with public safety and morality. Freedom of expression protects against censorship and prior restraints, but it does not grant immunity from punishment for disseminating views that are malicious, improper, and illegal. Such punishment is necessary for the preservation of peace and good order, religion and government; but no censor or licensor may be made the arbitrary and infallible judge of all debatable ideas and views. The guarantee permits freedom to speak or publish, to accept or reject ideas, but the public dissemination of views inimical to the ends of society may still be punished by society.

What theoretical foundation is there for the guarantee of freedom of speech and of the press? Is this freedom truly essential to an effective democracy? Ought its defense to be based on considerations of wisdom and desirability or upon arguments of legality? Should all categories of speech and writing receive the same degree of protection? If not, which should be preferred? Why? Is private speech and writing different from public? How far ought government to be allowed to go in suppressing dangerous or objectionable ideas? What is a "substantive" evil? How "clear," "present," "grave," "probable," "imminent" must it be to justify suppression of speech or publication? Can the American people be relied upon to examine ideas which are competing for acceptance and to reject those that are false and misleading? Or, ought the government to determine what ideas shall be allowed free play? Should motion pictures be censored by public authority; should library shelves be purged of materials of an objectionable nature? What is objectionable? Who is to say? By what standard? Is peaceful picketing genuinely an exercise of free speech, or is it a weapon of economic coercion? Should the police interfere with a soapbox speaker who arouses a crowd to anger, or stop the crowd from causing a disturbance in reaction to the speaker's statements?

These are but a few of the questions growing out of the First Amendment's protection of speech and of the press; but an effort to analyze a few of them should quickly indicate the difficulty of resolving the competing values which are involved in any situation of conflict between public interest or authority and private exercise of free speech or the press.

Freedom to Assemble Peaceably and to Petition.

The right of the people peaceably to assemble for the purpose of petitioning Congress for a redress of grievances, or for anything else connected with the powers or duties of the National Government, is an attribute of national citizenship, and, as such, under the protection of and guaranteed by, the United States. The very idea of a government, republican in form, implies a right on the part of its citizens to meet peaceably for consultation in respect to public affairs and to petition for a redress of grievances.[17]

Without the right of persons to assemble in peaceable groups, associations, clubs, and so on, freedom of speech and of the press could not serve its purpose, for men could not come together to discuss, criticize, and evaluate the information placed at their disposal. The pluralistic nature of American society rests upon this freedom of association. Free assembly is necessary so that common positions on public matters may be

---

[17] *United States* v. *Cruikshank* (1875), 92 U.S. 542. The freedoms of speech, of the press, and of religion are also privileges of United States citizenship.

worked out, grievances defined and stated, and petitions for their alleviation prepared. Accordingly, the right of peaceable assembly is a right cognate to those of free speech and a free press and is equally fundamental. Each is intimately related to the others and none would be meaningful if isolated from the others. The right of assembly is abused if it is used to incite others to crime, violence, or other unlawful acts, but that abuse may be punished if the right itself is not curtailed. The right of assembly and petition is essential to the existence of free institutions and free discussion of public matters; it is through it that government may be kept responsive to the will of the people and that changes, when desired, may be made by peaceful means.

The right of petition includes oral and written appeals to legislators or executive agents. Written petitions are in fact sent in great numbers, but the right to petition does not include the right to have them fulfilled. Hence, most only add to the nation's supply of trash. But, while petitions provide one means by which to transmit views to the government, the rights of the First Amendment retain most of their value because of their obvious relationship to the operation of democratic government by democratic political processes.

Communism and the First Amendment. The spectre of Communism in the United States in recent years has put the freedom of speech and of the press to severe tests. The question is: Can the freedoms of a democratic system be used by the enemies of that system to destroy it? These freedoms may be claimed only by persons who respect the rights of others to enjoy them, who exercise them in a peaceable and responsible fashion to win majority support for their point of view, and who permit the resulting minority to make itself a majority. The democratic freedoms are available only to those who accept the responsibilities of their use as the foundation of a political system. Communism does none of these things. It is an authoritarian, totalitarian ideology the avowed purpose of which is to destroy the political and governmental systems of what we know as democracy. It contemplates a closed and static political order, established and maintained by force, which tolerates no opposition. There seems to be no theoretical reason why democratic government should wait supinely until it is destroyed by its enemies, whether internal or external. Accordingly, Congress has not made belief in, or academic discussion of, the principles of Communism illegal, but it has proscribed the Communist Party and made criminal virtually all forms of overt action, including conspiracy, which might lead to the forcible overthrow or destruction of any government in the United States. Its purpose is

. . . to protect existing government, not from change by peaceable, lawful and constitutional means, but from change by violence, revolution and terrorism. That it is within the *power* of Congress to protect the Government of the United States from armed rebellion is a proposition which requires little discussion. Whatever theoretical merit there may be to the argument that there is a "right" to rebellion against dictatorial governments is without force where the existing structure of the Government provides for peaceful and orderly change. We reject any principle of governmental helplessness in the face of preparation for revolution, which principle, carried to its logical conclusion, must lead to anarchy. No one could conceive that it is not within the power of Congress to prohibit acts intended to overthrow the Government by force and violence. . . .

Congress did not intend to eradicate the free discussion of political theories, to destroy the traditional rights of Americans to discuss and evaluate ideas without fear of governmental sanction.[18]

The Second Amendment.

The Right to Keep and Bear Arms. The presence of the Second Amendment in the Bill of Rights is the result of colonial experience, with the confiscation of private arms by the British, and distrust of professional soldiers. The amendment states that

A well regulated Militia, being necessary to the security of a free State, the right of the people to keep and bear Arms, shall not be infringed.

It does not grant to anyone the right to keep and to bear arms[19] but merely forbids Congress to infringe the right. What is the meaning of the amendment? Does it prohibit Congress from making illegal the carrying of concealed firearms, switchblade knives, fully automatic weapons, or sawed-off shotguns?

In the absence of any evidence tending to show that possession or use of a "shotgun having a barrel of less than eighteen inches in length" at this time has some reasonable relationship to the preservation or efficiency of a well regulated militia, we cannot say that the Second Amendment guarantees the right to keep and bear such an instrument. Certainly it is not within judicial notice that this weapon is any part of the ordinary militia equipment or that its use could contribute to the common defense. . . .

The Constitution as originally adopted granted to the Congress power—"To provide for calling forth the Militia to execute the Laws of the Union, suppress Insurrection, and repel Invasions; to provide for organizing, arming, and disciplining, the Militia, and for governing such Part of them as may be employed in the Service of the United States. . . ." With obvious purpose to assure the continuation and render possible the effectiveness of such forces the declaration and guarantee of the Second Amendment were made. It must be interpreted and applied with that end in view.[20]

Since there is today no militia of the above description, the significance of the Second Amendment is a thing of the past. It leaves Congress and

---

[18] *Dennis* v. *United States* (1951), 341 U.S. 494. However, teaching or advocacy intended to *organize* or *incite to action* for the purpose of forcibly overthrowing the government in the United States is not protected by freedom of speech or of the press. See *Yates* v. *United States* (1957), 354 U.S. 298.

[19] See *United States* v. *Cruikshank, supra.*

[20] *United States* v. *Miller* (1939), 307 U.S. 174.

the states free to regulate the sale, possession, transportation, use, purchase or other activities that involve the keeping and bearing of weapons.

The Third Amendment.

Quartering of Troops. The Third Amendment states:

No Soldier shall, in time of peace, be quartered in any house, without the consent of the Owner, nor in time of war, but in a manner to be prescribed by law.

As with its immediate predecessor, inclusion of this amendment in the Bill of Rights was a direct consequence of colonial experience with British practices in the pre-Revolutionary period. The amendment is so thoroughly in agreement with our general ideals, particularly our subordination of the military to civilian control, that comment is unnecessary. The meaning of the amendment is self-evident, and the statutory authorization which it contemplates has never been enacted by Congress.

The Fourth Amendment. The rights included in amendments Four, Five, Six, Seven and Eight are procedural guarantees; hence, they determine not what the government does but how it may proceed in designated courses of action.

Unreasonable Searches and Seizures. The Fourth Amendment declares that

The right of the people to be secure in their persons, houses, papers, and effects, against unreasonable searches and seizures, shall not be violated, and no Warrants shall issue, but upon probable cause, supported by Oath or affirmation, and particularly describing the place to be searched, and the persons or things to be seized.

The language of this amendment indicates that search warrants were in common use at the time the Constitution was adopted. Its purpose is not to eliminate all searches and seizures, even ones conducted in the absence of a search warrant. It is merely intended to proscribe those which are "unreasonable" in character. Of course,

General searches have long been deemed to violate fundamental rights. It is plain that the amendment forbids them. . . . The requirement that warrants shall particularly describe the things to be seized makes general searches under them impossible and prevents the seizure of one thing under a warrant describing another. As to what is to be taken, nothing is left to the discretion of the officer executing the warrant.[21]

What is an "unreasonable" search and seizure? Not every search or seizure was intended by the framers of the Constitution to require a warrant, for

What is a reasonable search is not to be determined by any fixed formula. The Constitution does not define what are "unreasonable" searches and, regret-

[21] *Marron* v. *United States* (1927), 275 U.S. 192.

tably, in our discipline we have no ready litmus-paper test. The recurring questions of the reasonableness of searches must find resolution in the facts and circumstances of each case. . . .

A rule of thumb requiring that a search warrant always be procured may be appealing from the vantage point of easy administration. But we cannot agree that this requirement should be crystallized into a *sine qua non* to the reasonableness of a search. Whether there was time may well be dependent upon other considerations than the ticking off of minutes or hours. The judgment of the officers as to when to close the trap on a criminal committing a crime in their presence or who they have reasonable cause to believe is committing a felony is not determined solely upon whether there was time to procure a search warrant. Some flexibility will be accorded law officers engaged in daily battle with criminals. . . .

It is appropriate to note that the Constitution does not say that the right of the people to be secure in their persons should not be violated without a search warrant if it is practicable for the officers to procure one. The mandate of the Fourth Amendment is that the people shall be secure against *unreasonable* searches. . . . The relevant test is not whether it is reasonable to procure a search warrant, but whether the search was reasonable. That criterion in turn depends upon the facts and circumstances—the total atmosphere of the case. It is a sufficient precaution that law officers must justify their conduct before courts which have always been, and must be, jealous of the individual's right of privacy within the broad sweep of the Fourth Amendment. . . .[22]

The protections of the Fourth Amendment

. . . apply to all invasions on the part of the Government and its employees, of the sanctities of a man's home and the privacies of life. It is not the breaking of his doors and the rummaging of his drawers that constitutes the essence of the offense; but it is the invasion of his indefeasible right of personal security, personal liberty, and private property, where that right has never been forfeited. . . .[23]

In spite of this general language, however, the protection of the Fourth Amendment does not extend to some very important areas. For a search to be unreasonable, there must be a physical trespass; for a seizure to be illegal, there must be a wrongful taking of a tangible thing. Thus, what the eye can see or the ear can hear in the absence of the above elements does not violate the amendment. Portable recording devices, sensitive electric listening devices, eavesdropping, and keyhole peeping do not violate the Fourth Amendment, although their employment may very easily invade individual privacy.

The Fifth Amendment.
Immunity from Compulsory Self-Incrimination. The Fifth Amendment to the Constitution declares that no person "shall be compelled in any

[22] *United States* v. *Rabinowitz* (1950), 339 U.S. 56.
[23] *Boyd* v. *United States* (1885), 116 U.S. 616.

criminal case to be a witness against himself." This procedural safeguard incorporates within the fundamental law of the land

. . . an ancient principle of the law of evidence, that a witness shall not be compelled, in any proceedings, to make disclosures or to give testimony which will tend to incriminate him or subject him to fines, penalties, or forfeitures.[24]

Scope of the Privilege.

It is impossible that the meaning of the constitutional provisions can only be, that a person shall not be compelled to be a witness against himself in a criminal prosecution against himself. It would doubtless cover such cases; but it is not limited to them. The object was to insure that a person should not be compelled, when acting as a witness in any investigation, to give testimony which might tend to show that he himself had committed a crime. The privilege is limited to criminal matters, but it is as broad as the mischief against which it seeks to guard.[25]

Protection of the privilege against compulsory self-incrimination may be claimed by a witness in *any proceeding* whenever his answer might tend to subject him to criminal responsibility.

Testimony may be compelled, however, if Congress sees fit to trade complete immunity from prosecution for information about a crime known to an implicated witness. If an "immunity statute" protects the witness as fully as does the self-incrimination clause of the Fifth Amendment, he may be compelled to give evidence against himself. But the evidence so given cannot be used against him, directly or indirectly, and Congress may forbid its use against him in any way by state courts or officers, as well. This is so because

If . . . the object of the provision be to secure the witness against a criminal prosecution, which might be aided directly or indirectly by his disclosure, then, if no such prosecution be possible—in other words, if his testimony operate as a complete pardon for the offence to which it relates,—a statute absolutely securing to him immunity from prosecution would satisfy the demands of the clause in question.

It can only be said in general that the clause should be construed, as it was doubtless designed, to effect a practical and beneficent purpose—not necessarily to protect witnesses against every possible detriment which might happen to them from their testimony, nor to unduly impede, hinder, or obstruct the administration of criminal justice.[26]

Nevertheless,

Stringent as the general rule is, however, certain classes of cases have always been treated as not falling within the reason of the rule, and therefore con-

[24] *Counselman* v. *Hitchcock* (1892), 142 U.S. 547.
[25] *Ibid.*
[26] *Brown* v. *Walker* (1896), 161 U.S. 591.

stitute apparent exceptions. When examined, these cases will be found to be based upon the idea that if the testimony sought cannot possibly be used as a basis for, or in aid of, a criminal prosecution against the witness, the rule ceases to apply, its object being to protect the witness himself and no one else—much less that it shall be made use of as a pretext for securing immunity to others.

1. Thus, if the witness himself elects to waive his privileges, as he may doubtless do, since the privilege is for his protection and not for other parties, and discloses his criminal connections, he is not permitted to stop, but must go on and make a full disclosure. . . .

2. For the same reason, if the prosecution for a crime, concerning which the witness is interrogated, is barred by the statute of limitations he is compelled to answer. . . .

3. If the answer of the witness may have a tendency to disgrace him or bring him into disrepute, and the proposed evidence be material to the issue on trial, the great weight of authority is that he may be compelled to answer, although, if the answer can have no effect upon the case, except so far as to impair the credibility of the witness, he may fall back upon the privilege. . . .

4. It is almost a necessary corollary of the above propositions that, if the witness has already received a pardon, he cannot longer set up his privilege, since he stands with respect to such offense as if it had never been committed.[27]

Relationship of the Fourth and Fifth Amendments. The prohibition against unreasonable searches and seizures has been linked closely to the "self-incrimination" clause of the Fifth Amendment. The protection thus derived is broader than that afforded by either constitutional guarantee separately.

We have already noticed the intimate relation between the two Amendments. They throw great light on each other. For the "unreasonable searches and seizures" condemned in the Fourth Amendment are almost always made for the purpose of compelling a man to give evidence against himself, which in criminal cases is condemned in the Fifth Amendment; and compelling a man "in a criminal case to be a witness against himself," which is condemned in the Fifth Amendment, throws light on the question as to what is an "unreasonable search and seizure" within the meaning of the Fourth Amendment. And we have been unable to perceive that the seizure of a man's private books and papers to be used in evidence against him is substantially different from compelling him to be a witness against himself.[28]

Grand Juries. The Fifth Amendment also declares that

No person shall be held to answer for a capital, or otherwise infamous crime, unless on a presentment or indictment of a Grand Jury, except in cases arising in the land or naval forces, or in the Militia, when in actual service in time of War or public danger. . . .

[27] *Ibid.*
[28] *Boyd* v. *United States, supra.*

The grand jury is an informing and accusing tribunal of ancient English origin. It is a hearing, conducted by prosecuting officers before a panel of citizens constituting the grand jury, to determine whether there is sufficient evidence against an accused person to warrant bringing him to trial. It is a wholly one-sided procedure against the accused. Yet the grand jury is designed to protect the citizen against unfounded accusations, whether they come from government or are prompted by private enmity or political passion. Unless a grand jury, of from sixteen to twenty-three members selected from the community, shall declare under oath, and after careful deliberation, that there is good reason for his accusation and trial, no person shall be held to answer for a "capital, or otherwise infamous crime," except in the special cases provided. It is a valuable method of protecting individuals from open and public accusation of crime, and from the trouble, expense, and anxiety of a public trial before a probable cause is established. In the case of felonies it is one of the securities of the innocent against hasty, malicious and oppressive public prosecutions.

Whether or not the grand jury retains the value today that it was once thought to possess is a matter of some dispute. Of interest is the fact that in England its use has been discontinued since 1930. However, without amending the Constitution of the United States its use in connection with federal criminal trials for "capital, or otherwise infamous crimes" cannot be abandoned in favor of some other process.

Double Jeopardy. The Fifth Amendment declares that no person shall "be subject for the same offence to be twice put in jeopardy of life or limb."

This prohibition was designed to protect an individual from being subjected to the hazards of trial and possible conviction more than once for an alleged offense. The basic idea is that the government, with all its resources and power, should not be allowed to make repeated efforts to convict an individual, thereby subjecting him to embarrassment, expense, and ordeal, and compelling him to live in a continuous state of anxiety and insecurity, as well as enhancing the possibility that even though innocent he may be found guilty. He is in jeopardy once he is put on trial before a jury, and this prohibition prevents a judge or prosecutor from subjecting a defendant to a second, third, or fourth trial by discontinuing a prosecution whenever it appears that the jury may not convict.

However, there are in the United States two governmental jurisdictions, each with its system of criminal law and courts capable of dealing with the same subject matter within the same area. Each government, in defining in its law what shall be an offense against its peace and dignity, exercises its own authority. Hence,

It follows that an act denounced as a crime by both national and state sovereignties is an offence against the peace and dignity of both and may be punished by each. The Fifth Amendment, like all the other guaranties in the first eight amendments, applies only to proceedings by the Federal Government . . . and the double jeopardy therein forbidden is a second prosecution under authority of the Federal Government after a first trial for the same offence under the same authority. Here the same act was an offence against the State of Washington because a violation of its law, and also an offence against the United States under the National Prohibition Act. The defendants thus committed two different offences by the same act, and a conviction by a court of Washington of the offence against that State is not a conviction of the different offence against the United States and so is not double jeopardy.[29]

"The Due Process of Law" Clause. This clause of the Fifth Amendment is identical in form, and nearly identical in meaning, to that of the Fourteenth Amendment, examined in the preceding chapter. Two significant differences exist between them. The first involves their relationship to the Bill of Rights. It will be recalled that the "liberty" protected by the "due process" clause of the Fourteenth Amendment has been used to guarantee some rights of the Bill of Rights against infringement by state action. However, the "due process" clause of the Fifth Amendment does not embrace the prohibitions of the First or other amendments to the Constitution. The second difference arises from the fact that

The Fifth Amendment . . . does not contain an equal protection clause as does the Fourteenth Amendment which applies only to the states. But the concepts of equal protection and due process, both stemming from our American ideal of fairness, are not mutually exclusive. The "equal protection of the laws" is a more explicit safeguard of prohibited unfairness than "due process of law," and, therefore, we do not imply that the two are always interchangeable phrases. But . . . discrimination may be so unjustifiable as to be violative of due process.[30]

Congress, therefore, legislates unburdened by one major limitation which is applicable to the states. It may constitutionally enact discriminatory laws, unless these laws violate the due process clause. The limitation imposed upon Congress is not as restrictive as the guarantee of equal protection of the laws—made effective by the Fourteenth Amendment—is upon the states.

The Power of Eminent Domain. The Fifth Amendment also forbids Congress to take private property "for public use, without just compensation."

The power to take private property for public uses, generally termed the right of eminent domain, belongs to every independent government. It is an incident of sovereignty and . . . requires no constitutional recognition. The

---

[29] *United States* v. *Lanza* (1922), 260 U.S. 377.
[30] *Bolling* v. *Sharpe* (1954), 347 U.S. 497.

provision found in the 5th Amendment to the Federal Constitution . . . for just compensation for property taken, is merely a limitation on the use of the power. It is no part of the power itself, but a condition upon which the power may be exercised.[31]

Scope of the Power and Compensation.

If the United States has determined its need for certain land for a public use that is within its federal sovereign powers, it must have the right to appropriate that land. Otherwise, the owner of the land, by refusing to sell it or by consenting to do so only at an unreasonably high price, is enabled to subordinate the constitutional powers of Congress to his personal will. The Fifth Amendment, in turn, provides him with important protection against abuse of the power of eminent domain by the Federal Government. . . .

The considerations that made it appropriate for the Constitution to declare that the Constitution of the United States, and the laws of the United States made in pursuance thereof, shall be the supreme law of the land make it appropriate to recognize that the power of eminent domain, when exercised by Congress within its constitutional powers, is equally supreme. . . .

"The argument based upon the doctrine that the states have the eminent domain or highest dominion in the lands comprised within their limits, and that the United States have no dominion in such lands, cannot avail to frustrate the supremacy given by the constitution to the government of the United States in all matters within the scope of its sovereignty. That is not a matter of words, but of things. If it is necessary that the United States government should have an eminent domain still higher than that of the state, in order that it may fully carry out the objects and purposes of the constitution, then it has it. Whatever may be the necessities or conclusions of theoretical law as to eminent domain or anything else, it must be received as a postulate of the constitution that the government of the United States is invested with full and complete power to execute and carry out its purposes."[32]

The just compensation required by the Constitution to be made to the owner is to be measured by the loss caused to him by the appropriation. He is entitled to receive the value of what he has been deprived of, and no more. To award him less would be unjust to him; to award him more would be unjust to the public.[33]

The Sixth Amendment.

Right to a Speedy and Public Trial. The last three of the first eight amendments to the Constitution relate to various aspects of the civil and criminal judicial processes. As prohibitions on the exercise of governmental authority they restrict primarily the courts, but they may be in-

[31] *United States v. Jones* (1883), 109. U.S. 513.
[32] *United States v. Carmack* (1946), 329 U.S. 230.
[33] *Bauman v. Ross* (1897), 167 U.S. 548.

voked, as circumstances justify, against the executive and legislative branches of the government. Thus, the Sixth Amendment states:

In all criminal prosecutions, the accused shall enjoy the right to a speedy and public trial, by an impartial jury of the State and district wherein the crime shall have been committed, which district shall have been previously ascertained by law, and to be informed of the nature and cause of the accusation; to be confronted with the witnesses against him; to have compulsory process for obtaining witnesses in his favor, and to have the Assistance of Counsel for his defense.

The guarantee of a "speedy and public" trial protects accused persons from being held indefinitely in jail waiting for a trial that may never be held. A "speedy" trial is not one held within a specified period of time, but one that is held within a reasonable period after indictment. The interval between indictment and trial must be long enough to give the accused an opportunity to prepare his defense but not so long as to work an unjustifiable hardship upon him. To be a public trial it, or a significant portion of it—since some proceedings may take place behind closed doors—must be open to the public and especially to the relatives and friends of the accused. This protection assures that the interest of society in the fair administration of justice is being preserved, and that the rights of the accused are being protected.

What is embraced by the phrase "trial by jury?"

That it means a trial by jury as understood and applied at common law, and includes all the essential elements as they were recognized in this country and England when the Constitution was adopted, is not open to question. Those elements were—(1) that the jury should consist of twelve men, neither more nor less; (2) that the trial should be in the presence and under the superintendence of a judge having power to instruct them as to the law and advise them in respect of the facts; and (3) that the verdict should be unanimous. . . . The foregoing principles . . . demonstrate the unassailable integrity of the establishment of trial by jury in all its parts, and make clear that a destruction of one of the essential elements has the effect of abridging the right in controvention of the Constitution.[34]

The record of English and colonial jurisprudence antedating the Constitution will be searched in vain for evidence that trial by jury in criminal cases was regarded as a part of the structure of government, as distinguished from a right or privilege of the accused. . . . In the light of the foregoing it is reasonable to conclude that the Framers of the Constitution simply were intent upon preserving the right of trial by jury primarily for the protection of the accused. . . .

In other words . . . a person charged with a crime punishable by imprisonment for a term of years may, consistently with the constitutional provisions

[34] *Patton* v. *United States* (1930), 281 U.S. 276.

already quoted, waive trial by a jury of twelve and consent to a trial by any lesser number, or by the court without a jury.[35]

The well-settled rule is that, given a lawfully selected panel, free from any taint of invalid exclusions or procedure in selection and from which all disqualified for cause have been excused, no cause for complaint arises merely from the fact that the jury finally chosen happens itself not to be representative of the panel or indeed of the community. There is, under such circumstances, no right to any particular composition or group representation on the jury.[36]

Nature and Cause of the Accusation. Before a defendant can be tried in a national court he must be informed of the charges against him and the circumstances out of which they proceed. It is the function of the indictment or presentment to do this.

It is elementary that an indictment, in order to be good under the Federal Constitution and laws, shall advise the accused of the nature and cause of the accusation against him, in order that he may meet the accusation and prepare for his trial, and that after judgment he may be able to plead the record and judgment in bar of further prosecution of the same offense.[37]

If these requirements are met, the accused has received all the protection that he is entitled to under this provision of the Constitution.

Right to Counsel.

The Sixth Amendment guarantees that "In all criminal prosecutions, the accused shall enjoy the right . . . to have the Assistance of Counsel for his defense." This is one of the safeguards of the Sixth Amendment deemed necessary to insure fundamental human rights of life and liberty. . . . The Sixth Amendment . . . embodies a realistic recognition of the obvious truth that the average defendant does not have the professional legal skill to protect himself when brought before a tribunal with power to take his life or liberty, wherein the prosecution is presented by experienced and learned counsel. That which is simple, orderly and necessary to the lawyer, to the untrained layman may appear intricate, complex and mysterious. . . .

The "right to be heard would be, in many cases, of little avail if it did not comprehend the right to be heard by counsel. Even the intelligent and educated layman has small and sometimes no skill in the science of law. If charged with crime, he is incapable, generally, of determining for himself whether the indictment is good or bad. He is unfamiliar with the rules of evidence. Left without the aid of counsel he may be put on trial without a proper charge, and convicted upon incompetent evidence, or evidence irrelevant to the issue or otherwise inadmissible. He lacks both the skill and knowledge adequately to prepare his defense, even though he have a perfect one. He requires the guiding hand of counsel at every step of the proceeding against himself." The Sixth

---

[35] *Ibid.*, pp. 296-297, 290.
[36] *Frazier* v. *United States* (1948), 335 U.S. 497.
[37] *Bartell* v. *United States* (1913), 227 U.S. 427.

Amendment withholds from federal courts, in all criminal proceedings, the power and authority to deprive an accused of his life or liberty unless he has or waives the assistance of counsel.[38]

But the Constitution is not meant to be a procedural strait jacket. Therefore, although the right to have counsel may not be denied a defendant, he may be tried and convicted without legal assistance; for,

The short of the matter is that an accused, in the exercise of a free and intelligent choice, and with the considered approval of the court may . . . competently and intelligently waive his constitutional right to assistance of counsel. There is nothing in the Constitution to prevent an accused from choosing to have his fate tried before a judge without a jury, even though, in deciding what is best for himself, he follows the guidance of his own wisdom and not that of a lawyer. . . .

The right to assistance of counsel and the correlative right to dispense with a lawyer's help are not legal formalities. They rest on considerations that go to the substance of an accused's position before the law. The public conscience must be satisfied that fairness dominates the administration of justice. An accused must have the means of presenting his best defense. He must have time and facilities for investigation and for the production of evidence. But evidence and truth are of no avail unless they can be adequately presented. Essential fairness is lacking if an accused cannot put his case effectively in court. But the Constitution does not force a lawyer upon a defendant. He may waive his constitutional right to assistance of counsel if he knows what he is doing and his choice is made with eyes open.[39]

The Seventh Amendment.
Jury Trials in Civil Suits.

In suits at common law, where the value in controversy shall exceed twenty dollars, the right of trial by jury shall be preserved, and no fact tried by a jury, shall be otherwise re-examined in any Court of the United States, than according to the rules of the common law.

The essential aspects of this amendment to the Constitution are not different from those of the jury trial clause of the Sixth Amendment. It applies, however, only to civil suits at common law. Hence, the clause does not apply to any proceeding in a federal court in which jurisdiction in equity is invoked, or in which a jury is not authorized.

The Eighth Amendment.

Excessive bail shall not be required, nor excessive fines imposed, nor cruel and unusual punishment inflicted.

Cruel and Unusual Punishments. This prohibition came into the Constitution from English law. It is intended to apply primarily to courts which impose punishments on convicted criminals, but it also applies to

---

[38] *Johnson* v. *Zerbst* (1938), 304 U.S. 458.
[39] *Adams* v. *U.S. ex rel. McCann* (1942), 317 U.S. 269.

Congress which specifies the punishments in statutes defining the crimes. If the punishment prescribed for an offense against the laws of the United States was manifestly cruel and unusual, for instance crucifixion, burning at the stake, breaking on the rack or wheel, or live burial, it would be the duty of a court to state that such penalty was within the constitutional prohibition.

Excessive Bail.

The bail clause was lifted with slight changes from the English Bill of Rights Act. In England that clause has never been thought to accord a right to bail in all cases, but merely to provide that bail shall not be excessive in those cases where it is proper to grant bail. When this clause was carried over into our Bill of Rights, nothing was said that indicated any different concept. The Eighth Amendment has not prevented Congress from defining the classes of cases in which bail shall be allowed in this country. Thus in criminal cases bail is not compulsory where the punishment may be death. Indeed, the very language of the Amendment fails to say all arrests must be bailable.[40]

From the passage of the Judiciary Act of 1789 . . . to the present Federal Rules of Criminal Precedure, . . . Federal law has unequivocally provided that a person arrested for a non-capital offense *shall* be admitted to bail. This traditional right to freedom before conviction permits the unhampered preparation of a defense, and serves to prevent the infliction of punishment prior to conviction. . . . Unless this right to bail before trial is preserved, the presumption of innocence, secured only after centuries of struggle, would lose its meaning.

The right to release before trial is conditioned upon the accused's giving adequate assurance that he will stand trial and submit to sentence if found guilty. . . . Like the ancient practice of securing the oaths of responsible persons to stand as sureties for the accused, the modern practice of requiring a bail bond or the deposit of a sum of money subject to forfeiture serves as additional assurance of the presence of the accused. Bail set at a figure higher than an amount reasonably calculated to fulfill this purpose is excessive under the Eighth Amendment.[41]

Thus, the function of bail is a limited one, and since this is so, what constitutes reasonable bail in any given instance is to be decided by the officer, court, or judge, who is authorized to set bail according to the following standards fixed by the Federal Rules of Criminal Procedure:

Rule 46 (c). "Amount. If the defendant is admitted to bail, the amount thereof shall be such as in the judgment of the commissioner or court or judge or justice will insure the presence of the defendant, having regard to the nature and circumstances of the offense charged, the weight of the evidence against him, the financial ability of the defendant to give bail and the character of the defendant."

[40] *Carlson* v. *Landon* (1952), 342 U.S. 524.
[41] *Stack* v. *Boyle* (1951), 342 U.S. 1.

Justice is apt to be unequal where matters of bail are involved. Excessive bail is forbidden, but what is excessive bail? Bail which a wealthy defendant can supply with indifference may be prohibitive to a man of meager means. Bail of even a very modest amount may have the practical effect of denying the latter release. In the absence of bail an accused person held in jail will be handicapped in finding witnesses and in preparing his defense. His employment may be lost, but even if not, detention will prevent him from earning the funds necessary for his defense. If he is acquitted on trial or later appeal, the time he has spent in jail will have been unjustly extracted. Moreover, most bail is raised for all but wealthy defendants by resort to professional bondsmen, who for a high fee supply a surety bond for the amount fixed by the court. But the bondsman makes his decision to supply or deny the bond primarily on the defendant's financial status, not his character. Generally speaking, it is doubtful that the decision is made with major attention to the interest either of the defendant or of the public.

The bail system today may be unjust and certainly is anachronistic. Successful flight from justice, given modern methods of communication, identification, and detection, is difficult at best. Capture, return, and punishment of fugitives under bond is relatively easy and successful. Other non-monetary considerations might more equitably and just as effectively assure a defendant's appearance in court. The present system of bail seems too much at odds with the ideals of equal justice and presumed innocence to be perpetuated.

IN CONCLUSION

The precedural safeguards contained in the Bill of Rights and elsewhere in the Constitution impose upon agents and officers of the national government numerous standards of fairness that control their relationships with individuals. In their application, however, these clauses undoubtedly complicate many tasks of government, especially that of law enforcement. For this reason a considerable amount of criticism and dissenting opinion is voiced as to the wisdom of their continued implementation. Their critics argue that the burden which they impose upon the execution of governmental functions is not outweighed by effective protection against oppression, so that they are a luxury the constitutional system can no longer afford. Unhappily, this conclusion is reinforced in the public mind by the numerous accounts in the newspapers of unsavory characters who have escaped the reach of the law by taking advantage of some "loophole" or legal technicality. However, little or nothing is to be found in print about the large number of persons compelled to confess to crimes while under mental or physical duress. Not much is printed in the press about illegal invasions of privacy which are made by over-zealous law enforcement officers. Doubtless, some technicalities of the law have been made to benefit defendants who should have been pun-ished; but convictions gained by wrongful, though convenient, means would constitute miscarriages of justice of an even worse type.

The problem in these instances is not that of giving preference either to individual right or to the security of the community. Were the prob-lem this simple the security of the community, supported by the vast resources of the national government and its control of the courts, would undoubtedly triumph. But inasmuch as virtually all persons of democratic inclination agree that individual rights must be protected, the real prob-lem for which there is no ready solution becomes that of deciding how much protection is to be given to the freedoms of men and how much, at their expense, is to be given to the security of the community. This is no easy task, and its complexity as well as its importance to the survival of free government accounts for much of the respect that is paid by courts to the procedural safeguards of the Constitution. Implementation of the constitutional guarantees, therefore, is not undertaken by judges because of their liking for the technical niceties of legal rules, but because of their realization that, unless the indispensable but frequently misdirected coer-cive power of government is restrained and kept within established and acceptable bounds, there will soon remain to the people no freedom worth guarding by legal rules. "The history of liberty has largely been the history of observance of procedural safeguards."[42]

Time has not eliminated or significantly reduced the value of these pro-tections. Yet, an attitude of impatience with them has emerged, which may permit their interpretation in a hostile or niggardly spirit in order to ensure that they do not serve as shelters for wrongdoers.

The answer to critics of constitutional restraints is simple. If sufficient support can be obtained for the view that constitutional guarantees of individual liberty are outmoded by the conditions of the modern age in which we live, then the thing to do is to take them out of the Constitu-tion through the processes of amendment. No doubt the constitutional limitations on the authority of the national government may occasionally save a guilty person from his just deserts, but they were aimed at a more far-reaching evil:

. . . recurrence of the Inquisition and the Star Chamber, even if not in their stark brutality. Prevention of the greater evil was deemed of more importance than occurrence of the lesser evil. Having had much experience with a tendency in human nature to abuse power, the Founders sought to close the doors against like future abuses by law enforcing agencies.[43]

[42] *McNabb* v. *United States* (1943), 318 U.S. 332.
[43] *Ullmann* v. *United States* (1956), 350 U.S. 422.

CHAPTER VII

Public Opinion and Pressure Groups

The Bosses of the Senate

PUBLIC OPINION

Public opinion is commonly said to rule in democratic systems of government. What is public opinion? How is it made effective? To say that it is the "will of the people" (the will of voters expressed in elections) is to mislead and to confuse; government does many things upon which the voters never express an opinion, and when an opinion is expressed it is never unanimous. Many who vote have no opinion, and more than one-third of the potential electorate does not vote. All that can be hoped for is that a majority of the voters will agree upon a course of action to be followed by government; but most expressions of "public opinion" are made by a plurality, and sometimes by a minority, of the electorate. Hence, government by the "will of the people" can mean, realistically, only that voters periodically and freely indicate their acceptance or rejection of the candidates and policies of at least two political parties. The policies, however, between which the voter is asked to choose, are usually only those relating to the most controversial, serious, or dramatic public questions; minor issues go unnoticed and are judged in the arena of public opinion only in so far as they make up part of a party's record when it is submitted to the electorate for approval.

It is now generally agreed that there is no generic public opinion on any given issue. Instead, there are in the society at any given time many "publics" each of which consists of those persons who hold the same view on an issue of public policy. Each group constitutes a "public" in relation to that issue, and its "opinion" is its shared view which differentiates it from other "publics." Further, the issue upon which the opinion is held must be a public, as distinguished from a private, one—that is, an issue that can be decided by an appeal to the electorate. Public opinion on a given issue consists, therefore, of all opinions related to that issue which are held by various groups at any one time. Consequently, there are as many "publics" as there are groups holding opinions on public questions. Moreover, opinion, to be a trustworthy foundation for public policy and action, ought to be a sound judgment consciously formulated after examination of all available facts. Hence, a conclusion believed to be valid, held by a number of individuals, and pertaining to a matter of public concern, is entitled to be called public opinion, even though its supporters may number far fewer than a majority.

For example, on the issue of public versus private development of electrical facilities and services, the immediate division of opinion must be between those who have conclusions and those who do not. The latter greatly outnumber the former. Among the few who have conclusions on the issue a further division can be made between the people who take the side of private interests and those who take the side of government ownership and assistance. Each of these primary contestants in the controversy has behind it a group of secondary supporters who together constitute its "public." Each secondary group holds *an opinion* regarding the issue so that the major contestants are supported by allied groups, which, on this issue, include other utilities, railroads, taxpayers' associations, industries, municipalities, government agencies, consumers, conservation, recreation, and wildlife groups, and a host of others. Each such component "public" has its own view of what public policy ought to be that causes it to support one major contestant. Also, each side appeals to the public at large in an effort to win to its position a preponderance of the "effective" opinion of the community. Out of this interplay of political power will come policy decisions which are pertinent to the public versus private power question, but which will not produce a general "public opinion" on that issue. Thus, for several years, more than one hundred private electric power companies fought a running propaganda battle in national magazines with the National Rural Electric Cooperative Association. In their advertisements the former attacked, and the latter defended, the extension and continued operation of governmentally owned

RURAL ELECTRIFICATION
the "impossible job"
nobody really wanted!

Back in the early 30's, power companies looked upon electric service in thinly populated rural areas as a poor investment. They visualized limited use of electric power by the scattered customers beyond city limits, and high cost maintenance of rural lines.

When the Rural Electrification Administration was created, in 1935, these electric companies were urged to use REA loans to extend their lines to rural people. But most power companies decided against this move even though only about 11% of our farms had electricity. That's when rural people, themselves, got into the power business. They organized into groups, incorporated, borrowed money from REA, and built their own non-profit electric systems. Today, these locally owned electric systems operate 1.5-million miles of line serving 16 million rural people . . . and 97% of all farms have electric light and power.

To date, 984 cooperatives, 74 public utility districts —and a handful of power companies—have borrowed over $3½-billion from REA, and have paid more than $1-billion in principal and interest on these loans. They've turned the "impossible job" into one of the soundest investments our nation has ever made.

AMERICA'S
RURAL ELECTRIC
SYSTEMS

or aided electric power projects. Examine the appeal to general public opinion by the NRECA as it is reproduced here.[1]

Not all that passes for public opinion meets this test, however. Few persons have the time to acquire and digest the information necessary to

[1] Permission to reproduce an appeal by the independent light and power companies could not be obtained, but an example may be found in *Time*, October 19, 1959, p. 128. Compare the foundation of fact, emotion, and bias upon which they are based.

reach a deliberate judgment. On many matters information is lacking or is not available to the general public. Issues arise too quickly and are too far reaching, complex, or technical for the electorate to be able to form judgments about them. Force of habit, traditional attitudes of family or community, apathy, indifference, deference, lethargy, and preoccupation with private affairs combine to defeat the growth of an active public-wide opinion about even the most significant issues. The force of emotion and other non-rational factors which help determine individual reactions outweigh the element of reason. Public opinion, therefore, is neither a public-wide nor a reasoned judgment, and in practice any belief, conviction, opinion, or judgment, without regard to its truth or error, the extent of its support, or the method by which it gained acceptance, qualifies as public opinion if it relates to a public question.

Opinions are important for they influence all activities of men in every walk of life. In political and governmental matters, therefore, opinions of the public which influence their probable reactions to the policies and activities of parties, interest groups, or government are imponderables of great importance. They must be calculated and measured, for activities or policies that violate the opinions, beliefs, or convictions of mass men will arouse opposition, and possible defeat of the legislators and executives responsible for them. Disregard of public attitudes will also probably produce general resistance to the administration of objectionable policies or programs. Public opinion is a powerful limiting force in the body politic which must be ascertained and heeded by persons engaged in the political and governmental processes.

The Effect of Public Opinion. The effect of public opinion upon the thinking of persons engaged in politics or government depends upon various factors. Its weight varies with its appeal. Not all individuals react similarly to each issue. Those directly affected react strongly; those affected remotely, or not at all, react with varying degrees of response. How widely is the opinion held? Is it a matter of deep conviction or of superficial acceptance? Is it backed by powerful groups or by unorganized elements of the public at large? Are its proponents well organized, well led, and well financed? How many votes would be lost by acting contrary to the opinion? How many would be gained to offset those that were lost? Is the opinion founded on special knowledge and held by persons of prestige? Would the general public, voters and non-voters, accept and obey, or reject and resist, a contemplated policy or program? The answers to these and other similar questions make it possible for the probable public reaction to be calculated by the interested group and party leaders, candidates, legislators, and executives. To ignore public reactions is to invite trouble, and this is no less true for purely private groups than it is for political parties or governmental officers or agencies. The importance of public opinion is evidenced by the extent to which

"Oh Dear— Sometimes I Think They're Not Even Listening"

private groups, political parties, and governmental officers and agencies endeavor to cultivate and manipulate it in their favor.

Opinion Leadership. Some persons lead in the formation of public opinion; others are led by it. Some opinion leaders have large followings and much influence, but many do not. Their influence is determined by many factors, including their standing in the community, their access to listeners, the compatibility of their views with dominant sentiments, their knowledge of the subject, and their identification with the subject. The most influential opinion leaders include public affairs analysts, editors, clergymen, union officials, public officials, spokesmen for professional groups, business executives, and bankers. But, anyone who influences the opinion of one or more other individuals is an opinion leader to that extent. They emerge and fade within the community; none are wholly without influence; none are heeded on every issue, but their influence always depends upon the extent to which their views are accepted.

Their views will be most readily accepted if they can convince their hearers that they speak in the interests of all, whether "all" is the general public or the whole membership of a particular group. Usually, however, opinion leaders speak only for a minority of the general public or of their group. Many times the views expressed are those of the speaker only, although it will be implied or asserted that he represents a following and that he speaks in its name. The ideas that he utters may appeal to emotion or reason, be true or false, biased or objective, educational or propagandistic. Some of every type are usually employed; whatever their nature the aggregate of those accepted constitutes that body of opinion which is consulted by legislators and administrators, which determines the outcome of elections, and directly or indirectly influences the formation, enactment, and administration of public policy. Hence, much public "opinion" is not true opinion based on rational conviction.

Unevenness of Expression. Much that passes for public opinion is very unevenly expressed. Many, if not most, opinion leaders are spokesmen for vocal, well-organized groups comprising small segments of the general public, or are individuals who have access to the media for disseminating their views. In both instances the ideas expressed are usually of a particular and group-centered nature, and those representative of the general and public interest are too often poorly presented. Not infrequently the views of a small but vocal minority are accepted because the opinion of the majority is not heard and, therefore, does not make itself felt. Silent opinion carries little weight in the conduct of public business. Democracy assumes the existence of an intelligent, informed, and articulate opinion to guide government; but in the conditions of modern life there is usually nothing truly public about expressed views, nor are they real "opinion." The vehemence with which views are expressed is not a valid indicator either of their validity, or of the number of people who support them. Issues arise too fast and are too complex and technical for the average citizen to comprehend and formulate opinions upon. Issues are increasingly beyond his ability to grasp. His "opinions" are too often little more than emotional responses to oversimplified statements of problems. He has no time, little inclination, and inadequate information with which to familiarize himself with their complexities, to evaluate facts, derive alternatives, and arrive at reasoned conclusions. Hence, he is naturally susceptible to the slogans, labels, name-calling, generalities, and stereotypes thrown at him by opinion leaders who desire to influence his thinking and induce him to act in their interest. He is psychologically attuned to an acceptance of the ideas of the community figures whom he respects, because of the satisfaction and sense of status that he derives from doing so. Last, but not least, he is also the target of extensive "public education" efforts conducted by the agencies and officers of government whom his opinions are supposed to control and guide.

Agencies for Formulating Public Opinion. Public opinion in a democratic system of government is formulated by several agencies within society. These agencies almost always operate in conjunction one with another, and the aggregate of public opinion at a particular time is the product of their interaction. Chief among them are the media by which views and information pertaining to public issues are disseminated. Television, radio, newspapers, magazines, motion pictures, and books must be included in this category. Of great but subtle influence in the determination of individual reactions are the deeply ingrained behavioral patterns instilled through parental, school and church influence. A third major factor which helps shape public opinion is the existence of diverse groups in society. Groups both reflect and influence public opinion. They contribute to its formulation by engaging in educational and propaganda activities, using every means available to them to carry their message to their members, to the general public, Congress, and the administrative agencies. Fourth, are the efforts of political parties and their candidates to influence voter opinion. To gain votes, a party must sway the opinion of the voters, especially the "independent" voters, to accept its proposals of public policy. Between elections the parties continue to cultivate public opinion by searching for issues and policies, criticizing and attacking each other, holding press conferences, speaking in public, and addressing the country from the legislative chambers. At the same time they also respond to the ceaseless pressure of public opinion upon the political and governmental processes. Lastly, government agencies often unobtrusively but always significantly influence public opinion. Using all available techniques and media, including the talents of professional public relations men and the distribution or suppression of information, government agencies can and do mould a favorable or unfavorable public reaction as the one or the other suits their needs of the moment. Neither the media which influence or create public opinion, nor the forces using them, will achieve uniformity of success. Some media will be more successful than others, depending upon the time, the issue, and the group to be influenced; some forces employing the media will similarly meet with greater success than will others.

Expressing Public Opinion. Various methods are employed by the different "publics" within society to give expression to their opinions. Voting, writing letters to editors, legislators, and administrative officials, paid advertisements, public speeches, testimony before legislative committees, personal contacts with government agencies, radio and television talks, preparation of books and magazine articles, publication of group journals and papers, circulation and transmittal of petitions, and public demonstrations are among those commonly employed. Examine the matter printed in the *International Teamster*, house organ of the International Brotherhood of Teamsters, during and after consideration by Congress of the Labor-Management Reporting and Disclosure Act of 1959. The act was strongly opposed by the union as a "union busting" measure. Its proponents were as biased in its favor as the union was prejudiced against it.

A MESSAGE TO THE AMERICAN WORKER

LIVING and working under the Kennedy Strike-breaking Bill just passed by Congress, you will find out what has really happened to you.

► Your fellow citizens have been victimized by the propaganda mills of big business, aided by their willing accomplices, the nation's publishers.

These propaganda mills have shouted "labor corruption" so loud and long that few have bothered to question how false witness and innuendo have distorted the truth.

While this bill was supposed to be aimed at so-called "corruption," in fact corruption was not and has never been the issue.

This bill is aimed at the jugular vein of the American labor movement: the right of workers to aid each other in their fight for economic justice.

► Many of your fellow workers have been sold out by those so-called "labor leaders" who joined the witch-hunt in a desperate effort to preserve or to win a "good name" at the expense of the worker.

The collapse of the AFL-CIO in the face of this menacing legislation resulted from the uncertainty and panic of certain individuals who made their deals long ago and felt betrayed by the turn of events.

These individuals played the game of the labor-haters out of fear and confusion, and by cooperating in the strategy of "divide and conquer," they helped bring havoc to the house of labor.

► You have been dishonored by those whom you elected to Congress in 1958, when you defeated those candidates with anti-labor platforms, and sent the so-called "right-to-work" laws down to resounding defeat.

All but 52 Congressmen turned upon you because they believed that your vote was not as important as the support of big business and its lackey press.

Now the labor-haters, led for the past three years by McClellan of Arkansas and the two rich Kennedy boys, believe that they have devised a law which will turn one worker against the next, and force one union to break the strike of another.

It is yet too early to say how far the ramifications of this bill will go. Much will be left to the courts to decide.

But it is certain that the labor-haters hope, by outlawing "hot cargo" and secondary boycott, to destroy the historic solidarity of the organized worker.

I cannot tell you what will finally happen. I can tell you that the Teamsters will operate within the law. If that requires us to break the strike of another union, then the name of Kennedy must live in infamy in the minds of those who toil for the necessities of life.

But this I pledge to the American worker: we in the Teamsters Union shall do all that the ingenuity of man, operating within the law, can devise in order to uphold the highest traditions of the trade union movement.

The American worker will not long tolerate a situation in which he must break the strike of another. If the law is finally adjudged to mean that, then he will rise up in the free and orderly democratic process and change that law.

The American worker will not long abide by a requirement that he may not aid another worker in his fight for what is his due. If the law means this, he will change it, too.

No longer may anyone say that "labor does not belong in politics." Politics has struck down the labor movement severely in this year of 1959, and it must be through political action that we strike back.

You, the American worker, are the target of the most concentrated attack by big business in three decades.

The wealthy and privileged believe they now have the weapons they need to restore the sweat-shop days of giant profits and oppression of workers.

They are out to defeat you by destroying your unions.

Political action is one way to preserve your way of life against those who would take it away.

Unswerving loyalty to the high traditions of the trade union movement, insofar as the law permits, is the other.

Fraternally yours,

JAMES R. HOFFA
General President
International Brotherhood
of Teamsters

Elements of Public Opinion.

Propaganda. The chief tool that is used by groups and individuals to influence public opinion is propaganda.[2] Any idea, view, or information, which is expressed or disseminated with the intent deliberately to create, shape, or otherwise to manipulate opinion in a predetermined way, is propaganda. Its content may be true or false, or partly both; it may

[2] For a discussion of propaganda and its techniques see Donald L. Harter and John Sullivan, *Propaganda Handbook* (Philadelphia: Twentieth Century Publishing Co., 1953).

The crucial vote in favor of the Landrum-Griffin Labor-Killing Bill was 229 to 201. Yet the 229 Congressmen in favor of destroying labor represented fewer voters than the 201 who opposed the bill (see chart). Thus the NAM-Chamber of Commerce-Newspaper line about 'popular demand' is found wanting.

come from government or from a private source, an individual or a group, but as long as it is intended to control opinion, rather than to provide data upon which independent, objective judgments can be formed, it is propaganda.

To be effective in relation to national issues propaganda must have behind it extensive organization, be undertaken on a wide scale, and be well financed. It employs all the techniques and media for communicating and controlling ideas. Access to, or ownership of, the media of mass communications is limited to individuals or groups having considerable funds available for such purposes. Hence, the major facilities for disseminating propaganda are readily available only to political parties, important interest groups, unions, government agencies, corporations, and a few wealthy individuals. Except for the relatively few persons who write letters to editors, or who write and publish books and articles, the average citizen is virtually cut off from opportunities for large-scale propagandizing.

Agreement on Fundamentals. An important part of American public opinion consists of an underlying agreement upon the basic assumptions and institutions of American democracy. With significant exceptions, Americans accept such basic ideas as the equality of men, the sanctity of private property, the desirability of justice, individual freedom, and the rule of law, and admit the importance of individual personality. These are typical values upon which the political system rests. They are habits of mind which are seldom understood, and few persons can give a cogent statement of them. Nevertheless, they are deeply instilled in American opinion. They are the inarticulate premises upon which much opinion rests, and they go far to determine the standards of conduct and policy imposed by the electorate upon government through the political parties and the electoral process. They are seldom supported by organized groups established to secure their perpetuation and observance, and, along with other ideas, are often referred to as "unorganized interests." If they are not obscured by propaganda designed to weaken their force they are important determinants of the relationship between what government does and what public opinion feels it ought to do. These fundamental values are vague. They do not supply governed or governors with guides to the solution of public problems. However, they do provide a general framework of accepted ends or purposes with which the policies and programs of government or of private groups must be compatible. Although their existence in society does not exclude contradictory ideas or practices, it does eliminate most squabbling over basic considerations and provide a foundation of unity which accommodates differences and facilitates compromise. As a factor in public opinion, therefore, they limit the demands of individuals and groups upon government.

Concept of the Public Interest. References to the "public" or "general" interest are common, in spite of the vagueness of the concept invoked. The Constitution refers twice to the "general welfare," and most citizens will concede that the well-being of the body-politic is a value to be preferred. The public interest cannot be defined precisely, nor can violations of it be readily identified, yet acceptance of its existence is sufficiently general to exclude from public discussion policies or actions which are thought to be detrimental to it. In times of emergency the idea of the general welfare of the political body becomes the overriding consideration to which all but the most important private interests are largely and almost unquestioningly subordinated. Moreover, it is difficult to comprehend how any political organization could exist among men unless the restraints imposed by government upon private interests were generally felt to enhance the good of all. Belief in the idea of a public interest may, therefore, be an acknowledgement of this fact; but, in any event, the concept has sufficient strength to make it an important factor in any estimation of what public opinion will or will not stand for. In addition, the concept of the public interest is a variable which changes in content from time to time, and in the long run swings back and forth between liberalism and conservatism.

Role of Public Opinion. Hence, the role of public opinion in the American political system is that of arbiter. It cannot and does not express itself in specific terms or on any but the most important or controversial issues. Its force always bears on the governmental process and the conflict of interests in society. When it is articulate it decides between the claims of special interests and determines the extent to which they will be supported. In an inarticulate form public opinion constantly limits the exercise of public and private power over society, since, to the extent that it cannot be manipulated or controlled, it exists as a continuing determinant of what the people will permit or support. Public opinion seldom, if ever, devises the means by which the conflicting interests of society are to be adjusted, but it does determine the acceptability and adequacy of the ideas for reconciling them that are proposed by government, political parties, or private interests.

Public Opinion and Government. If the governmental process is to be controlled by and to be responsive to public opinion, the content of that opinion must be estimated and translated into public policy. The measurement of opinion is mainly undertaken by political leaders in and out of the government, but especially by the President and his political subordinates, and by the party leaders and organizations within the houses of Congress. Government officials, legislators, and party leaders must be sensitive to the demands of public opinion and to the limitations which it imposes upon fulfillment of those demands. Their function in the political process is to work out compromises between competing and conflicting interests within society which will adjust them compatibly with the public interest and acceptably to one another. This process of adjustment requires leaders sensitive to the origins, strength, and content of the beliefs and feelings within the body politic; and great ingenuity is involved in devising ways of accommodating conflicting interests in solutions that public opinion will support. Thus, political leadership, within and without government, endeavors to maintain a balance between contending forces in society by devising workable and acceptable public policies. These are given the force of law and carried into execution by the political branches of the national government. They are the result of negotiation and compromise carried on, within a framework of public opinion, between organized interests, political parties, and organs of government.

Public Opinion and Public Relations. Public opinion in a democracy is supposed to control the political and governmental processes, but a new force has emerged on the American political scene which jeopardizes this fundamental assumption. It is employed by political parties and by interest groups. It is the professional public relations expert.[3] His object, on behalf of a client, is to influence, mould, create, and manipulate public opinion. Pressure groups employ the minions of Madison Avenue to create attitudes in the public mind favorable to themselves; parties hire them to "sell" candidates and policies. Advertising agencies and public relations firms are experts in the understanding of public opinion, the use of mass media of communications, and the techniques of manipulating public attitudes.

In politics the professional's work is much the same as it is in his normal work. He must create a favorable public attitude for his client and an unfavorable attitude toward the opposition. To do so, he must create a "package" consisting of the ideas or personalities to be pushed, find their most attractive features and arguments in their support, and persuade the public to accept them in preference to competing ideas or personalities. Given a candidate or a policy to put across to the public, a public relations firm plans a detailed campaign to create a public image that will sell. It must figure out, within the limits of time and budget, an aggressive program designed to keep the opposition on the defensive. To do so the campaign should reach its peak immediately prior to election time. General principles and ideals must be reduced to catchy phrases, slogans, and symbols which can be drummed by repetition into the public mind, or be readily grasped and remembered because of their easy identification with familiar, accepted ideals or standards. "Return to

[3] For a more extended analysis of this subject see Stanley Kelly, Jr., *Professional Public Relations and Political Power* (Baltimore, Md.: Johns Hopkins Press, 1956).

Normalcy," "I like Ike," "Political Medicine is Bad Medicine" are examples of attention-holding trick phrases. Because there is great diversity in the interests and loyalties felt by individuals, public relations campaigns need to be kept flexible, and to be based on conditions of time and place. The appeal has to vary with the character of the group appealed to; it has to be, in effect, a many-pronged attack, so that if it fails to appeal to one interest or loyalty of an individual it may reach another responsive chord.

The use of professional public relations is too new to be fully or accurately evaluated so far. However, some advantages are thought to result from it. It has depersonalized politics and public opinion management by broadening the appeal to reach greater numbers of voters over a wider area. The appeal is to the general mass of the citizenry. It creates and presents to them a standardized image. It undermines the importance of voter control by political party units and by individuals able to "deliver" the vote. Handshaking, stump speaking, and other personal contacts as vote getting techniques have lost much of their value. The new technique also apparently places a greater emphasis on issues. The personality, the reputation, etc., of candidates are still valuable assets and can make the task of public relations men much easier, but the personal factor of politics is subordinated when an appeal is made on issues. National appeals must be made in terms of broad issues generalized to suit the audience, so that public relations employed on a national scale to influence a national electorate will emphasize national issues and minimize local considerations in national politics.

However, professional public relations in democratic politics is not wholly a blessing. It is a force not available equally to all, for its expense restricts its use to groups or parties with ample financial resources. More significantly, modern professional public relations plays on the weaknesses of democratic foundations. Its appeal is not directed to the reasoning of the people; it does not persuade by an appeal to reason. Instead, it plays on indifference, lassitude, and hero worship, on the habits, emotions, and prejudices of individuals. It puts the emphasis on catchwords and phrases, gimmicks, half-truths and slogans. It is primarily propaganda intended to mould, create, or manipulate the public response that is desired by its director. It is a substitute for thought. It is an attempt to control opinion which, according to democratic theory, is supposed to control public policy. From the nature of the endeavor the public relations expert must exercise considerable control over the substance and method of the group or party appeal. He knows what public opinion can be induced to accept and how best to conduct the public relations campaign. The result of these practices will not be the election of a candidate or the determination of public policy as a result of the informed, deliberative judgment of the voters; it will be manipulated consent, a consent given to what the manipulators desire.[4]

Public Opinion Polls. Efforts have been made for over a century to measure public opinion accurately. Modern techniques of polling make use of refined samples of opinion taken from scientifically ascertained groups. Depending upon the nature and scope of the issue to be polled, sample opinions of a limited number of individuals in each group are obtained. The sample may involve as few as two hundred persons or as many as fifty thousand. Their views are accepted as representative of those of the whole group. If all groups are validly constructed and the samples properly taken, the views expressed are assumed to indicate the attitude of the public at large. The larger the number of opinions solicited, the greater is the accuracy of the result, but the more expensive becomes the effort to obtain it; hence, the one must be balanced against the other.

The use of scientific polling is not a foolproof method for ascertaining public opinion, but it is a great improvement over the old "straw vote" technique of random sampling. It is founded, however, on two fundamental assumptions either of which, if incorrect, would destroy the validity of a poll: (1) that it is possible scientifically to construct a group that is representative of a cross-section of the community at large, and (2) that the responses given to the questions asked reflect the sound judgments of the interviewees. There are considerable grounds for doubting the validity of both, but although much has been done to substantiate the first, no infallible method is yet known. Moreover, opinion is not constant but dynamic and often erratic. Hence, accurate predictions make repeated surveys necessary in order to learn the direction and extent of opinion change.

The second assumption is open to serious challenge. The reliability of responses is affected by many factors which are difficult if not impossible to control. Ambiguity may cause a distorted response, and the phraseology of the questions, the interviewer's attitude or inflection may produce a conditioned response. Answers may amount to mere snap judgments, ill-considered emotional responses, or even lies. Indecision and lack of interest also affect answers in immeasurable ways.

Advantages of Polls. Experience with public opinion polls is relatively brief, but they do seem to offer certain limited advantages. Their utility for measuring short-range opinions on issues of limited scope seems to be considerable. They can be employed to measure opinion more frequently

---

[4] See Edward L. Bernays and others, *The Engineering of Consent* (Norman, Okla.: University of Oklahoma Press, 1956). For an analysis of public relations techniques in a senatorial campaign see *Maryland Senatorial Election of 1950,* Report of the Senate Committee on Rules and Administration, 82nd Congress, 1st session (1951).

and easily than can elections. They focus attention on public questions, and sharpen and stimulate discussion of them. They can be used with a timeliness, relative to the issue at hand, which elections often lack; and issues can be isolated and sharpened when made the subjects of polls. Their potential use by legislators, committees, and administrators to study opinions relating to policies and administrative matters is great but almost wholly undeveloped.

Disadvantages of Polls. The mass appeal of polls and their preparation for use by newspapers tend to make them superficial. The issues selected for attention are often those in which public interest is greatest, regardless of their importance. Numerous issues are handled at one time, so that no one of them can be treated in depth. Polls tend, therefore, to measure only surface opinion, and to ascertain that only once on each issue. Hence, they also fail to determine the solidity of opinion or to gauge the direction and extent of change. They afford no insight into the reasons for the answers given. Polls that indicate a strong opinion in favor of an issue or candidate can influence persons supporting another issue to abandon it and climb on the "bandwagon." They influence the opinion that they are supposed to measure. They do not measure the weight of opinions, but assume that every opinion is as important as every other in spite of differences of knowledge, experience, etc., among the persons questioned. Uninformed and unreflective opinions of persons who do not have to assume responsibility for their ideas, or to act upon them, are injected by polls into the decision of elections and policy questions.

PRESSURE GROUPS

Politics is fundamentally a process of interaction between *groups*. Men are seldom significant as individuals but have political importance as members of groups, for organization is essential to the attainment and exercise of political influence and governmental authority. Yet reactions of unorganized individuals, "unorganized interests," can have a negative significance as restraints on the political and governmental processes. The flagrant violation of a widely held value, such as "equality," might provoke a strong and immediate *organized* reaction. A latent power does reside in unorganized interests, but it is not adequate to prevent their violation, and it seldom gives a positive direction to the political and governmental processes. When it does, as when the "independent" voters decide an election, its effect is almost immediately lost on the legislators and administrators who make and implement policy. What is the interest of "independent" voters in "equality"? How is it to be determined? How is it to be given expression? "Unorganized interests" lack specific content. Hence, the ideal of "equality" will afford little guidance to the conduct of public business; it is, except in certain areas like race relations, generally unsupported by any organization to make it explicit and to work for its implementation. Therefore, the conduct of public business is left to the not so tender mercies of organized and concentrated interests which soon dominate or eliminate the vague and unorganized ones.

Parties and Interest Groups. Man long ago learned that he could better promote his own ends, protect his ideals, and further his welfare by entering into voluntary associations than he could be relying upon his own unaided efforts. In so far as his interests are compatible with public opinion and are of sufficient importance to command wide consideration, they will usually be supported by a political party. The parties, however, are able to represent only a few of the myriad interests extant within the country. Hence, individuals with similar experiences, knowledge, skills, and ideals, must band together to further their mutual aims and aspirations. Their efforts are for the most part legitimate ones, to gain acceptance of particular interests or views that are not sufficiently important or general to receive widespread popular support. The groups thus formed may be large or small, local, national or international in scope, wealthy or poor, active or lethargic, well led and unified or the reverse, dedicated or indifferent. They have a bewildering array of interests and purposes, but a majority of them could be included within one of the following categories: occupational, economic, professional, civic, patriotic, scientific, humanitarian, religious, educational, bureaucratic, philanthropic, ethnic, and reform. Their political activities are secondary to the enhancement of their particular interests, but a few are organized specifically to achieve political ends. However, all exist outside government and the political parties. All may be classified as interest groups. Those which attempt to influence the content of public policy, directly or indirectly, by acting on the legislative or executive branches, are known as pressure groups. Not all interest groups at a given time are pressure groups but and may qualify; and not all which attempt to exert pressure are equally important or successful. The objectives of most groups are usually selfish and intended to further the particular interests of their members, but they are not necessarily incompatible with the general welfare.[5]

Their strength and influence vary greatly. Those of an occupational, professional, or economic nature usually command high status, prestige, and the resources of money, talent, leadership, personnel, and organization necessary for successful propaganda and pressure activities. They are also the groups most interested in the social and economic policies of government. However, other groups, smaller and less well endowed with the material attributes of success, but which also possess prestige, special knowledge, zeal, determination, and unity have met with great success.

[5] For a more complete discussion of the types of pressure groups in the United States see Hugh A. Bone, *American Politics and the Party System* (New York: McGraw-Hill Book Co., 2nd edition, 1955), Chaps. 4-8.

Size and geographical distribution are also important determinants. Extensive dispersion promotes disunity by increasing the diversity of interests among members; however, concentration of members in too small an area diminishes bargaining power because only one or a few parochial interests are involved. They can be ignored by other groups. Doctrinal unity, flexibility, and public acceptance greatly enhance interest group power and influence. In the final analysis, however, it is large groups such as veterans' associations and labor unions which possess organization, money, and a specific shared interest that can exert a powerful influence at the polls. They will probably be most effective in attaining their goals.

Points of Pressure. They endeavor to serve the interests of their members by concentrating their promotional and protective efforts at four points. First, because virtually everything that is done by government requires legislative authorization or the appropriation of money, groups center their attention upon Congress. Each interest group has one or more unifying interests that hold its membership together. These are of major importance to it; therefore, it can be counted upon to support adoption by Congress of those policies which it favors, and to oppose the adoption of those that will do it injury. Second, the interest groups are fully aware that laws are not self-executing. They know that administrative personnel can do much, in the process of carrying it out, to change the meaning and effect of a statute. Therefore, interest groups concentrate their attention upon officials who administer the laws by which they are affected. Third, the groups appreciate fully that public opinion in the United States is the makeweight in the political and governmental systems. Hence, they endeavor through propaganda to "educate" public opinion to regard their interests favorably and to identify those interests with the general welfare. Fourth, the interest groups also work as far as possible through the political parties, and try to win their endorsement and support.

Interest Groups and the Democratic Process. Democracy assumes that all interests of individuals or groups must stand in a relationship of equality to the governmental process, and that no one will be able to secure for itself backstairs preference, privilege, or favoritism. Political parties afford the normal means contemplated by the democratic process for giving public notice to legitimate interests, for weighing them, and for recognizing their importance in the making of policy. However, the inability of the parties to recognize, serve, and translate into law the ideas or interests of all groups impels organizations to exert a direct influence upon government so far as they can.

Their right to do so is beyond question. The Constitution guarantees the freedom of peaceable assembly which makes possible the formation of interest groups; it guarantees freedom of speech and of the press by which the groups publicize their interests and try to gain acceptance for them; and it extends the right to petition the government for redress of their grievances. Their activities may be regulated in the public interest, but these essential rights may not be withdrawn without violating the Constitution. By utilizing the freedoms thus extended to them, interest groups are able at any time to bring their aspirations to the attention of government.

However, the role of interest groups is viewed with suspicion. The chief danger attendant upon their activities is that they will be able to insinuate or to buy their way into, to intimidate or otherwise to subvert, the governmental process to their own ends. Their effect upon that process is often too apparent for the ordinary citizen to ignore. Most groups are devoted to the service of private interests, and the public interests rarely have organized representation. In fact, what the public good is cannot be ascertained with facility or certainty. Moreover, there once was widespread use of bribery and other forms of corruption, and their occasional recurrences serve as reminders of past unsavory practices. These factors combine in the public mind to produce a strong scepticism as to the propriety of interest group activities.

Interest Groups and the Public Interest. What is the public interest in a democracy? It could be considered as non-existent. It could be the sum of particular interests. It could consist of considerations important to the general well-being combined with a compromise of private interests. The latter is the commonly accepted view. In any event, it can be *defined* authoritatively, or it can be *refined* by the competition, clash, and compromise of private and public interests. The first method of determining the public interest is obviously incompatible with democracy; the latter is the foundation on which it rests. Since Congress is the primary agency of the national government for translating the common interest into law, it is necessary that all interest groups have access to its councils so that their felt needs may be expressed, and petition made for their incorporation into the legislative declarations of public policy. Hence, Congress hammers out statements of policy, determining what government shall do, by compromising between the interest groups which attempt to influence it, the will of the voters when it has been made known, and its own judgment of the facts at hand and the prevailing climate of public opinion.

The Internal Character of Interest Groups. The unity of interest groups can easily be overstressed. Few can speak with one voice or can act in unison. Some are unified and dedicated, but most are merely loose associations of individuals who feel that they have or want something in common. Virtually all of them consist of a few active, articulate leaders and many inert, inarticulate followers. Thus, most interest groups act and speak through their leaders. The members are often divided among themselves and are not subject to the direction and control of the few. Hence, for example, labor leaders have seldom succeeded in delivering the "labor vote" in an election. The United States Chamber of Commerce finds a marked difference between the interests of "big" and "little" business. Moreover, few individuals who compose a group submerge themselves wholly in its affairs. Only the fanatic has a single interest to which he devotes his entire personality. Therefore, individuals usually belong to several or many groups among which they divide their attention, loyalties, and efforts. Their divided attention usually causes them to lessen the ardor with which they pursue each interest lest the attainment of one to an extreme degree should render impossible the realization of the others. A pluralistic society composed of multiple group interests and divided individual loyalties is most apt to be a society founded upon the firm basis of moderation. Furthermore, the internal division of interest groups, and the relatively small membership of even the largest, makes it impossible for any one of them fully to secure its aims and aspirations to the exclusion of other interests with which it conflicts. No group can impose its will. Consequently, every group is required to bargain with other groups and to make concessions to their interests in return for their support of its objectives. Finally, merely because they join groups, men do not throw off the restraining effect of the general consensus underlying American democracy nor do they always and fully lose sight of the ideal of the public interest. Interest group rivalry strengthens the democratic spirit of compromise.

Interest Groups in the United States. Interest groups which are active at the level of the national government in the United States are so numerous that no definitive listing of them has ever been made; although any person or group who endeavors directly to influence the legislative process is supposed to register with the clerk of the House of Representatives. It has been estimated that registrations increased by approximately 236 during 1960 to bring the total registrations under the Federal Regulation Lobbying Act[6] to 6,108; but it is well known that a large but indeterminate number of persons or groups who are subject to the registration requirement fail to place their identity and affiliations on the public record. Thus it is that the inadequacy of the political parties as comprehensive instruments of representation has brought into being a large number of organizations and persons whose sole, primary, or incidental purpose is to safeguard some special interest. More than five hundred interest groups maintain headquarters in Washington in order to be near the scene of national legislative and administrative activity.

Several factors contribute to the success of interest groups in the United States. The ideological climate is excellent for their propagation. It extends maximum protection to the freedom to act in one's own interests. It safeguards opinions and the dissemination of ideas through the formation of groups, and the right of the citizenry to have access to the political and governmental processes. The system is one where authority is divided between levels of government, between three branches within

6 60 *Statutes* 812.

REGISTERED LOBBYISTS SINCE 1946
(By Years)

1946*	222	1954	413
1947	731	1955	383
1948	447	1956	347
1949	599	1957	392
1950	430	1958	337
1951	342	1959	393
1952	204	1960	236
1953	296	1961**	336
			6108

* Last 4 mos. only.
** Jan. 1-Sep. 27.
Source: *Congressional Quarterly Almanac,* Vol. 17, 1961, p. 967.

each level, and between numerous subdivisions within each branch. Interest groups are thus afforded an almost unlimited number of points at which to work to attain their ends. Moreover, as will be revealed more fully later on American political parties are essentially weak, disunited, and undisciplined groups which are unable to agree or act cohesively on matters of policy. They are excessively susceptible to, and dependent upon, local pressures and interests, with the result that in the United States the common interest is left largely undefined, unorganized, and unprotected.

The instruments vary by means of which special interests seek recognition or favors. Many of the most powerful and well-financed interest groups with Washington headquarters—the National Association of Manufacturers, the American Petroleum Institute, the United States Chamber of Commerce, the American Medical Association, the National Association of Electric Companies, and the National Milk Producers' Association—maintain their own full-time, permanent, elaborately-organized staffs of researchers, propagandists, contact men, bill-drafters, and legislative counsel. These, and groups which are not as well organized or as affluent, also retain the services of professional legislative agents, who are often public relations consultants, lawyers, former members of the House or Senate, newspapermen, or onetime civil servants, all of whom know their way around the intricacies of official Washington.[7] Many legislative agents are men of honor and integrity; some are subject-matter experts; most undertake to serve the interests of their clients openly and legitimately, but others are charlatans who do nothing but claim credit for whatever crumbs of success may inadvertently fall their way.

Methods of Pressure Groups. As previously noted, interest groups endeavor to make their weight felt by concentrating their attention on

[7] See Lester W. Milbrath, "The Political Activity of Washington Lobbyists," *Journal of Politics,* Vol. 20 (May, 1958).

The Under-the-Bedside Manner

Congress, the administrative agencies, public opinion, and the political parties. However, any success that is achieved with respect to one of these will usually be felt by one or more of the others as well. The tactics used at one time against one point may be ill-advised at another time to influence the same or another point. Each instance of activity must be considered and dealt with on its own conditions.

Congress. Interest groups may work to secure the election or re-election of congressmen whose views are favorable to the group. Conversely, they may oppose the election of those whose views are hostile. Party affiliation is a matter that is secondary in importance to known attitude as a determinant for group support. Election support may take the form of direct money contributions to a candidate, often to candidates of both major parties in order to safeguard the group position. "Delivery" of votes, public endorsements, political education of members, fund raising, propaganda directed at the voting public, contributions of services, materials, radio and television time, preparation of speeches, and payment of campaign costs are but some of the methods groups employ to influence congressional elections. The AFL-CIO, the Farm Bureau Federation, and the National Grange have been especially successful in bringing about the election of friendly legislators and the defeat of others, for in particular constituencies their membership is sufficiently unified, disciplined, and numerous to influence the electoral result. Members of Congress whose political life is closely tied to a particular interest usually form a bloc and can be counted upon to support that interest and to oppose what it opposes. Party lines have little meaning in such cases and punishment at the polls awaits the member who betrays his trust.

The attentions given by legislative agents to congressmen include the traditional social activities, an important means of establishing friendly contacts, and the necessary preliminary to more important relations to follow. Complimentary travel and hotel accommodations, gifts, etc., make members receptive to arguments and to information that is supplied to them. In serving their clients' interests legislative agents seek to persuade legislators to accept their point of view by weight of argument, by winning their favor, by drafting bills, by following voting records and publicizing the results favorably or unfavorably, or by promising support or threatening retaliation at the polls. Members known to be sympathetic can usually be relied upon to lend a receptive ear and a helping hand. A well-placed member, especially a committee chairman, can often work wonders to aid a special interest. Hence, conferences to explain and justify the group's position are common. Great quantities of data, usually accurate and reliable as far as it goes, is supplied by interest groups to legislators who lack adequate personal information and the means to acquire it. Of course, the data supplied by a particular interest lacks objectivity in that it only tells the legislator what the group wants him to know; but by considering what all interests, pro and con, furnish him on a given issue he can learn something about many of its implications. In this way, the effect of one group's work may cancel that of another's.

However, the standing legislative committees of Congress, not the individual members, determine what the content of public policy shall be. They must have adequate information. Some information, but seldom enough, is secured by the staffs of the committees. The committees also normally invite all interested persons and groups to present arguments and data for their consideration and evaluation at hearings that they hold on measures under their consideration. It is, therefore, upon the committee responsible for a particular bill that interest groups concentrate their efforts. Data pertinent to the groups' interests are distributed in great quantity to committee members; prepared statements are submitted for consideration; legislative agents, propagandists, subject matter experts, and legal counsel set forth the views of the groups in open hearings. Administrative officials similarly present information, data, and views defining the position of interested and affected agencies. Their activities in this respect are not unlike those of private pressure groups, but their evidence and supporting data often go far to overcome the assertions, exaggerations, and half-truths presented by the latter.

At the same time that the above activities are carried on, interest groups do what they can to create an impression in the legislative mind that public opinion is in their favor. This they can do by organizing campaigns designed to deluge the members and committees with letters, postal cards, telegrams, memorials, petitions, delegations, and resolutions urging support of the group's position.

Public Opinion. Because the political and governmental processes are responsive to the force of public opinion, interest groups that are able to do so make every effort to "educate" public opinion to think favorably of, and to support, the groups' interests. Many successful campaigns have been waged to influence the formation of public policy.

In order to create a favorable public opinion groups employ every opportunity and device available to reach the public ear with propaganda. Advertising and public relations firms are retained, and books and pamphlets are written and published; speeches are delivered before any group which will serve as an audience, and material is fed to the newspapers, radio, and television outlets. An effort was even made once to rewrite textbooks in order to inculcate an attitude of opposition to public ownership of utilities in the minds of school children. In 1949 the American Medical Association retained a professional public relations agency, spent over $1,500,000, and distributed an estimated 55,000,000 pieces of literature in a successful effort to prejudice the public attitude against what was referred to as "socialized medicine."

A new force is developing among those who influence public opinion and the political parties. Numerous leading business corporations, including Boeing Airplane Company, Bell and Howell, Gulf Oil, DuPont, Glidden Paint Company, General Electric, Republic Steel, Ford Motor Company, and Johnson and Johnson, encourage their officers and employees to get into politics. The emphasis is twofold. First, they endeavor to instill in their employees and staffs the obligation to vote and take an active part in the political life of their communities by seeking public office. Second, corporations are using company papers, newsletters, reports and studies, advertising, and public speeches by executive and middle-management personnel to present their views on matters of public policy. The objective is stated to be a desire to make business a political force equal to that of labor and agriculture, so that it can actively promote its own causes as they are doing. More specifically the intent is to balance the political activity of labor with that of business, to defeat public policies which unduly restrict opportunities for profit and discourage investment, and to protect free enterprise from socialism. To promote these ends corporation executives are entering politics in increasing numbers, and approximately 20,000 businessmen have taken an eighteen-hour action course on practical politics sponsored by the United States Chamber of Commerce. The movement is still young but is gaining momentum. However, it is divided internally between those businessmen who feel that "business," *per se*, should abstain from political activity and those who favor such activity undertaken by businessmen *qua* individuals. Moreover, it must overcome a strong public aversion to business in politics which remains from the days of *laissez faire* economic and political practices and the failure of business-dominated government to solve its problems.[8]

Political Parties. Both political parties and interest groups endeavor to influence public policy, exercise political power, and mobilize votes, but in sum the effect of interest groups on the political process and the content of policy is probably greater than that of the political parties. Although pressure groups and parties have similar objectives, they differ in nature and methods. Interest groups exist outside the political parties, but they do not ignore the possibility of attaining their objectives by working through the parties. Campaign help that is extended to a candidate is also aid to the candidate's party, and direct aid and donations are given to the parties without regard for particular candidates. Pressure groups also attempt to persuade the parties to accept as policy statements in their platforms views favorable to the groups' interests; and they act through the parties when rewarding or punishing elected government officials. But, a political interest group is not a political party. It does not put up candidates for election, assume responsibility for the conduct of government, or attempt to control *general* public policy.

Administrative Officials. Interest groups understand that wide scope for the exercise of administrative discretion must be left by Congress to the executive, so that the latter can adapt statutes to the diverse conditions of modern society. They also know that use of discretion by administrative officials enables them to determine when and how particular laws are to be carried out. Therefore, administrative relations with interest groups are at least as extensive and as significant as are those of Congress, but they are less glamorous and more difficult to observe and analyze.

Some manifestations of the impact of interest groups upon government are apparent, however. Several agencies have been brought into being because of their demands for recognition, or because of public awareness of their need for special protection and service. Thus, the departments of Agriculture, Commerce, and Labor were created by Congress to serve the needs of obvious groups. The Veterans' Administration, the Childrens' Bureau, and the Bureau of Indian Affairs are but three of many more examples. Countless pieces of legislation have been passed to benefit particular groups. Agencies have been set up to regulate the activities of especially important groups, including the railroads, banks, utilities, securities exchanges, and radio and television broadcasters, in the public interest. They are intended to protect the public, but their creation acknowledges the public nature of the regulated groups, and the agencies serve, promote and protect *them* as well as the general public.

[8] Allen H. Center, editor, *Public Relations Ideas in Action* (New York: McGraw-Hill Book Co., 1957).

Other contacts exist between the executive and interest groups. Most important public laws enacted by Congress have their origin in the administrative agencies. They are usually formulated by a process of joint cooperative action and consultation between administrators and representatives of private interests. Proposals for policies to be submitted to Congress often are made to administrators by interest groups. Their representatives serve administrators in an advisory capacity, and supply them with great quantities of information and advice. They transmit group desires to the administrators, interpret statutes and administrative rules, orders, and regulations to their members, furnish specialists to aid administration, and occasionally perform functions on behalf of government. They endeavor to control the appointment of top-level executive and administrative officials so as to secure administrators whose views are favorable to them. Interest groups can reward or punish administrative agencies or officials. They rally to the support of these agencies in times of difficulty with Congress or the public, support or oppose policies before congressional committees, build or undermine their standing with Congress, and support or oppose their requests for funds, personnel, and authority, agitating always for expansion of services and functions beneficial to them and for the contraction or elimination of others. Every interest group has allies upon whom it can call for added support, and every administrative agency has one or more interest groups which are friendly to it and upon whose help it can depend. Hence, the support of interest groups is an important factor in the struggle of administrative agencies and officials for survival.[9] Both the interests and the agencies benefit from their relationships.

Regulation of Interest Group Activity. It is highly desirable that members of Congress should be able to identify pressure groups and legislative agents, and learn something of their purposes, interests, and clients. It is also important that legislators and administrators should not mistake the will of a highly vocal, organized, dedicated, and active interest for that of the people at large. There is more than a little indication that Congress is, to an excessive degree, becoming an instrument for registering the incessant and powerful demands of interest groups, to the detriment of its ability—which at best has never been very great—to develop and follow a sense of national interest. Little effort has been made to regulate the activities of interest groups that bring them into contact with the executive. Incompatibility of interest statutes, administrative dedication to the public interest, fair treatment, consultation and cooperation with affected interests, and judicially imposed controls are relied upon to

[9] See Harvey Fergusson, *People and Power: A Study of Political Behavior in America* (New York: William Morrow and Co., 1947); and Earl Latham, "The Group Basis of Politics: Notes for a Theory," *American Political Science Review*, Vol. XLVI (June, 1952).

protect the public from unjustifiable incursions by interest groups upon the administrative processes of government. But perhaps still less has been done to protect the legislative processes from the efforts of groups that are in contact with Congress. Pressure group activities are both necessary and legitimate, but some practices are intolerable. Bribery and other forms of corruption have been made illegal, as have objectionable electoral practices, but it was not until 1946 that Congress undertook to deal with the problem of lobbying. By doing so it gave belated recognition to the fact that

Present-day legislative complexities are such that individual members of Congress cannot be expected to explore the myriad pressures to which they are regularly subjected. Yet full realization of the American ideal of government by elected representatives depends to no small extent on their ability to properly evaluate such pressures. Otherwise the voice of the people may all too easily be drowned out by the voice of special interest groups seeking favored treatment while masquerading as proponents of the public weal. This is the evil which the Lobbying Act was designed to help prevent.

Toward that end, Congress has not sought to prohibit these pressures. It has merely provided for a modicum of information from those who for hire attempt to influence legislation or who collect or spend funds for that purpose. It wants only to know who is being hired, who is putting up the money, and how much. It acted . . . to maintain the integrity of a basic governmental process.[10]

1961 EXPENDITURES FOR LOBBYING BY CATEGORY AND NUMBER OF GROUPS REPORTING

Category Reporting	Number Reporting	Amount Reported
Business	171	$1,598,091.17
Citizens	52	437,695.26
Employee & Labor	40	857,788.55
Farm	22	365,887.57
Military & Veterans	10	133,734.52
Professional	17	376,911.89
TOTAL	312	$3,770,108.96

Adapted from data presented in *Congressional Quarterly Weekly Report*, Vol. 20, No. 15, p. 602.

The Regulation of Lobbying Act of 1946[11] was designed to apply chiefly to three distinct classes of lobbyists:

FIRST. Those who do not visit the Capital but initiate propaganda from all over the country in the form of letters and telegrams, many of which have been based entirely upon misinformation as to facts. This class of persons and organizations will be required . . . not to cease or curtail their activities in any respect, but merely to disclose the sources of their collections and the methods in which they are disbursed.

[10] *United States* v. *Harriss* (1954), 347 U.S. 612. See also, Donald C. Blaisdell, *American Democracy under Pressure* (New York: The Ronald Press Co., 1957), pp. 82-98.

SECOND. The second class of lobbyists are those who are employed to come to the Capital under the false impression that they exert some powerful influence over Members of Congress. These individuals spend their time in Washington presumably exerting some mysterious influence with respect to the legislation in which their employers are interested, but carefully conceal from Members of Congress whom they happen to contact the purpose of their presence. The [act] in no wise prohibits or curtails their activities. It merely requires that they shall register and disclose the sources and purposes of their employment, and the amount of their compensation.

THIRD. There is a third class of entirely honest and respectable representatives of business, professional, and philanthropic organizations who come to Washington openly and frankly to express their views for or against legislation, many of whom serve a useful and perfectly legitimate purpose in expressing the views and interpretations of their employers with respect to legislation which concerns them. They will likewise be required to register and state their compensation and the sources of their employment.[12]

The purpose of the Regulation of Lobbying Act is to make public the identities of persons and organizations by whom, or on whose behalf, efforts are made to influence the enactment of laws by Congress. To this end the Act requires that

Any person who shall engage himself for pay or for any consideration for the purpose of attempting to influence the passage or defeat of any legislation by the Congress of the United States shall, before doing anything in furtherance of such object, register with the Clerk of the House of Representatives and the Secretary of the Senate and shall give to those officers in writing and under oath, his name and business address, the name and address of the person by whom he is employed, and in whose interest he appears or works, the duration of such employment, how much he is paid and is to receive, by whom he is paid or is to be paid, how much he is to be paid for expenses, and what expenses are to be included. Each such person so registering shall, between the first and tenth day of each calendar quarter, so long as his activity continues, file with the Clerk and Secretary a detailed report under oath of all money received and expended by him during the preceding calendar quarter in carrying on his work; to whom paid; for what purposes; and the names of any papers, periodicals, magazines, or other publications in which he has caused to be published any articles or editorials; and the proposed legislation he is employed to support or oppose. The provisions of this section shall not apply to any person who merely appears before a committee of the Congress of the United States in support of or opposition to legislation; nor to any public official acting in his official capacity; nor in the case of any newspaper or other regularly published periodical (including any individual who owns, publishes, or is employed by any such newspaper or periodical) which in the ordinary course of business publishes news items, editorials, or other comment, or paid advertisements, which directly or indirectly urge the passage or defeat of legis-

---

[11] This is Title III of the Legislative Reorganization Act of 1946, to be found in 60 *Statutes* 812, 839.

[12] *Senate Report*, No. 1400, 79th Congress, 2nd session (1946), p. 27.

lation, if such newspaper, periodical, or individual, engages in no further or
other activities in connection with the passage or defeat of such legislation,
other than to appear before a committee of the Congress of the United States
in support of or in opposition to such legislation.[13]

The Act further requires that persons receiving or expending money to
influence directly or indirectly the defeat or passage of legislation must
file quarterly financial reports with the designated officers containing

1. The name and address of every donor of $500 or more.
2. The total sum of contributions made to or for the lobbyist.
3. The name and address of each person to whom an expenditure of
   $10 or more has been made, in one or more units, within the calen-
   dar year, and the amount, date, and purpose of such expenditure.
4. The total expenditures made by each lobbyist during the calendar
   year.

Defects of Regulation. In spite of the good intent of this legislation,
and in spite of the necessity for controlling the activities of lobbyists,
there is good reason to believe that the Regulation of Lobbying Act of
1946 represents only a sop thrown by Congress to the public in an effort
to relieve the pressure upon itself of adverse public opinion. The act does
not regulate the activities of lobbyists; it merely results, through the
operation of its reporting and registration provisions, in a greater amount
of information being collected on the scope of lobbying than had previously been the case. It probably has had a deterrent effect, but the information furnished in compliance with the statute is sketchy and virtually
worthless. The data supplied by respondents are unintelligible to all but
persons who specialize in their analysis, and they are available only in
Washington. The compilations published quarterly in the *Congressional
Record* are synoptic, unsupported by explanatory data, and almost meaningless. The law applies only to activities directed at Congress by groups,
individuals or organizations whose *principal purpose* is to influence legislation. Its language is confused and badly drafted; it all but invites
non-compliance. Many groups, obviously interested in the activities of Congress but which deny that their principal purpose is to influence legislation, have refused to register as lobbyists or have done so only under
pressure. It does not regulate the methods of influencing public policy
by permitting some and forbidding others, and it relates only to activities
of interest groups which bring them into *direct* contact with Congress. It
does not apply to the indirect methods of influencing the formulation of
public policy. Severe penalties have been provided in the form of fines up
to $10,000, imprisonment up to five years, and disqualification for three
years from pursuing the activities of a lobbyist at the Capitol. However,
no agency of the legislative or executive branches is responsible for enforcement of the statute.

[13] 60 *Statutes* 812, 841-842.

Thus, the interested student of lobbyists' activities can glean at best only a paltry knowledge of their financial affairs. He can obtain no insight into the specific uses to which money has been put, the measures which have been objects of the lobbyists' attention, whether the desire has been to promote or oppose passage, and the degree of success that has been attained. Nor can he gain insight into any other phases of lobbyists' efforts to influence the legislative process.[14]

Should lobbying activities be more stringently regulated? Public opinion would probably respond overwhelmingly in the affirmative, but the issue is not simple. The methods of lobbyists are now generally above reproach. The Buchanan investigation in the House of Representatives reported in 1950; it found few examples of objectionable activity and proposed no drastic modifications in the 1946 statute. How far could Congress go in regulating lobbying *activities* before it ran afoul of the constitutional guarantees of freedom of speech, of peaceable assembly, and of petition? Would not deprivation or serious infringement of those freedoms inflict greater harm upon the body politic than is caused by the occasional abuses of lobbies? Is the democratic representative process not best served by allowing the freest possible scope to the activities of pressure groups? If "good" lobbying is to be permitted and "bad" lobbying to be regulated or forbidden, what is the distinction between them? On what basis is the differentiation to be made? Venality and corruption versus self-sacrifice and honesty? Obscurity and obstruction versus clarity and helpfulness? Is too little lobbying more, or less, dangerous to the legislative process than too much lobbying? Does the legislative process really involve a struggle between the general welfare and selfish interests, or between one selfish interest and another? Do lobbies counteract one another and leave legislators relatively free to vote on principle? Are pressure groups "wicked" if they seek acceptance of their ideas by methods other than persuasion? Should a member of Congress vote so as to appease a powerful interest although by doing so he violates his conscience? Does a member who wholly subordinates particular interests to personal conviction fulfill his function more adequately than one who sells his vote? Should any group, by pressure exerted on a few key members, be able to bring about the passage or defeat of a measure because its own particular well-being is affected? What groups speak with the same authority and effectiveness for the interests of the general public?[15]

[14] For an account of the contribution and expenditures by labor in the 1958 Congressional campaigns, see "Labor Political Spending," *Congressional Quarterly*, Vol. 17, No. 15, pp. 509-515; a more general analysis of 1959 expenditures may be found under "Lobby Spending," *Congressional Quarterly*, Vol. 18, No. 11, pp. 404-408.

[15] For a thoughtful statement on the role of lobbies, see Emanuel Celler, "Pressure Groups in Congress," *Annals of the American Academy of Political and Social Science*, Vol. 319 (September, 1958).

CHAPTER VIII

Political Parties

'*I suppose you KNOW who your candidate will be?*'

GENERAL CONSIDERATIONS

Political parties in the United States are the product of the expansion of democracy. They are the indispensable adjuncts of the constitutional system, and the means for giving life and vigor to the legalistic framework within which the national government exists and functions. They are the heart of the democratic process, the political organ by means of which the lifeblood is pumped through the body politic. It is undemonstrable as an ultimate truth, but the weight of evidence supports the conclusion that they are indispensable to the existence of democracy. If this is not generally true, it is true with respect to democracy in the United States, for political parties in America stand mid-way between the people and the government. They are used to discover the desire of the majority. Hence, they are groups of individuals organized to formulate opinions and to direct behavior, functions which they share with most other associations that are not political parties. But, political parties are organized and maintained in recognition of the fact that isolated men and isolated ideas are politically impotent. Men cannot control the formu-

163

lation and implementation of public policy by their governors, as contemplated by democracy, until they are unified by organization and direction. Political parties in the United States serve to provide these elements and to make government responsive and responsible to the electorate.

Nature of a Political Party. Any effort to define a political party in the United States must be hedged about by exceptions and qualifications. No statement of common agreement on principles or common desire to gain public office, no single explanation of individual motivation to party membership, no pat statement of the relationship between member and party will neatly cover all the cases. The most that can be done is to point out in general terms the salient features of a political party. Thus, a political party in the United States can be described as a voluntary association of individuals who support the same principles, and who wish their party to gain access to public office through the electoral process in order to implement those principles. However, this description is adequate only to the point of conveying the general nature and purpose of a political party. Such a party in this country may normally be thought of as an undisciplined, loosely-joined organization which is without membership rolls, dues or initiation fees, identity cards, distinctive uniforms or other garb, qualifications for membership, probationary periods, or dogmatic creed.

Three levels of allegiance, not always sharply defined when applied to individuals, have been identified within a typical American party. The first consists of a few party members who maintain the permanent organization and functioning of the association, form the hard core of the party, and occupy the strategic positions of continuing responsibility. They are professional or semi-professional politicians who keep the party alive between elections, see to its finances, and exercise a great but immeasurable influence over the choice of its policies and the selection of its candidates. The second exceeds the first in number and consists of those persons who on a limited, non-professional basis contribute funds and services to the party's cause and publicly affirm their adherence to its principles and candidates. Greatest in number is the third level composed of voters who do no more than vote for the party. Between these three levels there may be wide disagreement about the principles of the party and the means of achieving them. Yet, between them all there must be at least that minimum agreement or acquiescence necessary to common action.

Democratic government should be based on the widest possible suffrage. The electorate should be the most important determinant of what government does. Therefore, it is important that the opportunity to vote should be made available to as many persons as possible. It is by means of elections that the popular will, as registered by the voters, is made known most directly, obviously, and strongly to legislators who enact the laws on which virtually all aspects of government are based. It is similarly impressed upon the political executive, the President, and through him on his political subordinates of the executive branch; he controls and directs them and they control and direct the administrative agencies which apply the laws to the people.

However, there is no uniform, clear, spontaneous, or fixed will of the people to which the political branches of the government are kept responsive and responsible. The will of the people is a composite of particular wills. Each voter who participates in its expression has many different interests. Each interest pulls him in its direction; for each interest he has a different will. His interests and desires may be contradictory, but he often supports them nevertheless. A great diversity of opinion exists in the American society. It is enhanced by the extensive literacy, the freedom of thought, expression, and association, and the widespread dissemination of information. All are essential to the formulation and expression of democratic majority opinion. The interests of voters reflect those of society, so that the electorate is not a homogeneous group always possessing, or easily able to formulate, a common view of what should be demanded of government. The American electorate, therefore, is an indeterminate, formless mass lacking direction, unity, and guidance. Without more agreement by it on questions of public policy, definition of the public interest, the popular choice of governors, or the enforcement of political accountability would be impossible. To solve these problems of democratic government is the mission of the political parties. And, to fulfill this mission political parties in the United States perform the following functions:

1. They select, clarify, and simplify questions of public concern, thereby making them comprehensible to the electorate, and focusing attention upon them.

2. They select candidates for public offices among whom the voters may make their choices.

3. They finance and conduct the campaigns.

4. They provide and operate the electoral machinery with which to register the will of the electorate.

5. They do much to harmonize relations between the legislative and executive branches.

6. They provide the basis for organizing the legislature into majority and minority groups which are necessary to define and enact a program of public policy.

7. They facilitate the orderly and peaceful change of government.

8. They provide rallying points around which persons of diverse views can find common ideological ground on which to agree, so that they can speak with one voice in elections.

9. They organize voters into conscious groups in advance of elections.

10. They provide the electorate with the instruments by which the popular control of government is made effective.

11. They educate the voters.

12. They overcome sectional and other differences by subordinating them to the common position that has been agreed upon.

13. They assume control of, and responsibility for, the conduct of government.

14. They serve as intermediaries between government and individuals.

Parties as Brokers of Ideas. From the ideas of individuals and groups which compete for acceptance a major political party selects those to be presented to the electorate. Its operation as a clearinghouse for ideas is affected by its necessity to attract the widest possible support among the electorate to its platform and candidates. It can select only the most important issues for support, and the form in which they are presented to the voters, and set out in the platform, represents a compromise of aims and ideals. On the basis of its platform a major party appeals to the voters to support its candidates, who are presented as standing for the platform and who, if elected, will bring about its enactment and implementation. Therefore, a major political party attempts to be all things to all people in order to attract voter support and gain control of public office. For that reason a major party can rarely afford to take a specific stand on a controversial public issue: specificity usually loses more votes than it attracts.

A major party must take a middle-of-the-road position on issues of public policy which will satisfy its candidates, its voter support, its leaders, and powerful or numerically large interests and groups. The process of choosing and refining its principles is a process of compromise which seldom gives full recognition to any set of ideals or desires, but which does give some recognition to many. Individuals and groups, party leaders and candidates must yield something of what they want in order to gain acceptance by the others. Each must give a little in order to get a little. By this process of reciprocal, peaceful accommodation conflicting ideas of what is for the general interest are harmonized. A middle position is hammered out by the party upon which it hopes a majority of the voters will stand in support of its candidates.

Majority Rule. How are the policies that are to be followed by government determined? The method most commonly used in the United States is designed to permit a decision by a numerical majority of the electorate. However, it does not guarantee and often does not produce a majority decision. Nor does consultation of the popular will necessarily produce a morally right or wise decision; the result may be either or both, but that would be a happy circumstance, not an inevitable result of the process. The voters can decide immorally and unwisely: a majority decision merely represents a position which is supported by more individuals than opposed it. Deciding issues by voting leaves the participants unharmed, whereas deciding them by physical combat does not. It is a process of counting heads, not cracking them, but it affords a result which is analogous to a display of physical strength on each side of the issue.

A system of majority rule rests upon several conditions which are necessary to its successful operation. First, the majority which makes decisions must not be a permanent one, so that the losing minority *always* loses. Majority rule, to be liberal and democratic, must be based on changing majorities, a different one being formed through the processes of compromise for the solution of each issue. Second, each minority must be left free to make itself a majority by winning converts to its point of view through peaceful persuasion. Unless it is free in this way it will be permanently at the mercy of the majority. Third, each majority must be willing to compromise its position to a degree necessary to admit the right of the minority to survive. Fourth, a minority must be willing to acquiesce in the decision of a majority. This it will do to gain concessions and to preserve for itself the opportunity of becoming a majority. Fifth, both sides must accept the fundamental ideals of democracy and the institutions of the constitutional system, although within this framework of consensus they agree to disagree. Thus, Americans agree that public power should be employed for the common good, but they disagree over what the common good is and how best to attain it. The general consensus in support of fundamental ideals and institutions, and the agreement to differ, prevent conflicts of ideas and interests from degenerating into violence destructive to society. It is through the political parties that decisions are made as to what government is to do, and who is to do it.

The Two-Party System. The traditional system which exists in the United States consists of two dominant parties, one of which can be expected to receive the support of an electoral majority for its policies and candidates, and thereby gain control of the Presidency and of Congress. The existence of other political parties, variously known as "third," "minor," or "splinter" parties is not incompatible with the two-party system, for it means only that there should be not more than two major political parties, and not that only two parties can exist within the system.

No incontrovertible explanation can be given for the existence of the two-party system in the United States. Numerous theories have been advanced. Among them must be counted the view that they are descended from the Whig and Tory parties in England in the seventeenth century; that Americans divided into Rebel and Loyalist groups during the American Revolution; that human nature divides men into two contending factions; that certain issues are so sharp that they allow for only two positions; that the electoral college system will not operate properly to choose a President should more than two major parties participate; that in the United States there are no politically conscious racial or religious groups that insist upon forming their own parties; and that the pressure of private affairs and the number and complexity of public questions militate against dissatisfied elements forming other parties with firmly fixed and uncompromising ideals. Whatever the reasons for its long tradition and firm existence, the American two-party system has several advantages to offer the cause of liberal democracy:

1. Its existence acknowledges that there are at least two sides to public questions, but it enables the voters to focus their attention upon only two major alternative programs of proposed governmental activity.

2. It offers the electorate an opportunity to experiment with public policy by supporting first one and then the other major party; to govern by trial and error rather than by imposed solutions.

3. It allows dissent to find an outlet for expression through the party not currently responsible for controlling the governmental process.

4. It promotes unity of thought and action by facilitating compromise and moderation based on free discussion of alternatives, acceptance of responsibility, and the mutual respect and good will of the contending parties.

5. It preserves the temporary character of political power while maintaining a high degree of stability and continuity in its employment.

6. It provides the group in control of government an outlet for its appeal for continued support and also affords its critics a rallying-point from which to challenge its right to govern.

7. It puts no great burden on the voter, requiring him at the least only to decide whether or not he is generally satisfied with the *status quo*, whether or not he desires a change.

8. It requires only a simplified electoral procedure.

9. It best enables the electorate to select and control its governors, and to enforce responsibility upon them for their rule.

10. It gives the electorate a maximum opportunity to influence public policy by encouraging compromises between competing interests and within the political parties before the issues are decided in elections.

One-Party Control. The two-party system of the United States is not the only form of political party system which might be employed. It is possible for only one party to exist within a political system. When this situation prevails within a democracy, as in the one-party South, or in one-party states such as Maine and Vermont, other parties can exist and opposition to the dominant group is possible. However, the possibility of securing political change or of holding the dominant party responsible by resort to the electoral processes is almost non-existent. To that extent democracy is impaired. In authoritarian one-party systems no outlet is provided the electorate for opposition to the governors. Hence, such a one-party system is not really a party *system,* for peaceful change is rendered impossible and is replaced by revolutionary action and purges. One program only is presented to the electorate for acceptance, by governors who have no faith in popular judgments, who demand obedience not opposition, and who deny that any other reasonable way exists by which to govern. An authoritarian one-party system is based upon rejection of the principle that the public interest can best be served by competition between political parties for the support of an electoral majority. The party machinery is merely the instrument by which the rulers perpetuate their authority built upon fraud, propaganda, intimidation, regulation, deceit, and censorship.

Multiparty Control. However, it is also possible for a party system to contain numerous political parties. Multiparty control serves the assumptions and interests of liberal democratic government. It offers the advantage of giving voters a better opportunity to choose and support a political party which has principles like or closely akin to their own. Voters need not compromise their ideals to the extent necessary in a two-party system, and therefore their party affiliation is made more meaningful to them; but it is also apt to confuse them, and to magnify factional and petty issues. Compromises of principle become more difficult, and decisions are usually reached by pluralities rather than by majorities. Legislatures may contain upwards of a dozen parties, so that the enactment of laws depends upon the uncertain support of coalitions of parties. Nevertheless, if decisions are to be reached compromises are necessary, but they are made between representatives of the party groups in the legislature after the elections have been held. Thus, the member-voter is afforded no chance to pass judgment on the position that his party has taken, although it may not be the one which led him to support the party. Public policy depends upon the cooperation of several parties, and it is virtually impossible for the voters to fix on any one of them the responsibility for what has been done or not done. Thus, a high degree of instability characterizes governments based upon multiparty systems, except when one party is disproportionately strong.

Minor Parties. "Minor," "third," or "splinter" parties exist only in a two-party system. They are not tolerated in an authoritarian one-party system and have no identity in a multiparty one. A "splinter" party consists of a faction which has broken away from a major party; "minor" or "third" parties are those which have developed outside the major parties. All are movements of protest and discontent composed of dissatisfied individuals who cannot obtain from a major party recognition for their aims or ideals. They therefore organize a party of their own and try to win sufficient electoral support to secure recognition for their policies. A minor party normally champions only one important policy, but sometimes more than one can be found in its platform. Its appeal for votes is couched in specific terms. A major party is vague and general in order not to alienate its supporters; a minor party is specific in order to attract the votes of persons similarly dissatisfied, for it has no vote to lose. But only one minor party has ever become a major party in American politics.

Minor parties seldom win public office, but they often attract enough votes to induce a major party to adopt their popular idea. Thereby the political life of the minor party is drawn off. This result is not unpleasing to most minor parties. Their leaders and supporters usually desire only recognition and fulfillment of their policies, and these ends can most often be achieved if a major party adopts them. Their importance is that they advocate unpopular reform ideas that lack appeal for the major parties. Few are able to survive long, for if success eludes them their support rapidly falls away. Hopeless causes are never popular.

Numerous obstacles stand in the path of effective minor parties. Lack of adequate financial support, voters' indifference to public issues, their preoccupation with private affairs, the irrational bases of party support, popular dislike of the techniques of partisan politics, political inexperience, the absence of effective organization, the compartmentalization of American politics, the intricacies and obstacles of state statutes governing the creation of parties, voter reluctance to support doubtful causes, and the uncertainty of reward for party service all tend to preclude the rise of minor parties and to hasten the demise of those few which are born.

Their activities are limited to the perimeter of politics, and their distance from success differentiates them from the major parties. Minor parties are seldom able to penetrate to the center of the political process and to gain control of public office. They usually have little or no expectation of winning elections, although those with a concentrated base have occasionally done so at a state or local level. They have only rarely won a House or Senate seat; a combined minor party vote of 5 per cent in a national election is a significant total. Although their effect is difficult to gauge, minor parties are thought to have altered the result of a presidential election only once in the twentieth century. This occurred in 1912, when they received 35 per cent of the popular vote. In subsequent elections they have polled as follows:

PERCENT OF POPULAR VOTE RECEIVED
BY MINOR PARTIES, 1916-1960

Year	Percentage
1916	4.6
1920	5.2
1924	17.0
1928	1.3
1932	3.1
1936	3.3
1940	0.5
1944	0.5
1948	5.6
1952	0.01
1956	1.1
1960	0.015

Yet their service as educational and propaganda associations is their primary contribution to the processes of political democracy. In this guise they have helped to force many policies upon the major parties, including unemployment insurance, old age and survivor's insurance, the eight hour day, a graduated income tax, a postal savings system, regulation of the railroads, direct election of senators, work relief, direct primaries, and maximum hours and minimum wage laws.

THEORIES OF PARTY ADHERENCE

One of the least understood phases of political party life in the United States concerns the reasons why individuals "join" these organizations. Many theories have been advanced in explanation, but although there is merit in many of them, no one of them fully answers the question. Thus, it has been argued that Americans divide naturally into liberals and conservatives, and are attracted for that reason into the Democratic and Republican parties, respectively. However, while it can scarcely be disputed that some individuals are attracted for this reason, neither major political party is wholly liberal or wholly conservative. Both have solid blocks of individuals of both persuasions within them. Furthermore, few if any individuals are consistently liberal or conservative. They normally hold liberal views on some matters and conservative ones on others. An estimated 75 per cent of the voters identify themselves with a party out of allegiance to traditional family political loyalties. Some few desire to become candidates, to influence policy on the choice of candidates, or to obtain favors from the party. Others join a party because of a psychological need for organizational ties, because it gives a satisfactory sense of being "on the inside," because of community pressures in one-party areas, because of loyalty to economic or class distinctions, or because of a sincere belief in its purposes and principles.

Because of the universality of their appeal, the major political parties in America are of cosmopolitan composition. They cannot induce sufficient electoral support to carry an appeal to the voters if they reject all but one or a few selected policies. They must appeal to as wide and diverse a cross section of the electorate as they can, for they are the primary means by which the electorate seeks to obtain public recognition for its myriad competing interests. Their composition is also affected by the characteristics of the American electorate. It probably would not, for example, countenance efforts to organize parties around religion. For that reason church parties have not been part of the American party system. Although religion has been a major factor in American politics, the major parties welcome members of every faith. Some effort has been made to create parties to promote the interests of particular economic, racial, nationalistic, occupational, or class groups, but voters who might be attracted to them have so far shown little inclination to secede from the major parties.

Independent Voters. Approximately 20 per cent of the American electorate professes to be independent of all party allegiance and loyalty, and to vote for the superior candidates and issues. These independent votes may decide a political contest between evenly balanced major parties. Hence, their support is assiduously cultivated, for a shift of from 5 to 10 per cent of the total vote is often sufficient to oust the incumbent party from office. The independent voter shifts his support from one party to the other according to the issues and the candidates. He is, typically, a white-collar, middle-income, suburbanite or small city dweller, a property owner and a mortgage-holder who is a moderate on domestic questions and an internationalist. His vote is influenced most strongly by the existence of prosperity, when he votes Republican or of adversity, when he votes Democratic. When the independent vote is given, as in the 1952 and 1956 presidential elections, to a single party, it can be the determining factor; however, it is usually split rather evenly between both major parties, so that its influence is diminished or lost.

Major American Parties. Since 1856 the major American political parties have been the Democratic and Republican organizations. They are moderate in outlook, and have frequently been accused of being so similar as to give the voter no real choice of alternatives. However, this similarity is the inevitable result of their role as agents of compromise; and to the extent that this compromise is successfully performed extreme differences disappear. Further, both parties support the fundamental ideals and institutions of America. Neither advocates the end of the "rule of law," the abolition of private property or the system of checks and balances, the transformation of the economic system, or the repeal of the Bill of Rights.

American political parties are not ideological parties characterized by tenaciously-held principles that are placed beyond compromise by their members. An American party serves its purpose and retains its value only as long as it can blend and harmonize narrow class, regional, and group interests through a process of give and take. Thus, the role of the parties is to soften and moderate the antagonisms which tend to divide a numerous people with diverse interests spread wide over a continent. To do this each must stimulate compromise among its supporters, who must express the widest possible diversity of viewpoints so that fanaticism cannot seize them and preclude moderation. Nevertheless, real differences in the policies of the Republican and Democratic parties become apparent when specific issues are examined.

The Republican Party. Each party tends to represent different groups and classes of people; their policies must reflect those interests. Modern

Republicanism tends to embrace voters who are well-to-do, of the Protestant faith, female, college educated, professional or executive, conservatively inclined (especially in economic affairs), and who are members of the older age groups. The party is strong in New England, throughout the rural Midwest, and in small towns generally. The Republican Party regularly favors limited governmental activity and reduced national expenditures, sound money, the interests of business, regulation and control of labor, state supremacy, individualism, economic *laissez faire,* limited executive authority, and curtailed foreign economic activity by government. It is the party of economic conservatism, private initiative and investment, and balanced budgets.

The Democratic Party. Since 1932 the Democratic Party has consisted regularly and mainly of male voters in the low to middle income range, non-college educated, white and blue collar, union and non-union workers, younger age groups, minority blocs (Negro, Jewish, Catholic, Irish-American, etc.), the unemployed, skilled and unskilled workers, and urban industrial populations. It supports the interests of labor, internationalism, a regulated economy, abundant currency, federal-state cooperativism, social and economic legislation, control of business, national authority, and executive ascendency. It is the party of economic liberalism, broad distribution of social welfare, and active government.

Party Support. Neither the issues nor the supporting groups are fixed aspects of the major parties. Accepting the Federalists of 1798-1817 as the antecedents of today's Republican Party, and the Jeffersonian Republicans of 1793-1824 as the predecessors of today's Democratic Party, the issues with which each began its life have changed, and are supported today by the opposition party. As the issues have changed, the allegiance of groups interested in the issues have also changed. The above analysis of issues and voter characteristics is suggestive of the usual situation only. No group is inseparably wedded to either major party, nor do the same voters of a group always support the same party. Voter allegiance shifts from party to party with the dominant issues, so that neither major party can hope to receive the solid vote of any group. All that can be said is that more voters of each group will usually support one party than the other. Until 1932 the Republican Party was the largest major party, but the shifting group support in subsequent decades has displaced its former electoral supremacy and has made the Democratic Party the party of the majority.

The complexion of party support continues to change in several important respects. First, a greatly expanded middle income group, basically conservative but leaning to the liberal side of the political spectrum, has developed in the last fifteen years. It has not yet become attached to either major party, but its spokesmen comprise the liberal wing of the Republican Party, which "Eisenhower Republicans" are trying to make

comfortable for it. Second, urban minority groups of the North have emerged as powerful elements within the Democratic Party. Third, organized labor is emerging as a political force; it is still within the ranks of the Democratic Party but threatens either to dominate it or to form a separate labor party to be employed as a makeweight in elections. Fourth, the demands of labor and urban minority groups threaten to alienate the conservative Southern wing of the Democratic Party and drive it toward the Republican fold. Fifth, Republican strength in the South continues to grow with the industrial growth and economic diversification of the region. Northern ideas, money, and leadership increasingly threaten Democratic supremacy, while the emergence of the Republican Party as the champion of Negro rights undermines the "white supremacy" of conservative Southern Democrats. Thus far, however, the record of the Democratic Party as the conqueror of the depression has proved sufficiently strong to keep the South safely within the Democratic fold. Sixth, the importance of the South to the Democratic Party is declining. Its strength tends to shift to the West and Southwest and to increase in the Midwest, so that electoral victory may become possible without a "solid South."

However, realignment of party support is not easily accomplished. Lack of internal unity, discipline, tightly knit organization, and centralized control from the top prevents party reconstruction by decision and command. The parties have weathered many fundamental economic and social changes since the Civil War without being shattered or reconstructed. The main levels of their organizations are so far removed from national issues and are so preoccupied with local and state electoral problems that often they are left untouched by the national issues which tend to split allegiance to the party. Moreover, party allegiance in America is commonly based only upon habit or family heritage and attachment. Because adherence is seldom a matter of belief in principle it requires a profound and deep-seated rift of national feeling to cause a split in party support. Again, evidence indicates that both parties tend to move in the same direction at the same time, but to different degrees and at different speeds; an example is the liberal movement in the ranks of current Republicanism.

PARTY ORGANIZATION IN THE UNITED STATES

In order to mobilize, educate, and accommodate a potential electorate of a hundred million persons the major political parties need to maintain an elaborate organization. Because political parties endeavor to gain control of public office, the structure of their organization is closely adjusted to existing political jurisdictions and electoral areas. However, the units of party organization and the units and agencies of government are entirely separate and distinct; acknowledged party leaders may occasionally secure election to public office, but the party organizations and leadership, as such, cannot dictate to or control the governmental organs. The latter depend in many respects upon the former, but are not subordinated to them.

The organizational structure, then, of the major political parties conforms closely to the structure of national, state, and local units of government and specific electoral areas. It is, therefore, federal in structure. The structure of a major political party consists of two cooperating but otherwise separate units of organization, the state and national divisions. Of these, the former is the more important for party success and survival.

Although the structures of the two major parties differ, a common pattern can be discerned. Some units of party organization are of a permanent type. This category includes committees, and officers and agents such as the national chairman, the treasurers, and the precinct captains. Others are temporary and include conventions, caucuses, and conferences. The permanent units provide leadership, plan matters of policy and campaign strategy, direct and conduct campaign activities, raise funds, maintain intraparty harmony, and in general keep the party in contact with the electorate. The temporary units are mainly concerned with approving matters of internal party policy, formulating and adopting the platform, nominating candidates, constituting committees, and settling intraparty disputes when necessary. Thus, at each level of the organization there is normally found a party committee which functions as the permanent directing authority in party affairs within its jurisdiction. Thus, a national committee, and congressional and senatorial campaign committees are found in the national structure of each major political party.

The state party organization is more complicated. Each party in each state has a state committee with a chairman, other officers, and subcommittees. A state committee sometimes exercises general supervision over all phases of state party affairs and activities, but when it lacks that broad authority it plans and directs the state campaigns, raises funds, carries on much of the campaigns for United States senators and representatives. It chooses or provides for the choice, by convention or primary, of the state's delegates to its national convention. It is closely regulated by state law, but it is not subject to direction and control by any national party unit. Its members are elected by primary, are chosen in state convention, or are the chairmen of county or city committees.

Below the level of the state committee in each state are numerous other committees. They are adjusted to the political subdivisions and electoral districts into which the state is divided. Of these the most important are the county and large city committees whose members are usually selected by county or city primaries but sometimes by conventions. More than three thousand counties possess county committees for one or both parties. They coordinate the lesser units of party organization in rural areas on a county-wide basis. The county chairmen are usually powerful figures in party councils, especially in relation to local political affairs; because the success of the state organization depends upon them, they often wield great influence at the level of state politics and serve as members of the state central committee.

The city committee and its chairman coordinate and give general direction to the work of the wards and of their subdivisions, the precincts. Those of large cities are usually linked directly to state committees, but those of small cities are usually subordinated to the county committee of the county within which they are located.

Below the county and city committees are found variously ward, town, township, village, or borough committees, depending upon the type of rural political subdivisions that exist in a particular state. Of these, wards, established in cities for the choice of city councilmen, are most common. Each has the usual committee, often composed of the precinct captains, which coordinates the party activities of the precincts. Town, township, and borough committees similarly coordinate local party activities in rural areas.

At the bottom of the party structures are the precincts, which are often subdivisions of wards. These number approximately 125,000, of which 100,000 are organized by one or both major parties. Each contains one

DEMOCRATIC PARTY ORGANIZATION IN INDIANA

At closed biennial primaries party members

nominate
Party candidates for
Congress
House of Representatives (2)
Senate (6)
State Legislature
House (2)
Senate*
County offices
Assessor
Auditor
Clerk
Commissioners (3)
Council
Coroner
Judges (6)
Prosecutor
Sheriff
Surveyor
Treasurer
Township offices
Trustee
Advisory Board

elect
a Precinct Committeeman who appoints a Vice-Committeewoman

The precinct committeemen and women of each county make up the County Central Committee.† It elects the County

| Chairman | Secretary |
| Vice-Chairman | Treasurer |

All county chairmen and vice-chairmen in each congressional district compose the District Committee, which elects a District

| Chairman | Secretary |
| Vice-Chairman | Treasurer |

All congressional district chairmen and vice-chairmen in the state make up the State Central Committee. It elects the State

Chairman	Treasurer
Vice-Chairman	National Committeeman
Secretary	National Committeewoman

elect
delegations to the State Convention from the counties

The State Convention

elects
delegations to the National Convention, nominated by caucuses of congressional district delegations.

nominates
all party candidates for statewide executive and judicial offices.

* All terms are for 4 years unless otherwise indicated.
† In cities, precinct committeemen and women make up the City Committee, which operates under direction and control of the County Chairman. City committees, for the most part, are active only in large cities.

polling place and from 100-400 voters, although extremes at each end of
the scale are not unknown. Each is headed by a precinct captain, committeeman, or leader. Occasionally precinct committees are to be found.
The precinct is the only level of the party structure that is in direct
contact with the voters, and it is the task of the precinct to "get out the
vote" on election day. On its success depends ultimately the success of
the party, for the voters in national, state and local elections are the
same. The local units of party organization must deliver the vote for the
highest as well as the lowest public offices if the party is to be successful
at the polls.

In the states, also, are special committees which have been established
to aid the election of designated officials. Thus, congressional district
committees, state senatorial district committees, and judicial district committees are common examples. They exist and function either as adjuncts
to or as integral parts of the usual structure of party units.

At the state level, conventions are held in a few states to nominate
candidates for various state offices, to decide matters of state-wide business, to adopt a platform, and to select state party officers and national
convention delegates. They possess little of the significance or authority
that they once enjoyed in the party structure. Conventions may occasionally be held at the congressional district, city, or county levels. When
party conventions are held, their authority is superior to that of the
corresponding committee, which functions subject to their direction and
control.

At the national level of the party structure conventions, composed of
locally selected delegates, are held every four years, for the purpose of
nominating candidates for the Presidency and Vice Presidency of the
United States, adopting or changing party rules, deciding matters of party
policy, and adopting the national platform. The content of the national
platform, and the selection of a presidential candidate, are not determined by open discussion and debate but are usually the result of bar-
gains, arrangements, deals, compromises, and threats made between and
by powerful state party leaders, elder statesmen of the party, legislative
party leaders, and powerful leaders of big city political organizations.
The convention will be discussed more fully later on.

The National Committee. The highest-ranking permanent organ of the
national party structure is its national committee, composed of one man
and one woman from each state and territory. The Republican Committee
also includes the state chairman of each state carried by the Republican
Party in the preceding election, or which has a Republican majority in
Congress, or which has a Republican governor. The Democratic National
Committee contains 108 members; that of the Republicans contains 146.
Members are nominated in the states by primary, by convention, by state
committee, or by delegations to the national convention. They are for-

mally elected by the national convention, but it invariably ratifies the nominations as made.

The committee is chosen for a term of four years, and serves from convention to convention. Its members take office when their first meeting is called after the adjournment of the convention, and they serve until the end of the following convention. It acts on behalf of the party in the interval between conventions. It is the creature of the national convention and is subject to its control and direction. Each national committee has its own set of officers, including a chairman, several vice-chairmen, a secretary and a treasurer, formally elected by the national committee but actually named by the party's presidential candidate and approved by the committee.

The duties of the Democratic National Committee are described by the *Democratic Manual* as follows:

DUTIES AND POWERS OF THE COMMITTEE

The duties and powers of the National Committee are derived from the Convention creating it and, while subject to variation as the Convention may provide, ordinarily include:

1. Control and direction of the national campaign.
2. Creation of committees and subcommittees deemed necessary to the proper prosecution of its work. . . .
3. Election or appointment of additional officers or committees . . . who may or may not be members of the National Committee. . . .
4. Adjudication of contests for membership on the National Committee. . . .
5. Maintenance of national headquarters at Washington and in the Convention city during the sessions of the Convention, supplying information, enlisting Party cooperation, carrying out Party mandates and contributing to fulfillment of Party pledges.
6. Maintenance of press, radio and television service, speakers' bureaus, club and organization supervision, supplying literature, speakers, organizers and Party representatives.
7. Financing of Convention and campaign expenses and supervision of related expenditures.
8. Provision for the National Convention, involving:

a. Selection of time and place. . . .
b. Authorization of call and determination within authority granted by last National Convention of representation from States, Territories and Districts. . . .
c. Preparation of temporary roll of delegates accepted as prima facie correct pending action on contests reported by the Committee on Credentials for disposition of the Convention. . . .
d. Physical arrangements for Convention, including hotel reservations, granting of concessions, adjustment of auditorium to requirements, installation of telephone, telegraph, radio, television, press and motion-picture facilities. . . .
e. Arrangements for seating of delegations, press, radio, television and visitors;

f. Designation of temporary officers, subject to the approval of the Convention, including the Temporary Chairman, who sounds the keynote of the campaign. . . .

9. Filling of vacancies on the national ticket occurring by reason of death, declination or resignation of any nominee of the Convention. . . .

10. . . . The duties and powers of the National Committee are derived from the Convention creating it and no Convention has authorized the formulation of proposals which might be construed to be in the nature of platform declarations. . . .

11. The National Committee is empowered to expel members for cause. . . .[1]

Both national committees work at top speed before, during, and after the convention until the general election is over. That of the winning party continues active during the next four years. That of the losing party must also work, but at repairing, rebuilding, or refinancing the party to ensure success in the off-year, and following presidential, elections.

The major political parties in the United States, therefore, are composed of fifty state organizations each of which is independent of the other. Within each of them various levels of party structure exist independent of one another in authority and activity. At the top of each party structure is a single set of national party organs which are concerned only with the nomination and election of national candidates. They have no formal powers of direction or control over the state party structures, but, since the ultimate success of the party depends upon the ability of the lower units to deliver the vote, the top organs are usually most anxious to cooperate with the lower ones. Moreover, the top controls much of the party's funds and by granting or withholding donations can exercise considerable influence over a state organization. Yet, it can seldom dictate, for the state structures are often self-supporting, have their own financial resources, and can reward faithful party service by the distribution of state and local patronage. The state and local levels of the party organization exist primarily to serve local party ends; but because there is no separate national electorate in the United States, candidates for national offices are almost entirely at the mercy of the state and local units for their success at the polls. Especially is this true of candidates for the United States House of Representatives and the Senate. Neither the congressional nor the senatorial campaign committees of the parties maintain independent machinery for promoting electoral success. Both, therefore, must work with and through the state organizations. Moreover, the representative must by custom be a local man, longtime resident of his district, familiar with its peculiar interests and problems and known to its electorate. Were it otherwise, opinion holds, a representative could not be depended upon to keep his constituents' interests at heart while serving

[1] Clarence Cannon, *The Official Manual of the Democratic National Convention* (1956), pp. 6-9.

in Congress. Thus, the selection and election of candidates to the House of Representatives is peculiarly a function of the local party machinery.

Independent Party Organizations. Outside the structure of the regular party organizations are to be found numerous party groups created to aid the cause of one or more candidates. To groups of this nature neither statute laws nor party rules are applicable. They take the form of caucuses, clubs, associations, etc., and a great variety of them have operated in recent elections. They have been especially important in presidential campaigns and elections, both primary and general, by virtue of their fund-raising activities, their cultivation of independent voters, and their success at inducing persons who normally remain aloof from partisan political activity to play a part in party politics. Among the more important of these groups have been the Aviation Club for Dewey, Minute Women, the Southern Anti-New Deal Association, the Committee for Constitutional Government, Volunteers for Stevenson, Harry Truman's Campaign Fund, Citizens for Eisenhower, and New Yorkers for Nixon. Disbursements by these groups in aid of a candidate or party in recent elections have become so great as virtually to annul the provisions of the state and national laws regulating party expenditures.

Thus, the Democratic and Republican parties are federally organized and lack integration. Their structural arrangement has the appearance of an integrated hierarchy with lines of authority running down from the top and lines of responsibility running upward from the bottom; but to view them in this way is to accept a false interpretation of their true nature. In general, the units of organization which exist at the various levels of the structure are formally independent of one another, except in so far as they may be dependent for financial support, distribution of patronage or other spoils, upon an officer or unit at a higher level. The least powerful units of the party structure are those at the national level, for the internal control, discipline and unity of policy that can be found in them exist only within the structure of the state organizations. Even there homogeneity is largely mythical. Each state organization is really a conglomerate of local factions contending for control of some 200,000 elective, local, state, and congressional positions and of the patronage that usually goes with them. Each faction has its attention concentrated on the task at hand and has only an indirect interest in the national success of the party. Moreover, parties are defined, given legal status, admitted to the ballot, and otherwise regulated in great detail by state laws.

Lack of Party Unity and Discipline. In theory, the electoral success by which a party gains control of Congress and the Presidency also ensures that it will be held responsible for its trusteeship of public authority. But, because of the lack of internal unity and discipline in American political parties this can be only partially accomplished. American voters do not vote by party principle but by personality and party label.

The parties have discovered that assumption of public office by their candidates, legislative or executive, does carry with it responsibility that is enforced through the political process. However, it is responsibility which falls upon individuals who bear the party label, not upon the party, *per se*. Party unity is so splintered that responsibility can be fixed in no other way. Thus the President is thought of as head of, and spokesman for, his party, but in reality a party has many heads and spokesmen who speak and act independently of his direction or control and often in opposition to him. In the American party system, the President is only a *symbol* of party unity and responsibility, and his ability to lead and direct is determined by many factors. He is not selected or elected to be the authoritative leader of the party, but his personality, his control of patronage, the prestige of his office, his constitutional authority, his ability to mobilize public opinion, his nation-wide constituency, and symbolic leadership can make him a potent factor in party councils. Yet, there is no standard unity or internal discipline which the party head can enforce upon elected recalcitrants who bear the party label.

American voters do not oust a party because they are dissatisfied with its policies; they turn out individuals, who are identified with the party machinery necessary for electoral success, but of whom each has presented his own ideas to the voters. The party does not stand or fall as a party, and presidential efforts to discipline and eliminate dissident elements from the party ranks usually fail because of the strength of local ties independent of national party control. No organ of the national party prepares a uniform platform that is imposed upon its candidates, or passes judgement upon the acceptability, in the light of its policy statements, of candidates running on its national ticket. The national convention is not a party legislative body. A statement of national party policy, to the extent that it does exist, is prepared by the platform committee of each national convention. But, its enactment into law depends upon members of Congress who are locally elected and whose attention is largely devoted to local matters.

Party unity and discipline is weakened by other factors. The federal nature of national party organizations, the near autonomy of the state party systems, the separation of legislative from executive powers under the national Constitution, and the fixed term of legislative and executive tenure with different modes of election, further divide party responsibility and insulate the various centers from centralized direction and control. Of particular importance is the fact that the parties in Congress maintain separate sets of legislative party machinery in each chamber. Each is independent of the regular structure of the party organs and of the President's control, except as political leadership and influence can induce cooperation and agreement on policies. Members of the President's own party in Congress are often able to maintain their character as free agents.

There is seldom a party "position" on legislation; in those few instances when an effort is made to define such a position the membership is not bound to support it. In truth, party leadership and legislative power are so divided in the chambers of Congress that it is possible for a single powerful personality occupying a key position in the legislative process to defeat the enactment of a measure backed by a President of his own party.

THE FUTURE OF THE
MAJOR POLITICAL PARTIES

There is currently a difference of opinion among students of party affairs, although not among politicians and party professionals, concerning the validity of the ideological orientation of the major political parties and the traditional pattern of their internal organization and operation. The critics allege that, given the problems of domestic and international life confronting government, a drastic realignment of both doctrine and organization is necessary.[2] Modern government demands leadership and control, but these are impossible without doctrinal consistency and structural centralization in the major parties. Supporters of the traditional system reply that the suggested changes would be undesirable and unwise, if not manifestly dangerous to democratic institutions.[3]

Immediately a number of important and controversial considerations are opened up. Are the two major American political parties really like Tweedledum and Tweedledee, alike in everything but candidates and name? Consider their respective positions on the issue of governmental action in the distribution of social welfare. Yet, history demonstrates that both do move in the same direction in the face of major changes in public opinion. Commentators have called for a realignment to make the parties stand for something definite, to give the voter a real choice of issues. What is the meaningfulness, they ask, of a party that lumps together under the same label men like Senator Goldwater and Senator Ives, or Senator Paul Douglas and Senator H. F. Byrd? In response it is said that factions have always existed and will probably always continue to exist within the

[2] James M. Burns, "Republicans, Democrats: Who's Who?" *The New York Times Magazine*, January 2, 1955, and *Roosevelt: The Lion and the Fox* (New York: Harcourt, Brace, 1956), pp. 466-467. See also the introduction to Volume 7 of *Public Papers and Addresses of Franklin Delano Roosevelt* (New York: The Macmillan Co., 1941), and especially the report by the Committee on Political Parties of the American Political Science Association, "Toward a More Responsible Two-Party System (1950)," *American Political Science Review*, Vol. 44, Supplement (September, 1950).

[3] In support of the *status quo* are such figures as Walter Lippman, Pendleton Herring, Sidney Hyman, D. C. Coyle, Herbert Agar, W. G. Carlton, and Robert Bendiner.

major parties; that representation of all major interests within each party makes of each an organ of compromise that is essential to political stability, reflects the fear of parties that was held by the framers, and blends sectional and local differences, thereby promoting the stability of the federal system. Moreover, although deep socio-economic changes have occurred domestically and internationally in earlier decades, the political parties have endured with only gradual and moderate responses to newly emergent values and institutions.

Thus, it can be asked: Are the traditional major party structural and doctrinal alignments essential to the system of government as we know it? Would a strengthening of internal discipline, control, and ideological unity along liberal-conservative lines jeopardize its continuance? Would a shaking up of the federal structure of the parties have a desirable or a detrimental effect upon the political and governmental systems? Do "me too" parties weaken the political interest of citizens, result in 60 per cent voter participation in presidential election years, and encourage a feeling that democratic political parties obstruct and evade rather than face up to difficult issues? American parties have not, traditionally—except for the period prior to the Civil War—been ideological parties. Does the resulting paucity of meaning in party labels produce a transfer of voter interest from issues to personalities, with an attendant danger of demagoguery, one-man rule, and enhancement of the executive power? Would a doctrinal realignment of our major parties drive out factions that are thus far satisfied to remain within them, and thereby weaken the two-party system by impelling them to form new parties more to their own liking? If a liberal-conservative realignment were accomplished would either side be in the position of a nearly permanent numerical inferior? Would a realignment be undone inevitably by the apparent necessity of democracy to be based upon a middle position between extremes? Is not the majority process founded on compromise? Would it be possible with strong ideological parties? Has the amorphous nature of the traditional parties brought to the system the degree of moderation, adaptability, and compromise that is attributed to it? Assuming that the parties could be given ideological consistency, would it be possible to operate a government, which had to function in a context of practical politics, on the basis of doctrinal consistency? Does emphasis on doctrine breed intransigence, inflexibility, and, perhaps, fanaticism within the party organization and ranks? Have not the traditional parties made significant contributions to the political system and our whole way of life? Are not changes in doctrinal position constantly taking place, especially in the corn and wheat states, the South and the Southwest? Urbanization and prosperity have had a great impact on the parties in the last twenty-five years, and both have made and continue to make significant adjustments to the pressure of social and economic issues that have all but displaced sectional issues.[4] Would not a party realignment now encourage extremism in the United States by repudiating moderation at a time of continuous stress and crisis psychology? Would the advantages of reform exceed the disadvantages of rejecting 160 years of party tradition, habit, and history?

In the end, it seems likely that doctrinal change and structural modification will come about not according to some design that is grandly conceived and executed, but in response to modifications of public opinion noted and accomodated by sensitive party leadership and ratified by party members.

PARTY FUNDS

Political party activities in the United States are wonderfully expensive phases of our national life. In 1952, the nomination and election of all public officers is estimated to have cost $140,000,000; the presidential and congressional races of 1956, $33,000,000. Non-accountable expenditures and those made by private groups or individuals would add many millions more if they could be ascertained. An hour of "prime" time on one national television network costs $65,000. It costs approximately $125-150 apiece to maintain the almost 140,000 polling places on election day. Like the cost of everything else, that of campaigning and of holding elections continues to rise.

Sources. Where does the money come from? Many resources have been tapped. Both parties rely heavily upon individual contributions. Personal financing of their campaign activities by the candidates is encouraged. Assessments are levied upon persons who want to become candidates. Assessments, often disguised as "voluntary" contributions, are commonly levied on the salaries of state and local employees. Fund-raising activities, loans that are never repaid by candidates or party organs, contributions or expenditures by interest groups, anonymous benefactors, or private associations help fill the party's coffers. Indirect aid in the form of public endorsements or paid advertising can be of great benefit to a candidate or party and can be more valuable than a monetary contribution. Finally, great quantities of unpaid labor are donated by volunteer workers in every campaign and election. These cost a party nothing but greatly aid in defraying the expenses of its activities.

Control of Money. The dependence of political parties upon outside sources of money, and the large sums necessitated by their expenses,

---

[4] An excellent analysis of these changes and the forces behind them may be found in Samuel Lubell, *The Future of American Politics* (Garden City, N.Y.: Doubleday and Co., 2nd edition, 1956).

Dark Alley

afford ample opportunity for corrupting the political process. If democracy is to fulfill its assumptions, it is important that no selfish individual or group should be able to purchase undue influence over, or otherwise subvert, the impartial operation of its agencies. Acceptance of contributions by a party creates an obligation to the donor which can be, and often is, used as a lever to secure preferential treatment. But party government, as the operating part of democracy, is predicated on the assumed equal right of individual and group interests to be judged impartially. The party, as an agency of compromise, accepts some group aims and rejects others for submission to the voters. The competition for party support should take place before campaigns and elections are held, so that the voters may judge the propositions submitted to them as the policies of the party. To the extent that the mechanism of compromise functions properly, the political process ensures that the successful candidates, as legislators or executives, will be free from obligations—to groups or individuals—which have not previously been passed on by the voters. Elected officials must be free to act for the well-being of all, according to standards openly determined by the electoral process and entrusted to them for realization. Therefore, in an effort to ensure that money shall not be employed by selfish interests to purchase undue influence over the governmental process, Congress and the several state

Parents of the problem child

legislatures have undertaken to regulate the financial activities of candidates and party organs in elections.

Congressional regulation of party finances supplements that of the states, but, by mutual consent of local party officials, the provisions of both sets of regulations are often ignored. Public indifference, lack of information concerning party finances, party interest in lax administration, and influence with local enforcement officers combine with the greatly decentralized nature of the electoral machinery to defeat effective regulation of party financial and electoral activity.

Congressional regulation of party finances leaves much to be desired. In general, it is designed either to control the amounts and sources of contributions and the amounts and purposes of expenditures, or to require candidates and party organs to make public their financial activities and records. Most of the enactments in each category are easily evaded with the ready and tacit consent of all. The opportunities for evasion are so numerous as to suggest that Congress intended the restrictions to be not fully effective and to serve only as deterrents. Few of them apply to primaries or to other party activities not directly related to the conduct of election campaigns; nor are activities or expenditures of private groups for partisan political purposes subject to regulation. Contributors may provide free office space, automobiles, airplanes, postage meter machines, office equipment and supplies, hotel suites, stationery, telephone and telegraph services, and even full-time paid employees of a private organization assigned to aid a candidate. No effective control is possible of the large indeterminable sums which are expended privately and often anonymously in aid of a party or a friend seeking office. The statutory limitations on expenditures of candidates and committees are unrealistically low, and this serves to encourage evasion. Financial reports, upon which publicity is supposed to be based, are submitted, if at all, with little scrupulous regard for the requirements of law. But, the crowning defect of congressional regulation of party finances consists in the fact that no enforcement machinery has been established in either political branch.

Proposed Changes. To remedy problems left untouched by existing legislation various proposals have been advanced. Among them are the following:

1. To extend free mailing privileges to all candidates for national office.
2. To encourage increased contributions to political parties by small donors by making these contributions deductible for income tax purposes, or by granting a direct credit of, for example $10, against taxes due.
3. To permit all candidates to list all campaign expenses as ordinary business costs, and thus make them deductible from gross income.
4. To impose and enforce under national law rigid but realistic limitations on the purposes and amounts of expenditures, and to have these paid in whole or in large part by the national government.
5. To reduce the cost of radio and television time to political parties by:

a. Requiring networks, as a condition of obtaining or renewing station licenses, to donate equal time to the candidates of the major political parties.
b. Providing time at reduced cost to the major party candidates for the Presidency.
c. Providing a governmental subsidy to each major party with which to defray the cost of network time charged for at the regular rate.[5]

In 1960, Congress by joint resolution on a "one-shot" basis suspended the "equal time" provision of the Federal Communications Act to permit the "Great Debates" between candidates Kennedy and Nixon.[6] That waiver of section 315 prevented eighteen minor party presidential candidates from demanding that the networks should give them free time equal to that donated for the debates. However, Congress has not made that waiver a permanent part of the law, although proposals to do so are pending. Neither has it shown great inclination to pass tighter regulations

[5] Perhaps the most thorough and detailed study of radio and television campaigning is that of the Freedom of Communications Subcommittee of the Senate Interstate and Foreign Commerce Committee, *Senate Report,* No. 994, Part 6, 87th Congress, 2nd session (1962).
[6] 74 *Statutes* 554.

to cover the reporting of campaign expenditures and contributions, or to limit the size of individual gifts. Provisions to achieve those ends were deleted from the 1961 "Clean Elections" Bill which was passed by the Senate but allowed to die in the House of Representatives.

Federal subsidization of national election campaigns might have far-reaching effects upon the existing patterns of intra-party influence and control. If funds were supplied to the national party units, especially if in large amounts, the result might easily be a loss of donations to the state and local units from private sources. Receipt of the subsidy would not only free the national party units from their present dependence upon money raised at the lower levels, but would also reverse that dependence, particularly if private donations dried up in the face of public financing. Moreover, the distribution of funds from the top of the party structure downward could be used to enforce upon the state organizations a greater degree of party unity, discipline, and support.

The present problem of campaign financing has attracted private attention and stimulated some efforts at solution. During the 1960 presidential campaign the American Heritage Foundation undertook an extensive publicity effort to induce small donors to contribute to the party of their choice. The Advertising Council, various newspapers, business organizations, and community associations have sought similarly to educate the public on the necessity of such support. In 1960, about 11,000 employees of Aero-jet Corporation raised approximately $23,000, divided equally between the two major parties.

Although these signs of public interest in the financial plight of the political parties are encouraging, the "rocketing costs of presidential campaigns, and the recurring difficulties parties encounter in meeting these costs, require us to seek new methods and incentives for financing our political parties." In these words President Kennedy's Commission on Campaign Costs summarized the situation in its report of April, 1962.[7] The Commission's proposals were intended to induce as many persons as possible to make small contributions to the financing of presidential campaigns, to increase public confidence in the ways that the campaigns are financed, and to instill respect among the general public for the legal regulations affecting that financing. To achieve these ends the Commission proposed:

1. To give contributors, during a trial period of not less than two presidential campaigns, a credit against their national income tax of 50 per cent of their contributions, up to a maximum credit of $10 per taxpayer per annum; or, alternatively, to let the taxpayer claim the full amount of his contribution as a deduction from taxable income up to a maximum of $1,000.

[7] *Financing Presidential Campaigns*, Report of the President's Commission on Campaign Costs (Washington, D.C.: U.S. Government Printing Office, 1962).

2. To repeal meaningless limitations on amounts that can be contributed and spent for political purposes.

3. To institute an effective system for disclosure and publicity of the sources and uses of money in politics.

4. To re-enact the 1960 waiver of the "equal time" clause.

5. To provide national funds to finance the successful presidential candidate and his future administration in the period between election and the assumption of office.

6. To enforce the present ban on contributions by labor unions and corporations.

Significantly, the report did not recommend direct government subsidies, but the Commission indicated that if its proposals proved inadequate after a period of reasonable trial it might be necessary to consider a matching system under which the national government would pay the parties up to $10 per voter. The total amount would then be paid into, held by, and disbursed from the United States Treasury. The tone of the Commission's report is thus moderate. It seeks to avoid government financing if possible. To that end the efforts of private bi-partisan business, labor, and individual groups should be substantially increased if the proposals are given legislative form by Congress. They should be authorized to sponsor bi-partisan fund-raising and registration drives, and other activities designed to get the views of candidates before the public on an impartial basis. If the two proposals for tax concessions become effective they should funnel into the party campaign chests a reasonable proportion of the private money that is given away each year in large amounts. Such donations would be channeled into a special unit to facilitate reporting and to preclude cheating by taxpayers in their declarations of tax exempt gifts; and, it is hoped, the proposals would put political contributions on the same basis of civic approval as is enjoyed by gifts to religious, educational, and charitable causes. The burden of responsibility is thereby left where it has historically been, upon the voluntary private contributions.

President Kennedy on May 28, 1962, submitted to Congress proposals for implementing the recommendations of the Commission on Campaign Costs. Except that his suggestions reduced the proposed tax deduction for contributions to $750, compared with the Commission's figure of $1,000, they followed the Commission closely. Both the Commission and the President have opted in favor of disclosure as the most effective, practical, and realistic check on campaign contributions and disbursements. Reporting requirements are to be tightened, and a central repository having authority to receive and examine all contributions has been proposed. Collections and expenditures by committees and other groups that figure so importantly in election campaigns have also been included in the coverage.

Who can argue cogently against a public policy that will free elected public officers from dependence upon a few large contributors, who all too often expect some special consideration in return. Reliance upon a wider range of more numerous small contributors would be much safer,[8] but whether Congress will enact an *effective* system of control over presidential campaign finances only time will tell.

[8] An interesting and informative popularized analysis of political fund-raising may be found in *Harper's Magazine*, May, 1962, "A Cure for Political Fund-Raising," by Philip M. Stern, former research director for the Democratic National Committee, 1952-1956.

CHAPTER IX

Citizenship in the United States

Welcome to all!

GENERAL CONSIDERATIONS

What is a citizen? Should that status, with its rights and obligations, be equally open and available to all? To a majority? To a minority only? If not to all, then to whom? What criteria for granting or withholding it should be employed? Can inequalities be avoided if distinctions are made between citizens and non-citizens? If inequality exists will it make democracy impossible or merely impair its realization? What are the privileges of citizenship? What are its obligations?

The principles governing acquisition and retention of citizenship in the United States are of utmost importance, for they determine the right of individuals to participate in the governmental process—to vote, to hold appointive, and to seek elective, offices, to serve on juries, and to enjoy the privileges and immunities that citizenship bestows. Without citizenship an individual is left subject to the authority of a government but is unable to govern himself by sharing in its power and influencing its policies. Citizenship, then, carries with it expectation of benefits and opportunities of an essentially political nature which are fundamental to

193

meaningful democracy, for they go far to determine the relationship which will exist between the governors and the governed. Who will be governors? How shall they be chosen? By whom? What rights will they possess? Will their rights be different from those of non-governors? Should all men, regardless of their relationship to the political order, possess a common minimum of political rights? Should all members of the state be citizens, or should citizens be a select group of members?

Citizenship, therefore, is a legal status of membership in a state which is shared by individuals who stand in the same relationship of duty, privilege, and patriotism to the body politic. In the United States citizenship is a status of privilege and obligation reserved for certain persons within the jurisdiction of the nation. Therefore, it is not conferred automatically upon everyone merely because he is physically present within its territory and subject to its authority. A citizen, then, is a member of the body politic, whose status imposes upon him the obligations of loyalty, allegiance, payment of taxes, performance of military service as required, obedience to law, and discharge of duties such as voting, holding office, and jury service, for democracy is founded on the fundamental assumption that the citizenry are able and willing intelligently to choose their governors and determine public policies. American citizens, especially, are obligated to inform themselves about matters of public concern.

The overwhelming proportion of persons in the United States are citizens and, therefore, eligible to share its offices and to participate in the determination and administration of its affairs. In return for the allegiance which he gives the political order the citizen receives its protection for his life, his property, and his liberty. They are regarded as reciprocal obligations, the one being compensation for the other.

In the United States at different times there have also been persons having the status of "nationals." A national is one who is not a full-fledged member of the political order, but who does not enjoy the full privileges of citizenship. He is not a citizen of another body politic; he is under the legal protection of and owes primary allegiance to the state which claims him as a national. The term is used mainly in international law and relations, but inhabitants of Puerto Rico prior to 1917, and inhabitants of the Phillipines before 1946, of Guam before 1950, of the Virgin Islands before 1927, and of American Samoa today, have had, or have, the status of nationals of the United States. However, today virtually all persons in relationship to the American political system are either citizens or aliens.

If an individual in the United States is neither a citizen nor a national, he is an alien. Alienage connotes the absence of relationship of the individual to the political order in which he finds himself. The laws of the United States, and of the states, may, and in fact do, grant him certain rights and guarantee them as long as he is in the country. But he has no *right* to be here, and his presence is at the suffrance of the national government. Therefore, his enjoyment of those rights that he is permitted is subject to termination at any time that he forfeits his good standing in the United States and is deported.

The Constitution of the United States refers to "citizens of the United States" and to "citizens of the several states." Thus, it recognizes within the American governmental system two types of citizenship, but it does not indicate what the relationship between them is. Which is primary? Can one be held without the other?[1]

Adoption of the Fourteenth Amendment, in 1868, answered these questions, for it declared unequivocally that

All persons born or naturalized in the United States, and subject to the jurisdiction thereof, are citizens of the United States and of the State wherein they reside.

In so declaring, it established that persons could be citizens of the United States whether or not they were citizens of a state.

That its main purpose was to establish the citizenship of the negro can admit of no doubt. The phrase "subject to its jurisdiction" was intended to exclude from its operation children of ministers, consuls and citizens or subjects of foreign states born within the United States. . . .

The next observation is more important. . . . It is that the distinction between citizenship of the United States and citizenship of a state is clearly recognized and established. Not only may a man be a citizen of the United States without being a citizen of a state, but an important element is necessary to convert the former into the latter. He must reside within the state to make him a citizen of it, but it is only necessary that he should be born or naturalized in the United States to be a citizen of the Union.

It is quite clear, then, that there is a citizenship of the United States and a citizenship of a state, which are distinct from each other and which depend upon different characteristics or circumstances in the individual.[2]

Thus, national citizenship was made paramount to, and independent of, citizenship of a state.

ACQUISITION OF CITIZENSHIP

The Fourteenth Amendment also declared that citizenship in the United States could be acquired only by birth or by naturalization.

Citizenship by Birth.

The Territorial Principle. Most American citizens are born in the United States. They acquire their citizenship according to the place of their birth by the ancient principle of *jus soli*, or "law of the soil." It is the primary rule governing acquisition of citizenship in the English-

[1] Prior to the Civil War these questions were the source of great dispute. See *Dred Scott* v. *Sanford* (1857), 19 Howard 393.

[2] *Slaughter-House Cases* (1873), 16 Wallace 36.

speaking countries and most of Latin America. By it the individual becomes a citizen of the country in which he is born without regard to the citizenship of his parents.

The 14th Amendment affirms the ancient and fundamental rule of citizenship by birth within the territory, in the allegiance and under the protection of the country, including all children here born of resident aliens, with the exceptions or qualifications . . . of children of foreign sovereigns or their ministers, or born on foreign ships, or of enemies within and during a hostile occupation of part of our territory. . . . The Amendment, in clear words and manifest intent, includes the children born within the territory of the United States, of all other persons, of whatever race or color, domiciled within the United States. Every citizen or subject of another country, while domiciled here, is within the allegiance and the protection, and consequently subject to the jurisdiction, of the United States. . . .

To hold that the 14th Amendment of the Constitution excludes from citizenship the children, born in the United States, of citizens or subjects of other countries, would be to deny citizenship to thousands of persons of English, Scotch, Irish, German, or other European parentage, who have always been considered and treated as citizens of the United States.[3]

The Parentage Principle. To supplement the principle of *jus soli* Congress has enacted that certain persons born outside the limits of the country may be citizens of the United States at birth, according to the principle known as *jus sanguinis,* or "law of the blood." By this principle citizenship is acquired at birth according to the nationality of the parents without regard to the place of birth. This ancient principle of Roman law is widely accepted, especially by the nations of Europe. The current act of Congress controlling acquisition of citizenship by parentage declares that the following shall be citizens of the United States at birth:

(3) a person born outside of the United States and its outlying possessions of parents both of whom are citizens of the United States and one of whom has had a residence in the United States or one of its outlying possessions, prior to the birth of such person;

(4) a person born outside of the United States and its outlying possessions of parents one of whom is a citizen of the United States who has been physically present in the United States or one of its outlying possessions for a continuous period of one year prior to the birth of such person, and the other of whom is a national, but not a citizen, of the United States; . . .

(7) a person born outside the geographical limits of the United States and its outlying possessions of parents one of whom is an alien, and the other a citizen of the United States who, prior to the birth of such person, was physically present in the United States or its outlying possessions for a period or periods totaling not less than ten years, at least five of which were after attaining the age of fourteen years; . . .

(b) Any person who is a national and citizen of the United States at birth under paragraph (7) . . . of this section, shall lose his nationality and citizen-

[3] *United States* v. *Wong Kim Ark* (1898), 169 U.S. 649.

ship unless he shall come to the United States prior to attaining the age of twenty-three years and shall immediately following any such coming be continuously physically present in the United States for at least five years: *Provided:* That such physical presence follows the attainment of the age of fourteen years and precedes the age of twenty-eight years.[4]

Thus, the more remote the allegiance of the parents to the United States, the more difficult it is for the child to acquire citizenship at birth. A person born in the United States or one of its outlying possessions is, of course, a citizen at birth by the principle of *jus soli;* the geographical United States includes the continental United States, Alaska, Hawaii, Puerto Rico, Guam, and the Virgin Islands, while Western Samoa and Swains Island are outlying possessions.

Dual Citizenship. In the United States the phrase "dual citizenship" has a special meaning in that most citizens of the United States are also citizens of a state. That this is a specialized use of the phrase is suggested by the widespread practice of referring to a "citizen" of the United States but to a "resident" or "inhabitant" of a state.

However, "dual citizenship" more properly refers to the condition that arises when the same individual is concurrently a citizen of two or more nations. The great majority of citizens of any country are born citizens by both the principle of place and of parentage, for most parents are citizens of the country in which their child is born. However, "dual citizenship" results when two nations at the same time lay equal claim to the allegiance of an individual. Thus, one nation may claim his allegiance because of his birth within its territory, and the second because his parents were citizens of it at the time of his birth. This situation arises from the inherent right of every nation to determine for itself, and according to its own constitution and laws, who its citizens shall be. Most governments insist that only a single allegiance is possible and either assert or relinquish their claims when disputes arise. Although the condition of "dual citizenship" may cause inconvenience to the individuals involved, it is not likely to produce serious consequences. Conflicting claims of allegiance are resolved by treaties between the United States and other governments. These treaties set forth the reciprocal rights and obligations of persons having "dual citizenship" which will be recognized by the claimant nations.

The United States does not attempt to exercise jurisdiction over dual citizens when they are within the jurisdiction of another claimant government. Their best protection from the other claimant government is to avoid its jurisdiction. Most governments recognize a right of choice vested in minors who have dual nationality, and one that they become eligible to exercise when they attain the age of twenty-one years. The United States permits a choice at age twenty-five.[5]

[4] *U.S. Code*, Title 8, sec. 1401.
[5] See *U.S. Code*, Title 8, sec. 1482.

Citizenship of Women. The citizenship of women in the United States is determined by their individual choice, apart from the status of their husbands. Since 1922 an American woman citizen has not lost her citizenship by marrying an alien; an alien woman has not gained citizenship by marrying an American citizen. The first category retains her citizenship unless she renounces it. The second must be naturalized to obtain it, although the process is simpler and speedier than that prescribed for other aliens.

Citizenship through Naturalization. There are but two ways of obtaining citizenship in the United States; one is by birth and the second is by naturalization. Naturalization can, therefore, be defined as the "conferring of the nationality of a state upon a person after birth, by any means whatever." In this country naturalization is exclusively regulated by Congress in the exercise of its constitutional authority to "establish an uniform Rule of Naturalization." Pursuant to that authority, Congress has provided for the collective naturalization of groups and the individual naturalization of persons.

Individual Naturalization. This process is jointly administered by the executive and judicial branches of government. Certificates of naturalization are conferred upon individuals by courts of law,[6] which usually act on each case as is recommended by an investigator from the Department of Justice.

Any alien, lawfully admitted to the United States for permanent residence, may petition for naturalization if he meets certain qualifications and has fulfilled certain requirements, and discrimination in the granting of citizenship because of the race, the sex, or the marital status of the petitioner is forbidden.[7]

The first stage in the process of individual naturalization begins when an alien, lawfully admitted to the United States for permanent residence, eighteen years of age or older, who has been five years in the country and six months a resident of a state, files a petition for naturalization with an appropriate court in that state. Thereafter, he may not leave the country until he has been admitted to citizenship; during the entire period of the process he must continue to be of good moral character, attached

---

[6] Jurisdiction to naturalize is vested in certain courts, as follows:

(a) Exclusive jurisdiction to naturalize persons as citizens of the United States is conferred upon the following specified courts: District courts of the United States now existing, or which may hereafter be established by Congress in any State, District Courts of the United States for the District of Columbia and for Puerto Rico, the District Court of the Virgin Islands of the United States, and the District Court of Guam; also all courts of record in any State or Territory now existing or which may hereafter be created, having a seal, a clerk, and jurisdiction in law or equity, or law and equity, in which the amount in controversy is unlimited. *U.S. Code*, Title 8, sec. 1421.

[7] *Ibid.*, sec. 1422.

to the principles of the Constitution of the United States, and well disposed to the good order and happiness of the United States. In addition to these qualifications, the prospective citizen must be able to read, write, and speak English,[8] understand the principles, history, and form of government of the United States, must repudiate totalitarianism, anarchy, and belief in the overthrow of government by force and violence, must not have advocated those principles, or belonged to organizations, or associated with individuals who did during the ten years prior to naturalization. These declarations must be witnessed by two citizens of the United States, who are required to sign each petition for naturalization, but their truth is also verified by an investigation made by agents of the Immigration and Naturalization Service. The investigator makes his recommendation to the court and reports his findings concerning the petitioner's qualifications for citizenship. The naturalization court need not, but usually does, act on the recommendation of the investigator that the applicant be granted or denied naturalization.

When at least thirty days have elapsed after the filing of the petition for naturalization, the court holds a public hearing, when it may examine the petitioner and his witnesses under oath, but if the usual prior investigation has been made this stage is a formality. In the latter case, the examination in open court is not made unless it is demanded by the candidate for citizenship or ordered by the court. At the end of this stage the court orders the petitioner admitted to citizenship, directs that letters of citizenship shall be issued, and the oath of renunciation and allegiance shall be administered, according to the following standards:

A person who has petitioned for naturalization shall, in order to be and before being admitted to citizenship, take in open court an oath (1) to support the Constitution of the United States; (2) to renounce and abjure absolutely and entirely all allegiance and fidelity to any foreign prince, potentate, state, or sovereignty of whom or which the petitioner was before a subject or citizen; (3) to support and defend the Constitution and laws of the United States against all enemies, foreign and domestic; (4) to bear true faith and allegiance to the same; and (5) (A) to bear arms on behalf of the United States when required by the law, or (B) to perform noncombatant service in the Armed Forces of the United States when required by the law, or (C) to perform work of national importance under civilian direction when required by the law. Any such person shall be required to take an oath containing the substance of clauses (1)-(5) of the preceding sentence, except that a person who shows by clear and convincing evidence to the satisfaction of the naturalization court that he is opposed to the bearing of arms in the Armed Forces of the United States by reason of religious training and belief shall be required to take an oath containing the substance of clauses (1)-(4) and clauses (5) (B) and (5) (C) of this subsection, and a person who shows by clear and convincing evidence

[8] Aliens over fifty years of age who have lived twenty years in the United States, and those physically unable to meet this test, are excused.

to the satisfaction of the naturalization court that he is opposed to any type of service in the Armed Forces of the United States by reason of religious training and belief shall be required to take an oath containing the substance of said clauses (1)-(4) and clause (5) (C).[9]

Clauses (5) (B) and (5) (C) represent the accommodation of demands made for the liberty of individual conscience which is the essence of liberal democracy. Religious liberty and freedom of thought, protected by the First Amendment and recognized by these clauses, acknowledges that in the domain of conscience there is an allegiance higher than that owed to the state. Thus, Congress has permitted aliens whose religion forbids them to bear arms in defense of the United States to be naturalized without being forced to sacrifice their religious beliefs.[10]

Upon completion of the oath of allegiance,

A person admitted to citizenship by a naturalization court . . . shall be entitled . . . to receive from the clerk of such court a certificate of naturalization, which shall contain substantially the following information: . . . statement that the court having found that the petitioner intends to reside permanently in the United States, . . . had compiled in all respects with all of the applicable provisions of the naturalization laws of the United States, and was entitled to be admitted a citizen of the United States of America, thereupon ordered that the petitioner be admitted as a citizen of the United States of America; attestation of the clerk of the naturalization court; and seal of the court.[11]

Collective Naturalization. This comes about when Congress, exercising its power to determine to whom, and the conditions under which, citizenship shall be extended, passes a statute naturalizing a group of people. Examples of this type of action are readily found, and one may be discovered in the granting of citizenship to the inhabitants of Alaska.

A person born in Alaska on or after March 30, 1867, except a noncitizen Indian, is a citizen of the United States at birth. A noncitizen Indian born in Alaska on or after March 30, 1867, and prior to June 2, 1924, is declared to be a citizen of the United States as of June 2, 1924. An Indian born in Alaska on or after June 2, 1924, is a citizen of the United States at birth.[12]

In accord with the rule that the acquisition of territory does not by itself extend citizenship of the United States to the inhabitants of the area, Congress has also passed statutes collectively naturalizing the inhabitants of Puerto Rico, Hawaii, the Virgin Islands, and, in 1950, Guam. In 1924 it extended citizenship to a distinct group of persons not identified with a particular geographical area when it collectively naturalized the American Indians.

[9] *U.S. Code,* Title 8, sec. 1448.
[10] See *Girouard* v. *United States* (1946), 328 U.S. 61.
[11] *U.S. Code,* Title 8, sec. 1449.
[12] *Ibid,* sec. 1404.

LOSS OF CITIZENSHIP

Citizenship may be lost as well as gained. If it is taken away against the will of the citizen, the loss is effected by "denaturalization." This is a process applicable only to naturalized citizens. If citizenship is voluntarily relinquished, the loss is known as "expatriation." Natural born and naturalized citizens may expatriate themselves.

Denaturalization. A naturalized citizen may have his citizenship revoked as a penalty or punishment, according to constitutional standards of protection. It is the duty of United States attorneys, when good cause is shown, to institute proceedings to revoke and set aside the order admitting naturalized citizens to citizenship, and to cancel their certificate of nationalization.

The power of revocation reserved to the United States is founded upon the firmly established principle that

An alien has no moral nor constitutional right to retain the privileges of citizenship if, by false evidence or the like, an imposition has been practiced upon the court, without which the certificate of citizenship could not and would not have been issued.[13]

An alien who seeks political rights as a member of this nation can rightly obtain them only upon terms and conditions specified by Congress. . . . No alien has the slightest right to naturalization unless all statutory requirements are complied with; and every certificate of citizenship must be treated as granted upon conditions that the government may challenge it . . . and demand its cancellation unless issued in accordance with such requirements.[14]

Such a certificate . . . is in its essence an instrument granting political privileges, and open like other public grants to be revoked if and when it shall be found to have been unlawfully or fraudulently procured.[15]

In its consequences, [denaturalization] is more serious than a taking of one's property, or the imposition of a fine or penalty. For it is safe to assert that nowhere in the world today is the right of citizenship of greater worth to the individual than it is in this country. . . . This does not mean that once granted to an alien, citizenship cannot be revoked or cancelled on legal grounds under appropriate proof. But such a right once conferred should not be taken away without the clearest sort of justification and proof. So . . . in an action instituted . . . for the purpose of depriving one of the precious right of citizenship previously conferred we believe the facts and the law should be confined as far as is reasonably possible in favor of the citizen. . . . It is not denied that the burden of proof is on the Government. . . . This . . . burden must be met with evidence of a clear and convincing character that when citizenship was conferred . . . it was not done in accordance with strict legal requirements.[16]

[13] *Johannessen v. United States* (1912), 225 U.S. 227, 242.
[14] *United States v. Ginberg* (1917), 243 U.S. 472, 474-475.
[15] *Johannessen v. United States*, p. 238.
[16] *Schneiderman v. United States* (1943), 320 U.S. 118.

Grounds for Denaturalization. A certificate of naturalization may be cancelled by appropriate judicial action if it can be shown that fraud was committed, or a material fact concealed or misrepresented, during the process of acquiring citizenship by naturalization. Moreover, a certificate may also be revoked if (1) within ten years following his naturalization a naturalized citizen refuses to testify as a witness before a congressional committee concerning his subversive activities; (2) if within five years after his naturalization he joins or becomes affiliated with any organization membership in, or affiliation with which, at the time of naturalization would have precluded him from naturalization; or (3) if within five years after his naturalization he returns to the country of his birth or to any other foreign country and takes up permanent residence there.[17]

For many decades Congress has treated the rights of naturalized citizens differently from its regulation of those of citizens at birth. Theoretically, the status of naturalized and natural-born citizens is the same in law, but in fact it is not. Citizenship obtained after birth is not worth as much as that acquired at birth, for naturalized citizens hold their nationality subject to limitations not applicable to natural-born ones. The former hold and enjoy their citizenship under restrictions of speech, travel, residence, and association, violation of which can result in loss of nationality. Moreover, acts showing bad moral character, as well as violations of law, may be grounds for denaturalization, which, when accomplished, is ordinarily followed by expulsion from the United States. Because a citizen at birth cannot be denaturalized, the same acts done or the same beliefs held by him cannot be followed by like consequences. Conviction for the violation of a law might be followed by loss of some or all of the rights of citizenship, but the citizen at birth would not loss his citizenship, except in a situation covered by the rules of expatriation. In that situation, he would become "stateless," unless another body politic claimed his allegiance; but, that possibility apart, it is doubtful that he could be expelled from the United States. Hence, not only can a naturalized citizen not become President of the United States, but he cannot do, without risking his citizenship, a considerable number of other things which a citizen at birth may do.

Expatriation. Expatriation is the voluntary relinquishment of citizenship by word or deed. Not all nations admit the right of expatriation, but the government of the United States has long made it available to naturalized and natural-born citizens.

Although Congress can attach loss of citizenship only to conduct voluntarily taken, it does not follow that a citizen must intend to lose his citizenship when he acts. Expatriation (denationalization) is not dependent upon the citizen's assent. Assent need not even be implied from his having engaged in conduct that amounts to an abandonment of citizenship.

[17] See *U.S. Code,* Title 8, sec. 1451 (a), (c), (d).

At present, a native-born or naturalized citizen may expatriate himself by (1) obtaining naturalization in a foreign state; (2) making an oath or other formal declaration of allegiance to a foreign state or a political sub-division thereof; (3) entering or serving in the armed forces of a foreign state without the prior authorization of appropriate American officials; (4) holding any office or employment under a foreign state if it requires that he should be a citizen of that state or take an oath of allegiance to it; (5) voting in a foreign election or plebiscite; (6) making a formal renuncia-tion of American citizenship before an official authorized to receive it; (7) deserting the military forces of the United States in time of war, if convicted and dishonorably discharged; (8) committing an act of treason, bearing arms against, or trying to overthrow the government of the United States by force or violence, or conspiring to do so, if convicted by court martial or a court of competent jurisdiction.[18]

Expatriation cannot be imposed. In all cases it is presumed to have been voluntarily assumed. Hence, these provisions contemplate voluntary actions performed with knowledge of their consequences, actions which by word, by deed or by a combination of both, demonstrate a lack of allegiance to the United States. But, the Constitution says nothing about loss of citizenship. It defines who are to be citizens and confers upon Congress the authority to regulate naturalization. Ought implementation of that grant to exhaust the power of Congress? *Should* Congress be able to provide for loss of individual citizenship, for any reason or as a con-sequence of any action, other than by deliberate, voluntary personal renunciation? An expressed, voluntary relinquishment before a court or a designated public officer, taking an oath of allegiance to, or being naturalized in, a foreign state, and holding a position under authority of a foreign state for which only its citizens are eligible, would clearly seem to imply a transfer or abandonment of one's allegiance to the United States. But can the same be said of voting in a foreign election or plebiscite, of deserting from the military forces, or of leaving the country to avoid military service or training? Even acts of treason might be im-pelled by considerations having nothing to do with one's allegiance. There can be no question of Congress' authority to deter commission of these acts by providing that their perpetrators shall be imprisoned, fined, de-prived of the *rights* of citizenship, even deprived of their lives. But, should the fact that conviction of treason may carry the death penalty justify stopping short of that and denationalizing the traitor? Does desertion from a military post when impelled by fear, anxiety, physical or nervous exhaustion, or even by a desire to get into the fighting, demon-strate a loss of allegiance or disloyalty? Is desertion to the enemy the same as desertion in the face of the enemy? Is desertion in peacetime different from that in war or national emergency? If a deserter must be convicted and dishonorably discharged first, is not denationalization merely addi-

[18] *Ibid.*, sec. 1481.

tional punishment? Does that process transfer control of the individual's citizenship to the military officers composing the court martial that tried him? Should the military have authority to determine anyone's citizenship?[19]

The threat of denationalization, for most persons, probably has a very strong deterrent effect. To attach it to acts such as voting in a foreign election, or to desertion, is doubtless a convenient and effective way of inducing American citizens to refrain from specified types of activity. It is certainly convenient for Congress to be able to attach loss of citizenship to individual conduct that it has sought to regulate under its legislative authority. But, *should* it do so? Does the act of voting in a foreign election or plebiscite, for example, necessarily demonstrate a lack of that loyalty and allegiance to the United States that is the essence of citizenship? If foreign electoral law permits aliens to vote, how can participation by American citizens create a reasonable danger of embarrassments and dangers to our foreign relations? Or, suppose that the action resulting in forfeiture of nationality was taken to aid the United States and out of loyalty to it, as when Italian-Americans voted in post World War II Italian elections to help defeat the Communist Party in Italy.[20] Are there no means by which Congress could attain its ends without imposing a disability of such far-reaching and unusual consequences upon citizens of the United States?

[19] See *Trop* v. *Dulles* (1958), 356 U.S. 86, in which sec. 401 (g) of the Nationality Act of 1940, as applied to a natural-born citizen, was held to be void. That section provided that a citizen would lose his nationality "by deserting the military or naval forces of the United States in time of war, provided he is convicted thereof by court martial and as a result of such conviction is dismissed or dishonorably discharged from the service." Only five justices were able to agree on the result, but they could not agree among themselves on why they thought so. Four thought that to deprive of his citizenship a dishonorably discharged soldier convicted by a military court of desertion in wartime was a cruel and unusual punishment that violated the Eighth Amendment. Two of them went on to hold sec. 401 (g) void because it vested control over citizenship in the military without giving the accused the protection of the Bill of Rights during his trial. The fifth member of the majority felt that there was no reasonable relation between the war power and denationalization. The four dissenters felt that loss of citizenship here was not a cruel and unusual punishment, since the death penalty could be imposed upon conviction. They also felt that loss of citizenship was sufficiently related to the war power to sustain the statute as a necessary and proper means to its effective execution.

In *Kennedy* v. *Martinez* and *Rusk* v. *Cort*, Nos. 2 and 3, October Term, 1962, decided February 18, 1963, the Supreme Court invalidated the provisions of the 1940 and 1952 Nationality Acts prescribing loss of citizenship by a natural-born citizen who left, or who refused to return to, the United States to avoid military training or service during war or a period of national emergency. The Court disposed of the cases on grounds of procedural due process of law, and left unanswered the basic question whether Congress could cause revocation of a natural-born citizen's nationality for any reason. However, the grounds relied upon suggest that if the proper procedure is employed such revocation can be constitutionally achieved.

[20] See *Perez* v. *Brownell* (1958), 356 U.S. 44, which upheld sec. 401 (e) of the Nationality Act of 1940.

How valid is it to reason that a citizen, natural-born or naturalized, voluntarily relinquishes his nationality, although he does not assent to or intend that result or know that it will occur because of what he does? Is not the burden of the magnitude and nature of denationalization really *imposed on*, rather than being voluntarily *assumed by*, the citizen? Moreover, if Congress can employ loss of citizenship to make one of its legislative powers more effective, why can it not do so in aid of any or all of them? Obedience to the laws of the United States and payment of its taxes, like military service in its defense, are obligations of citizenship. Fulfillment of them is evidence of loyal attachment and allegiance to it. Why should one who fails to render military service be deprived of his nationality, when an embezzler of national funds, an evader of national taxes, or a robber of a national bank is not? Do not espionage and sabotage also endanger paramount national interests and the safety of the body politic? Yet, conviction on a charge of espionage or sabotage does not result in loss of nationality. Why does the first show a lack of allegiance, loyalty, and attachment to the United States, when the others do not?

Consider the thoughts of Chief Justice Warren on the subject of denationalization:

Citizenship is not a license that expires upon misbehavior. The duties of citizenship are numerous, and the discharge of many of these obligations is essential to the security and well-being of the Nation. The citizen who fails to pay his taxes or to abide by the laws safeguarding the integrity of elections deals a dangerous blow to his country. But could a citizen be deprived of his nationality for evading these basic responsibilities of citizenship? In time of war the citizen's duties include not only the military defense of the Nation but also full participation in the manifold activities of the civilian ranks. Failure to perform any of these obligations may cause the Nation serious injury, and, in appropriate circumstances, the punishing power is available to deal with derelictions of duty. But citizenship is not lost every time a duty of citizenship is shirked. And the deprivation of citizenship is not a weapon that the government may use to express its displeasure at a citizen's conduct, however reprehensible that conduct may be.[21]

PRIVILEGES AND IMMUNITIES OF UNITED STATES CITIZENSHIP

Citizenship of the United States imposes duties but it also extends to those who hold it privileges and immunities which cannot be abridged by any law made or enforced by a state. These are enjoyed equally by native-born and naturalized citizens, but they are nowhere enumerated. If the Supreme Court had, *ab initio*, interpreted the "privileges and immunities of United States citizenship" in an inclusive manner, it could have made them comprehend all of the freedoms of the Bill of Rights, but it did not do so.

[21] *Trop* v. *Dulles* (1958), 356 U.S. 86.

Both state and national citizenship carry privileges and immunities, but only the latter are protected from state action by the Fourteenth Amendment. However, the declaration that "No state shall make or enforce any law which shall abridge the privileges or immunities of citizens of the United States" was not intended to transfer to Congress the power to protect all civil rights in the United States. It can protect only those which owe their existence to the national government, its national character, its Constitution, or its laws.

One of these . . . is said to be the right of the citizen of this great country, protected by implied guaranties of its Constitution, "to come to the seat of government to assert any claim he may have upon that government, to transact any business he may have with it, to seek its protection, to share its offices, to engage in administering its functions. He has the right of free access to its seaports, through which all operations of foreign commerce are conducted, to the sub-treasuries, land offices, and courts of justice in the several states." . . .

Another privilege of the citizen of the United States is to demand the care and protection of the Federal government over his life, liberty and property when on the high seas or within the jurisdiction of a foreign government. Of this there can be no doubt, nor that the right depends upon his character as a citizen of the United States. The right to peaceably assemble and to petition for a redress of grievances, the privilege of the writ of habeas corpus, are rights of the citizens guaranteed by the Federal Constitution. The right to use the navigable waters of the United States, however they may penetrate the territory of the several states, and all rights secured to our citizens by treaties with foreign nations, are dependent upon citizenship of the United States, and not citizenship of a state. . . . To these may be added the rights secured by the 13th and 15th articles of Amendment and by the [due process] clause of the Fourteenth.[22]

The privileges of United States citizenship also include the right to vote for national officers, to enter the public lands, to pass freely from state to state, to be protected against violence while in the custody of a United States marshall, to petition Congress for a redress of grievances, and to inform United States authorities of violations of its laws.[23]

However, most of the ordinary rights of everyday life are privileges of state citizenship. This bestows "nearly every civil right for the establishment and protection of which organized government is instituted," including the right to marry, establish a home, raise a family, buy, hold and sell property, make contracts, pursue a lawful occupation, and inherit money or property.

Since 1873 there has been a consistent refusal to enumerate the privileges and immunities of United States citizenship or to increase their number. Instead, the "due process" and "equal protection" clauses of the Fourteenth Amendment have provided much of the constitutional basis for controlling state authority and protecting individual rights.

[22] *Slaughter-House Cases* (1873), 16 Wallace 36.
[23] Enumerated in *Twining* v. *New Jersey* (1908), 211 U.S. 78.

Exclusion and Expulsion of Aliens. Although this subject involves control of alienage rather than the regulation of citizenship, it is sufficiently closely associated with the latter to justify setting out a few of the fundamental principles which guide the exercise of national power.

It is an accepted maxim of international law, that every sovereign nation has the power, as inherent in sovereignty, and essential to self-preservation, to forbid the entrance of foreigners within its dominions, or to admit them only in such cases and upon such conditions as it may see fit to prescribe. . . . In the United States, this power is vested in the national government, to which the Constitution has committed the entire control of international relations, in peace as well as in war. It belongs to the political department of the government, and may be exercised either through treaties made by the President and Senate, or through statutes enacted by Congress. . . .[24]

The right of a nation to expel or deport foreigners, who have not been naturalized or taken any steps towards, becoming citizens of the country, rests upon the same grounds, and is as absolute and unqualified as the right to prohibit and prevent their entrance into the country. . . .

Vattel says: "Every nation has the right to refuse to admit a foreigner into the country, when he cannot enter without putting the nation in evident danger, or doing it a manifest injury. What it owes to itself, the care of its own safety gives it this right; and in virtue of its natural liberty, it belongs to the nation to judge whether its circumstances will or will not justify the admission of the foreigner." "Thus, also, it has the right to send them elsewhere if it has just cause to fear that they will corrupt the manners of the citizens; that they will create religious disturbances, or occasion any other disorder, contrary to the public safety. In a word, it has a right, and is even obliged, in this respect, to follow the rules which prudence dictates. . . ."

The right to exclude or to expel all aliens, or any class of aliens, absolutely or upon certain conditions, in war or in peace, [is] an inherent and inalienable right of every sovereign and independent nation, essential to its safety, its independence and its welfare. . . .[25]

In spite of the harsh ring of these statements of sovereign authority, the policy of the national government toward immigrants and alienage in the United States can scarcely be surpassed in its leniency.[26]

[24] *Ekiu* v. *United States* (1892), 142 U.S. 651.
[25] *Fong Yue Ting* v. *United States* (1893), 149 U.S. 698.
[26] The student may pursue this subject farther by consulting William Spencer Bernard, C. Zeleny, and H. Miller, editors, *American Immigration Policy* (New York: Harper Bros., 1950); the report of the President's Commission on Immigration and Naturalization, *Whom Shall We Welcome?* (Washington, D.C.: U.S. Government Printing Office, 1953); Max James Kohler, *Immigration and Aliens in the United States* (New York: Bloch Publishing Co., 1936); Marcus L. Hansen, *The Immigrant in American History* (Cambridge, Mass.: Harvard University Press, 1940); Milton R. Konvitz, *The Alien and the Asiatic in American Law* (Ithaca, N.Y.: Cornell University Press, 1946); and William M. Gibson, *Aliens and the Law* (Chapel Hill, N.C.: University of North Carolina Press, 1940).

CHAPTER X

Suffrage in the United States

GENERAL CONSIDERATIONS

Although in a liberal democratic system of government many ways are open to the individual through which he can influence government, the key to promotion of self-government is participation in the franchise. It quickly registers the opinions of all enfranchised segments of the population. It is the primary means afforded by the liberal political mechanism for holding one's governors to account. It is a means of obtaining equality, social, political, and economic, among the classes and groups comprising the membership of the body politic. It is a stabilizing force within the political order, for men will more readily obey laws which they have had a share in making than they will those that are imposed upon them. If they feel confident that their grievances can be made known through use of the legitimate channels of protest, they will not feel impelled to throw up the barricades and resort to violence. Extension of the suffrage, it seems, must precede achievements in other areas.

The evolution of voting in the United States shows that the strength and vigor of democracy has increased in direct proportion to the expansion of the suffrage and the resulting effectiveness of the peoples' voice in choosing their public officers. This has been especially true for the place in society and the well-being of certain identifiable groups. Consider the political awakening and liberation of women and Negroes that have occurred, mainly in the twentieth century. Politicians have little need, and no disposition, to concern themselves with the plight or interests of any class of citizens that cannot or will not vote. In a liberal representative democracy the balance of power within the electorate conditions the balance of power within the communities and among the political parties and the politicians. Each modification of suffrage qualifications, each shift in the composition of the electorate, is reflected in a shift of political power within and between the parties. The franchise, and individual and group self-interest, are seemingly inseparable, but whereas a broadly based suffrage is indispensable to democracy, the existence of democracy is no assurance that universal suffrage will prevail. Great advances have been made since 1789 in the democratization of American political life, but backsliding has occurred. The mere act of voting is without significance, as recent experience with authoritarianism teaches, unless the whole political system is oriented to give meaning to the vote. In the United States since the Civil War disfranchisement in practice has grown at the same time that legal qualifications for voting have been relaxed. The imbalance of urban-rural populations, corrupt practices, tricky registration procedures, gerrymandering both deliberate and silent, the restrictive effects of poll taxes, literacy tests, understanding and character tests, residence requirements, and of fear, intimidation, and physical and economic coercion combine to keep large numbers of American citizens from the polls, or to distort the representative character of their votes.

To be in harmony with the democratic ethic qualifications for voting should be as devoid of restrictions and limitations as possible, so that the maximum number of persons can participate. However, probably no political order has ever permitted everyone to vote. Aliens are generally excluded by contemporary practice, as also are certain categories of citizens. The problem is to admit all qualified persons while excluding all unqualified ones, but the absence of precise standards of eligibility makes the solution difficult. Therefore, it is of primary importance to discover who may vote in the United States, and how that determination is made.

Synoptic History of Voting in the United States. A survey of the history of suffrage in America, however brief, reveals a constantly broadening basis of popular participation. When the Constitution was adopted only a small percentage of the people could qualify to vote under the then existing state laws. Distrust of popular government was strong and was reflected in a wide variety of financial qualifications for voters. Religious tests were not unknown. The framers incorporated no uniform requirements into the Constitution because of their inability to agree upon a common set. In spite of the number and diversity of limitations on the suffrage, the percentage of voters in America in 1789 was higher than in other countries, although the suffrage was not democratic by present standards.

Viewed in its broadest perspective the suffrage has been steadily extended since 1789, as one after another of the barriers to voting has been removed. Until about 1835 there was a gradual elimination of financial, religious, and property-owning qualifications. Thereafter, the franchise was available to most free white, male, citizens, over twenty-one years of age, and, although this was a far cry from universal suffrage, it represented a great step toward the practical realization of democratic theory. It brought about a shift of political power to the common man from the semi-aristocratic control of the earlier federalist period. This condition of the suffrage prevailed until adoption of the Fifteenth Amendment by which all legal impediments to Negro voting were theoretically removed. In 1920, after fifty years of agitation a similar step was taken to end discrimination based on sex when the Nineteenth Amendment was added to the Constitution.

Once the most liberalized in the world, the American suffrage is now surpassed by those of several foreign nations—Australia, New Zealand, Norway, Sweden, Denmark, England, Holland, France, and Canada. A substantial minority of American citizens are for various reasons, some entirely legitimate, ineligible to vote. In general, felons, aliens, lunatics, and minors are barred from voting. However, at the same time that suffrage qualifications in most of our states have been revised to admit more persons, those of other states have been made more restrictive. Persons of Oriental descent, Mexican-Americans, Puerto Ricans, American Indians, and Negroes have been the subjects of discriminatory legislation and practice in those states where they live in considerable numbers. An impressive list of devices and schemes, some sophisticated, some simple minded, have been added to the voter qualification laws of a few states. Probably no state today is administering its electoral system with wholly clean hands; but by far the most widely-known object of discrimination is the southern Negro. To a large extent the history of voting in the United States for nearly a century has been the history of the effort to gain equality of voting rights for the Negro. Only the women's suffrage movement has a comparable history, and that was concluded forty years ago.

The History of Negro Suffrage in the South. At the conclusion of the Civil War, the southern states were occupied militarily by the northern states. Carpetbaggers moved in to pick at the corpse of the South. The newly-freed Negro was a new citizen as well, untutored, inexperienced, without any awareness of the obligations or responsibilities of self-government. Military defeat brought with it political disqualification of the former white plantation and urban semi-aristocratic leadership, and thus created a vacuum into which moved the carpetbagger and the newly en-franchised Negro. Supported by the military regime, reconstruction governments were established in the former confederacy by Radical Re-constructionists in Congress, and until 1876 maintained control. Negro voters, legislators, and administrators figured prominently in the affairs of the time. Unable to vote or hold office themselves, southern whites of the earlier leadership class formed terrorist organizations to fight the political ascendency of the Negro. The Ku Klux Klan, the Knights of the Golden Horseshoe, the Knights of the White Camellia, and other similar groups came into being to terrorize, intimidate, coerce, and brutalize the Negro into political quiescence. With the end of Reconstruction in 1876, however, northern military forces were withdrawn. Having regained their political rights, the whites, who regarded the Negro as politically in-competent and intellectually inferior, sought ways to evade the Fifteenth Amendment. Use of force and terrorism continued widespread. Control of the state governments was regained from the carpetbaggers and Negroes, and laws, copied mainly from those of big city political machines in the North, were enacted to render the Negro politically harmless. Legislatures encouraged discrimination by private individuals and public officers, and the ingrained servility of the Negro was played on to its maximum worth.

However, southern whites have always been divided into moderates and extremists in their attitude toward the place of the Negro in the political order. Some of the post-Civil War leadership was embarrassed by the extensive and enduring use of violence, and sought more subtle, legal, and non-violent means to exclude or control Negro voting. Illegal methods had largely driven the Negro out of southern political life, so that in the 1880's and 1890's the southern states began to enact laws establishing elaborate literacy tests, residence requirements, financial qualifications, and intricate registration procedures. In 1890 came Mississippi's constitutional amendment combining a literacy test, tax paying requirement, and an understanding test tied to a system of voter registra-tion. Its purpose and net effect were to increase the powers of discretion of registration officers, who now without difficulty could exclude Negroes but enroll whites who were no better qualified. Tests of good character that could be administered with complete subjectivity, requirements of property ownership, and the "grandfather clause" (of short but infamous duration) followed.

The effectiveness of the methods for disenfranchising the Negro was largely dependent upon the skill of legislators, registrars, and voting officers in giving them both an appearance of generality devoid of racial bias and a content capable of application in a highly arbitrary and discriminatory manner. Moreover, once violence had abated, courts of law showed no great initiative in looking behind the letter of the laws to examine their spirit and the manner of their execution. If no discrimination was contained in their language, courts for several decades showed no disposition to ruffle the serenity of racial relations by inquiring into their application. Not until 1915 did the Supreme Court invalidate, because of its design and result,[1] a state statute aimed at disenfranchising the Negro, and that decision did nothing to aid Negro suffrage in the South. Then came the "white primary," the device *par excellence* to exclude Negroes but admit whites to an effective role in the political process. Most Negroes who voted were members of the Republican Party. The Democratic Party in the South became the avowed white party by excluding Negroes from membership. Thus, it became a simple matter to make nominations at closed primaries in which only whites participated and in which the only effective political choice could be made in the South.

In the last twenty years a revival of interest in the political rights of the Negro has developed out of a combination of factors. Industrialization in the North has caused many southern Negroes to migrate there. The Negro populations of industrial areas have increased, and with increased numbers has come increased political strength. Both major political parties in the North have been forced to seek, in effect bargain for, their support. Perhaps post-World War II "humanism" in America has augmented concern for the Negro at home, but certainly the impact of racial discrimination in America upon the cold war position of the United States and its ability to appeal to new nations, especially African ones, in the name of liberty and equality has emphasized the urgency of reform. Also, and of great significance, the Supreme Court in 1944 demonstrated a new attitude and willingness to use the judicial power to protect the voting rights of Negroes.[2] Supported by the added impact of legal actions, the enactment of the Civil Rights Acts of 1957 and 1960, and investigations of southern voting practices, Negroes in increasing numbers are beginning to vote, particularly in urban areas of the South; but the fight to end discrimination against the Negro voter is far from won.

Since the days of the New Deal, the Negro vote in America has been

---

[1] *Guinn* v. *United States* (1915), 238 U.S. 347.
[2] *Smith* v. *Allwright*, 321 U.S. 649.

TWENTY CONGRESSIONAL DISTRICTS WITH
LARGE NON-WHITE POPULATIONS

Rank	District	Member	% of Non-white Population	Winner's % 1960 Total Vote
1	Ill. 1 (U)	Dawson (D)*	92.1%	77.8%
2	N.Y. 6 (U)	Powell (D)*	88.5	71.6
3	Pa. 4 (U)	Nix (D)*	73.8	78.4
4	Haw. (AL + 1)	Inouye (D)	68.0	74.4
5	Miss. 3 (R)	Smith (D)	65.5	92.7
6	Ill. 2 (U)	O'Hara (D)	51.7	66.6
7	N.C. 2 (R)	Fountain (D)	50.5	87.8
8	Mich. 13 (U)	Diggs (D)*	50.3	71.4
9	Miss. 2 (R)	Whitten (D)	49.6	X
10	Va. 4 (R)	Abbit (D)	48.0	X
11	Mich. 15 (U)	Dingell (D)	46.6	79.4
12	S.C. 6 (R)	McMillan (D)	46.6	X
13	Miss. 4 (R)	Williams (D)	46.4	X
14	Ohio 21 (U)	Vanik (D)	46.4	73.0
15	Md. 4 (U)	Fallon (D)	45.5	65.5
16	S.C. 1 (R)	Rivers (D)	44.0	X
17	N.C. 1 (R)	Bonner (D)	43.8	86.5
18	Mich. 1 (U)	Nedzi (D)	41.4	85.5#
19	Ga. 6 (R)	Vinson (D)	41.3	X
20	Miss. 5 (R)	Winstead (D)	41.2	X

U   Urban
R   Rural
AL At large
*   Negro member
+   A majority of the non-white population is non-Negro
1   46.5% urban; 44.5% rural; 9% suburban
X   No major party opposition
Post-1960 special election

Of the remaining 76 congressional districts with non-whites forming over 20 per cent of the total population, only one (43 Calif. 15 (U), McDonough, 32.4, 51.3) was captured by a Republican in the 1960 congressional election. Of those above, 11 are southern, 9 are non-southern districts. Of the remaining 76, 58 are southern, 18 are non-southern.

Adapted from *Congressional Quarterly Weekly Report*, Vol. 20, No. 13, p. 507.

solidly behind the Democratic Party in and outside the South, except in the presidential elections of 1952 and 1956. In 1960 an estimated 70 per cent of all Negroes voting in 1960 cast their ballots for the Democratic Party.

Senator Thruston Morton, then Republican National Chairman, blamed Nixon's loss on the failure of the party to capture a larger portion of the Negro vote.[3] Of the 96 congressional districts having populations over 20 per cent non-white only one returned a Republican to the House, and in a study released by Representative William H. Ayres, Republican of Ohio,

[3] *The New York Times*, November 10, 1960, p. 35.

of 86 *non-southern* districts with populations 10 per cent non-white only 15 elected Republican representatives.[4] Judged by the results of the New York City mayoralty, and the New Jersey gubernatorial, elections of 1961 the peak of Negro support has not yet been reached. Probably the economic status of the Negro, which is lower than that of all other major population groups, is the primary reason for his support of the Democrats. He badly feels the need for such things as public housing, and welfare legislation, issues that are stressed by the Democratic Party programs, while the Republican Party stresses economy, limited government, balanced budgets, and individual self-sufficiency. The parties' stands on civil rights have some importance, but they are thought to be secondary to the influence of economic issues. Wooing of the Negro vote by the Democratic Party began with President Franklin Roosevelt, whose legislative program won the southern Negro away from his Republican background. The programs and policies of the northern liberal Democrats have held the support of the newer generations of Negro voters. The Kennedy administration was very active in appointing Negroes to high office and in publicizing that fact, has vigorously enforced the voting rights laws, it is claimed, and has sought to speed up public school desegregation, and to end racial discrimination on the facilities of interstate commerce and in public housing.

CONTROL OF VOTING QUALIFICATIONS

Voting in the United States is a privilege reserved at present to citizens. It is an obligation of citizenship. The privilege becomes the legal right of persons who can meet the qualifications set by law; and its use to choose congressmen and presidential electors is a right protected by the Constitution of the United States.

The power to fix qualifications for voting is left by the Constitution to the states. Choice of presidential electors is controlled by the state legislatures, and representatives and senators are chosen by voters qualified to elect members "of the most numerous Branch of the State Legislature."[5]

Thus the states determine the qualifications for voting in the United States. Considerable variation exists from state to state, although within each state the qualifications are the same for all elections.[6]

[4] Reported in *Congressional Quarterly Weekly Report*, Vol. 20, No. 13, p. 508.

[5] See Article I, sec. 2, Article II, sec. 1, and Amendment XVII of the Constitution.

[6] A tabulation of state voting qualifications may be found in *The Book of the States, 1962-1963* (Chicago: Council of State Governments, 1958), pp. 20-21.

SUFFRAGE QUALIFICATIONS IN THE STATES

State	Age	U.S. Citizen	Residence Requirements			Poll Tax	Literacy Test	Loyalty Oath
			State	County	Precinct, etc.			
Alabama	21	Yes	1 yr.	6 mos.	3 mos.	$1.50[12]	Yes	Yes
Alaska	19	Yes	1 yr.	—	30 days	—	Yes	—
Arizona	21	Yes	1 yr.	30 days	30 days	—	Yes	—
Arkansas	21	Yes	1 yr.	6 mos.	1 mo.	1.00[14]	—	—
California	21	90 days	1 yr.[1]	90 days[1]	54 days	—	Yes	—
Colorado	21	Yes	1 yr.	90 days	15 days[8]	—	—	—
Connecticut	21	Yes	1 yr.	—	[10]	—	Yes	Yes
Delaware	21	Yes	1 yr.	3 mos.	30 days	—	Yes	—
Florida	21	Yes	1 yr.	6 mos.	—	—	—	Yes
Georgia	18	Yes	1 yr.	6 mos.	6 mos.	—	Yes	—
Hawaii	20	Yes	1 yr.	—	3 mos.	—	Yes	—
Idaho	21	Yes	6 mos.	30 days	—	—	—	Yes
Illinois	21	Yes	1 yr.	90 days	30 days[21]	—	—	—
Indiana	21	Yes	6 mos.	60 days	30 days	—	—	—
Iowa	21	Yes	6 mos.	60 days	10 days[8]	—	—	—
Kansas	21	Yes	6 mos.	30 days	—	—	—	—
Kentucky	18	Yes	1 yr.	6 mos.	60 days	—	—	—
Louisiana	21	Yes	1 yr.	1 yr.	3 mos.[9]	—	Yes[16]	—
Maine	21	Yes	6 mos.	3 mos.	[17]	—	Yes	—
Maryland	21	Yes	1 yr.	6 mos.	6 mos.	—	—	—
Massachusetts	21	Yes	1 yr.	—	[10]	—	Yes	—
Michigan	21	Yes	6 mos.	—	[20]	—	—	—
Minnesota	21	3 mos.	6 mos.	—	30 days	—	—	—
Mississippi	21	Yes	2 yrs.	1 yr.	1 yr.[11]	2.00[13]	Yes	Yes
Missouri	21	Yes	1 yr.[2]	60 days	[21]	—	—	—
Montana	21	Yes	1 yr.	30 days	30 days	—	—	—
Nebraska	21	Yes	6 mos.	40 days	10 days	—	—	—
Nevada	21	Yes	6 mos.	30 days	10 days[10]	—	Yes[16]	—
N. Hampshire	21	Yes	6 mos.	—	—	—	—	—
New Jersey	21	Yes	6 mos.	60 days	—	—	—	—
New Mexico	21	Yes	1 yr.	90 days	30 days	—	—	—
New York	21	90 days	1 yr.	4 mos.	30 days	—	Yes	—
N. Carolina	21	Yes	1 yr.	4 mos.	30 days	—	Yes	Yes
N. Dakota	21	Yes	1 yr.	90 days	30 days	—	—	—
Ohio	21	Yes	1 yr.[3]	40 days	40 days	—	—	—
Oklahoma	21	Yes	1 yr.	6 mos.	30 days	—	—	—
Oregon	21	Yes	6 mos.	30 days	30 days	—	Yes	—
Pennsylvania	21	1 mo.	1 yr.[4]	—	2 mos.	—	—	—
Rhode Island	21	Yes	1 yr.	—	[10]	—	[18]	—
S. Carolina	21	Yes	2 yrs.[5]	1 yr.	4 mos.	—	—	—
S. Dakota	21	Yes[19]	1 yr.	90 days[7]	30 days[7]	—	—	—
Tennessee	21	Yes	1 yr.	6 mos.	—	—	—	—
Texas	21	Yes	1 yr.	6 mos.	—	1.75[13]	—	—
Utah	21	90 days	1 yr.	4 mos.	60 days[6]	—	—	—
Vermont	21	Yes	1 yr.	—	—	—	—	Yes
Virginia	21	Yes	1 yr.	6 mos.	30 days	1.50[15]	Yes	—
Washington	21	Yes	1 yr.	90 days	30 days	—	Yes	—
W. Virginia	21	Yes	1 yr.	60 days	—	—	—	—
Wisconsin	21	Yes	1 yr.[3]	—	10 days	—	—	—
Wyoming	21	Yes	1 yr.	60 days	10 days	—	Yes	—

Adapted from *Congressional Quarterly Weekly Report*, Vol. 18, No. 8, p. 256.

This situation reflects the fact that the framers of the plan could not agree upon a uniform set of qualifications. Each state had its own and different qualifications and was unwilling to compromise them. Hence, the matter was left in the control of the states, and subject only to a few constitutional limitations.

First, the Fifteenth Amendment declares:

The right of citizens of the United States to vote shall not be denied or abridged by the United States or by any State on account of race, color, or previous condition of servitude.

What effect did this amendment have upon the power of the states to control the qualifications of voters?

The Fifteenth Amendment does not confer the right of suffrage upon anyone. It prevents the States, or the United States, however, from giving preference, in this particular to one citizen of the United States over another, on account of race, color, or previous condition of servitude. Before its adoption, this could be done. It was as much within the power of a State to exclude citizens of the United States from voting on account of race, etc., as it was on account of age, property or education. Now it is not. If citizens of one race having certain qualifications are permitted by law to vote, those of another having the same qualifications must be. Previous to this Amendment, there was no constitutional guaranty against this discrimination; now there is. It follows that the Amendment has invested the citizens of the United States with a new constitutional right which is within the protecting power of Congress. That right is exemption from discrimination in the exercise of the elective fran-

---

[1] 54 days residence for presidential elections if person a qualified voter of former state.

[2] Only 60 days for presidential elections.

[3] None for presidential elections.

[4] Six months if previously a native of the state.

[5] Clergy, public school teachers and spouses, may vote after six months residence.

[6] Three months in the township.

[7] Retains voting right in former county or precinct until establishes one at new residence.

[8] 30 days in city or town.

[9] Four months in municipality.

[10] Six months in city or town.

[11] Six months for clergy and wives.

[12] Poll taxes for 2 years must be paid. Veterans exempt.

[13] On citizens 21-60.

[14] Servicemen exempt.

[15] Poll taxes for 3 years must be paid.

[16] Exceptions allowed.

[17] Three months in city, town, or plantation.

[18] Property ownership an alternative to literacy.

[19] Five years residence in the U.S.

[20] 30 days in the election district.

[21] 60 days in town.

chise on account of race, color or previous condition of servitude. This . . . Congress may enforce by appropriate legislation. . . .[7]

The right to vote in the States comes from the States; but the right of exemption from the prohibited discrimination comes from the United States. The first has not been granted or secured by the Constitution of the United States; but the last has been.[8]

The Fifteenth Amendment does not confer authority upon Congress to punish discrimination practiced by private individuals against other individuals. It relates solely to action "by the United States or by any State" and does not contemplate wrongful individual acts.

The Nineteenth Amendment admonishes that:

The right of citizens of the United States to vote shall not be denied or abridged by the United States or any State on account of sex.

Neither amendment fixes qualifications for voters. Prior to their adoption the states were free to permit, and some did permit, voting by Negroes and women. The amendments only limited the exercise by the states of their power to fix the qualifications of voters in the United States.

There is, therefore, no "national electorate" in the United States, if by this term is meant a body of voters qualified by Congress to choose national officers. The electorate is composed of fifty separate groups of voters each of which has been required to meet a different set of qualifications. The issue is not fully resolved, but it is widely believed that Congress lacks the authority to determine the qualifications that voters in national elections should meet.

Democratic Suffrage Requirements. There is no fixed pattern of "proper" qualifications for voting. Indeed, the number and rapidity of changes in qualifications have made this one of the most dynamic aspects of our political life. In the absence of any ideal qualifications, however, certain vague standards are widely accepted. It is felt that a voter ought to be devoted to the democratic processes of government, to be intelligent and informed about public issues, to be free from subservience to any force that threatens to destroy his independence of expression and action, and to be imbued with the spirit of the Constitution. These values cannot be legislated, and the specific qualifications are determined more by expediency and politics than by considerations of morality and justice.

The movement toward political democracy in the United States has led to general acceptance of the conclusion that the only qualifications for voting that are consistent with the principles of democracy pertain to the age, citizenship, and residence of the voters. Although many other qualifications are to be found in the laws of the various states, only these are compatible with the ideal of "one man, one vote."

[7] *United States* v. *Reese* (1876), 92 U.S. 214.
[8] *United States* v. *Cruikshank* (1876), 92 U.S. 542.

Uniform Qualifications—Age. Voters should possess the maturity, experience, and awareness of community values which are largely the products of age. Possession of these attributes is necessary if the voter is to make responsible choices upon issues of public importance. Therefore, forty-six states assume that persons otherwise qualified who have attained the age of twenty-one years are capable of making such responsible choices. The states of Georgia and Kentucky permit the assumption to be made at age eighteen, Alaska at age nineteen, and Hawaii at age twenty. The ages thus fixed are largely the product of arbitrary selection; uniformity is purely conventional, if not coincidental.

Uniform Qualifications—Citizenship. All states require voters to be citizens of the United States. It is uniformly agreed at present that none but legal members of the body politic should participate in the determination of its affairs. However, there is no necessary relationship between citizenship and the right to vote.[9]

Thus, citizenship and suffrage are entirely separable. At one time aliens were able to vote; yet today not all citizens can vote. Minors under the legal voting age of their states, persons detained in asylums, residents of the District of Columbia and of the territories, and criminals deprived of their political rights are usually citizens of the United States, but none of them are able to vote.

Uniform Qualifications—Residence. The voting laws of every state require potential electors to live within the state, county, and district for a prescribed period of time. Residence varies from six months to two years in the state; from thirty days to one year in the county, town, township, or other unit of local government; and from ten days to six months in the voting precinct. The purpose of the requirement is to ensure that voters are attached to the community where they help elect the officers and help determine policies. Residence requirements disfranchise those persons who have to move about without long remaining in one place, but they also prevent "floating votes" being brought into a community to influence an election.

Diverse Qualifications—Property. Voters in former times were required to own varying amounts of property. It was assumed that all voters should possess a substantial material interest in the community. The best evidence of such interest was ownership of a sizable accumulation of wealth, and the payment of taxes to support the community. Possession of property was accepted as proof of the superior merit, character, and ability of its owners which made them stand out from the undistinguished masses. Only minor forms of property qualifications exist in several of the states at the present time.

Diverse Qualifications—Payment of Taxes. A surviving property qualification is the requirement that a potential voter should have paid all of his taxes. Another requires the payment of a poll tax. The poll tax is

[9] See *Minor* v. *Happersett* (1875), 21 Wallace 162.

The poll tax reflects the opposition of the southern states to the Fifteenth Amendment. To defeat its letter and its spirit, they used devices

levied on each individual at a uniform rate. However, five states (Alabama, Arkansas, Mississippi, Texas, and Virginia) make its payment a prerequisite for voting, and in this form it is a property qualification. Thus, the Constitution of Virginia declares:

ARTICLE II

ELECTIVE FRANCHISE AND QUALIFICATIONS FOR OFFICE

Sec. 20. Who May Register.—Every citizen of the United States, having the qualifications of age and residence required . . . shall be entitled to register, provided:

First. That he has personally paid to the proper official all state poll taxes legally assessed or assessable against him for three years next preceding that in which he offers to register. . . .

Sec. 21. Conditions for Voting.—A person registered . . . shall have the right to vote for all officers elective by the people, subject to the following conditions:

That . . . he shall, as a prerequisite to the right to vote, personally pay, at least six months prior to the election, all state poll taxes assessed or assessable against him, under this Constitution, during the three years next preceding that in which he offers to vote. . . .

The poll tax reflects the opposition of the southern states to the Fifteenth Amendment. To defeat its letter and its spirit, they used devices to escape fulfillment of its intent. Among these was the poll tax. Its undeclared purpose was to discriminate against Negro voters who, it was hoped, could not pay the tax and, hence, could not vote. It was hoped that if, perchance, some Negroes were able to pay their taxes, they would forget to do so six months in advance of the election, for no effort was made to publicize the due date or to collect the tax.

Another modification of this device is to require the voter to produce his poll tax receipt when he requests his ballot. It is assumed that Negro voters are careless and will be more apt than white voters to lose their poll tax receipts. Yet another refinement is to require back payment of all accumulated poll taxes. An impecunious prospective voter who neglects to pay his poll tax finds it annually more difficult to do so should he desire to exercise his franchise.

On its face the tax is a general statewide levy which does not discriminate on account of race.[10] In fact, however, it does prevent large numbers of poor Negroes, and whites, from voting. It is an effective device where it survives. After several Congresses had made unsuccessful attempts to end its use as a test of eligibility for registration, the 87th Congress approved and submitted to the states for ratification an amendment to the Constitution forbidding its use in connection with national elections.

Diverse Qualifications—Literacy Tests. An informed electorate must be literate. Literacy, or "education" tests, therefore, are intended to ensure that democratic government will be controlled by intelligent and informed voters. The assumption is that men have, or can obtain, the information necessary to reach sound conclusions on what is in the best interest of all and, through the processes of democratic government, can govern themselves better than one or a few men can govern them. The literacy test is properly used to verify which potential voters are capable of acquiring the knowledge of public affairs that is necessary to their intelligent and informed participation in self-government. To that end the literacy test is currently used in twenty-one states.

Is the literacy test one of intelligence or of educational attainment? Can it not be used to evade the Fifteenth Amendment? An effective method of discriminating against voters must be selective. It must exclude those to be discriminated against but admit all others to the vote. It must be fair in form but available for discriminatory administration, for that, although unconstitutional, is very difficult to detect and prove if achieved in an artful manner. The literacy test meets these standards.

Its effectiveness as an instrument of discrimination depends upon the discretion of the registrars. These officers prepare the official lists of qualified voters. A person wishing to be registered must satisfy the registrar that he meets the qualifications set by law. The discretion of the

[10] See *Breedlove* v. *Suttles* (1937), 302 U.S. 277.

registrar to concede or deny possession of the qualifications claimed is usually almost unlimited. Therefore, when a literacy test must be taken and the registration officer chooses to discriminate on racial or other grounds, members of the objectionable group mysteriously but almost automatically become illiterate; other applicants become sufficiently literate to pass the test.

One form of the literacy test was the "grandfather clause" which was employed at various times by several southern states so that they could have illiterate white persons permanently registered by exempting them from literacy tests which Negroes were required to take. This was a patently unconstitutional attempt to evade the Fifteenth Amendment, and it was so declared by the courts; but it survived long enough to achieve the intended result. Once this end was realized, the fate of the test became unimportant.

The nature of the "grandfather clause" is illustrated by the following one, formerly a part of the Constitution of Oklahoma:

No person shall be registered as an elector of this state or be allowed to vote in any election held herein, unless he be able to read and write any section of the Constitution of the state of Oklahoma; but no person who was, on January 1st, 1866, or any time prior thereto, entitled to vote under any form of government, or who at that time resided in some foreign nation, and no lineal descendant of such person, shall be denied the right to register and vote because of his inability to so read and write sections of such Constitution.[11]

Concerning this provision it was said:

We have difficulty in finding words to more clearly demonstrate the conviction we entertain that this standard has the characteristics which the government attributes to it than does the mere statement of the text. It is true it contains no express words of an exclusion from the standard which it establishes of any person on account of race, color, or previous condition of servitude, prohibited by the 15th Amendment, but the standard itself inherently brings that result into existence since it is based purely upon a period of time before the enactment of the 15th Amendment, and makes that period the controlling and dominant test of the right of suffrage. In other words, we seek in vain for any ground which would sustain any other interpretation but that the provision, recurring to the conditions existing before the 15th Amendment was adopted and the continuance of which the 15th Amendment prohibited, proposed by in substance and effect lifting those conditions over to a period of time after the Amendment, to make them the basis of the right of suffrage conferred in direct and positive disregard of the 15th Amendment.[12]

However, literacy tests can be worthwhile in form and application. Thus, the Constitution of the State of New York provides

[11] *Guinn* v. *United States* (1915), 238 U.S. 347.
[12] *Ibid.*, pp. 364-365.

ARTICLE II

Section 1. . . . After January first, one thousand nine hundred and twenty-two, no person shall become entitled to vote on attaining majority, by naturalization or otherwise, unless such person is also able, except for physical disability, to read and write English.

The test has been established and is administered by the educational authorities of the state. Thus:

CHAPTER 17

ELECTION LAW

ARTICLE 7—REGISTRATION AND ENROLLMENT OF VOTERS

Sec. 168. Proof of literacy and regulations.

1. The Board of Regents of the state of New York shall make provision for the giving of literacy tests. A certificate of literacy issued to a voter under the rules and regulations of the board of regents of the state of New York to the effect that the voter to whom it is issued is able to read and write English save for physical disability only, and to the extent of such physical disability, which shall be stated in the certificate, shall be received . . . as conclusive of such fact, except as hereinafter provided.

2. . . . But a new voter may present as evidence of literacy a certificate or diploma showing that he has completed the work of an approved eighth grade elementary school or of a higher school in which English is the language of instruction. But the genuineness of the certificate and the identity of the voter shall remain questions of fact to be established to the satisfaction of the election inspectors and subject to challenge, like any other fact relating to the qualification of a voter.

3. The inability of a voter, save for physical disability only, obvious to the election inspectors, to write his name in a register or poll book, shall be deemed conclusive proof of inability to read and write English, notwithstanding the presentation of proof of literacy as herein provided. . . .

The most recent effort by Congress to abolish discriminatory literacy tests was a proposed bill which sank under waves of senatorial oratory in May of 1962. Under its terms any state would have been able to employ a literacy test, but any person who could demonstrate completion of a sixth grade education would have been presumed literate for purposes of participation in national elections. Both the majority and minority leaders backed the measure and the endeavor to cut off filibustering against it, but the membership rejected a closure motion, and a motion to table the bill, because: (1) senators are traditionally reluctant to terminate debate in that fashion; (2) the bill was vulnerable to the charge of unconstitutionality; (3) it was felt that the 1960 Civil Rights Act had not been enforced with sufficient vigor to justify further legislation which would compel respect for the voting rights of Negroes; (4) neither the administration nor advocates of civil rights made a determined effort to save the measure; (5) some Republicans were interested in keeping alive an issue that split the Democratic Party wide open; (6) the vote against tabling, in the face of the filibuster, was a meaningless gesture, but it was popularly interpreted as a vote in favor of civil rights and a credit to any senator making it. Hence, liberals, conservatives, northern and southern Democrats, virtually any member regardless of his real feelings could appear to favor the bill but really vote to kill it.

Assuming that the measure would have stood up in court, loss of the bill was regarded as a major setback for Negro voting rights. Impatience and dissatisfaction is building up among Negroes in the South, particularly among college students of voting age, who in some counties cannot obtain registration but who see white applicants being enrolled who are obviously less well qualified. The literacy test bill was intended to attack the situation in two ways: (1) it would have made the use of literacy tests as a cover for discrimination impossible, and (2) it would greatly have increased prospects for success in voter registration cases that were taken into courts. It would not have solved all problems that involved discrimination in voting, and it would also have applied in states outside the South.

Diverse Qualifications—Understanding Tests. A variant of the literacy test requires that potential voters should read, understand, and interpret any designated section of the state or national Constitution to the satisfaction of the registration authority. This arrangement vests great discretion in the voting registrar to determine subjectively who can, and who cannot, understand and interpret the assigned passage satisfactorily. It is very easy to deny the acceptability of a man's interpretation if his skin happens to be of the wrong color.

Since 1946, however, the discriminatory administration of an otherwise valid understanding test can cause the test to fall before the Fourteenth and Fifteenth Amendments. Such a test authorized by the Constitution of Alabama provided that only voters who could "understand and explain" any provision of the Constitution of the United States should be registered. Its adoption was clearly within the power of the state; therefore, its validity turned upon its compatibility with the Fourteenth and Fifteenth Amendments.

The words "understand and explain" do not provide a reasonable standard. A simple test may be given one applicant; a long, tedious, complex one to another; one applicant may be examined on one article of the Constitution; another may be called upon to "understand and explain" every article and provision of the entire instrument.

To state it plainly, the sole test is: Has the applicant by oral examination or otherwise understood and explained the Constitution to the satisfaction of the particular board? To state it more plainly, the board has a right to reject one applicant and accept another, depending solely upon whether it likes or dislikes the understanding and explanation offered. To state it even more plainly, the

board, by the use of the words "understand and explain," is given the arbitrary power to accept or reject any prospective electors that may apply . . . The board has the power to establish two classes, those to whom they consent, and those to whom they do not—those who may vote and those who may not. Such arbitrary power amounts to a denial of equal protection of the law within the meaning of the Fourteenth Amendment to the Constitution. . . .

Furthermore, the administration of the Boswell Amendment by the defendant board demonstrates that the ambiguous standard prescribed has, in fact, been arbitrarily used for the purpose of excluding Negro applicants for the franchise, while white applicants with comparable qualifications were being accepted. The evidence is without dispute that this Amendment has been used to disqualify many Negro applicants for registration while it does not definitely disclose that it has been used to disqualify a single white applicant. It is further shown that as a rule the Boswell test of "understand and explain" is required of Negroes while no such exaction is made of white applicants.

It, thus, clearly appears that this Amendment was intended to be, and is being used for the purpose of discriminating against applicants for the franchise on the basis of race or color. Therefore, we are necessarily brought to the conclusion that this Amendment to the Constitution of Alabama, both in its object and the manner of its administration, is unconstitutional, because it violates the Fifteenth Amendment. . . .[13]

[13] *Davis* v. *Schnell* (1949), 81 F. Supp. 872. The Supreme Court of the United States affirmed this decision of the district court in 336 U.S. 933 (1949).

Hence, the principle seems to be established that an "understanding" test as a prerequisite for registration may not be discriminatory either on its face or in the manner of its administration.

The "White Primary". The southern political leadership interested in keeping the Negro away from the polls has shown great determination and ingenuity in its ability to create new means by which to attain this end. In the states of the South the Democratic Party is the dominant one. Consequently, nomination as the candidate of that party for any state or national office virtually guarantees election. The primary election is the most widely used method for selecting candidates in the South. If the "right" candidates are to be nominated it is imperative that Negro party members should be kept away from the polls not on election day, when the voters are presented with a list of previously chosen candidates, but on primary day when the choice of candidates is made. Therefore, considerable effort has been made to make the primaries "all white" by excluding Negroes from participation in them.

To do this without violating the Constitution, however, has not proved easy. Success has depended upon showing that a primary is not an election within the meaning of the Constitution. The power to regulate primaries and to determine who can participate in them has had to be separated from the authority to control general elections and to fix the qualifications of voters. Consequently, the proponents of "white primaries" in the South have endeavored to prove that the conduct of a primary is a purely private activity of a purely private organization. Since the Fourteenth and Fifteenth Amendments give no protection against discrimination by private parties, it has been asserted that the exclusion of Negroes from primaries does not violate either of them. However, in spite of a long history of attempted evasion of constitutional principle and of discrimination against Negro voters in the South,

It may now be taken as a postulate that the right to vote in . . . a primary for the nomination of candidates without discrimination by the State, like the right to vote in a general election, is a right secured by the Constitution. By the terms of the Fifteenth Amendment that right may not be abridged by any State on account of race. Under our Constitution the great privilege of the ballot may not be denied a man by the State because of his color. . . .

The party takes its character as a state agency from the duties imposed upon it by state statutes; the duties do not become matters of private law because they are performed by a political party. . . . When primaries become a part of the machinery for choosing officials, state and national, as they have here, the same tests to determine the character of discrimination or abridgement should be applied to the primary as are applied to the general election. If a state requires a certain electoral procedure, prescribes a general election ballot made up of party nominees so chosen and limits the choice of the electorate in general elections for state offices, practically speaking, to those whose names appear on such a ballot, it endorses, adopts and enforces the discrimination against Negroes, practiced by a party entrusted by . . . law with the determination of the qualifications of participants in the primary. This is state action within the meaning of the Fifteenth Amendment.

The United States is a constitutional democracy. Its organic law grants to all citizens a right to participate in the choice of elected officials without restriction by any State because of race. This grant to the people of the opportunity for choice is not to be nullified by a State through casting its electoral process in a form which permits a private organization to practice racial discrimination in the election. Constitutional rights would be of little value if they could thus be indirectly denied.

The privilege of membership in a party may be . . . no concern of a State. But when, as here, that privilege is also the essential qualification for voting in a primary to select nominees for a general election, the State makes the action of the party the action of the State.[14]

Thus, it seemed no longer possible for the states to argue that a political party is a private organization and that a primary sponsored by it is a private activity. The prohibitions and protections of the Constitution apply to primaries to prevent discrimination just as they apply to elections.

The states of the South have sought by further devious tactics to exclude Negroes from primary elections, but none has successfully evaded the fact that the primary is an election. It does not matter what form elective practices take; if they produce discrimination, based solely upon race or color, in the enjoyment of the right freely to participate in the electoral process, they are forbidden by the Constitution. Thus, it has become increasingly difficult for states to evade the Fifteenth Amendment. The poll tax, literacy, and understanding tests which are not discriminatory on their face and are not made so by the mode of their administration, remain valid. The "white primary" is unconstitutional. What new and ingenious schemes the states will be able to devise only the future will make known. It is probably too much to hope that they will abide by the letter and spirit of the Constitution.

Moreover, the most effective source of discrimination, and the most difficult to control, still remains. This is the great discretion vested by the law of many states in voter registration officials. Registration is not a qualification for voting. Rather, it is a means of identifying and recording qualified voters. However, in the last analysis, the right to vote is of little value unless one can be registered; for unless the voter's name appears on the registration book, he cannot obtain a ballot on which to express his choice. It is, therefore, as important to eliminate discrimination from the registration process as it is from the voting process.

[14] *Smith* v. *Allwright* (1944), 321 U.S. 649. See also *Rice* v. *Elmore* (1947), 165 F. (2nd) 387.

RECENT CIVIL RIGHTS LEGISLATION

Civil Rights Act of 1957. In 1957 Congress for the first time in eighty-two years overcame southern opposition to civil rights legislation affecting Negroes. From 1875 to 1957 a small Civil Rights Unit in the Department of Justice had tried to protect the enjoyment of voting and other civil rights by all eligible persons in the United States on the basis of a few inadequate fragments of post-Civil War statutes which had been enacted to protect the rights of former slaves.

The 1957 Civil Rights Act was intended to prevent the southern states from discriminatorily enforcing their many suffrage qualifications against Negro voters when the unconstitutionality of the white primary was finally established beyond evasion. New authority was granted to the Attorney General to bring civil suits in appropriate federal courts on behalf of individuals who were about to be, or had been, deprived of their right to vote. Such suits could be brought against *any* person, whether or not he acted in an official capacity.

By this procedure the Justice Department, when it possesses adequate evidence that state officials have deprived, or are about to deprive, qualified persons of their right to vote, can bring an action to enjoin them. The court then issues a temporary restraint during which the individual who has been discriminated against is allowed to register or vote and the case is heard. If the court's ruling favors the Justice Department the restraint is made permanent, and the state officials are ordered to register the person affected and to allow him to vote. Any state official who refuses to obey can be convicted of civil and/or criminal contempt.

The law created a Civil Rights Commission and authorized it to investigate alleged deprivations of voting rights, other voting practices, and discrimination in public housing and education. The Commission was to report its findings and recommendations within two years to the President. The Act also expanded the old Civil Rights Unit of the Department of Justice into the Civil Rights Division, under the direction of an Assistant Attorney General. Since its status was acquired the Division has successfully brought several actions in the South to protect the voting rights of Negroes from denial or abridgement.

However, in the face of the new legislation southern resistance to Negro voting and school desegregation continued along traditional lines accompanied by increased violence. Bombings of churches, schools, homes, automobiles, and businesses, beatings of Negroes, intimidations, and conspiracies to intimidate Negroes, became prevalent. Lack of adequate statutory authority upon which to punish such acts, as well as flight across state lines to avoid prosecution by state authorities, the interstate shipment of explosives or their possession or use for such purposes, the obstruction of national court orders, and the refusal by state authorities to protect Negroes or to prosecute recalcitrant whites led to a heightened demand by officials and the public for new and stronger laws. Meanwhile, between 1957 and 1959, the Civil Rights Commission conducted extensive investigations throughout the South. It met with constant harassment and refusal to cooperate on the part of state and local officials. In September, 1959, it filed a report setting out its difficulties;[15] but successful judicial actions have established the constitutionality of suits brought against state officials,[16] and have done much to overcome the more blatant forms of obstruction and hindrance.

On the basis of its findings the Commission recommended that voting registrars should be required to keep voting and registration records for at least five years and that federal registration of voters for national elections should be established when it is shown that state officials have discriminatorily refused to enroll them.

In 1959 President Eisenhower requested Congress to enact extensive supplementary civil rights legislation, but although measures were introduced in both houses nothing was accomplished. However, in 1960 a combination of Republicans and northern Democrats, in the face of impending elections, succeeded in enacting the Civil Rights Act of that year. Proponents of the revision, however, could not break down southern racial and general states' rights opposition to obtain enactment of authority for the Civil Rights Division to protect all rights of the individual guaranteed by the Constitution.

In essence the 1960 Civil Rights Act makes it a crime against the United States (1) to obstruct by threat or by force *any* order of a United States court; (2) to flee across a state line to avoid prosecution, punishment, or requirement to testify about any actual or attempted bombing or burning of a building, vehicle, or other facility; (3) to transport or possess explosives with intent or knowledge that they would be used to blow up any building or vehicle; (4) to use any interstate facility to threaten a bombing or to create a false bomb scare. Further, all voting records and registration papers relating to national elections must be preserved against mutilation, theft, or destruction for twenty-two months and be open to federal inspection.

Most important, however, the Act increased national authority to protect Negro voters' rights by providing that when the Attorney General wins a voting rights case under the 1957 law he can request a second proceeding by the trial court to ascertain whether a "pattern or practice"

[15] See *Congressional Quarterly Weekly Report,* Vol. 17, No. 37, pp. 1258-1259. See also the *Report of the United States Commission on Civil Rights, 1959* (Washington, D.C.: U.S. Government Printing Office, 1959); and also the report for 1961.
[16] See *United States* v. *Raines* (1960), 362 U.S. 17; *United States* v. *Alabama* (1960), 362 U.S. 602; and *Hanna* v. *Larche* (1960), 363 U.S. 420.

of discrimination against Negro voters exists in the area specified in the suit. If prohibited discrimination does exist, any Negro voter in the area can request the federal court to issue an order declaring that he is qualified if (1) he can show his qualification under state law; (2) he has tried to register after the "pattern or practice" of discrimination was found to exist; and (3) he has been denied the right to do so by a state official acting under pretense of law. If the national court issues an order directing registration of the petitioning voter, the appropriate state official is required to complete the registration, upon penalty of contempt of court for refusal to comply. The national court may appoint one or more voting referees, who are to receive applications for registration, hold hearings, take testimony, and report to the court. State officials cannot stop this process. The decision of a referee is final in all questions involving the literacy of voters seeking registration, but findings of the referees relating to other qualifications can be challenged by the state officials. If a challenge is disallowed by the court, it or a referee can issue a certificate declaring that the party is qualified to vote.

The measure as finally approved satisfied few interests, and little has been accomplished under the legislation. It was strongly criticized by both proponents and opponents. Many of the first felt that "We have a watered-down bill that has been so further diluted that it will wash right out of this chamber and hardly be noticed in the mainstream of American life. . . . We were beaten before we started—beaten by the committee seniority system, beaten by the combined strength of the leadership of both parties, and beaten by the usual voting coalition."[17] Senator Douglas stated: "The bill . . . sets up an elaborate obstacle course which the disfranchised Negro in the South must successfully run before he will be permitted to vote at all. . . ."[18] The measure was soundly condemned by spokesmen for the National Association for the Advancement of Colored People who called it a "fraud" and "not worth the paper it's written on." More restrained and probably more accurate was the statement of Senator Kenneth Keating (R., N.Y.) who said that the Civil Rights measure was "not a victory for anyone. It is a compromise measure. . . . This kind of half-way measure is a compelling invitation to a renewal of the struggle for effective civil rights legislation at the very next opportunity."[19]

In the two years since enactment of the 1960 Civil Rights Act the Justice Department has initiated twenty-three actions in various southern states. Fourteen of these have been brought to achieve freedom of registration and voting for Negroes. Approximately one hundred counties are under investigation by the Civil Rights Commission for irregularities in

[17] Senator Pat McNamara (D. Mich.), April 8, 1960, *Congressional Record*, 86th Congress, 2nd session (1960), p. 7190.
[18] *Congressional Record*, 86th Congress, 2nd session, (1960), p. 7261.
[19] *Ibid.*, p. 7223.

registration and voting practices. Experience with the civil rights legislation has brought to light the fact that some federal district court judges are less than enthusiastic about taking action in voting cases. The 1960 provision authorizing the appointment of voting referees has rarely been applied, but it should be noted that threatened or actual legal action against local officials has resulted in several instances, as in Macon County, Alabama, home of Tuskeegee Institute, in increased Negro registrations. White candidates in Macon County have actively campaigned for Negro votes, and those elected have been racial moderates.

Although progress is being made, it is slow, and the Department of Justice asserts that with existing authorization and available manpower, no faster legal action can be undertaken. Two courses are open: one is legal action to prevent or abate intimidation of registrants; the second is a suit to compel registration of qualified Negroes. The first requires proof of intimidation and has been successfully undertaken in a few counties, but the second requires proof that a "pattern of discrimination" exists and this, even in a friendly court, is a complicated and tedious job to fulfill. In a given county all the voter registration records must be analyzed. In Montgomery County, Alabama, 36,000 applications were processed by a Justice Department lawyer and four aides. The task lasted three months. The trial required a week, 160 witnesses, two months of legal preparation, and the time and talents of five lawyers. Alabama alone has sixty-seven counties, but the Justice Department has only ten lawyers to work on voting cases.

With a constitutional literacy test statute or a constitutional amendment thousands of Negroes and other disfranchised voters could quickly gain registration. Under existing practice an estimated 80 per cent of those rejected have more than a sixth grade education. It would be necessary to prove only educational facts for each applicant in order to obtain a court order directing his registration. In the last two years only six final orders have been directed against local officers in those of the hundred counties selected because of their records of extensive discrimination against the voting rights of Negroes.

Negro Voting in the South Today. Coercive and restrictive practices intended to discourage registration and voting by Negroes are operative in approximately one hundred counties in eight states of the deep South; how significant they are it is difficult to ascertain, but the Civil Rights Commission reports that in its estimation substantial discriminatory disfranchisement of Negroes does exist. The over-all effect of the Negro vote is still so small as to suggest strongly that it is almost an inert political force. The 1961 Commission report showed that of southern congressional districts for which data were available there were seventy in which Negroes of voting-age constituted 10 per cent or more of the population, but in only forty of these did they equal 10 per cent of the electorate.

Over-all in the South Negroes comprised 19 per cent of the voting-age population but only 10.6 per cent of the registered voters. Only 28.2 per cent of the voting-age Negroes were registered in the South, compared with 56.3 per cent of the eligible whites. Tennessee was the only southern state in which registered Negroes equaled as much as 40 per cent of the state-wide voting-age Negro population. In only fourteen congressional districts distributed across the region were more than 50 per cent of the Negro voting-age population registered, and in only *three* districts did they equal as much as 20 per cent of all registered voters.

The over-all Negro registration levels remain low in congressional districts throughout the South. In a few, mainly in urban areas, numbers have increased to the point at which the Negro vote has become an important "bloc" vote whenever a genuine party contest develops. However, there is not yet any measurable effect of the Negro vote upon incumbents of districts with heavy Negro populations, but there is some suggestion that a concentration of Negro votes may drive the incumbent more tightly into the embrace of the conservative southern Democrats.

Why do more Negroes not register and vote? There are many contributing causes, but fundamental to them all is the existence in the South of a power structure put together over a long period of time by whites, run by themselves according to their own value system, and neither the structure, nor the value system, nor many of the white leaders have any regard for the Negro as a political entity. The power and the machinery used to be, and largely continue to be, available to intimidate, threaten, harass, and persecute Negroes who threaten to disrupt the traditional value system. Although the Negro is associated with the South, the South is a white man's area; in 129 southern counties where Negroes are a substantial part of the population, fewer than 10 per cent are registered, and in 23 counties none are registered. In very few counties does the number of Negroes exceed the number of whites, but invariably the whites control the machinery of government and coercion. Moreover, to complement its use other forms of constraint and intimidation are available. Negroes who register or vote, or attempt to do so, may find that the result is loss of employment, pressure for rent and loan payments, cancellation of insurance policies, eviction from housing or land, denial of credit for food, rent, or clothes, repossession of articles bought under time payment plans, or refusal of "run" or "furnish" money traditionally supplied to sharecroppers and tenants to tide them over between crops. Informal community "blacklisting" is effective. Loss of employment is a particularly effective sanction when held over the heads of Negro school teachers, the group that provides much of the leadership in the movement to end discrimination of all types. In order to register Negro applicants are required to fill out forms with a degree of meticulousness not demanded of whites. They are denied aid in registration although this is frequently given to white applicants, and they are often rejected for formal, technical, and inconsequential errors while whites who make the same mistakes are enrolled as voters. When educated Negro leaders, teachers, and students are repeatedly turned away the very act of trying seems useless and wasteful. Negroes have been made to provide three registered voters to affirm their identity, a hurdle arbitrary on its face and not easy to overcome when there are very few registered Negroes at hand. Literacy and understanding tests are common obstacles. Negroes are made to yield their places in registration lines to whites, to submit to other deferential requirements, and for one reason or another are subjected to the embarrassments and frustrations of repeated denials. All of this takes place in communities of predominantly hostile white opinion, in some of which citizens' groups and legislative action openly endorse deliberate discrimination. Mobs, police action, economic coercion, physical brutality, and community hostility create situations throughout the South in which fear, apathy, and intimidation make it almost impossible for a conspicuous minority to qualify for and to exercise its rights of suffrage.

Increase in Negro Voting. Prodding by the Supreme Court and the Civil Rights Commission, the publicity given to unconscionable southern electoral practices, and a gradually awakening public opinion within and without the South have produced an increase in the number of Negro votes cast in the South. But although these figures are encouraging, they are apt to be misleading. In the one-party South only the primary counts as an effective part of the electoral process, and no great increase in Negro voting at primaries has occurred. Furthermore, increased Negro voting adds to the stature of southern leadership in the eyes of the country; as long as the Negro votes for the "right" candidate little effort will be made to keep him from the polling place. The number of Negro voters has been so low that a relatively small numerical increase will show as a large percentage increase. Some gain has been made to be sure, but much remains to be done. However, inertia, accommodation to the *status quo,* and opposition make doubtful any immediate solution of the problem of discrimination against Negro voters.[20]

THE PROBLEM OF NON-VOTING

The most serious problem confronting the effort to promote democracy through an expanded suffrage is not the exclusion of any particular class or group, but the failure of many qualified voters to exercise their vote.

[20] See V. O. Key, *Southern Politics* (New York: Alfred A. Knopf, 1949); and the 1959 and 1961 reports of the United States Commission on Civil Rights (Washington, D.C.: U.S. Government Printing Office).

An election decided by 50 to 60 per cent of the *qualified voters* is accepted as in tune with the "will of the people." This proportion is usually realized, moreover, only in presidential elections. State and local elections produce results based on the votes of between 10 and 50 per cent of the electorate. General elections in the South, and primaries everywhere except in the South, often result in less than 25 per cent of the qualified voters going to the polls. Because of the importance of the southern primary the voter turnout there is considerably higher than it is for the general election.

What causes so few Americans to exercise the right that is so essential to democratic government? No one cause can be pointed to, but among the many are indifference, inertia, discrimination, disqualification, the weather, preoccupation with private affairs, illness, absence, one party domination, dissatisfaction with the candidates, issues, or parties, faulty registration systems, lengthy ballots, and too frequent elections. These are but a few.

Compulsory voting laws, employed in several foreign countries, are incompatible with the heritage and spirit of American democracy. Moreover, mere increased numbers would add little that would improve the quality of the result.

Voter Behavior. Voting must be carried on within a legal and institutional framework, but the existence of that framework does not guarantee that voters will exercise the franchise. Votes are worthless unless they are cast. Whether and how they are cast are determined by a multitude of factors, psychological, personal, economic, rational, emotional, geographic, etc., and not by laws and institutions of the political system. Little is known about the factors that motivate or influence *individual* voting, although a great quantity of data has been collected to explain the voting behavior of *groups*. However, most voting behavior is determined by associational influences that are brought to bear through membership in groups.

The attitude of the voter is the major determinant of voting behavior, but it represents the product of many influences. Thus, people most regularly vote who have a direct interest in what government does, who are aware of that interest, and are informed on the subject, people who are not pulled variously by competing interests of nearly equal importance, and who are subjected to external pressure to vote. One of the main stimuli to voting is economic pressure. Most individuals feel a need for economic security. Low-income groups hope to improve their lot to obtain a greater share of life's goods, by supporting the party, policies, and candidates promising them greater social, economic, and political advantages. Voters in the upper income groups tend to vote to maintain advantages already possessed. Economic factors are not the only determinants of voter behavior. Their influence may be overridden occasionally or regularly by one or more considerations such as race, culture, class, education, professional or social contacts, family, section, or other factors. Each issue calling for an expression of voter opinion bears on the voter according to the facts and circumstances that gave rise to it, how these are brought home to him through the media of communication and through contacts with family, friends, and associates, how he interprets the impact of events upon himself, how candidates appeal to him, how they and their parties react to the issues, and how he responds to the influences which exert pressure upon him. A voter lacking personal interest will not vote at all or will vote as he is influenced by one or more of these pressures. Voters of weak conviction are easily influenced by strong external pressures. Those of strong conviction are most apt to make up their own minds; but they may decide to vote as independents or traditionally as group members according to the direction of their personal convictions. They may lead or be led to the poll, but at least they vote.[21]

[21] On the subject of voting behavior see: Gardner Lindzey (editor), Handbook of Social Psychology (Cambridge, Mass.: Addison-Wesley Publishing Co., 1954); Paul K. Lazarsfeld, Bernard Berelson, and Hazel Gaudet, The People's Choice (New York: Columbia University Press, 1948); Wesley and Beverly Allinsmith, "Religious Affiliation and Politico-Economic Attitude," Public Opinion Quarterly, Vol. 12 (Fall, 1948); Lawrence P. Fuchs, "American Jews and the Presidential Vote," American Political Science Review, Vol. 49 (June, 1955); Angus Campbell and Homer C. Cooper, Group Differences in Attitudes and Votes: The 1954 Congressional Elections (Ann Arbor, Mich.: University of Michigan Press, 1956); Herbert Hyman and Paul B. Sheatsley, "The Political Appeal of President Eisenhower," Public Opinion Quarterly, Vol. 17 (Winter, 1953); Angus Campbell, Gerald Gurin, and Warren E. Miller, The Voter Decides (Evanston, Ill.: Row, Peterson and Co., 1954).

CHAPTER XI

The Characteristics and
Organization of Congress

GENERAL COMMENT

The Congress of the United States consists of persons assembled and organized to perform certain functions. When first chosen these persons have the identity of members-elect of Congress. That status gives them a unity which sets them apart from all other persons. It is fortified by numerous arrangements, made within their group, which determine the organization of the legislative body that they compose. Hence, an understanding of Congress necessitates an understanding of the manner of its composition and organization. These are determined to no little extent by constitutional and statutory law, but they also presuppose the existence of political parties, many of the aspects of which are wholly extra-legal.

Form. Article I of the Constitution declares that

All legislative Powers herein granted shall be vested in a Congress of the United States, which shall consist of a Senate and House of Representatives.

Therefore, Congress is bicameral in form, an organizational type that was suggested by the English Parliament and by the colonial assemblies and state legislatures; but the decisive factor in its adoption was a desire to provide a non-elected Senate composed of conservative men who could curb the democratic excesses of the House. Bicameralism has been justified as being more representative, more compatible with the federal nature of the governmental system, more consonant with the theory and practice of democratic government, more permissive of thorough debate from different points of view, and more safe, since it permits one chamber to act as a check upon the other.

However, the case for bicameralism is not without weaknesses. Congress is bicameral because of convenience and a need to compromise, and not because of regard for bicameralism as a principle. Representatives are no less disposed to protect the interests of their states than are the senators. By providing two arenas bicameralism encourages representation of, and emphasis upon, local interests at the expense of national ones. It is more expensive and more vulnerable to outside pressures than is unicameralism, and it is slow, cumbersome, complex, and less responsible and responsive. It can be pointed out that the differences between the states today are essentially economic, not political as in 1789; that the Senate was designed as a stronghold to protect the interests of wealth and privilege from assaults by popularly elected representatives; that it was to restrain democracy, and not to increase it; that judicial review, the executive veto, and the electoral process restrain the abuse by Congress of its powers; that each house has passed measures on the theory that the other will kill them, only to find that the second is no more able or willing than the first to resist powerful political forces. The Senate *does* contribute additional deliberation prompted by different attitudes and interests than those that characterize the House of Representatives, but when both houses are controlled by the same party, the effectiveness of the Senate as a curb on the House is often greatly reduced. When different parties control the two chambers, friction and deadlocks too commonly result.

This is not to suggest that bicameralism will be abolished during the lifetime of any reader of these pages. Its incorporation in the Constitution, long familiarity with its strengths and weaknesses, and the difficulty of constitutional amendment will probably result in its continuance.

Size. The size of the Senate is determined by the principle of state equality. Thus:

> The Senate of the United States shall be composed of two Senators from each State.

The size of the House of Representatives is determined in a somewhat more complex manner. It was originally fixed by the Constitution at sixty-five members, subject to the requirement that

. . . Representatives and direct Taxes shall be apportioned among the several States which may be included within this Union, according to their respective Numbers, which shall be determined by adding to the whole Number of free Persons, including those bound to Service for a Term of Years, . . . three fifths of all other Persons. The actual Enumeration shall be made within three Years after the first Meeting of the Congress of the United States, and within every subsequent Term of ten years, in such Manner as they shall by Law direct. The Number of Representatives shall not exceed one for every thirty Thousand, but each State shall have at Least one Representative; and until such enumeration shall be made, the State of *New Hampshire* shall be entitled to chuse three, *Massachusetts* eight. . . .

After the first census the number was set at 105 and was thereafter increased as the population grew. Abolition of slavery made the three-fifths clause obsolete, so that the Fourteenth Amendment omitted reference to "three fifths of all other persons."

The Amendment also contained a penalty clause which declared that:

Representatives shall be apportioned among the several States according to their respective numbers, counting the whole number of persons in each State, excluding Indians not taxed. But when the right to vote at any election for the choice of electors for President and Vice-President of the United States, Representatives in Congress, the Executive and Judicial officers of a State, or the members of the Legislature thereof, is denied to any of the male inhabitants of such State, being twenty-one years of age, and citizens of the United States, or in any way abridged, except for participation in rebellion, or other crime, the basis of representation therein shall be reduced in the proportion which the number of such male citizens shall bear to the whole number of male citizens twenty-one years of age in such State.

It was aimed at the southern states, but no state sends members to Congress with spotlessly clean hands. An occasional member may propose that the penalty should be invoked, but it has never been applied to reduce the representation of a state. What is sauce for the goose is also sauce for the gander.

Apportionment of Representatives. Seats in the House are assigned to the states according to their respective populations, although the Constitution guarantees each state at least one seat however small its population. Hence, every member of the House is chosen in a state. So that the states may know how many members they are entitled to in the House it is necessary to determine their population by the decennial census. Hence, the implication is strong that every ten years, following a census, the membership of the House will be redistributed among the states, so that for the next ten years representation and population will be in accord.[1] However, the Constitution does not expressly state that a decennial reapportionment is obligatory.

[1] For an analysis of census uses and activities, see *Congressional Quarterly Weekly Report,* Vol. 18, No. 14, pp. 578-581.

In 1912, Congress by statute arbitrarily fixed the size of the House at 435 members. Following the admission of Alaska and Hawaii to the Union, Congress increased the size of the House to 437 members until the next reapportionment. Rather than permit the House to become larger and more unwieldy than it is, Congress has kept its size constant, and each ten years takes away representatives from states whose populations have declined or have failed to increase as rapidly as have those of other states, and assigns them to the latter.

Reapportionment is assured, for Congress has provided by statute for a process that is essentially automatic. Thus:

On the first day, or within one week thereafter, of the first regular session of the Eighty-second Congress and of each fifth Congress thereafter, the President shall transmit to the Congress a statement showing the whole number of persons in each State, excluding Indians not taxed, as ascertained under the seventeenth and each subsequent decennial census of the population, and the number of Representatives to which each State would be entitled under an apportionment of the then existing number of Representatives by the method known as the method of equal proportions, no State to receive less than one Member.

. . . It shall be the duty of the Clerk of the House of Representatives, within fifteen calendar days after the receipt of such statement, to send to the executive of each State a certificate of the number of Representatives to which such State is entitled under this section.[2]

Each plan is prepared for the President by the Bureau of the Census. It becomes effective if within sixty days after receiving it Congress fails to enact a different one.

Term. The terms of the House and the Senate are fixed by the Constitution at two and six years, respectively.

The length of the term for senators enables them to gain considerable legislative experience, to "learn the ropes," to establish a record upon which to be judged by the voters. It facilitates the exercise of independent judgment, supplies continuity and stability to the legislative process, and de-emphasizes local interests and provincial attitudes in favor of broader domestic and foreign interests of the nation.

The term for representatives is probably the optimum length to ensure maximum correspondence of views between the people and their representatives and to provide opportunity for reaffirming or correcting that correspondence. However, the advantages provided by the longer terms of senators are lost to members of the House of Representatives.

Renewal. Since all members of the House are chosen every second year, the membership is wholly renewed at each election. The Senate is only

[2] *U.S. Code,* Title 2, sec. 2a.

	REAPPORTIONMENT OF HOUSE SEATS			NET CHANGE
States	*1940*	*1950*	*1961*	*1950-1961*
Alabama	9	9	8	−1
Alaska	—	—	1	+1
Arizona	2	2	3	+1
Arkansas	7	6	4	−2
California	23	30	38	+8
Colorado	4	4	4	—
Connecticut	6	6	6	—
Delaware	1	1	1	—
Florida	6	8	12	+4
Georgia	10	10	10	—
Hawaii	—	—	2	+2
Idaho	2	2	2	—
Illinois	26	25	24	−1
Indiana	11	11	11	—
Iowa	8	8	7	−1
Kansas	6	6	5	−1
Kentucky	9	8	7	−1
Louisiana	8	8	8	—
Maine	3	3	2	−1
Maryland	6	7	8	+1
Massachusetts	14	14	12	−2
Michigan	17	18	19	+1
Minnesota	9	9	8	−1
Mississippi	7	6	5	−1
Missouri	13	11	10	−1
Montana	2	2	2	—
Nebraska	4	4	3	−1
Nevada	1	1	1	—
New Hampshire	2	2	2	—
New Jersey	14	14	15	+1
New Mexico	2	2	2	—
New York	45	43	41	−2
North Carolina	12	12	11	−1
North Dakota	2	2	2	—
Ohio	23	23	24	+1
Oklahoma	8	6	6	—
Oregon	4	4	4	—
Pennsylvania	33	30	27	−3
Rhode Island	2	2	2	—
South Carolina	6	6	6	—
South Dakota	2	2	2	—
Tennessee	10	9	9	—
Texas	21	22	23	+1
Utah	2	2	2	—
Vermont	1	1	1	—
Virginia	9	10	10	—
Washington	6	7	7	—
West Virginia	6	6	5	−1
Wisconsin	10	10	10	—
Wyoming	1	1	1	—

Adapted from *Congressional Quarterly Weekly Report,* Vol. 17, No. 15, p. 516; Vol. 18, No. 47, p. 1883.

partially renewed, for it is a continuing body. Approximately two thirds of its members are always in office, because

Immediately after they shall be assembled in Consequence of the first Election, they shall be divided as equally as may be into three Classes. The Seats of the Senators of the first Class shall be vacated at the Expiration of the second Year, of the second Class at the Expiration of the fourth Year, and of the third Class at the Expiration of the sixth Year, so that one-third may be chosen every second Year. . . .

Eligibility. The Constitution declares that

No Person shall be a Representative who shall not have attained the Age of twenty-five Years, and been seven Years a Citizen of the United States, and who shall not, when elected, be an Inhabitant of that State in which he shall be chosen.

It similarly prescribes the qualifications for senators:

No Person shall be a Senator who shall not have attained to the Age of thirty Years, and been nine Years a Citizen of the United States, and who shall not, when elected, be an Inhabitant of that State for which he shall be chosen.

The Constitution refers only to qualifications of age, citizenship, and residence. There is no *essential* reason why they should be specified, but reference to them might limit the power of the people to elect a popular, demagogic, and unqualified figure to the Congress. However, it can be argued that democracy implies a right to choose poorly as well as wisely. The qualifications need not be met until the oath is administered. Persons chosen to the houses before attaining them are not seated until they meet the prescribed qualifications.

The Fourteenth Amendment added another condition of eligibility, for it asserted that

No person shall be a Senator or Representative in Congress . . . who, having previously taken an oath, as a member of Congress, or as an officer of the United States, or as a member of any State legislature, or as an executive or judicial officer of any State, to support the Constitution of the United States, shall have engaged in insurrection or rebellion against the same, or given aid or comfort to the enemies thereof. But Congress may, by a vote of two-thirds of each House, remove such disability.

Discipline and Qualifications. Each house is the judge of the elections, returns, and qualifications of its own members. Each may punish them for disorderly behavior and by a two-thirds vote expel a member. These powers extend to all cases where the offense is inconsistent with the trust and duty of membership. Each may deny seats to members-elect or expel members found to lack the requisite qualifications. Does its power to judge enable each house to deny a seat or expel a member on other than constitutional grounds when the prescribed ones are possessed? Both have done so in spite of the apparent imposition of qualifications for membership, additional to those of the Constitution, implied by their actions. Disloyalty to the Union, violation of incompatibility-of-interest statutes, and belief in polygamy have been grounds for exclusion or expulsion. Thus, in exercising its power to judge its members, each house has in fact extended its authority to include their pre-election conduct.

The best method of procedure is to seat a member whose qualifications are in dispute and then, by the required two-thirds vote, to expel him. However, it requires only a simple majority to deny a seat to a member-elect, and the recent practice of both houses indicates a tendency to follow the simpler procedure.[3]

Either house may censure a member by a formal rebuke of his words or acts. Censure is a milder form of discipline than expulsion, but it is more severe than being called to order for disorderly behavior or being required by force, if necessary, to attend the sittings of the chamber. Censure may be accompanied by expulsion or by a milder form of penalty.

Qualification by Custom. Custom requires each member of the House of Representatives to be a resident of his district. Although this requirement is no guarantee of effective representation, it does lead to over-emphasis of local issues, to excessive concern with pleasing "the folks back home," with keeping the political machinery of the district in smooth operating condition, and to neglect of the broader perspective of public policies. More important, it militates against the most effective use of political talent by eliminating all persons who are not residents of a congressional district.

Incompatible Offices. Persons otherwise qualified for the House or Senate must observe the constitutional directive that

. . . no Person holding any Office under the United States, shall be a member of either House during his Continuance in Office.

This provision of the Constitution applies the doctrine of the separation of powers to the relationship of the legislative and executive authorities. This clause makes it impossible for officers of the executive branch to be at the same time members of the legislative branch. An officer of the executive who wishes to sit in Congress must first resign his executive position. The problem, therefore, is not one of ineligibility but of incompatibility.

[3] See *Congressional Record*, 66th Congress, 2nd session (1920), pp. 1339-1343, for the refusal of the House to seat Victor L. Berger on November 10, 1919.

Forbidden Offices. A member of Congress may accept an office in the executive branch if he first resigns his seat in the legislature, but exceptions to this rule arise from the fact that

No Senator or Representative shall, during the Time for which he was elected, be appointed to any civil Office under the Authority of the United States, which shall have been created, or the Emoluments whereof shall have been encreased during such time. . . .

Hence, civil offices may exist which members of Congress are forbidden to fill.

What is a civil office under the authority of the United States? A civil office is one possessing duration and permanency, excluding special employment in temporary service. The word "office" expresses the idea of tenure, duration, emoluments, and duties. Its duties must be continuing and permanent. Special positions of an advisory nature are not civil offices. However, members of Congress may accept temporary appointments to positions when the duties are not incompatible with their membership in Congress, are auxiliary to their work as congressmen, and better qualify them to aid and guide their colleagues.

The prohibition prevents Congress from creating offices which its members would seek to fill upon resigning their seats. It also prevents the President from appointing members of Congress to offices which have been created during their membership.

CHOICE OF SENATORS AND REPRESENTATIVES

The original body of the Constitution stated that

The Senate of the United States shall be composed of two Senators from each State, chosen by the Legislature thereof, for six Years; and each Senator shall have one Vote.

Dissatisfaction with this method of choice and gradual recognition of its undemocratic nature led, in 1913, to the adoption of the Seventeenth Amendment, which declares that

The Senate of the United States shall be composed of two Senators from each State, elected by the people thereof, for six years; and each Senator shall have one vote. The electors in each State shall have the qualifications requisite for electors of the most numerous branch of the State legislatures.

Thus, senators are chosen to *represent states*. The character of the Senate is in keeping with federalism and is perpetuated by a constitutional guarantee of the equal representation of the states.

Senators are elected at-large and, with rare exceptions, those from the same state are not elected at the same time. In practice a state is never divided into two constituencies from each of which a single senator is chosen, although the persons selected by the parties to be candidates for the office may be required by extra-legal arrangement to be residents of different parts of the state.

Members of the House of Representatives may *represent* the *people* of an entire state or those of a portion of it. Only a few are chosen at-large, for choice of representatives by single-member districts has prevailed since 1842. By normal practice those states which are entitled to more than one representative are divided into a corresponding number of districts in each of which a member is chosen. This method is simple to operate and will usually produce a bipartisan delegation to the House. However, it also leads to gerrymandering, to repeated failures to re-district, and to localism.

Redistricting. The task of redividing a state into congressional districts, known as redistricting, is done by the state legislature after the state has been informed of the number of representatives to which it is entitled. National law implies that redistricting will be done but does not expressly require it. However, Congress has declared, in effect, that

1. If the number of Representatives is equal to the number of Congressional Districts within a state, each Representative shall be chosen from a district;
2. If the number of districts exceeds the number of Representatives, all Representatives shall be chosen from the states at-large; or
3. If the number of Representatives exceeds the number of districts, one representative shall be chosen from each available district with the number of Representatives in excess being chosen from the state at-large.[4]

State legislatures redistrict free from congressional control. Congress no longer requires that districts should be as nearly as possible equal in population and composed of compact and contiguous territory. Hence, the states are largely free to draw the lines of the congressional districts as they see fit.

Gerrymandering. How the task is done is determined in part by the desire of the majority party in the state legislature to elect the maximum number of its own candidates to Congress. This it can do by creating the districts so as to consolidate its opponent's strength in the fewest possible districts, which it then concedes as lost. Alternatively, it can create them so as to divide the opposition vote into segments and nullify each with a preponderance of its own strength. Both practices involve what is known as "gerrymandering," and constitute deliberate attempts to distort the representative character of the state's delegation in the House of Representatives. A "silent" gerrymander comes about when the same political party controls the state legislature for a long period of time and fails to re-district the state to reflect population changes because it does not wish to lose an advantage that it already holds.

[4] *U.S. Code,* Title 2, sec. 2a (c).

Relief from either situation is difficult to obtain. Some may be had from state constitutions that require districts to be equal in population and composed of compact and contiguous territory; but few contain such requirements, and some which do are ignored. Change forced by public opinion has always been possible, but since the majority party has the votes and holds the advantage not much can be accomplished by that means. Until recently no relief could be obtained through the judiciary; but in a major departure from established principle and law the Supreme Court of the United States recently gave its consent for a district court to accept jurisdiction over a case involving apportionment. The controversy involved the failure of the Tennessee legislature, in violation of its own state constitution, to reapportion for the selection of its own members since 1901.[5] Although no challenges have yet entered the national courts, there now seems to be no reason why the judicial power cannot be invoked against mal-apportionment of congressional districts by a state legislature.

At best redistricting is a difficult and complicated task for which no objective formula affords a ready solution. The larger the number of districts to be provided, the more complex the task becomes. It is a political function and the interests to be considered are numerous and varied. Urban demands compete with rural, industrial with agricultural. Natural geographical or economic areas must be reconciled with units such as counties, towns, townships, cities, wards, and even streets. Districts should be constructed of contiguous territory, be compact, and contain a population approximating the national quota of representation.[6] Considerations of advantage to the majority party must be served. The task is never easily accomplished, but when one party controls the cities and another the rural areas, when the chambers of the state legislature are controlled by different parties, or when rural delegates outnumber those from the cities, it becomes still more complex.[7]

Nomination. Party candidates for congressional seats are nominated by party caucus, convention, petition, declaration, or primary. Only one provision of a national statute refers to the subject, and it declares:

Candidates for Representative or Representative to be elected at large in any State shall be nominated in the same manner as candidates for governor, unless otherwise provided by the laws of such States.[8]

Therefore, nominating methods are determined by state law.

[5] *Baker* v. *Carr* (1962), 369 U.S. 186.

[6] Obtained by dividing 435 into the population of the United States.

[7] A measure to eliminate gerrymandering was considered by the House of Representatives in 1959 in anticipation of the 1961 reapportionment, but it did not become law. See *Congressional Quarterly Weekly Report*, Vol. 17, No. 27, pp. 900-901.

[8] *U.S. Code*, Title 2, sec. 5.

The result of the nominating process controls the choice open to the voter. His effective choice is limited to names on the ballot, and those nominated by caucus, convention, or primary are usually those approved by the party leaders. Nominations by petition or declaration lack party support and are usually futile. Some independence from party domination can be obtained when write-in votes are cast, but this, too, is usually a futile effort.[9] In the South nomination is tantamount to election, but in one-fourth of the congressional districts outside the South, also, it is a virtual guarantee of election. Hence, in almost one-half of the congressional districts nomination by the "right" party is the key to electoral success.[10]

The Direct Primary. The "direct primary" is intended to enable the rank-and-file members of a political party to nominate their candidates. The names of persons selected in the primary are placed on the election ballot. Primaries are regulated in great detail by state law and are usually conducted in the same manner and by the same officials as the regular elections.

"Open" Primary. The direct primary is usually either "open" or "closed." In open primaries a qualified voter may express his choice of candidates regardless of party affiliation. He is given either a blanket ballot on which are printed the names of all candidates for nomination, or separate ballots prepared for each party. The voter marks one choice for each office; only in Washington may he cross party lines. When more than one ballot is used he deposits the unmarked ones in a separate box. The "open" primary is used in only three states; it is said to promote an independent choice by primary voters, and to safeguard the secrecy of their party affiliation. However, it weakens the party "regularity" of participants, it permits members of one party to "raid" the primaries of the opposition in order to nominate the latter's weakest candidates, it permits members of one party to participate in the determination of the business of the opposition party, it gives no assurance that the nominee will be a "vote getter" with general popular appeal, and it is, therefore, heartily disliked by the party leaders.

"Closed" Primary. A participant in a "closed" primary may be challenged and required to reveal his party affiliation to obtain a ballot. Thus, the primary is "closed" to all but members of the party conducting it, who may be required to affirm their membership in the party or take an oath of party loyalty, or, though not registered members, promise to support its candidates in the general election. A voter's party affiliation is normally recorded at the time of his registration, but failing this, the system of

[9] However, Senator Strom Thurmond (D., S.C.) and Representative Dale Alford (D., Ark.) were elected by write-in votes in recent elections.

[10] An account of the nominating methods employed in the states can be found in *The Book of the States, 1962-1963* (Chicago: Council of State Governments, 1962), p. 22.

challenge and oath-taking at the primary polling place is available to test the party loyalty of participants. Needless to say, voters in "closed" primaries are supplied only with the ballot of the party in whose primary they participate. The "closed" primary is highly popular with party leaders for reasons that should be obvious.

Congressional Control of Primaries. A primary is an election within the meaning of the Constitution; the right of qualified voters to participate and to have their votes counted as cast is protected by the Constitution. This must follow although the Constitution makes no mention of primaries, which were unknown at the time of its writing, because:

> Unless the constitutional protection of the integrity of "elections" extends to primary elections, Congress is left powerless to effect the constitutional purpose, and the popular choice of representatives is stripped of its constitutional protection save only as Congress, by taking over the control of state elections, may exclude from them the influence of the state primaries. Such an expedient would end that state autonomy with respect to elections which the Constitution contemplated that Congress should be free to leave undisturbed, subject only to such minimum regulations as it should find necessary to insure the freedom and integrity of the choice.[11]

Congressional and Senatorial Campaign Committees. To aid candidates seeking election to the House or Senate each political party maintains a special campaign committee in each house of Congress. These are the Democratic (Republican) Congressional Campaign Committee and the Democratic (Republican) Senatorial Campaign Committee. They are permanent units of the national party organizations composed, respectively, of representatives and senators of each party. They receive contributions, disburse funds, act in advisory capacities, provide speakers, publicity, voting records, and reports on issues and candidates, conduct research, and do what else they can to elect their candidates to Congress. Each cooperates closely with its national committee and with other party units at all levels of the structure, but each is organizationally independent of them. However, their financial dependence upon the national committees reduces their actual independence.

Control of the Electoral Process. The election of congressmen is mainly controlled by state law, but Congress can make or alter state regulations governing the times, places, and manner of holding elections. Under it Congress has legislated to control the raising and spending of money in congressional primaries and elections, to facilitate absentee voting in the armed forces, to establish a nationally-uniform election day, to require the use of printed ballots or voting machines, and to provide for the filling of vacancies in the House.

[11] *United States* v. *Classic* (1941), 313 U.S. 299.

The Control of Money in Congressional Elections. Congress, under the "times, places, and manner" clause has enacted extensive legislation pertaining to the raising, spending, and reporting of party funds in national elections. The power to enact legislation to safeguard such elections from the improper use of money to influence the results is essential to national self-protection. This power Congress possesses just as it possesses every other power essential to the preservation of the departments and institutions of the national government from impairment and destruction, whether through force or corruption. The electoral process is the foundation upon which is built the edifice of the governmental system; and in a republican government, where political power is vested in elected representatives of the entire population, chosen at short intervals by popular elections, it is essential to eliminate from the electoral process temptations to control the process by fraudulent and corrupt use of money.

Therefore,

(b) Unless the laws of his State prescribe a less amount as the maximum limit of campaign expenditures, a candidate [for Congress] may make expenditures up to—

(1) The sum of $10,000 if a candidate for Senator, or the sum of $2,500 if a candidate for Representative, Delegate, or Resident Commissioner; or

(2) An amount equal to the amount obtained by multiplying three cents by the total number of votes cast in the last general election for all candidates for the office which the candidate seeks, but in no event exceeding $25,000 if a candidate for Senator or $5,000 if a candidate for Representative, Delegate, or Resident Commissioner.

(c) Money expended by a candidate to meet and discharge any assessment, fee, or charge made or levied upon candidates by the laws of the State in which he resides, or expended for his necessary personal, traveling, or subsistence expenses, or for stationery, postage, writing, or printing (other than for use on billboards or in newspapers), for distributing letters, circulars, or posters, or for telegraph or telephone service, shall not be included in determining whether his expenditures have exceeded the sum fixed by paragraph (1) or (2) of subdivision (b) of this section as the limit of campaign expenses of a candidate.[12]

Other provisions of national law exist pertaining to the control of money in elections.[13] No funds of a corporation chartered by Congress may be contributed to *any* campaign fund, nor may any funds of a cor-

[12] Corrupt Practices Act, 1925, sec. 248, 43 *Statutes* 1073.

[13] See also *1956 General Election Campaigns,* Senate Subcommittee on Privileges and Elections, 85th Congress 1st session (1957), for an account of the increasing cost of elections; and Herbert E. Alexander, *Money, Politics, and Public Reporting* (Princeton, N.J.: Citizen's Research Foundation, 1960) which sets forth a study of existing national and state reporting procedures, and analyzes present and proposed levels of disclosure and publicity.

poration chartered by a state be contributed to any campaign fund used in a national election. However, corporation officers may make contributions of private funds. The Labor Management Relations Act imposed on labor organizations a blanket prohibition against contributions or expenditures of union dues made in furtherance of any *national election,* and *all* primaries, conventions, and caucuses related to such election. The Hatch Act of 1939 prohibits the acceptance by *any* party organization or candidate of contributions from any person on relief. No individual, committee, or organization may donate more than $5,000 per year to aid the campaign of any candidate for national office, but any number of different candidates or committees may be aided by donations from the same giver. Moreover, any number of members of the same family may make separate contributions of $5,000 to the same candidate or committee. This prohibition does not apply to contributions made to state or local candidates or committees, and since some of this money is sent up to the national party committees the full effect of the $5,000 limitation can be easily evaded. No political committee which functions in two or more states may spend more than $3,000,000 in any national campaign, but no limit exists on the number of such committees a party may create or on the ability of a committee to transfer funds to another committee. No employees of the national government may solicit contributions of money, kind, or services within, or outside, government buildings whether during office hours or not. No officer or employee may use his position to intimidate, threaten, or punish any other officer or employee for giving, or failing to give, any contribution of money, service, or kind to any party, organization, committee, agency or person for political purposes. However, national employees may make voluntary contributions. These limitations apply also to state and local employees whose compensation is derived in whole or in part from the national government.

Although these seemingly extensive provisions have some regulatory and a considerable deterrent effect, they are but a hesitant step in the direction of effectively controlling money in national elections. They are full of "loopholes" some of which have been noted above. They do not regulate contributions to, and expenditures by, representatives and senators in the interval between elections. Most of them do not extend to primaries. Important and sizeable expenditures are not subject to regulation, although made by or on behalf of a candidate or his committee; but more important is the impossibility under existing law of ascertaining the sources and amounts of private expenditures that are made to aid a candidate when neither he nor his committee have received the money or know of the expenditure. Loans made to aid a campaign are not covered by the regulations, although they may ultimately prove to be contributions since repayment may be neither demanded nor made. Accountings are required to be made before the financial affairs of campaigns are concluded, but many candidates—even successful ones—and committees supply only incomplete or no information as required by law, and no enforcement machinery exists to secure compliance or to bring about the desired publicity. The problem remains and grows more serious as the costs of campaigning increase. Provisions of current law are inadequate for its solution, and successive Congresses seem little disposed to enact more realistic and comprehensive controls or to provide for the enforcement of existing ones.

In May of 1962 President Kennedy recommended to Congress the repeal of the $3,000,000 and $5,000 limitations referred to above as part of a more general attack on the problem of regulating money in elections. However, the President made no proposals relating to the raising or spending of funds for between-campaign expenses for numerous trips home, radio and television tapes, etc., by which members of Congress keep in touch with their states and districts. Members have an obligation to be available to constituents, to make their views known on public questions, and to be available for questioning. Lack of provision for these expenses puts great pressure on members to take money from private contributors. Sooner or later they find themselves under pressure to return the favor at the expense of the public interest. Publicity is not adequate protection against this sort of conflict of interest, and there is at present no effective control whatever over it. The statutes outlaw the giving and taking of money to perform services or to support legislation, but they are silent on the propriety of taking money when services are not delivered or promised. At the very least the statutes ought to call for reports from donors and recipients of interim contributions and expenditures. Constituents are entitled to know from whom such contributions have come so that they can judge their propriety. Nothing is more fundamental in a democratic society than absolute public confidence in the integrity of its political institutions. That confidence will be badly shaken if it is known that elected officials have recourse to secret financial support from private individuals.

Contested Elections. Each house of Congress can judge the elections and returns of its members. It does so whenever a contested election occurs.[14] A member-elect whose election is in doubt usually stands aside when the oath is administered. A contest in the House is referred to the Committee on House Administration to be resolved, and in the Senate to the Committee on Rules and Administration. The process of decision may be lengthy, and is often decided in a partisan fashion. During this period the contested member-elect participates in the proceedings and draws his salary. If he loses the contest, he retains his salary but is displaced by the winner of the contest who is sworn as a member.

[14] *U.S. Code*, Title 2, secs. 201 and 202, governs the procedure for bringing about a contest.

Pay and Perquisites of Members. The Constitution guarantees that members of Congress shall receive a salary, fixed by law, and paid out of the Treasury of the United States. In spite of complaints to the contrary, the following enumeration of pay and perquisites suggests that congressmen ought to be able to avoid destitution:

Pay—$22,500.

Taxation—No national income tax on first $3,000 if the member maintains two residences, one in Washington and another in his district.

Communications—Free first-class mailing privileges, plus $400 (senators, $450) per year for purchase of airmail and special-delivery stamps, $1,800 yearly for stationery, and substantial allowances for long-distance telephoning (senators, $1,800 for calls originating outside Washington, plus 7200 minutes of long-distance conversation from Washington) and for telegrams (senators, $2,000 per year).

Pensions—By 7½ per cent annual contribution from his pay a member can qualify for a yearly pension up to $18,000 if he has 30 years service, including military service and time in other federal jobs. Payments are in addition to social security or other retirement income.

Group Life Insurance—At a cost of $10.83 per month a member can purchase a $20,000 life insurance policy without medical certification.

Travel—Three round trips per year (senators, two) between home and Washington at 20¢ per mile. While traveling on official business at home and abroad, members and employees receive a $12 per diem allowance for food and lodging.

Local Office—Supplied in federal building if space is available, plus $600 expense allowance. If no public space can be furnished an allowance of $1200 is granted instead.

Health and Medical Care—Members enjoy use of two gymnasiums, steam rooms, a congressional physician and staff to provide medical advice and some medicines without cost. Members can obtain hospitalization, treatment, and surgery at military hospitals at reduced costs. One Senate office building has a swimming pool.

Staffs: Representatives—One administrative assistant per member plus an average of $35,000 per year to pay other aides and office help, who are frequently relatives. Nepotism is common in both chambers.

Staffs: Senators—Dependent upon the population of the senator's state. Eighteen staff members and $100,000 allowance are not unusual. One in five senators in November, 1961, had one or more relatives on his staff.

Offices: Representatives—A suite of at least two rooms, storage space, closets, and lavatory. New members are assigned to old, less desirable quarters. A third House office building is under construction and will provide additional expanded and modern space.

Offices: Senators—A minimum of five rooms per suite. A new Senate office building provides members with wall-to-wall carpeting, refrigerators, and built-in wall safes.

Members also enjoy the comforts or advantages of lounges, library facilities, low-cost radio recordings and motion pictures for "home town"

"Yes Sir — We Have to Keep Hunting Waste in Those Foreign Aid Programs"

use, discount prices on stationery and miscellaneous gift items, free flowers for offices and official functions, low-cost meals and haircuts, and free parking.

Since Congress controls its own purse strings and has no "watchdog" to which it must answer, the opportunities for questionable practices are abundant. The chambers fix their own standards and rules of conduct. Many members are scrupulous in their regard for the proprieties of public office, but there is much evidence to suggest that some are not. At the time of this writing the spending habits of members are the subject of a newspaper inquiry but of little official concern, and no significant action. Attention centers upon the House of Representatives.

The annual budget of Congress is now approximately ninety-two million dollars. It employs about 7,500 persons. All members operate unaffected by the hampering restrictions of "conflict of interest" laws, (which have embarrassed the executive branch on numerous occasions and forced more than one official to resign), since none of these apply to congressmen.[15] A member with important private economic interests may introduce legislation or vote on that of another member which is favorable to those interests.

[15] See Joseph L. Rauh, "Conflict of Interest in Congress," *Conference on Conflict of Interest, February 20, 1961* (Chicago: The School of Law, University of Chicago) Conference Series No. 17, pp. 1-13, especially p. 5.

In theory the guarantee of adequate standards of conduct is that the electorate will repudiate any member who abuses his position for private benefit or gain. Although flagrant cases are dealt with in that manner, the electorate cannot take action without information, and convincing data are almost impossible to obtain. Legitimate perquisites of office include tours to foreign places to inspect military bases, aid programs, or anything else of concern to the committee on whose behalf the trip is made. Military air transportation is easily obtained and the red carpet is always rolled out for a congressman, (especially if he represents a key committee or is a powerful senator or representative) by the bureaucrat, diplomat, or commanding officer at the destination. Counterpart funds can be obtained by congressmen at many American embassies merely for the asking. Only conscience guides their expenditure, for only nominal accounting is required. Cut-price ocean cruises can be had on vessels of steamship lines subsidized by Congress or seeking other favors from it. The stationery allowance given each member has been the source of purchases falling within that class of article only by the wildest interpretation of the term. When, however, enterprising newspapermen began to reveal in print the results of examination by them of thousands of expense vouchers on file with the House disbursing office, the records were ordered closed to public examination. But this was not before they had uncovered evidence of public funds being used to rent unnecessary Cadillacs in New York City, and to pay for luxury hotel suites, the travel expenses of wives and friends, and nightclub entertainment.

These revelations have prompted new efforts to require full accounting of congressional members' and employees' spending, and to open the records to public view. Several earlier bills have passed the two chambers, but such measures seem unable to survive the ministrations of the conference committee. Congress watches the executive, but who watches Congress?

BOX SCORE—CONGRESSIONAL JUNKETS—1959

Travelers				Destination					
					Senators		Represents.		
	D	R			D	R	D	R	Total
Senators	30	21		Africa and the					
Representatives	83	56		Near East	4	4	17	12	37
	113	77		Western Europe	13	8	56	25	102
				Far East	10	6	20	15	51
				Latin America	7	10	18	10	45
				Pacific Islands	6	4	12	11	33
				Russia and Eastern Europe	6	1	14	10	31
				Total	46	33	137	83	299

Adapted from data collected and presented by *Congressional Quarterly Weekly Report*, Vol. 18, No. 9, p. 298.

Privileges of Members. The members of Congress enjoy broad immunities designed to guarantee their independence of action. Thus:

They shall in all Cases, except Treason, Felony and Breach of the Peace, be privileged from Arrest during their Attendance at the Session of their respective Houses, and in going to and returning from the same; and for any Speech or Debate in either House, they shall not be questioned in any other Place.

In the American constitutional scheme of things these protections enable members of Congress to perform their duties free from fear, intimidation, restraint or constraint.

The immunity from arrest is of no value. Originally it applied only to arrests in civil actions, but these have long been discontinued. It affords no exemption from arrest in any criminal case. The clause is therefore practically obsolete with respect to the immunity from arrest which it appears to give.

However, other protections for members grow out of its language. They may not be held to answer in any place, at any time, or to any person for things said or done in the performance of their legislative duties, although these may have been unnecessary to the fulfillment of those duties, irregular, and against the rules. Their immunity extends to the floors of the chambers, committee proceedings, written reports, votes, resolutions, or any other aspect of their legislative capacity within or without the United States. Should a member, however, say or do something when acting in a purely private capacity, his membership in Congress would not save him from prosecution.[16]

Vacancies. Deaths and resignations bring about numerous vacancies in the Senate and House during the life of each Congress. To facilitate representation of each state at all times by its full delegation a constitutional amendment provides that

When vacancies happen in the representation of any State in the Senate, the executive authority of such State shall issue writs of election to fill such vacancies: *Provided,* That the legislature of any State may empower the executive thereof to make temporary appointments until the people fill the vacancies by election as the legislature may direct.

Vacancies in the House of Representatives are filled by elections as prescribed by the laws of the states.

Sessions. The Twentieth Amendment controls the sessions of Congress by declaring that the terms of its members shall begin at noon on the third day of January and that:

The Congress shall assemble at least once in every year, and such meeting shall begin at noon on the 3d day of January, unless they shall by law appoint a different day.

[16] See *Kilbourn* v. *Thompson* (1881), 103 U.S. 168.

The life of a Congress is two years, divided into two annual sessions known as the first and second sessions, but one or more special sessions may be called by the President. Congresses also are numbered consecutively. The date fixed for the opening of a session is regularly varied to avoid weekends, but once begun each session lasts as long as the houses desire to sit. According to law,

> Sec. 132. Except in time of war or during a national emergency proclaimed by the President, the two Houses shall adjourn sine die not later than the last day (Sundays excepted) in the month of July in each year unless otherwise provided by the Congress.[17]

But this date is commonly ignored.

ORGANIZATION OF CONGRESS

Having disposed of these external aspects of Congress, we can now turn our attention to its internal organization. The houses of Congress have two sets of machinery, of essentially different types, both of which are necessary to the performance of their functions. Through the informal (party) machinery the political parties endeavor to control the process and substance of legislation. These units are held together by the common desire of their members to attain success, power, and influence over the course of legislation, and thereby to enhance their chances of re-election. To these ends party members tend to accept leadership over the law-making process, and are often persuaded by considerations of party unity and harmony, unless the dictates of their consciences or the demands of their constituents determine otherwise.

The formal, or parliamentary, organization is composed of the officers and committees provided for by the rules, statutes, or the Constitution. Some agents of the formal organization function in a highly partisan manner; but it is through the formal structure that the decisions of party leadership are implemented. Hence, it is on the formal machinery that the political forces which shape public policy are concentrated. The ability of a party in the House or Senate to attain its ends requires the successful use of both types of legislative machinery. Consequently, the members of each house are vitally interested in their positions within its units.

Informal Organization of the Houses. The newly elected members of the houses normally belong to the major political parties. Hence, they may be divided into two groups, each of which is united by a bond of party allegiance. That bond is an important element in the organization of the house to undertake its work.

[17] Legislative Reorganization Act, 1946, Title I, to be found in 60 *Statutes* 812, 831.

The simplest evidence of this unity is the seating of the members in each chamber. As seen from the Chair, Democrats sit to the right, Republicans to the left of the center aisle. Whichever party has most members is the "majority" party; the other is the "minority." Furthermore, some members have been re-elected. They know, and newly elected members soon learn, that the new organization of the chamber will differ little, if any, from the old. All that is needed to set it in motion is the completion of a few formalities, but these formalities are of great importance to the process of law making.

The problem of organizing the Senate is simplified by the fact that it is a continuous body. Its organization, informal and formal, is in continual existence, so that only vacancies in the various units need to be filled. This task is simplified because re-elected members are normally returned to their old places within these units.

When organized for business, the members of each chamber assume the character of the parts of a collegiate body. Each new member will find that he is not a free agent, but is subject to considerable direction and control and to great pressure from the leaders of his party. He will find, particularly in the House, rules and procedures that make it difficult for him to serve on important committees, be recognized to speak from the floor, secure consideration of his bills, or do any of the other things he might expect to do as a member of Congress. He will be subjected to restraint and constraint which he must accept if he is to gain the influence and power which good standing with his party leaders will assure him. He will find that laws are not passed in an atmosphere of calm deliberation and lofty intellectualism but in response to pressures and deals by men who originate few of the measures that they introduce, and who seldom understand or are interested in more than a handful of the laws that they enact. He will find that regard for the "general welfare" all but disappears during the process of making laws and emerges, if at all, as a vaguely perceived amalgam of parochial interests, all demanding recognition. He will find, in other words, that the legislative process is a political process. Hence, an understanding of the forms and authority of the party organization in the houses of Congress is essential.

General Role of Party in Legislation. The party ties of members and the influence of parties over them serve to regularize, not greatly, perhaps, but to some extent, the individual's propensity to unpredictable action. The political party in Congress moderates, steadies, and disciplines, not necessarily punitively, but within general principles. It can emphasize the broad aspects of policy, perhaps wean the member away from narrow parochial interests of a selfish and self-serving nature and induce him to serve a broader, even a national, interest. By accommodating the divergent factions of the modern political party in the same Republican or Democratic fold, it can promote tolerance of differing viewpoints, not only within, but also between, parties. Hence, in the daily operations of the chambers members of either major party are not apt to balk at supporting an issue because by doing so they will be brought into the ideological company of opposition members. Further, membership in a national political party exerts an influence, however subtle and slight, that inclines members to overlook the local and regional forces which promote factionalism and cloaks all with dedication to a common cause. Because the parties are composed of men and women who embrace different principles on public issues, albeit with differing degrees of conviction and conscientiousness, without self-assumed infallibility, each party tacitly concedes the wisdom and practicality of pitting its views against those of the opposition. Out of the competition will normally emerge a middle position acceptable to a majority of the membership, though almost never to all. Thus, while the parties inject some order, steadiness, and uniformity into the legislative process, they leave room for the accommodation of individual differences, loyalties, commitments and consciences. But, excessive independence among the membership is incompatible with the role of a national, representative law-making body in the governmental system. It must, therefore, be tempered by the restraints which frequent elections and the necessity for party support impose. And so the parties in Congress curb tendencies on the part of their memberships toward egoistic, self-righteous independence by serving as agents of mediation and adjustment between conflicting local, state, regional, and national demands.

Caucuses or Conferences. In each house of Congress each party maintains a caucus (conference) to which all of its members in the chamber belong. The caucus is the largest and most basic unit of party organization. Its function is to weld its members into an harmonious group able to present a united front and to act in concert and harmony to secure the passage of favored legislation and the defeat of that which is opposed. The caucuses have lost much of their former power over legislation and party members, but they serve as arenas for the settlement of intra-party disputes. Only the House Democratic caucus makes a pretense of binding its members, by vote of the caucus, to support the party's position on pending legislation. However, the power is seldom used; when invoked it leaves each member free on questions of constitutional interpretation, questions on which he has made a contrary pledge to his constituents prior to his election, or on which he has received contrary instructions from his nominating authority.[18]

To enact its legislation a party must win control of the organization

---

[18] For the voting record of northern Republicans and southern Democrats in 1957, 1958, and 1959 see *Congressional Quarterly Weekly Report,* Vol. 17, No. 47, pp. 1491-1496; and for a record of bipartisan voting, 1956-1959, see *Ibid.,* Vol. 17, No. 46, pp. 1477-1480.

of the houses every two years. On matters of organization the parties in both houses demand absolute "regularity" from their members. However, only the majority party in each House possesses the votes necessary to control the process of organization. That party always elects its candidates to the positions of leadership and power, and controls the standing legislative committees of each chamber.

Each conference meets before the start of a session. Other meetings may be called by party leaders as needed, but the conferences seldom assemble. Most work to maintain party unity and harmony is carried on outside the conferences.

The influence and importance of a conference is proportional to its character as a compact majority of party members who agree on questions of public policy that are of interest to their party. However, because few caucuses are composed of compact homogeneous majorities, because few issues are decided on strictly party lines, and because members insist upon remaining independent so that they can respond to local demands, the caucuses cannot abuse the power they represent. The caucus is no longer the potent instrument of party control that it once was; yet, it affords party members of each house a means to confer jointly on important measures of policy, to "dicker" for support on lesser bills of interest to individuals or blocs, to smooth differences of opinion, and to reach common agreement on the basis of which many members will stand together even though not bound to do so.

Floor Leaders. Each party in each house has a floor leader, who in many respects is the most important unit of the informal organization of the houses. He is chosen by his caucus and is the legislative "general" of his faction. All are usually senior members, skilled parliamentarians, masters of persuasion and compromise, and men of demonstrated leadership who are respected by their colleagues. A majority party leader supported by a solid superiority of the votes determines in cooperation with other units of party leadership what measures will be called up for debate and when, how they will be amended, how much time will be allotted to them, what procedure will be used to consider them, who may speak for or against them, and a host of other details which make up the legislative process.

However, seldom is the floor leader backed by such support. He must work through what amounts to a coalition composed of some of his own and some of the minority party's members. In this situation he must pay heed to the wishes not only of his fellow leaders but also of the rank and file of his party, and to the likes and dislikes of the minority group whose aid he must have. He must see to it that the majority-controlled legislative process hammers out a measure acceptable to all these diverse elements. Moreover, he cannot ignore the known attitudes of the other house, which must also accept each measure, or of the executive whose veto always looms in the background. The floor leader of the President's party is the recognized spokesman in his chamber for the legislative program of the administration.

Whips. The floor leaders must have help if they are to perform their tasks. It is supplied by assistant floor leaders (whips) appointed by the floor leaders (Democrats), or elected by the conference (Republicans). The chief whips in the House usually appoint one or more assistant whips. The whips function, subject to the floor leaders' direction and control, to see that members are present when votes are anticipated or are to be taken, and when debate on controversial measures of interest to the party is scheduled. They aid the floor leader by ascertaining the attitudes of members on pending bills; on the basis of that information the floor leader gauges the chances for their passage and decides what compromises must be made to bring them through. The whips relay information, attitudes, and decisions from the floor leader, the Speaker, and the President to the members. In the House of Representatives the chief whip of each party publishes a weekly newsletter informing the membership of the probable legislative program outlined by the floor leaders for the coming week. Thus, the whips are the eyes and ears of the floor leaders.

Steering Committees. The conference of each party in each house elects a steering committee. In the House the floor leaders chair these party units, which serve as executive committees of the conferences. They determine, in detail, the legislative program set out in general terms by the conferences, serve as centers of collective party leadership, guide the individual leaders and members, make recommendations for conference action on measures, and coordinate party legislative plans with the powerful Rules Committee whose help is necessary for their execution. However, in the House of Representatives only the steering committee of the majority party possesses the votes to make its weight felt in the legislative process, and yet the Speaker, floor leader, and whip, who control the business of the House, so dominate it that it merely reaffirms their decisions and has become largely superfluous. The minority steering committee of the House helps to determine the legislative policies of its party and to unify the ranks of its members.

The steering committees of the Senate have been displaced as organs of effective party leadership and control. That of the Democrats acts as their committee on committees, while that of the Republicans serves no purpose and seems to endure because its membership also serves on the Republican policy committee to which the steering committee has given its power.

Policy Committees. These committees exist only in the Senate. They have a foundation in law, but they function no less as units of party control because of that. The policy committees are very active; that of the majority holds weekly meetings. The legislative powers and responsibilities of the steering committees have been transferred to them. They do not control the floor proceedings or exact binding commitments to support particular bills or actions, but they do coordinate the work of standing committees, obtain intra-party agreement upon the general principles of legislation, sharpen party responsibility, and formulate over-all legislative policy for the parties.

Their composition illustrates the interlocking leadership in the houses of Congress. Thus, the Republican policy committee is composed of the first seven members named by the chairman of the conference to the steering committee. They include the chairman himself, the floor leader, the whip, and four of the most respected, influential, senior members of the party in the Senate. To them are added other key Republican senators to make a total of twenty-three. The Democratic policy committee is appointed by the Democratic floor leader and includes seven of the most influential Democratic senators, together with the secretary of the caucus and the whip.

Committees on Committees. Each party in each House has a committee on committees. They function as party agents and are responsible to their caucuses. They assign the members of their respective parties to the standing legislative committees. Except for those of the Senate Democratic committee on committees, the assignments must be approved by the caucus of the party.

Their size and composition varies. The House Republican committee is composed of one representative from each state having a Republican member. One is elected by the Republican members of the state's delegation and has as many votes as there are Republicans from his state. The Senate Republican committee on committees consists of from five to eight members appointed by the chairman of the Senate Republican conference. The House Democratic committee on committees is made up of the Democratic members of the House Committee on Ways and Means chosen by the Democratic caucus. Depending upon the party strength in the House, therefore, the committee on committees may vary from about seven to seventeen members, each of whom has a single vote. The Senate Democratic committee on committees is the old steering committee.

Arranging the assignments of members to standing committees is not a simple task. Seats on each are roughly apportioned according to the strength of the parties in the chamber, but the precise number to be given each party is fixed by the majority leadership. Seniority governs, and members once placed on a committee are continued in their existing assignments unless they request a change. In making initial assignments, efforts are also made to consider the members' states of origin, their legislative interests, their special knowledge, their party standing, and other data pertinent to the assignments. Presidential influence may be strongly felt. Much weight is traditionally given to the reaction of the committee chairmen. Further, Senate Democratic leadership tries to ensure every member a major committee assignment, but all other assignments there and in the House conform almost wholly to the seniority rule.

The slates of proposed assignments are given to the floor leaders who first submit them for caucus approval and thereafter present them to their chambers during the period of organization at the start of a Congress. Each slate is proposed to and voted upon by the proper house without debate or opposition. By this means the important standing legislative committees are constituted. The process is one involving strict party regularity and is firmly controlled by the majority in its own interest. Failure to organize its house will ruin its ability to control the legislative process, but organizational success does not guarantee the latter.

Without the informal party units the formal ones would be almost useless; for it is the informal machinery that breathes life into the legislative process, that staffs and sets in motion the formal machinery, that gives some direction and purpose to its efforts. The two sets of machinery are closely entwined. The informal part provides the common purpose, deliberation, planning, responsibility, and responsiveness to what in its absence would be little more than the uncoordinated, irresponsible, and frantic efforts of individual members to serve their own particular ends.

Formal Organization of the Houses.

Rules. Of great importance to the regularity, order, control, predictability of action, and rights of the minority, are the rules of the houses. Each house determines the rules of its proceedings. The rules govern the organization and procedures of each house and prescribe a progression of stages through which bills and resolutions must pass to become law. However, some details of organization and procedure rest on statutes and the Constitution. The latter provides that "a Majority of each [House] shall constitute a Quorum to do Business," and further states:

Each House shall keep a Journal of its Proceedings, and from time to time publish the same, excepting such Parts as may in their Judgment require Secrecy; and the Yeas and Nays of the Members of either House on any question shall, at the Desire of one fifth of those Present, be entered on the Journal.

Because it is a continuous body, the rules of the Senate are continuous and remain binding from one Congress to the next, but they may be altered at the beginning of a session. The House of Representatives, however, is not continuous, so its rules must be re-adopted at the beginning of each Congress. The procedure is usually only a formality, but occasionally controversy is stirred up by efforts to bring about alterations. The size of the House and the complexities of its procedures require more numerous and detailed rules than in the Senate. They conserve time, increase the power of the Speaker, and enhance the prospect for the legislative success of the majority party. But some argue that the rules of both houses excessively constrain the processes of representative government.

"You're Out Of Order"

Officers.

Senate. The Constitution stipulates that

The Vice President of the United States shall be President of the Senate, but shall have no Vote, unless they be equally divided.

The Senate shall chuse their other Officers, and also a President pro tempore, in the Absence of the Vice President, or when he shall exercise the Office of President of the United States.

The Vice President is not, of course, a member of the Senate, and is therefore regarded as an outsider. His decisions are often appealed to the floor, he is unable to address the Senate from the floor in debate, and he has been denied authority comparable to that of the Speaker of the House. He cannot be as overtly partisan as can the Speaker. Moreover, the political complexion of the President of the Senate may be opposite to that of the majority party in that assembly.

The President *pro tempore* of the Senate is a constitutional officer. He is nominated by the majority party conference and elected when the Senate is organized. The office is one of some power and prestige but of no great importance. The "pro tem" is one of several partisan functionaries of the majority party, but he lacks the commanding position of the Speaker of the House, and is completely overshadowed by the majority floor leader.

The Senate has officers other than its President and President *pro tempore,* but they are not provided for in the rules. They include the secretary, sergeant-at-arms, doorkeeper, and chaplain. Nominees to these positions are designated by the caucus of each party at the beginning of a Congress and voted upon by the senators during the process of organization. The candidates of the majority party always win. These officers, and the President *pro tempore,* are chosen for an indefinite term, so that it is only necessary to make choices when vacancies occur or when party control of the Senate shifts after an election.

Officers.

House of Representatives. The Constitution states that "The House of Representatives shall chuse their Speaker and other Officers. . . ." Hence, Rule II of the House provides:

ELECTION OF OFFICERS

There shall be elected by a viva voce vote, at the commencement of each Congress, to continue in office until their successors are chosen and qualified, a Clerk, Sergeant-at-Arms, Doorkeeper, Postmaster, and Chaplain, each of whom shall take an oath to support the Constitution of the United States, and for the true and faithful discharge of the duties of his office to the best of his knowledge and ability, and to keep the secrets of the House; and each shall appoint all of the employees of his department provided for by the law.[19]

These officers are chosen at the beginning of each Congress.

On the day set for the first meeting of a new Congress, the members-elect assemble at the appointed hour in the Hall of the House of Representatives, where they are called to order by the clerk of the former House. The clerk reads the roll, following the alphabetical order of the states, and the members-elect answer to determine whether a quorum is present. The first order of business is election of the Speaker. The candidates have been chosen by the party caucuses. Their names are put in formal nomination on the floor and voted upon by the members-elect. The candidate of the majority party is elected Speaker. His defeated opponent invariably becomes the minority floor leader. The Speaker-elect is escorted to the chair where he takes his oath of office. He then administers the oath of office to the members-elect who rise and respond in unison.

Soon after the Speaker is chosen by the House and the members are sworn, the House chooses its other officers. Nominations for these positions have also been prepared by the caucus of each party and are reported as a slate by a member designated to act on behalf of his group. By this means the majority party nominees for clerk, sergeant-at-arms,

[19] *Rules and Manual, United States House of Representatives, 1961* (Washington, D.C.: U.S. Government Printing Office, 1961), p. 310, printed as House Document No. 459, 86th Congress, 2nd session. Hereafter cited as *House Rules and Manual.*

doorkeeper, postmaster, and chaplain are elected. The House formally observes the constitutional requirement that it must elect its Speaker and other officers, although in fact the election is a mere formality the outcome of which is well known in advance.

Speaker of the House. The Speaker of the House of Representatives is one of the most powerful figures in the structure of the national government and possesses political power second only to that of the President. He invariably is, although he need not be, a member of the House. However, the powers vested in his office by the rules make it unlikely that any but a member of long service, skilled in the techniques of the legislative process, highly respected by his colleagues, and of proven character and ability, would be entrusted to exercise them. A Speaker can normally expect to be re-elected as long as he himself remains a member, his party remains in the majority, and he retains the confidence of his colleagues.

RULE I

DUTIES OF THE SPEAKER

1. The Speaker shall take the chair on every legislative day precisely at the hour to which the House shall have adjourned at the last sitting, immediately call the Members to order, and on the appearance of a quorum, cause the Journal of the proceedings of the last day's sitting to be read, having previously examined and approved the same.

2. He shall preserve order and decorum, and, in case of disturbance or disorderly conduct in the galleries, or in the lobby, may cause the same to be cleared.

3. He shall have general control, except as provided by rule or law, of the Hall of the House, and of the corridors and passages and the disposal of the unappropriated rooms in that part of the Capitol assigned to the use of the House, until further ordered.

4. He shall sign all acts, addresses, joint resolutions, writs, warrants, and subpenas of, or issued by order of, the House, and decide all questions of order, subject to an appeal by any Member, on which appeal no Member shall speak more than once, unless by permission of the House.

5. He shall rise to put a question, but may state it sitting; . . .

6. He shall not be required to vote in ordinary legislative proceedings, except where his vote would be decisive, or where the House is engaged in voting by ballot; and in cases of a tie vote the question shall be lost.

7. He shall have the right to name any member to perform the duties of the Chair, but such substitution shall not extend beyond three legislative days: *Provided, however,* That in case of illness, he may make such appointment for a period not exceeding ten days, with the approval of the House at the time the same is made; and in his absence and omission to make such appointment, the House shall proceed to elect a Speaker pro tempore to act in his absence.[20]

The Speaker is the leader of the majority party although he is seldom its senior member. He is a parliamentary officer, but he openly uses and

[20] *Ibid.,* pp. 303-307.

is expected to use the authority of his position to aid the majority in the enactment of its legislative program. He is a key member of the majority leadership, a member of its steering committee. He is aided in the discharge of his party responsibilities by the efforts of the majority floor leader, who often functions as his assistant on the floor, and he cooperates with the Rules Committee and the chairmen of the standing committees. Nevertheless, as a parliamentary officer of the House, the Speaker must function within the rules and precedents of the assembly.

Committees. The houses of Congress function through systems of committees. Committees lend themselves to the performance of special functions; permanent ones with continuing memberships permit the development of *expertise* among the members of the assembly; they permit a great division of labor, which not only enables more thorough work to be done but also speeds up the legislative process by relieving members from the necessity of attending to every matter.

Because of the flexibility and the adaptability of committees to the needs of the legislative process the houses of Congress make extensive use of several different types. There are *special* or *select committees* which are occasionally created for the purpose of undertaking special tasks not within the jurisdiction of existing committees. They are established by resolution of the House or Senate, and appointed by the appropriate presiding officer. An *investigating committee* is occasionally a select group appointed to conduct an inquiry into some matter of interest, but investigations are usually made by all or part of one of the permanent legislative committees. They are identified by the function they perform. A phenomenon known as the Committee of the Whole is used in the House of Representatives only. It is the House sitting as a committee composed of all the representatives. *Conference committees* are *ad hoc* committees composed of members from each house to reconcile differences between the House and Senate versions of the same act. *Joint committees* are permanent non-legislative committees consisting of an equal number of members from each chamber created to deal with specific matters of interest to both. Thus, joint committees exist to deal, *inter alia,* with atomic energy, printing, internal revenue taxation, the economic report of the President, and the Library of Congress.

The most important committees of Congress are the *standing committees.* They are the main cogs in the legislative machinery of the houses. Each is a miniature legislative body whose power over legislation it is difficult to exaggerate. There are twenty committees in the House and sixteen in the Senate. Those of the House largely duplicate those of the Senate. Titles vary but they deal generally with agriculture, appropriations, armed services, banking and currency, the post office and the civil service, government operations, taxation, foreign affairs, commerce, labor, the judiciary, and the District of Columbia. The House has a unique Rules Committee unparalleled by any Senate committee. House commit-

Return of the dictator

tees range in number from a low of nine to a high of over fifty, but average about twenty-five members. Those of the Senate vary from a low of nine to a high of twenty-three, but a membership of fifteen is most common.

Each senator may serve on two standing committees, with the exception that not more than sixteen majority and five minority members of committees on the District of Columbia, Government Operations, and Post Office and Civil Service, may serve on three. Representatives may serve on only one standing committee, except that members of the committees on the District of Columbia, Government Operations, Un-American Activities, and House Administration may serve on two.

The manner of their establishment has been noted, but the rules of the House further provide that

2. The Speaker shall appoint all select and conference committees which shall be ordered by the House from time to time. . . .

3. At the commencement of each Congress, the House shall elect as chairman of each standing committee one of the Members thereof; in the temporary absence of the chairman the member next in rank in the order named in the election of the committee, and so on, as often as the case shall happen, shall act as chairman; and in case of a permanent vacancy in the chairmanship of any such committee the House shall elect another chairman.

4. All vacancies in standing committees in the House shall be filled by election by the House.[21]

[21] *Ibid.*, Rule X, pp. 326-327.

Seniority Rule. When the committees on committees prepare the slates of members for election by the respective chambers, they designate that member of their party who has served longest on each standing committee. This senior member automatically becomes chairman, if he is not already chairman of another committee that he prefers to head, although his position is dependent upon the formality of election.

Committee chairmen can control the substance of legislation. In spite of their power, strict observance of the "seniority rule" places entire emphasis upon length of service and ignores all qualifications of fitness except that of age. The seniority rule puts in these positions of great authority and control over the legislative process members from "safe" constituencies who need not worry about re-election. They are often out of step with, and indifferent to, the opinions of their constituents and of the country at large. Many times they are at odds with the leadership of their own party. Seniority means that most committees are controlled by southern Democrats or Midwest Republicans whenever the respective parties control the houses. With changes of party control the same men rotate between the committee chairmanships and the position of ranking minority members. Hence, large areas of the nation are unrepresented among the committee chairmanships. Seniority excludes from the chairs young members with new ideas and fresh contacts with voter opinion. It may work to keep them off committees for which they are more qualified than are members senior to them in service but inferior in knowledge and ability. It tends to keep members in positions of great responsibility until they are past their prime years of service.

However, the seniority rule does have some compensating advantages. It permits long service which fosters the growth of subject-matter expertness. It develops familiarity with the intricacies of the legislative process. It provides an easy solution to the otherwise very difficult problem of selecting committee chairmen. It holds out the prospect of reward for long and faithful service.

Whatever its advantages and disadvantages there is little likelihood that the seniority rule will be abandoned by either chamber. Committee chairmanships are highly desirable prizes. Their possession impresses constituents, carries great weight with voters, and, in general, is popularly accepted as evidence of the responsibility, statesmanship, ability, and character of their possessors. They vest in their holders power far in excess of that enjoyed by their less fortunate colleagues. Therefore, it is probable that any method of selection other than an automatic one would precipitate great conflict and party strife and might easily become a popularity contest.

Publicity. Democracy requires that the representatives of the people should conduct their deliberations in open session so that adequate publicity may be given to their actions and the reasons for them. Otherwise, the responsibility and responsiveness of those to whom the authority to make laws has been delegated would be difficult if not impossible to enforce. Accordingly, the daily sittings of the houses usually begin at noon and are open, in principle, to the public. However, sessions closed to all but members and officers may be held by either house for the consideration of confidential communications which ought to be kept secret.

Written accounts of various types are printed to cover the events that take place within the halls of Congress. The Constitution provides that

Each House shall keep a Journal of its Proceedings, and from time to time publish the same, excepting such parts as may in their Judgment require Secrecy. . . .

Copies of the *Journal* have to be deposited at the Library of Congress where they may be examined by interested parties. The *Journal* is not very informative, for it contains only a bare outline of the actions of the houses, but detailed accounts of the proceedings can be found in other publications. What purports to be a verbatim account of the proceedings of the House and Senate is published daily under the title of the *Congressional Record*. Although this publication does contain a reliable account of what is said, and what transpires, it also contains much material that is inserted, with the consent of the chambers, at the appropriate place as though it had been said. Yet, the *Congressional Record* makes a sitting of the House or Senate as public in principle as though the reader had been present in the gallery.

A great mass of printed material is made available to the public. Much of it pertains to the activities of the committees.

Publications ordered printed by Congress, or either House thereof, shall be in four series, namely: One series of reports made by the committees of the Senate, to be known as Senate reports; one series of reports to be made by the committees of the House of Representatives, to be known as House reports; one series of documents other than reports of committees, the orders for printing which originate in the Senate, to be known as Senate documents; and one series of documents other than committee reports, the orders for printing which originate in the House of Representatives, to be known as House documents. . . . Hearings of committees may be printed as congressional documents only when specifically ordered by Congress or either House thereof.[22]

Finally, the legislative product is first published in the form of "slip laws." These consist of copies of an act or resolution printed as soon as it has been signed by the President. They are numbered according to the order of their enactment. When the life of each Congress has ended all laws, resolutions, and treaties are published in volumes known as the *United States Statutes at Large*.

[22] *U.S. Code*, Title 44, sec. 142.

CHAPTER XII

The Powers of Congress

GENERAL CONSIDERATIONS

The power of the national government is not restricted to that of Congress. That of Congress is extensive, but other authority is possessed by the executive and judicial branches. However, since the authority, structure, and functions of the judiciary and the executive depend on Congress, its powers are for most purposes equivalent to those of the national government, and *vice versa*. In large measure the primacy of legislative authority arises from the first sentence of the Constitution, which states that

All legislative Powers herein granted shall be vested in a Congress of the United States. . . .

Hence, no such power is granted to any other part of the national government. This power of Congress may be exercised only by it, and may not be delegated to another branch. The phrase "powers herein granted" refers mainly to eighteen powers of Congress enumerated in the eighth section of Article I, but other provisions of the Constitution expressly or

271

by implication also delegate power to it. These powers have been adequate to meet all contingencies which have confronted the nation since 1789. There have been emergencies, however, when its authority has been bent, if in truth it has not been broken. Nevertheless, in theory if not in fact, emergencies have been met by action within the scope of acknowledged constitutional authority, for, by established theory

Emergency does not create power. Emergency does not increase granted power nor diminish the restrictions imposed upon power granted or reserved. The Constitution was adopted in a period of grave emergency. Its grants of power to the federal government and its limitations of the powers of the states were determined in the light of emergency and are not altered by emergency. What power was thus granted and what limitations were thus imposed are questions which have always been, and will always be, the subject of close examination under our constitutional system.

While emergency does not create power, emergency may furnish the occasion for the exercise of power. . . . The constitutional question presented in the light of an emergency is whether the power possessed embraces the particular exercise of it in response to particular conditions. Thus, the war power of the federal government is not created by the emergency of war, but it is a power given to meet that emergency. It is a power to wage war successfully, and thus it permits the harnessing of the entire energies of the people in a supreme cooperative effort to preserve the nation. . . . When the provisions of the Constitution, in grant or restriction, are specific, so particularized as not to admit of construction, no question is presented. . . . But, where constitutional grants and limitations of power are set forth in general clauses, which afford a broad outline, the process of construction is essential to fill in the details.[1]

MAJOR POWERS OF CONGRESS

The Taxing Power.

The Congress shall have Power . . . To lay and collect Taxes, Duties, Imposts and Excises, to pay the Debts and provide for the common Defence and general Welfare of the United States; but all Duties, Imposts and Excises shall be uniform throughout the United States; . . .

Under the Articles of Confederation (1781-1789) lack of a national taxing power caused much embarrassment and difficulty. A desire to remedy that defect was one of the main incentives leading to the eventual replacement of the Articles. Perhaps for this reason the taxing power is the first enumerated power of Congress set out in the Constitution.

The authority to tax that was granted Congress is broad, but it is not without limitations. One of these arises from the purposes for which the power was granted. But what is meant by "purposes?" Several possible meanings are available. The obvious purpose of taxation is to raise

[1] *Home Building and Loan Association* v. *Blaisdell* (1934), 290 U.S. 398.

revenue, and a tax is a compulsory exaction, presumably for support of a government. Although some money is raised other results may also occur, and they may be the real ends for which taxation was imposed. Also, the use to which tax money is put may be regarded as a purpose of its levy and collection. Thus, the power to tax is limited by the words "to pay the Debts and provide for the common Defence and general Welfare." The preposition "to" is to be read as meaning "for the purpose of," so that Congress may use its power only for those very broad purposes.

The Tax Power and the General Welfare. Was Congress given a separate power to enact any laws it deemed necessary and proper to promote the general welfare? That question was not answered until 1936, when it was declared that

. . . the phrase "to provide for the general welfare" qualifies the power "to lay and collect taxes." The view that the clause grants power to provide for the general welfare, independently of the taxing power, has never been authoritatively accepted. Mr. Justice Story points out that if it were adopted "it is obvious that under color of the generality of the words, to 'provide for the common defense and general welfare,' the government of the United States is, in reality, a government of general and unlimited powers, notwithstanding the subsequent enumeration of specific powers." The true construction undoubtedly is that the only thing granted is the power to tax for the purpose of providing funds for payment of the nation's debts and making provision for the general welfare. . . .

While, therefore, the power to tax is not unlimited, its confines are set in the clause which confers it, not in those of § 8 which bestow and define the legislative powers of Congress.[2]

Although the "general welfare" clause is a limitation upon the taxing power, it is not much of a restriction, for the proceeds of taxation are rarely segregated for specific purposes. They are held in the Treasury of the United States until their expenditure is authorized by Congress for whatever purposes fall within the scope of national power. The "general welfare" clause limits the power of Congress to spend as well as to tax. Furthermore, it is not easy to recall a purpose for which Congress might tax or spend that is unrelated to the common defense or the general welfare of the nation.

Uniformity of Indirect Taxation. Indirect taxes "shall be uniform throughout the United States." What does this mean? Does it mean that only a flat tax of, say, $10 may be assessed on any estate, regardless of its size? Or does it mean that estates may be taxed progressively according to their size as long as the tax paid in New York is the same as that paid on one of the same amount in Sacramento? The second alternative conveys the proper meaning. "Uniform throughout the United States" requires geographical, not intrinsic, uniformity. It means that if a subject

[2] *United States* v. *Butler* (1936), 297 U.S. 1.

is taxed anywhere, it must be taxed everywhere throughout the United States, and at the same rate.

Apportionment of Direct Taxation. Direct taxes have to be apportioned among the several states according to their population as determined by the decennial census. Little use has been made by the national government of direct taxes. It was clearly understood in 1789 that such taxes consisted of levies on real property and persons, capitation, or poll, taxes, the burden of which could not be shifted, and the apportionment and collection of which, therefore, was not difficult. However, when Congress attempted in 1895 to levy a tax on income, part of which was derived from land and buildings, this was held to be a direct tax which would have to be apportioned among the several states according to population. That destroyed the potential value of the income tax as a source of revenue, because no necessary relation exists between individual income, which may be very low, and the population of a state, which may be very large.

The Sixteenth Amendment. Hence, the effect was temporarily to deprive the national government of one of its most productive sources of revenue. It placed beyond the effective taxing power of Congress a significant part of the wealth of the nation, but it so aroused public opinion that the Sixteenth Amendment was added to the Constitution in 1913. Thereafter it was determined that

The Congress shall have power to lay and collect taxes on incomes from whatever source derived, without apportionment among the several States, and without regard to any census or enumeration.

What was the effect of the Sixteenth Amendment on the taxing power of Congress? It made the power to tax income a lucrative source of revenue by eliminating the question of whether such an exaction was a direct levy.

It is clear on the face of this text that it does not purport to confer power to levy income taxes in a generic sense—an authority already possessed and never questioned—or to limit and distinguish between one kind of income taxes and another, but the whole purpose of the Amendment was to relieve all income taxes when imposed from apportionment from a consideration of the source whence the income was derived.[3]

Implied Limitation. The national and state governments are each immune from the tax power of the other. Hence, this "intergovernmental immunity" limits the taxing power of Congress.

It is admitted that there is no express provision in the Constitution that prohibits the general government from taxing the means and instrumentalities of the states, nor is there any prohibiting the states from taxing the means and instrumentalities of that government. In both cases the exemption rests upon

[3] *Brushaber* v. *Union Pacific Railroad Co.* (1916), 240 U.S. 1.

necessary implication, and is upheld by the great law of self-preservation; as any government whose means employed in conducting its operations, if subject to the control of another and distinct government, can exist only at the mercy of that government. Of what avail are these means if another power may tax them at discretion.[4]

The need for some degree of reciprocal immunity has never been disputed, but how broad it should be has been the source of much uncertainty. As government activities have increased, and the complexities and rivalries of taxing systems have grown, two guiding principles have emerged by which to gauge the restraining effect of "intergovernmental immunity" upon the national tax power.

The one, dependent upon the nature of the function being performed by the state or in its behalf, excludes from the immunity activities thought not to be essential to the preservation of governments even though the tax be collected from the state treasury. The state itself was taxed for the privilege of carrying on the liquor business in South Carolina v. United States . . . and a tax on the income of a state officer engaged in the management of a state-owned corporation operating a street railroad was sustained in Helvering v. Powers . . . because it was thought that the functions discouraged by these taxes were not indispensable to the maintenance of state government. The other principle . . . forbids recognition of the immunity when the burden on the state is so speculative and uncertain that if allowed it would restrict the federal taxing power without affording any corresponding tangible protection to the state government. . . .

The basis on which constitutional tax immunity of a state has been supported is the protection which it affords to the continued existence of the state. . . . The state and national governments must co-exist. Each must be supported by taxation of those who are citizens of both. The mere fact that the economic burden of such taxes may be passed on to a state government and thus increase to some extent . . . the expense of its operation, infringes no constitutional immunity. Such burdens are but normal incidents of the organization within the same territory of two governments, each possessed of the taxing power.[5]

Miscellaneous Limitations on the Tax Power. No taxes or duties can be laid on articles exported from a state. This restriction has denied to the national government a potentially lucrative source of revenue. It refers only to goods and commodities sent out of the United States to a foreign country. It does not refer to things sent out of one state into another. Moreover,

No Preference shall be given by any Regulation of Commerce or Revenue to the Ports of one State over those of another: Nor shall Vessels bound to, or from, one State, be obliged to enter, clear, or pay Duties in another.

These limitations, it will be noted, also restrict the power of Congress to regulate interstate and foreign commerce.

[4] *Collector* v. *Day* (1871), 11 Wallace 113.
[5] *Helvering* v. *Gerhardt* (1938), 304 U.S. 405.

Federal Police Power—Taxation. Congress can use its taxing and spending powers to protect or enhance the health, safety, morals or well-being of the people. By means of the taxing power it can often do indirectly what it cannot do directly; for every tax has some regulatory effect, however slight it may be, and:

> It is beyond serious question that a tax does not cease to be valid merely because it regulates, discourages, or even definitely deters the activities taxed. . . . The principle applies even though the revenue obtained is obviously negligible . . . or the revenue purpose of the tax may be secondary. . . . Nor does a tax statute necessarily fall because it touches on activities which Congress might not otherwise regulate. As was pointed out elsewhere: "From the beginning of our government, the courts have sustained taxes although imposed with the collateral effect of attaining ulterior ends which, considered apart, were beyond the constitutional powers of the lawmakers to realize by legislation directly addressed to their accomplishment.[6]

Moreover, Congress can use its taxing power to induce compliance with, and thus aid the exercise of, its other powers. In theory, however, if the regulatory feature of an exaction outweighs its character as a tax, the alleged tax is not a tax but a penalty, and is void. The relationship between revenue and regulation is essentially a question of whether passage of the contested measure is within the scope of Congress' power. If the power to tax exists, its use is not rendered invalid because of the effects it may produce. A tax may even destroy the thing taxed; but if a need for revenue can be demonstrated, the burden it imposes will not make it void. Neither will elaborate regulations accompanying a tax that have no relationship to its collection.

Congress has used the regulatory effect of taxation to accomplish many important economic results which it would not have achieved directly. It has taxed out of existence state bank notes which once competed as money with notes issued and circulated under its authority. It has destroyed the traffic in poisonous white phosphorus matches, and opium. It has regulated and restricted the sale and distribution of dangerous and noxious drugs by a licensing system based upon payment of a one dollar tax. By means of taxation it has undertaken to regulate dealings in firearms to destroy the traffic in machine guns, sawed-off shot guns, and silencers. The Social Security and Unemployment Compensation programs are based upon the taxing powers. Estate and income taxes are used to make more difficult the accumulation of large fortunes. In 1936, the taxing power was used to force corporations to distribute a greater part of their earnings. The protective tariff is of ancient age.

Spending Power. Taxes are not collected for their own sake, but to finance activities of the national government. Limitations on the power

[6] *United States* v. *Sanchez* (1950), 340 U.S. 42.

to spend are few. Funds in the treasury may be withdrawn only as a consequence of appropriations made by law, and expenditures for supporting the army cannot be made for a longer term than two years. Otherwise the power to spend is as broad as the power to tax, and is implied from it, from the power to borrow, and from grants to do things which are impossible unless money can be spent. The necessary implication of the taxing power is that funds may be spent "to pay the Debts and provide for the common Defence and general Welfare of the United States." But, in sum, the spending power of Congress, like the taxing power, is a power separate and distinct from the direct grants of legislative power found in the Constitution, and is not restricted by them. Congress consequently has a substantive power to spend.[7] Expenditures may be made, but are not restricted to those necessary to implement the enumerated powers of Congress; however, they must be for the common defense or general welfare, for purposes general and not local, public and not private, in nature.

The Commerce Power.

The Congress shall have Power . . . To regulate Commerce with foreign Nations, and among the several States, and with the Indian Tribes.

Of great significance is the power to regulate commerce "among the several States," for more than any other it has enabled Congress to cope with changing social and economic conditions, and has provided much of the flexibility of the Constitution.

It is the most extensive power Congress possesses. Its scope is so vast as virtually to defy description. Since 1824 it has steadily expanded, yet its limits are but vaguely defined. By its use Congress can regulate virtually any phase of life in the United States that is part of, affects, or is related in any way to interstate or foreign commerce. It extends to every type of movement of persons and things, every type of communication, every mode of transmitting intelligence, and every type of negotiation that results in a flow of services or power, or an act of transportation of persons or things, across state lines. It controls some subjects purely local in character and confined wholly to one state; in truth there is virtually nothing wholly beyond the reach of the commerce power. Much of the "centralization" of governmental responsibility in Washington, D.C. has occurred through its use by Congress.

Nature of the Commerce Power. In 1824 the commerce clause was construed in the broadest possible terms to include, within the power it grants, commercial intercourse between nations and parts of nations in all its branches. The words of the clause comprehend every species of interstate and foreign commercial activity. No sort of trade can be carried on between this country and any other, or between states or parts of

[7] See *United States* v. *Butler* (1936), 297 U.S. 1.

states, to which this power does not extend, for "commerce," as the word is used in the Constitution, is a unit, every part of which is indicated by the term. In regulating that commerce, the power of Congress does not stop at the jurisdictional lines of the several states. Interstate and foreign commerce is that of the whole United States, in which every part has a right to participate, and the power of Congress to regulate it can be exercised wherever the subject exists. If it exists within a state the power of Congress can be exercised there also. The power to regulate that commerce is the power to prescribe the rules by which it is to be governed, and, like all others vested in Congress, is complete in itself, may be exercised to its utmost extent, and acknowledges no limitations other than are prescribed in the Constitution. However, this is not intended to imply that the power comprehends commerce which is completely internal to a state and which does not extend to, or affect, other states.

Growth of the Commerce Power. The Constitution endures because of its adaptability to the changing conditions of American society. The "commerce clause" has made its contribution to that flexibility because it possesses a capacity for indefinite growth. Thus:

> Both commerce and the postal system are placed within the power of Congress, because, being national in their operation, they should be under the protecting care of the national government.
> The powers thus granted are not confined to the instrumentalities of commerce known or in use when the Constitution was adopted, but they keep pace with the progress of the country, and adapt themselves to the new developments of time and circumstances. They extend from the horse with its rider to the stagecoach and the steamboat to the railroad, and from the railroad to the telegraph, as these new agencies are successively brought into use to meet the demands of increasing population and wealth. They were intended for the government of the business to which they relate, at all times and under all circumstances. As they were intrusted to the general government for the good of the nation, it is not only the right, but the duty, of Congress to see to it that intercourse among the States and the transmission of intelligence are not obstructed or unnecessarily encumbered. . . .
> The Government of the United States, within the scope of its powers, operates upon every foot of territory under its jurisdiction. It legislates for the whole nation, and is not embarrassed by state lines. Its peculiar duty is to protect one part of the country from encroachment by another upon the national rights which belong to all.[8]

By relying on the commerce power and the "necessary and proper" clause Congress has enacted legislation dealing with a wide variety of subjects. More and more persons and things have been brought under its control, as it has applied the commerce power to such diverse subjects as

[8] *Pensacola Telegraph Co.* v. *Western Union Telegraph Co.* (1878), 96 U.S. 1.

pleasure yachts, sailing, driving, swimming, viewing motion pictures across state lines, railroads, motor trucks, airplanes, production and marketing of agricultural commodities, oil, gas, and water moved through pipelines, immigration, transmission of electric power, telegraph, radio, telephone, television, and wigwag signals, stolen automobiles and other property, women taken across state lines for immoral purposes, production, distribution and labeling of foods, drugs, and cosmetics, wages and hours, kidnapped persons, lotteries, the interstate grain trade, stockyards, shipment of livestock, highways, dealings in securities and insurance, correspondence schools, agricultural production and marketing, flammable fabrics, fraudulent advertising, prices, collective bargaining and unionization, fair trade, labor and management practices, and countless other subjects "in," "related to," or "affecting" interstate commerce.

The Commerce Power—Federal "Police Power." Reference to these subjects should indicate that the commerce power is also an important source of national "police power."

We have frequently said that in the exercise of its control over interstate commerce, the means employed by the Congress may have the quality of police regulations. . . . "Congress can certainly regulate interstate commerce to the extent of forbidding and punishing the use of such commerce as an agency to promote immorality, dishonesty or the spread of any evil or harm to the people of other states from the region of origin. In doing this it is merely exercising the police power for the benefit of the public, within the field of interstate commerce."

The anticipated evil or harm may proceed from something inherent in the subject of transportation as in the case of diseased or noxious articles, which are unfit for commerce. . . . Or the evil may lie in the purpose of transportation, as in the case of lottery tickets, or the transportation of women for immoral purposes. . . .[9]

The commerce power is a more fruitful source of national "police power" than is the authority of Congress to tax. Thus, Congress has required installation of safety devices on interstate trains, closed the channels of commerce to impure foods and drugs, improperly-inspected meat, misbranded commodities, adulterated foods, prize-fight films, lottery tickets, prison-made goods, products made by labor working under substandard conditions, livestock having infectious diseases, liquor when forbidden by state law, moths, plant lice and other insect pests injurious to plants and trees, slot machines, and switchblade knives, to mention but a few objectionable articles. Some of these are bad in themselves; others, although not harmful, will produce or perpetuate harmful or undesirable conditions in the state of origin or destination.

[9] *Kentucky Whip and Collar Co., v. Illinois Central Railroad Co.* (1937), 299 U.S. 334.

The basic doctrine on which the broad application of the "commerce power" rests has been stated by one eminent scholar as follows:

The early and not uncommon idea that the use by Congress of its commerce power to deal with broad social problems was not quite honest, that it amounted to "covert" or "backstairs" legislation, was largely forgotten. We had come to realize that serious evils which menace the health, safety, and welfare of the nation are spread and even generated by our vast national system of transportation and communication, and by our continent-wide network of interstate markets. It was clear that interstate commerce could be used for the public injury as well as for the public welfare. The commerce clause makes Congress the guardian of interstate commerce—and the only guardian. It is therefore not only the right of Congress, but its clear duty, to see to it that the facilities of interstate commerce are not used by anyone, in any manner, to do any kind of harm.[10]

Relation of the States to the Commerce Power. The grant of power to Congress over interstate and foreign commerce is not accompanied by any express prohibition on the exercise of state power, but the states were probably not expected to share in this authority of Congress. This fact does not mean that the power of Congress is exclusive. The grant of authority does not, of itself, settle the question of what power is left to the states to adopt legislation regulating foreign or interstate commerce. As a general proposition control of commerce among the states is vested in Congress; control of intrastate commerce is left to the states. Yet, much overlap between the two spheres of regulation has developed, so that Congress now regulates many *intrastate* activities and the states assert a degree of influence over *interstate* commerce.

Congress may regulate productive or other activities which have a close relationship to interstate commerce although the subjects when viewed separately are wholly local, because

The power of Congress over interstate commerce is not confined to the regulation of commerce among the states. It extends to those activities intrastate which so affect interstate commerce or the exercise of the power of Congress over it as to make regulation of them appropriate means to the attainment of a legitimate end, the exercise of the granted power of Congress to regulate interstate commerce.[11]

The exercise of state power over local internal affairs often affects interstate commerce. In such circumstances

[10] Robert E. Cushman, editor, *Leading Constitutional Decisions* (New York: Appleton-Century-Crofts, 9th edition, 1950), p. 333. *United States* v. *Darby Lumber Co.* (1941), 312 U.S. 100, contains an example of the application of these views.

[11] *United States* v. *Darby Lumber Co.*, p. 100.

. . . the States have their police and taxing powers and may use them as their own views of sound public policy may dictate even though interstate commerce may be "incidentally" or "indirectly" regulated, it being understood that such "incidental" or "indirect" effects are always subject to Congressional disallowance.[12]

The problem is one of protecting the free movement of commerce among the states from burdens, impediments, and discriminations while leaving to the states adequate discretion in dealing with local affairs, the control of which touches interstate commerce in some way.

Although the commerce clause conferred on the national government power to regulate commerce, its possession of the power does not exclude all state power of regulation. . . . It has been recognized that, in the absence of conflicting legislation by Congress, there is a residuum of power in the state to make laws governing matters of local concern which nevertheless in some measure affect interstate commerce or even, to some extent, regulate it. . . . When the regulation of matters of local concern is local in character and effect, and its impact on the national commerce does not seriously interfere with its operation, and the consequent incentive to deal with them nationally is slight, such regulation has been generally held to be within state authority. . . .

But . . . the states have not been deemed to have authority to impede substantially the free flow of commerce from state to state, or to regulate those phases of the national commerce which, because of the need of national uniformity, demand that their regulation, if any, be prescribed by a single authority. . . .

There has thus been left to the states wide scope for the regulation of matters of local state concern, even though it in some measure affects the commerce, provided it does not materially restrict the free flow of commerce across state lines, or interfere with it in matters with respect to which uniformity of regulation is of predominant national concern.[13]

In general, therefore, state power over commerce falls into one of three categories. First, the states may not regulate some subjects of commerce even though Congress has not provided needed regulation. These are the types of subjects which need to be regulated by a nationally-uniform rule. Their nature does not permit diverse state regulations. The absence of congressional regulation is taken to mean that they are not to be regulated at all. Second, the states under some circumstances may regulate local aspects of interstate commerce in the absence of congressional regulation of the same subject. However, Congress can withdraw from state control *any* phase of interstate commerce, and its action, by virtue of the supremacy clause, can displace any state law. Third, there is, in theory at least, purely intrastate commerce over which the power of the

[12] *Simpson* v. *Shepherd* (1913), 230 U.S. 352.
[13] *Southern Pacific Railway Co.* v. *Arizona* (1945), 325 U.S. 761.

states is unquestioned. Thus, in practice the authority of Congress over interstate commerce can be made exclusive, for either the use or non-use of that authority may bar the direct regulation of interstate commerce by the states.

Use of the Commerce Power in Aid of State Authority. Congress may use its prohibitory powers over the subjects and facilities of interstate commerce to prevent violation or evasion of state laws. For example, Congress has forbidden the shipment, in interstate or foreign commerce, of goods made by convict labor into any state where they are to be received, possessed, used, or sold in violation of state law. Concerning such use it has been said that

. . . while the power to regulate interstate commerce resides in the Congress, which must determine its own policy, the Congress may shape that policy in the light of the fact that transportation in interstate commerce, if permitted, would aid in the frustration of valid state laws for the protection of persons and property. . . .

The pertinent point is that where the subject of commerce is one as to which the power of the state may constitutionally be exerted by restriction or prohibition in order to prevent harmful consequences, the Congress may, if it sees fit, put forth its power to regulate interstate commerce so as to prevent that commerce from being used to impede the carrying out of the state policy.

In the congressional action there is nothing arbitrary or capricious. . . . Nor has the Congress attempted to delegate its authority to the states. The Congress has not sought to exercise a power not granted or to usurp the police powers of the states. . . . The Congress has exercised its plenary power which is subject to no limitation other than that which is found in the Constitution itself.[14]

Control of Foreign Commerce. In general all that has been said about the power of Congress over interstate commerce pertains to the control of foreign commerce. The authority of Congress over foreign commerce is also complete, and acknowledges no limitations other than those prescribed in the Constitution. Therefore, it may only be carried on subject to the terms set by Congress. Congress controls without restriction what articles may be imported and the terms upon which the importation may take place. Its power over foreign commerce has been called on more than one occasion "exclusive." Important manifestations of this power are total or partial embargoes, export quotas, the exclusion or admission of aliens, protective tariffs, export and import licensing, trade and other commercial treaties and agreements, and numerous restrictions upon foreign trade. The control of foreign commerce is an important adjunct to the inherent authority of the national government over foreign affairs.

Commerce with the Indian Tribes. Congress has exclusive and unfettered power to regulate commerce with the Indian tribes, a power as

[14] *Kentucky Whip and Collar Co.* v. *Illinois Central Railroad Co.*

broad as that to regulate commerce with foreign nations. When the Constitution was drafted this was a serious problem that it left to Congress, but the power today, though it still exists, is of no consequence. Commerce with the Indians is no longer of importance or the source of many problems.

The Postal Power.

The Congress shall have Power . . . To establish Post Offices and post Roads; . . .

The simplicity of this statement gives no hint of the extensive uses to which this power has been put. The postal system is said to be the largest business undertaking in the world. It employs about 500,000 persons, approximately one-fifth of all national personnel.

By use of the postal power, Congress has maintained the postal system, has financed a system of national highways, created and operated a banking system, a package delivery service, and a philatelic store. It has provided below-cost rates for handling publications that disseminate information of a useful public nature because an intelligent, informed public is essential to democracy. This benefit is passed on to advertisers as lowered costs for advertising space. One popular picture magazine is thus subsidized annually to the extent of almost $10,000,000. The postal power is also used to subsidize the nation's railroad, steamship, bus, and airline companies by paying them more than the actual cost of transporting the mails to help maintain them in an up-to-date and financially solvent condition in the interests of national well-being.

The Postal Clause—Federal "Police Power." The postal power is a major source of federal "police power." By its use Congress excludes from the mails objects considered dangerous or injurious to the public, to postal employees, or to the mails. Excluded items include liquor, firearms, ammunition, flammable objects and substances, obscene pictures, books and magazines, explosives, lottery tickets, extortion and blackmail demands, and matter employed in perpetrating fraud.

When the power to establish post-offices and post-roads was surrendered to the Congress it was as a complete power, and the grant carried with it the right to exercise all the powers which made that power effective. It is not necessary that Congress should have the power to deal with crime or immorality within the States in order to maintain that it possesses the power to forbid the use of the mails in aid of the perpetration of crime or immorality. . . .[15]

Monetary Powers of Congress. Congress possesses exclusive authority to establish and protect a monetary system for the United States. It may borrow money on the credit of the United States, coin money and

[15] *Ex parte Rapier* (1892), 143 U.S. 110.

regulate both its value and that of foreign coin, and provide for the punishment of those counterfeiting the securities and current coin of the United States. These and other powers conferred upon Congress must be seen as related means to achieve a common end. No single purpose is the end for which the Constitution was adopted. The powers to levy and collect taxes, to coin money and to regulate its value are means for the establishment of a government sovereign in its sphere, with the capacity of self-preservation. Thus, through use of its monetary powers Congress provides a nationally-uniform currency system, determines the circulating media which compose the currency, and punishes counterfeiting; it has chartered banks, set up a system of national banks and replaced them by the present federal reserve system; it has made paper money, unbacked by gold or silver, legal tender in payment of debts; it manipulates the value of the currency to maintain economic stability; it can control the credit structure of the economy by controlling the currency system; it has withdrawn gold from circulation and made its private ownership, except for minor purposes, illegal; it has denied the quality of legal tender to foreign currency; it has restrained the circulation as money of notes and coins not issued under its own authority.

The Borrowing Power. The first of the monetary powers of Congress is its power to borrow money on the credit of the United States. This virtually unlimited power of Congress may be used to borrow any amount, at any time, under any terms, and in any form that it finds practicable. The borrowing power and the power to coin money and to "regulate the Value thereof" provide the basis of the currency system of the country. Together these powers authorize Congress to print paper money and make it legal tender, a prevailing method by which the government borrows at the same time that it places money in circulation, because:

The power "to borrow money on the credit of the United States" is the power to raise money for the public use on a pledge of the public credit, and may be used to meet either present or anticipated expenses and liabilities of the government. It includes the power to issue, in return for the money borrowed, the obligations of the United States, in any appropriate form, of stock, bonds, bills or notes; and in whatever form they are issued, being instruments of the National Government, they are exempt from taxation by the governments of the several states. . . .

It appears . . . to follow, as a logical and necessary consequence, that Congress has the power to issue the obligations of the United States . . . and to impress upon them such qualities as currency for the purchase of merchandise and the payment of debts, as accord with the usage of sovereign governments. . . .

This position is fortified by the fact that Congress is vested with the exclusive exercise of the analogous power of coining money and regulating the value of domestic and foreign coin, and also with the paramount power of regulating foreign and interstate commerce. Under the power to borrow money on the credit of the United States, and to issue circulating notes for the money borrowed, its power to define the quality and force of those notes as currency is as broad as a like power over metallic currency under the power to coin money, and to regulate the value thereof. Under the two powers taken together, Congress is authorized to establish a national currency, either in coin or in paper and to make that currency lawful money for all purposes, as regards the National Government or private individuals.[16]

Coinage Power. The power to coin money and regulate its value is separate from the borrowing power, and great discretion is left to Congress in its use.

The Constitution does not ordain what metals may be coined, or prescribe that the legal value of the metals, when coined, shall correspond at all with their intrinsic value in the market. Nor does it even affirm that Congress may declare anything to be a legal tender in payment of debts. Confessedly, the power to regulate the value of money coined, and of foreign coins, is not exhausted by the first regulation. More than once in our history has the regulation been changed without any denial of the power of Congress to exchange it, and it seems to have been left to Congress to determine alike what metal shall be coined, its purity, and how far its statutory value, as money, shall correspond, from time to time, with the market value of the same metal as bullion.[17]

But the full extent of Congress' power over the monetary system of the United States is to be found in all the related powers granted to it by the Constitution. Its broad and comprehensive authority over revenue, finance, and currency is derived from the powers to lay and collect taxes, to borrow money, to regulate interstate and foreign commerce, to coin money and regulate its value in relation to that of foreign coins, to fix the standards of weights and measures, and "To make all Laws which shall be necessary and proper for carrying into Execution" the other enumerated powers.[18]

Furthermore, although Congress is expressly given power to punish counterfeiting of the securities and coin of the United States, this power would surely have been derived by necessary implication from the power to coin money and regulate its value. If the genuine coinage created by Congress could be displaced by one it had neither created, established, nor authorized, and which had little or no intrinsic value, the constitutional power would be rendered wholly worthless. Having established a system of coinage indispensable for the purposes of the community and of the government itself, Congress would be obligated to prevent its debasement.

The War Powers of Congress. As an independent member of the international community of nations, the United States possesses the power to

---

[16] *Julliard* v. *Greenman* (1884), 110 U.S. 421.
[17] *Knox* v. *Lee* (1871), 12 Wallace 457.
[18] See *Norman* v. *Baltimore and Ohio Railroad Co.* (1935), 294 U.S. 240.

declare and wage war. The "war power" is one of the inherent powers which exist in it as inescapable attributes of its status of nationality. The clause giving to Congress the power to *declare* war is merely confirmatory, and eliminates any doubt as to which part of the government shall exercise it. The power to conduct war, however, is vested in the President, subject to congressional control. Hence, the war powers of Congress are but part of those belonging to the national government.

In addition to taxing, borrowing, and spending for the common defense, other grants of authority relating to the preparation for and the waging of war are delegated to Congress. It must protect the states against invasion, it may suspend the privilege to the writ of *habeas corpus,* and it may declare the punishment for treason and other acts against the United States, but more importantly, it is authorized:

To declare War, grant Letters of Marque and Reprisal, and make Rules concerning Captures on Land and Water;

To raise and support Armies, but no Appropriation of Money to that Use shall be for a longer Term than two Years;

To provide and maintain a Navy;

To make Rules for the Government and Regulation of the land and naval Forces;

To provide for calling forth the Militia to execute the Laws of the Union, suppress Insurrections and repel Invasions;

To provide for organizing, arming and disciplining, the Militia, and for governing such Part of them as may be employed in the Service of the United States, reserving to the States respectively, the Appointment of the Officers, and the Authority of training the Militia according to the discipline prescribed by Congress. . . .

These powers must be read in conjunction with the "necessary and proper" clause of the Constitution. The result of so associating them is to acknowledge that there resides in Congress a power the vast scope of which it is difficult to exaggerate.

The Power to Declare War. Only Congress can declare war, but its power is of little importance in the light of modern conditions and techniques of war. War today is becoming increasingly dependent upon the element of surprise, and since the existence of a condition of war is a state of fact, it is not dependent upon the nicety of a formal declaration. Moreover, the President can dispose the armed forces so as to precipitate a situation in the face of which Congress is left with no alternative but to declare war. War as a condition arrived at only after deliberation and formal action by the representatives of the people has become virtually devoid of meaning.

Army and Navy. The enumerated power of Congress to raise and support armies and to provide and maintain a navy is virtually without limit. It has exclusive and plenary authority to determine what military forces shall be raised, how this shall be done, at what age members of the armed forces shall be received, what compensation shall be paid, and to which service each individual shall be assigned. This authority overrides that of parents over minors who are needed for military service. It is possible to imply almost anything from these grants of authority, for any measure "necessary and proper" to carry them into effect can be sanctioned by them. When read in conjunction with the power to wage war, interpreted in the light of the necessities of modern "total" war which embraces almost all parts of the national life, these clauses bestow power which knows only theoretical bounds.

The unusual denial of funds to the army for periods longer than two years can be explained in historical terms since a fear of military power was widely felt at the time that the Constitution was drafted. No such limitation applies to appropriations for the navy.

Military Laws. Congress has enacted elaborate bodies of rules for the governance of the military forces of the United States. These regulations constitute the law by which their internal affairs are governed. Hence, they are known as military law. Military law is not to be confused with martial law, which is rule by military forces over civilians in areas where the normal processes and agencies of government have broken down. Either or both of these terms may be confused with the term "military government," which is properly applied only to the government of conquered territory by military forces.

Militia. The militia, known since 1916 as the National Guard, is a state organization when not in the service of the United States. Congress prescribes how the Guard shall be armed, trained, organized, and disciplined, authorizes the President to call it or designated portions of it into national service, and while it is in such service exercises the same control over it as it exercises over the components of the regular armed forces of the United States. The power of the states over the Guard is held and exercised in subordination to the paramount power of Congress to raise and support armies; the power of Congress over it is unlimited except in the two areas of selecting its officers and training its men.

Extent of the War Powers of Congress.

In express terms Congress is empowered "to declare war," which necessarily connotes the plenary power to wage war with all the force necessary to make it effective; and "to raise . . . armies," which necessarily connotes the like power to say who shall serve in them and in what way.

From its very nature, the war power, when necessity calls for its exercise, tolerates no qualifications or limitations, unless found in the Constitution or in applicable principles of international law. In the words of John Quincy Adams, —"This power is tremendous; it is strictly constitutional; but it breaks down every barrier so anxiously erected for the protection of liberty, property and of life." To the end that war may not result in defeat, freedom of speech may, by act of Congress, be curtailed or denied so that the morale of the people and the spirit of the army may not be broken by seditious utterances; freedom of the press curtailed to preserve our military plans and movements from the knowledge of the enemy; deserters and spies put to death without indictment or trial by jury; ships and supplies requisitioned; property of alien enemies, theretofore under the protection of the Constitution, seized without process and converted to the public use without compensation and without due process of law in the ordinary sense of that term; prices of food or other necessities of life fixed or regulated; railways taken over and operated by the government; and other drastic powers, wholly inadmissible in time of peace, exercised to meet the emergencies of war.[19]

The power to wage war is the power to initiate it and to fight it to a successful conclusion. To this end Congress has used the full measure of its vast authority. During periods of modern war scarcely a facet of American life has been left undisturbed by wartime legislation that authorized compulsory military service, rationing, price, rent, and travel controls, restrictions on wages and mobility of labor, the allocation of strategic and scarce materials, extensive controls of aliens—especially of enemy aliens—and seizure of their property, control of the importation, manufacture, storage, mining, or distribution of necessaries, the requisitioning of foods, fuels, and feeds, the seizure and operation of factories, packing houses, pipelines, mines, and other installations, the limitation, regulation, or prohibition of the use of food materials in the production of alcoholic beverages, the regulation of the production, sale, and distribution of fuels, the allocation of priorities in use of transportation facilities, the seizure and operation of the rail and water transportation systems and the telephone and telegraph communications systems of the nation, the seizure and operation of any defense plant closed by a strike, the displacement of citizens from homes and businesses, and curfews and blackouts.

Considering the activities brought on by World War I, former President Hoover has written:

After a few weeks of muddling and resisting, we accepted the inexorable fact that no democracy can fight a modern war with the processes of democracy. They are made for peace. They are too slow in action; there is no time for debate and the meeting of minds. We became an effective dictatorship. We had to do it if we were to bring quick strength upon the front. We conscripted all our boys. By direct and indirect means the government took control of production, of prices, of labor. It rightly seized about 85% of war profits. The government took over the railways. It directed credit, and by direct and indirect means it partially suppressed free speech and free press. It told the people what to eat and wear.[20]

[19] *United States* v. *MacIntosh* (1930), 283 U.S. 605.
[20] Former President Hoover writing in *The Saturday Evening Post,* October 28, 1939. Reprinted by special permission of *The Saturday Evening Post,* © 1939, The Curtis Publishing Company.

The relationship of the Constitution to the necessities of total war has been expressed as follows:

With the advent of such warfare, mobilized property in the form of equipment and supplies became as essential as mobilized manpower. Mobilization of effort extended not only to the uniformed armed services but to the entire population. . . . The language of the Constitution . . . places emphasis upon the supporting as well as the raising of armies. The power of Congress as to both is inescapably express, not merely implied. The conscription of manpower is a more vital interference with the life, liberty and property of the individual than is the conscription of his property or his profits or any substitute of such conscription of them. For his hazardous full-time service in the armed services a soldier is paid whatever the Government deems to be a fair but modest compensation. . . . The constitutionality of the conscription of manpower for military service is beyond question. The constitutional power of Congress to support the armed forces with equipment and supplies is no less clear and sweeping.

The war powers of the Congress and the President are only those which are to be derived from the Constitution but . . . the primary implication of a war power is that it shall be an effective power to wage the war successfully. Thus, while the constitutional structure and controls of our Government are our guides equally in war and peace, they must be read with the realistic purposes of the entire instrument in mind.[21]

The War Power in Time of Peace. The war powers of Congress convey authority not only to prepare for and fight a war but also to deal with problems created by war which continue after its termination. The war power

. . . is not limited to victories in the field. . . . It carries with it inherently the power to guard against the immediate renewal of the conflict, and to remedy the evils which have arisen from its rise and progress. . . .[22]

By virtue of this principle, Congress legislated in peacetime to cope with a postwar housing deficit,

. . . which in considerable measure was caused by the heavy demobilization of veterans and by the cessation or reduction in residential construction during the period of hostilities due to the allocation of building materials to military projects. Since the war effort contributed heavily to that deficit, Congress has the power even after the cessation of hostilities to act to control the forces that short supply of the needed article created. If that were not true, the Necessary and Proper Clause . . . would be drastically limited in its application to the several war powers. . . . The result would be paralyzing. It would render Congress powerless to remedy conditions the creation of which necessarily followed the mobilization of men and materials for successful prosecution of the war. So to read the Constitution would be to make it self-defeating.[23]

21 *Licter* v. *United States* (1948), 334 U.S. 742, 754-756, 782.
22 *Stewart* v. *Kahn* (1817), 11 Wallace 493, 507.
23 *Woods* v. *Miller* (1948), 333 U.S. 138.

LESSER POWERS OF CONGRESS

Establishment of Uniform Standards of Weights and Measures. Under its constitutional authority to fix standards of weights and measures, Congress has created in the Department of Commerce the National Bureau of Standards.

The functions of the bureau shall consist in the custody of the standards; the comparison of the standards used in scientific investigations, engineering, manufacturing, commerce, and educational institutions with the standards adopted or recognized by the Government; the construction, when necessary, of standards, their multiples and subdivision; the testing and calibration of standard measuring apparatus; the solution of problems which arise in connection with standards; the determination of physical constants and the properties of materials, when such data are of great importance to scientific or manufacturing interest and are not to be obtained of sufficient accuracy elsewhere.

The bureau shall exercise its functions for the Government of the United States; for any State or municipal government within the United States; or for any scientific society, educational institution, firm, corporation, or individual within the United States engaged in manufacturing or other pursuits requiring the use of standards or standard measuring instruments.[24]

The Bureau of Standards fixes uniform standards of weights and measures. The content of No. 2 cans or of quart bottles, the size of No. 16 electric wire, the thickness of 20 gauge sheet metal, units of an ounce, yard, foot, barrel, bushel, peck, etc., are uniform in this country. Standardization is of great advantage to business, industry, science, and invention. The metric system of weights and measures is also legal in the United States. Modular units approved by the Bureau are preserved by it, and duplicate sets are presented to each state for use in its enforcement activities. The Bureau of Standards also tests products to verify quality, undertakes container and packaging standardization to eliminate unnecessary sizes and shapes and to reduce costs, and also to protect the buying public.

Congress is authorized to *fix* the standards. The national government, therefore, does not undertake to enforce them except in interstate commerce, and in the District of Columbia, the territories, and the dependencies. It otherwise leaves this function to the states.

Regulation of Bankruptcy. When a person (or corporation) becomes financially insolvent he may voluntarily surrender his assets to be distributed equitably among his creditors, or his creditors may force him to do so. In either event, he is said to be bankrupt.

The Federal system of bankruptcy is designed not only to distribute the property of the debtor, not by law exempted, fairly and equally among his creditors, but as a main purpose of the act, intends to aid the unfortunate

[24] *U.S. Code*, Title 15, secs. 271-273.

debtor by giving him a fresh start in life, free from debts, except of a certain character, after the property which he owned at the time of bankruptcy has been administered for the benefit of creditors. Our decisions lay great stress upon this feature of the law as one not only of private but of great public interest, in that it secures to the unfortunate debtor, who surrenders his property for distribution, a new opportunity in life.[25]

Congress is authorized "To establish . . . uniform Laws on the subject of Bankruptcies throughout the United States." This power of Congress is paramount and unrestricted and has pre-empted the subject to the virtual exclusion of state laws.

Congress and the Law of Nations. When the United States became an independent member of the international community of nations, it became subject to the system of rules which reason, morality, and custom had established among the states of the world to guide their relations in the absence of a more definite body of enacted law. Acceptance of this system of rules known as "international law," or "the law of nations," is a condition of membership in the international community of states. It was implied in the Constitution where the document granted Congress exclusive power "To define and punish Piracies and Felonies committed on the high Seas, and Offences against the Law of Nations." Accordingly, Congress has passed numerous acts to give effect to the rules of "international law" and to prevent any wrong being done within its dominion to another nation, with which it is at peace, or to the people of such nation.

The United States has dealt extensively in its own laws with its rights and duties as a sovereign nation. Thus, Congress has provided for the definition and punishment of piracies, murders, and other felonies committed on the high seas, for the counterfeiting of bonds, notes and other securities of a foreign nation, its political subdivisions, or its corporations. It has provided for the enforcement and preservation of the neutral relations of the United States with other nations, for the punishment of violations of the law of war, and for a host of other purposes. Congress alone determines what subjects of international law it shall legislate upon; but the United States is responsible to foreign nations for all violations of their rights, whether committed by public or private action. It is bound to observe and enforce all rules of international law, whether or not they have been enacted by Congress into the law of the United States, unless they have been excluded from operation as part of the law of the United States by statute, treaty, or constitutional provision.

Sciences and the Useful Arts. The Constitution vests in Congress power

To promote the Progress of Science and useful Arts, by securing for limited Times to Authors and Inventors the exclusive Right to their respective Writings and Discoveries. . . .

[25] *Stellwagen* v. *Clum* (1918), 245 U.S. 605.

Patents. A patent is an exclusive grant, awarded to an inventor, to manufacture, use, sell, lease, withhold or otherwise dispose of his invention within the jurisdiction of the United States. It endures for seventeen years and is not renewable. Its duration and other conditions are determined by Congress in its discretion.

Letters patent are . . . to be regarded . . . as public franchises granted to the inventors of new and useful improvements for the purpose of securing to them, as such inventors, for the limited term therein mentioned, the exclusive right and liberty to make and use and vend to others to be used their own inventions, as tending to promote the growth of science and the useful arts, and as matters of compensation to the inventors for their labor, toil, and expense in making the inventions, and reducing the same to practice for the public benefit, as contemplated by the Constitution and sanctioned by the laws of Congress. . . .

. . . Persons who have made an invention and desire to obtain an exclusive property therein, may make application in writing to the Commissioner of Patents, and the provision is that the Commissioner, on due proceedings had, may grant a patent for the said invention.[26]

Patents may be issued only for new and useful inventions, including machines, manufactures, arts, the composition of matter, and plants other than tuberous ones, which are the creation of mental processes displaying "ingenuity," "inventive" or "creative genius."

This test is often difficult to apply; but its purpose is clear. Under this test, some substantial innovation is necessary, an innovation for which society is truly indebted to the efforts of the patentee. . . . The primary purpose of our patent system is not reward to the individual but the advancement of the arts and sciences. Its inducement is directed to disclosure of advances in knowledge which will be beneficial to society; it is not a certificate of merit, but an incentive to disclosure.

It has never been the object of [the patent] laws to grant a monopoly for every trifling device, every shadow of a shade of an idea, which would naturally and spontaneously occur to any skilled mechanic or operator in the ordinary progress of manufacture. Such an indiscriminate creation of exclusive privileges tends rather to obstruct than to stimulate invention. It creates a class of speculative schemers who make it their business to watch the advancing wave of improvement, and gather its foam in the form of patented monopolies, which enable them to lay a heavy tax upon the industry of the country, without contributing anything to the advancement of the arts.[27]

The Patent Office of the Department of Commerce is supposed to ascertain, prior to the granting of a letter patent, that a claimed invention is in fact original and new, is not patented or described in any publication in this or any foreign country, and does not infringe any patent previously

[26] *Seymour* v. *Osborne* (1871), 11 Wallace 516.
[27] *Atlantic Works* v. *Brady* (1882), 107 U.S. 192.

granted. Because of this intensive examination, a letter patent once issued becomes legal evidence of the originality of the patented item and may be used to protect the inventor's rights in it.

Copyrights. The privilege of copyright extends to all books, including composite and cyclopedic works, directories, gazetteers, and other compilations and periodicals, including newspapers; but English language books must be set and printed in the United States. Also included, however, are lectures, sermons, and addresses, musical, dramatic and dramatico-musical compositions, maps, works of art, reproductions of works of art, drawings or plastic works of a scientific or technical character, photographs, prints and pictorial illustrations (including prints or labels used for articles of merchandise), motion picture photoplays, motion pictures other than photoplays, and television scripts as used in oral presentation.

The copyright is granted for an initial period of twenty-eight years, and may be renewed once for an equal period in most cases. It is issued by the Register of Copyrights in the Copyright Office of the Library of Congress to every applicant upon payment of the required fees and the deposit of two copies of the work to be copyrighted. Like a patent, a copyright is a form of property and is transferable. It conveys to the proprietor the exclusive right to print, reprint, publish, copy and sell, translate, arrange, dramatize, or convert into a novel or other non-dramatic work, to present the work in public for profit, and to receive a royalty from its performance if it is a musical or dramatico-musical composition presented for profit. However, a copyright is granted as a matter of course upon proper application and conveys no protection to the proprietor. No effort is made to verify that the copyrighted work is original; therefore, a copyright is not evidence of authenticity as a patent is.

Control of the Territories and Other Property of the United States. Congress holds power

> To exercise exclusive Legislation in all Cases whatsoever, over such District (not exceeding ten Miles square) as may, by Cession of particular States, and the Acceptance of Congress, become the Seat of the Government of the United States. . . .

Moreover,

> The Congress shall have Power to dispose of and make all needful Rules and Regulations respecting the Territory or other Property belonging to the United States . . .

Authority to Acquire Territory. The Constitution makes no mention of how territories shall be acquired. It assumes that they will exist. However, it is well established that the authority to acquire territory may be implied from the power to admit new states, from the war and treaty powers, from the power to spend, and from the inherent powers of nationality which attach to the United States as a nation. It may be exercised by discovery and occupation, by purchase, conquest, annexation, or cession by a state; and the authority to govern territory is implied from the power to acquire it, the provision of the Constitution giving that power to Congress being confirmatory in character.

The Territories are not political subdivisions or the outlying dominions of the United States. They bear much the same relation to the General Government that counties do to the States, and Congress may legislate for them as States do for their respective municipal organizations. The organic law of a Territory takes the place of a constitution as the fundamental law of the local government. It is obligatory on and binds the territorial authorities; but Congress is supreme and, for the purposes of this department of its governmental authority, has all the powers of the People of the United States, except such as have been expressly or by implication reserved in the prohibitions of the Constitution.[28]

Hence, Congress possesses complete authority over the territories. It may legislate with regard to all or some of their local affairs, or it may, as it has usually done, transfer that function, subject to its superior control, to a locally-elected legislative assembly created by it. The territorial legislature then becomes vested with all legislative power that is not prohibited by the Constitution of the United States or by acts of Congress.

Territorial Self-Government. Since its organization of the Northwest Territory in 1787 Congress has been guided whenever practicable by the principle that people everywhere should be allowed self-government. It has followed the practice of establishing local governments for the territories belonging to the United States, but the inhabitants, except as Congress might provide otherwise, have no right to participate in political authority until the territory becomes a state. Meanwhile, they are in a condition of temporary pupilage and dependence. Although Congress can be expected to recognize the principle of self-government to whatever extent it believes to be wise, its discretion alone determines the issue.

In spite of the fact that it is under no compulsion to do so,

Congress has from time to time established governments in the various territories that have come under federal control. Territorial government in the continental United States was customarily viewed as a transition step to statehood, and statehood in fact resulted. The Spanish-American War opened a new chapter. Beginning with the Treaty of Paris, the United States acquired by conquest, treaty or purchase outlying territories for which statehood was not contemplated. The position of these territories in our national scheme gave rise to lively political controversy. . . .[29]

At present, the major territories include the "free," self-governing

[28] *First National Bank of Brunswick* v. *Yankton* (1880), 101 U.S. 130, 133.
[29] *Granville-Smith* v. *Granville-Smith* (1954), 349 U.S. 1.

commonwealth of Puerto Rico, the Virgin Islands, and Guam. These are more or less organized for purposes of local self-government but, with the possible exception of Puerto Rico, they are far from qualifying for statehood or independence. Other areas known as outlying possessions have little or no organization for local self-government. These include Kingman, Johnston, Swain's, Palmyra, Baker, Jarvis, Howland, Canton, Enderbury, Wake, Midway and Ocean islands.

Land and Property Within the States. Congress exercises exclusive jurisdiction

. . . over all Places purchased by the Consent of the Legislature of the State in which the same shall be, for the Erection of Forts, Magazines, Arsenals, dock-Yards, and other needful Buildings. . . .

Land within a state may also be acquired by purchase or condemnation, for other than these purposes, with or without the state's consent, and will be subject to the concurrent jurisdiction of both governments. With respect to jurisdiction over them, the states and Congress can come to any terms they find to be mutually agreeable, and thereby adjust cooperatively problems arising from the federal nature of our governmental system. Consent of the state need not be given without reservation or qualification. The states in the Union are competent to refuse to make, or to qualify, concessions of jurisdiction when the national government acquires property within their boundaries by purchase or condemnation without their consent.

The United States has large bodies of public lands (within the several States). These properties are used for forests, parks, ranges, wildlife sanctuaries, flood control, and other purposes not covered by (the Constitution over which the States retain some jurisdiction). In other instances, it may be deemed important or desirable by the National Government and the State Government in which the particular property is located that exclusive jurisdiction be vested in the United States by cession or consent. . . . As the National Government may, "by virtue of its sovereignty" acquire lands within the borders of the states by eminent domain and without their consent, the respective sovereignties should be in a position to adjust their jurisdictions. There is no constitutional objection to such an adjustment of rights. It follows that jurisdiction less than exclusive may be granted the United States.[30]

However, concurrent state authority does not extend to any matter which conflicts with the power of Congress to protect the property, control its occupancy and use, and prescribe how others may acquire rights in it. To these ends Congress has extensively regulated use of its lands and other property, has prohibited and made punishable acts harmful to them or which prevented their use in the manner, or for the purposes intended.

[30] *Collins* v. *Yosemite Park Co.* (1908), 204 U.S. 518.

CHAPTER XIII

Functions of Congress:
Legislative Control of the Executive

GENERAL CONSIDERATIONS

In a representative democracy the legislature is the political embodiment of the sovereign people. Therefore, it is thought properly to be vested with a degree of control over the executive (although in practice the extent of this varies considerably). This is to say that the executive is more or less accountable to the legislature. In the United States, the answerability of the executive is but slightly developed. The equality of the two branches of government, the choice of the executive by what amounts to popular election, and a fixed term of office, go far to create an artificially stable and independent executive. However, control by Congress of the executive is by no means absent and responsibility does exist.

297

INFORMATION

Little effective control can be exercised by Congress over the executive unless the legislature is informed about its activities. Congress constantly probes its activities to make the executive prudently cautious in the discharge of its responsibilities. Information underlies all intelligent criticism, and criticism is admitted to have a salubrious influence in a democracy.

Sources of Information. Congress acquires an enormous mass of information, much of it pertaining to the executive branch. Some is supplied in the form of regular reports to Congress as required by statute; some is transmitted by the executive at the request of members or committees. Requests are complied with, unless a refusal can be defended on grounds of public interest, national security, or administratively-privileged communications.

Testimony by executive officials before the standing committees is extensively relied upon to obtain data concerning legislation pending or contemplated, especially in connection with matters of public finance. The committees of Congress maintain close relations with appropriate administrative agencies, and depend upon them for information on matters of policy. Agencies are regularly consulted about pending legislation; their top personnel spend many hours before committees explaining their stand on policies or defending their programs and activities. These committees exert a pervasive influence over administration which, to be intelligent and constructive, must be informed. Further, the hearings on appropriations afford an unsurpassed opportunity to impress legislative views on policy and administration upon the minds of administrative officers.

Investigations. Special investigations also provide data usable for criticizing the executive and for enforcing its responsibility to the legislature. The power to investigate is an ancient one, but only in recent decades has its use by Congress been extensive. The rules of the House of Representatives direct that in order[1]

To assist the House in appraising the administration of the laws and in developing such amendments or related legislation as it may deem necessary, each standing committee of the House shall exercise continuous watchfulness of the execution by the administrative agencies concerned of any laws, the subject matter of which is within the jurisdiction of such committee; and for that purpose shall study all pertinent reports and data submitted to the House by the agencies in the executive branch of the Government.[2]

[1] See "Congressional Expenditures for Investigations, 84th-86th Congresses," *Congressional Quarterly Weekly Report*, Vol. 17, No. 18, pp. 597-598. Senate authorizations for the 86th Congress, 2nd session (1960), may be found in *ibid.*, Vol. 18, No. 7, p. 246.

[2] *House Rules and Manual*, p. 368.

'Maybe I'll Do a Little Spying of My Own!'

An investigation is usually ordered by simple resolution of a chamber. It may be made by a standing committee, a subcommittee, or a specially created investigating committee. Use of special committees has declined since 1946, but they have been replaced by subcommittees to such an extent in the House that the Rules Committee has undertaken to police their employment.

Recent Congresses have seen an outburst of investigations. Most have been of serious and well-intentioned purpose, but some have been the opposite. Use of nation-wide television coverage has created a feverish competition for chairmanships or places on committees that have brought with them prestige, appropriations, patronage, and publicity. A more legitimate cause of the increased use of investigations is available for consideration. However inadequately it may serve to do so, resort to the investigatory power by Congress is regarded by it as a means of recovering for the legislative branch some of the power that has passed to the executive. To the extent that it can control executive actions and policies by controlling agencies and officers of the executive branch, it can regain some of its lost initiative and redress the balance of legislative-executive power in its own favor.

The extensive powers of investigative committees make it imperative that they should be subjected to adequate and effective controls. The essential premise of a resolution authorizing an investigation is that it, on behalf of the parent chamber, shall have clearly and definitely instructed the committee members on what they are to do with the authority granted to them. It is the responsibility of the authorizing chamber to ensure that the committee's powers will be used only in pursuance of a purpose within the scope of Congress' legislative power. This means that the instructions given to an investigative committee should spell out the committee's jurisdiction and purpose with particularity and clarity. The authorizing resolution is the charter of a committee; it should grant authority, define its scope of application, and place limitations upon it so that the members conducting the inquiry, and persons subjected to the powers and processes employed by them, can determine within a reasonable doubt what it is proper for the committee to do. Too often, however, the resolutions authorizing investigations are broadly drafted and loosely worded, so that they leave tremendous latitude and discretion to the investigators.[3]

Power Over Witnesses. The position of a witness before an investigating committee is not an enviable one. He can be placed under oath, by any member of a committee and prosecuted for perjury or contempt if he lies or refuses to answer. His presence, and the production of books, papers, and other materials of an evidential nature can be compelled by subpoena. He cannot refuse to testify as to any fact, or to produce any paper about which he is questioned, on the ground that he may be disgraced or otherwise rendered infamous thereby. If two-thirds of the committee members vote, the Attorney General is notified, and a United States district court approves, he may be deprived of the privilege against compulsory self-incrimination in return for immunity from prosecution based on the testimony that he has been constrained to give.[4] He must decide on the spot whether or not to invoke constitutional or other protections for his rights, subject to the knowledge that to do so may result in his prosecution by the Justice Department. He is protected by none of the traditional rules governing the admissibility of evidence, right of confrontation, credibility of witnesses, or of cross-examination.

The investigative powers of Congress are theoretically employed subject to the full protection of the First and Fifth Amendments and of the doctrine of the separation of powers, but powers of subpoena, compulsory testimony and production of evidence, administration of oaths, and prosecution for perjury and contempt are characteristics of process usually associated with courts of law rather than with legislatures. Their abuse has been too frequent, and more than one investigation has taken on the aspect of a legislative trial, without the niceties of trial procedure.

[3] For a full discussion of this problem see *Watkins* v. *United States* (1957), 354 U.S. 178.

[4] See *Ullman* v. *United States* (1956), 350 U.S. 422. See also *U.S. Code*, Title 2, secs. 191-194.

"Yes, Master. Whom Do You Wish Me to Strike Down?"

More than one inquiry has lacked a purpose more evident than a desire to blacken character, impugn motive, or propagate ideas. Compulsory process confronts the witness at every turn; few specific rights protect him. He may be subjected to abuse and ridicule and be disgraced in the eyes of his neighbors. He may be tried by the newspapers and suffer loss of job and reputation so that his standing in the community is destroyed to a degree that would not result if he were convicted of even serious crimes.

But, the question must be asked: Are such results legitimate consequences of the investigative function? Do they aid the legislative power of Congress? Should a small group of legislators, for whatever reasons, be permitted to do what no court of law and no executive agency or officer can do?

Rules of Committee Procedure. Each chamber should control its committees sufficiently to protect the rights of witnesses, but this is inadequately done. Few uniform rules exist in either house to achieve this end. The rules of the House of Representatives merely state:

26(a) The rules of the House are the rules of its committees so far as applicable. . . . Committees may adopt additional rules not inconsistent therewith.

(b) Each committee shall keep a complete record of all committee action. . . .

(i) The chairman at an investigative hearing shall announce in an opening statement the subject of the investigation.

(j) A copy of the committee rules, if any, . . . shall be made available to the witness.

(k) Witnesses at investigative hearings may be accompanied by their own counsel for the purpose of advising them concerning their constitutional rights. . . .

(m) If the committee determines that evidence or testimony at an investigative hearing may tend to defame, degrade, or incriminate any person, it shall

> (1) receive such evidence or testimony in executive session;
> (2) afford such person an opportunity voluntarily to appear as a witness; and
> (3) receive and dispose of requests from such persons to subpoena additional witnesses. . . .

(o) No evidence or testimony taken in executive session may be released or used in public sessions without the consent of the committee. . . .

(q) Upon payment of the cost thereof, a witness may obtain a transcript copy of his testimony given at a public session, or if given in an executive session, when authorized by the committee.[5]

These rules give some protection to witnesses, but their content and application leave much to be desired. They do not guarantee the fairness and relevance of questions, prevent "fishing expeditions" to see what can be turned up of interest to the investigators, preserve the rights of witnesses, prevent exposure to ridicule, defamation, degradation, or destruction of the good name and standing of witnesses in the community, guard against waste of public funds, headline-seeking, exposure for the sake of exposure, abuse of power, violation of rules, half-truths, or innuendoes. Investigative committees function almost completely in the absence of effective supervision and control by their parent assemblies.

Nature and Scope of the Investigative Power. The houses of Congress may investigate anything about which they can legislate. Today, most investigations concern the activities, policies, and personnel of the executive branch; and the knowledge that he and his agency can be investigated at any time lies close to the surface of every administrator's consciousness. Such awareness can have a salutary effect, but it can also breed undue caution, fear, and excessive reliance on precedent and rules, and can stifle administrative initiative and imagination.

Investigations are a control over the executive and enforce its answerability to the popularly-chosen representatives of the people. They have become a primary method of achieving this end. Accordingly:

It is the proper duty of a representative body to look diligently into every

[5] *House Rules and Manual,* pp. 364-368.

affair of government and to talk much about what it sees. It is meant to be the eyes and the voice, and to embody the wisdom and will of its constituents. Unless Congress have and use every means of acquainting itself with the acts and the disposition of the administrative agents of the government, the country must be helpless to learn how it is being served; and unless the Congress both scrutinize these things and sift them by every form of discussion, the country must remain in embarrassing, crippling ignorance of the very affairs which it is most important that it should understand and direct. The informing function of Congress should be preferred even to its legislative function.[6]

But, the assumption is always that legislation can result if a need for it is revealed. The power to investigate is regarded as essential to the legislative process. The theory of a committee inquiry is that the committee serves as a representative of the parent assembly in collecting information upon which the full legislature can act. To discharge this mission, a committee or subcommittee is endowed with the full power of Congress to compel testimony. Congress may investigate the administration of the laws by any or all agencies of the executive branch, seek out inefficiency and wrongdoing, determine the need for new, or the modification of old, laws, influence public opinion to suit legislative or executive needs or purposes, examine any phase of the policies or operations of any department, agency, or officer of the national government, or virtually any phase of the social, economic, or political system.

A legislative body cannot legislate wisely or effectively in the absence of information respecting the conditions which the legislation is intended to affect or change; and where the legislative body does not itself possess the requisite information—which not infrequently is true—recourse must be had to others who do possess it. Experience has taught that mere requests for such information often are unavailing, and also that information which is volunteered is not always accurate or complete; so some means of compulsion are essential to obtain what is needed. All this was true before and when the Constitution was framed and adopted. In that period the power of inquiry—with enforcing process—was regarded and employed as a necessary and appropriate attribute of the power to legislate—indeed, was treated as inherent in it. Thus, there is ample warrant for thinking, as we do, that the constitutional provisions that commit the legislative function to the two houses are intended to include this attribute to the end that the function may be effectively exercised.[7]

New laws need not originate from an investigation. Many inquiries produce much information and attract public attention, but little legislation usually results from them. However, they have been responsible for the enactment of several important statutes.

[6] Woodrow Wilson, *Congressional Government* (Boston: Houghton Mifflin Company, 3rd edition, 1885), p. 303.
[7] *McGrain* v. *Daugherty* (1927), 273 U.S. 135.

Hence, the major problem involving congressional investigations is how to accommodate the interest of the Government with the rights of the individual. It must be continually emphasized that

. . . broad as is this power of inquiry, it is not unlimited. There is no general authority to expose the private affairs of individuals without justification in terms of the functions of the Congress. . . . Nor is Congress a law enforcement or trial agency. These are functions of the executive and judicial departments of the government. No inquiry is an end in itself; it must be related to, and in furtherance of, a legislative task of the Congress. Investigations conducted solely for the personal aggrandizement of the investigators or to "punish" those investigated are indefensible.

It is unquestionably the duty of all citizens to cooperate with the Congress in its efforts to obtain the facts needed for intelligent legislative action. It is their unremitting obligation to respond to subpoenas, to respect the dignity of the Congress and its committees, and to testify fully with respect to matters within the province of proper investigation. This, of course, assumes that the constitutional rights of witnesses will be respected by the Congress as they are in a court of justice. The Bill of Rights is applicable to investigations as to all forms of governmental action. Witnesses cannot be compelled to give evidence against themselves. They cannot be subjected to unreasonable search and seizure. Nor can the First Amendment freedoms of speech, press, religion, or political belief and association be abridged.

We have no doubt that there is no congressional power to expose for the sake of exposure. The public is, of course, entitled to be informed concerning the workings of its government. That cannot be inflated into a general power to expose where the predominant result can only be an invasion of the private rights of individuals. . . .

It is manifest that despite the adverse effects which follow upon compelled disclosure of private matters, not all such inquiries are barred. . . . Such an investigation into private affairs is invalid if unrelated to any legislative purpose. That is beyond the powers conferred upon the Congress in the Constitution. . . . The critical element is the existence of, and the weight to be ascribed to, the interest of the Congress in demanding disclosures from an unwilling witness. We cannot simply assume, however, that every congressional investigation is justified by a public need that overbalances any private rights affected.[8]

CONTROL OF PUBLIC FINANCES

Control of the finances of the national government is a function divided between Congress and the executive. The executive proposes and Congress disposes. In general, the executive plans the expenditures and estimates the income; Congress authorizes the expenditures and raises the revenue. The process is one of great complexity but constitutes an under-

[8] *Watkins* v. *United States* (1957), 354 U.S. 178.

standable and responsible system. Ultimate control of the public moneys rests with Congress. It controls the public purse and, thereby, the executive branch. Because virtually nothing can be done by government without spending funds, the appropriations committees are the most powerful instruments of Congress for scrutiny and control of the executive.

All branches of the national government must spend funds to operate, and, with the total requested expenditures approximating ninety billion dollars, the mechanism of the appropriations process has become of great practical importance. On the legislative side of the arrangement, the key features are the appropriations acts, by which Congress authorizes expenditures and in effect *determines* what the executive may do. These acts do not *order* that moneys authorized be spent, but they do limit what is spent to the amount appropriated, the purposes stated, and the details prescribed.

Nevertheless, although the power of final decision resides in Congress, it cannot provide the leadership and direction necessary to successful and intelligent financial planning and execution. The executive, through whose agencies laws are administered and money is expended, is best able to fulfill the planning function. Congress after many years of unsuccessfully trying to perform the planning function, has imposed responsibility for preparing estimates of expenditure known as the "executive budget," upon the President. It is upon this document that the deliberations of Congress are based. Hence, executive action both precedes and follows the appropriation of public money by Congress. Finally, an audit of the expenditure accounts of the executive made by an agency of Congress, with the enactment of remedial or punitive legislation by Congress, if necessary, completes the process and returns final authority to the legislature. The relation between the functions of the two authorities is so close that consideration of the financial functions of Congress necessitates consideration of certain functions of the executive.

The Budget and Budgeting. An executive budget is the comprehensive financial plan of the government prepared by the executive for submission to the legislature. It sets out in advance the fiscal plan of the government for a definite period of time. It is a planned program for future operation; it is not a random list of proposed expenditures but a resolution of competing programs and policies expressed in dollars. There are many things government might do, but the financial, human, and material resources available to do them are limited. Decisions must be made about what is to be done, what the order of priority shall be, so that a share of the resources available can be apportioned to each. Thus, every proposal to spend that is contained in the budget represents a decision on a question of public policy. Hence, the process of budget preparation affords the President an excellent opportunity to control the substance and priority of the activities of every administrative unit. If budgeting is properly used, the budget document should represent to Congress an integrated statement of the President's policies, and of the programs necessary to implement them, for the entire executive branch during the coming fiscal year.

Budgeting is far more important than preparing figures and estimates of expenditures. The budgeting functions are vital to the whole conduct of our Government. In the preparation of the estimates lies not only the control of departmental expenditures but the power to insist on efficient methods of management in the spending agencies. And within an effective budgeting system lies the restoration of the full control of the national purse to the Congress.[9]

What should be the content of the executive budget? It should be drawn up to show clearly, fully, and understandably the functions and activities of the government, what has been done and what it cost, the future estimated receipts of the government under existing and proposed revenue laws, all essential facts concerning the financial condition of the government, its indebtedness, and the financial position of the Treasury at the end of the last fiscal year, its estimated condition at the end of the current year in progress, and what its condition will be if the proposals contained in the budget are approved by Congress. But most importantly, the budget should contain a full statement of the estimated expenditures and proposed appropriations which the President judges necessary for the support of the government during the coming fiscal year. This is the essence of the budget and should reveal to any interested party *what* is to be done, how it is to be accomplished, by whom, and at what cost. To aid Congress in making comparisons between past, present, and future activities and plans, the President must also show in his budget the actual appropriations, expenditures, and receipts of the government for the last completed fiscal year, as well as the estimated expenditures and receipts, and the actual or proposed appropriations during the current fiscal year. To some extent the executive budget meets these standards, but in several important particulars it fails to do so.

The President is required to transmit to Congress a budget which, on paper at least, is in balance. If estimated expenditures exceed estimated receipts and cash in the Treasury, the President must make recommendations to Congress for new taxes, loans, and other appropriate action to overcome the expected deficit, but Congress can, and usually does, ignore these proposals. If a surplus of income over expenditure is anticipated, the President can make to Congress whatever recommendations he feels are in the public interest.

[9] The Commission on Organization of the Executive Branch of the Government, *Budgeting and Accounting*, June, 1955, p. ix.

All this information, plus the President's message to Congress on the budget, the summary data and supporting detail, comprise the executive budget of the national government.

Because foresight and planning can never be perfect, because unanticipated emergencies arise, and because Congress authorizes many expenditures not contemplated by the President's budget, he is authorized to transmit to Congress from time to time proposed supplemental or deficiency appropriations that he believes to be necessary and in the public interest. But, he must explain to Congress why the action is necessary and why the proposed expenditures were omitted from the budget.

To protect the integrity of the President's budget from being undermined by the expansionist tendencies and the financial gluttony of administrative agencies Congress has provided that

No estimate or request for an appropriation and no request for an increase in an item of any such estimate or request, and no recommendation as to how the revenue needs of the Government should be met, shall be submitted to Congress or any committee thereof by any officer or employee of any department or establishment, unless at the request of either House of Congress.[10]

Bureau of the Budget. The President does not personally prepare the budget. He has been provided with a special unit, subject to his immediate and complete control, which performs the function for him. Thus:

There is created in the Executive Office of the President a bureau to be known as the Bureau of the Budget. There shall be in the bureau a Director and a Deputy Director, who shall be appointed by the President. . . . The Bureau, under such rules and regulations as the President may prescribe, shall prepare the Budget, and any proposed supplemental or deficiency appropriations, and to this end shall have authority to assemble, correlate, revise, reduce, or increase the requests for appropriations of the several departments or establishments. . . .

The bureau, when directed by the President, shall make a detailed study of the departments and establishments for the purpose of enabling the President to determine what changes (with a view of securing greater economy and efficiency in the conduct of the public service) should be made in (1) the existing organization, activities, and methods of business of such departments or establishments, (2) the appropriations therefor, (3) the assignment of particular activities to particular services, or (4) the regrouping of services. The results of such study shall be embodied in a report or reports to the President, who may transmit to Congress such report or reports or any part thereof with his recommendations on the matters covered thereby. . . .

Under such regulations as the President may prescribe (1) every department and establishment shall furnish to the bureau such information as the bureau may from time to time require, and (2) the director and the assistant director,

[10] *U.S. Code,* Title 31, secs. 11, 13-15.

or any employee of the bureau when duly authorized, shall, for the purpose of securing such information, have access to, and the right to examine, any books, documents, papers, or records of any such department or establishment. . . .

The head of each department and establishment shall prepare or cause to be prepared in each year his requests for regular, supplemental, or deficiency appropriations. . . .

The head of each department and establishment shall submit his requests for appropriations to the Bureau on or before a date which the President shall determine. In case of his failure to do so, the President shall cause such requests to be prepared as are necessary to enable him to include such requests with the Budget in respect to the work of such department or establishment.[11]

The budget covers one fiscal year, which begins July 1, and ends at midnight of the following June 30. The budget system is geared to these dates. Budget planning must be completed by the day set for transmitting the document to Congress. About May-June of one year, the spending agencies begin their financial planning for a fiscal year that starts more than one calendar year and ends more than two calendar years in the future. The President transmits the budget to Congress during the first fifteen days of each regular session, approximately six months before the beginning of the fiscal year. Congress should enact the financial proposals into law by July 1.

Formulation of the Budget. Requests for appropriations are compiled by the executive agencies requiring them according to instructions issued by the Bureau of the Budget. These are based upon a financial program prepared by the President and his aides and advisers.

After the requests for appropriations have been prepared, reviewed, correlated, increased, cut, and justified at the successively higher levels of section, division, bureau and department, they are transmitted to the Bureau of the Budget, where they undergo further searching analysis. The process lasts for months and is marked by severe competition for acceptance at every stage. Unit heads must decide between alternative lines of policy for which to request funds, for they know that money to implement all of them cannot be obtained; units compete with one another for funds. Increased appropriations mean increased staffs, more activity, greater organizational security; reduced appropriations mean the reverse. New policies compete for recognition with established ones. Pressure groups vie with one another, and with agencies of government, to gain acceptance for the policies and programs they favor and to block support for those they oppose. Behind every item of appropriation in the budget are the urgings of interest groups, consultations between heads of smaller units and chiefs of larger ones, hearings held by agency financial officers, appearances of departmental heads before the Estimates Review

---

[11] *U.S. Code*, Title 31, secs. 16, 18, 21-22.

Committee of the Bureau of the Budget and before the Policy Review Committee, and behind the whole process, almost daily conferences between the Director of the Bureau of the Budget and the President. The budget, therefore, is very largely a political document.

The entire process of budget formulation vests in the President extensive control over his branch of the government; for, with the exception of certain fixed charges on the Treasury, and the legislative and judicial estimates, nothing is included in the budget which is not approved by him. At the same time, the budget is the basis upon which congressional control of the executive branch, through manipulation of the purse strings, is primarily based.

Procedure in Congress. The congressional share in the appropriations process is based upon the constitutional declaration that

No Money shall be drawn from the Treasury, but in Consequence of Appropriations made by Law; and a regular Statement and Account of the Receipts and Expenditures of all public Money shall be published from time to time.

By custom appropriation measures originate in the House of Representatives. In consequence of this the budget document, required by law to be transmitted to the "Congress," is submitted to the House of Representatives. It is not a law and does not become a law except as parts of

'Hold It—He Can't Fly on One Wing!'

it are incorporated into appropriations or revenue bills. Hence, one part of the budget pertains to expenditures and another to income. Expenditures are traditionally considered first by Congress.

Appropriations. When the budget is transmitted to the House of Representatives, it comes as a communication from the President and is laid on the table. The parts relating to appropriations are referred by the Speaker to the Committee on Appropriations. This committee operates through subcommittees, the full committee usually meeting only to approve the draft measure proposed by the smaller body. Members of the subcommittees gain considerable familiarity with the organization, personnel needs, and other special features of the agency or agencies whose expenditure estimates they review. On the basis of their analyses of the estimates, they prepare a dozen appropriations bills. These are amended and adopted by the full Appropriations Committee and reported to the House, by which they are treated as highly privileged bills. Ideally, their passage should be completed before July 1, but their consideration in the Senate often runs into late July or early August. Moreover, those for the ensuing year are not the only ones with which Congress is concerned. It will also probably be called upon to pass supplemental and deficiency appropriations acts providing additional funds for the current or last completed fiscal year.

Congressional Power Over Appropriations. Congress retains complete authority to alter the estimates of expenditures proposed by the President's budget. Its committees can, and often do, reduce or increase them. Presidential influence can only be exerted through the appearances and testimony of his agency heads before the appropriations committees, through the advice and information supplied them by the Bureau of the Budget, and through his appeals to public opinion, his personal influence, and his leadership as head of the political party. If Congress emasculates his fiscal proposals, there is little the President can do to prevent it. He lacks the power to veto objectionable *parts* of an appropriations measure; he must accept the bad with the good or reject the good in order to eliminate the bad. The latter course he can follow only if he is willing to deprive the affected agency or agencies of their funds until Congress takes some further action. Veto of an appropriations act is rarely done.

Congressional power over appropriations contradicts the executive budget system. To be consistent with that system, Congress should refrain from increasing estimates proposals and making unplanned expenditures, but should exercise the power to reduce or eliminate expenditures.

However, such self-denial would amount to abdication by Congress of much of its power over policy and expenditures. Worse, it would greatly increase the authority of the executive in relation to that of the legislative branch. That result is unacceptable to Congress. It will never accede in principle to such highly developed executive leadership.

Instead, Congress tries to strengthen its control over the appropriations process. It once tried to fix a ceiling to appropriations above which it would not authorize expenditures, but found that it could not prevent the total from exceeding its own maximum figure. Since that sole effort at implementation this method of control has lapsed into disuse and is now obsolete.

In 1950 it again tried to strengthen its control over the appropriations process by incorporating all appropriations into a single bill. However, in 1951 the experiment was abandoned. It did not enable Congress to reduce appropriations; it resulted in the attachment of riders and unanticipated expenditure authorizations supported by outside groups or blocs of members; and, the omnibus act was so large and complicated that it made full comprehension and careful consideration impossible.

Revenue. At approximately the same time that the Bureau of the Budget prepares the estimates of expenditures, the Treasury Department is busy estimating what the income of the national government under existing laws will be during the coming fiscal year. These estimates, together with recommendations to increase the revenue if it is thought that expenditures will exceed income, are transmitted by the President as part of the budget document.

The Constitution expressly gives the House of Representatives priority in the control of revenue by stating that

All Bills for raising Revenue shall originate in the House of Representatives; but the Senate may propose or concur with Amendments as on other bills.

The Senate has extended its authority until it encompasses considerably more than this ability to amend revenue bills. The power to amend implies that revenue proposals originate in the House of Representatives and are then sent to the Senate. The power to propose new or increased taxation in excess of that originated in the House looks as if it is not the power to amend, but the power to initiate. Even so, the Senate has gone farther, and in the guise of making amendment, at times has struck out all but the enacting clause of a House tax bill and substituted a wholly new set of proposals of its own creation.

In the House of Representatives proposals for raising revenue are assigned to the Committee on Ways and Means, whose counterpart in the Senate is named the Committee on Finance. It is a highly privileged committee whose power and practices closely parallel those of the Appropriations Committee. Moreover, the enactment of revenue measures follows the same procedure that is applied to appropriations bills.

Ultimate Congressional Control of Finances. Congress exercises final control of the purse through its power to call to account the expenditures of any spending agency of the executive branch. Thus:

There is created an establishment of the Government to be known as the General Accounting Office, which shall be independent of the executive departments and under the control and direction of the Comptroller General of the United States. . . .

There shall be in the General Accounting Office a Comptroller General of the United States and an Assistant Comptroller General of the United States, who shall be appointed by the President with the advice and consent of the Senate. . . .

Except as hereafter provided by this section, the Comptroller General and the Assistant Comptroller General shall hold office for fifteen years. The Comptroller General shall not be eligible for reappointment. The Comptroller General or the Assistant Comptroller General may be removed at any time by joint resolution of Congress after notice and hearing, when . . . permanently incapacitated or has been inefficient, or guilty of neglect of duty, or of malfeasance in office, or of any felony or conduct involving moral turpitude, and for no other cause and in no other manner except by impeachment. . . .

(a) The Comptroller General shall investigate, at the seat of government or elsewhere, all matters relating to the receipt, disbursement, and application of public funds, and shall make to the President, when requested by him, and to Congress at the beginning of each regular session, a report in writing of the work of the General Accounting Office, containing recommendations concerning the legislation he may deem necessary to facilitate the prompt and accurate rendition and settlement of accounts and concerning such other matters relating to the receipts, disbursement, and application of public funds as he may think advisable. In such regular report, or in special reports at any time when Congress is in session, he shall make recommendations looking to greater economy or efficiency in public expenditures.

(b) He shall make such investigations and reports as shall be ordered by either House of Congress or by any committee of either House having jurisdiction over revenue, appropriations, or expenditures. . . .

(c) The Comptroller General shall specifically report to Congress every expenditure or contract made by any department or establishment in any year in violation of law. . . .

All departments and establishments shall furnish to the Comptroller General such information regarding the powers, duties, activities, organization, financial transactions, and methods of business of their respective offices as he may from time to time require of them; and the Comptroller General, or any of his assistants or employees, when duly authorized by him, shall, for the purpose of securing such information, have access to and the right to examine any books, documents, papers, or records of any such department or establishment. . . .[12]

Criticism of Congressional Control over Appropriations. Although it cannot do so in fact Congress can, theoretically, withhold from the executive all funds for operating the government, and force the President and his administration to conform to its will. By granting or denying funds requested by the executive agencies, Congress certainly can determine not only how much is spent but also the goals, programs, structure, status, operating procedures, personnel ceilings, and countless other aspects of executive business. It is also true that appropriations may be legally spent only for purposes intended by Congress; and more than one administrative unit has been terminated or crippled because an appropriations committee took revenge upon it or its administrative head for failing to heed the will of Congress. The hearings on the budget requests provide unlimited opportunity for legislative interrogation of executive officers concerning any phase of their unit's existence. Yet, in spite of this seemingly great power, legislative control of the executive through control of the purse is often largely ineffective.

Its failure is in part due to the separation of powers, which prevents it from being pushed to its logical extreme. In a dispute between the political branches over funds, the President can point to the fact that he too is popularly elected and that he is also the only officer of the general government who represents the people and interests of the entire nation. He is better able to marshall popular opinion in support of his position than Congress is. Congress is not ignorant of that possibility,

[12] *U.S. Code,* Title 31, secs. 41-43, 53, 54.

particularly since the responsibility of the executive to the legislative authority is vague and indefinite, and their respective spheres of authority and leadership are not clearly established. The President, therefore, is usually able to advance arguments for popular acceptance of his position which are as sound as those that Congress directs against him.

Other factors undermine congressional power derived from control of the purse. The budgets are large and complicated. Congress lacks the time and ability to deal effectively with them. Its members lack the technical knowledge necessary to make intelligent judgments about the reasonableness of the executive's requests for funds. The monetary committees lack assistance adequate to their tasks. There is as yet no over-all review of the expenditure proposals by Congress; the magnitude and complexity of the budget virtually precludes it. Consideration of the budget is hopelessly divided, so that the procedures of Congress do not permit a comprehensive view. The committees of the House operate separately from those of the Senate; the subcommittees operate separately one from the other, and the tendency of a full committee to adopt without review the proposals of its subcommittees puts great power in their hands. Revenue measures are considered by one set of committees, appropriations by another, within and between the houses of Congress. Excessive attention is paid to details. More than a dozen fiscal measures are passed each year. Moreover, many ordinary statutes are enacted which require the expenditure of funds not included in the budget. Hence, the current appropriations system divides responsibility among numerous groups and encourages every member to obtain from the "porkbarrel" by the techniques of reciprocal assistance all the public funds he can for "the folks back home."

Requests for appropriations represent policy decisions translated into the numbers of dollars thought necessary to put them into effect; but their consideration in Congress gives little evidence of an awareness there that appropriations are also political, not just financial, decisions. Recognition that appropriations reflect policy decisions, that only the executive can prepare an integrated program of policy, and that Congress is virtually helpless to resist executive direction in this field is tacitly given by the fact that Congress seldom manages to make any major reduction in the requests of the President and, when it does endeavor to do so, usually restores the cuts in supplemental and deficiency appropriations. Congress is not really economy minded; its members are under strong and numerous pressures to obtain all they can for their constituencies. In the entire area of public policy, and especially in the matter of appropriations, Congress can follow, disrupt, oppose, and dispose, but it cannot provide, effective leadership.

The efforts by Congress to implement a legislative budget and to enact an omnibus appropriation act, the hearings of the standing legislative committees, the efforts of investigations to call executive agents to account, and the hearings of the appropriations committees are probably evidence of a desire on the part of Congress to control policy but without knowing of an effective means for doing it. It is compelled by the doctrine of the separation of powers to share the function with the executive, but it lacks sufficient faith in the system of checks and balances to do it with a strong sense of confidence. It continues to place its faith in legal arrangements at the expense of the further development of political sanctions over the executive.

Thus, although power over the public purse provides the best possible foundation for the exercise of political control by Congress over the executive, although debate of proposed appropriations affords an excellent opportunity for criticizing executive policies, little advantage is taken by Congress of either possibility. Because Congress cannot determine the tenure of the executive in the American system, it is without a fully effective political sanction to apply against it. The executive is somewhat less than fully responsible to the legislature in our scheme of governmental arrangements. It is accountable to Congress, but accountability is one thing and responsibility backed by effective sanction is something very different.

Knowledge that they may at any time become the subject of a congressional investigation, that audits will be made of their handling of expenditures, that impeachment may be instituted against them for violation of penal law does have a deterrent effect upon officers of the executive branch of the national government. But these legal processes and legal sanctions constitute arrangements very different from those of a political nature which are employed to enforce executive responsibility to the legislature.

Moreover, the machinery available to Congress for controlling the executive does not permit it to discharge this function with thoroughness. The administrative units of the executive are too numerous, the committees of Congress too few, too small, and too under-staffed; the members commonly lack the technical knowledge to challenge the assertions of executive experts; there is inadequate leadership and unity of outlook in Congress; its members are too concerned with other duties to give much thought to the supervision of executive activities.

The lawmaking, appropriations, and investigate powers of Congress, therefore, afford but partial control of the executive. The first, as will be seen in the following chapter, has largely succumbed to the influence and leadership of the executive branch. The second is ineffective for any but piecemeal controls. The third remains but cannot cope with the immensity of the problem.

In sum:

The indictment against the existing system of congressional control is impressive. It is basically control over details, not over essentials. It is negative and repressive rather than positive and constructive. It reflects fear rather than confidence. It is sometimes irresponsible. It is based on no rational plan, but is an accumulation of particulars whose consequences are seldom seen in perspective.[13]

However, the criticisms are criticisms of detail and procedure; the principle of legislative control over the executive remains unchallenged.

SANCTION OF LEGISLATIVE-EXECUTIVE CONTROL

For its control of the executive to be fully effective Congress should be able to command the resignation or dismissal of the policy-making executive at its will. This, however, is not compatible with the doctrine of the separation of powers. Congress may investigate, inform the public, and criticize the President and his administration, but it cannot determine the tenure of the executive and his political subordinates. In the American national government the controls of Congress over the executive are primarily legal, not political.

Impeachment. Nothing better illustrates the inefficiency of legal sanctions as means of controlling the policy-making executive than does the disuse into which the process of impeachment has fallen. Impeachment is the means by which Congress may remove from office top-ranking members of the executive. To this end:

The House of Representatives . . . shall have the sole Power of Impeachment.

The Senate shall have the sole Power to try all Impeachments. When sitting for that Purpose, they shall be on Oath or Affirmation. When the President of the United States is tried, the Chief Justice shall preside: and no Person shall be convicted without the Concurrence of two thirds of the Members present.

Judgment in Cases of Impeachment shall not extend further than to removal from Office, and disqualification to hold and enjoy any Office of honor, Trust or Profit under the United States, but the Party convicted shall nevertheless be liable and subject to Indictment, Trial, Judgment and Punishment according to Law.

The President, Vice President, and all civil Officers of the United States, shall be removed from Office on Impeachment for, and Conviction of, Treason, Bribery, or other high Crimes and Misdemeanors.

[13] Leonard D. White, "Congressional Control of the Public Service," *American Political Science Review,* Vol. 39 (February, 1945), pp. 2-3.

Use of the impeachment process as a means of controlling the executive is limited by the Constitution to instances in which civil officers commit crimes. Two circumstances render the process ineffective. First, very few civil officers commit crimes, and those who do are invariably removed from office by the President to whom they are responsible and who, in turn, is responsible to the people through the electoral process. Second, it is very difficult to secure conviction. Hence, impeachment, invoked because of a difference of view between the two authorities as to the policies and programs that will best serve the general interest, affords no control of the executive by the legislature. It is useless as a political sanction and unnecessary as a legal one. Congress is, therefore, forced to control the executive on a piecemeal basis by means of statutes regulating the myriad details of executive business, machinery, authorizations, and finances.

CHAPTER XIV

Functions of Congress: The Legislative Process

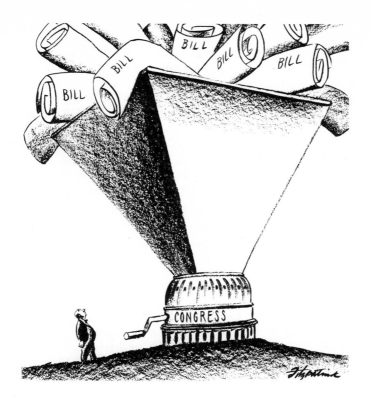

GENERAL CONSIDERATIONS

A visitor in the gallery of the House or Senate sees merely the most formal and superficial aspects of the process of legislation. He gains no comprehension of the sources from which the measures introduced originate, of the consequences of committee action, of the political pressures that determine the content of legislation, of the compromise necessary to its enactment, or of the controls exercised behind the scenes by the party leadership. These and many other highly important features of the legislative process are invisible and unknown to the casual observer. Yet, their impact upon the quantity, content, and character of laws cannot be overestimated.

Party Control in the House. Decisions concerning the course and content of legislation are made by key members in positions of authority who are motivated by considerations of partisanship. The ostensible legislative program of each party is determined in its broad outlines by a steering or policy committee and occasionally by the caucus. Each committee, to promote party unity and harmony, maintains close contact with

319

its party's members and consults them on issues of importance. The decisions of these committees are not binding, but they exert much influence upon the members. Their function is to work out a legislative program which the members will support. The steering committee of the President's party must work for the enactment of his legislative proposals.

The floor leader is the link binding virtually all units of party leadership, decision, and control. Aided by the whip, he determines what support party members will give to a particular bill and what form the bill must be given if it is to obtain the necessary votes to pass. This information he passes on to the chairmen of the standing committees, wherein the real process of shaping legislation goes on. He serves as chief spokesman for his party in the House, works closely with all units of party control, with the Speaker and committee chairmen in their party capacity, and controls the legislative process.

However, the majority leader does not always have his way without opposition. On more than one occasion his own party members have thwarted his plans. Under the most ideal circumstances he and his fellow party leaders must consult the minority and consider the demands of their own members. They must work with, not dictate to, the minority. By unwritten rule they must not oppress the minority. Moreover, they can accomplish little without at least the acquiescence of the minority. Rarely can the minority defeat majority control, but it often obstructs and frustrates its efforts to enact its legislative program. For its cooperation, the minority can demand compromises and concessions from the majority.

Much the same situation prevails in the Senate, although party control is not as vigorously asserted. The Senate is a more manageable body that has developed a tradition of freedom not found in the House. Senators do not react graciously to formalized restraints. Hence, decisions affecting the content and priority of legislation in the Senate are concluded through informal personal discussions and compromises reached by a few trusted leaders. However, a policy committee for each party controls the course of legislation and includes the floor leader among its membership. The floor leaders, too, are their parties' spokesmen and link all the agencies of party control. The Democratic leader is chairman of his policy committee. Each floor leader works closely with his policy committee and with the ranking members of his party on each standing committee. Each chairman must gauge the reactions of committee members to proposed legislation. The floor leader's task is lightened by the work of the whips and by the evaluations and advice of the committee chairmen. The majority floor leader must consider the attitudes of his party members and conciliate them and the minority leaders if he expects to gain the enactment of his party legislation.

Lack of Party Responsibility in Congress. However, members of Congress are not guided by a strong sense of party allegiance. Such responsibility as exists is individual. It is not enforced by the party in the name of party unity and responsibility, but by the voters in the constituencies against individual members, often on the basis of local values and parochial judgments. Except for those cast during the organization of the houses of Congress, votes are not cast on strictly party lines. Decisions reached on the floor or elsewhere seldom represent the collective judgments of the majority party members for which they stand answerable to the country as a party.

Party responsibility in the House and Senate is spread so thin among so many different centers of power and influence that it cannot be fixed. Congress possesses many leaders but little centralized leadership and control. This is, perhaps, its chief characteristic. Party leadership in the houses does not exist to make party responsibility for the formulation of public policy a feature of the legislative process. It facilitates and expedites the legislative function and, when possible, the enactment of a majority party President's policies. These measures are introduced as "administration," not party, measures, although the President is its chief and its spokesman. Presidential leadership and influence are brought into play, but never perfectly; for even though the necessary votes are commanded by his party's members, the party, *per se*, neither assumes responsibility for the President's proposals nor endeavors to exert firm party discipline over its members to enact them. The proposals are his in his capacity as the executive. Although party unity of the executive and Congress contributes to harmony between the branches of government, it adds little to the ideological responsibility of parties in American political life.

The Legislative Product. The product of congressional effort is composed of various elements, some of which have the character of law and some of which do not. Those which do, in addition to treaties, are known as bills or joint resolutions.

These measures make law and must be signed by the President in order to become effective. The difference between them is difficult to make plain. Perhaps it is sufficient to state that usage has accustomed Congress to "enacting" in some instances and to "resolving" in others. Thus, statutes are enacted; resolutions are resolved. Bills may be classed according to whether they are "private" and apply to one person, an identifiable small group, or a designated community, or are "public" and make law of general application to all persons in the United States who come within the scope of their terms. Joint resolutions are customarily used to propose amendments to the Constitution, to extend the applicability of an existing law, to annex territory, and in other ways to guide administrative action. They are characteristically measures relating to a single subject which cannot be considered to make general law.

Orders and other resolutions also occupy the attention of the houses.

An order of a house (*"Ordered,* That the hour of daily meeting of the House shall be 12 am."), a simple resolution (*"Resolved,* That the House declines to consider any bill which violates its constitutional prerogative of originating revenue bills."), and concurrent resolutions ("Resolved by the House of Representatives [the Senate concurring], That the President ought to declare the week of March 11-19 to be National Love Thy Neighbor Week.") are used to express the intent, sense, directive, or purpose of the houses. In no case is law made or is the signature of the President required to give them effect, for they comprehend only the authority of the Congress or of the house involved, but not that of the government of the United States. In recent years, concurrent resolutions have been invoked to terminate statutory grants of power to the executive, thus evading the possibility of a veto.

Congressional Record

United States of America — PROCEEDINGS AND DEBATES OF THE 87th CONGRESS, SECOND SESSION

Vol. 108   WASHINGTON, FRIDAY, NOVEMBER 2, 1962   *No. 194*

Daily Digest

RÉSUMÉ OF CONGRESSIONAL ACTIVITY OF EIGHTY-SEVENTH CONGRESS

	FIRST SESSION January 3 through September 26, 1961			SECOND SESSION January 10 through October 13, 1962		
	Senate	House	Total	Senate	House	Total
Days in session	146	147	..	177	157	..
Time in session	1,005 hrs., 00'	569 hrs., 43'		1,159 hrs., 22'	656 hrs., 48'	
Congressional Record:						
Pages of proceedings	12,755	7,489	20,244	13,704	8,548	22,252
Appendix	..	..	8,435	..	..	8,077
Public bills enacted into law	145	256	401	167	317	484
Private bills enacted into law	99	185	284	141	259	400
Bills in conference	..	7		2	15	..
Bills through conference	14	41		15	50	..
Measures passed, total	1,133	1,234	..	1,212	1,190	..
Senate bills	459	245	..	375	284	..
House bills	433	678	..	576	623	..
Senate joint resolutions	25	11	..	33	26	..
House joint resolutions	27	31	..	25	29	..
Senate concurrent resolutions	23	19	..	19	13	..
House concurrent resolutions	23	25	..	38	34	..
Simple resolutions	143	225	368	146	181	327
Measures reported, total	*1,239	*1,159	..	*1,312	*1,143	..
Senate bills	501	179	..	425	228	..
House bills	433	772	..	575	683	..
Senate joint resolutions	27	6	..	35	16	..
House joint resolutions	26	24	..	25	33	..
Senate concurrent resolutions	29	11	..	19	12	..
House concurrent resolutions	23	19	..	38	26	..
Simple resolutions	200	148	348	195	145	340
Special reports	35	54	..	29	61	..
Conference reports	..	62	..	..	70	..
Reported measures not acted on	**36	**60	..	**50	**88	..
Measures introduced, total	3,071	10,955	14,026	1,494	4,796	6,290
Bills	2,644	9,480	12,124	1,166	3,940	5,106
Joint resolutions	145	593	738	93	315	408
Concurrent resolutions	55	401	456	43	184	227
Simple resolutions	227	481	708	192	357	549
Quorum calls	33	115	148	82	169	..
Yea-and-nay votes	207	116	323	227	124	..
Bills vetoed	2	6	..	4	8	12
Vetoes overridden	..			..		

*These figures on measures reported include all placed on calendar or acted on by Senate even if there was no accompanying report. In the Senate 1,117 reports were filed during the first session and 1,173 in the second session; while the House filed 1,283 in the first session and 1,273 in the second session.
**This figure does not agree with the total difference between bills reported and bills passed, because resolutions and bills placed on the House Calendar without having been formally reported were not included in figures of measures reported to the House; the difference in the case of Senate figures is due to uncounted bills "laid on the table" or "indefinitely postponed." Reported measures not acted on include measures reported during first session. These data include bills on calendar and in conference at the end of the first session.

THE LEGISLATIVE PROCESS

Thousands of bills, resolutions, and orders are introduced each year. Relatively few are passed. Important ones are lost; unimportant ones are enacted. Some retain their original form; others are so changed as to be unrecognizable.

A bill is the typical object of legislative attention. However, simple resolutions and orders involve only the house of origin. The stages of passage are basically the same in both houses and have been summarized as follows:

STAGES OF A BILL IN THE CONGRESS

1. Introduction.

By a member dropping the bill in the hopper on the Clerk's table informally. A Member sometimes introduces a petition only, leaving to the committee the drawing of a bill, such a petition referred to a committee having jurisdiction of the subject giving authority to report a bill. Sometimes communications addressed to the House from the executive departments or from other sources are referred to committees by the Speaker and give authority for the committees to originate bills. Messages from the President also are referred by the Speaker or the House and give jurisdiction to the committees receiving them to originate bills.

2. Reference to a standing or select committee:

Public bills are referred under direction of the Speaker; private bills are indorsed with the names of the committees to which they go under the rule by the Members introducing them. Senate bills are referred under direction of the Speaker. A bill is numbered and printed when referred.

3. Reported from the committee:

Committees having leave to report at any time make their reports from the floor; other committees make their reports by dropping them in the hopper on the Clerk's table informally. The bill and the report are printed when reported.

4. Placed on the Calendar:

Occasionally a privileged bill is considered when reported; but usually it is placed with the unprivileged bills on the Calendar where it belongs under the rule by direction of the Speaker.

5. Consideration in Committee of the Whole:

Public bills which do not raise revenue or make or authorize appropriations of money or property do not go through this stage. All other bills are considered in Committee of the Whole. The stages of consideration in Committee of the Whole are: General debate; reading for amendment under the five-minute rule; order to lay aside with a favorable recommendation, or to rise and report; reporting of to the House.

6. Reading a second time in the House:

Bills not requiring consideration in Committee of the Whole are read a second time in full, after which they are open to debate and amendment in any part. Bills considered in Committee of the Whole are read a second time in full in that committee and when reported out, with or without amendments, are not read in full again, but are subject to further debate or amendment in the House unless the previous question is ordered at once.

7. Engrossment and third reading:

The question of House bills is taken on ordering the engrossment and third reading at one vote. If decided in the affirmative, the reading a third time usually takes place at once, by title. But any Member may demand the reading in full of the engrossed copy, in which case the bill is laid aside until it can be engrossed. Senate bills come to the House in engrossed form, and the question is put on third reading alone. When the question on engrossment and third reading of a House bill or third reading of a Senate bill is decided in the negative the bill is lost as much as if defeated on the final passage. The question on engrossment and third reading is not made from the floor, but is put by the Speaker as a matter of course.

8. Passage:

The question on the passage of a bill is put by the Speaker as a matter of course, without awaiting a motion from the floor.

9. Transmission to the Senate by message:

10. Consideration by the Senate:

In the Senate House bills are usually referred to committees for consideration and report, after which they have their several readings, with opportunities for debate and amendment. The same procedure takes place in the House as to bills sent from the Senate.

11. Return of, from the Senate without amendments:

If the Senate passes a House bill without amendment it returns it to the House, where it is at once enrolled for signature. A bill thus passed without amendment goes into possession of the clerk, and is not laid before the House prior to enrollment. If the Senate rejects a House bill the House is informed. Similar procedure occurs when the House passes a Senate bill without amendment.

12. Return of, from the Senate with amendments:

House bills returned with Senate amendments go to the Speaker's table. If any Senate amendment requires consideration in Committee of the Whole the bill is referred by the Speaker informally to the standing committee having jurisdiction, and when that committee reports the bill with recommendations it is referred to Committee of the Whole House on the state of the Union, to be there considered and reported to the House itself. When no Senate amendment requires consideration in Committee of the Whole the bills come before the House directly from the Speaker's table.

13. Consideration of Senate amendments by the House:

When a bill with Senate amendments comes before the House, the House takes up each amendment by itself and may vote to agree to it, agree to it with an amendment, or disagree to it. If it disagrees it may ask a conference with the Senate or may send notice of its disagreement, leaving it to the Senate to recede or insist and ask the conference.

14. Settlement of differences by conference:

When disagreements are referred to conference, the managers embody their settlement in a report, which is acted on by each House as a whole. When this report is agreed to the bill is finally passed, and is at once enrolled for signature.

15. Enrollment:

The House in which a bill originates enrolls it.

16. Examination by the Committee on House Administration:

The chairman of the Committee on House Administration or the Secretary of the Senate as the case may be affixes to the bills examined a certificate that the bill has been found truly enrolled.

17. Signing by the Speaker and President of the Senate:

The enrolled bill is first signed by the Speaker, whether it be a House or Senate bill, after which it is transmitted to the Senate and signed by the president of that body.

18. Transmittal to the President of the United States:

The Chairman of the Committee on House Administration or the Secretary of the Senate as the case may be carries the bills from his House to the President. In the House of Representatives a report of the bills taken to the President each day is made to the House and entered on its Journal.

19. Approval by the President:

If the President approves he does so with his signature.

20. Disapproval by the President:

When the President disapproves a bill he returns it to the House in which it originated, with a message stating that he disapproves, and giving his reasons therefor.

21. Action on, when returned disapproved:

The House to which a disapproved bill is returned has the message read and spread on its Journal. It may then consider at once the question of passing the bill notwithstanding the President's objections, or may postpone to a day certain, or refer to a committee for examination. The vote on passing the bill, notwithstanding the President's objections, must be carried by two-thirds and the question must be determined by yea and nay vote. If the bill fails to pass in the House to which it is returned it remains there; but if it passes it is sent to the other House for action.

22. Filing with the Administrator of General Services:

When approved by the President a bill is deposited in the office of the Administrator of General Services; and when the two Houses have passed a bill, notwithstanding the President's objections, the presiding officer of the House which acts on it last transmits it to the Administrator of General Services.[1]

This process by which laws are made may be reduced to a few relatively simple stages. These are introduction and referral, committee stage, debate stage, and final passage.

Legislation: (i) Introduction and Referral. Bills may be introduced only by members of the House and Senate, who enjoy the right of unlimited initiative. Introduction is, however, largely a formality.

Bills originate from many sources, but when a member introduces one, it becomes his whether or not it originated with him, with an administrative agency, an interest group, a constituent, or some other source. Most public bills originate in the executive branch; most others stem from a source other than the minds of the membership.

The executive plays an important role in the origin and passage of legislation. The President and his congressional leaders meet weekly to discuss pending or future measures, problems of legislative-executive relations, strategy of enactment, and like subjects. The President can exert great influence over the substance of legislation, and enjoys some important legislative powers of his own. He or his agencies can often create a desired public reaction to proposed acts. The President makes numerous legislative recommendations to Congress, and normally attempts to pressure their enactment. Public bills are submitted to the appropriate executive agencies for analysis and criticism, and thereafter go to the Bureau of the Budget for analysis in the light of the President's program and known views. Bills which originate in the executive are thus cleared before being sent to Congress for introduction. Few measures can withstand the concerted opposition of the executive.

In the Senate introduction of a bill must be preceded by recognition, and is often accompanied by a brief statement of purpose, but a bill may be introduced simply by being sent to the Secretary's desk.

Readings. Measures are "read" three times in each house. However, they are not read each time in their entirety. Senate bills and joint resolutions are normally read twice *by title* immediately upon being introduced. Objection made to an immediate second reading causes the bill to lie over for one day, but no proposal can be amended or referred until it has been read twice. A third reading occurs on consideration.

In the House of Representatives bills and resolutions are theoretically read the first time by title, a requirement met by printing them in the

[1] *House Rules and Manual,* pp. 517-520.

Journal and the *Congressional Record.* Second reading in the House, as distinguished from the Committee of the Whole, is had when the bills are called up for debate. Those considered in the Committee of the Whole are read a second time in the Committee of the Whole. Third reading is by title only, but a member *can* demand a full reading.

After a bill is introduced, it is numbered for ease of identification, ordered printed, entered upon the *Journal,* and referred to a standing committee according to the subject matter of the bill. Referral in the Senate is by the President; but the member who introduces a measure may indicate the committee that he would like it referred to. In the House, bills are referred by direction of the Speaker, but the Parliamentarian[2] makes the choice, except in cases of dispute when the Speaker decides.

Legislation: (ii) Committee Stage. Choice of a committee may be very important to the fate of a bill. Party leaders can kill a bill they oppose by sending it to a hostile committee. It may inadvertently be assigned to a hostile committee; and that, too, may bring on its end. However, most bills are referred without incident or regret.

Role of the Committees. The standing committees are the filters through which opposed, unwise and unimportant bills are screened out. Thus, their elimination is accomplished early in the legislative process, for the standing committees receive a great many more measures than they can possibly consider. Their first task is to determine which should be given further consideration. This is a source of much power, for during the life of a Congress approximately 20,000 measures will be introduced. About ten per cent will pass. Most of the remaining ninety per cent die because they are never reported out of the standing committees to which they were referred.

It is in the standing committees that laws are written, and the houses often only approve what is proposed to them. Every significant measure undergoes some changes not approved by the committee, but major changes not proposed by a standing committee are rarely made by the chambers. A house usually accepts the suggestions of its committees, so that these exercise almost unchallenged control over the substance of legislation.

Party Control in Committee. Party control is supposed to be enforced in committee by the chairman. He is expected to keep committee action commensurate with the aims of his party by using his great personal power and influence to support his party leadership. But that power and influence also enables him to fight his party if he is so inclined. He knows the attitudes of the majority members toward bills of interest to the leadership, and should keep his leaders informed of the support they can expect from the committee. The ranking minority member does the same for his leaders. Thus, they are the spokesmen for their parties and the

[2] An expert on matters of legislative rules and procedure.

immediate party leaders. The members are supposed to follow their lead, which they nominally take from their party leadership outside the committee. Within this context of party control, the work of the committees is carried on.

Powers of the Chairman. The chairman usually determines the measures to be considered, whether to hold public hearings, and their duration if held. He appoints and controls the committee staff, reports measures to the floor or can refuse to do so, appoints sub-committees, can control debate and the amendment of measures, and serves on conference committees. Although the chairman is formally subject to control by the committee majority, he is often strong enough to defeat the wishes of his committee and even of his party leaders. Hence, for a measure to get through committee it must gain his approval and have party support, but while the chairmen are vital cogs of the legislative process, they do not form a collegiate group. They take no consultative, cooperative action to adopt an integrated legislative program. Their committees proceed independently and at their own pace. Consequently, no common purpose exists between the measures of one committee and those of another except what the party leaders can secure.

Procedure in Committee. A bill remains the business of a committee for the life of a Congress, until the committee disposes of it, or is discharged of further responsibility for it. Its power over a bill or resolution is absolute. It may refuse to consider it, or it may consider and reject it; in either case the effect is to kill it in committee.

Legislative Committee Hearings. Inconsequential bills are read by committee clerks and disposed of expeditiously by the committee. An important bill accepted for consideration is usually assigned to a subcommittee, and a decision to hold hearings is usually taken, although the details of their conduct are controlled by the committee, and particularly by its chairman. It is during the legislative hearings that administrative officials and other interested persons attempt to influence the legislative process. This seldom amounts to more than a struggle of special interests competing for recognition and acceptance.

It is at this point that legislative-executive relations are closest. Committee hearings provide the best opportunity for executive officers to express their views on matters of public policy. Hours of testimony may be given by representatives of administrative agencies interested in or affected by proposed legislation. They supply vast quantities of data on which to base legislation. Their specialists advise the committee and even participate in their secret sessions. They reportedly attach themselves to members in charge of particular bills and follow them through to passage. The agencies of the executive branch influence legislation at least as much as do the private lobbyists and legislative "agents."

If extensive hearings are held by a committee of the house in which a major bill originates, the corresponding committee of the second house will often not hold them. However, there are always a few important measures each session on which duplicate hearings are held.

Executive Sessions. When the hearings are ended, the subcommittee reports to its parent group, which will usually meet in secret (executive) session while it considers the bill in the light of information obtained from the hearings. During this time the content of the bill will be amended. What the committee does is determined largely by consultations between its chairman and his party leadership. Here the bill is made acceptable to the party members and leaders and as little offensive as possible to the minority. The committee may decide to kill the measure, but usually it will adopt the bill with amendments, explain in detail what was done and give the reasons therefor, prepare a report on the measure, and send it to the floor of the chamber. If the committee membership divides over the bill, the minority group may prepare a report setting forth its views for the edification and enlightenment of the assembly. However, nothing done in committee takes effect until adopted by its parent chamber.

Each reported measure has a "manager" to guide it through the legislative process. He is backed by majority control, unless the bill is unacceptable and endeavors to secure the adoption of committee amendments —and the defeat of any opposed by the committee. This is usually accomplished with little difficulty, for the houses of Congress seldom repudiate the preparatory work done by the standing committees.

All of this means, of course, that the relative handful of men who compose a particular committee exercise a tremendous influence over the formulation of public policy. Laws are not made by debate and persuasion in full and open assembly, but by a closely guarded weighing and compromising of competing values and pressures upon virtually every part of the legislative machine, and especially upon the standing committees.

Committee Report. The report of a bill sent to the floor will most frequently recommend favorable action, but it may state the adverse opinion of the committee or indicate lack of any committee sentiment. The Senate rules assume that reports will be made directly to the floor, but those of the House require that

All reports of committees, except as provided in clause 21 of Rule XI, together with the views of the minority, shall be delivered to the Clerk for printing and reference to the proper calendar under the direction of the Speaker, in accordance with the foregoing clause, and the titles or subject thereof shall be entered on the Journal and printed in the Record: *Provided,* That bills reported adversely shall be laid on the table, unless the committee reporting a bill, at the time, or any Member within three days thereafter, shall request its reference to the calendar, when it shall be referred to the proper calendar.[3]

[3] *House Rules and Manual,* Rule XIII, clause 2, p. 374.

Seven committees in the House of Representatives have the privilege of reporting at any time.[4] Their privilege carries with it the right to have the report taken up by the House at any time.

Calendars. When measures are reported from committee they are assigned to a calendar in the chronological order in which they have been reported. Thus, a calendar is merely a chronological listing of measures that have been reported from the various standing committees and that are awaiting further consideration. A calendar records the calendar number of the measure, the bill or resolution number, the name of the senator or representative who introduced it, the committee that reported it, and the date and number of the report.

The Senate's is the Calendar of Bills and Resolutions. Measures pending are classified as "Unfinished Business," "Resolutions and Motions Over Under the Rule," "General Orders," "Executive," "Special Orders," etc. Each category of items comprises a separate list maintained for the convenience of the Senate, but for purposes of describing the procedure of the Senate, only one calendar is used in that chamber.

In the House of Representatives, however, there are three major calendars to which all bills reported from committees are assigned according to their subject matter, as follows:

First, a Calendar of the Committee of the Whole House on the state of the Union, to which shall be referred bills raising revenue, general appropriation bills, and bills of a public character directly or indirectly appropriating money or property.

Second, a House Calendar, to which shall be referred all bills of a public character not raising revenue nor directly or indirectly appropriating money or property.

Third, a Calendar of the Committee of the Whole House, to which shall be referred all bills of a private character.[5]

In addition, there are the Consent Calendar, the Discharge Calendar, and the District of Columbia Calendar. With few exceptions measures reported to the House go on one of the main calendars. However, neither assignment of a measure to a particular calendar nor its position thereon necessarily determines the procedure by which, or the order in which, it is considered. The houses may do anything they desire by unanimous consent. Any rule of the House may be suspended by a two-thirds vote, and all rules may be suspended by the same vote at certain designated times. Adoption of a special rule for a particular purpose will permit the doing of anything at any time in any way if the Rules Committee consents to the innovation. Here it is not possible to do more than describe the usual method of procedure and take note of the fact that departures from it are not only easily brought about but extensively employed.

[4] *Ibid.*, Rule XI, clause 21, pp. 357-358.
[5] *Ibid.*, Rule XIII, clause 1, p. 373.

Legislation: (iii) Assembly Debate. The stages of the legislative process thus far have occupied none of the time of either house of Congress. All that has been accomplished has been done in the standing committees. The House and Senate consider a measure by calling up its committee report, usually from its place on the calendar. Such consideration is referred to as debate.

Debate in the halls of Congress probably changes few votes, for it possesses a formal, rather than a persuasive character. In neither house is there much need for real debate intended to carry the issue by the weight of its logic and principle; most major policy decisions are made in committee, or by party agency, so that in the lower house much that is done in debate almost amounts to *pro forma* approval of committee proposals. Therefore, much of the basis for real debate is eliminated. There, more than in the Senate, the membership is conditioned to the restraints imposed on individual initiative in the name of discipline. The individual is dominated by the necessities of the lawmaking process in that chamber. Under such circumstances effective debate is rendered extremely difficult, and much that is said is irrelevant. The rules of the House require that debate should be germane, but a reading of the *Congressional Record* reveals that the requirement is not enforced. In the Senate the rules contain no such requirement, and debate may range freely over any subject. Moreover, Senate debate rambles and jumps rapidly from one subject to another.

Time is the pressing factor in the halls of Congress. This is especially true in the House of Representatives. Control of debate mainly takes the form of control over the time available for it. Increments of time allotted for different purposes make up the daily schedule of the House. Common examples include the "Morning Hour;" a definite period, usually two hours, assigned for general debate in Committee of the Whole; reading for debate under the five-minute rule; ten minutes of debate, five for and five against, on a motion to dispense with Calendar Wednesday; forty minutes of debate on a motion to suspend the rules. The member in charge of a bill is assigned one hour of time when it is called to the floor of the House. He controls that hour, may use all or part of it himself, or may assign portions of it in periods of minutes to other members. On vote he is entitled to another hour. No one in the House may speak more than once on the same issue or for more than one hour on any question in the House or in committee. Time in the House is controlled more stringently than in the Senate; the rules of the House seem to be based on the theory that success of the legislative process depends upon a careful allocation of time.

The Senate rules impose very few restrictions upon debate, but nevertheless it is frequently limited by self-imposed unanimous consent agreements. The Senate rules do provide for a means to end debate by invoking a difficult and largely ineffective procedure. This will be considered below.

Procedure in the Senate. Senate procedure is more simple, and its rules are less formal, precise, and rigid than are those of the House. Custom and precedent largely determine its work habits. Its rules are easily modified by a motion to adopt a course of action "without objection" of the membership, that is, by unanimous consent, and much of what is accomplished there is brought about by such agreements.

In the Senate many measures are called up in their chronological order. The procedure is simple:

RULE VIII

MORNING BUSINESS

At the conclusion of the morning business for each day, unless upon motion the Senate shall at any time otherwise order, the Senate will proceed to the consideration of the Calendar of Bills and Resolutions, and continue such consideration until 2 o'clock: and bills and resolutions that are not objected to shall be taken up in their order, and each Senator shall be entitled to speak once and for five minutes only upon any question; and the objection may be interposed at any stage of the proceedings. . . .[6]

By this method the calendar is called for consideration of "unobjected to" bills and resolutions. Measures are called in their correct order, and each called without objection becomes the order of business until passed or rejected; or if neither occurs, it is carried over as unfinished business until the calendar is next called. If objection is made to a bill when the calendar is called, it is passed over. In practice only non-controversial, usually unimportant bills can be taken up in this expeditious manner; but there are many such bills. By this procedure the Senate conserves its time for important measures.

Important bills in the Senate are seldom taken up in their chronological order from the calendar. Some are considered immediately upon report from committee; some are called up by unanimous consent, but most of those objected to on call of the calendar are brought to the floor by a motion made and passed to consider a specified bill.

Senate bills are never considered in Committee of the Whole. When called up, they are read in full, or are considered as having been read, and are opened for debate and amendment, which proceed apace. Committee amendments take precedence over others. Debate is allowed to range freely and virtually without limitation.

At any time that two-thirds of the senators present so vote, any matter before the Senate may be made the subject of a special order, so that when the time fixed for its consideration arrives, it becomes the order of

---

[6] *Rules and Manual, United States Senate, 1961* (Washington, D.C.: U.S. Government Printing Office, 1961), p. 8, printed as Senate Document No. 2, 87th Congress, 1st session. Hereafter cited as *Senate Manual.*

STICKY WICKET

business. If not finally disposed of on that day, it takes its place on the Calendar of Special Orders, to await final disposition when that calendar is next called. By these procedures virtually all important measures are taken up in the Senate.

Procedure in the House of Representatives—Public Bills. In theory, measures on the calendars of the House are taken up in their chronological order. However, with the exception of bills on the Private Calendar this is rarely true; those on the "public" calendars are virtually never considered in their regular order.

Special Rules. The power to call a bill from a calendar is the power of life or death over it. Normally the Rules Committee will report a "special rule" to set aside the regular course of procedure. Its use has increased greatly over time, and rarely is a non-privileged public bill enacted without a rule. Only the Rules Committee can move adoption of a special rule. Therefore, it can determine which bills it will favor with a rule, but its decisions are usually those of the majority party leadership.

The Rules Committee may be asked to grant a special rule by any member of the House, but it usually responds only to requests by the majority leadership. Since a special rule is one that is made to suspend the regular rules, the resolution proposing it is referred to the Committee on Rules.

This committee is not a legislative committee; it is supposed to be an agency of majority party leadership which regulates the flow of business in the chamber. It is dominated by the majority party and acts in coordination and harmony with its steering committee of the House.[7] However, because of its domination by the majority party and its power to grant or withhold favors, it can not only regulate legislative traffic but also control the content of bills that it is asked to assist. It can determine which measures the House will debate, and upon threat of denying a special rule, compel a committee to put into, or take out of, a measure virtually anything it demands; it determines how much time shall be given to debate; it can specify what amendments may be offered, and in many other ways determine the substance of a measure and the authority of the standing committee over it. It may hold hearings on the *substance* of a bill for which a special rule has been asked; this suggests that it regards itself as a superior legislative committee.

A special rule is not granted automatically. The Rules Committee proceeds in much the same manner as standing committees do in handling bills submitted to them. Applications for rules must be based on either the necessity or the importance of the affected bill. It is the duty of the Rules Committee to facilitate the passage of a public bill which is thought, by the leadership, to have a higher priority than other measures longer on the calendar.

The report of a special rule is placed on the House Calendar, if its privileged status is not invoked to secure immediate consideration. When it has been seven days on the calendar without being called up, any member of the Rules Committee may call it to the floor of the House. Its effect, if adopted, is as follows:

DEPARTMENT OF DEFENSE REORGANIZATION
ACT OF 1958

Mr. Thornberry: Mr. Speaker, by direction of the Committee on Rules, I call up House Resolution 579 and ask for its immediate consideration.

The Clerk read the resolution as follows:

Resolved, That upon the adoption of this resolution it shall be in order to move that the House resolve itself into the Committee of the Whole House on the State of the Union for the consideration of the bill (H.R. 12541) to promote the national defense by providing for reorganization of the Department of Defense, and for other purposes. After general debate, which shall be confined to the bill and continue not to exceed 4 hours, to be equally divided and controlled by the chairman and ranking minority member of the Committee on Armed Services, the bill shall be read for amendment under the 5-minute rule. At the conclusion of the consideration of the bill for amendment, the Committee shall rise and report the bill to the House with such amendments as may have been adopted, and the previous question shall be considered as

[7] *Congressional Record,* 71st Congress, 3rd session (1930), pp. 3699-3700.

ordered on the bill and amendments thereto to final passage without intervening motion except on motion to recommit.[8]

Committee of the Whole. The House of Representatives considers a large proportion of its public bills in what is called Committee of the Whole House on the State of the Union. Thus:

All motions or propositions involving a tax or charge upon the people, all proceedings touching appropriations of money, or bills making appropriations of money or property, or requiring such appropriation to be made, or releasing any liability to the United States for money or property, or referring any claim to the Court of Claims, shall be first considered in a Committee of the Whole, and a point of order under this rule shall be good at any time before the consideration of a bill has commenced.[9]

The Committee of the Whole House is the entire membership of the House, with a chairman presiding. It is a creature of the House. It is what the House makes it; it does what the House permits it. Nothing it does has any binding character until adopted by the House, yet its use has advantages. It enables all members to listen to and participate in debate and amendment of bills. It has certain time-saving characteristics. Debate is both general and detailed. A specified period is set for general debate and is followed immediately by a reading in detail for amendment. No member may then speak for more than five minutes, no time-consuming roll-call votes may be taken, and no delaying motions may be made. Precedence in debate is given to the chairman, to the ranking minority member of the standing committee, to its other members, and then to the House membership. Procedure is more formal than in the House, and a quorum consists of only a hundred members. Bills are considered and amended by the Committee and reported to the House. It may devote several days to one bill or approve several bills on the same day, but once begun, consideration of a bill usually becomes its unfinished business until completed. At the end of a day's sitting the chairman may report:

Mr. Speaker, the Committee of the Whole House on the State of the Union, having had under consideration the bill H.R. 12541, directs me to report that it has come to no resolution thereon.

If the Committee has come to a resolution on the bill, the chairman reports to the Speaker of the House:

Mr. Speaker, the Committee of the Whole House on the State of the Union, having had under consideration the bill H.R. 12541, directs me to report the same with (an amendment or amendments), with the recommendation that the amendment(s) be agreed to and that the bill do (not) pass.

[8] *Congressional Record,* 85th Congress, 2nd session (1958), p. 10883.
[9] *House Rules and Manual,* Rule XXIII, paragraph 3, p. 449.

Bills favorably reported to the House are usually passed by it in from five to thirty minutes. Upon passage of one bill, the House goes on to consider the next that has been agreed upon by the party leadership.

Special Legislative Days. Not all non-privileged public bills obtain a special rule. Many measures reported from committee die on the calendars, but many are benefitted by one of the "special legislative day procedures." On the first and third Mondays of each month public bills to which there is no objection may be called up and passed by unanimous consent. Bills in committees may be forced out and brought to the floor for immediate consideration and passage when the Discharge Calendar is called on the second and fourth Mondays of each month. On Wednesdays, unless dispensed with by a two-thirds vote, opportunity is afforded to the standing committees to call up any measure reported on a previous day and which is on the House or Union Calendar. However, current practice has all but dispensed with this procedure. On the second and fourth Mondays of the month the House Committee on the District of Columbia may call up any measure from the calendar to which it has been assigned. Finally, on the first and third Mondays of the month, and during the last six days of a session, the rules may be suspended by a two-thirds vote. On the first Monday preference is given to individuals, on the third to committees. Use of these special procedures is also largely determined by agreement of the party leadership.

Procedure in the House of Representatives—Private Bills. The enactment by Congress of private bills remains one of its most time-consuming tasks; but it has reduced their number by providing in the Legislative Reorganization Act of 1946 that

No private bill or resolution (including so-called omnibus claims or pension bills), and no amendments to any bill or resolution, authorizing or directing (1) the payment of money for property damages, for personal injuries or death for which suit may be instituted under chapter 171 of the Judicial Code, or for a pension (other than to carry out a provision of law or treaty stipulation); (2) the construction of a bridge across a navigable stream; or (3) the correction of a military or naval record, shall be received or considered in either the Senate or the House of Representatives.[10]

The procedure for enacting private bills is a "special day" procedure limited to private measures. Thus:

On the first Tuesday of each month after disposal of such business on the Speaker's table as requires reference only, the Speaker shall direct the Clerk to call the bills and resolutions on the Private Calendar. Should objection be made by two or more Members to the consideration of any bill or resolution so called, it shall be recommitted to the committee which reported the bill or resolution. . . .

[10] 60 *Statutes* 812, 831.

On the third Tuesday of each month after the disposal of such business on the Speaker's table as requires reference only, the Speaker may direct the Clerk to call the bills and resolutions on the Private Calendar, preference to be given to the omnibus bills containing bills or resolutions which have previously been objected to on a call of the Private Calendar. All bills and resolutions so called, if considered, shall be considered in the House as in Committee of the Whole.[11]

On the first Tuesday of each month private bill procedure is mandatory, but on the third Tuesday the Speaker may use his discretion and substitute other business. Objected-to private bills are returned to committee; they may later be reported as paragraphs of an omnibus bill to be called up on the third Tuesday of each month. The same procedure is used for them as for individual bills, but they are considered by paragraph, each paragraph consisting of a private bill previously objected to, returned to committee, and being reported out for the last time.

An unusual feature of this procedure is the use of "objectors' committees," composed of three or more members of the majority and minority parties respectively. Their task is to read each private bill called up and to register objection on behalf of their party. They are instructed by their respective party leaders which measures or types of measures to oppose, and they object or remain silent accordingly. The majority party objectors screen the bills and the minority party objectors check on their actions. Without the protection given by them it would, theoretically, be possible for huge amounts of public money or property to be given to private persons or corporations contrary to the common good.

Legislation: (iv) Final Passage. Final passage of bills is implicit in the procedure of both the House and the Senate. In the House, bills are called and considered in Committee of the Whole or in the House, according to their characters. In each instance passage is pushed to completion or defeat as soon as possible. When the process of debate and amendment is completed, the question "to engross and read a third time" is put automatically. If it carries, third reading by title only is had immediately, and the final version of the measure with all amendments is printed; but if a member demands a third reading in full, the reading must be delayed until a printed copy of the bill in amended form can be obtained. The bill is engrossed and signed by the Speaker and clerk and sent to the Senate. It is now an "act" and goes through the special procedure employed by the Senate.

If the measure is a Senate bill passed by the House without amendment, it goes back to the Senate to be enrolled (printed in the form as passed by both houses, and signed by the Speaker of the House and the President of the Senate), and is then sent to the White House for the

[11] *House Rules and Manual*, Rule XXIV, p. 4661.

President's signature. It is by this procedure that Congress carries out its lawmaking function.

Conference. In order for a bill to become law, it must pass both houses of Congress in exactly the same form. This frequently is the case when both houses have completed action, but for virtually every controversial piece of legislation the House and Senate versions will differ. The house that alters a bill originated by the other chamber may request it to accept the changes. If the changes are rejected, the house responsible for them may withdraw them. However, if the one will not accept the changes and the second will not relinquish them, and if no way can be found to reconcile the differences, the measure will be lost. Coincidence cannot be relied upon to achieve agreement. Hence, Congress employs a more deliberate procedure to obtain it.

This procedure utilizes *ad hoc* committees, called conference committees. A separate one is established for each bill over which the House and Senate have disagreed. Members of the committees are called managers. Each represents the opinion of its house in a conference held to compromise differences. Their nature and procedure is controlled as follows:

Statement of principles governing the selection of Conferences on the part of the House . . . namely:

The House members of conference committees, called the managers on the part of the House, are appointed by the Speaker.

They are usually three in number, but on important measures the number is sometimes increased. In the selection of the managers the two large political parties are usually represented, and, also, care is taken that there shall be a representation of the two opinions which almost always exist on subjects of importance. Of course the majority party and the prevailing opinion have the majority of the managers. . . .

It is also almost invariable practice to select managers from the members of the committee which considered the bill. . . . But sometimes in order to give representation to a strong or prevailing sentiment in the House the Speaker goes outside the ranks of the committee. . . .

The managers of the two Houses while in conference vote separately, the majority determining the attitude to be taken toward the propositions of the other House. When the report is made the signatures of a majority of each board of managers are sufficient. The minority managers frequently refrain from signing the report, and it is not unprecedented for a minority manager to endorse his protest on the report.

When conferees have disagreed or a conference report has been rejected, the usual practice is to reappoint the managers. . . .

Conferees having been appointed, it is too late to reconsider the vote whereby the House has disagreed to a Senate amendment. . . .

CONFERENCE COMMITTEES AND REPORTS
Authority of Conference Committees

A conference committee is practically two distinct committees, each of which acts by a majority. . . .

Conference reports must be signed by a majority of the managers on the part of each House. They are made in duplicate for the managers to present to their respective Houses, the signatures of the managers of each House appearing first on the report that is to be presented to the House they represent. . . .

Conferees may not include in their report matters not committed to them by either House. . . .

Conferees may not strike out in conference anything in a bill agreed to and passed by both Houses. . . .

A conference committee may report agreement as to some of the matters of difference, but inability to agree as to others. . . .

Presentation and Privilege of Conference Reports

A conference report is made first to the House agreeing to the conference. . . .

Conference reports are in order in the Senate . . . as follows:
The presentation of reports of committees of conference shall always be in order, except when the Journal is being read or a question of order or a motion to adjourn is pending, or while the Senate is dividing; and when received, the question of proceeding to the consideration of the report, if raised, shall be immediately put, and shall be determined without debate. . . .

Conference reports are in order in the House . . . as follows:
The presentation of reports of committees of conference shall always be in order except when the Journal is being read, while the roll is being called, or the House is dividing on any question. And there shall accompany any such report a detailed statement sufficiently explicit to inform the House what effect such amendments or propositions shall have upon the measures to which they relate. . . .

A conference report may not be received by the House if no statement accompanies it. . . .

The rejection of a conference report leaves the matter in the position it occupied before the conference was asked. . . .

Amendment of Conference Report

It is not in order to amend a conference report, and it must be accepted or rejected as an entirety.[12]

[12] See Cleaves' Manual of the Law and Practice in Regard to Conferences and Conference Reports as reproduced in *Senate Rules and Manual*, pp. 141-156. See also "How Conference Committees Work," *Congressional Quarterly*, Vol. 17, No. 18, pp. 597-598.

When the conference committee has fulfilled its function the houses may accept the report and discharge the managers. If continued disagreement prevails, the committee report may be accepted in so far as it reflects agreement, and instruction may be given to continue conferring on the remaining points of difference; or the committee may be discharged, the effort abandoned and the bill lost; or the committee may be discharged and replaced by a new one.

The importance of the conference committees to the legislative process is inverse to their small size. Their essential function is to bring about compromise, but compromise frequently is dependent upon delicately balanced considerations. Hence, upon the ability of these committees to perform their function rests not only the successful completion of the legislative process but also the provision of public policy to enhance and safeguard subjects of common interest. Moreover, the small size of the committees, and the secrecy which surrounds their activities, make them favorite points upon which lobbyists, public or private, bring to bear their efforts to influence the legislative process. This is especially true when the disagreement of the two houses is wide, for then the conferees are able virtually to write a new bill.

OTHER FEATURES
OF THE LEGISLATIVE PROCESS

Of Decorum and Debate. The procedure in the House and Senate is orderly; it is orderly because the rules of the houses regulate what may be done and said. With few exceptions, the requirements of the House of Representatives are typical of those of the Senate also; they state:

1. When any Member desires to speak or deliver any matter to the House, he shall rise and respectfully address himself to "Mr. Speaker," and, on being recognized, may address the House from any place on the floor or from the Clerk's desk, and shall confine himself to the question under debate, avoiding personality. . . .

2. When two or more Members rise at once, the Speaker shall name the Member who is first to speak; . . . and no Member shall occupy more than one hour in debate on any question in the House or in committee, except as further provided in this rule. . . .

4. If any Member, in speaking or otherwise, transgress the rules of the House, the Speaker shall, or any Member may, call him to order; in which case he shall immediately sit down, unless permitted, on motion of another Member, to explain, and the House shall, if appealed to, decide on the case without debate; if the decision is in favor of the Member called to order, he shall be at liberty to proceed, but not otherwise; and, if the case require it, he shall be liable to censure or such punishment as the House may deem proper. . . .

6. No Member shall speak more than once to the same question without leave of the House, unless he be the mover, proposer, or introducer of the matter pending, in which case he shall be permitted to speak in reply, but not until every Member choosing to speak shall have spoken. . . .

7. While the Speaker is putting a question or addressing the House no Member shall walk out of or across the hall, nor, when a Member is speaking, pass between him and the Chair; and during the session of the House no Member shall wear his hat, or remain by the Clerk's desk during the call of roll or the counting of ballots, or smoke upon the floor of the House; and the Sergeant-at-Arms and Doorkeeper are charged with the strict enforcement of this clause. Neither shall any person be allowed to smoke upon the floor of the House at any time.

8. It shall not be in order for any Member to introduce to or bring to the attention of the House during its sessions any occupant in the galleries of the House; nor may the Speaker entertain a request for the suspension of this rule by unanimous consent or otherwise.[13]

Every member is required to be present within the hall of the House during its sittings, unless excused or necessarily prevented, and he must vote on each question put, unless he has a direct personal or pecuniary interest, although personal interest rarely prevents voting.

Closure. To protect the time of legislative assemblies from waste, and to enable the majority to protect its legislation from the delaying tactics of a vigorously obstructive minority, the rules usually provide some method whereby debate can be terminated at the will of a majority of members. That process is known as closure or cloture.

Closure—Senate. Because Senators may speak as long as they are capable, the practice of filibustering has developed.[14] Senators opposed to a pending measure endeavor to secure its modification by obtaining and holding the floor until concessions are made to their demands. If this occurs at the end of a session when the pressure of time is greatest, they are often able to force the abandonment of a bill so that the Senate can consider other legislation.

Although the Senate cherishes the tradition of free debate which it has established, closure can be invoked by fulfilling certain conditions:

. . . At any time a motion signed by sixteen Senators, to bring to a close the debate upon any measure, motion, or other matter pending before the Senate, or the unfinished business, is presented to the Senate, the Presiding Officer shall at once state the motion to the Senate, and one hour after the Senate meets on the following day but one, he shall lay the motion before the Senate and direct that the Secretary call the roll, and, upon the ascertainment that a quorum is present, the presiding officer shall, without debate, submit to the Senate by a yea-and-nay vote the question:

[13] *House Rules and Manual,* Rule XIV, pp. 377-386.
[14] See "History, Techniques of Senate Filibusters," *Congressional Quarterly Weekly Report* Vol. 18, No. 10, pp. 337-339.

"Is it the sense of the Senate that the debate shall be brought to a close?"

And if that question shall be decided in the affirmative by two-thirds of the Senators present and voting, then said measure, motion, or other matter pending before the Senate, or the unfinished business, shall be the unfinished business to the exclusion of all other business until disposed of.

Thereafter no Senator shall be entitled to speak in all more than one hour on the measure, motion, or other matter pending before the Senate, or the unfinished business, the amendments thereto, and motions affecting the same, and it shall be the duty of the Presiding Officer to keep the time of each Senator who speaks. Except by unanimous consent, no debate shall be in order after the motion to bring the debate to a close, unless the same has been presented and read prior to that time. No dilatory motion, or dilatory amendment, or amendment not germane shall be in order. Points of order, including questions of relevancy, and appeals from the decision of the Presiding Officer shall be decided without debate.[15]

Freedom of debate is the rule; closure is the rare exception, and the former may triumph over the latter although votes are available to cut off debate.

Closure—House of Representatives. The House of Representatives possesses a very effective, simple, and long-established method of closing debate. It takes the form of a motion to "put the previous question," the previous question being whatever the question then before the House might be. Thus:

There shall be a motion for the previous question, which, being ordered by a majority of Members voting, if a quorum be present, shall have the effect to cut off all debate and bring the House to a direct vote upon the immediate question or questions on which it has been asked and ordered. The previous question may be asked and ordered upon a single motion, a series of motions allowable under the rules, or an amendment or amendments, or may be made to embrace all authorized motions or amendments and include the bill to its passage or rejection.[16]

Voting. Several forms of voting are used. Votes are taken *viva voce,* the "Aye's" and "No's" being called out by the members upon the request of the chair, who says: "As many as are in favor (as the question may be), say 'Aye'"; and after the affirmative voice is expressed: "As many as are opposed, say 'No'." If the presiding officer is in doubt of the outcome, or if the members would like the matter to be voted on by another method, a vote by division, tellers, or roll call may be had. On division, the Speaker says: "As many as are in favor will rise and stand until counted." After the affirmative votes have been counted, the members wishing to vote in the negative are directed to stand and be counted. The Presiding Officer counts and announces the result to the chamber.

[15] *Senate Rules and Manual,* Rule XXII, p. 23.
[16] *House Rules and Manual,* Rule XVII, pp. 411-412.

However, if one-fifth of a quorum are dissatisfied with these procedures they may order a vote by tellers or by roll call. When tellers are employed, the chair names one member from each side of the question to tell the votes in the affirmative and those in the negative. The tellers stand on either side of the center aisle and count members who pass between them. After those in the affirmative have been counted, the tellers report the number to the chair; then the chair announces: "As many as are opposed will now pass between the tellers and be counted." The number of those in the negative is then reported, after which there is an opportunity for additional members to vote on either side, the tellers reporting the additions. Then the chair reports the vote.

If a roll call vote is ordered in the House, the Speaker directs:

As many as are in favor (as the question may be) will, as their names are called, answer "Yea;" and as many as are opposed will answer "Nay." The Clerk will call the roll.

To take a vote by roll call in the House an average of six hundred names must be read, and the time required approximates one half hour. The average time for roll call in the Senate is about eight minutes. Therefore, the roll call is used more frequently there than in the House. This time-consuming method of voting is the only method which enables a permanent record of the individual votes of members to be obtained.

CHAPTER XV

The Presidency: Office and Choice

'Primary's Anyone?'

THE PRESIDENCY OF THE UNITED STATES

The first sentence of Article II of the Constitution establishes the office, position, and authority of the President by declaring that

The executive Power shall be vested in a President of the United States of America.

Thus, he alone holds the great, undefined, and largely unlimited executive power. He is *head* of the executive branch and is *the* executive of the United States. No other officer can challenge his position. Only the Vice President is independent of the President's removal power.

Qualification of the President. The Constitution declares that

No Person except a natural born Citizen, or a Citizen of the United States, at the time of the Adoption of this Constitution, shall be eligible to the Office of President; neither shall any Person be eligible to that Office who shall not have attained to the Age of thirty five years, and been fourteen Years a Resident within the United States.

Naturalized citizens are disqualified, as may also be citizens at birth by the principle of *jus sanguinis,* although that is not probable. The residence requirement is satisfied by any period or periods totaling fourteen years lived within the United States prior to the assumption of the office of President. These qualifications are intended to protect the people against the folly of their own action, but they have not yet been of practical importance.

The question may be asked whether every person who possesses these qualifications is suitable to be President of the United States. Congress has in fact enacted statutes which, *inter alia,* disqualify from "holding office under the United States" persons guilty of inciting to rebellion or insurrection against the United States, and officers of the United States convicted of taking bribes. Hence, such persons may not be elected President.

Term of Office. The Constitution sets the President's term of office at four years, to begin at noon, January 20, following each presidential election. The four-year term represents a compromise reached at Philadelphia between the alternatives of life tenure, one seven-year term, and a four-year term with re-eligibility. However, re-eligibility has been modified by the Twenty-Second Amendment to be considered below.

The Two-Term Tradition and the Twenty-Second Amendment. Sentiment at Philadelphia favored indefinite re-eligibility for the President, although the Constitution is silent on the subject. From 1789 to 1940 custom decreed that a President should not serve more than two terms, but the intervening years involved the two-term tradition in weakening confusion. Finally, in 1940 and 1944 it was shattered by the third and fourth elections of Franklin Roosevelt.

Adoption of the Twenty-Second Amendment followed. It states:

No person shall be elected to the office of the President more than twice, and no person who has held the office of President, or acted as President, for more than two years of a term to which some other person was elected President shall be elected to the office of the President more than once. But this Article shall not apply to any person holding the office of President when this Article was proposed by the Congress, and shall not prevent any person who may be holding the office of President, or acting as President, during the term within which this Article becomes operative from holding the office of President or acting as President during the remainder of such term.

Thus, a President may succeed himself once and serve two terms totaling eight years. A Vice President who has filled a vacancy may serve a maximum of ten years less one day, or a minimum of six years plus one day. On the death of a President-elect, the Vice President becomes President and may be elected only once in his own right.

Opinion on the Amendment is divided. Some persons hail it as a necessary safeguard against the rise of demagogues and men on horseback; others regard it as an undemocratic and foolish restriction on the processes of self-government. It is condemned as the product of a partisan attack upon a deceased President and an example of political tampering with the Constitution. It is said to ignore the intent of the framers of the Constitution and to displace a flexible custom, strongly supported by public opinion, with an inflexible law. A President desired by the people or demanded by national emergency cannot be retained. Limited experience with the amendment has somewhat demonstrated the weakening effect which ineligibility has upon a President during the last years of his term.

Succession to the Presidency. In the event that the Presidency becomes vacant by

. . . the Removal of the President from Office, or of his Death, Resignation, or Inability to discharge the Powers and Duties of the said Office, the Same shall devolve on the Vice President, and the Congress may by law provide for the Case of Removal, Death, Resignation or Inability, both of the President and Vice President, declaring what Officer shall then act as President, and such Officer shall act accordingly, until the Disability be removed, or a President shall be elected.

The words "shall act as President" suggests that a Vice President who succeeds to the Presidency should remain Vice President but act as President. However, precedent has firmly established that he becomes the President.

The Twentieth Amendment to the Constitution has supplemented the provisions of the above section by stating that

If, at the time fixed for the beginning of the term of the President, the President elect shall have died, the Vice President elect shall become President. If a President shall not have been chosen before the time fixed for the beginning of his term, or if the President elect shall have failed to qualify, then the Vice President elect shall act as President until a President shall have qualified; and the Congress may by law provide for the case wherein neither a President elect nor a Vice President elect shall have qualified, declaring who shall then act as President, or the manner in which one who is to act shall be selected, and such person shall act accordingly until a President or Vice President shall have qualified.

The Congress may by law provide for the case of the death of any of the persons from whom the House of Representatives may choose a President whenever the right of choice shall have devolved upon them, and for the case of the death of any of the persons from whom the Senate may choose a Vice President whenever the right of choice shall have devolved upon them.

Removal is possible by means of impeachment, but no President has been convicted. Eight have died in office. None has resigned. On three occasions the President has been unable "to discharge the powers and duties" of his office. But, what constitutes "inability," and who is to determine its existence and termination? Is a disabled President permanently ousted from office or displaced only until the "inability" is, removed?

The questions remain unanswered, and so far no Vice President has assumed the powers and duties of the office. Congress seemingly feels the matter is so complicated and politically charged that no effort to resolve it should be made.

Succession Beyond the Vice President. Congress may also provide for succession to the Presidency beyond the Vice President. Succession has not gone beyond the Vice President; but this is mere chance, for any one of the several Vice Presidents who have become President could have suffered the fate of his predecessor. The current law provides that after the Vice President succession passes first to the Speaker of the House, the President *pro tempore* of the Senate, and thence to the heads of the executive departments in the order of their creation. If the eligible successor meets the constitutional qualifications for President, he acts as President until the end of the term. However, if his discharge of the powers and duties of the office is based on the failure of the President-elect and Vice President-elect to qualify, or on the disability of the President or Vice President, he acts only until one or the other qualifies, or the disability is removed from one of them.

This scheme has advantages and disadvantages. It provides for the filling of vacancies caused by failure of the President and Vice President to qualify. It continues the principle that an elected official should succeed to the Presidency, if succession does not progress further than two places after the Vice President. It would, at least during the time of a succession, strengthen legislative-executive relations. However, it permits Congress to designate the successor after the Vice President. And, it is questionable that the Speaker and President *pro tempore* are "officers" within the meaning of the Constitution. It could precipitate a change of party control of the executive without an election. It is more than possible that a Speaker, or a President *pro tempore,* since each is a senior member of his chamber, will be out of step with opinion in the country and the party.

Oath of the President. The Constitution requires that a President should take an oath of office, which it prescribes as follows:

Before he enter on the Execution of his Office, he shall take the following Oath or Affirmation:—"I do solemnly swear (or affirm) that I will faithfully execute the Office of President of the United States, and will to the best of my Ability, preserve, protect and defend the Constitution of the United States."

Remuneration of the President. The Constitution also provides that

The President shall, at stated Times, receive for his Services, a Compensation, which shall neither be encreased nor diminished during the Period for which he shall have been elected, and he shall not receive within that Period any other Emolument from the United States, or any of them.

However, Congress has fixed the amount of presidential remuneration subject to the prescribed safeguards, as follows:

Compensation of the President.

The President shall receive in full for his services during the term for which he shall have been elected compensation in the aggregate amount of $100,000 a year, to be paid monthly, and in addition an expense allowance of $50,000 to assist in defraying expenses relating to or resulting from the discharge of his official duties, for which expense allowance no accounting other than for income tax purposes, shall be made by him. He shall be entitled also to the use of the furniture and other effects belonging to the United States and kept in the Executive Mansion.

Traveling expenses.

There may be expended for or on account of the traveling expenses of the President of the United States such sum as Congress may from time to time appropriate, not exceeding $40,000 per annum, such sum when appropriated to be expended in the discretion of the President and accounted for on his certificate only.[1]

In addition to the cash remuneration authorized by Congress, the President enjoys numerous perquisites of office.

NOMINATION OF THE PRESIDENT

When the voter goes into the polling place on election day he is presented with a ballot upon which appear the names of two or more candidates for the office of President of the United States. For one or another of these candidates the average voter casts his vote. The effective choice which he is able to make is thus restricted within exceedingly narrow limits. In practice, therefore, paramount importance attaches to the means by which the candidates, whose names appear upon the general election ballots, have been selected. This process is known as nomination. As applied to presidential and vice presidential candidates it is accomplished at present through the national conventions of the two major political parties.

Pre-convention Campaigning. Before the national nominating conventions meet in early summer, persons seeking nomination engage in ex-

[1] *U.S. Code*, Title 3, secs. 102-103.

tensive campaigning. They try to prove their popularity and vote-getting ability, make themselves known, win over party leaders and influential personages, gain the support of party organizations, and secure the support of delegates to the national conventions. However, hopefuls of the in-party whose President is able to succeed himself have no problem of this nature. They must wait until he does not or cannot run. Even then they may be "frozen out" by the President's personal endorsement of an aspirant, as President Eisenhower's grooming and endorsement of Vice President Nixon in 1960 virtually eliminated all other Republican aspirants to the presidential nomination. Aspirants of the out-party must seek its nomination. They must be "available," that is they must possess the "right" legal, moral, and political qualifications to win.

After "availability" however, the usual key to success is organization. A well-organized, smoothly operating, extensive and well-financed campaign machine is essential. It must possess brains, imagination, personnel, political "savvy," leadership, and enthusiasm. That of Senator John F. Kennedy in the 1960 pre-convention campaign will serve as an illustration. It included a chief political adviser, a foreign policy adviser, an experienced political strategist, a polling specialist, and several advance observers. The Senator and his strategist traveled over a million miles gathering knowledge of the peculiarities of American politics, people, and problems, and formulating ideas. Election laws, electoral jurisdictions, and local situations were studied in detail and at first hand. A card file of some 29,000 names and addresses of influential Democrats and party leaders was assembled. In the spring of 1959, more than twelve months before convention time, the advance men, using the card file, began to build organizations to aid Senator Kennedy's drive for the nomination. By the following November, seven months before convention time, a trusted leader had been placed in every state, and organizations built in the ones in whose primaries the Senator intended to participate.

In Washington a headquarters for the campaign was established, and staffed with a general manager, a publicity director, advance men, and secretaries and switchboard operators. It was stocked with campaign buttons, bumper stickers, photographs, film clips, news releases, and other assorted paraphernalia. A fourteen-page manual on "Kennedy for President State Organizational Procedure," a kind of organizational masterplan, was prepared in detail, but flexibility was the keynote of local operations to adapt each effort to local needs.

During the campaign period the Senator was seen publicly on every occasion possible. He walked the streets moving in and out of cafes and businesses shaking hands and greeting persons casually encountered, he spoke to delegations and groups, made impromptu television appearances, addressed rallies, held press meetings, made statements on current public issues, formulated policy positions, made numerous trips to states whose primaries had been entered, "stumped" them extensively prior to primary day, and contacted scores of local and state politicians whose support was indispensable to success. Meanwhile, state organizations had to be built. Leaders were chosen for congressional districts, appeals to various interests were planned, campaign paraphernalia were procured for the state and local units, volunteer workers located, meetings and rallies held, literature prepared and distributed, and funds raised.

Prior to the Wisconsin primary on April 5, Senator Kennedy campaigned to win the Democratic vote and delegate support from Senator Hubert Humphrey, a native of the region and a rival aspirant. He "stumped" the state extensively, aided by his wife, two cousins, a brother-in-law, three sisters, two brothers, and his mother, a veteran of senatorial election and the New Hampshire primary fights. His sisters, aiming for the women's vote, made "Coffee with the Kennedys" a popular slogan in Wisconsin by conducting "coffee hour receptions" in private homes across the state. Hostesses were selected from various backgrounds, political, social and economic. Each invited about fifty friends to "meet the Kennedys." A "Kennedy Kit" containing campaign buttons, a statement of Senator Kennedy's views, an account of his war record, a "business reply" letter requesting the names of women who would support him, an attack upon him by the President of the Teamsters' Union, and a postal card to be returned by any lady willing to sponsor a "coffee hour," was given to each guest. The Senator's brothers directed the primary campaign, stuffed envelopes, ran the headquarters and organizational machinery, made numerous speeches, distributed literature at factory gates, and shook thousands of hands. They visited many small, out-of-the-way places that otherwise could not have been contacted. The aspirant visited dozens of small towns, speaking to audiences wherever he could find them. Often he was preceded or followed by another Kennedy. Throughout the feverish activity, however, ran the "soft sell." Conversation at coffees ran to small talk, with politics injected subtly and at their conclusion. In some speeches the primary was left unmentioned.[2]

All of this must be done by or for a serious aspirant to the presidential nomination. Seldom is the effort as extensive or as well-organized as was that of the Kennedy forces, for most hopefuls lack the appeal and support necessary to the endeavor. They may enter a "key" primary or two and try to keep their names in the public mind, but most hope that the lightning will strike them at the national convention. At the convention the aspirants trade on the strength they have built and vie with one another to gain the nomination. A deadlock there may throw the prize to a rela-

---

[2] Pre-convention campaigning is expensive. Costs are, for the most part, not paid out of party funds but are met out-of-pocket, by fund-raising activities, by generous friends, and by public contributions. Reliable estimates of expenditures are supplied by Alexander Heard, an authority on the subject, in an interview reported in *U.S. News and World Report*, May 28, 1962, p. 75.

"On to the Next State, Boys"

tive unknown who has not actively sought it. On the other hand, one man may have so outdistanced the others as to make the conferring of the nomination "no contest." When these conditions do not prevail, however, pre-convention efforts usually entail six to eight months of planning, organizing, and campaigning. So successful was Kennedy in his build-up of strength in the primaries that interest in its preservation and use was stimulated anew.

Based upon his experiences with the pre-convention campaigns of 1952 and 1956, Adlai Stevenson declared that the object is "to win friends and influence people." This requires the candidate to bow to local interests and whims to the extent of wearing "silly hats" and eating "indigestible food," "denouncing the Japanese beetle," "fearlessly attacking the Mediterranean fruit fly," speaking on every subject from "nuclear bomb tests to the tariff on tuna," with much repetition and small audiences. The effort neither clarifies national issues nor embraces those deserving the attention of a presidential candidate. It necessitates beginning in January and continuing until June, moving directly into the national convention contest, and then plunging immediately into the general election campaign. Hence, the rules of the game require extensive "perambulating, incessant exposure and talk," a grueling, exhausting experience involving ten months of total effort, 300 speeches, and 75,000 miles of travel, during which the candidate becomes "weary, frustrated and bored." Emphasis is mainly on appeals to party workers and small groups of voters in "halls, hotels, and picnic grounds." A premium attaches to local, parochial issues unrelated to the Presidency. Effort is concentrated on the "key" primary states where the candidate feels he can make a good showing. Hence, the campaigning becomes localized and is directed to audiences not much interested in national issues, but concerned with immediate party matters, and with "meeting the candidate."[3]

Composition of the National Convention. The parties regulate the composition of their national conventions by rules applied by the national committees. Six months prior to the convention they send to their respective state chairmen a "call" to the convention, informing them of the time and place of its meeting and the number of votes their states will have.

ALLOCATION OF VOTES IN THE NATIONAL CONVENTIONS BY GEOGRAPHICAL AREAS

Number of Votes				
Democrats			Republicans	
1956	1960		1956	1960
392	412	South	325	327
364	410	East	372	378
356	404	Midwest	378	372
242	271	West	238	242
18	24	Territories	10	12
1372	1521	TOTAL	1323	1331

Percent of Votes				
Democrats			Republicans	
1956	1960		1956	1960
28.6%	27.1%	South	24.6%	24.6%
26.5	26.9	East	28.1	28.4
26.0	26.6	Midwest	28.6	27.9
17.6	17.8	West	18.0	18.2
1.3	1.6	Territories	.7	.9
100.0%	100.0%	TOTAL	100.0%	100.0%

Adapted from *Presidential '60,* a *Congressional Quarterly* special report (November, 1959), p. 33.

The composition of the 1960 Democratic national convention was determined by the following method of apportioning votes among the states:

[3] Adlai Stevenson, "Choice by Hullabaloo," reprinted from *This Week Magazine,* February 28, 1960. Copyright 1960 by the United Newspapers Magazine Corporation. An interesting modern political document came to light in 1959 consisting of the views of the late Senator Robert A. Taft on the primary and convention fights of 1952. It is printed in *U.S. News and World Report,* December 7, 1959, pp. 109-111.

1. Delegates and alternates: two delegates and one alternate could be selected for each vote to which a state was entitled in convention, except for votes reserved to members of the Democratic National Committee. The maximum number of delegates was 3,042; alternates, 1,467. There were 1,521 votes, with 761 necessary to nominate.

2. Votes were allocated to the states thus: for each senator and representative the state received 2½ votes, plus an additional ½ vote in any instance when this formula yielded a fractional result. Each state was given an additional vote to be divided between the national committeeman and woman, or to persons they designated.

3. The District of Columbia was allotted eight votes, Puerto Rico six, and the Canal Zone and the Virgin Islands three votes each.

4. No state was allowed to have fewer votes in the 1960 convention than it had had in 1956. When necessary the total votes of a state were increased by the addition of at-large votes until the greater number was attained.

The 1960 Republican national convention contained 1,331 votes, each cast whole by one delegate.[4] The number of votes necessary to receive nomination was 666. Delegates were chosen according to the following formula:

1. Delegates-at-large: two for each senator and two for each representative-at-large to which a state was entitled in Congress. Six bonus delegates-at-large for each state which had cast its electoral votes for Eisenhower in 1956, or which had elected a GOP senator or governor in 1956 or later.

2. District delegates: one district delegate for each congressional district casting two thousand (2,000) votes or more for any Republican elector in the last preceding presidential election or for the Republican nominee for Congress in the last preceding congressional election.

3. One additional district delegate for each congressional district casting ten thousand (10,000) votes or more for any Republican elector in the last preceding presidential election or for the Republican nominee for Congress in the last preceding congressional election.

4. The District of Columbia was allowed eight delegates-at-large and four additional if the delegate to Congress elected at the last election had been a Republican. Puerto Rico was allowed three delegates-at-large and the Virgin Islands one.[5]

Thus the Republican Party distributes its at-large votes among the states so as to give each an approximately equal voice in convention, but district votes are added in rough proportion to the party's strength in each state. In this way state party organizations are encouraged to work for the election of candidates for national office, and those states in which the efforts are successful are rewarded with a greater voice, in convention, in the determination of party business.

[4] The Republican Party does not permit splitting of votes, so that the number of votes and the number of delegates is the same. The Democratic convention permits half votes.

[5] Adapted from *Presidential '60,* a *Congressional Quarterly* special report (November, 1959), p. 33.

CHOICE OF NATIONAL CONVENTION DELEGATES

	Democrats		Republicans			Democrats		Republicans	
	District	At Large	District	At Large		District	At Large	District	At Large
Alabama	P	P	Co.C D.C.	S.C.	Montana	S.C.	S.C.	S.C.	S.C.
Alaska	S.C.	S.C.	S.C.	S.C.	Nebraska	P	P	P	P
Arizona	S.C.C.	S.C.C.	S.C.C.	S.C.C.	Nevada	S.C.	S.C.	S.C.	S.C.
Arkansas	S.C.C.	S.C.C.	D.Cm.	S.C.C.	New Hampshire	P	P	P	P
California	P	P	P	P	New Jersey	P	P	P	P
Colorado	D.C.	S.C.	D.C.	S.C.	New Mexico	S.C.	S.C.	S.C.	S.C.
Connecticut	S.C.	S.C.	D.C.	S.C.	New York	P	S.C.C.	P	S.C.C.
Delaware	S.C.	S.C.	S.C.	S.C.	North Carolina	S.C.	S.C.	D.C.	S.C.
Florida	P	P	P	P	North Dakota	S.C.	S.C.	S.C.	S.C.
Georgia	S.C.C.	S.C.C.	D.C.	S.C.	Ohio	P	P	P	P
Hawaii	S.C.	S.C.	S.C.	S.C.	Oklahoma	½ D.C.	½ S.C.	D.C.	S.C.
Idaho	S.C.	S.C.	S.C.	S.C.	Oregon	P	P	P	P
Illinois	P	S.C.	P	S.C.	Pennsylvania	P	S.C.C.	P	S.C.C.
Indiana	S.C.	S.C.	D.C.	S.C.	Rhode Island	S.C.	S.C.	S.C.	S.C.
Iowa	S.C.	S.C.	D.C.	S.C.	South Carolina	S.C.	S.C.	S.C.	S.C.
Kansas	S.C.	S.C.	D.C.	S.C.	South Dakota	P	P	P	P
Kentucky	D.C.	S.C.	D.C.	S.C.	Tennessee	S.C.	S.C.	D.C.	S.C.
Louisiana	S.C.C.	S.C.C.	D.C.	S.C.	Texas	S.C.	S.C.	S.C.	S.C.
Maine	S.C.	S.C.	D.C.	S.C.	Utah	S.C.	S.C.	D.C.	S.C.
Maryland	S.C.	S.C.	S.C.	S.C.	Vermont	S.C.	S.C.	S.C.	S.C.
Massachusetts	P	P	P	P	Virginia	S.C.	S.C.	D.C.	S.C.
Michigan	D.C.	S.C.	D.C.	S.C.	Washington	S.C.	S.C.	D.C.	S.C.
Minnesota	D.C.	S.C.	D.C.	S.C.	West Virginia	P	P	P	P
Mississippi	S.C.	S.C.	S.C.	S.C.	Wisconsin	P	P	P	P
Missouri	S.C.	S.C.	D.C.	S.C.	Wyoming	S.C.	S.C.	S.C.	S.C.
District of Columbia	P	P	P	P	Puerto Rico	C.C.	C.C.	C.C.	C.C.
Canal Zone	T.C.	T.C.	—	—	Virgin Islands	T.C.	T.C.	T.C.	T.C.

Adapted from data compiled and presented by *Congressional Quarterly*, Vol. 18, No. 7, p. 225.

C.C.—Commonwealth Convention   S.C.C.—State Committee
D.C.—District Convention   C.C.—County Convention
T.C.—Territorial Convention   D.Cm.—District Committee
S.C.—State Convention   P—Primary

Selection of Delegates to the National Convention. Various methods are used to select delegates to the national conventions. Fifteen states and the District of Columbia elect about one-third of the delegates by primary;[6] thirty states select approximately two-thirds by state and district conventions, and a small minority are appointed in six states by state committees. Use of state and district conventions and of state committees for this purpose removes selection of the national nominees several steps away from individual party members.

[6] See *Congressional Quarterly Weekly Report,* Vol. 18, No. 10, pp. 341-348, for a detailed state-by-state analysis of presidential primaries.

DEMOCRATIC NOMINEE FOR PRESIDENT
761 Votes Needed

DEMOCRATIC NATIONAL CONVENTION
Los Angeles, July 11
2,934 Delegates With 1,521 Votes
(Kentucky: 62 Delegates With 31 Votes,
Including 2 National Committee Members)

DEMOCRATIC STATE CONVENTION
Louisville, June 25, at 2 p.m. C.D.T.
(2,381 Delegates With 1 Vote Each)

Elects 12 Half-Vote National Convention Delegates-At-Large;
May Ratify 48 Half-Vote Delegates Chosen At District Convention

All District Conventions To Be Held At 10 A.M. C.D.T. In Louisville June 25

EIGHTH DISTRICT CONVENTION
169 Delegates
Elects Six Half-Vote National Convention Delegates

Bell	22
Clay	5
Clinton	4
Cumberland	5
Harlan	35
Jackson	3
Knox	13
Laurel	12
Leslie	3
McCreary	4
Monroe	6
Owsley	2
Pulaski	19
Rockcastle	7
Russell	6
Wayne	11
Whitley	13

SEVENTH DISTRICT CONVENTION
368 Delegates
Elects Six Half-Vote National Convention Delegates

Bath	11
Boyd	43
Breathitt	16
Carter	11
Elliott	11
Floyd	40
Greenup	25
Johnson	12
Knott	20
Lawrence	12
Lee	5
Letcher	21
Magoffin	11
Martin	3
Menifee	6
Morgan	16
Perry	23
Pike	57
Rowan	12
Wolfe	8

SIXTH DISTRICT CONVENTION
336 Delegates
Elects Six Half-Vote National Convention Delegates

Bourbon	16
Boyle	17
Casey	8
Clark	18
Estill	10
Fayette	68
Franklin	32
Garrard	9
Harrison	18
Henry	16
Jessamine	10
Lincoln	15
Madison	28
Montgomery	13
Nicholas	8
Owen	15
Powell	7
Robertson	4
Scott	14
Woodford	10

FIFTH DISTRICT CONVENTION
244 Delegates
Elects Six Half-Vote National Convention Delegates

Boone	15
Bracken	8
Campbell	52
Carroll	11
Fleming	13
Gallatin	6
Grant	11
Lewis	8
Mason	18
Oldham	9
Pendleton	9
Trimble	9

Kenton—Will choose 75 delegates at 4 legislative-district conventions

FOURTH DISTRICT CONVENTION
228 Delegates
Elects Six Half-Vote National Convention Delegates

Adair	12
Anderson	10
Barren	26
Bullitt	11
Green	9
Hardin	22
Hart	16
Larue	9
Marion	15
Meade	14
Mercer	14
Metcalfe	10
Nelson	16
Shelby	20
Spencer	5
Taylor	12
Washington	10

THIRD DISTRICT CONVENTION
417 Delegates
Elects Six Half-Vote National Convention Delegates

Jefferson—11 Separate legislative-district conventions will be held. Time and place to be set by county chairman and advertised in newspaper at least four days prior to meetings. These will choose 417 delegates.

SECOND DISTRICT CONVENTION
247 Delegates
Elects Six Half-Vote National Convention Delegates

Allen	10
Breckinridge	14
Butler	6
Daviess	33
Edmonson	5
Grayson	10
Hancock	5
Henderson	28
Hopkins	33
McLean	10
Ohio	14
Simpson	14
Union	14
Warren	36
Webster	15

FIRST DISTRICT CONVENTION
372 Delegates
Elects Six Half-Vote National Convention Delegates

Ballard	15
Caldwell	12
Calloway	31
Carlisle	10
Christian	32
Crittenden	7
Fulton	15
Graves	50
Hickman	12
Livingston	9
Logan	26
Lyon	8
McCracken	71
Marshall	22
Muhlenberg	24
Todd	15
Trigg	13

The opposite photo-chart indicates how Democrats in the non-primary state of Kentucky select their delegates to the national convention. The procedure affords the rank-and-file party member his only opportunity to influence the choice of his party's presidental nominee. That influence is expended four places removed from the actual choice, however.

First phase: On June 11, in each county of the state and in the 11 legislative districts of Jefferson County (Louisville), and the 4 of Kenton County mass meetings of "all known Democrats who are registered voters" were held at the courthouses under direction of the county Democratic chairman (or legislative district chairman). These meetings had the sole purpose of electing delegates (the respective numbers indicated in the lower boxes of the chart) to represent each county at the district and state Democratic conventions. The number was determined by dividing by 200 the Democratic vote in each county for President in 1956. The record of the proceedings, names of delegates, and other accomplishments of the mass meetings had to be filed with the secretary of the Democratic State Executive Committee prior to the meeting of the state convention.

Phase Two: Two weeks later (June 25) eight district Democratic conventions assembled simultaneously but separately. They represented the eight congressional districts into which 120 counties of the state are divided. Each was called to order by the Democratic chairman of that county in the district which cast the largest Democratic presidential vote in 1956. The functions of the district Democratic conventions were to elect:

1. Six national convention delegates, each with ½ vote, and three alternates;
2. One presidential elector and one assistant;
3. Two men and two women to serve for four years on the State Executive Committee; and
4. Four persons to serve one each on the organization, credentials, rules, and resolutions committees of the state Democratic convention. Other aspects of party business of a local nature could also be handled by the conventions, subject to review and final decision by the Democratic state convention.

Finally, the record of each convention and the names of delegates, had to be filed with the secretary of the state convention.

Phase Three: The afternoon of June 25, the chairman of the state party called the state Democratic convention to order. Its functions and duties were:

1. To elect 12 national convention delegates from the state-at-large, each to cast ½ vote, and 6 alternate delegates;
2. To reject or approve any or all of the national convention delegates and alternates selected by district conventions and elect new ones as required;
3. To elect two presidential electors-at-large and two assistants and reject or approve those selected by the district conventions, or elect new ones as required;
4. To elect a new chairman of the Democratic State Executive Committee;
5. To elect 8 members-at-large to serve on the State Executive Committee;
6. To designate one man and one woman to serve on the Democratic National Committee;
7. To adopt such rules and regulations for the Democratic Party in Kentucky as were felt to be necessary and proper by the convention.

The state convention also possessed power to invoke the unit rule upon the national convention delegates and instruct them to support a particular presidential candidate.

Finally, the Democratic state convention gave final approval to the state's 10 presidential electors and 10 assistant electors, the state chairman and vice chairwoman of the Executive Committee, the national committeeman and woman, and the eight members-at-large of the State Executive Committee.

Phase Four: On July 11, at Los Angeles, the delegates to the Democratic national convention chose a presidential candidate whom it was hoped the rank-and-file Democratic Party member in Kentucky would support.[7]

Use of the primary affords the party member a more direct voice in party business. He may choose the delegates to the national convention, express his preference for a presidential candidate, or both. When both are permitted the delegates chosen may or may not be bound to support the most popular candidate for the nomination. This arrangement is known as the Presidential, or Preferential, Primary. Of the eleven states using the preference poll, seven permit write-in votes. These may serve as important indicators of popular sentiment and the strength of unavowed aspirants to the nomination.

When state law binds convention delegates to support the candidate receiving the largest preferential vote in the primary, the obligation endures only until it appears that the candidate has no chance of being nominated, until he frees them from their pledge, or fails to receive as much as ten per cent of the vote on a given ballot. Some states permit an expression of preference but no selection of delegates; others permit the reverse. The number of possible variations of the presidential primary is considerable.[8]

Presidential primaries are a subject of controversy. They have been attacked for being only a small part of presidential nominating politics, for being misrepresentative because they exclude independent voters, for being parochial, too prodigal of time and money, exhausting, and for lacking binding force. Their purpose is defeated by "favorite son" candidates, and they may give the "kiss of death" to a good prospect who fails to win in a primary that has been ballyhooed as a "key" contest. Aspirants to the nominations are not required to enter primaries. Hence, they usually pick them carefully to avoid unfavorable circumstances and results. Preferential primaries that bind delegates may be avoided for such reasons while others, though not binding, and, therefore, of little real value, may be entered only because circumstances favor success. Seldom do more than 25 per cent of the voters participate.

[7] Adapted, by permission, from an article by Hugh Morris in *The Courier-Journal*, June 12, 1960.

[8] See *Congressional Quarterly Weekly Report*, Vol. 18, No. 10, pp. 341-348 for an analysis of the various primaries in use.

1960 PRESIDENTIAL PRIMARIES

States and Delegate Strength*	Primary Date	Filing Deadline	Consent of Candidate	Type of Primary	Voter Qualification
New Hampshire (11D; 14R)	Mr. 8	Jan. 27	Not reqd.; may withdraw in 10 days	Non-binding preference poll; election of delegates who may be pledged to a candidate; Vice Presidential preference permitted.	Closed
Wisconsin (3D; 30R)	Ap. 5	Mr. 4	Required	Preference poll only by voting for pledged delegate slate, pledge binding on first ballot and on additional ballots unless ⅔ of delegates vote to change, or candidate withdraws.	Open
Illinois (69D; 60R)	Ap. 12	Jan. 25	Required but may withdraw	Non-binding preference poll; election of unpledged district delegates; at-large delegates selected by state convention.	Closed
New Jersey (41D; 38R)	Ap. 19	Mr. 10	Not required and may withdraw	Non-binding preference poll; election of delegates who may be pledged; write-in votes permitted.	Closed
Massachusetts (41D; 38R)	Ap. 26	Mr. 8	Required	Non-binding; write-in preference poll; election of delegates who may be pledged.	Closed
Pennsylvania (81D; 70R)	Ap. 26	Feb. 23	Not required	Preference poll; election of district delegates who may state willingness to be bound by preference poll; at-large delegates selected by party committees; write-in votes permitted.	Closed
District of Columbia (9D; 8R)	May 3	Ap. 1	Required	Preference poll; election of officially unpledged delegate slates.	Closed
Indiana (34D; 32R)	May 3	Mr. 24	Required	Binding (on first ballot) preference poll; all delegates chosen by conventions; no write-in preference votes.	Closed
Ohio (64D; 56R)	May 3	Feb. 3	Required	Election of delegates; delegates' 1st & 2d preferences appear on ballot; preference of voter expressed by voting for delegates.	Closed
Nebraska (16D; 18R)	May 10	Mr. 11	Required	Non-binding preference; election of unpledged delegates; write-in votes permitted.	Closed
West Virginia (25D; 22R)	May 10	Feb. 6	Required	Non-binding preference poll; election of unpledged delegates; no write-in votes.	Closed
Maryland (24D; 24 R)	May 17	Mr. 14	Required	Binding preference poll; delegates chosen by convention; no write-in votes permitted.	Closed
Oregon (17D; 18R)	May 20	Mr. 11 (for petitions)	Not reqd.; may withdraw if entered by Sec. of State but not if by petition	Binding preference poll; election of delegates who may state preference for candidate; write-in votes permitted.	Closed
Florida (29D; 26R)	May 24	Mr. 1	Not required	Election of slate of delegates which may be pledged to a candidate.	Closed
California (81D; 70R)	June 7	Mr. 9	Required	Election of slate of pledged delegates.	Closed
South Dakota (11D; 14R)	June 7	May 8	Required	Election of slate of delegates which may be pledged.	Closed

* Alabama Democrats on May 3, and both parties in New York on June 7, 1960, elected unpledged delegates, but no preference vote was taken.
Adapted from Congressional Quarterly Weekly Report, Vol. 18, No. 10, p. 348.

On the other hand, the use of primaries has been defended as a means of forcing the candidates for nomination to express their ideas on public issues and to explain their records. They also give the individual party member his only opportunity to influence the selection of his party's presidential nominee.

When delegates have been chosen in a state their names are forwarded with their credentials to the national committee of their party, which prepares a temporary roll of the members of its convention.

Rules of the National Conventions. The advent of radio and television has made the proceedings of the national convention, held during July or August, familiar to most persons. The highlight of the meeting is its nomination of a presidential candidate, but it must also organize, adopt a platform, and nominate a vice presidential candidate. Whatever is done is accomplished under the rules of the convention formulated and adopted by itself. The rules are prepared by the Committee on Rules and Order of Business, one of the four major committees of the convention. Major changes are seldom made in them, but each national convention is the highest organ of party authority and may do to its rules whatever it desires.

Proceedings of the National Convention. The organizations and procedures of the national conventions are very similar. The proceedings appear to be those of a political circus, full of noise, confusion, demonstration and oratory. Behind the facade of color, however, are months of planning and organization. From the first to the last rap of the gavel little occurs that has not been planned in advance. The conventions are not intended to be deliberative bodies, and much that takes place has no significance. The numerous speeches provide time for organization and decision making behind the scenes. Time-consuming roll calls enable floor managers of presidential hopefuls to scurry about trying to line up support, within state delegations, for their respective aspirants to the nomination. Much that is of significance takes place beyond the convention hall. The delegates are aware of the almost superfluous nature of much of what they do. They pay little attention to anything apart from the nominations. They have been selected by their respective party members in primaries, by their party organizations in conventions, or by their state committees. Their choice is usually a reward for faithful party service. The task at hand has its serious moments, to be sure, but on the whole the trip to the convention is a lark, and the work to be done can be accomplished in an atmosphere of gaiety and relaxation. Not even coverage by nationwide television facilities has made the convention proceedings less circus-like and more serious and deliberative. Nevertheless, the activities of the conventions possess a certain sanity instilled by a regular order of business.

The Platform. The statement of party principles and positions on current political issues of the campaign is known as its "platform." The platform is the official statement of the party's and the candidate's attitudes toward questions of public importance. It becomes general almost to the point of obscuring the differences of ideology supposed to distinguish Democrats from Republicans. This results because the essence of platform drafting is compromise. Both parties agree basically upon the fundamentals of the American political system and compete for the support of the groups which make up the electorate. Their appeals for votes must be general or run the risk of alienating blocs of voters. Thus, it comes about that the platforms of the major parties resemble "letters of recommendation written by the body recommended."

Drafting begins well in advance of the convention. Subcommittees of the resolutions committee hold hearings and prepare "planks," or statements of party position, on one or more issues. Many pressures are exerted upon their efforts. Presidents tend to dominate the process of their party; senators and representatives exert a major influence on that of a party out of power. Representatives of major interests submit prepared statements of party position which they urge the committees to adopt. Leading contenders for the nomination may bring their own platforms to the convention.

The major function of the committee, therefore, is to decide which issues the party shall support and what position it can take on each. Each "plank" must compromise conflicting points of view. Hence, generality is the common characteristic of major party platforms; their purpose is to attract as many votes as possible and to hold on to those already "in the fold." Specificity tends to alienate votes and is avoided if possible. Hence, major parties either ignore controversial issues or treat them as delicately as possible.

Platforms are probably of little value. Few voters know or care what is in them. They have little effect upon presidential candidates, who depart widely from them as the need demands, or upon the administration when a candidate is elected. The position of the candidate as he defines and explains it carries far more weight with the voters.[9]

Nomination of the Presidential Candidate. When the convention is organized and the reports of the four major committees approved, it proceeds to a consideration of the nominations. The secretary of the convention reads the roll of the states alphabetically (beginning with Alabama). Each state in turn may place a name in nomination, second a nomination already made, yield to another state further down the list so that it may have the honor of nominating some candidate, or pass without doing anything. Nominating speeches are limited to fifteen or twenty

[9] For an analysis of the extent to which the major parties fulfilled their 1956 platform planks see *Congressional Quarterly Weekly Report,* Vol. 17, No. 52, pp. 1573-1585.

minutes duration; seconding speeches to five minutes. Nominating speeches represent the highest attainment of political oratory. They are carefully prepared and flamboyantly delivered. The name of the person to be nominated is a poorly-kept secret, but it is not mentioned until the end of the speech when it serves as the cue for a "spontaneous" demonstration to break out on the floor of the convention. These are, of course, thoroughly prepared in advance, with signs, banners, noise-makers, and demonstrators arranged for and on hand at the proper moment.

When all the states have been polled for nominations, and the seconding speeches, usually two or three for each nomination, have been completed, the roll is again called for voting by state delegations. On the first ballot votes are frequently given to "favorite sons" or other persons whom it is desired to honor but who are not expected to win. This move has the advantage, also, of permitting a state to hold back its vote until it has a chance to see which candidate the winds of political fortune are favoring. Votes can always be changed at the end of the ballot, so that a state retains the opportunity to climb on the "bandwagon" of a winning candidate if one is designated on the first ballot.

The Democratic convention permits use of the "unit rule," by which all members of a delegation must cast their votes for the aspirant favored by a majority of them. This rule has never been used by the Republicans.

The number of ballots required to nominate varies. The Democrats have nominated on the first ballot in about one-half of their conventions since 1856. The Republicans have done so approximately three-fourths of the time. But 103 ballots were required by the Democrats to nominate John W. Davis in 1924, and 36 were required by the Republicans to nominate James A. Garfield in 1880.

A nominee is not chosen by careful, deliberate, and judicious canvassing of qualifications on the part of the delegates at the convention. The choice of all but incumbent Presidents is the result of negotiations, deals, maneuvers and agreements between candidates, their managers, powerful city bosses, governors, senators, state and county chairmen, and other acknowledged personalities of the party. Nomination of a candidate to be President of the United States is accomplished by a process resembling a Roman circus.

Nomination of the Vice Presidential Candidate. Interest in the convention lapses when the presidential candidate has been nominated, but a vice presidential candidate must also be selected. The same method is employed, but several new factors are significant in influencing the choice. The presidential candidate may dictate the choice of his running mate. However, that choice is often influenced by factors other than personal preference. One may be a desire to balance the ticket by choosing a candidate from a geographical area where the vote-getting power of the presidential candidate is weak. Another may be a desire to put a growing political rival "on the shelf" by getting him into the dead-end of the Vice Presidency. The second prize may go to the runner-up for the presidential nomination. It may be given to the leader of a faction so as to heal a breach in party unity. These are some of the factors that determine the choice of the vice presidential candidate.

Chronology of the 1960 Democratic Convention

Monday, July 11

5:14 p.m. (PDT)—National Chairman Paul M. Butler calls the convention to order in Los Angeles' Memorial Sports Arena. . . . Invocation is given. . . . With 761 votes needed to nominate a candidate, Senator John F. Kennedy (Mass.) is reported to have close to 700 votes, with Senator Lyndon B. Johnson (Tex.) second with under 450 votes. Senator Stuart Symington third with less than 100, and a scattering for Adlai Stevenson. . . . Film stars parade before the convention. The secretary of the Democratic National Committee reads the official call of the convention to a half-empty hall. . . . Temporary rules adopted without dissent. . . .

5:57 p.m.—Mayor Norris Poulson, a Republican, given cool reception as he welcomes the delegates to Los Angeles.

6:03 p.m.—Delegates warm up for first time as Governor Brown, first Democratic governor of California in 20 years, welcomes delegates to California, attacks administration foreign policy. Brown is followed by the California national committeeman.

6:30 p.m.—National Chairman Paul Butler accounts for his stewardship.

7:02 p.m.—Convention adopts slate of temporary officers. Temporary chairman of the convention introduced. Begins keynote address. Short demonstration for the temporary chairman, Frank Church, senator from Idaho. Kennedy announces his consideration of Freeman, Loveless, Docking, and Jackson as candidates for vice presidential nomination but does not eliminate Symington or Johnson.

8:01 p.m.—At the Ambassador Hotel, after a nine-hour session, Platform Committee Chairman Chester Bowles emerges to announce unanimity on civil rights plank could not be reached, that a strong civil rights plank has been adopted, 66-24, over strong southern opposition. . . . Senator John Stennis (Miss.) announces nine southern states dissent on the plank they consider "extreme, radical, unconstitutional," but says they will not walk out of the convention.

8:30 p.m.—On the floor, permanent rules, including 1956 party loyalty rule, adopted by the convention. First session adjourned at 8:40 p.m.

Tuesday, July 12

3:00 p.m.—Kennedy and Johnson engage in colorful presentation of views before meeting of Texas and Massachusetts delegations. Caucus of California delegation jolts Kennedy forces by reporting 31½ votes for Stevenson in spite of Governor Brown's endorsement of Kennedy. Minnesota reportedly holding aloof from Kennedy bandwagon. Kennedy forces reassert assurance of nomination.

4:06 p.m.—Second session convened by temporary chairman Church.

4:42 p.m.—Report of Committee on Permanent Organization adopted. Governor Leroy Collins (Fla.) made permanent chairman; holders of other positions made permanent.

5:22 p.m.—Collins introduced by Church. Collins addresses convention. Interrupted several times by demonstrations for late entering Democratic personages.

6:06 p.m.—Report of Committee on Credentials approved.

6:17 p.m.—Adlai Stevenson enters—first major demonstration begun; lasts seventeen minutes; delegates and galleries cheer and chant "We want Stevenson."

6:27 p.m.—Bowles introduced; begins presentation of platform, really the report of the Resolutions Committee. Delegates applaud civil rights plank.

7:52 p.m.—At end, Collins announces that Resolutions Committee has filed two minority reports. Georgia delegation chairman reads minority report on behalf of southern states.

8:19 p.m.—Senator Ervin (N.C.) moves that adopted civil rights plank should be stricken from the platform. A minority report on fiscal responsibility presented by Virginia delegate.

8:25 p.m.—One hour of debate, divided equally for and against, announced.

9:30 p.m.—Minority report on fiscal responsibility rejected by voice vote.

9:42 p.m.—Southern states fail in demand for roll call vote on minority civil rights report. Collins declares report rejected on voice vote.

9:43 p.m.—Full platform adopted by voice vote.

9:56 p.m.—Second session adjourns. Kennedy forces claim enough votes to win. Other sources say Kennedy camp admits to close first vote. Iowa reported to hold off from Kennedy on first ballot—to back favorite son. Johnson camp claims Kennedy faltering in California, Kansas, Minnesota, North Dakota, Canal Zone. Press association estimate places Kennedy 20 short of first ballot nomination.

Wednesday, July 13

3:16 p.m.—Third session convened. Will select presidential nominee. Candidate withdrawals and vote changes to be permitted after roll call in strict alphabetical order of the states.

3:43 p.m.—Collins directs roll call of states for nominations for President. Alabama yields to Texas. Speaker Sam Rayburn nominates Lyndon Johnson. twenty-four-minute demonstration and three seconding speeches follow.

4:34 p.m.—Alaska yields to Minnesota. Governor Orville Freeman nominates Kennedy. Sets off twenty-three-minute demonstration; six seconding speeches follow.

5:27 p.m.—Arkansas yields to Florida. Senator Spessard Holland (Fla.) nominates favorite son Senator George Smathers (Fla.); followed by demonstration and two seconding speeches.

6:09 p.m.—Delaware yields to Missouri. Stuart Symington nominated—twenty-four-minute demonstration and four seconding speeches.

7:02 p.m.—Favorite son, Governor Loveless, a Kennedy seconder, nominated by Iowa but gains floor and withdraws for Kennedy.

7:31 p.m.—Same thing occurs when Governor George Docking (Kan.) nominated as favorite son. Rumors circulate that Symington is ready to withdraw in favor of Kennedy in return for the vice presidential nomination. Symington camp denies rumors.

7:57 p.m.—Kentucky yields to Minnesota for nomination of Adlai Stevenson. Most enthusiastic demonstration follows with Stevenson supporters in galleries making most noise. Lasts twenty-eight minutes, followed by seconding speeches.

9:00-10:06 p.m.—Maine yields to New Jersey for favorite-son nomination of Governor Meyner (N.J.); Mississippi nominates its Governor Ross Barnett as favorite son. Roll of states completed. No candidates withdraw.

10:07 p.m.—Balloting starts. Roll of states called. Alabama casts 20 of 29 votes for Johnson. . . . Kennedy shows surprising strength in mountain states. Holds majority of votes during most of balloting. With 13 delegations out at 10:43, vote stands Kennedy 680½, Johnson 267, Symington 80, Stevenson 70. . . . At 10:51 Wyoming gives 15 votes to Kennedy, giving him 765 and the nomination. At end, Kennedy 806, Johnson 409, Symington 86, Stevenson 79½, with a scattering for others.

10:55 p.m.—Missouri recognized. Switches vote to Kennedy; moves nomination by acclamation. So declared by chairman of convention.

11:50 p.m.—Kennedy appears briefly before convention. Thanks Johnson and Symington supporters for making nomination by acclamation. Predicts victory in November.

12:00 p.m.—Third session adjourned.

Thursday, July 14

4:05 p.m.—After day of conferences with party leaders, Kennedy announces Johnson is personal choice for Vice President.

5:23 p.m.—Fourth session opened. Governor Luther Hodges (N.C.) addresses convention. Party notables introduced. Speeches praising achievements of the party.

8:23 p.m.—Vice presidential nominations. Roll of states called. Alabama yields to Pennsylvania for nomination of Lyndon Johnson. Seconding speeches.

9:09 p.m.—Motion made to suspend rules and make nomination by voice vote. Collins rules motion in order. Vote taken and Collins announces necessary two-thirds in favor. Rules Johnson nominated by acclamation, despite audible boos.

9:14 p.m.—Johnson appears on podium.

9:34 p.m.—Fourth session adjourned.

Friday, July 15

6:44 p.m.—Fifth and final session convened outdoors in Los Angeles Coliseum.

6:52 p.m.—Long series of congratulatory speeches begun—Rayburn, Humphrey, G. Mennon Williams, James Roosevelt, Symington.

7:30 p.m.—Johnson accepts vice presidential nomination. Calls for and pledges a united party.

7:47 p.m.—Kennedy's mother, brothers, sisters, and other relatives introduced.

8:02 p.m.—Kennedy introduced by Adlai Stevenson. Accepts nomination. Says: "With a deep sense of duty and high resolve, I accept your nomination. . . ."

He announces his intention "to lead our party back to victory and our Nation back to greatness." Warns that the road to the "New Frontier" offers more sacrifices, not more luxuries, promises social welfare programs, implementation of party platform. Reaffirms his intention, if elected, not to be swayed by religious pressures in his exercise of office.

8:34 p.m.—Following end of Kennedy speech, benediction and the national anthem, Collins adjourns the convention *sine die*.[10]

General Election Campaign. Following a brief interlude for rest and planning strategy the presidential nominees must hit the trail again in an effort to win the support of the general electorate in the election. The problem, therefore, is to reach them. Traditional methods include the "whistle stop" tour, radio and television talks, press releases and public statements, public rallies, party dinners, newspaper advertising, and barbecues; the process of the pre-convention campaign is duplicated, but with an appeal directed to a wider audience and supported by the machinery and finances of the party organization.

Every means of getting the candidate and his ideas before the voters is employed. Of these the use of television reaches the largest audience with the least expenditure of effort and energy. However, television in politics is not an undisguised blessing. One great drawback is its expense. In 1956 the Republicans spent $4,036,935, and the Democrats $2,971,143 for the use of television in the presidential campaigns. Thus, the best-financed party enjoys a great advantage over its rivals; but television has been condemned for other reasons. The most effective presentation is a one-minute "spot identification," a five-minute speech is long enough, and no television speech should exceed fifteen minutes. None of these permits a candidate to deal adequately with a complex question. Mr. Adlai Stevenson concluded that the candidate "is reduced to sloganeering, to huckstering, to oversimplifying." Television fosters "producing" the candidate, entertaining the viewers, and heightening their apathy. Providing free television time would ease the problem of cost to the parties, but how can this be done? At the expense of the national government? By forced contributions from the networks? And for whom? The Republican and Democratic parties only? For all national candidates? How should free time be controlled to ensure that it is used wisely? Would voters grow tired of listening to an hour-long debate on a national question and tune out? Should all channels be pre-empted to prevent that? If not, who will determine what candidate appears opposite which regular show, and at what time? These are questions for which no ready answers are available, but their solution will have an important effect on campaigning through the medium of television.[11]

---

[10] Adapted from *Congressional Quarterly Weekly Report*, Vol. 18, No. 29, pp. 1231-1232; No. 30, p. 1307.

[11] Adlai Stevenson writing in *This Week* Magazine, February 28 and March 6, 1960. Copyright 1960 by the United Newspapers Magazine Corporation.

Trumpet Call

OPENING OF REPUBLICAN CAMPAIGN

DEMOCRATIC SENATE MAJORITY

DEMOCRATIC HOUSE MAJORITY

LePelley

ELECTION OF THE PRESIDENT

Theory and Practice. The quadrennial choice of the President and the Vice President is an event of great interest and importance, for the Presidency is the most powerful political office within the free political systems of the world. Hence, great importance attaches to the method by which the incumbent of this office is selected. However, there is a vast difference between the theory and the process of the choice. This divergence is attributable almost entirely to the emergence and growth of political parties.

The constitutional plan for choosing a President was intended to ensure the choice of outstanding statesmen who would be above party and popular passions. It was a scheme for indirect choice by electors who stood between the voters and the selection of a President and Vice President. They were to be outstanding men of their states who would independently, and judiciously, select acknowledged national figures qualified to be President and Vice President of the United States.

Method of Choosing Electors. The Constitution states that the President shall

. . . together with the Vice President . . . be elected, as follows

Each State shall appoint, in such Manner as the Legislature thereof may direct, a Number of Electors, equal to the whole Number of Senators and Representatives to which the State may be entitled in the Congress: but no

Senator or Representative, or Person holding an Office of Trust or Profit under the United States, shall be appointed an Elector.

Electors have been chosen in various ways. Some have been "appointed" by the legislatures; some have been popularly elected by congressional districts with two elected from the state at large. Currently all states provide for popular election on the general ticket system. The political party which polls a majority or plurality of the popular vote automatically elects all of its presidential electors and wins the entire electoral vote to which the state is entitled.

Voters in a presidential election vote for a slate of presidential electors nominated by their party in the number to which their state is entitled. However, the average voter *feels* that he is voting directly for a presidential candidate, because he knows that electors will cast their votes for the candidates of the party which designated them. Because of this, when the distribution of the popular vote in each state is known, the choice of a President and Vice President can be known by anticipation.

The presidential electors have become figureheads and the President is, in effect, directly elected by the voters of the states. The popularly-chosen presidential electors do not exercise discretion in choosing a President of the United States. It is assumed that the electors will not make independent judgments, but will follow the expressed preferences of the voters of the state by whom the elector was chosen.

Although the theory of the system remains unaltered, the laws of the several states regulating the choice of the electors recognize that theory and practice do not completely coincide. One fifth of the states place on the ballots only the names of persons to be electors. Another fifth also list the party nominees to be President and Vice President. The remainder print only the names of the presidential and vice presidential candidates of the parties. The following provision of the electoral law of the State of Illinois is typical of this last and most realistic view of the process of presidential selection:

> The names of the candidates of the several political parties or groups for electors of President and Vice President shall not be printed on the official ballot to be voted in the election. . . . In lieu of the names of the candidates for such electors of President and Vice President, immediately under the appellation of party name of a party or group in the column of its candidates on the official ballot, to be voted at said election first above named . . . there shall be printed within a bracket the name of the candidate for President and the name of the candidate for Vice President of such party or group with a square to the left of such bracket. Each voter in this State from the several lists or sets of electors so chosen and selected by the said respective political parties or groups, may choose and elect one of such lists or sets of electors by placing a cross in the square to the left of the bracket aforesaid on one of such parties or groups. Placing a cross within the square before the bracket enclosing the

names of President and Vice President shall not be deemed and taken as a direct vote for such candidates for President and Vice President, or either of them, but shall only be deemed and taken to be a vote for the entire list or set of electors chosen by that political party or group so certified to the Secretary of State as herein provided. . . .[12]

Time for Choosing Electors. The state legislatures regulate the method of choosing electors, but it was stated in the Constitution that

The Congress may determine the Time of chusing the Electors, and the Day on which they shall give their Votes; which Day shall be the same throughout the United States.

By virtue of this authority to legislate, Congress has provided that

The electors of President and Vice President shall be appointed, in each State, on the Tuesday next after the first Monday in November, in every fourth year succeeding every election of a President and Vice President.[13]

Casting the Electoral Vote.

The Twelfth Amendment. As originally provided in the Constitution the electors were each to make two choices. The person receiving the highest number of electoral votes was to be President; the person receiving the next highest number was to become Vice President. As long as the electors voted independently all went well, but in the election of 1800 the fact that electors faithfully supported the candidates of their party produced a tie. Jefferson and Burr each received 73 votes, although Jefferson was intended by the electors to be President and Burr to be Vice President. Because no candidate obtained a majority of the electoral votes, the choice was thrown into the House of Representatives, where each state had one vote.

To preclude another tie vote, the Twelfth Amendment was added to the Constitution. It states:

The Electors shall meet in their several states, and vote by ballot for President and Vice-President, one of whom, at least, shall not be an inhabitant of the same state with themselves; they shall name in their ballots the person voted for as President, and in distinct ballots the person voted for as Vice-President, and they shall make distinct lists of all persons voted for as President, and of all persons voted for as Vice-President, and of the number of votes for each, which lists they shall sign and certify, and transmit sealed to the seat of the government of the United States, directed to the President of the Senate;— The President of the Senate shall, in the presence of the Senate and House of Representatives, open all the certificates and the votes shall then be counted;— The person having the greatest number of votes for President, shall be the President, if such number be a majority of the whole number of Electors appointed; and if no person have such majority, then from the persons having the

[12] *Illinois Revised Statutes,* 1949, Chapter 46, Article 21.
[13] *U.S. Code,* Title 3, sec. 1.

highest numbers not exceeding three on the list of those voted for as President, the House of Representatives shall choose immediately, by ballot, the President. But in choosing the President, the votes shall be taken by states, the representation from each state having one vote; a quorum for this purpose shall consist of a member or members from two-thirds of the states, and a majority of all the states shall be necessary to a choice. And if the House of Representatives shall not choose a President whenever the right of choice shall devolve upon them, before [noon of the 20th day of January] next following, then the Vice-President shall act as President, as in the case of the death or other constitutional disability of the President.—The person having the greatest number of votes as Vice-President, shall be the Vice-President, if such number be a majority of the whole number of Electors appointed, and if no person have a majority, then from the two highest numbers on the list, the Senate shall choose the Vice-President; a quorum for the purpose shall consist of two-thirds of the whole number of Senators, and a majority of the whole number shall be necessary to a choice. But no person constitutionally ineligible to the office of President shall be eligible to that of Vice-President of the United States.

Procedure. Congress and the states collaborate in controlling the time and manner of casting the electoral vote. Thus, Congress has provided:

The electors of President and Vice President of each State shall meet and give their votes on the first Monday after the second Wednesday in December next following their appointment at such place in each State as the legislature of such State shall direct. . . .

The electors shall make and sign six certificates of all of the votes given by them, each of which certificate shall contain two distinct lists, one of the votes for President and the other of the votes for Vice President, and shall annex to each of the certificates one of the lists of the electors which shall have been furnished to them by direction of the executive of the State.

The electors shall seal up the certificates so made by them, and certify upon each that the lists of all the votes of such State given for President, and of all the votes given for Vice President, are contained therein.

The electors shall dispose of the certificates so made by them and the lists attached thereto in the following manner:

First.   They shall forthwith forward by registered mail one of the same to the President of the Senate at the seat of government.

Second.   Two of the same shall be delivered to the secretary of state of the State, one of which shall be held subject to the order of the President of the Senate, the other to be preserved by him for one year and shall be a part of the public records of his office and shall be open to public inspection.

Third.   On the day thereafter they shall forward by registered mail two of such certificates and lists to the Administrator of General Services at the seat of government, one of which shall be held subject to the order of the President of the Senate. The other shall be preserved by the Administrator of General Services for one year and shall be a part of the public records of his office and shall be open to public inspection.

Fourth.   They shall forthwith cause the other of the certificates and lists to be delivered to the judge of the district in which the electors shall have assembled.[14]

The regulation of other details of the assembly of electors and the casting of their votes are left to control by state authority.

Counting the Electoral Votes. When the votes of the electors have been cast in their respective states and forwarded to the seat of the government, they are counted before a joint session of the houses of Congress. For purposes of counting the electoral votes, except when it is necessary to fix another day by law,

Congress shall be in session on the sixth day of January succeeding every meeting of the electors. The Senate and House of Representatives shall meet in the Hall of the House of Representatives at the hour of 1 o'clock in the afternoon on that day, and the President of the Senate shall be their presiding officer. Two tellers shall be previously appointed on the part of the Senate and two on the part of the House of Representatives, to whom shall be handed, as they are opened by the President of the Senate, all the certificates and papers purporting to be certificates of the electoral votes, which certificates and papers shall be opened, presented, and acted upon in the alphabetical order of the States, beginning with the letter A; and said tellers having read the same in the presence and hearing of the two Houses, shall make a list of the votes as they shall appear from the said certificates; and the votes having been ascertained and counted in the manner and according to the rules in this sub chapter provided, the result of the same shall be delivered to the President of the Senate, who shall thereupon announce the state of the vote, which announcement shall be deemed a sufficient declaration of the persons, if any, elected President and Vice President of the United States, and, together with a list of the votes, be entered on the Journals of the two Houses. . . .[15]

Disputed Elections. If more than one set of returns is received from a state a disputed election results, like that of 1876. However, because of that experience Congress has provided that disputes growing out of the appointment of electors are to be settled by the state concerned according to the method it has established. Its settlement is conclusive, and governs the counting of the electoral votes so far as determination of the electors is concerned.[16]
However:

If more than one return or paper purporting to be a return from a State shall have been received by the President of the Senate, those votes, and those votes only, shall be counted which shall have been regularly given by the electors who are shown by the determination mentioned in section 5 of this title to

[14] *U.S. Code*, Title 3, secs. 7, 9-11.
[15] *U.S. Code*, Title 3, sec. 15.
[16] *U.S. Code*, Title 3, sec. 5.

PRESIDENTIAL ELECTIONS
1928-1960

Year and Candidates	Electoral Vote	Popular Vote	% Electoral Vote	% Popular Vote
1928				
Hoover (R)	444	21,391,381	83.61	58.1
Smith (D)	87	15,016,443	16.38	40.8
Others	0	337,115		1.1
1932				
Roosevelt (D)	472	22,821,857	88.88	57.4
Hoover (R)	59	15,761,841	11.11	39.7
Others	0	1,160,615		2.9
1936				
Roosevelt (D)	523	27,751,597	98.41	60.2
Landon (R)	8	16,679,583	1.50	36.5
Others	0	1,201,052		3.3
1940				
Roosevelt (D)	449	27,244,160	84.57	54.8
Wilkie (R)	82	22,305,198	15.42	44.8
Others	0	203,620		.4
1944				
Roosevelt (D)	432	25,602,504	81.37	53.4
Dewey (R)	99	22,006,285	18.62	45.9
Others	0	336,051		.7
1948				
Truman (D)	303	24,105,812	57.06	49.4
Dewey (R)	189	21,970,065	35.59	45.0
Others	39	1,589,794	7.34	5.6
1952				
Eisenhower (R)	442	33,778,963	83.23	54.9
Stevenson (D)	89	27,314,992	16.76	44.4
Others	0	457,964		.7
1956				
Eisenhower (R)	457	35,584,135	86.07	57.4
Stevenson (D)	73	26,036,080	13.74	41.9
Others	1	417,090	.18	.7
1960				
Kennedy (D)	303	34,221,531	56.42	49.7
Nixon (R)	219	34,108,474	40.78	49.6
Others	15	502,773	2.79	.7

Sources:
  1928-1944—*Historical Statistics of the United States, 1789-1945*, p. 228.
    1948—*The World Almanac, 1960*, p. 586.
    1952—*Statistics of the Presidential and Congressional Election of November 4, 1952* (Washington, D.C.: U.S. Government Printing Office, 1953) p. 53.
    1956—*Encyclopaedia Britannica Book of the Year, 1957*, p. 294.
    1960—*Encyclopedia Americana, 1961 Annual*, p. 334.

have been appointed, if the determination in said section provided for shall have been made . . . but in case there shall arise the question which of two or more such authorities, determining what electors have been appointed, . . . is the lawful tribunal of such State, the votes regularly given of those electors, and those only, of such State shall be counted whose title as electors the two Houses, acting separately, shall concurrently decide is supported by the decision of such State. . . . But if the two Houses shall disagree in respect of the counting of such votes, then, and in that case, the votes of the electors whose appointment shall have been certified by the executive of the State, under the seal thereof, shall be counted. . . .[17]

REFORM OF THE ELECTORAL SYSTEM

Weaknesses of the Existing Electoral System. Proposals to reform or abolish the electoral college system are common. They attack the present method of choosing a President as being seriously defective. Among criticisms voiced are the following. The electoral college will elect a President who has received only a plurality of the popular vote. More rarely, it will elect one who has received fewer votes than his major opponent. It distorts the electoral vote in a way favorable to the winner and unfavorable to the loser. The electoral vote is meaningless since its out-

[17] *Ibid.*, sec. 15.

come is known two months in advance. Distribution of the electoral votes favors the small and thinly populated states. The general ticket system discourages active campaigning in states regarded as hopelessly lost or "in the bag." The large blocs of votes assigned to populous states make them "key" or "swing" states upon which the parties concentrate their efforts, to the neglect of the others. The parties are encouraged to woo excessively the vote of minority blocs whose support is necessary to carry a closely divided key state. Present practice amounts to popular election of the President, so why hide that fact behind the electoral college? There is no assurance that the electors will cast their electoral votes for the candidate of their party.[18] Candidates tend to be drawn from important states in which a party's strength is doubtful on the theory that a local favorite will draw votes away from the opposition.

ELECTORAL VOTES OF THE SEVEN LARGEST STATES
(After 1961)

New York	43
California	40
Pennsylvania	29
Illinois	26
Ohio	26
Texas	25
Michigan	21

The gain by these states of seats in the House of Representatives entitles them to a net gain of five electoral votes, and thereby increases their influence in the choice of future Presidents. Any nominee who carries all seven of them in 1964 or 1968 will need only 58 additional electoral votes to gain the White House.

Adapted from *Congressional Quarterly Weekly Report*, Vol. 17, No. 15, p. 517.

Direct Popular Election. For these reasons, it has been suggested that direct popular election should be substituted for the current system. This proposal, however desirable, is probably impracticable because:

1. The states, *qua* states, would lose their voice in the election of the President and Vice President.
2. The small states would lose their relative advantage over the large state in the choice of a President.
3. The parties would be forced to campaign actively in every state since every popular vote they could obtain would be to their advantage.
4. It would compel the conservatively-oriented Democratic party of th South to lower the bars to voting.
5. Because of the light vote in the southern states, it would reduce the impact upon the choice of a President.
6. The Democratic Party would gain more advantage in the North than th Republican Party would gain in the South.

[18] But see *Ray* v. *Blair* (1952), 343 U.S. 214.

7. It could only be accomplished by a constitutional amendment which for the above reasons could never receive the necessary votes for proposal.

Distribution of Electoral Vote by District. It has been proposed that presidential electors should be abolished, and the electoral vote should be distributed by awarding one vote for each congressional district, or special district laid out by Congress, to the presidential candidate who won that district, and two "at-large" votes to the candidate who carried the state. The electoral vote would thereby be distributed between the parties in rough proportion to the popular vote received by each. This solution would be more democratic than the current system, but it would have to overcome objections based on the following points:

1. It would merely lower the level of party campaign activity from the state to the district, but would not eliminate "swing" states. To them it would probably add "swing" districts.
2. It would perpetuate the advantage enjoyed by the less populous states.
3. It would do little to stimulate the growth of a two-party system in the South.
4. By tending to equalize the distribution of popular and electoral votes it would lessen the character of the winner as President of all the people.
5. The Democrats would probably gain more electoral votes in northern states than Republicans would gain in southern ones. Hence, it would be strongly opposed by the latter.

Proportional Distribution of Electoral Votes by States. Of the specific plans for reform the one that has been most favorably received is the Lodge-Gossett proposal. It's features are as follows:

The Electoral College system of electing the President and Vice President of the United States is hereby abolished. The President and Vice President shall be elected by the people of the several States. The electors in each State shall have the qualifications requisite for electors of the most numerous branch of the State Legislature. Congress shall determine the time of such election, which shall be the same throughout the United States. Until otherwise determined by the Congress, such election shall be held on the Tuesday next after the first Monday in November of the year preceding the year in which the regular term of the President is to begin. Each State shall be entitled to a number of electoral votes equal to the whole number of Senators and Representatives to which such State may be entitled in the Congress.

Within forty-five days after such election, or at such time as Congress shall direct, the official custodian of the election returns of each State shall make distinct lists of all persons for whom votes were cast for President and the number of votes for each, and the total vote of the electors of the State for all persons for President, which lists he shall sign and certify and transmit sealed to the seat of the Government of the United States, directed to the President of the Senate. The President of the Senate shall in the presence of the Senate and the House of Representatives open all certificates and the votes shall then be counted. Each person for whom votes were cast for President in each State shall be credited with such proportion of the electoral votes thereof as he received of the total vote of the electors therein for President. In making the computations, fractional numbers less than one-thousandth shall be discarded unless a more detailed calculation would change the result of the election. The person having the greatest number of electoral votes for President shall be President. If two or more persons shall have an equal and the highest number of such votes, then the one for whom the greatest number of popular votes were cast shall be President. . . .[19]

A plurality of forty per cent of the electoral vote would be sufficient to elect a President. If no candidate received that number, the election would be decided by a joint session of Congress, each *member* having one vote, which would choose a President and Vice President from the two candidates having the highest totals of electoral votes.

Advantages of the Lodge-Gossett Plan. This proposal would realize a more exact reflection of the will of the voters by its distribution of the electoral votes. Direct popular election would best do that, but it is impossible to obtain. Hence, this is the next best remedy. The plan retains the electoral vote and thus overcomes the opposition which its abolition would engender; it is in keeping with the principle of federalism. Its division of the electoral vote would reflect the popular vote with great mathematical accuracy. It would force the parties to campaign actively in every state. The phenomenon of "swing" states would disappear. Every popular vote would count for something. It would stimulate voter interest in the electoral process and break down one-party areas by giving the second party an incentive to fight for votes. It would reduce the importance of minority bloc votes. It would eliminate the useless office of electors. It would provide an element of fair play and electoral justice not present in the current system. By emphasizing the importance of every popular vote cast, it would bring all states into presidential politics, and would encourage the expansion and strengthening of the two party system.

Disadvantages. Opponents of the plan argue that it would weaken the two party system. They feel that by guaranteeing to a party as little as 1/1000th of one per cent of the electoral vote for a corresponding per cent of the popular vote the plan would end the incentive of minor parties to compromise their demands with, and to work within, the major parties. Compromise is essential to the attainment of a middle ground and is the essence of the two party system. If the incentive to compromise now produced by the hopeless situation of a minor party is taken away it would, it is feared, produce a tendency toward political extremism and a multiplication of political factions. Entry of numerous candidates into the

[19] House Joint Resolution 9, January 3, 1947, and Senate Joint Resolution 91, March 19, 1947, 80th Congress, 1st session.

competition would increase the dispersion of the popular vote and make the necessary forty per cent more difficult to obtain. It would throw an increased number of elections into Congress. It would have the effect of increasing the number of plurality Presidents and of weakening the status and prestige of the Presidency, and it would do nothing to end the relative advantage now enjoyed by the small states.

Neither the Lodge-Gossett nor any other reform has sufficient support to be accepted. Liberals, conservatives, southerners, northerners, political parties, and state officials concede the need for change, but none trust the suggestions of the others enough to give them the support necessary for adoption. All prefer the weaknesses of the current system to the unknown results of proposed reforms.

CHAPTER XVI

Powers of the President

GENERAL CONSIDERATIONS

The American Presidency places upon its incumbent the greatest political power, prestige, and legal authority vested in any head of a democracy. However, the personality of its incumbent largely determines how its powers and influence are exercised. History records as "strong" those Presidents who bring to their position a vigorous personality, a determination to make the most of their office, a willingness to assume the initiative and take the responsibilities of leadership, and a more or less well-developed mastery of practical politics. The "weak" Presidents have been irresolute, lacking a finely-tuned political sense, unimaginative, and unable or unwilling to assert the powers and prestige of their office.

The office surrounds its incumbent with ample power, prestige, and influence to meet virtually any situation with which he may be confronted. A President is irremovable except by impeachment, and is subordinate to no other executive officer. He is head of the administration of government and has the assistance necessary to enable him to exercise reasonably effective control over it. He is head of personnel and of fiscal administration. He appoints the political, non-permanent members of the executive and can discharge all but a few of them without let or hindrance. He is the sole repository of the executive power, subject only to the authority of Congress to enact laws "necessary and proper" for carrying it into execution. He is commander-in-chief of the armed forces and chief of foreign affairs. Through the combination of constitutional authority, practical necessity, and popular demand he has assumed leadership in the formulation of national policy. He and the Vice President are the only national officers elected by all qualified voters, and he is, therefore, able to claim that he represents and is obligated to protect the general welfare more clearly than is a member of either house of Congress. He is spokesman for the national interest in affairs both foreign and domestic. He is the head of his political party, he controls the dispensation of patronage, mobilizes public opinion, and focuses attention upon any question which he sees fit to make into a national issue.

Authority and Power. The executive power of the President is a combination of legal *authority* and political *power*. The first is authority granted in statutes or by the Constitution. Some of it is executive in the strict sense of the word and is of the type that executives almost always possess. However, some authority of the President is not executive strictly speaking, for his office has lodged in it some authority which is legislative and some which is judicial in character. The political power of the President is derived principally from the fact that he is head of his political party; it includes all of his informal sources of influence and control.

WHOLLY EXECUTIVE AUTHORITY AND FUNCTIONS

The Constitution declares:

The executive Power shall be vested in a President of the United States of America. . . .

The President shall be Commander in Chief of the Army and Navy of the United States, and of the Militia of the several States, when called into the actual Service of the United States. . . .

. . . He shall take Care that the Laws be faithfully executed. . . .

By the first of these provisions *the* executive power is vested entirely and exclusively in the President. His duty is to use it to carry out the essential function of governing, that of enforcing, administering, or *executing* the laws. Other clauses make specific grants of authority to the President, but they are mentioned only to affirm that they are included in the general grant of executive power. The President also possesses much authority given to him by acts of Congress.

Discretionary Power of the President. Further authority originates in the President's duty to see that the laws are *faithfully* executed, for the meaning of a "faithful" discharge of this responsibility varies. Hence, it leaves the President wide discretion that affords him great political and legal power. Politically, he can use it to define the policies of his administration as determined by his idea of what best serves the general interest. Legally, he can use it to enforce or fail to enforce a law. He may or may not intervene at Little Rock or prosecute monopolies, but if he exceeds his authority, he may be held accountable through his subordinates, although he cannot be judicially constrained or restrained.[1]

How is the Authority of the President Exercised?: Some powers of the President must by their nature be exercised by that officer personally. The Attorney General of the United States has ruled:

It may be presumed that he, the man discharging the presidential office, and he alone, grants reprieves and pardons for offenses against the United States, . . . So he, and he alone, is the supreme commander in chief of the Army and Navy of the United States, and of the militia of the several states when called into the actual service of the United States. That is a power constitutionally inherent in the person of the President.[2]

In general, however, the President may delegate duties imposed by statute upon him, and these duties if performed within the limits of the law are regarded as the acts of the President himself.

The President, in the exercise of his executive powers under the Constitution, may act through the head of the appropriate executive department. The heads of departments are his authorized assistants in the performance of his executive duties, and their official acts, promulgated in the regular course of business, are presumptively his acts.[3]

This rule is necessary because:

It is manifestly impossible for the President to execute every duty, and every detail thereof, imposed upon him by the Congress. The courts have recognized this and have further recognized that he usually and properly acts through the several executive departments. Every reasonable presumption of validity is to be indulged with respect to the performance by the head of a department of a duty imposed upon the President and executed by the department head ostensibly in behalf of the President. Nevertheless, the authorities indicate that the President cannot, without statutory authority, delegate a discretionary duty, relieving himself of all responsibility, so that the duty when performed will not be his act but wholly the act of another.[4]

Immunity of the President from Judicial Process. Government rests ultimately upon physical force, for the functions of all of its branches may

---

[1] See *Youngstown Sheet and Tube Co.* v. *Sawyer* (1952), 343 U.S. 579, and *Mississippi* v. *Johnson* (1867), 4 Wallace 475.
[2] *13 Opinions of the Attorney General* 453, 464-465.
[3] *Wilcox* v. *Jackson* (1839), 13 Peters 498.
[4] *Williams* v. *United States* (1843), 1 Howard 290.

depend upon its use for their execution. However, it is assumed that the citizenry will do what is required of them, and the use of force will not be necessary except to control outlaws. Nevertheless, a monopoly of force is always available to make the processes of government effective should the need arise. It is controlled by the President, who can use it to enforce the administrative process or to isolate himself from the judicial process.

Suppose the Supreme Court ordered the President not to execute an act of Congress that it alleged to be unconstitutional. What consequences might follow?

If the President refuse obedience, it is needless to observe that the Court is without power to enforce its process. If, on the other hand, the President complies with the order of the Court and refuses to execute the acts of Congress, is it not clear that a collision may occur between the Executive and Legislative Departments of the Government? May not the House of Representatives impeach the President for such refusal? And in that case, could this Court interfere, in behalf of the President, thus endangered by compliance with its mandate, and restrain by injunction the Senate of the United States from sitting as a court of impeachment? Would the strange spectacle be offered to the public world of an attempt by this Court to arrest proceedings in that court?

These questions answer themselves. . . .

But we are fully satisfied that this Court has no jurisdiction of a bill to enjoin the President in the performance of his official duties; and that no such bill ought to be received by us.[5]

However, the President's immunity from judicial process is carefully restricted. He is protected even when performing an illegal act, but his subordinates or agents who obey or execute his illegal order are not. They may be prosecuted and may not plead the commands of their superior as a defense. Further, subordinates may be stopped from performing illegal acts or may be ordered to perform those required by law.

The Appointing Power. The President cannot personally discharge the duties of his office. Therefore, history and logic combine to give him power to appoint subordinates. This power is essentially executive. Hence, the Constitution declares that the President

. . . shall nominate, and by and with the Advice and Consent of the Senate, shall appoint Ambassadors, other public Ministers and Consuls, Judges of the Supreme Court, and all other Officers of the United States, whose Appointments are not herein otherwise provided for, and which shall be established by Law; but the Congress may by Law vest the Appointment of such inferior Officers, as they think proper, in the President alone, in the Courts of Law, or in the Heads of Departments.

Persons appointed in accordance with these procedures are "officers" of the United States. Within the meaning of this provision they are either

[5] *Mississippi* v. *Johnson* (1867), 4 Wallace 475.

"superior" or "inferior." The first are nominated and appointed by the President with the approval of the Senate. The second are appointed by some other method.

Among the "superior" appointments which the President makes those to positions of "cabinet level" stand apart from the rest, for the consent of the Senate is given in most instances as a matter of course. History affords but a few examples of presidential nominations to "cabinet level" positions which have been rejected by the Senate. The most recent occurred in 1959 when the nomination of Admiral Lewis Strauss to be Secretary of Commerce was turned down.

Senatorial Courtesy. By presenting a united front to Presidents, senators have converted their constitutional power to approve presidential nominations into an ability to dictate nominees to him. That ability has been made effective by "senatorial courtesy"; its nature and operation are made clear by the following colloquy:

NOMINATION OF NAT GOLDSTEIN

Mr. Harrison. May I ask the Senator another question? Has any action been taken touching the Nat Goldstein nomination? . . .

Mr. McCumber. Oh, no. Let me state to the Senator what is the usual course in such matters. The moment any nomination is sent to the committee, the chairman hands that nomination to some Senator and asks him to consult with both the Senators from the State of the nominee to ascertain whether the nomination is satisfactory to them.

That is the first step to be taken, and it is the step which always has been taken, whether the Democratic Party or the Republican Party has been in control. If the nomination is satisfactory and if it is so reported to the committee, the committee acts upon it. If, however, any extraneous matters have come to the attention of the committee to indicate that there will be opposition to the nomination, then, of course, the nomination is held in abeyance until such opposition may be heard.[6]

Presidents usually nominate the persons recommended by senators of their own party for appointments to vacancies in the senators' states. If the President fails to do so and his nominee is personally objectionable to the senator or senators involved, that objection need only be made known to the whole Senate and the latter will refuse approval of the President's choice.

"Senatorial courtesy," therefore, involves the "courtesy" of the Senate to the senator who finds the President's nominee obnoxious. If no senator of the President's party is involved, practice suggests that he should consult the representatives of his party, and, failing that, the state party leaders. Names are often advanced to repay political debts and from motives of friendship. Moreover, the good party standing of nominees

[6] *Congressional Record,* 67th Congress, 2nd session (1922), pp. 6555-6556.

must be established, and this often involves clearance by the party's national headquarters. Since both headquarters are within a few blocks of the White House, that is easily done.

Thus, the President's power to appoint "superior" officers is limited by extralegal practices. There are an estimated 25,000 of them; about 750 fill top-level policy-making positions in Washington, D.C. Senators, representatives, and the party headquarters have found the remainder, located throughout the country, to be of great value in paying off political obligations, maintaining political fences, and keeping the state party machinery in good operating order. They are filled politically and constitute modern-day "patronage."

Many "inferior" offices also constitute "patronage." With respect to them the practice is also well established that "politically right" congressmen of the states in which the offices are located should be consulted. In unusual circumstances, it may even be highly expedient for the President to consult members of the opposite party who are friendly to him and upon whose aid his own party in Congress relies.

Recess Appointments. Because vacancies may occur in "superior" offices when the Senate is not in session,

The President shall have Power to fill up all Vacancies that may happen during the Recess of the Senate, by granting Commissions which shall expire at the End of their next session.

A "recess" appointment is made without senatorial approval, is temporary, and is permitted so that the office need not remain vacant and its duties unexecuted. The Senate is afforded an opportunity to accept or reject the appointee, but if it rejects or fails to consider him, his recess appointment terminates as provided.

However, a President can violate the spirit of the Constitution by granting successive "recess" appointments. To make it as difficult as possible for the President to circumvent the will of the Senate in this way Congress has declared:

No money shall be paid from the Treasury, as salary, to any person appointed during the recess of the Senate, to fill a vacancy in any existing office, if the vacancy existed while the Senate was in session and was by law required to be filled by and with the advice and consent of the Senate, until such appointment has been confirmed by the Senate. The provisions of this section shall not apply (a) if the vacancy arose within thirty days prior to the termination of the session of the Senate; or (b) if, at the time of the termination of the session of the Senate, a nomination for such office, other than the nomination of a person appointed during the preceding recess of the Senate, was pending before the Senate for its advice and consent; or (c) if a nomination for such office was rejected by the Senate within thirty days prior to the termination of the session and a person other than the one whose nomination was rejected thereafter receives a recess commission: *Provided,* That a nomination to fill such vacancy under (a), (b), or (c) of this section, shall be submitted to

the Senate not later than forty days after the commencement of the next succeeding session of the Senate.[7]

Moreover, Congress has excluded from succession to the Presidency a
department head serving on the basis of a recess appointment.

Removal Power. The Constitution bestows upon the President no
power to remove administrative subordinates. Its only reference to removal is to impeachment. Moreover, impeachment is inappropriate for
use by the executive to control the administration; it is a power of the
legislature for control of the executive. It applies only to "treason,
bribery and other high crimes and misdemeanors" which administrators
seldom commit; it cannot be used to remove persons who are inept, disloyal, or insubordinate, or whose acts prove politically embarrassing to a
President but are not illegal.

Nevertheless, since 1789 Presidents have removed subordinates. Congress has attempted to limit the power of the President to remove "superior" officers by requiring that such removals should have the consent
of the Senate, by fixing definite terms of office, or by prescribing the
causes for which removals can be made. But, can Congress restrict the
removal power of the President? If it could it would weaken the President's ability to control the executive branch.

The power to remove executive officers is implied from the power of
the President to appoint. But is this an exclusive power? Cogent arguments have been advanced to support the conclusion that it is. Thus:

It is reasonable to suppose that had it been intended to give to Congress
power to regulate or control removals . . . it would have been included among
the specifically enumerated legislative powers in Article I, or in the specified
limitations on the executive power in Article II. . . . The fact that the executive power is given in general terms strengthened by specific terms where emphasis is appropriate, and limited by direct expressions where limitation is
needed, and that no express limitation is placed on the power of removal by
the executive is a convincing indication that none was intended. . . .

Made responsible under the Constitution for the effective enforcement of the
law, the President needs as an indispensable aid to meet it the disciplinary
influence upon those who work under him of a reserve power of removal. . . .
The degree of guidance in the discharge of their duties that the President may
exercise over executive officers varies with the character of their service as
prescribed by the law under which they act. The highest and most important
duties which his subordinates perform are those in which they act for him. In
such cases they are exercising not their own but his discretion. This field is a
very large one. . . . Each head of a department is and must be the President's
alter ego in matters of that department where the President is required by law
to exercise authority.

But this is not to say that there are not strong reasons why the President
should have a like power to remove his appointees charged with other duties

[7] *U.S. Code,* Title 5, sec. 56.

than those above described. The ordinary duties of officers prescribed by statute come under the general administrative control of the President by virtue of the general grant to him of the executive power, and he may properly supervise and guide their construction of the statutes under which they act in order to secure that unitary and uniform execution of the laws which Article II of the Constitution evidently contemplated in vesting general executive power in the President alone. Laws are often passed with specific provision for the adoption of regulations by a department or bureau head to make the law workable and effective. The ability and judgment manifested by the official thus empowered, as well as his energy and stimulation of his subordinates, are subjects which the President must consider and supervise in his administrative control. Finding such officers to be negligent and inefficient, the President should have the power to remove them.[8]

However, Congress may provide that members of the Federal Trade Commission, appointed by the President with the consent of the Senate for terms of seven years, shall be removable by him only "for inefficiency, neglect of duty or malfeasance in office."

The Federal Trade Commission is an administrative body created by Congress to carry into effect legislative policies embodied in the statute . . . and to perform other specified duties as a legislative or as a judicial aid. Such a body cannot in any proper sense be characterized as an arm or an eye of the executive. Its duties are performed without executive leave and, in the contemplation of the statute, must be free from executive control. In administering the provisions of the statute . . . the commission acts in part quasi-legislatively and in part quasi-judicially. In making investigations and reports thereon for the information of Congress in aid of the legislative power it acts as a legislative agency. Under §7, which authorized the commission to act as a master in chancery under rules prescribed by the court, it acts as an agency of the judiciary. To the extent that it exercises any executive function—as distinguished from executive power in the constitutional sense—it does so in the discharge and effectuation of its quasi-legislative or quasi-judicial powers, or an agency of the legislative or judicial departments of the government. . . .

The authority of Congress, in creating quasi-legislative or quasi-judicial agencies, to require them to act in discharge of their duties independently of executive control, cannot well be doubted; and that authority includes, as an appropriate incident, power to fix the period during which they shall continue, and to forbid their removal except for cause in the meantime. For it is quite evident that one who holds his office only during the pleasure of another cannot be depended upon to maintain an attitude of independence against the latter's will. . . .

The result of what we now have said is this: Whether the power of the President to remove an officer shall prevail over the authority of Congress to condition the power by fixing a definite term and precluding a removal except for cause will depend upon the character of the office. The *Myers* decision, affirming the power of the President alone to make the removal, is confined to purely executive officers. And as to officers of the kind here under consideration, we hold that no removal can be made during the prescribed term for

[8] *Myers* v. *United States* (1926), 272 U.S. 52.

which the officer is appointed, except for one or more of the causes named in the applicable statute.[9]

Foreign Affairs Power. The conduct of foreign relations is an inherent power of the national government; its use is vested exclusively in the President, but Congress can influence its exercise. The President is, of course, assisted by the Department of State and the other agencies of the executive branch, and by the diplomatic and consular services. He nominates, and with the consent of the Senate appoints the policy-making officers of the Department of State as well as ambassadors, other public ministers, and consuls.

Presidential Diplomatic Agents. Ambassadors and ministers conduct the diplomatic relations of the United States in the name of the President and through the machinery of the Department of State. However, the President may personally participate, or he may utilize the services of a personal agent to represent and speak for him. Such agents are appointed on an *ad hoc* basis by the President alone, exercise authority granted by him, are paid out of funds at his disposal, and serve at his pleasure. They are his personal representatives; because they are not "civil officers" they are not subject to approval by the Senate. Nevertheless, they can take any action within the scope of a regular diplomatic representative.

Receiving Ambassadors. The Constitution also declares that the President "shall receive Ambassadors and other public Ministers. . . ." This authority extends to all diplomatic and consular agents sent to the United States. It implies the power to refuse to receive them, to request their recall, or to dismiss them. Moreover, it is this simple statement of authority which makes the President the sole medium of contact between the United States and foreign nations.

The power to send and receive ambassadors and ministers can be used to produce several results. By sending an American diplomat to, or by receiving the diplomatic representative from, a newly established government or state the President extends the recognition and therewith the implied blessing and approval of the United States to it. He may refuse to do either, thereby declining to extend American recognition and implying disapproval, an action which may produce considerable adverse effect. He may also grant recognition by making a treaty; but the acts of sending ambassadors and concluding treaties are less favored than is recognition granted by receiving a diplomatic representative, for the latter course alone excludes Congress from the recognition power. By recalling American representation or by dismissing the representative from a foreign government he may sever diplomatic relations.

The Role of Congress. Congress plays an important part in the conduct of foreign affairs. Its support is indispensable to any foreign policy. Through its powers to tax and spend, to create armies and navies, to provide for the common defense, to declare war, to define offenses against

[9] *Rathbun* v. *United States* (1935), 295 U.S. 602.

the law of nations, and to legislate on many subjects it exerts a great influence upon external relations.

It makes pronouncements upon questions of foreign affairs which are often accepted by unknowing foreign statesmen as expressions of the official policy of the United States. It can investigate, debate, and otherwise educate public opinion. It can urge upon the President various actions which it feels he should take. Moreover, the Senate must approve treaties and confirm ambassadors, other public ministers, and consuls.

Nevertheless, the role of Congress is essentially negative, and the Senate Foreign Relations Committee once summed up its relation to the conduct of foreign affairs and to the power of recognition as follows:

> The "recognition" of independence or belligerency of a foreign power, technically speaking, is distinctly a diplomatic matter. . . . The reception of the envoy, as pointed out, is the act of the President alone. The next step, that of sending a public minister to the nation thus recognized, is primarily the act of the President. The Senate can take no part in it at all, until the President has sent in a nomination. Then it acts in its executive capacity, and, customarily, in "executive session." The legislative branch of the Government can exercise no influence over this step except, very indirectly, by withholding appropriations. . . . Nor can the legislative branch of the Government hold any communications with foreign nations. The executive branch is the sole mouthpiece of the nation in communication with foreign sovereignties. . . . Resolutions of their legislative departments upon diplomatic matters have no status in international law. In the department of international law, therefore, properly speaking, a Congressional recognition of belligerency or independence would be a nullity.[10]

It is in the area of foreign affairs that Congress has been least able to withstand presidential leadership, so that its powers have been employed more often in aid of presidential primacy than in opposition to it.

Courts and the Conduct of Foreign Affairs. Questions arising within the sphere of external relations can be answered only by Congress and the President, for

> The President, both as Commander-in-Chief and as the Nation's organ for foreign affairs, has available intelligence services whose reports are not and ought not be published to the world. It would be intolerable that courts, without the relevant information, should review and perhaps nullify actions of the Executive taken on information properly held secret. Nor can courts sit *in camera* in order to be taken into executive confidence. But even if courts could require full disclosure, the very nature of executive decisions as to foreign policy is political, not judicial. Such decisions are wholly confided by our Constitution to the political departments of the government, Executive and Legislative. They are delicate, complex, and involve large elements of prophecy. They are and should be undertaken only by those directly responsible to the people whose welfare they advance or imperil. They are decisions of a kind

[10] Senate Document 56, 54th Congress, 2nd session (January 11, 1897), pp. 20-22.

for which the judiciary has neither aptitude, facilities nor responsibility and which has long been held to belong in the domain of political power not subject to judicial intrusion or inquiry.[11]

The Treaty-Making Power of the President.

The Constitution empowers the President to make treaties by prescribing that

He shall have Power, by and with the Advice and Consent of the Senate, to make Treaties, provided two thirds of the Senators present concur. . . .

The treaty power so granted by the Constitution

. . . is in terms unlimited except by those restraints which are found in that instrument against the action of the government or of its departments, and those arising from the nature of the government itself and that of the States. It would not be contended that it extends so far as to authorize what the Constitution forbids, or a change in the character of the government or in that of one of the States, or a cession of any portion of the territory of the latter, without its consent. . . . But with these exceptions, it is not perceived that there is any limit to the questions which can be adjusted touching any matter which is properly the subject of negotiations with a foreign country.[12]

The process of making treaties is divisible into three parts: the first is negotiation, which the President alone controls; the second is that of obtaining senatorial consent. A draft treaty is presented to the Senate in final form, but the President need not submit it merely because it has been negotiated. Once submitted, he may withdraw it, and he may refuse to ratify it, although it has been approved, if he feels ratification would not be in the national interest. On its part, the Senate must be content with whatever information concerning a draft treaty the President supplies it.

Obviously the treaty must contain the whole contract between the parties, and the power of the Senate is limited to a ratification of such terms as have already been agreed upon between the President, acting for the United States, and the commissioners of the other contracting power. The Senate has no right to ratify the treaty and introduce new terms into it, which shall be obligatory upon the other power, although it may refuse its ratification, or make such ratification conditional upon adoption of amendments to the treaty.[13]

Changes or reservations must also be accepted by the President. If any party fails to accept the conditions, the treaty will fail. The third part of the process is ratification, or the exchange of signed and sealed copies of the treaty among the signatory parties. It is exclusively an executive act.

[11] *Chicago and Southern Airlines* v. *Waterman Steamship Corp.* (1948), 333 U.S. 103.

[12] *Geofroy* v. *Riggs* (1890), 133 U.S. 258, 267.

[13] Justice Brown concurring in *Fourteen Diamond Rings* v. *United States* (1901), 183 U.S. 176. The term "ratify" is here used as a synonym for "approve."

Treaties as Supreme Law of the Land. The Constitution, statutes "made in pursuance thereof," and treaties made under authority of the United States are the supreme law of the land. Nevertheless, treaties are subordinate to the overriding supremacy of the Constitution and may not conflict with or amend its provisions, for the authority of the national government, like water, cannot rise higher than its source. It cannot make a treaty repugnant to the Constitution. Treaties "made under authority of the United States," and statutes "made in pursuance" of the Constitution are of equal force and effect as internal law of the United States. Hence, the more recent takes precedence over the earlier.

Treaties make law that is superior to the law or public policies of any state which conflict with it. Moreover,

Treaties are to be liberally construed, so as to effect the apparent intention of the parties. . . . And as the treaty-making power is independent of and superior to the legislative power of the states, the meaning of treaty provisions so construed is not restricted by any necessity of avoiding possible conflict with state legislation, and when so ascertained must prevail over inconsistent state enactments.[14]

Termination of Treaties. Treaties are terminated by their own provisions, by war, by substitution of another treaty, by mutual consent of its signatories, by legislation that conflicts with it, or by authorization for the President to denounce it. If the President finds that action by another signatory has violated a treaty he may proclaim that it has lapsed, but the declaration of its abrogation by the United States must come from Congress.

Unilateral abrogation of a treaty by the United States ends its character as internal law but does not destroy its effectiveness as an international instrument unless agreed to by the other signatory. Other parties could acknowledge the withdrawal of the United States but continue the treaty in effect among themselves.

Executive and Other Agreements. The Constitution implies a difference between "treaties" and "agreements" but gives no clue as to what it is. Practice has established that agreements do not require approval by either house of Congress, but the need for implementing legislation or for spending authority may dictate that the President has to consult Congress before or after their conclusion. They may be made by the President in execution of his foreign affairs or command powers, but Congress may direct him to conclude an agreement and submit it for approval. In the absence of legislative direction, however, the President is free to act as he desires. Major matters are dealt with by executive agreements; but minor ones arising from the conduct of routine foreign affairs are regulated by agreements of a non-executive type. The treaty process is too

[14] *Neilson* v. *Johnson* (1929), 279 U.S. 47.

cumbersome and slow for their settlement, and their importance does not warrant the President's concern. An executive agreement theoretically binds only the President who makes it and should be used to settle matters of an immediate and specific nature.

Effect of Executive Agreements. Executive agreements are regarded as provisional arrangements of temporary duration, but they have increasingly been used to deal with matters of great importance to the well-being of the nation, and have assumed a legislative character. Many determine future policy and impose lasting obligations without being subject to approval by Congress, acting on behalf of the American people. Therefore, they are pledges of the national faith pertaining to a specific matter of an external nature, and have the same force as treaties.

Plainly, the external powers of the United States are to be exercised without regard to state laws or policies. The supremacy of a treaty in this respect has been recognized from the beginning. . . . And while this rule in respect of treaties is established by the express language of the Supremacy Clause of the Constitution, the same rule would result in the case of all international compacts and agreements from the very fact that complete power over international affairs is in the national government and is not and cannot be subject to any curtailment or interference on the part of the several states. . . . In respect of all international negotiations and compacts, and in respect of our foreign relations generally, state lines disappear. . . . Within the field of its powers, whatever the United States rightfully undertakes, it necessarily has warrant to consummate. And when judicial authority is invoked in aid of such consummation, state constitution, state law, and state policies are irrelevant to the inquiry and decision. It is inconceivable that any of them can be interposed as an obstacle to the effective operation of a federal constitutional power.[15]

Use of Joint Resolutions. Practice has demonstrated that a joint resolution of Congress passed by a simple majority vote of both houses can accomplish what the Senate would not permit by treaty. Thus, Texas and Hawaii were annexed by joint resolution after the Senate had refused its consent to the two treaties negotiated for that purpose. Peace was concluded at the end of World War I, and the United States became a member of the International Labor Organization, by joint resolution.

POWERS OF THE PRESIDENT RELATED TO LEGISLATION

Relations between the political branches of the national government virtually defy prediction, and are never static. They depend only in part upon the powers of the President, and at any time range in tenor from harmony, sweetness, and light to bitter conflict, discord, and stalemate. If the President's party controls Congress good feeling and cooperation may

[15] *United States* v. *Belmont* (1937), 301 U.S. 324.

prevail, but that circumstance has not always been sufficient to calm troubled political waters. If one or both houses of Congress have been lost to the party of the President, the probability of legislative-executive harmony is greatly diminished.

Other factors affect relations between Congress and the President: the personality of the chief executive; the presence or absence of strong personal leadership in Congress whether friendly or hostile toward the executive; his ability to mobilize public opinion on his side of any dispute with the legislature; his personal popularity; his ability to influence voters for or against legislators whom he desires to reward or punish, and to dispense patronage artfully; his eligibility to succeed himself and to be elected if he is eligible; the attitude toward him and his policies held by "senior" senators and representatives; and the presence or absence of an emergency, foreign or domestic, military or economic. Nor is this list intended to be more than illustrative.

Of the factors mentioned, that of emergency exerts the greatest impact upon legislative-executive relations, for it greatly enhances the position of the President and reveals the inability of Congress to provide leadership and initiative in government. Emergency in theory does not create power or remove limitations to its exercise, but in practice it often enables a President to exercise his powers in virtually any manner and to any ends made necessary by the exigencies of the time. Whether he can rise to the occasion will largely depend upon his personality. He must be willing to exercise initiative, assume responsibility, and provide positive leadership. A weak, irresolute, and indecisive President will not meet the exigencies of modern government.

Moreover, the constitutional system neither provides an effective means of compelling him to furnish the needed leadership and initiative, nor does it supply another source from which they may be had. They must come from the President. Congress ably fulfills its functions of opposing and criticizing, but it is incapable of governing. The cabinet is powerless. The judiciary is beyond the pale of politics. It is because of the necessity for positive leadership that his influence and prestige have grown while those of Congress have tended to diminish.

Many of the links between the legislative and executive branches are built upon the powers of the President relating to legislation. These include the power to call special sessions of the chambers, or either of them; to adjourn them; to recommend measures to their attention; to exercise a suspensory veto over measures enacted by them; and to issue rules and regulations having the force of law.

Control of the Sessions of Congress. The President "may, on extraordinary occasions, convene both houses, or either of them." This power is invoked only on emergency occasions. Presidents are reluctant to call special sessions, for while Congress sits, they are compelled to share public attention with it. When it is assembled, it possesses all of its legisla-

'If I Told You Once, I Told You a Thousand Times . . .'

tive power and independence. The President can call it back, but he cannot control its deliberations thereafter. The House of Representatives has never been called back alone; the Senate on several occasions has been convened to consider treaties and nominations.

Although it has never been exercised, the President also has authority to adjourn the houses of Congress, "in case of disagreement between them, with respect to the time of adjournment," to such time as he may think proper.

Proposal of Legislation by the President. The President is charged with the authority and duty of recommending legislation to Congress. Thus, the Constitution states:

He shall from time to time give to the Congress Information of the State of the Union, and recommend to their Consideration such Measures as he shall judge necessary and expedient. . . .

In accordance with this duty, the President regularly delivers, by recent practice in person, a Message on the State of the Union soon after Congress convenes. In this message, he outlines his general program and makes recommendations for legislation to carry it out. Delivery of this message affords the President an opportunity to appeal not only to Congress but also to the nation and to the world. It is one of his finest opportunities to focus public attention on his program.

Congress requires that the President should transmit to it two other annual messages. His Budget Message accompanies transmission of the budget and contains his recommendations for appropriation and tax legislation. The second message accompanies his Economic Report and sets forth his legislative recommendations for achieving and maintaining maximum employment, purchasing power, and production.

In addition, the President may suggest legislation in special messages, through personal contacts with members, at weekly meetings with the leadership of his party, in veto messages, at press conferences, and in public addresses. Of course, no member of the executive branch may introduce measures in Congress, but a friendly legislator can usually be found to accommodate the President. Also, it will be recalled that communications from the President may be referred directly to a standing committee and carry with them authority for the committee to draft a bill.

The Veto Power. The President may exercise a suspensory veto power over acts of Congress which often in fact turns out to be final. Four courses of action are open to him when he receives an act for his signature:

1. He may veto it and return it to the house of its origin together with a statement of his objections. Thus:

Veto Message of the President[16]

To the House of Representatives:

I am unable to approve H. R. 6645, to amend the Natural Gas Act as amended. This I regret because I am in accord with its basic objectives.

Since the passage of this bill, a body of evidence has accumulated indicating that private persons, apparently representing only a very small segment of a great and vital industry, have been seeking to fulfill their own interests by highly questionable activities. These include efforts that I deem to be so arrogant and so much in defiance of accepted standards of propriety as to risk creating doubt among the American people concerning the integrity of the Governmental process.

Legally constituted agencies of Government are now engaged in investigating this situation. These investigations cannot be concluded before the expiration of the 10-day period within which the President must act upon the legislation under the Constitution.

I believe I would not be discharging my duty were I to approve this legislation before the activities in question have been fully investigated by the Congress and the Department of Justice. To do so under such circumstances could well create long-term apprehension in the minds of the American people. It would be a disservice both to the people and to their Congress. Accordingly, I return H. R. 6645 without my approval.

At the same time I must make quite clear that legislation conforming to the basic objectives of H. R. 6645 is needed. It is needed because the type of regulation of producers of natural gas which is required under present law will discourage individual initiative and incentive to explore for and develop new sources of supply.

In the long run this will limit supplies of gas which is contrary not only to the national interest but especially to the interest of consumers.

[16] *Congressional Record*, 84th Congress, 2nd session (1956), p. 2793.

I feel that any new legislation, in addition to furthering the long-term interests of consumers in plentiful supplies of gas, should include specific language protecting consumers in their right to fair prices.

The White House   Dwight D. Eisenhower

February 17, 1956.

2. He may sign it, in which case it immediately becomes law, although Congress may adjourn within the ten days stipulated for his action.

3. He may hold it for ten days without signing, in which case it also becomes law if Congress remains in session. This course is followed to indicate mild disapproval of a measure.

4. The President may "pocket veto" the act. If it is presented to him less than ten days before the adjournment of Congress, it cannot become law automatically. Hence, if he does not sign it, the measure is automatically killed. This result amounts to an absolute veto, for no opportunity is provided to the houses of Congress to reverse his decision.

The veto power may be used because the President doubts the validity of an act or disagrees with its policy. He may threaten to use the power if Congress passes an act in a form unacceptable to him. A threat of veto can be used to induce compromise, and is often a greater influence over the legislative process than is an actual veto. Few measures are repassed over a veto because of the difficulty of mustering a two-thirds vote of the full membership of both houses of Congress against the President.

PRESIDENTIAL VETOES: 1913-1960

		Vetoed Bills			Vetoes	Vetoes
Periods	*Presidents*	*Total*	*Regular*	*Pocket*	*Upheld*	*Reversed*
1913-1921	Wilson	44	33	11	38	6
1921-1923	Harding	6	5	1	6	—
1923-1929	Coolidge	50	20	30	46	4
1929-1933	Hoover	37	21	16	34	3
1933-1945	F. Roosevelt	631	371	260	622	9
1945-1953	Truman	250	180	70	238	12
1953-1960	Eisenhower	201	83	118	198	3

Source: *Statistical Abstracts of the United States, 1961* (Washington, D.C.: U.S. Department of Commerce, 1961), p. 356.

Item Veto. The item veto is one that applies to a particular section of an act. The President does not possess this power but has to invalidate an entire measure in order to eliminate its objectionable parts. Proponents of a presidential item veto point out that it would enable him to protect the integrity of his budget by striking out appropriations at odds with his financial requests. It could also be used against "riders" to appropriations acts, unrelated sections tacked on the end in the hope that the need for funds will preclude their veto.

However, it is argued that a presidential item veto would encourage irresponsible appropriations by Congress on the assumption that the President would veto them and incur the blame of the voters for doing so, that it would augment an already inflated executive power and reduce to virtually nothing the power of Congress to control the public purse strings, and that Congress would enact key appropriations in general acts to which the item veto would not apply. Therefore, nothing would be gained.

Rule-making Power of the President. Congress is increasingly constrained by the process of legislation, and the scope and complexity of the problems of modern government, to enact statutes in general terms, leaving to the President and his subordinates the task of refining their provisions in the course of applying them to particular circumstances. If Congress attempted to prescribe in the statutes every possible detail of their application, they would apply only to those details. The laws would be unworkably rigid and would quickly become outmoded. Hence, they are enacted in general terms, and much discretion is left to those who administer them. By issuing rules and regulations as authorized by Congress, the executive can give specific meaning to the general policies prescribed in statutes by the legislative branch. Authority to issue rules and regulations with the force of law may be granted to the President alone, to him for delegation to a subordinate, or directly to a subordinate executive officer. So great is the quantity of "subordinate legislation" which issues from the executive branch that Congress has required that it should be specially printed in the *Federal Register* so that the public can ascertain its content.

JUDICIAL POWERS AND FUNCTIONS
OF THE EXECUTIVE

The Pardoning Power. The pardoning power of the President is related to the administration of justice. Thus:

. . . he shall have Power to grant Reprieves and Pardons for Offences against the United States, except in Cases of Impeachment.

The pardoning power is not subject to legislative control. Congress cannot limit the effect of a presidential pardon nor exclude from its application any class of offenders.

This power of the President extends only to crimes defined by act of Congress, may be exercised before or after conviction, but does not extend to convictions of impeachment. If it did, an impeached President could pardon himself. A pardon may be granted absolutely or conditionally, but the power may not be exercised in anticipation of a crime.

A pardon is an act of executive clemency which usually has the effect of cancelling

. . . both the punishment prescribed for the offence and the guilt of the offender; and when the pardon is full, it releases the punishment and blots out of existence the guilt, so that in the eye of the law the offender is as innocent as if he had never committed the offence. If granted before conviction, it prevents any of the penalties and disabilities consequent upon conviction from attaching; —if granted after conviction, it . . . restores him to all his civil rights; it makes him, as it were, a new man, and gives him a new credit and capacity.[17]

However, a pardon cannot

. . . make amends for the past. It affords no relief for what has been suffered by the offender in his person by imprisonment, forced labor, or otherwise; it does not give compensation for what has been done or suffered, nor does it impose upon the government any obligation to give it. The offence being established by judicial proceedings, that which has been done or suffered while they were in force is presumed to have been rightfully done and justly suffered, and no satisfaction for it can be required. Neither does the pardon affect any rights which have vested in others directly by the execution of the judgment for the offence, or which have been acquired by others whilst that judgment was in force.[18]

Executive clemency under this power may take other forms. The President may grant a reprieve, which suspends a legally imposed penalty, or a commutation of sentence to substitute a lesser for a more severe penalty. However, neither removes the stigma of guilt nor restores civil or political rights. He may grant a presidential amnesty, a pardon granted to a group or class of individuals. Although neither Congress nor the courts may interfere with or limit an act of executive clemency, Congress may enact statutes granting amnesty by remitting penalties imposed under national laws.

Quasi-adjudication. In the course of administering laws, agents of the executive power are called upon to make frequent decisions to settle controversies between the government and individuals or groups to whom regulatory laws are applied. Hence, many rights and duties are determined by administrative action. The phenomenon of "administrative justice" arises when executive officers perform functions similar to those of a court. When an administrative officer enforces laws and determines rights and duties without recourse to courts, adjudicative power is exercised. This exercise of decision-making power represents a blending of executive and judicial authority in apparent violation of the doctrine of the separation of powers.

Administrative justice implemented by officers and units of the executive branch is an inescapable feature of modern government. It cannot be avoided; it has been recognized by Congress and the courts. Therefore, the only intelligent course of action is to learn to live with it, to subject it to sufficient controls, and to perfect its processes to produce administrative justice that is responsible to Congress and fair to the public.

---

[17] *Ex parte Garland* (1867), 4 Wallace 333, 380.
[18] *Knote* v. *United States* (1877), 95 U.S. 149, 153-154.

CHAPTER XVII

Theory and Structure of the Executive Branch

POLICY AND ADMINISTRATION

Agencies of the executive branch execute the laws. A law embodies a policy enacted by Congress as necessary or desirable. Its fulfillment is the responsibility of administration. Laws are seldom self-executing; they must be administered or remain inert. But the wisest laws and most statesman-like policies can be rendered ineffectual by improper implementation.

Thus, according to theory, the legislative branch formulates policies and the executive branch administers them. In practice, however, the activities of the political branches are inseparable. The impact of administration upon policy formulation occurs at many points and is irresistible by Congress. Policy formulation and administration are connected steps equally necessary to fulfillment of the general welfare. Hence, policy formulation has come under strong executive influence. Many policies originate in the executive branch. The President's legislative powers have been noted above. Vast numbers of executive or administrative rules, orders, regulations, and directives make policy by

399

filling in the details of statutes enacted in general terms. Further, what administration does is largely determined by statutes which set its goals, bestow its authority, provide its machinery, appropriate its funds, and prescribe its procedures, organizational forms, and personnel limits.

If a statute is general and legislative intent is not clear, administrators must exercise their judgment as to its meaning and application. Such discretion often permits the executive to determine what laws will be rigorously enforced, against whom, and when. It is sometimes broad enough to enable administrators to defeat the legislative intention. Interest groups seeking to influence the implementation of laws and the recommendations of executive agents to Congress to enact, amend, or repeal statutes also focus on administration. This latter recognizes and mitigates their special demands, and transmits and explains their proposals to Congress and the policies of Congress to them. Administrators serve as consultants to Congress and its committees, draft bills, supply information, and testify before legislative committees.

Administration and policy formulation are essentially political in nature and are conducted in a social milieu of which government is an important part. The enactment and administration of laws ought to be responsive to the pressures and demands emanating from that milieu. Administration is not carried on in a vacuum. It ameliorates social and economic conflict, perceives changing community values, and transforms them into programs to give them reality. It promotes harmony and unity in a society of myriad interests; it seeks to attain social, economic, and legal justice. It acts pursuant to legislative commands, and seeks to provide an atmosphere of order and stability in society so that peaceful change can take place.

The activity of administration varies according to the demands made upon it. "Big government" is a modern phenomenon. It is not the development of greedy, empire-building administrators. Congress has met the demand for remedial legislation. And the enactment of this has produced an expansion of administration, because administration transforms legislative intent into governmental action and gives permanence and continuity to the conduct of public functions.

Control of Administration by the President. As head of the executive branch the President should be able to control and direct administration. However, his powers of direction and control are far from complete. The great size of the executive branch works to defeat them. He must contend with nullifying forces like grants of statutory authority to subordinates, administrative independence, and congressional interference. His control is implemented through staff organization and cabinet meetings, appointments and removals, through his control of budget preparation and of policy and expenditure, through his personal prestige and leadership, his reorganization power, his delegation of authority, and the issuance of rules, orders, commands, and regulations. Nevertheless, the scope and effectiveness of his directive authority fails to approach that which his constitutional position implies should exist.

Control of Administration by Congress. The dependence of administration upon Congress is so thorough that the power of the legislature over the executive is almost unlimited. Few phases or subjects are beyond the scope of its concern. Congress has been likened to a national board of directors which controls and holds accountable the national general manager, the President. By its investigatory, appropriations, auditing, and general legislative powers Congress oversees the enforcement of the law and the fulfillment of the legislative intent. However, the defects of congressional structure, the pressure of legislative business, the necessary compromises of politics, and the size and complexity of the executive branch go far to negate its theoretical power to oversee the executive.

SOME GENERAL PRINCIPLES OF ORGANIZATION

Although the President is head of administration, he is not an operating officer; he does not administer the law, but he sees that others faithfully do so. Most administration is carried out by ten departments, but other non-departmental units exist. Whatever the type, however, the organization of an administrative unit is basically the same.

Organization is basic to all collective human effort. When even two people undertake a simple project some organization is necessary. The need varies with the size and complexity of the endeavor, for organization is the arrangement of personnel and tasks into integrated systems of relationships which will enable a maximum use of resources to obtain the desired objective in the most efficient and economical manner.

The Position. The basic unit of any organization is the position. It may be described as a job, office, or employment, full or part-time, filled or vacant, paid or unpaid, having certain duties, authority, and responsibility that distinguish it from other positions. As long as they remain the same, the position does also. It is different from the person who occupies it. Positions are grouped into small units which are combined into successively larger ones.

Top Management. Positions at the top of an organization demand general knowledge, insight, leadership, tact, imagination, and managerial skill. Incumbents determine broad policies within the limits of statutory authority, prescribe internal operating procedures and structure, resolve major conflicts, delegate authority, fix responsibility, conduct public relations, coordinate, provide leadership, and see to planning, staffing, budgeting. They are filled by the President with the consent of the Senate, are frequently referred to as "top management," and are the policy-determining group.

Middle Management. Below them are the "middle management" positions, the bureau and division chiefs, the branch, section, and unit heads, career supervisory personnel whose special competence is administrative ability. They receive directives, orders, regulations from the top and translate them into operating plans and programs, plan the work of their units, apportion tasks to personnel within them, check progress of work, and maintain smooth operations.

Supervision is a primary function of middle management. Hence, it operates to control individuals, to direct their actions, and to reduce the irrational behavior of employees. It channels the conduct of employees by deciding what to do and how to do it, by improving morale and motivating workers, and by directing the group effort.

Hierarchy. An organization, therefore, is composed of positions arranged in groups and assigned to different levels in the structure. A few at the top exercise extensive authority. Those of lower levels are more numerous, but their authority decreases and their responsibility increases. Thus, organizational hierarchy consists of positions arranged into superior-subordinate relationships. Each employee assumes the authority, duties, and responsibility vested in his position. He is the superior of positions subject to his authority, but he is responsible to persons who are his superiors.

Hierarchy serves other purposes. Lines of command and communications run through the key points of authority from top to bottom. Responsibility moves up from lower to higher positions, and authority flows down by delegation from the top to successively lower positions. The delegation of authority forces decision-making into the lower levels of the structure; it helps develop leadership and initiative in the junior positions. Most important, hierarchy makes division of labor possible and aids the use of available special skills and knowledge.

Coordination and Control. Organization is essential to coordination. If the units of an organization are assembled in their proper relationships, each will make a coordinated contribution to attainment of their common goal. The better constructed an organization is, the better will its parts work together. However, since coordination can never be perfectly achieved, control is necessary. It is exercised throughout the structure; any organization is a pattern of supervisory relationships. Control (supervision) is exercised at every level where authority is exerted. Thus, both coordination and control seek to direct administrative conduct into desired channels.

Span of Control. An administrator can control only a limited number of persons. That ability is known as his "span of control." It varies according to his ability, the number and location of the persons supervised, what they do, and other factors. Hence, proper regard for the limit of effective supervision is essential to sound organization and effective administration

Location of Authority. Ultimate authority ought to reside in the head of an organization. Thus, the President should control administration with lines of command running to the unit and away from it throughout the entire service. All responsibility should run upward to the President. In practice, however, this ideal is only partially realized.

The relationship of an organization head to his unit is not significantly different from that of the President to the executive branch. The President is *the* executive, and in law an agency head is *the* agency. The organization head is responsible for general administration and for budgetary and personnel management. His subordinates act largely in his name and subject to his control. Unlike the President, he is the subject of legal actions against the organization, receives processes issued against it, and signs processes issued in its name against others.

Delegation of Authority. The head of an organization cannot personally exercise the authority vested in his position by law. He must have subordinates. Their authority should not be vested in their positions by law but should be delegated to them from above. When necessary, subdelegations to the next lower levels of authority may be made. Each subdelegation of authority is narrower than the one received and may be modified at the will of the delegator. It may be a blanket authority or power to act for a specific purpose only. A delegation of authority to perform the duties of a specific position is most common. Thus:

The President of the United States is authorized to designate and empower the head of any department or agency in the executive branch or any official thereof who is required to be appointed by and with the advice and consent of the Senate, to perform without approval, ratification, or other action by the President (1) any function which is vested in the President by law, or (2) any function which such officer is required or authorized by law to perform only with or subject to the approval, ratification, or other action of the President: *Provided:* That nothing contained herein shall relieve the President of his responsibility in office for the acts of any such head or other official designated by him to perform such functions. Such designation and authorization shall be in writing, shall be published in the Federal Register, shall be subject to such terms, conditions, and limits as the President may deem advisable, and shall be revocable at any time by the President in whole or in part.[1]

The virtues of delegation are numerous. Without it organization could not exist; division of labor would be impossible. All decisions would have to be made at the top; top management would be swamped and the organization would flounder. Instead, dispersion of authority by delegation spreads responsibility throughout the organization, forces decision making into the lower levels where it can be made by subordinates close to the problem at hand. It develops subordinates by encouraging them to accept responsibility, exercise initiative, and show resourcefulness. It is an

[1] *U.S. Code,* Title 3, sec. 301.

expression of confidence in the junior, and usually generates a sense of appreciation and loyalty toward the superior.

Thus, it is the backbone of administration, but it does not relieve the superior of responsibility for its use. Responsibility also goes with delegation, for acceptance of delegated authority implies willingness to exercise it properly and when necessary. Finally, its pattern must be constantly modified, for no pattern once adopted will always meet every administrative need. Structure and delegated authority must be adapted to each change of organizational purpose.

Function in Organization. Administrative units are set up to perform a function or group of related functions. Each should exist to attain a single goal and should be so structured and coordinated with the rest that it makes its maximum contribution to the total effort. Normally, the lower a unit is in the over-all structure, the more specific is its function and the clearer is its unity of purpose.

In major units the largest functional subdivisions having a distinct unity of purpose are usually known as bureaus. Ideally, each bureau should function harmoniously as part of a whole, but in fact each tends to become an autonomous unit, with a strong sense of self-identity, cohesiveness, and pride. Its personnel develop divergent values about its worth and tend to think of *its* functions as most important, to demand more personnel and a greater share of the appropriations. Cooperation, harmony, subordination, teamwork, and sacrifice essential to attainment of the departmental goals are each opposed by a tendency toward empire building and organizational aggrandizement. Each bureau tends to become a department within a department. Its chief may possess statutory authority which he can exercise independently of superior control; he builds his own support with interest groups and members of Congress; he appears as the rival of the department head rather than as his loyal subordinate. Thus, the lines of authority from, and responsibility to, the President are seriously weakened.

Single versus Plural Executive. Should there be one man or several at the head of an organization? The proper reply depends upon circumstances not revealed by the question. It is generally conceded that a plural executive should not be vested with administrative duties. Confusion, delay, buck-passing, and lack of responsibility will result from dividing administrative power among several people. When a plural body is felt to be necessary, all purely administrative functions should be assigned to a general manager. This officer would implement the policies of the group subject to its control. Nevertheless, plural executives may be used for performing quasi-legislative and quasi-judicial functions, for reaching collective judgments, for serving as an appellate body, for working out new policy on a trial-and-error basis, for insulating administration from politics, or for representing diverse interests.

However, when an organization is established, its policies, procedures and standards worked out, the public interest defined and protected, and when the influence of politics is not a problem, a single executive is best. He will best provide the unity, the clear focus of responsibility, the energy of decision and action, and the firmness of direction and leadership necessary for effective administration.

Caveat. The ideas of these paragraphs should be regarded only as bases for discussing organization. Span of control, hierarchy and its attendant ramifications, delegation and coordination, etc., are helpful conceptions for discussing and analyzing organization. They reveal that it is not wholly or even mainly the product of accident but is a relatively permanent and stable arrangement of parts upon rational considerations guided by standards of general but not wholly absolute validity. With this admonition in mind, attention is turned to the active structure of the executive branch.

THE EXECUTIVE BRANCH—STRUCTURE

General Comment. The executive branch is the largest of the three constitutional divisions. Its employees number approximately two and one-half million. Its structure is complex, its functions numerous and technical. Its general task is to execute the laws. To do this it operates through a bewildering array of departments, agencies, corporations, and commissions.

Some units known as "line" agencies serve or regulate the public, or in other ways administer the laws upon them. Others serve the "line" units by performing common functions on their behalf such as records storage and maintenance, and purchasing. They have incidental contact with the public and are known as "auxiliary" agencies. Finally, "staff" organizations have no contact with the citizenry but exist to advise, study, recommend, supervise, and otherwise aid the President in his control of the executive branch.

The executive branch ought not to be thought of as a neat monolithic structure. Even the nomenclature used to designate its parts is unstandardized. Titles such as department, board, commission, service, administration, authority, corporation, agency, and office distinguish, often without apparent difference, the units of the executive branch. In theory, they serve a major purpose or a small number of related purposes; they are arranged in a neat hierarchy spreading out below the President, to whom they are represented as being effectively subordinated and controlled. The impression conveyed is one of unity, cooperation, and integration between them and the President. He controls policy and the administrative units do his bidding, so that policies and programs are nicely integrated, and each unit coordinates its activities and objectives with others similarly concerned. They execute laws without prejudice or preference, and the "general welfare" shines before their eyes to be served and striven for. To its realization they are unswervingly dedicated. However, reality falls considerably short of theory.

Political and Routine Executive. The "political executive" numbers approximately one per cent of the total, and consists of officers elected or appointed to office who comprise the policy-forming executive. They and "top management" are almost identical. They include the President and the "superior" officers of the many administrative units of the executive branch. They are temporary wielders of public authority whose tenure is directly or indirectly dependent upon the will of the people expressed through the electoral process.

The second group of executive agents includes more than two million employees, who comprise the "routine," or career, executive, known as the civil service. The "routine" executive should be politically neutral, should be chosen by competitive processes, and should possess permanence of tenure as long as satisfactory service is rendered. This group provides stability and continuity to government operations in spite of the impermanence, lack of knowledge and ability, and unfamiliarity with government procedures often characteristic of the political executive.

The President may be thought of as on a plane of authority above other political agents, these agents as being above other lesser ones, and so on down. Again, the political executives may be thought of as above the numerous routine executives. The positions of the routine executives can be arranged into various classes and grades according to their duties, responsibilities, and authority. Hence, the executive branch can be ideally seen as a number of positions differentiated by their political or non-political nature and arranged into a vast pyramid. At the top in solitary splendor stands the President. Beneath him are the political heads of departments and their assistants, still relatively few in number. Beneath them, and usually subject to their direction and control, are the various levels into which the routine positions of the executive are arranged. The lower levels of agents are successively responsible to those above them, and all are ultimately responsible to the President, and he to the voters.

The Vice President. The Vice President is the second-ranking political executive. His term and qualifications are the same as those of the President. His office exists to provide a successor to the Presidency. His constitutional duties are to preside over meetings of the Senate and to vote in case of a tie. His office has traditionally been held in low esteem as a reward for faithful party supporters, as a burying ground for political rivals, and as a make-weight in presidential elections.

Knowledge that eight Vice Presidents have succeeded to the Presidency, the sudden death of President Kennedy, and recent experiences with the poor health of President Eisenhower have combined to emphasize the potential importance of the Vice Presidency. Without any change in their constitutional status recent Vice Presidents have been given increased responsibilities and have been brought into closer contact with the Presidency. Vice President Nixon was a member of the National Security Council, and regularly attended cabinet meetings and presided over them when the President was absent. He chaired the President's Commission on Government Contracts. He made statements on foreign policy as administration spokesman; he was consulted on policy statements to be included in the State of the Union address. He emerged as a major political strategist of the administration. His activities added to the status of his office in the public mind; the Twenty-second Amendment made him the heir apparent to the presidential nomination. However, these changes have been based upon personalities rather than law, so that a future President could reverse the trend and return to the former view of the office as a virtually useless appendage of the executive branch.

Change the Nature of the Vice Presidency? To relieve the burdens reposing upon the President, the Vice President might be made formally more useful to his chief. To relieve him of his legislative duty would require a constitutional amendment but would emphasize his character as an executive officer and facilitate the vesting of executive duties in his office. Again, administrative duties might be added to the present office. Or, a statutory administrative Vice President might be created to provide administrative aid. Such changes would, however, raise one or more of the following objections and would doubtless be defeated. First, the services of the Vice President in promoting better legislative-executive relations would be greatly impaired or lost. Second, Vice Presidents have more than once differed strongly with their President's major policies. Third, the bases upon which the choice of Vice Presidents rests are not of the sort to promote a relationship of harmony and confidence between the two officers. Fourth, great care, not now taken, would be required to ensure that Vice Presidents possessed ability, talent, and stature. Fifth, it would be very difficult to transform the Vice Presidency into an effective office compatible with the necessary and the undoubted power of the President to choose his immediate aides and chief subordinates and hold them responsible to him.

The Executive Office of the President. The President must have help in performing the duties of his office. He is aided by every agency of his branch, but help is also furnished by special units located in the Executive Office of the President. They aid him in the formation and execution of policy and in the control of the executive branch.

A staff unit serves the President in an advisory or facilitative capacity, and functions to control and coordinate the "line" agencies. It may have been created by an act of Congress or by executive order, but it is subject to the direct command of the President. Its authority to issue orders, directives, and rules to "line" agencies is held by statutory grant or by delegation from the President.

In general, the following functions are typical of those performed by staff units to assist the President: (1) to make studies of contemplated organizational and procedural changes; (2) to conduct investigations, collect, analyze, and evaluate data, and formulate recommendations thereon for consideration by the President; (3) to keep the President informed; (4) to aid in anticipating new developments and making plans to meet them; (5) to protect their principal from hasty or ill-tempered judgments; (6) to see that only matters proper for decision by their principal reach him, after full study and analysis, and in a form suitable for intelligent and quick decision; (7) to receive, explain, and pass on to subordinates the decisions of their principal; (8) to examine and report to their principal upon the implementation of his decisions by subordinates.

Hence, staff activities lighten the President's burden by freeing him from details and by conserving his time and energy.

Within the Executive Office of the President are several units responsible for aiding the President in the formulation of policy. They include the policy aides of the White House staff, the National Security Council which integrates and advises on all matters of foreign, military, and domestic policies related to national security, the Office of Emergency Planning which advises on policy for the full preparedness and mobilization of the nation's nonmilitary resources, the National Aeronautics and Space Council, the Office of Science Technology, and the Council of Economic Advisers which

. . . analyzes the national economy and its various segments; advises the President on economic developments; appraises the economic programs and policies of the Federal Government; recommends to the President policies for economic growth and stability; and assists in the preparation of the economic reports of the President to the Congress.[2]

The Bureau of the Budget is mainly a facilitative staff agency; it serves the President by enforcing service-wide coordination and control. Nevertheless, it exerts a strong influence over the formulation and implementation of policy. The Bureau standardizes accounting forms and procedures used to control administration; reviews for approval or disapproval all legislature proposals which originate within the executive branch before they are sent to Congress; prepares executive orders for the President; reviews and analyzes all legislation sent by Congress to the President; advises what action should be taken thereon; prepares or advises on veto messages; keeps the President and administrative agencies informed of

[2] *United States Government Organization Manual, 1962-1963* (Washington, D.C.: Office of the Federal Register, 1962), p. 56.

the implications of legislation pending in Congress; and studies, evaluates, and prepares plans for improving the organization and management of the executive branch.

Although the Bureau is a staff agency the fact that it acts in the President's name causes the distinction between a recommendation and a command to become so blurred as to be lost. Moreover, it is given frequent grants of authority to direct specific actions, with the result that its advisory character is lost sight of. Rarely does a department or agency challenge the Bureau of the Budget.

The Cabinet. The cabinet is extra-legal and extra-constitutional. It is wholly subordinate to the President; his subordination to it would divide responsibility within the executive branch and undermine his position as head of administration.

The cabinet is composed of the President's "official family," and consists of persons asked by him to meet with him. The heads of the executive departments are invariably included. Recent Presidents have also requested the Vice President, the Director of the Bureau of the Budget, the Chairman of the Civil Service Commission, and even personal friends whose advice was desired, to attend. It is purely advisory and shares none of the executive power. The President is responsible politically for the acts of its members. Its members ought to be persons who agree with his policies and in whom he has trust. Hence, they are seldom carried over from one administration to another. Each President prefers to choose his own advisors, but they need not be members of his party.

Some factors limit the composition of the cabinet, however. Senatorial confirmation must be obtained. Appointments to reward party service, to placate the leader of a rival party faction, to compensate a losing candidate for the presidential nomination, to reward or appease a member of Congress, or to represent diverse areas or interests may have to be made. They are seldom chosen from Congress and need not be party leaders. Understanding of governmental methods and law, knowledge of subject-matter, and administrative ability only occasionally receive serious consideration as qualifications for appointment to cabinet-level position.

Because the cabinet is wholly advisory, formal decisions are not taken. Votes merely reveal the sense of the groups. The President is free to consult or ignore it. He can call meetings as he desires. Mr. Kennedy rarely convened his cabinet, but preferred to consult members individually or in small groups. He can create a "super cabinet" which swallows up the regular one. Meetings are informal, leisurely, and secret, without formal rules of debate and with a free exchange of views. Subjects are presented by the President or, with his consent, by the members. The discussions often improve morale, coordinate policies and programs, promote uniform understandings, and bring out useful views and information.

Members are individually responsible to the President for the administration of their respective agencies but collectively give him advice. They thus have a dual status. However, they are neither collectively nor individually responsible to the Congress or to either chamber.

The cabinet is a less than ideal advisory body. Department heads are too immersed in the affairs of their agencies to have the time to serve the President to his maximum advantage. They know they will be judged by their administrative achievements, not by their cabinet service. Agency loyalty occasionally conflicts with loyalty to the President when budget cutbacks, loss of programs, personnel reductions, or other aspects of departmental status are involved. They too often lack administrative ability, political acumen, and knowledge of the subject. Therefore, their advice may be less than fully reliable. Hence, Presidents often turn for aid and advice to a more selective "kitchen cabinet" of trusted friends and advisers.

The importance of the cabinet varies according to the personality of the President and his conception of his office. "Weak" Presidents tend to rely heavily upon its advice; "strong" ones give little or no heed to it. Its importance is also determined by the frequency of its meetings and the issues submitted to its consideration. Its character is of considerable importance. Mediocre cabinets have been most common in American history, but an able one can add great strength to the executive.

Interdepartmental problems are assigned to committees of cabinet members whose knowledge and experience bear on their solution. They have been used to form foreign and domestic policies concerning transportation, natural resources, security, finances, manpower, and other pertinent considerations.

The Institutionalization of the Presidency. The Presidency and the President interact. Each conditions the other in various ways and to different degrees. The President to some extent makes the office what he wants it to be; conversly, the office exerts a strong influence over its incumbent. When the problems of government that demanded the personal attention of the President were few in number, relatively simple in nature, limited in scope, and mainly confined to domestic affairs, he was able to keep in reasonably close touch with their details and to take a personal hand in as many phases of their solution as he cared to. His cabinet was available to give advice, as were a few close personal associates and trusted advisers. The administrative staff of the executive branch numbered a few thousand employees, all of whom were subject to his partisan political control in his capacity as party leader. Then, if he desired to, a President could be President in fact as well as in name.

However, among the concomitants of modern government is to be counted not only an increase in the authority and prestige of the Presidency but also a great increase in the number and size of the units that comprise his office. The constitutional position of the President in the system of government remains the same if measured by the written document, but the aggrandizement of executive power and influence has in part caused, and in part been caused by, a proliferation of the units which help him to be President. The Presidency has become institutionalized. Both the structure and the functions of the executive branch and the institutions of his immediate office threaten to escape his domination and to dominate him instead. The President more and more finds himself dependent upon the planning, recommendations, knowledge, resources, and experiences of his subordinates and advisers. To that extent he becomes their captive, dependent, unless he wishes to act blindly, capriciously, or arbitrarily, upon what they tell him and what they advise. The power of decision, of course, belongs to him alone, but he is at the center of a great swirl of influences and pressures, originating from within as well as from outside the government, which seek to determine how his decision-making power will be used. Moreover, the power to decide is confronted by times that demand sound decisions in rapid succession, and carries with itself a tremendously wide area of discretionary action. These factors together with a condition of chronic emergency, the prevalence of foreign and military affairs, and the ease with which a President can mobilize public opinion in his favor, all tend to stimulate the exercise of executive authority, and at the same time to encourage a relaxation of the traditional controls upon it by making their effective operation more difficult. Perhaps never before in the history of the American Presidency has the President of the United States relied so heavily upon his advisory units and aides as have the incumbents of the office since the end of World War II. Within the White House staff, the Bureau of the Budget, the Council of Economic Advisers, the National Security Council, and the Office of Emergency Planning are almost 1,500 political aides and confidantes, economic planners, military strategists, coordinators, budget analysts, special assistants, and a host of others. All combine their efforts to keep the President informed, to anticipate problems, to find and propose solutions to existing ones, to transmit orders, to evaluate their implementation, to plan policy programs, and to present matters to him in a form suitable for speedy and intelligent decision and action.

Although the institutionalization of the Presidency is probably an inevitable consequence of the times and conditions in which it functions, it is a disguised blessing at best. It does inject an element of evenness into the office that, on the one hand, can go far to bridge the depths of presidential lethargy, naïvete, indifference, and lack of ability, or on the other hand, to tone down an excess of presidential exhuberance, zeal, and demagoguery. It does increase the range and variety of experiences, viewpoints, resources, etc., at the command of the President, all of which he cannot be expected to have acquired himself. It does serve to mitigate the tendency of the body politic to overvalue and to undercritize the President, thereby encouraging the growth of irresponsible leadership.

But the institutionalization of the Presidency also has undesirable consequences. It makes the President excessively subject to the influences of those persons who prepare recommendations, propose alternative courses of action, supply information. Responsibility for supplying information affords the opportunity to withhold it as well; an opportunity to propose alternatives is an opportunity to emphasize one in preference to better ones and to weight data in its favor; knowledge of the President's plans and thoughts enhances the ability to cater to them; the ability to control access to him carries with it the ability to control the ideas he hears, the persons he sees, and the advice he gets. It provides a setting in which presidential aides, from whatever motive or reason, can act to usurp authority, derive personal gain, exert undue influence over the processes of administration, or indulge in some other questionable activity. It tends to produce discordant and conflicting recommendations and advice, and if the President permits it to do so, it can isolate him from the political realities of his office and encourage him to take an artificial view of his position and functions as being "above politics." Therefore, although the President is but one man, the modern Presidency is the sum of many men, an institution.

Executive Departments. The Constitution made no direct provision for administrative units within the executive branch, but assumed that those developed during the Confederation would continue to administer the business of government. Hence, it merely declared that

The President . . . may require the Opinion, in writing, of the principal Officer in each of the executive Departments, upon any Subject relating to the Duties of their respective Offices. . . .

. . . The Congress may by Law vest the Appointment of such inferior Officers, as they think proper, in the President alone, in the Courts of Law or in the Heads of the Departments.

The "necessary and proper clause" gives Congress power to create, alter, or abolish administrative units necessary to execute the duties and responsibilities of the President. The best known of the agencies that it has provided are the executive departments. They are ten in number; and in order of seniority they are the departments of State, Treasury, Defense, Justice, Post Office, Interior, Agriculture, Commerce, Labor, and Health, Education and Welfare. Their functions are the oldest or most widely accepted of those performed by the national government. Each is headed by a single officer of the "superior" type who is traditionally a member of the cabinet; it is normally composed of several single-purpose functional subdivisions called bureaus. Each is directly subject to control by the President.

The Constitution leaves the type and number of departments to be fixed according to the needs of time and circumstance. Congress has sporadically established the various departments. It may prescribe their internal organization, operations, and procedures, but it usually leaves them to control by the executive. Because they are created by statute they may not be added to, altered, or abolished by the President acting without authority granted by Congress.

Independent Establishments. Congress has created outside the departments numerous "independent agencies"; they report to the President, are subject to his control, but are not of cabinet rank. Some, like the Veterans Administration, are headed by single, others by plural, executives. Some exceed in size several of the departments; others, such as the American Battle Monuments Commission, possess fewer than fifty employees. The powers and functions of some rival those of the departments in scope and importance. In other instances their significance is imperceptible. They perform the newer, temporary, or experimental undertakings of government which are regulative, administrative, or entrepreneurial in nature. Most were created by act of Congress, a few, for example the old Office of Price Administration, by executive order. Most endure as permanent parts of the executive branch; a few have been abolished, and others, like the many World War II offices—Censorship, War Information, etc.— lapsed at the expiration of their authorized life.

The causes of their creation are varied. Among pertinent considerations may be noted the political factors which influence Congress, the temporary nature of units, the novelty of their functions, their failure to fit into an existing department, the distrust of or desire to chastise a department head, the auxiliary, staff or clientele nature of a unit, the desire to utilize a plural executive, and the unwillingness of Congress to entrust power over important rights to a single politically responsive executive. Moreover, these factors have exerted their influence in endless combination. These independent agencies adversely affect the unity, integration, and facility of presidential direction and control.

Independent Regulatory Commissions. Another group of non-departmental agencies nominally within the executive branch consists of the uniquely-American independent regulatory commissions. They are intended to be wholly removed from politics, and resemble no other unit in power, function, and relationship to the President. They are legally independent of presidential control. Their function is to regulate complex interests which require the attention of experts, involve important segments of the national economic system, and transcend state power. Their regulation by independent commissions is intended to ensure fairness, to permit control by experts, and to eliminate political pressures and influences. However, not all governmental regulation is effected by independent commissions, and not all commissions are regulatory.

The regulatory commissions and the areas of activity which they supervise are the Federal Reserve Board (money supply, credit, and national and many state commercial banks); the Federal Power Commission (gas and electrical utilities); the Federal Communications Commission (radio, telephone, television, and telegraph); the Interstate Commerce Commission (interstate carriers by rail, water, and motor); the Civil Aeronautics Board (interstate carriers by air); the Federal Maritime Board (ocean carriers); the Securities and Exchange Commission (buying and selling of securities, and operation of stock exchanges); the National Labor Relations Board (unionization, collective bargaining, and unfair labor practices in interstate commerce); and the Federal Trade Commission (unfair trade practices).

Among the more important reasons for these agencies the following may be cited: Congress is unable to provide, effectively, the necessary regulation; the interests regulated oppose control by politically responsive units; regulation must be fair and impartial and must protect private and public interests; representation of diverse interests and views and collective judgments by experts are made possible. The independent commissions and their staffs of experts are intended to meet these requirements.

The independent regulatory agencies are headed by plural executives consisting of from five to eleven members appointed by the President with the consent of the Senate. Their terms of office are fixed by statute at from five to fourteen years, and expire on a staggered basis. Most are required to be bipartisan, on the false theory that non-partisanship will be achieved. Members may usually be removed by the President only for causes stated in law, of which malfeasance in office, inefficiency, and neglect of duty are examples.

These arrangements are intended to isolate the commissions from political interference, but their effectiveness is open to question. They are not immune to political pressures or influence, especially from outside government. A "two-term" President can "stack" their memberships and thereby influence the substance and administration of their policies. Bipartisanship is easily circumvented, for a President can select appointees from the liberal or conservative wing of the pertinent political party. He can mobilize public opinion against them, can control them through the Bureau of the Budget and the Civil Service Commission, and can veto certain commission actions. Congress has insulated them from the legal control but not from the influence of the President. However, they are not at all independent of Congress, for they are created to aid it and are its creatures subject to its full control. Their chief accountability, therefore, is to Congress, not to the President.

No immunity from control by the judiciary is possessed by them. The courts will not hesitate in a proper instance to inquire into their jurisdiction, procedures, or the substance of their action.

Finally, they do not escape the influence of outside interests. They respond to the suggestions of congressmen and other public figures. Their institutional well-being is aided by the support of interest groups, often the ones they control. The choice of their members from the interests

regulated has led to partiality in their favor and to sacrifice of the public interest.

Case for the Independent Regulatory Commissions. A fairly strong case can be made out for the independence of these commissions. The tradition and mechanics of independence have undoubtedly insulated them to some extent from presidential and congressional pressures. It has aided the gradual definition of rules by a process of trial and refinement. The Hoover Commission study group in 1949 stated the case for the independent commission as follows:

The wide latitude inherent in effective regulation opens the door to favoritism and unfairness in administration. The regulated interests are powerful and often politically influential. The privileges which the regulatory agencies can grant or withhold are often of great value, and regulation will obviously have a tremendous impact on the profits, service, and finances of the industry involved.

This combination of wide discretion on the part of officials, and strong motives for influencing the officials on the part of the regulated industry, involves serious risks of corruption and unfairness. If the agency is subject to partisan or political influence or control, this will not only defeat the public purposes of regulation and unfairly benefit the influential, but will also tend to impair public confidence in the democratic process and the effectiveness of governmental action generally. Thus, in the interests of fairness to the individuals concerned, of the attainment of the public objectives, and of the maintenance of the integrity of government, there is a vital necessity for assuring that such regulatory agencies are insulated from partisan influence or control to the maximum extent feasible.

The independent commission was designed to meet this need. The number of members and their security of tenure are intended to assure freedom from partisan control or favoritism. The group is able to resist outside influence more effectively than an individual and each member is free from a threat of removal as a source of pressure. Moreover, since the activities of the commission may be more subject to public scrutiny than would be a single bureau in a large department there is greater opportunity for exposure of pressures or improper actions. Finally, while provisions for hearings or similar safeguards against arbitrary actions are not peculiar to commissions, they may be more effective when combined with group action.[3]

Functions of the Commissions. The commissions perform two types of function. Within the scope of their authority they fix policy, prescribe standards, and lay down rules and regulations for future application. This is the essence of the legislative function and is referred to as "quasi-legislative." Regulatory commissions also enforce these policies, standards, and rules by procedures resembling those used in courts of law. This activity is designated as "quasi-judicial." Hence, the commissions are frequently referred to as being quasi-legislative and quasi-judicial in character. Their unique feature, therefore, is the degree to which they combine the functions of making, executing, and interpreting rules and regulations that have the force of law.

The independent regulatory commissions create a confusing and difficult situation in the field of national administration. There is a conflict of principle involved in their make-up and functions. They suffer from an internal inconsistency, an unsoundness of basic theory. This is because they are vested with duties of administration and policy determinations with respect to which they ought to be clearly and effectively responsible to the President, and at the same time they are given important judicial work in the doing of which they ought to be wholly independent of Executive control. In fact, the bulk of regulatory commission work involves the application of "legislative" standards of conduct to concrete cases, a function at once discretionary and judicial, and demanding, therefore, responsibility and independence.

The evils resulting from this confusion of principles are insidious and far-reaching. In the first place, governmental powers of great importance are being exercised under conditions of virtual irresponsibility. . . . Power without responsibility has no place in a government based on the theory of democratic control, for responsibility is the people's only weapon, their only insurance against abuse of power.

But though the commissions enjoy power without responsibility, they also leave the President with responsibility without power. Placed by the Con-

[3] The Commission on Organization of the Executive Branch of the Government, *Task Force Report on Regulatory Commissions* (January, 1949), p. 20.

stitution at the head of a unified and centralized Executive Branch, and charged with the duty to see that the laws are faithfully executed, he must detour around powerful administrative agencies which are in no way subject to his authority and which are, therefore, both actual and potential obstructions to his effective over-all management of national administration. The commissions produce confusion, conflict, and incoherence in the formulation and in the execution of the President's policies. . . .

THE ADMINISTRATIVE PROBLEM

The independent commissions present a serious immediate problem. No administrative reorganization worthy of the name can leave hanging in the air . . . irresponsible agencies free to determine policy and administer law. Any program to restore our constitutional ideal of a fully coordinated Executive Branch responsible to the President must bring within the reach of that responsible control all work done by these independent commissions which is not judicial in nature. That challenge cannot be ignored.

Therefore:

The following proposal is put forward as a possible solution of the independent commission problem. . . . Under this proposed plan the regulatory agency would be set up, not in a governmental vacuum outside the executive departments, but within a department. There it would be divided into an administrative section and a judicial section. The administrative section would be a regular bureau or division of the department. . . . It would be directly responsible to the Secretary and through him to the President. The judicial section, on the other hand, would be "in" the department only for purposes of "administrative housekeeping," such as the budget, general personnel administration, and material. It would be wholly independent of the department and the President with respect to its work and its decisions. Its members would be appointed by the President with the approval of the Senate for long, staggered terms and would be removable only for causes stated in the statute.

This proposed plan meets squarely the problem presented by the independent commissions. It creates effective responsibility for the administrative and policy determining aspects of the regulatory job and, at the same time, guarantees the complete independence and neutrality for that part of the work which must be performed after the manner of a court. It facilitates and strengthens administrative management without lessening judicial independence.[4]

Efforts to carry this recommendation into execution were defeated by Congress.

The first Hoover Commission, established to study reorganization of the executive branch, in its final report to Congress stated its belief

. . . that the independent regulatory commissions have a proper place in the machinery of our Government, a place very like that originally conceived, but

[4] The President's Committee on Administrative Management, *Report with Special Studies* (1939), pp. 39-40.

that the role of these commissions as originally established has not been adequately fulfilled.[5]

It proposed in 1949 that non-regulatory functions vested in several commissions should be transferred to an appropriate department. This has been accomplished. The American Bar Association has supported the transfer of all adjudicative functions to a special court presided over by judges. This proposal was seconded by the second Hoover Commission of 1955. In 1957 Congress undertook to review the problem of the commissions, but the analysis presented twenty years ago still remains as pertinent as it was when made.

Government Corporations. The final type of agency is the corporation wholly owned and operated by the national government. Each of the approximately two dozen units has a distinct legal existence and offers the advantages of a private corporation. It possesses a corporate charter, a board of directors makes policy, and a manager supervises its administration subject to the board's control. It can buy, sell, and own property, sue and be sued, reinvest earnings, and have continual existence.

The Government corporation is a useful and efficient means of carrying out powers granted the Federal Government under the Constitution. It has proved to be an effective device not only for emergency purposes but for the continuing operation of a variety of economic services. Its peculiar value lies in freedom of operation, flexibility, business efficiency, and opportunity for experimentation. . . .

PURPOSES OF THE CORPORATION

The corporate device presents factors of flexibility and business efficiency not often obtainable under the typical bureau form of organization. Corporations are generally expected to be self-supporting enterprises and to be no burden upon the Treasury, even in cases where it has subscribed to their initial capital. They usually have the right to borrow on their own obligations and to use the income derived from charges for their services for payment of their necessary expenses. Freedom from the necessity of appropriations carries with it freedom from various governmental controls and restrictions, such as budget procedures . . . and various governmental rules regarding purchase, travel, space, and property. Ordinarily they devise their own system of accounts, and, within the limits of their enabling statutes, may incur obligations and settle claims.

Citizens, particularly when they participate in their ownership, are more inclined to expect businesslike procedures from corporations than from direct Governmental activity. Corporations have demonstrated their business efficiency in such fields as the making and collection of loans, the management of property, and the operation of transportation facilities. They can be held responsible for an entire result by the accomplishments reflected in their annual reports and balance sheets rather than by a minute scrutiny of their detailed transactions.

[5] The Commission on Organization of the Executive Branch of the Government, *A Report to the Congress, Regulatory Commissions* (March, 1949), p. 3.

The corporation affords considerable opportunity for regional decentralization and local autonomy. Authority and responsibility can be devolved upon patrons by representation on regional boards. In a Nation so large and varied in its natural conditions and habit patterns, this device brings into play a mechanism which can respond to a regional need more adequately than conventional governmental form. Its regional boundaries need not coincide with political areas but can conform to economic and social factors of homogeneity relevant to its purposes. These purposes can be unitary, such as providing home loans or farm loans. The Tennessee Valley Authority has demonstrated that they can be multiple in the broad field of regional development, including such varied elements as river control, conservation, power production and transmission, and national defense. So broad a program affects every aspect of regional and governmental activity for its advancement.

The corporate form provides a particularly convenient means for achieving various degrees of limitation of sovereign immunity when the Federal Government undertakes to foster business-like activities in fields it may properly enter. A Federal corporation can be specifically authorized to pay State taxes, to sue and be sued in Federal courts, and by appropriate legislation can be made subject to certain State laws that have reference to its particular activities. . . .

The use of the corporate device is by no means new. Since 1791, when the Congress authorized the creation of the first Bank of the United States, the Federal Government has frequently used corporate devices to carry out its powers under the Constitution. . . . The history of the establishment of Government corporations indicates that those of a permanent nature have been for the most part financial and banking institutions established under the fiscal powers of the Congress. Authority for the creation of most of the other Federal corporations has been derived from the war power or from the power to regulate interstate commerce. Most Federal corporations have been authorized during periods of national emergency, such as economic depressions and wars.[6]

The activities of corporations require operating freedom, opportunity to experiment with forms and procedures adapted to business-like enterprises. Restrictive rules applicable to regular departments and agencies often do not apply to them. They enjoy greater freedom to escape the control policies, programs, and procedures. They are freer to act according to their peculiar needs.

Abatement of Corporation Freedom. The original freedom of corporations has been slowly reduced by extending to them overhead controls of personnel, budgeting, accounting, and auditing. By 1939 they numbered almost a hundred. The problems of coordinating and integrating their policies with those of the President had grown apace. They had failed to provide efficient, economical administration and immunity from political influence. Experience showed not only that independence was not essential to their operation but also that their freedom weakened the administrative position and authority of the President. Great pressures developed to place them within supervising agencies where they would be

[6] The President's Committee on Administrative Management, *Report with Special Studies* (1939), pp. 43-44.

subject to control by the President. In 1939 all except the Tennessee Valley Authority and the Federal Deposit Insurance Corporation were brought within the structure of a regular department or agency, and the civil service system was extended to all but the TVA, whose independent system was retained. In 1945 the Corporation Control Act further reduced their independence. It provided: (1) that no corporations should be created, acquired, or organized except by act of Congress; (2) that the General Accounting Office should audit their accounts, applying to them a "business type" audit to show the sources of corporate funds, the amounts and purposes of expenditures, financial status, and profits and losses; (3) that they should submit budgets to the Bureau of the Budget, to Congress, and to the President, and should go annually to Congress to obtain operating funds; and (4) that they should manage all accounts in excess of $50,000 through the Treasury. The corporations today have less financial, legal, and managerial freedom than they enjoyed prior to 1945, but Congress has not fully destroyed their operating freedom and flexibility.

However, the relationship of the corporation to the President remains a problem. The ideal of corporate freedom, flexibility, and adaptability continues to compete with that of order, unity, symmetry and integration within the executive branch under authority of the President.

Field Services. The structure of the national government consists of the "departmental service" located at Washington, D.C., and of the "field service" located throughout the country with heavy concentrations in major cities. Most major departments and agencies have established field services, which include approximately 92 per cent of the employees of the national government. Most of the contacts that the average citizen has with government take place through agents and officers located in the "field." It is in the "field" that services are rendered, laws are enforced, and regulations are imposed.

Field services provide a means of decentralizing administration whenever operational uniformity is not essential. They enable personnel in direct contact with a situation to administer broad policy at a local level, so that it can be adapted to local needs and conditions, and direct contact with the people involved can be maintained. Private citizens may take part in administration or be consulted in advisory capacities. Decentralization brings the citizen and his government together, facilitates public understanding of policies and programs, and stimulates cooperation and coordination between national, state, and local governments.

The "departmental service" at Washington is not primarily operational. It has little direct contact with the public. Instead, it sets general policy, develops operating procedures and programs, fixes standards of performance, establishes, perfects, and supervises the field services, and performs the housekeeping functions.

However, neither the "field" nor the "departmental" service can operate in isolation from the other. Each must understand and appreciate the problems of the other. If close contact is not maintained between them, the center will distrust the field service, will not delegate sufficient discretion and authority to it, and will impose unrealistic policies, programs, and standards upon it. The field will be out of sympathy with and will fail to comprehend the decisions of the center, and the operative part of government will be greatly hindered.

REORGANIZATION OF THE EXECUTIVE BRANCH

The need for reorganization arises from the fact that administration is dynamic; it is government in action. To avoid stagnation it must vary its activities as public needs shift. Hence, organization must be altered, for a structure adequate for one time and purpose will probably not serve others. Reorganization should maintain effective government, and because change always goes on in the social, economic, and political environment, a need for continual reorganization exists.

In more specific language it has been pointed out that

It is almost impossible to comprehend the organization and management problem of the Federal Government unless one has some concept of its hugeness and complexity. The sheer size, complexity and geographical dispersion of its operations almost stagger the imagination. As a result of depression, war, new needs for defense, and our greater responsibilities abroad, the Federal Government has become the largest enterprise on earth. In less than 20 years its civil employment has increased from 570,000 to over 2,000,000. Its bureaus, sections, and units have increased fourfold to over 1,800. Annual expenditures have soared from $3 billion to over $42 billion. It now costs more each year to pay the interest on the national debt than it did to pay the total cost of the Federal Government sixteen years ago.

Only 10 per cent of the over 2,000,000 Federal employees are located in Washington; the balance are in the field service. In September, 1948, more Federal civilian employees were working outside the continental limits of the United States than in the city of Washington. The Federal Government of today is markedly different from the Government of 20 years ago. It is a Government almost 4 times larger in terms of agencies and employees, and 12 times larger in terms of expenditures. Such rapid growth could not take place without creating serious problems of organization and management. Methods, procedures, and controls effective two decades ago cannot cope with the management needs of today.[7]

A primary essential for the better organization of the whole executive branch is consolidation and unification into a more simple structure. This is the first necessity for the establishment of efficient and economical functioning of the Government. This step is also necessary in order to relieve the President of onerous administrative detail which arises from lack of unification.

[7] The Commission on Organization of the Executive Branch of the Government, *Concluding Report* (May, 1949), pp. 3-4.

At the present time there are 65 departments, administrations, agencies, boards, and commissions engaged in executive work, all of which report directly to the President—if they report to anyone. This number does not include the "independent" regulatory agencies in their quasi-judicial and quasi-legislative functions. It is manifestly impossible for the President to give adequate supervision to so many agencies. Even one hour a week devoted to each of them would require a 65-hour work week for the President, to say nothing of the time he must devote to his great duties in developing and directing major policies as his constitutional obligations require.[8]

Yet, the effort to meet the reorganizational need has been half-hearted. Only since 1937, when the President's Committee on Administrative Management began its work, has serious attention been devoted to the modernization of the executive branch. Two years later the Bureau of the Budget was made responsible for improving organization in the executive branch, but its effort has been mainly directed toward making changes internal to the departments and agencies and has been closely related to its powers of budgetary review and execution. It also prepares reorganization plans for the President, receives proposals from the administrative agencies, and clears plans with them. Of course, within the departments and agencies continuous reorganization of an unspectacular, often routine, type does go on.

Congress has declared many times in similar language that its policy is to

. . . promote economy, efficiency, and improved services in the transaction of the public business in the departments, bureaus, agencies, boards, commissions, offices, independent establishments, and instrumentalities of the executive branch of the Government by—

(1) limiting expenditures to the lowest amount consistent with the efficient performance of essential services, activities, and functions;

(2) eliminating duplication and overlapping of services, activities, and functions;

(3) consolidating services, activities, and functions of a similar nature;

(4) abolishing services, activities, and functions not necessary to the efficient conduct of government; and

(5) defining and limiting executive functions, services, and activities.[9]

To implement that policy Congress in 1947 created the Commission on Organization of the Executive Branch of the Government.[10] This commission reported that any effort to improve the organization and admin-

---

[8] The Commission on Organization of the Executive Branch of the Government, *General Management of the Executive Branch* (February, 1949), pp. 35-36.

[9] *Ibid.*, pp. vii-viii.

[10] For details of this commission's composition and mandate see *U.S. Code*, Title 5, sec. 138 (a)-(i). Its findings and recommendations can be found in nineteen reports published as public documents.

istration of the executive branch in keeping with the policy of Congress must:

1. Create a more orderly grouping of the functions of Government into major departments and agencies under the President.

2. Establish a clear line of control from the President to these departments and agency heads and from them to their sub-ordinates with correlative responsibility from these officials to the President, cutting through the barriers which have in many cases made bureaus and agencies partially independent of the Chief Executive.

3. Give the President and each department head strong staff services which should exist only to make executives more effective, and which the President or department head should be free to organize at his discretion.

4. Develop a much greater number of capable administrators in the public service, and prepare them for promotion to any bureau or department in the Government where their services may be most effectively used.

5. Enforce the accountability of administrators by a much broader pattern of controls, so that the statutes and regulations which govern administrative practices will encourage, rather than destroy, initiative and enterprise.

6. Permit the operating departments and agencies to administer for themselves a larger share of the routine administrative services, under strict supervision and in conformity with high standards.

Only by taking these steps can the operations of the executive branch be managed effectively, responsibly, and economically.[11]

Congress has usually directed the President to implement the recommendations of the various study commissions that it has established, and to that end has authorized him to prepare reorganization plans. However, the authorizing legislation has invariably imposed numerous limitations upon his freedom to make changes. His authorization is for a specified term only, and provides that Congress may reject any reorganization plan if either chamber by a majority of its full membership votes against it within sixty days of its receipt. However, current reorganization legislation leaves the President much greater freedom than did earlier laws, and Congress seems more willing than in the past to permit the President's proposals to become effective.

Thus, it appears that Congress is tacitly and slowly conceding its inability to cope with the problem of keeping the executive branch modern; but it is careful to retain authority to substitute its judgment for that of the President, although it has not abused this power. However, Congress has not admitted that the principal responsibility for reorganization rests with the President, that politics must be subordinated to considerations of good government, that the need for reorganization is a continuing one, and that reorganization is as important as stability. In the last analysis the process of reorganizing the executive branch is dependent upon the intelligent cooperation of President and Congress.

[11] The Commission on Organization of the Executive Branch of the Government, *General Management of the Executive Branch* (February, 1949), pp. 7-8.

Difficulties of Reorganization. Everyone favors reorganization, but no one wants to be reorganized. The process is a difficult one, full of pitfalls and frustrations. It must overcome the jealousy characteristic of legislative-executive relations. Congress is not prone to abandon its creatures to the not-so-tender mercies of the executive. Reorganization enhances the President's power and control over administration; relatively, therefore, that of Congress diminishes. Agencies faced with loss of authority, personnel, structure, money, and prestige, invoke the aid of their legislative angels. Private groups bring their political influence to bear upon Congress to protect agencies in which they are interested. Reorganization upsets the *status quo* and threatens the vested interests of affected employees; hence, it arouses the opposition of employee associations. The threat of loss to agencies, to personnel, and to interest groups is more obvious and comprehensible than is the uncertain hope of gain which reorganization offers.

Accomplishments. Yet, the reorganization movement has met with considerable success. Results have been obtained by four methods: executive order, reorganization plans, acts of Congress, and intra-agency action. 72 per cent of the first Hoover Commission's 273 proposals have been adopted. Approximately 40 per cent of them required implementing legislation. In addition, between 1949 and the middle of 1957, 56 reorganization plans were submitted to Congress; approximately four-fifths of them became effective. Significant changes have been achieved by executive order, and the heads of all departments and agencies have been directed to analyze their internal organization and procedures to ascertain what improvements could be made to achieve greater effectiveness and economy of operation. Approximately one-third of the Commission's recommendations can be implemented by this means. However, some of its major proposals will probably never be adopted because of their controversial or political nature.

Second Hoover Commission. A second Hoover Commission similar to the first was created by act of Congress in July, 1953 and terminated on June 30, 1955. It was mainly concerned with functions, programs, and policies, and was directed to study the desirability of "eliminating nonessential services, functions, and activities which are competitive with private enterprise." It, therefore, was authorized to inquire into the functions that the national government *ought* to perform, and to recommend the discontinuance of some others. Organization and reorganization were of only incidental interest to it. In the words of the Commission:

> The major difference between the method of operation of the two Commissions is that the first Commission concerned itself chiefly with reorganization of departments and agencies and their relations with each other. That Commission's proposals were directed to removing the roadblocks to more effective organization and the reduction of expenditures.

This Commission has dealt more extensively with the functional organization of the executive branch and with questions of policy than the first Commission. We have therefore based recommendations on examination of related functions straight across the executive branch. . . . We have dealt more intensively with policy questions than did the previous Commission because of the wider authorities in the law and the expressed wish of Congress.[12]

The second Commission set forth its findings and conclusions pertaining to the relocation of agencies in its final report as follows:

PART IV

RELOCATING AGENCIES

Among the duties assigned to the Commission by the Congress was "relocating agencies now responsible directly to the President in Departments of other agencies." We deal with it here as we have made no special report on the subject. A study revealed that there are 64 agencies of this character. Of these, the President has the unavoidable direct responsibility for about 31, but the remaining 33 are of such diverse character and duties that few of them lend themselves to relocation in other existing agencies.

To solve the problem arising out of the sheer inability of the President to give them adequate personal supervision, and to lighten the load upon him, we make the following recommendation:

Recommendation

(a) That the President direct such as he may approve of these 33 remaining agencies to report to some official in the executive office whom he may designate.

(b) That such agencies be required to report regularly upon such matters as organizational activities, proposed programs, appointments of staff, expenditures and their proposed appropriations.

(c) This designated official to be authorized to advise the President and the Bureau of the Budget of his conclusions in respect to such questions.[13]

The second commission studied sixty of the sixty-four executive agencies in detail, and made 362 recommendations; of these, legislation would be required to implement 167; 145 could be adopted by the departments and agencies; reorganization plans and executive orders could be used to implement 50. Both commissions made numerous administrative recommendations to agencies while investigating them. The task forces which investigated them on the ground made many more. Many were immediately put into practice, so that the full effect of the studies is considerably greater than indicated by the changes brought about by formal administrative action, executive order, reorganization plan, or legislation.

[12] The Commission on Organization of the Executive Branch of the Government, *Final Report to the Congress* (June, 1955), p. 5.
[13] *Ibid.*, p. 17.

CHAPTER XVIII

The National Judiciary

GENERAL CONSIDERATIONS

In the United States the citizen lives under two systems of laws and courts, national and state. Each is relatively independent of the other. Thus, state courts enforce state laws, and national courts enforce national laws. However, some reciprocal authority exists, and Congress has provided in specific instances for the trial in state courts of cases arising under national laws. The laws of the United States are not alien in relation to the state courts; for the states of the Union constitute a nation, and their officials are sworn to support the supreme law of the land.[1]

However, a single act which constitutes a crime under the laws of both jurisdictions may be punished by each in its own courts without placing the defendant in double jeopardy. No rule or practice determines which jurisdiction shall prosecute first. Great hardship can result if both invoke their authority, especially if one secures a conviction after the other has acquitted an accused person; but the potential evil is mitigated by the cooperation of state and national authorities. Prosecutions are usually left

[1] *Testa* v. *Katt* (1947), 330 U.S. 386.

to the states, and the Attorney General of the United States has instructed his subordinates to prosecute, when a state also prosecutes, only in extreme situations.

Independence of the Judicial Process. The task of courts is to administer legal justice, to decide cases and controversies according to rules of law. The traditions of democratic government dictate that its administration should be fair and impartial, and the Constitution undertakes to protect the integrity of the judicial process. The manner in which it does so is regarded as the best example of the application of separated powers.

The Constitution guarantees the independence and integrity of the judiciary by extending it certain protections, the first of which declares that "The Judges, both of the supreme and inferior courts, shall hold their Offices during good Behavior. . . ." "Good behavior" is, in most instances, the equivalent of "life tenure," for "good behavior" endures as long as a judge is not convicted after his impeachment. Impeachment is the only means by which judges may be removed from office, but the guarantee of tenure does not prevent Congress from abolishing a court. Its judges, however, continue to hold their office and may be assigned to another court or may be left to do nothing.

Judges of national courts are also protected against financial coercion. If Congress could arbitrarily adjust the salary of judges, these officials would perform their duties subject to the constant threat of financial coercion applied or favoritism bestowed by the legislative branch. Instead,

> The judges, both of the supreme and inferior Courts, . . . shall, at stated Times, receive for their Services, a Compensation, which shall not be diminished during their Continuance in Office.

However, judges may be required to pay income taxes.[2]

It is an easy matter to over-emphasize the reality of judicial independence, for many contacts between the political and judicial branches exist. Congress determines the salary to be paid a judge, although it may not vary his compensation once he has assumed office. It creates and may abolish all courts except the Supreme Court, though it may vary the size and regulate other details of the existence of even this Court. Congress determines by statute, and can adjust at its pleasure, all of the jurisdictions of lower national courts and can similarly define and adjust the appellate jurisdiction of the Supreme Court. It appropriates funds for the judiciary. The judiciary cannot enforce its own decisions but must ultimately depend upon the executive. Moreover,

> The President . . . shall nominate, and by and with the Advice and Consent of the Senate, shall appoint . . . Judges of the Supreme Court. . . .

as well as those of courts inferior to it. Hence, "senatorial courtesy" limits

---

[2] *O'Malley* v. *Woodrough* (1939), 307 U.S. 277.

the choice of nominees to lower court judgeships, as does the practice of choosing them from within the jurisdictions to be served, but it does not apply to the choice of justices of the Supreme Court. Presidents are careful to scrutinize the social and economic philosophy of their nominees; for experience has demonstrated that party affiliation is a poor indication of how they will decide social and economic questions. Nevertheless, most Presidents nominate members of their own party to judgeships on national courts, and, withal, the caliber of judges is high.

THE STRUCTURE OF THE JUDICIARY

General Comment. The decisions of 1789 to apply national power directly to the people of the several states, and to include the "supremacy clause," made provision for national courts virtually indispensable. Adjudication of conflicts of authority might have been entrusted to state courts only, or to state courts with a right to appeal questions involving the supreme law to a single national court; but it is probably essential in the American federal system to enable the national government to decide such questions in its own courts. Otherwise, it would have no way to protect its limited powers from usurpation by the states.

Other reasons supported the decision to create a separate system of national courts. A uniform national law can best be developed by a single system of integrated courts; application of national law by national courts can do much to eliminate local bias and prejudice. State courts are not suitable instruments for deciding suits involving the authority of the national government, its property, and ambassadors accredited to it by foreign governments, nor for deciding suits between states, between citizens of different states, and suits involving admiralty and maritime matters, treaties, or international law.

Constitutional Courts. The Constitution, which mentions only the Supreme Court, leaves its creation to Congress. But it also in two places gives Congress power "To constitute Tribunals inferior to the supreme Court." Congress has employed that authority to call the Supreme and inferior courts into being and to regulate the details of their existence. The size of the Supreme Court has been fixed at one Chief Justice and eight associate justices, who are compensated annually in the amounts of $35,-500 and $35,000 respectively. Congress may increase the size of the Court at any time, but it may reduce it only by requiring that vacancies are not to be filled until the desired decrease has occurred. It has required that the Court is to meet annually at the seat of the government, beginning on the first Monday in October, and has authorized such special terms as may be necessary. It has set the order of precedence of the justices. The powers and duties of the Chief Justice, when that office is vacant or its incumbent cannot discharge them, devolve upon the senior associate justice, who may exercise them until a new Chief Justice takes office or the disability of the old one is removed. Associate justices have precedence according to the seniority of their commissions.

Resignation and Retirement. Justices and judges of national courts may avail themselves of a liberal retirement and pension plan. They may resign or retire on full salary for the remainder of their lifetimes upon reaching the age of seventy if they have served for ten years, or upon half salary after ten years service at any age. The same standards govern retirement for disability, but without regard to age.

Courts of Appeals. Below the Supreme Court are the courts of appeals of the United States, which have from three to nine judges each. Each judge, except those in the District of Columbia, must be a resident of the circuit for which he is appointed. Each receives a salary of $25,500 per annum.

Courts of appeals meet annually at places within each circuit as designated by law. The judges may sit *en banc* or in division, but cases may not be heard or determined by fewer than two judges. There is one appellate court in each of the ten judicial circuits into which the United States is divided and an eleventh in the District of Columbia. These intermediate tribunals each year review several thousand decisions of the district courts, and serve as a barrier to hold from the Supreme Court the flood of litigation which otherwise would swamp it.[3] Justices of the Supreme Court are assigned to circuits but seldom participate in the decision of cases.

United States District Courts. The ten regular judicial circuits of the United States are subdivided into 86 judicial districts each having a district court. There are 289 judges who decide cases only under national jurisdiction. The districts are so defined that twenty-five states each constitute a district; sixteen states are divided into two districts, seven into three, and two into four. Courts of comparable trial jurisdiction serve the District of Columbia and Puerto Rico, and others of the same name but different jurisdiction are found in Guam, the Virgin Islands, and the Canal Zone. The latter are territorial courts. District courts are at the base of the judicial hierarchy and are the only ones to employ juries. They are the most important courts in terms of the number of cases handled; in fiscal 1960 about 200,000 actions of all types were filed.

Each court has from one to twenty-four judges assigned to it, but cases are usually decided by a single judge, who may hold session at the same

[3] There are now a total of eighty-eight judges on these courts. During fiscal 1960, 3,899 cases were filed and 3,715 were disposed of. As of June 30, 1960, 2,220 cases were pending. The median time from filing to disposition was 6.8 months. More complete statistical data on all national courts can be found in the *Annual Report of the Director, Administrative Office of United States Courts, 1960* (Washington, D.C.: U.S. Government Printing Office, 1961).

UNITED STATES DISTRICT COURTS

Time Interval from Filing to Disposition
of Civil Cases Terminated

Time Interval	1950		
	Total Cases	Non-Jury	Jury
TOTAL	5,020	3,320	1,700
Less than 6 months	1,118	721	397
6 months to 1 year	1,574	1,011	563
1 to 2 years	1,448	937	511
2 years and over	880	651	229
Less than 1 year—%	53.6	52.2	56.5
Median interval—mos.	11.2	11.5	10.4

Time Interval	1960		
	Total Cases	Non-Jury	Jury
TOTAL	4,979	2,500	2,479
Less than 6 months	499	228	271
6 months to 1 year	1,100	480	620
1 to 2 years	1,677	891	786
2 years and over	1,703	901	802
Less than 1 year—%	32.1	28.3	35.9
Median interval—mos.	17.8	18.8	16.6

Time Interval	1955		
	Total Cases	Non-Jury	Jury
TOTAL	5,239	2,806	2,433
Less than 6 months	866	398	468
6 months to 1 year	1,308	617	691
1 to 2 years	1,561	865	696
2 years and over	1,504	926	578
Less than 1 year—%	41.5	36.2	47.6
Median interval—mos.	14.6	16.7	12.6

Includes only cases in which a trial was held, excluding
condemnation, forfeiture, and habeas corpus proceedings.
Excludes territorial district courts and that for the District of Columbia.

Source: *Statistical Abstracts of the United States, 1961*
(Washington, D.C.: U.S. Department of Commerce,
1961), p. 148.

time that other sessions are held by fellow judges of his court. Each receives a salary of $22,500 and is required to reside in the district for which he is appointed. Attached to each court are a United States attorney, a marshal, and one or more commissioners.

The attorneys are appointed by the President for a term of four years. Their duties include prosecutions for all offenses against the United States; representation of the United States in civil suits arising under the revenue laws; prosecutions to collect fines, penalties, and forfeitures under the revenue laws; and prosecution or defense on behalf of the government in all civil actions, suits, or proceedings in which the United States is concerned. Their work is supervised and controlled by the Attorney General.

The marshals are also appointed by the President for four year terms and must reside within the district for which they are appointed. Each may appoint deputies to help him assist the national courts, and to execute lawful writs, processes, and orders issued under authority of the United States. A marshal may also "command all necessary assistance to execute his duties." He is supervised and directed by the Attorney General in the performance of his duties, and when executing the laws of the United States within a state, may exercise the same powers which a sheriff of the state may exercise in executing the state's laws.[4]

United States commissioners are appointed by each district court in such number as it deems advisable for a term of four years, unless sooner removed by the court. Their duties include the taking of bail, acknowledgements, affidavits, and depositions, the issuing of attachments on property to recover unpaid taxes, and the holding of preliminary hearings in criminal cases to determine whether to hold accused persons for grand jury action, to discharge them or to bind them over.[5]

Each United States district court also has a clerk of the court, a secretary and law clerk for each judge, and one or more reporters, at least one of whom shall

. . . attend at each session of the court . . . and shall record verbatim by shorthand or mechanical means: (1) all proceedings in criminal cases had in open court; (2) all proceedings in other cases had in open court, unless the parties with the approval of the judge shall specifically agree to the contrary; and (3) such other proceedings as a judge of the court may direct. . . .

The original notes or other original records and the transcript in the office of the clerk shall be open during office hours to inspection by any person without charge.[6]

Special Constitutional Courts. The above courts comprise the regular system of United States courts which have been created under Article III

[4] *U.S. Code*, Title 28, Chapter 33.
[5] *Ibid.*, Chapter 43.
[6] *U.S. Code*, Title 28, sec. 753.

of the Constitution to exercise the judicial power of the national government. Apart from them, however, are other tribunals which can only be described as "special" constitutional courts. They were originally created by Congress under its "necessary and proper" power to aid in the administration of its enumerated authority. But, in recent years Congress has changed their status by declaring that they are Article III courts, so that their existence is presumably the result of Congress' authority to create tribunals inferior to the Supreme Court. The independence of their judges is protected by the Constitution, but their jurisdiction does not conform to that which, according to Article III of the Constitution, it is within the power of Congress to assign to the courts created by it.

The first of these "special" courts is the United States Customs Court of nine judges, no more than five of whom may be from the same political party. This court ranks on the same level with the regular district courts but has very different jurisdiction. It sits at the port of New York, and hears and decides requests for reappraisement of imports, protests against the decisions of collectors of customs, and actions to regain duties that are alleged to have been wrongfully collected.[7] In 1956 Congress declared that it was a court established under Article III of the Constitution.

The second of the "special" constitutional tribunals is the United States Court of Claims, established in 1855 under the monetary powers of Congress to pay the debts of the United States and to appropriate its moneys. It consists of five judges, who decide claims of private parties against the United States which arise under contractual relations, torts, and private claims. In 1953 it was also declared to be a court created under Article III.[8]

In an appellate relationship to the Customs Court, the United States Tariff Commission, and the Patent Office, stands the Court of Customs and Patent Appeals, first created by Congress in 1910 under the commerce and patent powers. It now is on a par with courts of appeal in the regular judicial structure, and consists of five judges. In 1958, Congress declared that it too was a court created under the judiciary article of the Constitution.[9]

THE ADMINISTRATION OF JUDICIAL BUSINESS

The effective, speedy, and uniform dispensing of justice by an extensive judicial system requires much coordination, cooperation and integration. To help attain this goal conferences and councils of participating judges are held. The Judicial Conference of the United States meets annually

[7] See *U.S. Code*, Title 28, secs. 251, 252, 254.
[8] *Ibid*, sec. 1491. Concerning the status of the Court of Claims see *Glidden Co.* v. *Zdanok* (1962), 268 U.S. 815, and also *U.S. Code*, Title 28, secs. 171, 173-175.
[9] *U.S. Code*, Title 28, secs. 211, 213.

and is attended by the Chief Justice of the United States, the chief judge of each circuit, the chief judge of the Court of Claims, and a district judge from each circuit. All those designated are required to attend and to advise on the needs of their courts and on any matters where the administration of justice can be improved. The conference also makes a comprehensive survey of the condition of business in the courts, and submits suggestions to them in the interests of uniformity and the speedy accomplishment of business. It surveys the rules of practice and procedure, recommends changes to promote simplicity in procedure, fair administration, and just determination of litigation, and refers cases of unjustifiable expense and delay to the Supreme Court for its consideration and adoption.

At least every six months the chief judge of each circuit calls a judicial council of the judges of the circuit. Each council makes all necessary orders for the effective and expeditious administration of the judicial business within the circuit. District judges are required to carry into effect promptly all orders of the council.

An annual Judicial Conference of the Circuit attended by all judges of of the circuit considers the business of the courts within it and the means for improving their administration of justice. Members of the bar also attend and participate in these conferences.[10]

Administrative Office of the United States Courts. The Administrative Office of United States Courts was created to regulate the work of the courts and to provide for their common needs. It aids the Chief Justice in the discharge of his duties as the directing authority of the judicial system. Its director is appointed and removed by the Supreme Court. He is the administrator of the courts under the supervision and direction of the Judicial Conference of the United States. His office supervises the administrative work of the clerks and administrative personnel of the courts, examines the state of their dockets, studies their needs for assistance, reports quarterly to the chief judge of each circuit statistical data on the status of business of the courts therein, sends that data and an account of the activities of the Administrative Office, and of the state of business in all courts, to the Judicial Conference of the United States, together with his recommendations. These reports, data and recommendations also go to the Attorney General and to Congress. The Administrative Office also performs numerous incidental functions common to the courts.[11]

Hence, by means of the conferences and councils and the work of the Administrative Office continuous effort is made to modernize and expedite the conduct of judicial business in the courts of the United States.

[10] *U.S. Code,* Title 28, secs. 331-334.
[11] These may be found *in extenso* in the *U.S. Code,* Title 28, secs. 601, 604.

Mobility of Judges. "Justice delayed is justice denied"—so holds a maxim of the legal profession. Therefore, it is desirable that the judicial system should provide for the transfer of judges from court to court as the pressure of litigation varies from time to time and place to place. Accordingly circuit judges may be moved temporarily from one circuit court to another, to the Court of Claims, or to a district court within the circuit. District court judges may be assigned to serve on the court of appeals for their circuit or a division of it whenever its business requires, to any district court, court of appeals, or to the Court of Claims.[12]

"Legislative" Courts.

General Comment. From time to time Congress has created courts by using its implied power, on the ground that such courts were "necessary and proper" to carry into execution one or more of its enumerated powers. Such courts are known as "legislative" courts to distinguish them from those of the regular system of "constitutional" courts—described above— established under Article III of the Constitution.

It bears repeating here that the essential point of distinction is that "constitutional" courts are, and "legislative" courts are not, established under authority of Article III of the Constitution. Judges of the former are necessarily protected in their independence by the Constitution, but those of "legislative" courts are not. Congress may prescribe "life" tenure for judges of "legislative" courts and it may refrain from reducing their salaries; but the point is that it *can* give them shorter tenure and it *can* reduce their salaries at any time. And, it should also be noted that judges of "constitutional" courts may not render advisory opinions but those of "legislative" courts may be directed by Congress to do so.[13]

Examples of "legislative" courts have never been numerous, but several, mostly now defunct, have existed over time. Territorial courts are "legislative" courts, as also are the local courts of the District of Columbia and the United States Court of Military Appeals. In times past, the United States Court for China, consular courts at various places in foreign countries, the Commerce Court, the Court of Claims, the Customs Court, the Court of Customs and Patent Appeals, the Choctaw and Chickasaw Citizenship Court, and others existed as "legislative" courts.

Administrative Tribunals. Congress from time to time has established within the executive branch administrative tribunals, which, although executive in nature, are more judicial in character and procedure than the

[12] For a more explicit statement of this transferability of judges consult the *U.S. Code*, Title 28, secs. 292, 293.

[13] For a statement of the differences between these types of courts see *Ex parte Bakelite Corporation* (1929), 279 U.S. 438. However, the clarity of this distinction has been clouded by the creation, by Congress, of the unusual "special" Article III courts out of what previously, and by the standards of the *Bakelite* case, were "legislative" courts.

independent agencies designated "quasi-judicial." They mark a tendency toward the creation of administrative courts. Thus, the present Tax Court of the United States was known until 1942 as the Board of Tax Appeals, plainly an agency of the executive, but in 1942 Congress enacted that

The Board of Tax Appeals shall be continued as an independent agency in the Executive Branch of the Government, and shall be known as the Tax Court of the United States. The members thereof shall be known as chief judge and the judges of the Tax Court.

The Tax Court and its divisions shall have such jurisdiction as is conferred on them. . . .

The Tax Court shall be composed of 16 members.

Judges of the Tax Court shall be appointed by the President, by and with the advice and consent of the Senate, solely on the grounds of fitness to perform the duties of the office. Each judge shall receive salary at the rate of $22,000 per annum, to be paid in monthly installments. . . .

The terms of office of all judges of the Tax Court shall expire 12 years after the expiration of the terms for which their predecessors were appointed; but any judge appointed to fill a vacancy occurring prior to the expiration of the term for which his predecessor was appointed shall be appointed only for the unexpired term of his predecessor.

Judges of the Tax Court may be removed by the President, after notice and opportunity for public hearing, for inefficiency, neglect of duty, or malfeasance in office, but for no other cause.[14]

JURISDICTION

General Comment. Two distinct systems of courts function in the same territory over the same people. How they can function without conflict and confusion is a pertinent query. A similar one may be raised as to the manner in which conflict and confusion between the various national courts is avoided. The simple answer is that each system and each type of court can hear and decide only certain cases and controversies.

Cases (criminal) and controversies (civil) may come before a court in either of two ways. The power of a court to decide cases and controversies is its jurisdiction. "Original" ones are initiated and tried there, and the authority of the court to hear them is its "original" jurisdiction. Others are brought to a higher court for review after they have been decided by a lower one. These are "appellate" cases or controversies, and the authority to review them is "appellate" jurisdiction. Any court may have jurisdiction to hear and decide actions "civil" or "criminal" in nature, originally or on appeal. Not every court possesses jurisdiction of each type, however.

Thus, national and state courts may be differentiated by analyzing the

14 *U.S. Code,* Title 26, secs. 7441-7443.

authority by which they were created and the jurisdiction they respectively possess; one national court may be distinguished from another by the same means. Our concern now is with the jurisdiction of the national judiciary as a whole, and of the individual courts within it considered severally.

General Jurisdiction. Cases and controversies not included within the following enumeration are within the judicial power of the states, for, under Article III of the Constitution, that of the United States

. . . shall extend to all Cases, in Law and Equity, arising under this Constitution, the Laws of the United States, and Treaties made, or which shall be made, under their Authority;—to all Cases affecting Ambassadors, other public Ministers and Consuls;—to all Cases of admiralty and maritime Jurisdiction;—to Controversies to which the United States shall be a Party;—to Controversies between two or more States;—between a State and Citizens of another State;—between Citizens of different States;—between Citizens of the same State claiming Lands under Grants of different States, and between a State, or the Citizens thereof, and foreign States, Citizens or Subjects.

Several points deserve mention. First, these categories are not mutually exclusive. Several are broad enough to include one or more of the others. Second, this is a statement of the *maximum* authority which *may* be entrusted to national courts. Congress may, as it sees fit, distribute among the various courts authority to hear and decide actions only of these types. Third, these categories are not conferred *exclusively* on the national courts or on any one of them. Congress may restrict them to the national courts, but it may permit some or all of them to be decided by state courts also. Jurisdiction is then "concurrent." But the enumerated types of cases and controversies are those which may be, and for the most part have been, placed within the cognizance of the national courts. The relative lack of friction and conflict between the national and state judicial systems is principally due to this simple method of distribution.

Examination of the enumerated cases and controversies reveals that they fall within the scope of national judicial power either because of the subject matter of the dispute or because of the character of the parties to it.

Cases National Because of Their Subject Matter.

1. Cases arising under the Constitution, laws, and treaties of the United States.

Questions of right based upon the Constitution, a law, or a treaty are known as "federal questions," and cases involving them are within the jurisdiction of the national courts, regardless of the parties involved. However, state courts decide such questions in great numbers, but their answers may be reviewed by the Supreme Court of the United States.

2. All cases of admiralty and maritime jurisdiction.

Disputes arising under rules of international usage that control commerce and navigation on the high seas, and under acts of Congress, and treaties regulating certain aspects of interstate commerce which take place upon the waterways of the United States, are within the scope of the national judicial power.

Cases and Controversies National Because of the Character of the Parties.

1. Cases affecting ambassadors, other public ministers, and consuls.

Ambassadors or ministers accredited to this country have immunity from the laws of the United States and of the states comprising it. They may consent to be sued, however, or bring suit against another party. If they consent to suit it is particularly appropriate that the suit should be tried in a court of the United States; if they sue, they may do so in either a national or a state court. Consuls do not possess diplomatic immunity and may appear as plaintiff or defendant in either a state or a national court. This category is of little importance.

2. Controversies to which the United States is a party.

Two reasons can be advanced for not vesting jurisdiction over this category of controversies in state courts. First, the interpretation and enforcement of national law, especially in the light of the "supremacy" clause, ought not to be left to state courts. Second, a government ought to make itself liable in suits brought against it by injured citizens, but such suits ought not to be tried in the courts of another government.

In a general sense, the United States is a party to the criminal prosecution of the violators of its laws, and such prosecutions, with minor exceptions, are in its own courts. As plaintiff in a civil action it will also initiate suit in its own appropriate court. If it is defendant, the extent of its liability will be determined by statute in keeping with the principle that it cannot be sued without its own consent. Congress, therefore, has granted permission for suit to be brought against it only in actions of tort and contractual liability and damage.

3. Controversies between two or more states.

Decision of a controversy of this type ought not to be left to the courts of one of the party states. To decide it thus would leave the procedure and result open to suspicion of favoritism or prejudice. Hence, such suits were wisely brought within the authority of the national courts.

4. Controversies between a state and citizens of another state.

This category if liberally interpreted would include controversies in which a state was defendant as well as those in which it was plaintiff. However, there is reason to believe that the framers of the Constitution did not intend that the former type should come within national cognizance. Yet, when the first such suit was brought before the Supreme Court of the United States, it accepted jurisdiction and explained:

"The judicial power of the United States shall extend to controversies between a state and citizens of another state." If the Constitution really meant to extend these powers only to those controversies in which a State may be plaintiff, to the exclusion of those in which citizens had demands against a State, it is inconceivable that it should have attempted to convey that meaning in words, not only so important, but also repugnant to it; if it meant to exclude a certain class of those controversies, why were they not expressly excepted; on the contrary, not even an intimation of such intention appears in any part of the Constitution.[15]

This decision that national courts could decide controversies brought against a state, without its consent, by a citizen of another state quickly led to the Eleventh Amendment to the Constitution:

The Judicial power of the United States shall not be construed to extend to any suit in law or equity, commenced or prosecuted against one of the United States by Citizens of another State, or by Citizens or Subjects of any Foreign State.

Therefore, suits may not be brought in national courts against a state. A citizen may sue his own state only with its consent, in its own courts, and upon the terms which it establishes. A citizen of another or foreign state may sue it only on the same terms. A state, therefore, may be sued in a national court only by the United States or by another state.

5. Controversies between citizens of different states.

This largest class of controversies decided by the national courts involves "diversity of citizenship" of the parties involved. It was brought within the competence of the national courts to avoid the possibility that a state court might be prejudiced in favor of its own citizen party to a suit with the citizen of another state. The law applied by the national courts in these suits is state law, and these suits would have been tried in a state court but for the fact that the parties were citizens of different states. However, to reduce the number of this type of suit brought into national courts, Congress has enacted that

(a) The district courts shall have original jurisdiction of all civil actions where the matter in controversy exceeds the sum or value of $10,000, exclusive of interests and costs, and is between—
(1) citizens of different States;
(2) citizens of a State, and foreign states or citizens or subjects thereof; and
(3) citizens of different States and in which foreign states or citizens or subjects thereof are additional parties.[16]

When the amount or value in controversy is less than $10,000 it may be tried only in the appropriate state court.

6. Controversies between citizens of the same state claiming the same lands under grants from different states.

[15] Opinion of Chief Justice Jay in *Chisholm* v. *Georgia* (1793), 2 Dallas 419.
[16] *U.S. Code*, Title 28, sec. 1332.

When the Constitution was adopted, and for some time thereafter, suits of this type were common and the source of much difficulty. However, for obvious reasons, controversies of this class have not been of importance for many years. They may still be tried, however, should they arise from time to time.

7. Controversies between a state or its citizens and a foreign state or its citizens or subjects.

The Eleventh Amendment also restricted the scope of this class of suits by withdrawing from the cognizance of national courts those instituted against a state by a foreign state or by its citizens or subjects.

Separate Jurisdiction of National Courts. In similar fashion the national courts have their respective individual jurisdictions which determine their places in the system.

The Supreme Court of the United States. Within the nine categories of cases and controversies discussed above Congress grants, withdraws, or denies appellate jurisdiction to the Supreme Court as it sees fit. Its regulations are far too complex and extensive to be examined here. However, the bulk of the Court's business arises under this appellate jurisdiction.

The Supreme Court also possesses original jurisdiction. This is set forth in the Constitution as follows:

In all Cases affecting Ambassadors, other public Ministers and Consuls, and those in which a State shall be a Party, the supreme Court shall have original Jurisdiction.

Congress has defined its original jurisdiction to differentiate between that which is original *and* exclusive and that which is original only.

(a) The Supreme Court shall have original and exclusive jurisdiction of:

(1) All controversies between two or more states;

(2) All actions or proceedings against ambassadors or other public ministers of foreign states or their domestics or their domestic servants, not inconsistent with the law of nations.

(b) The Supreme Court shall have original but not exclusive jurisdiction of:

(1) All actions or proceedings brought by ambassadors or other public ministers of foreign states or to which consuls or vice consuls are parties;

(2) All controversies between the United States and a State;

(3) All actions or proceedings by a State against the citizens of another State or against aliens.[17]

Few actions originate under these classes in a year.

Jurisdiction of the Court of Appeals. Courts of appeals have appellate jurisdiction only. They review the decisions of district courts, except for a few which may be taken directly to the Supreme Court. Most appeals, however, must go to a court of appeals, and for all but a few its decision is final. Thus, the ability to take a case or controversy to the Supreme

[17] *U.S. Code,* Title 28, sec. 1251.

SUPREME COURT OF THE UNITED STATES

Cases Filed, Disposed of, and Remaining on the Dockets during October Terms 1951-1960

	1951	1952	1953	1954	1955	1956	1957	1958	1959	1960
Total Cases										
Remaining from prior term	119	146	151	160	205	219	351	225	281	356
Filed	1234	1283	1302	1397	1644	1802	1639	1819	1862	1940
Disposed of	1207	1278	1293	1352	1630	1670	1765	1763	1787	1911
Remaining at end of the term	146	151	160	205	219	351	225	281	356	385
Original Cases										
From prior term	8	9	11	11	11	11	11	12	12	12
Filed	1	2	–	–	4	3	2	3	–	–
Disposed of	–	–	–	–	4	3	1	3	–	1
Remaining at end of the term	9	11	11	11	11	11	12	12	12	11
Appellate Cases										
From prior term	96	113	121	121	122	155	260	137	155	187
Filed	716	742	684	713	891	974	826	886	857	842
Transferred	15	8	10	9	7	31	18	18	35	17
Disposed of	714	742	694	721	865	900	967	886	860	887
Remaining at end of the term	113	121	121	122	155	260	137	155	187	159
Miscellaneous Applications										
Remaining from prior term	15	24	19	28	72	53	80	76	114	157
Filed	517	539	618	684	749	825	811	930	1005	1098
Disposed of	493	536	599	631	761	767	797	874	927	1023
Transferred to appellate docket	15	8	10	9	7	31	18	18	35	17
Remaining at end of the term	24	19	28	72	53	80	76	114	157	215

Source: *Annual Report of the Director, Administrative Office of United States Courts, 1961* (Washington, D.C.: U.S. Government Printing Office, 1962), p. 218.

Court is not a right of citizenship or an essential part of American democracy. Courts of appeals also review decisions of the territorial district courts in all cases involving the Constitution, the laws, or the treaties of the United States, and serve as reviewing authorities of the regulatory procedures and orders of numerous executive agencies.

Jurisdiction of United States District Courts. The district courts are trial courts and have no appellate jurisdiction; their original jurisdiction is extensive and highly complex, for they have to decide approximately forty types of civil cases, exercise review and enforcement powers over administrative orders issued by administrative agencies and officers, and in criminal matters decide offenses against the laws of the United States.

CRIMINAL PROCEEDINGS BEGUN IN U.S. DISTRICT COURTS IN THE FISCAL YEAR 1960 BY NATURE OF THE OFFENSE

Total Original Proceedings	*28,137*
Transportation, etc., of stolen motor vehicle	3,796
Fraud and other theft, total	9,184
Theft, interstate commerce	518
Breaking and entering	114
Embezzlement	1,096
Forgery	2,589
Fraud	
Income tax	605
Other tax	428
Other fraud	1,580
Transportation, etc., of stolen property	978
Other theft	1,221
White slave traffic	176
Narcotics, total	1,450
Marijuana Tax Act	411
Other narcotics	1,039
Liquor, Internal Revenue	3,948
Other liquor, total	13
Indian liquor laws	8
Smuggling liquor	5
Antitrust violations	27
Food and Drug Act	378
Immigration laws	2,293
Impersonation	135
Juvenile delinquency	1,194
Migratory bird laws	556
Motor Carrier Act	653
National defense laws	
Selective service	198
Illegal use of uniform	76
Alien registration	3

Treason
Espionage
Sabotage 2
Sedition
Other 45
All other United States offenses, total 2,030
   Robbery 247
   Assault 58
   Counterfeiting 101
   Prison escape, riot, mutiny 156
   Extortion, racketeering and threats 119
   Fair Labor Standards Act 119
   Nationality laws 33
   Perjury 45
   Lottery 15
   Postal laws 255
   Homicide 2
   Bribery 30
   Customs laws 72
   Contempt 45
   Kidnaping 26
   Maritime 29
   Stowaways 40
   Firearms and weapons 184
   Other offenses 454
Local offenses, total 1,882
   Murder 74
   Manslaughter 43
   Robbery 162
   Assault 233
   Burglary 315
   Auto theft 95
   Embezzlement, forgery & fraud 175
   Larceny 304
   Rape 109
   Other sex offenses 56
   Gambling 65
   Other offenses 251

Source: *Statistical Abstracts of the United States, 1961* (Washington, D.C.: U.S. Department of Commerce, 1961), p. 147.

Interrelationship of the Courts. How do cases and controversies move from one court to another? How can a suit be taken from a state court to a national court? To which of the latter can it be taken? To answer these questions fully is far beyond the scope of this inquiry, but some effort at comprehension is essential. Basic relationships are determined by the jurisdiction of the separate systems and courts. It is possible to take a case from a state to a national court. Assuming the existence of jurisdiction, three methods are available.

The first method is by transferring it. A case may be transferred at the defendant's discretion to the proper United States district court *before trial* in the state court, when the plaintiff has decided to *bring* it in a state court.

This right of transfer enables a defendant to offset any advantage that the plaintiff expected to gain by bringing the action in a state instead of a national court. But, cases may not be transferred from a national to a state court. *After decision* by a state court of "last resort"—that is, the highest state court *from which a decision can be obtained*—a case may be taken only to the Supreme Court of the United States. It may be taken by right of appeal or after petition for a writ of certiorari. Appeal can be *made* as a matter of right; therefore, to reduce their number the grounds for appeals are narrowly limited to two: (1) a final decision of a "state court of last resort" against the validity of a treaty or statute of the United States; or (2) a final decision which sustains the validity of a state statute or constitutional provision alleged to violate the "supreme law of the land." In both instances the claim of right derived from national authority has been denied by a state court. To guard against the possibility that state courts might take too narrow a view of the validity of such claims, Congress has provided for the appeal to the Supreme Court of decisions denying them. But, the right to *take an appeal* does not in practice include a right to have it *heard* by the Supreme Court.

The second method of taking a final decision of a state court into the national judicial system involves use of a *petition for a writ of certiorari.* This writ is an order of a higher court directing a lower one to send up the record of a case so that its decision can be reviewed. It is used on occasions when a "federal question" is raised but no right of appeal is open to the dissatisfied party. That party asks the Supreme Court to review the decision, but the latter is not required to grant the request. In fact, most requests are not granted.

The rule of the Supreme Court regulating the matter states:

1. A review on writ of certiorari is not a matter of right, but of sound judicial discretion, and will be granted only where there are special and important reasons therefor. The following while neither controlling nor fully measuring the court's discretion, indicate the character of reasons which will be considered:

(a) Where a state court has decided a federal question of substance not theretofore determined by this court, or has decided it in a way probably not in accord with applicable decisions of this court.

(b) Where a court of appeals has rendered a decision in conflict with the decision of another court of appeals on the same matter; or has decided an important question of local law in a way probably in conflict with applicable local decisions; or has decided an important question of federal law which has not been, but should be, settled by this court; or has decided a federal question in a way probably in conflict with applicable decisions of this court; or has so far departed from the accepted and usual course of judicial proceedings, or so far sanctioned such a departure by a lower court, as to call for the exercise of this court's power of supervision.

(2) The same general considerations outlined above will control in respect of petitions for writs of certiorari to review judgments of the Court of Claims, of the Court of Customs and Patent Appeals, or of any other court whose determinations are by law reviewable on writ of certiorari.[18]

By means of the writ of certiorari, therefore, the Supreme Court is able to accept for review those decisions of state courts which it feels are sufficiently important to justify the expenditure of its time. At the same time, the discriminating character of the writ enables it to protect itself against being overburdened. Nevertheless, the writ serves as an important means of facilitating the exercise by the Supreme Court of its supervisory powers over the inferior national courts, and it is through the use of its discretionary power that the Court is able to dispose of many cases each year.

Movement of Cases and Controversies from District Courts. Since the district courts have no appellate jurisdiction no cases are reviewed by them, but ones that have been decided by them can be reviewed by a higher court. If an action involves an anti-trust, interstate commerce, or communications statute, or an order of a district court granting or denying an injunction to restrain enforcement, operation, or execution of a statute of the United States or of a state, or an order of a state administrative agency alleged to be unconstitutional it can be appealed directly to the Supreme Court. The consequences of the decision or the importance of the issue involved dictate this expeditious process. In all other instances decisions of the district courts may be appealed to the courts of appeals.

Movement of Cases and Controversies from the Courts of Appeals. In the vast majority of instances decisions by the courts of appeal are not appealable. Only two grounds of appeal to the Supreme Court by right exist: (1) a party who relies upon a state statute held unconstitutional by a court of appeals may appeal, and (2) either party to a civil action holding an act of Congress void may appeal, if one party is the United States government or an agency, officer, or employee thereof. Also, if judges of the intermediate court disagree on points of law, they may certify a case to the Supreme Court. It may direct how the case is to be decided below, or it may call up the entire record and render a decision. The only other avenue of approach to the Supreme Court is by petition for a writ of certiorari.

[18] *Revised Rules of the Supreme Court of the United States,* 346 U.S. 951, Part V, No. 19, pp. 967-968.

METHOD OF DISPOSING OF CASES BY THE
SUPREME COURT

	1951	1952	1953	1954
By written opinion	96	122	84	86
Per curiam (total)	101	71	86	102
After argument	25	10	23	16
By final decree-original cases	–	–	–	–
By denial or dismissal of certiorari	904	970	1029	1026
By dismissal of appeals	–	–	–	8
By motion to dismiss or by stipulation	5	11	2	4

	1955	1956	1957
By written opinion	103	112	125
Per curiam (total)	127	134	184
After argument	18	23	27
By final decree-original cases	4	3	1
By denial or dismissal of certiorari	1222	1248	1318
By dismissal of appeals	16	20	14
By motion to dismiss or by stipulation	3	3	4

	1958	1959	1960
By written opinion	116	110	125
Per curiam (total)	135	122	136
After argument	23	20	22
By final decree-original cases	3	–	1
By denial or dismissal of certiorari	1357	1388	1499
By dismissal of appeals	26	17	21
By motion to dismiss or by stipulation	3	4	4

Source: *Annual Report of the Director, Administrative Office of United States Courts, 1961* (Washington, D.C.: U.S. Government Printing Office, 1962), p. 221.

JUDICIAL REVIEW
AND THE JUDICIAL PROCESS[19]

Establishment of the Power-Acts of Congress. Does the power of judicial review extend to acts of Congress? As often happens the passage of years has supplied the answer, for in 1803 part of an act of Congress was declared unconstitutional.

It is a proposition too plain to be contested, that the constitution controls any legislative act repugnant to it; or, that the legislature may alter the constitution by an ordinary act.

Between these alternatives there is no middle ground. The constitution is either a superior paramount law, unchangeable by ordinary means, or it is on a level with ordinary legislative acts, and, like other acts, is alterable when the legislature shall please to alter it.

If the former part of the alternative be true, then a legislative act contrary to the constitution is not law; if the latter be true, then written constitutions are absurd attempts, on the part of the people, to limit a power in its own nature illimitable.

Certainly all those who have framed written constitutions contemplate them as forming the fundamental and paramount law of the nation, and, consequently, the theory of every such government be, that an act of the legislature, repugnant to the constitution, is void.

This theory is essentially attached to a written constitution, and is consequently to be considered, by this Court, as one of the fundamental principles of our society. It is not, therefore, to be lost sight of in the further consideration of this subject.

If an act of the legislature, repugnant to the constitution, is void, does it, notwithstanding its invalidity, bind the courts, and oblige them to give it effect? Or in other words, though it be not law, does it constitute a rule as operative as if it was a law? This would be to overthrow in fact what was established in theory; and would seem, at first view, an absurdity too gross to be insisted on. It shall, however, receive a more attentive consideration.

It is emphatically the province and duty of the judicial department to say what the law is. Those who apply the rule to particular cases, must of necessity expound and interpret that rule. If two laws conflict with each other, the courts must decide on the operation of each.

So if a law be in opposition to the constitution; if both the law and the constitution apply to a particular case, so that the court must either decide that case conformably to the law, disregarding the constitution; or conformably to the constitution, disregarding the law; the court must decide which of these conflicting rules governs the case; this is of the very essence of judicial duty.

If, then, the courts are to regard the constitution, and the constitution is superior to an ordinary act of the legislature, the constitution, and not such ordinary act, must govern the case to which they both apply. . . .

---

[19] Consideration of this topic was begun in Chapter 3. It is suggested that the material found there should be reviewed before the present section is considered.

The judicial power of the United States is extended to all cases arising under the constitution.

Could it be the intention of those who gave this power, to say, that in using it, the constitution should not be looked into? That a case arising under the constitution should be decided, without examining the instrument under which it arises?

This is too extravagant to be maintained. In some cases, then, the constitution must be looked into by the judges. And if they can open it at all, what part of it are they forbidden to read or to obey? . . .

It is not entirely unworthy of observation, that in declaring what shall be the supreme law of the land, the constitution itself is first mentioned; and not the laws of the United States generally, but those only which shall be made in pursuance of the constitution, have that rank.

Thus, the particular phraseology of the constitution of the United States confirms and strengthens the principle, supposed to be essential to all written constitutions, that a law repugnant to the constitution is void; and that courts, as well as other departments, are bound by that instrument.[20]

Establishment of the Power-Acts of State Legislatures. The power of judicial review extends also to acts of state legislatures. The "supremacy clause" clearly assumes this application of the power, for by declaring what shall be the supreme law, it anticipates the application of the power to state statutes as they bear a relation to the Constitution, to laws made in pursuance of it, and to treaties made under authority of the United States; and the appellate jurisdiction of national courts extends to the classes of controversies to which states are parties.

The first Congress authorized the Supreme Court to review decisions or decrees of state courts of last resort, in cases of law or equity,

. . . where is drawn in question the validity of a treaty or statute of, or of an authority exercised under the United States, and the decision is against their validity; or where is drawn in question the validity of a statute of, or an authority exercised under any State, on the ground of their being repugnant to the Constitution, treaties or laws of the United States, and the decision is in favor of such their validity, or where is drawn in question the construction of any clause of the Constitution, or of a treaty, or statute of, or commission held under the United States, and the decision is against the title, right, privilege or exemption specially set up or claimed by either party, under such clause of the said Constitution, treaty, statute or commission, may be re-examined or reversed or affirmed in the Supreme Court of the United States upon a writ of error. . . .[21]

Judges in every state are sworn to support the Constitution, "any thing in the Constitution or Laws of any State to the Contrary notwithstanding." Thus, the state courts are supposed to be the first line in the defenses of

---

[20] *Marbury* v. *Madison* (1803), 1 Cranch 137.
[21] 1 *Statutes* 73, 85-86. This is the basis for appeals by right from state courts of last resort to the Supreme Court.

the Constitution; but to guard against the possibility that state judges might be prejudiced in favor of the constitution or laws of their respective states, the first Congress enacted the above-quoted section of the Judiciary Act of 1789.

From earliest times there was no serious doubt that the national government would, of necessity, have power to determine the validity of state statutes. Absence of that power over acts of Congress would perhaps not have been a defect fatal to the federal system, but its application to state statutes is probably indispensable to the preservation of federalism in our constitutional system.

The states strongly opposed the extension of judicial review to decisions rendered by their courts. State judges, it was asserted, were bound to recognize the "supreme law of the land" only so far as was necessary to dispose of cases in the state courts, and the national power of judicial review extended only to cases which began in national courts. Supporters of state immunity maintained

. . . that the nation does not possess a department capable of restraining peaceably, and by authority of law, any attempts which may be made, by a part, against the legitimate powers of the whole; and that the government is reduced to the alternative of submitting to such attempts, or of resisting them by force. They maintain that the constitution of the United States has provided no tribunal for the final construction of itself, or of the laws or treaties of the nation; but that this power may be exercised in the last resort by the courts of every state of the Union. That the Constitution, laws and treaties may receive as many constructions as there are states; and that this is not a mischief, or, if a mischief, is irremediable. . . .[22]

Arguments such as these, however, ignored the fact that

The mischievous consequences of the construction contended for . . . are also entitled to great consideration. It would prostrate, it has been said, the government and its laws at the feet of every state in the Union. And would not this be its effect? What power of the government could be executed by its own name, in any state disposed to resist its execution by a course of legislation? The laws must be executed by individuals acting within the several states. If these individuals may be exposed to penalties, and if the courts of the Union cannot correct the judgments by which these penalties may be enforced, the course of the government may be, at any time, arrested by the will of one of its members. Each member will possess a *veto* on the will of the whole. . . .

No government ought to be so defective in its organization, as not to contain within itself the means of securing the execution of its own laws against other dangers than those which occur every day. Courts of justice are the means most usually employed; and it is reasonable to expect that a government should repose on its own courts, rather than on others. . . .

America has chosen to be, in many respects, and to many purposes, a nation; and for all these purposes, her government is complete; to all these objects it is

[22] *Cohens* v. *Virginia* (1821), 6 Wheaton 264.

competent. The people have declared, that in the exercise of all powers given
for these objects, it is supreme. It can, then, in effecting these objects, legitimately control all individuals or governments within the American territory.
The constitution and laws of a state, so far as they are repugnant to the constitution and laws of the United States, are absolutely void. These states are
constituent parts of the United States; they are members of one great empire. . . .

The exercise of the appellate power over those judgments of the state tribunals which may contravene the constitution or laws of the United States, is,
we believe, essential to the attainment of those objects. . . . "Thirteen independent courts," says a very celebrated statesman, . . . "of final jurisdiction
over the same causes, arising upon the same laws, is a hydra in government,
from which nothing but contradictions and confusion can proceed."[23]

The extension of judicial review to decisions of state courts greatly
strengthened the authority and position of the national government by
securing to one of its institutions the power to guard the Union against
the predatory actions of states. It made possible the review by the highest
court in the Union of all cases involving the supreme law, and it vested
in the national government the power to resolve all questions concerning
the extent of its own authority.

Effect of Judicial Review. Why do decisions of national courts bind
Congress in the future enactment of statutes? It is, perhaps, only a
practical necessity acquiesced in by the legislature which abides by the
spirit of the system. That Congress regards itself as bound by decisions of
the Supreme Court is an important feature of judicial review; for if it did
not, it would be free to disregard their effects. Judicial decisions would
then apply only to laws already passed and would have no effect upon
measures to be passed in the future.

To explain this feature of judicial review it is necessary to accept the
premise that judges stand in a relation to the Constitution which is not
permitted to legislators. It must be assumed that judges are able to *know*
what the law of the Constitution is, whereas legislators are only able to
hold informed opinions. This, apparently, is what Justice Roberts meant
when he wrote that

When an act of Congress is appropriately challenged in the courts as not
conforming to the constitutional mandate, the judicial branch of the Government has only one duty, to lay the article of the Constitution which is invoked
beside the statute which is challenged and to decide whether the latter squares
with the former. All the court does, or can do, is to pronounce its considered
judgment upon the question. The only power it has, if such it may be called, is
the power of judgment.[24]

[23] *Loc. cit.*
[24] *United States* v. *Butler* (1936), 297 U.S. 1.

The claim that judges alone are competent to ascertain the true meaning of the Constitution has never received unanimous support. It has been strenuously opposed by Presidents and Congress on various occasions. Congress has, under the Constitution, full control over the appellate jurisdiction of the Supreme Court, and it has used that control on at least one occasion to withdraw the authority to decide a case which it feared would be decided contrary to its wishes. The size of the Supreme Court is also determined by Congress, and it has been altered on several occasions under circumstances strongly suggesting that Congress was endeavoring to influence the Court's opinion. There is considerable evidence, also, that Presidents in nominating and appointing justices, and the Senate in confirming them, carefully scrutinize the social and economic ideas of candidates in order to place men on the highest court who hold "proper" views on the questions of policy that might come before that court for decision.

Limitations on the Power of Judicial Review. Numerous restraints upon judicial review exist. The Supreme Court is restrained by the limits of its jurisdiction, by opinion, by the nature of the judicial function, and by its own sense of self-restraint. It cannot go abroad and seek out legal conflicts to be settled, and it has no power to initiate action or to render advisory opinions on the constitutionality of laws. Moreover, the necessity to declare a law unconstitutional arises only because a statute relied upon by a party to a dispute is alleged to conflict with the fundamental law. The theory of the process is that the purported law has always been void. The Court does not make it void by its decision; it merely discovers that it has never been a law and announces the fact.

Further, the Supreme Court employs judicial review subject to a number of self-imposed limitations, some of which it has stated as follows:

1. The Court will not pass upon the constitutionality of legislation in a friendly, non-adversary, proceeding, declining because to decide such questions "is legitimate only in the last resort, and as a necessity in the determination of a real, earnest, and vital controversy between individuals. It never was thought that, by means of a friendly suit, a party beaten in the legislature could transfer to the courts an inquiry as to the constitutionality of the legislative act." . . .

2. The Court will not "anticipate a question of constitutional law in advance of the necessity of deciding it." . . . "It is not the habit of the Court to decide questions of a constitutional nature unless absolutely necessary to the decision of the case." . . .

3. The Court will not "formulate a rule of constitutional law broader than is required by the precise facts to which it is to be applied." . . .

4. The Court will not pass upon a constitutional question although properly presented by the record, if there is also present some other ground upon which the case may be disposed of. This rule has found most varied application. Thus, if a case can be decided on either of two grounds, one involving a constitutional

question, the other a question of statutory construction or general law, the Court will decide only the latter. . . .

5. The Court will not pass upon the validity of a statute upon complaint of one who fails to show that he is injured by its operation. . . . Among the many applications of this rule, none is more striking than the denial of the right to challenge to one who lacks a personal or property right. . . .

6. The Court will not pass upon the constitutionality of a statute at the instance of one who has availed himself of its benefits. . . .

7. "When the validity of an act of Congress is drawn in question, and even if a serious doubt of constitutionality is raised, it is a cardinal principle that this Court will first ascertain whether a construction of the statute is fairly possible by which the question may be avoided."[25]

Further, judicial review is limited because the courts presume that statutes are constitutional; because they will invalidate only a portion of a statute if what remains makes sense; because the validity of many statutes is never properly challenged in a court; because the courts refuse to inquire into the wisdom of specific legislation, the motives of the legislative body in enacting it, or other matters likely to involve the judiciary in the political processes of the people.

Political Questions. An apparent limitation on the exercise of judicial review arises from the nature of judicial power, and from the relation of the judiciary to the legislative and executive branches under the Constitution. The courts of the United States are granted by the Constitution only *judicial power,* the power to decide real cases and controversies. Since courts possess only judicial power, they cannot properly concern themselves with matters of *policy,* that is, with questions, even though they arise under the Constitution, that involve problems of a *political* as distinguished from a legal nature.

A complete list of "political questions" cannot be compiled, for the Supreme Court determines in its wisdom what are and what are not such questions. Several have been noted in the foregoing chapters. In these and other instances it has refused to assume jurisdiction because the questions raised could be settled by the legislative and executive branches under the Constitution.

Political questions are unsuited to settlement by judicial processes, for the training of judges, the procedures of judicial action, and the precedents that guide courts are not adapted to their solution. Moreover, courts adhere to the principle of separated powers when they refuse to invade authority left to the political branches.

Reasonable Doubt. The Supreme Court persistently takes the position that it will not hold an act of Congress unconstitutional as long as there is a reasonable doubt about its invalidity, and that all reasonable doubts will be resolved in favor of constitutionality. However, almost one-half

---

[25] *Ashwander* v. *Tennessee Valley Authority* (1936), 297 U.S. 288.

Above and beyond the call of politics

of the decisions holding acts of Congress unconstitutional, and many of the uncounted number declaring state statutes invalid, have not been unanimous, and on more than one occasion, a single vote has stood between validity and invalidity. There can be no question but that a strong doubt exists in the minds of justices who find themselves outvoted. What this limitation of the exercise of judicial review amounts to, therefore, is that a statute will not be held unconstitutional unless a majority of the justices are convinced that it is. The doubts that a minority might entertain carry no weight, even though they are based on the strong misgivings of equally intelligent and learned men.

Importance of Judicial Review. The limitations upon judicial review have had no great effect on its importance, for they are ignored about as often as they are observed. The importance of judicial review depends mainly on the use to which it is put. Most clauses of the Constitution have not been of signficance to the development of the American political system. All of them possess equal force as law, but judicial review has grown largely out of the Court's attitude toward fewer than a dozen of them. Its general tendency has been to permit the aggrandizement of both national and executive power. Through its decisions the Supreme Court has firmly established itself as the supervisor of the American constitutional system.

Jefferson's fear that exclusive possession by the judiciary of authority to interpret the Constitution would give it a despotic power over the political branches, has not been realized. Only about 80 of an estimated

35,000 acts of Congress have been held in whole or in part to violate the Constitution. Two of these have led eventually to constitutional amendments that have reversed them, and some have applied only to parts of statutes, the remaining portions having been left unaffected. Some have declared statutes of only minor importance invalid, and some have been reversed by later decisions of the Court. Therefore, the total impact of judicial review upon the Congress has not been very great.

Judicial review has significance as a method of protecting individual rights, of maintaining federalism, and curbing governmental power; but its main importance arises from the difficulty of amending the Constitution and its use therefore to keep that document "flexible." Its chief mode of adaptation is by judicial amplification. In the light of its often vague provisions, the judges have to consider the validity of legislation passed to accommodate demands for service or regulation by the national government. They have to refine the meaning of constitutional provisions relevant to cases brought to them for decision, ascertain the existence or nonexistence of authority necessary for action, as well as the scope, if any, of that authority.

THE JUDICIAL PROCESS

In theory, a judge acts as a dispassionate mouthpiece of the law, enunciating whichever legal rule is to be applied in each case. When a court exercises its power of judicial review, it merely finds that a rule relied upon by one of the parties to a dispute lacks the force of law and cannot be applied.

Stated in these terms the exercise of judicial review seems to present no problems of uncertainty or imprecision. However, there is no touchstone that can always be counted upon to reveal to judges the solutions to legal disputes. This is particularly true of disputes which come before the Supreme Court, for that court receives only the most difficult cases and controversies. The less important and more easily settled ones are decided by lower courts.

The chief aid in the settlement of suits is the use of precedent. As courts decide cases their decisions become part of the permanent record of the judiciary. Each decision involves a set of facts that constitute the basis of a conflict. To those facts the court applies a legal rule, and the dispute and the rule of law applied to its solution create a precedent which is then available for application to subsequent cases. Therefore, when a judge has to decide a dispute he turns to the precedents and endeavors to find one as similar as possible to the case before him. If he is successful in his search, he may find that the rule of law established earlier will also dispose of the existing conflict.

Judges interpret and apply law, but what law? The answers to many questions are not governed by obvious rules of established law. Often many rules might apply to a given question, but no one of them does so clearly to the exclusion of the others. Which, then, should be selected. If none applies directly, one might be made to apply if the judges give it a new twist of meaning. If that cannot be done, a new rule can usually be created by the judges to answer the question at hand.

Thus, the task of the judge is not an easy one. No two disputes are ever exactly the same; therefore, no precedent is ever precisely applicable, and resort to precedent may fail to provide a legal rule by which to decide a present case. Decision is not a matter of rote.

Judges do not feed facts into a legal machine out of which pops a rule of law that exactly fits the dispute at hand. They are not automatons and the judicial process is not an automatic one. As human beings judges are subject to the same influences that affect other persons. Their special training in the law, their age and experience, their isolation from the stresses and strains of partisan politics, and the prestige of their office enable them to perform their function with a maximum of impartiality. But, whether they are interpreting statutes or constitutional provisions there is great opportunity in most important disputes for the exercise of judicial discretion. Judges can and do make law. They create new rules of law, reject old ones, and give new meaning to existing ones.

They are not, of course, completely free agents. Decisions of the courts are closely watched by the general public, lawyers, bar associations, other judges, interest groups of all types, Congress, the President, and government officers. When problems of constitutional or statutory interpretation are involved, judges are constrained to work within the limits of the written instrument, for there is a core of meaning, however small, within every provision. They must also have before them the general public attitude, for in the last analysis law is obeyed and courts are respected because they are supported by the public. Public support will continue to bolster them as long as their rulings do not antagonize too strongly the force of public opinion. Within the framework of good character, impartiality, judicial integrity, and the limitations imposed by the above factors, judges must make value judgments. They are popularly regarded as being guided in their decisions by the specific facts of the situation pending before them; but while a dispute affects the parties to it, it also affects the interests of great numbers of persons who are not actual parties. Hence, there is considerable evidence that judges are influenced in their decisions by the nature and scope of the broad interests affected by them, by their impact upon society or on some major interest within it, as well as by the narrow interests of the parties to the dispute.

Constitutional interpretation, then, is not automatic or objective. No doubt most judges make every effort to subordinate the subjective forces that might affect their judicial determinations, but no person can do so with assurance of complete success. Accordingly, judges who are equally learned, equally impartial, and equally experienced often arrive at opposite conclusions as to the proper interpretation of the Constitution that should be applied to a given set of facts.

The process of constitutional interpretation also involves the judges in the determination of questions that are not legal in nature, no matter how skillfully they may be disguised by legal language. Whether or not an exercise of power is sanctioned by the Constitution is very apt to depend upon the judge's individual conception of what the extent of national power *ought* to be. A judge can find legal support for virtually any position he desires to take in deciding a case before his court. The answer at which he arrives will depend upon the premises from which he starts his process of reasoning. If he is disposed to think that the Constitution ought to be interpreted broadly as a grant of powers to the general government, if he believes that the Constitution supplies power to the national government adequate to the solution of any problem, he will probably begin his process of reasoning from the premise that a challenged statute is valid. However, if he views the Constitution primarily as a statement of limitations on the authority of the national government, if he believes that the national government *ought* to be restricted to the performance of only a few essential functions, if he feels that it *ought not* to meddle in the free operation of an economic system governed by "natural" laws, he will doubtless begin his reasoning from the premise that the legislature lacked power to enact the statute under consideration.

Occasionally, justices of the Supreme Court have characterized the judicial function in realistic terms, for instance when Justice John Harlan declared, "If we don't like an act of Congress we don't have much trouble to find a ground for declaring it unconstitutional."[26] There can be little doubt that the meaning of the Constitution and its application through judicial review is as much dependent upon "human" factors as it is upon the principles and precedents of the law.

As applied to the exercise of judicial review the method by which the judicial process is conducted assumes great importance. The Constitution is not intended to be a strait jacket with which to confine the exercise of authority by the general government. It is a synoptic document that was meant to provide in general terms for a durable and flexible system of government. Judges who are called upon to exercise the power of judicial review are able, if they will, to find through the interpretation of its clauses the authorization to meet the needs of an expanding nation. The alternative to judicial amplification of national power by constitutional

---

[26] Quoted in E. S. Corwin, *Constitutional Revolution, Ltd.* (Claremont, Calif.: Claremont College, 1941), p. 38.

interpretation is resort to the formal process of amendment. That the latter would be more in harmony with popularly controlled government is scarcely debatable, but that it would prove practicable is subject to serious doubt. The fact that the Constitution has remained flexible and has endured longer than any other "written" constitution is attributable in no little degree to the scope that has been permitted to the exercise of national power by the Supreme Court.

Lack of Unanimity. In about one-third of the cases which they decide after hearing the justices of the United States Supreme Court are unable all to agree on a single principle of law with which to dispose of the case at hand. The Court has been subjected to criticism for its lack of unanimity, because, it is argued, the expression of divergent views undermines public confidence in the judicial process, reveals doctrinal differences within the Court, complicates the task of lawyers by muddying the waters of legal principle, and increases unrest and uncertainty in society. The right of any justice to register his disagreement with his colleagues on the Court over any issue is well established, but some chief justices have endeavored to persuade all to take a common position for the sake of appearance alone. Chief Justice Warren apparently makes no such demands upon the present members of the Supreme Court, for not only are dissenting opinions frequent but the language employed in them is often frank and bitter.

Reasonable differences of opinion are inevitable among the justices. On virtually every other difficult subject controversy is permitted and often encouraged. Why should it be discouraged when difficult legal questions which have no obvious answers are involved? Seldom does a problem of any difficulty come before the Supreme Court to which only one legal principle can be applied. Read what Justice Frankfurter has said of the judge's role in the determination of cases:

> The decisions in the cases that really give trouble rest on judgment, and judgment derives from the totality of a man's nature and experience. . . .
>
> Judges are men, not disembodied spirits. Of course, a judge is not free from preferences or, if you will, biases. But he may deprive a bias of its meritricious authority by stripping it of the uncritical assumption that it is founded on compelling reason or the coercive power of a syllogism. He will be alert to detect that though a conclusion has a logical form it in fact represents a choice of competing considerations of policy, one of which for the time has won the day.
>
> . . . For judges it is not merely a desirable capacity to "emancipate their purposes" from their private desires; it is their duty. [A judge] brings his whole experience, his training, his outlook, his social, intellectual, and moral environment with him when he takes a seat on the supreme bench. But a judge worth his salt is in the grip of his function. . . .[27]

[27] Felix Frankfurter, "Some Observations on the Nature of the Judicial Process of Supreme Court Litigation," *Proceedings of the American Philosophical Society*, Vol. 98, p. 233.

The Impact of the Legislative Process on Judicial Interpretation. The necessities of the legislative process complicate the judge's task in judicial review. (1) Statutes often lack specificity because they are the products of compromise. Democratic government and society are built on uncertainty, on trial and error. They deny that any authority is entitled to unquestioning absolute obedience, because they deny that any authority possesses infallible insight into the one right course of action. Law in a democracy is the product of compromise between competing and differing views, each of which is thought to contain a share of truth but none of which is admitted to embody a monopoly of it. If the spirit of compromise endures the product of the democratic interplay of forces is a law stating a new rule and representing a middle position by which the conflicts of society can be peacefully and lawfully resolved. (2) On more than one occasion, however, the compromise necessary to obtain results has been possible only by incorporating in an act two or more differing, if not conflicting, principles as the price for securing any law at all. (3) An act may be deliberately drafted to omit a controversial feature certain to arise in the course of its administration, or (4) for reasons of party expediency a politically touchy issue may be dealt with in vague, ambiguous, and undefined terms. Review and interpretation of statutes are further complicated by the fact that (5) Congress cannot provide for every situation in the text of an act, so that judges must ask "What would Congress have done if it had provided a specific rule for this situation?" (6) Construction and application of statutory language must be carried on in a context of linguistic ambiguity. The same words have different meanings in different situations at different times or to different persons. Words are symbols with mutable content. They do not always convey the meaning that was intended by their use. (7) Moreover, a statute is the product of no one mind or individual effort; it is the result of a group effort undertaken by many people and accommodating diverse points of view. (8) A statute is a practical thing intended for the practical affairs of men and government, but the subjects of concern to modern government are often beyond the scope of legislative knowledge and ability to anticipate; therefore, present-day enactments are often deliberately couched in vague terms so as to bestow upon administrative agencies adequate authority to apply them to unanticipated developments with a minimum of difficulty.

In the face of these complicating factors statutory construction cannot be executed according to the rules of Aristotelian logic. The function becomes an exercise in determining the meaning and the scope of the permissible application of the act at hand. It is not to be undertaken by ritualistic procedures but by the use of every available legitimate aid suitable to the occasion. The meaning of the public policy embodied in the act must be discovered and applied. It is a function that involves the judge in the exercise of wide discretion. The consequences of the legislative struggle surrounding its enactment are incorporated in its terms, so that what the legislators were unable, or unwilling, to do to make its meaning specific the judges must now try to accomplish.

In spite of great latitude for the injection of personal views into the law, no judge "worth his salt" will draw from, or read into, the language of an act whatever his predilections or biases suggest. Judges operate within the restraints imposed upon them by their place in the democratic structure of society and its governmental organization. For them to read into an act what its makers did not include, or for them to read out what was clearly expressed or implied, is to impinge upon the legislative power. The courts, and especially the Supreme Court, can never, except at their peril, lose sight of the fact that they are subject to the general superintending powers of Congress, in spite of the theoretical equality of the three branches of government. Self-imposed restraint is the essence of judicial prudence.

The major work of the national courts is concerned not with questions of constitutional law but with the less glamorous problems of statutory interpretation. Statutory law is at the base of most controversies that come before these courts. Within the language of the statutes the judges must find the meaning that Congress incorporated, not what it meant to say but what it did say. And all the while the judiciary must have respect for the legislative power and the presumption that its enactments reflect the legislature's regard for the established principles and values of the social and political order. Further, the judges must have constant regard for what Congress *did not say;* its omissions will often aid in making meaningful what it did express. They may also find that *the law* is determined not by a single act but by several pertaining to the same or related subjects, all adding to its meaning and making it intelligible in the light of history, usage, social necessity, and the attitude of Congress at the time of its enactment. To aid the judiciary Congress may include in its acts definitions of terms, but sometimes it does no more than supply a general standard to assist the courts and administrators in applying its provisions. Most perplexing of all for a judge are those acts or clauses that have constitutional implications, for they inevitably bring into the task of construction some aspect of federalism, or the separation of powers, or some other constitutional uncertainty. Therefore, the inherent nature of the judicial function, the human element involved, the nature of statutes and of the legislative process all encourage judicial subjectivity and undermine unanimity. They demonstrate conclusively the error of the widely held myth that the law is fixed, comprehensive, and unfailing in its ability to provide a specific and obvious answer to every problem.

On the other hand, it is essential to the democratic process that the judiciary should impose tight standards of statutory construction upon the enactments of Congress and, as occasion arises, upon those of the

state legislatures. Rigorous standards of statutory validity keep the legislatures on their toes and discourage sloppy draftsmanship, the assumption
of unlawful authority, and the abdication of responsibility to the courts
or to the executive. Concerning uncertainty in the law it has been said:

> So it is that the law will always teem with uncertainty. It has always been
> the case—and it always will remain that way under the democratic scheme of
> things. The truth is that the law is the highest form of compromise between
> competing interests; it is a substitute for force and violence—the only path to
> peace man has yet devised. It is the product of attempted reconciliation be-
> tween the many diverse groups in a society. The reconciliation is not entirely a
> legislative function. The judiciary is also inescapably involved. When judges
> do not agree it is a sign they are dealing with problems on which society itself
> is divided. It is the democratic way to express dissident views. Judges are to
> be honored rather than criticized for following that tradition, for proclaiming
> their articles of faith so that all may read.[28]

Interplay Between Congress and the Supreme Court. Although emo-
tionalism in Congress may, periodically, run high against the Supreme
Court, as it did when the non-sectarian prayer approved by New York
State for recitation in the public schools was declared unconstitutional in
June, 1962, there is, over the long run, a healthy interplay between Congress and the Supreme Court. The decisions of the Court are studied by
the legislative committees, and their implications evaluated. Thus, between 1945 and 1957 Congress tried to modify by later enactment the
rules of law enunciated by the Supreme Court in twenty-six instances of
statutory interpretation.[29] It may on occasion be moved to do so to correct
an interpretation at odds with what it intended its enactment to mean, or,
in the light of experience, to modify the impact upon its declared policy
of circumstances unforeseen at the time of enactment. It may wish to
restrict the full impact of a judicial pronouncement, to alter an enactment
of a preceding Congress, or to deal with a subject not appropriate for
judicial power.

Stare Decisis and the Rule of Precedent. The place of precedent in the
judicial process has been briefly noted above. Regard for it is an important element in the Anglo-American legal system, and the Supreme Court
is subjected periodically to strong criticism because it has overruled or
ignored some previously decided case, thus flaunting the rule of *stare
decisis* which teaches that cases today are to be decided according to the
principles that settled similar cases yesterday. To ignore precedent, it is
argued, is to inject a disquieting degree of flux and uncertainty into the
law, whereas to observe it will promote stability and uniformity and
assure men that like law will govern like situations. Because most of our

[28] Felix Frankfurter, *op. cit.*
[29] See "Congressional Reversal of Supreme Court Decisions: 1945-1957."
Harvard Law Review, Vol. 71, p. 1324.

daily affairs are governed by statute law, regard for *stare decisis* in the disposition of cases involving enacted law is especially relevant to a realization of the general desire of men for predictability, order, and security. Hence, disregard of precedent is less common in cases arising from enacted law than in those arising from the Constitution.

This is probably as it should be, for the essential natures of statutes and constitutions are different. The former are products of *ad hoc* efforts to solve specific problems, are narrow in scope and particular in purpose. The latter are synoptic, skeletal, of general purpose and broad scope, intended to accommodate changing and diverse values, institutions, and conditions of men over long periods of time. That the language of a constitution should be given variable meaning should occasion no great surprise or consternation if viewed realistically. Rigid adherence to precedent in the area of constitutional law would probably inflict a disservice upon society. In the words of Justice Frankfurter:

> A judge who is asked to construe or interpret the Constitution often rejects the gloss which his predecessors have put on it. For the gloss may in his view offend the spirit of the Constitution or do violence to it. That has been the experience of this generation and of all those that have preceded. It will likewise be the experience of those to follow. And so it should be. For it is the Constitution which we have sworn to defend, not some predecessor's interpretation of it. *Stare decisis* has small place in constitutional law. The Constitution has written for all times and all ages. It would lose its great character and become feeble if it were allowed to become encrusted with narrow, legalistic notions that dominated the thinking of one generation.[30]

This is the philosophy by which the political branches of the national government have generally operated, and the one to which a majority of the present Supreme Court adheres. But a different majority in the future might accept, and past Courts have adhered to, other viewpoints. Some have attempted to conform rigidly to what they thought was the original meaning of the framers, ignoring the changed conditions of social, economic, and political life in America since 1789. Another viewpoint has advocated a present-day interpretation based upon the original meaning of words as they were understood in 1789. Both viewpoints are treacherous, because the meaning of the framers or the original meaning of the words used cannot in many instances be ascertained with any certainty. More objectionable, however, is the fact that both bases for interpretation would tie the present too tightly to the past.

Therefore, it is probably less desirable for judges to adhere rigidly to precedent when interpreting the Constitution of the United States than when interpreting acts of Congress. Of course, the meaning of some clauses of the Constitution is definite and clear, and the legal boundaries

---

[30] *Loc. cit.*

are firmly fixed; but these conditions do not prevail for many other clauses, unless it is assumed that every particular of the document means now exactly what it meant in 1789. That assumption, however, cannot be made if the fundamental law is to endure as a flexible, adaptable scheme of government. So, to the extent that precision of meaning is lacking, each judge must ascertain for himself what a particular provision of the Constitution signifies. To that end he may be guided by evidence of what its framers intended, by his own best judgment, by precedent, or by his emotions and feelings about what *ought* to be. To the extent that he accepts precedent he accepts the conclusions of a predecessor who was faced with the same problem in a bygone time. Perhaps the principle then adopted retains its applicability to the changed conditions and problems of contemporary times; but if it is thought by him to have lost its relevancy it should and probably would be ignored, distinguished, or reversed without hesitation. The institutions and problems of contemporary life cannot be forced into conformity with constitutional principles devised to suit those of yesterday. An attempt to make them do so would only promote the very insecurity and conflict which adherence to precedent is supposed to diminish. The same authority that enabled judges in previous decades to establish the law of constitutional precedents would authorize those of today to abandon them in favor of new doctrines. To argue to the contrary is to take a position in favor of freezing the Constitution in a pattern given it by an earlier generation that was no better equipped than our own to know definitely *the* meaning of the document. Is it not better that each succeeding generation should be permitted to work out its own destiny on the basis of its whole accumulated experience within the general principles of the fundamental law and the basic assumptions of democracy?

The Present Supreme Court. The present Supreme Court of the United States has been involved in more political controversy and criticism, and has generated more proposals to curb its powers of judicial review than has any preceding Court since that of the mid-1930's which gave rise to the court-packing plan of President Franklin Roosevelt. That was a "conservative" Court under attack by "liberals" because it thwarted the major efforts of the New Deal to cope with the economic and social problems of the depression era. Today's Court, however, is a "liberal" one under attack by "conservatives" because, in their opinion, it tries to go too far too fast, usurps legislative power, and reduces the Constitution to whatever the justices say it is at the moment. As a "liberal activist" Court it has aroused criticism from interests concerned with the control of subversive activities, but not so concerned with the law of civil liberties, when it has rendered decisions which they regard as favorable to disloyal elements. It precipitated a further storm of criticism when it declared that desegregation in public education was in violation of the Constitution.

"States' righters" raised their voices against it as a consequence of several decisions which they felt invaded the powers of the states and further weakened their position in the Union. Between 1953 and 1959 the furor was at its height, but in the latter year the appointment of Justice Potter Stewart gave the more "conservative" bloc within the Court a majority. Although the attacks upon the Court did not cease, much of the initial storm subsided as a result of the Court's shift to a more "conservative" position; but in mid-1962 the appointments of Justices Byron White and Arthur Goldberg, presumably "liberals," to replace Justices Whittaker and Frankfurter, both "conservatives," have probably shifted the balance back to the "liberal" side once again.

Since 1959, then, the ideological split among the justices has been most evident. Each session of the Court has been marked not only by conflicts of law but also by a conflict of philosophy governing the place of the

Court in the constitutional system. Dissension, often in the open and sharply expressed, has been common. Split decisions, many 5-4, have been the rule in most important cases. From 1959 until Justice White replaced Justice Whittaker, the group in the majority was headed by Justice Felix Frankfurter, who was usually supported by Justices Harlan, Clark, Stewart, and Whittaker. This group was notable for its advocacy of judicial self-restraint, for its regard for the binding effect of precedent in constitutional cases, for its unwillingness to decide a constitutional question if a way could be found to avoid doing so, for its tendency to decide such a question on the narrowest possible grounds when it could not be avoided, for its deference to the legislative branch, for its preference for a go-slow attitude in the evolution of constitutional principles, and for its apparent desire to avoid controversial issues whenever possible. The decisions of this group tended to favor administrative actions, to hold against claims of civil rights, especially freedom of speech and of association, to uphold assertions of legislative investigatory power against claims of individual rights, to sustain state statutes alleged to deny due process of law or to conflict with national authority, and to sustain the independence of states to control the processes of their criminal courts without tight restraint imposed by standards of procedural due process.

In opposition to them on the above issues were Justices Black, Douglas, Warren, Brennan, and, now, clearly, Goldberg. This new "liberal activist" majority feels that the Court fails to fulfill its proper role in the constitutional scheme unless it moves vigorously in shaping and applying constitutional principles. Its members are willing to assume a share of the responsibility for the development of public policy. They are willing to search for and to declare judicial remedies for current problems, for they tend to regard government as a positive force with a mission to accomplish and the Court as an agent for aiding its accomplishment whenever possible. Therefore, the "activists" believe that the Court should facilitate the efforts of the political branches by formulating new rules of constitutional doctrine whenever desirable results cannot be obtained from old ones. The "activists" have not been reluctant to uphold individual rights, even though by doing so they have been brought into conflict with Congress, the states, the executive, and public opinion. They are, apparently, not over-impressed by the virtues of judicial self-restraint or the moderating effect of precedent. During the periods when it has been controlled by the "activist" group, the Court has precipitated criticism for its open endorsement of the view that the Constitution should be adapted to the needs of the present day to the maximum extent reconcilable with its language. Critics of the "activists" assert that they have not maintained the degree of consistency and logic in their decisions that is necessary and desirable; they have exceeded the proper bounds of judicial discretion; and they have violated popular expectations of order and stability in the law, thereby weakening the prestige and authority of the judiciary.

The controversy leaves unanswered many basic questions: Should the Supreme Court exercise the function of judicial review? If not, what substitute can be found for it? Can the amending process be used satisfactorily as an alternative arrangement to achieve the same end? If so, should Congress have the power to reverse a decision of the Court on a point of constitutional law? Should its decisions be mandatorily binding on state courts? Should the states have authority to negate a decision of the Court by action of a stipulated number of their legislatures, or conventions? Should the Court fulfill an active or a passive role in relation to the political branches and the states? In a democracy should any group of politically irresponsible men wield the power that is exercised by the justices? How does their power compare with that of congressional committee chairmen, pressure groups, etc.? Did the framers really authorize the judiciary to make interpretations of the Constitution that would be binding on Congress and the executive? Has the role of the Court in the constitutional system subtly changed from that of a judicial body to that of a policy-making group which responds to political pressures? Should the judiciary, particularly the Supreme Court, seek to preserve the original relations of federalism and of separated powers in the face of conditions calling for centralized power and a strong President? Should the Court assume the role of preserver and teacher of the nation's political heritage, refurbishing and emphasizing the principles of the Constitution by the test of "original intent of the framers" or by the standard of "concurrent meaning?"

Bibliography

The interested student will find among the following works many that will further his knowledge of American Government, in particular, and of political science, in general. In this enumeration are several sections pertaining to subjects not treated in the body of this book but which might be usefully pursued as topics of independent study or for term papers or special class reports. The entries in none of these sections are presented as complete listings of all titles available on the respective topics considered, but once a beginning is made, consultations of bibliographical entries will carry the inquirer as far as he needs or desires to go with his study. Various general research tools are available. Topics of a current nature can usually be found indexed in the *Reader's Guide to Periodical Literature*, the *New York Times Index*, Bulletin of the *Public Affairs Information Service, International Index to Periodicals, Index to Legal Periodicals*, Legal Periodical Digest, and the United States Government Publications Monthly Catalog. The *Congressional Quarterly Weekly Report*, and *Almanac*, and *Facts on File* are also very useful aides. The former is especially valuable for matters pertaining to Congress and legislation.

Numerous professional journals and learned society publications are available for advanced inquiry. Law journals and quarterlies should not be overlooked, nor should those in the areas of economics, anthropology, history, psychology, and sociology. Among the better known ones within the area of political science, however, are: *American Political Science Review, Annals of the American Academy of Political and Social Sciences, Political Science Quarterly, Midwest Journal of Political Science, Journal of Criminal Law, Criminology and Political Science, Journal of Political Economy, Journal of Politics, Public Administration Review, Public Personnel Review, Review of Politics*, and the *Western Political Quarterly*. In the area of international relations are *International Organization, Journal of Asian Studies, Journal of Central European Affairs, Mid East Journal, Middle Eastern Affairs, Pacific Affairs*, and the *Quarterly Journal of International Relations*.

The student will probably experience terminological difficulties at some time. He will find helpful E. C. Smith and A. J. Zurcher, *Dictionary of American Politics* (Barnes and Nobel, revised ed. 1955) and M. Tallman, *Dictionary of Civics and Politics* (Philosophical Library, 1953). Law dic-

467

tionaries are also very useful on occasion. A unique study guide and dictionary of American government has been prepared by Jack Plano and Milton Greenberg, *The American Political Dictionary* (1962).

Official Government Publications: Many aides useful to the student of American national government are published by its agencies. For others not mentioned here he should consult the documents librarian of his school's library. Among the more useful government documents are: annual reports of administrative agencies and officers, and of the Administrative Office of the United States Courts; the *Congressional Directory* for the current Congress which also contains much data on the executive and judicial branches; *Historical Statistics of the United States, 1789-1945* and supplements and the current edition of the *Statistical Abstracts; Opinions of the Attorney General; Rules and Manual of the House of Representatives* (current volume), and the same for the Senate; *United States Statutes at large,* a chronological presentation of the texts of laws, resolutions, and treaties of the United States; the *United States Code, Annotated* sets out in codified form existing national public law by subject. The *United States Government Organization Manual* contains some data on Congress and the judicial system but is mainly devoted to the structure of the executive branch and its agencies. Opinions of the Supreme Court may be found in the *United States Reports. The Congressional Record* presents what purports to be a verbatim account of the debates in Congress. The *Journals* of the chambers are a record of the actions taken. House and Senate *Reports* contain the printed reports of the standing committees, and the House and Senate *Documents* contain special studies made by or on behalf of the chambers. In the *Federal Register* are to be found all administrative rules, orders, regulations, and procedural changes as they are instituted.

Students interested in the ideological side of American government will find these works of aid and interest; F. W. Coker, *Democracy, Liberty, and Property* (1947); M. E. Curti, *The Growth of American Thought* (1943); A. P. Grimes, *American Political Thought* (1955); J. M. Jacobson, *The Development of American Political Thought* (1932); A. T. Mason, *Free Government in the Making* (1947); C. E. Merriam, *A History of American Political Theories* (1936); V. L. Parrington, *Main Currents of American Political Thought* (1939); F. G. Wilson, *The American Political Mind* (1949); B. F. Wright, *A Source Book of American Political Theory* (1929).

Supplementary Works: Numerous compilations of documents, essays, judicial opinions and other materials exist which are useful supplementary commentaries on American national government. Among them are: H. M. Bishop and S. Hendel, *Basic Issues of American Democracy: A Book of Readings* (1956); A. R. Chandler, ed., *The Clash of Political Ideas* (1949); A. N. Christenson and E. M. Kirkpatrick, *The People, Politics, and the*

Politician (1953); R. E. Cushman, *Leading Constitutional Decisions* (11th ed., 1959); R. G. Dixon and E. Plischke, *American Government: Basic Documents and Materials* (1950); T. H. Eliot, *et al, American Government: Readings and Problems for Analysis* (1959); D. Fellman, *et al, Readings in American National Government* (1950); G. B. Huszar, *et al, Basic American Documents* (1952); R. E. Lane, *Problems in American Government: An Introduction to Political Analysis* (1957); E. W. Lefever and W. V. Hohenstein, *Profile of American Politics* (1960); H. M. MacDonald, *et al, Readings in American Government* (1957); J. M. Mathews and C. A. Berdahl, *Documents and Readings in American Government* (1940); J. W. Peltason, *et al, American Government Annual, 1959-1960* (1959); N. Riemer, *Problems of American Government* (1952); C. W. Shull and N. D. Grundstein, *Workbook in American Government Organization and Institutions* (1955); W. B. Stubbs and C. B. Gosnell, *Select Readings in American Government* (1948); G. Stourzh and R. Lerner, *Readings in American Democracy* (1959); J. M. Swarthout and E. R. Bartley, *Materials on American National Government* (1952).

Works introductory to the study of political science may be useful in explaining terms, principles, and alternatives. They include: E. Barker, *Principles of Social and Political Theory* (1952); O. Butz, *Of Man and Politics* (1960); J. A. Corry and H. A. Abraham, *Elements of Democratic Government* (3d. ed., 1958); O. H. Flechtheim, ed., *Fundamentals of Political Science* (1953); C. J. Friedrich, *Constitutional Government and Democracy* (1950); J. W. Garner, *Political Science and Government* (1935); A. de Grazia, *The Elements of Political Science* (1952); R. M. MacIver, *The Web of Government* (1951); R. Rienow, *Introduction to Government* (1952); J. P. Roche and Murray Stedman, *The Dynamics of Democratic Government* (1954); C. C. Rodee, *et al, Introduction to Political Science* (1957); J. S. Roucek, *et al, Introduction to Political Science* (1950); E. B. Schultz, *Essentials of Government* (1958).

Particularly fruitful areas for extended independent study are the colonial background and the political antecedents of the Constitution. Many of the works here mentioned contain some material on pre-Revolutionary America. Of special interest are C. M. Andrews, *The Colonial Background of the American Revolution* (1924); H. Osgood, *The American Colonies in the Seventeenth Century*, 4 vols. (1924-1925); D. J. Boorstin, *The Americans: The Colonial Experience* (1958). For the advent of the Revolution see E. P. Douglass, *Rebels and Democrats* (1955); L. H. Gipson, *The Coming of the Revolution* (1954); J. E. Jameson, *The American Revolution Considered as a Social Movement* (1950); C. H. McIlwaine, *The American Revolution: A Constitutional Interpretation* (1923); J. C. Miller, *Origins of the American Revolution* (1943); L. Montress, *The Reluctant Rebels, the Story of the Continental Congress* (1950); C. L. Rossiter, *Seedtime of the Republic* (1953); C. H. Van Tyne, *The Causes of the War for Independ-*

ence (1922). The political ideas of the Revolutionary period are well treated in R. G. Adams, *The Political Ideas of the American Revolution* (1922) and in most of the works referred to above which discuss the ideological side of American Government. The outstanding analysis of the Declaration of Independence is Carl Becker's *The Declaration of Independence* (1922), but valuable also are E. Latham, ed., *The Declaration of Independence and the Constitution* (1949), and E. Dumbauld, *The Declaration of Independence and What It Means Today* (1950). For the pediod of the Revolution see J. R. Alden, *The American Revolution, 1775-1783* (1954); A. Nevins, *The American States During and After the Revolution, 1775-1789* (1924); M. M. Jensen, *The Articles of Confederation* (1940), and *The New Nation: A History of the United States During the Confederation* (1950). The classical analysis of the Confederacy is by J. Fiske, *The Critical Period of American History* (1888).

Literature abounds on the framing of the Constitution of the United States. Among the primary sources which should be consulted are: M. Farrand, *Records of the Federal Convention*, 2nd ed., 4 vols. (1937). The somewhat sketchy *Notes* of the proceedings kept by James Madison at Philadelphia is included in this, as are other documentary materials. The *Notes* may also be found in G. Hunt and J. B. Scott, editors, *The Debates in the Federal Convention of 1787 Which Framed the Constitution of the United States* (1920). Much documentary material may also be found in C. C. Tansill, *Documents Illustrative of the Formation of the Union of the American States* (House Document, No. 398, 69th Congress, 1 session, 1927). The debates and proceeding of the state ratifying conventions are set out in J. Elliot, *The Debates in the Several State Conventions on the Adoption of the Federal Constitution* (1920).

The work of the Philadelphia Convention is treated in A. N. Holcomb, *Our More Perfect Union* (1950); A. T. Prescott, *Drafting the Federal Constitution* (1941); W. U. Solberg, *The Federal Convention and the Formation of the Union of the American States* (1958); M. Farrand, *The Framing of the Constitution* (1913); C. Warren, *The Making of the Constitution* (1928). Much can be learned of the period from biographies of the leading figures of the day. Of value in this respect are also: H. Lyon, *The Constitution and the Men Who Made It* (1936); F. Rodell, *Fifty Five Men* (1936); N. Schachner *The Founding Fathers* (1954); and C. Van Doren, *The Great Rehearsal: the Story of the Makin ; and Ratifying of the Constitution of the United States* (1948).

The most authoritative and complete ana.ysis of the Constitution by contemporaries is *The Federalist,* a collection of papers written in defense of the new plan by Alexander Hamilton, John Jay, and James Madison. Many editions exist. Of interest also is P. Ford, *Essays on the Constitution, 1787-1788* (1892) containing contemporary arguments for and against the Constitution.

What the framers of the Constitution intended their work to mean has been the subject of much speculation and interpretation. Clues may be found in most of the above cited references. However, of specific attempts to answer the question, the following are worthy of attention: Most controversial, perhaps, is C. A. Beard's *The Economic Interpretation of the Constitution* (1913); the Beard thesis has recently been challenged in detail by R. E. Brown, *Charles Beard and the Constitution: A Critical Analysis of "An Economic Interpretation of the Constitution"* (1956), and F. McDonald, *We the People: The Economic Origins of the Constitution* (1958). B. F. Wright, *Consensus and Continuity, 1776-1787* (1958) also disputes the Beard thesis, as do general treatments of constitutional growth and expansion by A. C. McLaughlin, *Constitutional History of the United States* (1935), and C. Warren, *Making of the Constitution* (1937). Socio-political economic studies of the Constitution which illustrate its expanding flexible character are E. S. Corwin, *The Constitution and What It Means Today,* 12th ed. (1959); L. Hartz, *The Liberal Tradition in America* (1955); H. L. McBain, *The Living Constitution* (1942); C. H. McIlwaine, *Constitutionalism and the Changing World* (1939); C. B. Swisher, *American Constitutional Development* (1954). A highly provocative interpretation of the Constitution which stresses its framers' intention to establish a strongly centralized national government is W. W. Crosskey, *Politics and the Constitution* (1953). The most definitive treatment from a legal point of view is E. S. Corwin, ed., *The Constitution of the United States of America, Revised and Annotated* (Senate Document 170, 82nd Congress 2nd session, 1953). B. Schwartz, *A Commentary on the Constitution of the United States* (1963), Part I, deals in two volumes with the powers of the national government and with those of the President.

The Bill of Rights receives special attention in Z. Chafee, *How Human Rights Got into the Constitution* (1952); L. Hand, *The Bill of Rights* (1958); and A. Rutland, *The Birth of the Bill of Rights* (1955).

CITIZENSHIP AND IMMIGRATION

No recent general study of citizenship in the United States is available. The standard work on the subject, outdated but useful, is L. Gettys, *The Law of Citizenship in the United States* (1934). H. F. Gosnell, *Democracy, the Threshhold of Freedom* (1948) advances some theories of citizenship and of the right to vote. The conflict of private conscience and public duty is treated in H. M. Roelofs, *The Tension of Citizenship: Private Man and Public Duty* (1957). Pertinent decisions of the Supreme Court should be consulted.

Materials dealing with immigration are more numerous. See *Statistical Abstracts of the United States* (current edition), and *Historical Statistics of the United States*. Other works include: F. L. Auerbach, *Immigration*

Laws of the United States (1955); W. C. Bernard, C. Zelney, and H. Miller, (eds.), *American Immigration Policy* (1950); J. C. Bruce, *The Irony of Our Immigration Policy* (1954); J. P. Clark, *The Deportation of Aliens from the United States to Europe* (1931); R. A. Diving, *American Immigration Policy, 1924-1952* (1957); H. P. Fairchild, *Immigration: A World Movement and Its American Significance* (1928); O. Handlin, *Race and Nationality in American Life* (1957), *The American People in the Twentieth Century* (1954), and *The Uprooted* (1951); M. L. Hansen, *The Immigrant in American History* (1940); "History of American Immigration Policy" in M. R. Davie, *World Immigration with Special Reference to the United States* (1936); Immigration and Nationality Act, 1952, Public Law 414, 82d Congress, 2nd session, in 66 *Statutes* 163; E. P. Hutchinson, *Immigrants and Their Children* (1956); S. Kansas, *United States Immigration, Exclusion, Deportation, and Citizenship* (1940); M. J. Kohler, *Immigration and Aliens in the United States* (1936); M. R. Konvitz, *The Alien and Asiatic in American Law* (1946), and *Civil Rights in Immigration* (1953); H. H. Laughlin, *Immigration and Conquest* (1939); E. Lowenstein, *The Alien and Migration Law* (1959); J. C. Messersmith, *Illegal Entrants and Illegal Aliens in the United States* (1958); C. A. Peters, *The Immigration Problem* (1948); Report of the President's Committee on Immigration and Naturalization, *Whom We Shall Welcome* (1953); Report of the Senate Committee on the Judiciary, *Immigration and Naturalization Systems of the United States* (1950), 81st Congress, 2nd session; P. Tyler, *Immigration and the United States* (1956); B. M. Ziegler, ed., *Immigration: An American Dilemma* (1953).

FEDERALISM

On the general subject of federalism see R. R. Bowie and C. J. Friedrich, *Studies in Federalism* (1954); A. McMahon, ed., *Federalism, Mature and Emergent* (1955); K. C. Wheare, *Federal Government* (1953). Two government publications set forth a detailed and extensive study of federalism in the United States: *Federal-State Relations,* Senate Document 81, 81st Congress, 1st session (1949), and *Report to the President* (1955) of the President's Commission on Intergovernmental Relations which also contains an enumeration of special studies bearing upon this topic.

Recent titles on federalism include W. Anderson, *Federalism and Intergovernmental Relations* (1946) and *The Nation and the States* (1955); G. C. S. Benson, *The New Centralization* (1941); J. P. Clark, *The Rise of the New Federalism* (1938); J. B. Fordham, *A Larger Concept of Community* (1955); W. S. Livingston, *Federalism and Constitutional Change* (1956); M. J. C. Vile, *The Structure of American Federalism* (1961) presents a reexamination of American federalism intended to present the whole system as an integrated structure. L. D. White, *The States and the Nation* (1953).

Special studies of particular aspects of federalism include E. S. Corwin, *The Commerce Power versus State Rights* (1936); W. B. Graves, *Uniform State Action* (1934); J. A. Maxwell, *The Fiscal Impact of Federalism* (1946).

On the subject of interstate compacts see Council of State Governments, *Interstate Compacts, 1783-1956* (1956); S. Zimmerman and M. Wendell, *The Interstate Compact Since 1925* (1951); V. V. Thursby, *Interstate Cooperation: A Study of the Interstate Compact* (1953); R. H. Leach and R. S. Sugg, *The Administration of Interstate Compacts* (1959).

Regarding grants-in-aid see: Council of State Governments, *Federal Grants-in-Aid* (1949); House Committee on Government Operations, Reports on Federal-State-Local Relations, *Federal Grants-in-Aid*, 85th Congress, 2nd session (1955); V. O. Key, *The Administration of Federal Grants to the States* (1937); R. L. Notz, *Federal Grants-in-Aid to States* (1956); R. L. Roettinger, *The Supreme Court and State Police Power: A Study in Federalism* (1957); J. R. Schmidhauser, *The Supreme Court as Final Arbiter in Federal-State Relations* (1958).

Constitutional adaptability is largely the product of judicial review, which is considered below in this bibliography. Critical of the role of the Supreme Court in relation to the present topic is L. B. Boudin, *Government by Judiciary* (1932); somewhat critical is the attitude of C. G. Haines, *The American Doctrine of Judicial Supremacy* (1932); his study *The Role of the Supreme Court in American Government and Politics, 1789-1832* (1944) is a detailed history of the Court to the death of John Marshall. The analysis is continued in L. B. Boudin and F. H. Sherwood, *The Role of the Supreme Court in American Government and Politics, 1835-1864* (1957). The classical account of the Court's role is C. Warren, *The Supreme Court in United States History* (1937). Related to the period after 1937 not covered by Warren are: F. V. Cahill, *Judicial Legislation, A Study in American Legal Theory* (1952); E. Cahn, *The Supreme Court and Supreme Law* (1954); E. S. Corwin, *Court over Constitution* (1938), and *Constitutional Revolution, Ltd.* (1941); E. M. Eriksson, *The Supreme Court and the New Deal* (1940); R. S. Hirschfield, *The Constitution and the Court* (1962); J. W. Peltason, *Federal Courts in the Political Process* (1955); C. H. Pritchett, *The Roosevelt Court: A Study in Judicial Politics and Values, 1937-1947* (1948), and *Congress and the Supreme Court 1957-1960* (1961); B. Schwartz, *The Supreme Court: Constitutional Revolution in Retrospect* (1957). Personality and political factors bearing on constitutional growth through interpretation are examined in L. P. Beth, *Politics, the Constitution, and the Supreme Court* (1962); J. P. Frank, *Marble Palace* (1958); A. T. Mason, *The Supreme Court from Taft to Warren* (1958); W. F. Murphy and C. F. Pritchett, *Courts, Judges and Politics* (1961); T. R. Powell, *Vagaries and Varieties in Constitutional Interpretation* (1955); F. Rodell, *A Political History of the Supreme Court of the United*

States from 1790 to 1955 (1956); J. R. Schmidhauser, *The Supreme Court: Its Politics, Personalities, and Procedures* (1960); B. R. Twiss, *Lawyers and the Constitution: How Laissez Faire came to the Supreme Court* (1942). The role of constitutional custom is treated in B. C. Rodick, *American Constitutional Custom: A Forgotten Factor in the Founding* (1953); H. Horwill, *Usages of the American Constitution* (1925). For further references on the judiciary see below.

Regarding formal amendment of the Constitution see: H. V. Ames, *The Proposed Amendments to the Constitution,* House Document 353, 54th Congress, 2nd session (1897); M. A. Musmanno, *Proposed Amendments to the Constitution,* House Document 551, 70th Congress, 2nd session (1929); A. Hehmeyer, *Time for a Change: A Proposal for a Second Constitutional Convention* (1943); D. P. Meyers, *The Process of Constitutional Amendment,* Senate Document 314, 76th Congress, 3rd session (1941); L. B. Orfield, *The Amending of the Federal Constitution* (1942).

CIVIL RIGHTS

The most authoritative sources for the study of civil rights are the opinions of the Supreme Court of the United States found in the United States Reports, but collections of these classified by subject may be found in tables of cases, in footnotes, in constitutional law texts, and especially under the appropriate headings in E. S. Corwin, ed., *The Constitution of the United States, Revised and Annotated* (1952). *American Jurisprudence, Corpus Juris Secundum* and the *Index to Legal Periodicals* should also be consulted if available. The *Annual Reports* of the American Civil Liberties Union are valuable current sources.

There are many books on the subject, but among the more valuable ones are: C. Becker, *et al, Safeguarding Civil Liberty Today* (1944), and *Freedom and Responsibility in the American Way of Life* (1945); Z. Chafee, *The Blessings of Liberty* (1956); H. S. Commager, *Civil Liberties Under Attack* (1951), and *Majority Rule and Minority Rights* (1943); R. E. Cushman, *Civil Liberties in the United States* (1956); T. I. Emerson and D. Haber, *Political and Civil Rights in the United States,* 2 vols., 2nd ed. (1958); O. K. Fraenkel, *Our Civil Liberties* (1944); W. Gellhorn, *Individual Freedom and Governmental Restraint* (1956); L. Hand, *The Bill of Rights* (1958); R. A. Horn, *Groups and the Constitution* (1956); R. G. Kauper, *Frontiers of Constitutional Liberty* (1957); A. H. Kelly, ed., *Foundations of Freedom* (1958); M. R. Konvitz, *Fundamental Liberties of a Free People* (1957); S. L. Morrison, *Freedom in Contemporary Society* (1956); R. L. Perry, ed., *Sources of Our Liberties* (1959); L. Pfeffer, *The Liberties of An American: The Supreme Court Speaks* (1956); R. Pound, *The Development of Constitutional Guarantees of Liberty* (1957); C. H. Pritchett, *Civil Liberties in the Vinson Court* (1954), and *The Political*

Offender and the Warren Court (1958); *Report of the Civil Rights Commission, 1959* (1959); Report of the President's Committee on Civil Rights, *To Secure These Rights* (1947); J. M. Smith, *Freedom's Fetters* (1956); Leon Whipple, *Our Ancient Liberties* (1927).

The category of specially preferred liberties of the First Amendment may be found treated in the following works as are some ancillary aspects of the topic: P. Blanshard, *The Right to Read* (1955); J. W. Carghey, *In Clear and Present Danger* (1958); Z. Chafee, *Free Speech in the United States* (1946), and *Government and Mass Communications* (1947); W. L. Chenery, *Freedom of the Press* (1955); W. E. Hocking, *Freedom of the Press* (1947); R. A. Inglis, *Freedom of the Movies* (1947); A. W. Johnson and F. H. Yost, *Separation of Church and State in the United States* (1948); M. R. Konvitz, *Fundamental Liberties of a Free People* (1957); A. Meikeljohn, *Free Speech and Its Relation to Self-Government* (1948); L. Pfeffer, *Church, State, and Freedom* (1953); M. O. Sibley and P. E. Jacobs, *Conscription and Conscience* (1952); G. W. Spicer, *The Supreme Court and Fundamental Freedoms* (1959); A. P. Stokes, *Church and State in the United States* (1950); L. White, *The American Radio* (1947).

Procedural rights have attracted much attention. The more important ones have been considered in: W. M. Beaney, *The Right to Counsel in American Courts* (1955); A. R. Beisel, *Control Over Illegal Enforcement of the Criminal Law: Role of the Supreme Court* (1955); E. DeHaas, *Antiquities of Bail: Origin and Historical Development* (1940); D. Fellmen, *The Defendent's Rights* (1958); E. N. Griswold, *The Fifth Amendment Today* (1955); F. H. Heller, *The Sixth Amendment to the Constitution of the United States* (1951); B. P. Patterson, *The Forgotten Ninth Amendment* (1955); V. Wood, *Due Process of Law, 1932-1949* (1951).

Two special topics of great interest to the application of civil rights protections are race relations and loyalty. The first of these is treated in: C. Abrams, *Forbidden Neighbors* (1955); A. P. Blaustein and C. C. Ferguson, Jr., *Desegregation and the Law* (1957); R. K. Carr, *Federal Protection of Civil Rights: Quest for a Sword* (1947); J. Greenberg, *Race Relations and American Law* (1960); D. McEntire, *Residence and Race* (1961); D. Shoemaker, *With All Deliberate Speed* (1957); A. S. Miller, *Racial Discrimination and Private Education: A Legal Analysis* (1957); B. Muse, *Virginia's Massive Resistance* (1961); M. M. Tumin, *et al, Desegregation: Resistance and Readiness* (1958); R. M. Williams and M. W. Ryan, eds., *Schools in Transition* (1954); C. Vann Woodward, *The Strange Career of Jim Crow* (1947); C. E. Vose, *Caucasions Only* (1955).

The loyalty program is treated in the following work. Those openly critical of its handling are marked with an asterisk (*): *A. Barth, *The Loyalty of Free Men* (1951); E. Bontecou, *The Federal Loyalty-Security Program* (1952); R. S. Brown, *Loyalty and Security* (1958); R. K. Carr, *The House Committee on Un-American Activities, 1945-1950* (1952); H. Chase,

Security and Liberty 1947-1955 (1955); H. S. Commager, *Freedom, Loyalty and Dissent* (1954); Committee on Government Security, hearings before the Subcommittee on Reorganization of the Committee on Government Operations, Senate, 84th Congress, 1st session, on S. J. 21. (1955); T. I. Cook, *Democratic Rights versus Communist Activity* (1954); *E. Davis, *But We Were Born Free* (1954); M. Grodzins, *The Loyal and the Disloyal* (1956); S. Hook, *Common Sense and the Fifth Amendment* (1957), and *Political Power and Personal Freedom* (1959); *C. Lamont, *Freedom Is as Freedom Does* (1956); H. D. Lasswell, *National Security and Individual Freedom* (1950); *J. L. O'Brian, *National Security and Individual Freedom* (1955); Father A. R. Ogden, *The Dies Committee*, 2nd ed., (1945); Report of the Subcommittee on Constitutional Rights, 84th Congress, 2nd session (1955); J. H. Schaar, *Loyalty in America* (1957); Senate Judiciary Committee, *The Communist Party of the United States*, Senate Document No. 117, 84th Congress, 2nd session (1956); S. A. Stouffer, *Communism, Conformity and Civil Liberties* (1955).

THE POLITICAL PROCESS

This section contains materials relating to public opinion, pressure groups, lobbying, and political parties.

Public Opinion: Among the periodicals dealing with public opinion the *Public Opinion Quarterly* and the *International Journal of Opinion and Attitude Research* are especially valuable.

Many works of a general nature consider public opinion, but among the more useful are W. Albig, *Modern Public Opinion* (1956); B. Berelson and M. Janowitz, eds., *Reader in Public Opinion and Communication* (1951); L. W. Doob, *Public Opinion and Propaganda* (1948); A. O. Hero, *Opinion Leaders in American Communities* (1959); D. Katz, *et al*, eds., *Public Opinion and Propaganda: A Book of Readings* (1954); C. D. MacDougall, *Understanding Public Opinion* (1952); M. G. Ogle, *Public Opinion and Political Dynamics* (1950); N. J. Powell, *Anatomy of Public Opinion* (1951); C. A. Siepmann, *Radio, Television and Society* (1950); M. B. Smith, *et al*, *Opinions and Personality* (1956). B. L. Smith, *et al*, *Propaganda, Communications, and Public Opinion* (1946), and B. L. Smith and C. M. Smith, *International Communications and Public Opinion* (1956) both contain excellent bibliographies as well as valuable subject matter; F. G. Wilson, *A Theory of Public Opinion* (1962). Closely related to public opinion but primarily concerned with propaganda are: L. W. Doob, *Propaganda, Its Psychology and Technique* (1935); D. L. Harter and J. Sullivan, *Propaganda Handbook* (1953); W. Hummel and K. Huntress, *The Analysis of Propaganda* (1949); F. C. Iron, *Public Opinion and Propaganda* (1950).

The techniques of polling are considered in: L. H. Bean, *How to Predict Elections* (1948); H. Cantril, *Gauging Public Opinion* (1944); M. C. Meier and H. W. Saunders, *The Polls and Public Opinion* (1949); M. Partens, *Surveys, Polls, and Samples* (1950); L. Rogers, *The Pollsters* (1949); F. F. Stephen and P. J. McCarthy, *Sampling Opinions: An Analysis of Survey Procedure* (1958).

Pressure Groups: The nature, roll, techniques, and operation of pressure groups upon the political process are discussed in general in A. F. Bentley, *The Process of Government* (1949); D. C. Blaisdell, *American Democracy Under Pressure* (1957), and ed., *Unofficial Government: Pressure Groups and Lobbies* (1959); H. A. Bone, *American Politics and the Party System* (1949); S. Chase, *Democracy Under Pressure* (1945); K. G. Crawford, *The Pressure Boys* (1939); H. Fergusson, *People and Power* (1947); B. Cross, *The Legislative Struggle* (1953); P. Herring, *Group Representation Before Congress* (1929), and *Politics of Democracy* (1940); D. D. McKean, *Party and Pressure Politics* (1949); C. E. Merriam, *Private and Public Government* (1944); K. Schriftsgiesser, *The Lobbyists* (1951); D. B. Truman, *The Governmental Process* (1951).

Among the special studies of pressure group activity are to be noted R. Baker, *The American Legion and American Foreign Policy* (1954); D. C. Blaisdell, *Economic Power and Political Pressure* (TNEC Monograph, No. 26, 1941); F. Caulkins, *The CIO and the Democratic Party* (1952); M. R. Dearing, *Veterans in Politics* (1952); L. E. Ebersole, *Church Lobbying in the Nation's Capital* (1951); Federal Trade Commission, *Summary* Report on Publicity and Propaganda, *Efforts by Associations and Agencies of Electric and Gas Utilities to Influence Public Opinion,* Senate Document No. 92, 70th Congress, 1st session (1934); O. Garceau, *The Political Life of the American Medical Association* (1941); J. Gray and V. H. Bernstein, *The Inside Story of the Legion* (1948); E. Gruening, *The Public Pays* (1931); O. Handlin, *Race and Nationality in American Life* (1957); C. M. Hardin, *The Politics of Agriculture* (1952); M. Karson, *American Labor Unions and Politics* (1958); L. C. Kesselman, *The Social Politics of FEPC* (1948); O. M. Kile, *The Farm Bureau Through Three Decades* (1948); E. Latham, *The Group Basis of Politics* (1952); W. McCune, *The Farm Bloc* (1943), and *Who's Behind Our Farm Policy* (1956); P. Odegard, *Pressure Politics: The Story of the Anti-Saloon League* (1928); F. W. Riggs, *Pressures on Congress: A Study of the Repeal of Chinese Exclusion* (1950); M. L. Rutherford, *The Influence of the American Bar Association on Public Opinion and Legislation* (1937); E. E. Schattschneider, *Politics, Pressures, and the Tariff* (1935); U. S. Senate, *Hearings* on S. Res. 219, 84th Congress, 2nd session and on S. Res. 47, 85th Congress, 1st session, by Special Committee to Investigate Political Activities, Lobbying, and Campaign Contributions, Oil and Gas Lobby.

POLITICAL PARTIES

The studies available of the American party system and its details are almost without number. However, some of a general nature and others of more specific concern can be singled out for special notice. They include D. J. Boorstin, *The Genius of American Politics* (1958); M. Duverger, *Political Parties: Their Organization and Activities in the Modern State* (1954); W. Goodman, *The Two-party System in the United States* (1960); I. Hinderaker, *Party Politics* (1956); S. Lubell, *The Future of American Politics* (1953), and *Revolt of the Moderates* (1956); S. Neumann, ed., *Modern Political Parties* (1956); M. Ostrogorski, *Democracy and the Organization of Political Parties* (1902); H. A. Turner, ed., *Politics in America* (1956); V. O. Key, *Politics, Parties, and Pressure Groups* (1958); A. Leiserson, *Parties and Politics: An Institutional and Behavioral Approach* (1958); C. E. Merriam and H. F. Gosnell, *The American Party System* (1949); H. R. Penniman, *Sait's American Parties and Elections* (1952); A. Ranney and W. Kendall, *Democracy and the American Party System* (1956).

Party History: Considerable attention is paid in many of the above titles to the subject of party history in America. However, others are available which are devoted more exclusively to this subject. See: C. A. Beard, *The American Party Battle* (1928); W. E. Binkley, *American Political Parties: Their Natural History*, 3rd ed. (1958); I. Howe and Lewis Coser, *The American Communist Party: A Critical History* (1958); R. E. Pinchott, *A History of the Progressive Party, 1912-1916* (1958); M. B. Schnappes, *The G.O.P.: A Pictorial History* (1956); D. A. Shannon, *The Socialist Party of America: A History* (1955); E. Stanwood, *A History of the Presidency*, 2 vols. (1916). Two contemporary studies of the major parties are by D. Acheson, *A Democrat Looks at His Party* (1956), and A. Larson, *A Republican Looks at His Party* (1956).

Many studies are also available concerning special aspects of party affairs and activities. Among the more current are: S. D. Allbright, *The American Ballot* (1942); H. A. Bone, *Party Committees and National Politics* (1958); P. David, R. Goldman and R. C. Bain, *The Politics of National Party Convention* (1960); A. de Grazia, *The Western Public, 1952 and Beyond* (1954); J. P. Harris, *Election Administration in the United States* (1934); J. Redding, *Inside the Democratic Party* (1958); E. H. Rosenbloom, *A History of Presidential Elections* (1957); A. Heard, *A Two-Party South?* (1952); W. B. Hesseltine, *The Rise and Fall of Third Parties from Anti-Masonic to Wallace* (1948); A. F. Lovejoy, *LaFollette and the Establishment of the Direct Primary in Wisconsin, 1890-1904* (1941); H. J. Abraham, *Compulsory Voting?* (1955); J. B. Johnson and J. J. Lewis, *Registration for Voting in the United States* (1946); P. Lewinson, *Race, Class and Party* (1932); D. McGovney, *The American Suffrage Medley* (1949); T. H. McKee, ed., *National Conventions and Platforms of All Political Parties*,

1789-1904 (1904); H. P. Nash, Jr., *Gadflies of American Politics* (1955), and *Third Parties in American Politics* (1959); M. Stedman and S. Stedman, *Discontent at the Polls* (1950); K. H. Porter and D. B. Johnson, *National Party Platforms, 1840-1956* (1956); L. F. Schmeckebier, *Congressional Apportionment* (1941); V. Torrey, *You and Your Congressman* (1944).

Party Leadership: Studies on party leadership include many biographies not listed among these general works on the subject: H. A. Bone, *Grass Roots Party Leadership* (1952); J. Farley, *Behind the Ballots* (1938); S. Forthal, *Cogwheels of Democracy: A Study of the Precinct Captain* (1946); H. F. Gosnell, *Machine Politics: Chicago Model* (1937); D. McKean, *The Boss* (1940); R. Moley, *27 Masters of Politics* (1949); J. T. Salter, *Public Men In and Out of Office* (1946), and *The American Politician* (1938); R. A. Tugwell, *The Art of Politics As Practiced by Three Great Americans* (1958); H. Zink, *City Bosses in the United States* (1930). Of significance also are: W. F. Whyte, *Street Corner Society* (1943) and A. W. Gouldner, ed., *Studies in Leadership* (1950). The employment of professional public relations in elections is a relatively new phenomenon. There are but few works that deal with it, among which are: E. L. Bernays, *The Engineering of Consent* (1955); S. Kelly, Jr., *Professional Public Relations and Political Power* (1956); V. Packard, *Hidden Persuaders* (1957); W. H. Whyte, Jr., *Is Anybody Listening?* (1952).

Whether political parties should be loose and amorphous or tight and disciplined is a subject of dispute. On the side of the former are H. Agar, *Price of Union* (1950), and P. Herring, *Politics of Democracy* (1950). Favoring the latter are A. Ranney, *The Doctrine of Responsible Party Government* (1954); Report of the Committee on Political Parties of the American Political Science Association, *Toward A More Responsible Two-Party System* (1950); E. E. Schattschneider,*The Struggle for Party Government* (1948).

Money in Politics: On the interesting subject of money in politics see N. E. Alexander, *Money, Politics, and Public Reporting* (1960); A. Heard, *Money and Politics* (1956), and *The Costs of Democracy* (1960); L. Overacker, *Presidential Campaign Funds* (1946); J. B. Shannon, *Money and Politics* (1958); *Report of the Committee on Rules and Administration on the Federal Elections Act, 1959,* to accompany S. 2436, July 23, 1959; *Report of the Special Committee to Investigate Political Activities, Lobbying and Campaign Contributions,* Senate Report No. 395, 85th Congress, 1st session (1957); Report of the Senate Subcommittee on Privileges and Elections, *1956 General Election Campaigns,* 85th Congress, 1st session (1957); J. R. White and J. R. Owens, *Parties, Group Interests and Campaign Finance: Michigan 1956* (1960).

Voting Behavior: Studies in political behaviorism: Much has been learned in recent decades about the motivations and responses of voters in America. Among studies which present such analyses are: D. Anderson and P. E. Davidson, *Ballots and the Democratic Class Struggle* (1943); H. M. Bain and D. S. Hecock, *Ballot Position and Voter's Choice* (1957); B. R. Berelson, *et al, Voting* (1954); E. Burdick and A. J. Brodbeck, eds., *American Voting Behavior* (1959); W. D. Burnham, *Presidential Ballots, 1836-1892* (1955); A. Campbell and H. C. Cooper, *Group Differences in Attitudes and Votes* (1956); A. Campbell, *et al, The Voter Decides* (1954), and *The American Voter* (1960); P. T. David, *et al, Presidential Nominating Politics in 1952*, 5 vols. (1954); C. A. M. Ewing, *Congressional Elections, 1896-1944* (1947), and *Primary Elections in the South* (1953); L. C. Ferguson and R. H. Smuckler, *Politics in the Press: An Analysis of Press Content in 1952 Senatorial Elections* (1954); E. J. Flynn, *You're the Boss* (1947); L. P. Fuchs, *The Political Behavior of American Jews* (1956); L. Harris, *Is There a Republican Majority?* (1954); A. Heard and D. S. Strong, *Southern Primaries and Elections* (1950); H. H. Hyman, *Political Socialization: A Study in the Psychology of Political Behaviorism* (1959); F. Kent, *The Great Game of Politics* (1923); V. O. Key, *Southern Politics* (1949); A. Kornhauser, *et al, When Labor Votes: A Study of Auto Workers* (1956); R. E. Lane, *Political Life* (1959); H. Lasswell, *The Analysis of Political Behavior* (1948); P. K. Lazarsfeld, B. Berelson, and H. Gaudet, *The People's Choice* (1948); S. M. Lipset, *Agrarian Socialism* (1950); C. E. Merriam and H. F. Gosnell, *Non-voting* (1924); S. A. Mitchell, *Elm Street Politics* (1959); H. L. Moon, *The Balance of Power: The Negro Vote* (1948); E. A. Moore, *A Catholic Runs for President* (1956); M. C. Moos, *Politics, Presidents and Coattails* (1952); F. D. Ogden, *The Poll Tax in the South* (1958); R. M. Scammon, ed., *America Votes*, 4 vols. (1956-1962); C. A. H. Thomson, *Television and Presidential Politics: The Experience in 1952 and the Problems Ahead* (1956); C. A. H. Thomson and F. N. Shattuck, *The 1956 Presidential Campaign* (1959).

CONGRESSIONAL ORGANIZATION AND PROCEDURE

Law-making is central to the governmental process. The theoretical side of legislation and representation is examined in R. Luce, *Legislative Principles* (1930). But see also: J. C. Wahlke and H. Eulau, eds., *Legislative Behavior: A Reader in Theory and Research* (1959). A. de Grazia, *Public and Republic: Political Representation in America* (1951) contains an historical account of the theory and practice of American representative government. The legislative process is analyzed in J. P. Chamberlain, *Legislative Process: National and State* (1936).

General studies of the organization and procedure of Congress include: S. K. Bailey, *Congress Makes a Law* (1950). The case method of analysis is also used in S. K. Bailey and H. D. Samuel, *Congress at Work* (1952); D. A. Berman, *A Bill Becomes A Law: The Civil Rights Act of 1960* (1962); *The Story of the 1959 Labor Reform Bill, Congressional Quarterly*

Special Report (September, 1958); valuable also are G. B. Galloway, *The Legislative Process in Congress* (1953); Harvey Walker, *The Legislative Process* (1948). The process of legislative policy making is considered as a struggle of power centers in B. Gross, *The Legislative Struggle: A Study in Social Combat;* Sen. E. Kefauver advocates organizational and procedural reform in *A Twentieth Century Congress* (1947), but E. S. Griffith, *Congress: Its Contemporary Role* (1951) defends the status quo. F. M. Riddick presents a technical study of the legislative process in *The United States Congress: Organization and Procedure* (1949). A comparative study can be found in G. B. Galloway's *Congress and Parliament* (1955). R. Young examines the strengths and weaknesses of the decision-making process in *This Is Congress* (1943) and *The American Congress* (1958).

Relations of Congress with other parts of the government are examined in D. Acheson, *A Citizen Looks at Congress* (1956). W. E. Binkley, *President and Congress* (1947) is a history of legislative-executive rivalry. Less controversial is S. Horn, *The Cabinet and Congress* (1960). Lost Congressional leadership is regretted in J. Burnham, *Congress and the American Tradition* (1959), but J. W. Burns, *Congress on Trial* (1949) wants more executive leadership. L. H. Chamberlain, *The President, Congress, and Legislation* (1946) examines problems of legislative-executive relations, and W. Y. Elliot, *The Need for Constitutional Reform* (1935), T. K. Finletter, *Can Constitutional Government Do the Job?* (1945), J. L. Freeman, *The Political Process: Executive Bureau-Legislative Committee Relations* (1955), and H. Hazlitt, *A New Constitution Now* (1942) propose reforms.

Congressional investigations have come in for their share of attention: see A. Barth, *Government by Investigation* (1955); C. Beck, *Contempt of Congress* (1961); *Congressional Power of Investigation*, Senate Document No. 99, 83rd Congress, 2nd session (1954); E. M. Dimmock, *Congressional Investigating Committees* (1929); E. J. Eberling; *Congressional Investigations* (1928); J. E. Johnson, *Investigating Powers of Congress* (1951); M. N. McGeary, *The Development of Congressional Investigative Power* (1940); A. R. Ogden, *The Dies Committee* (1945); R. K. Carr, *The House Un-American Activities Committee* (1952); and T. Taylor, *Grand Inquest* (1955).

Special studies of Congress include H. R. Carroll, *The House of Representatives and Foreign Affairs* (1958); R. Dahl, *Congress and Foreign Policy* (1950); E. Huzar, *The Purse and the Sword* (1950); E. V. Huntington, *Methods of Apportionment in Congress*, Senate Document 304, 76th Congress, 3rd session (1940); A. Simpson, *A Treatise on Federal Impeachments* (1916); D. R. Matthews, *United States Senators and Their World* (1960); A. C. McCown, *The Congressional Conference Committee* (1927); G. Y. Steiner, *The Congressional Conference Committee* (1951); M. Thomas and R. M. Northrup, *Atomic Energy and Congress* (1956); J. A. Robinson, *Congress and Foreign Policy Making* (1962); T. V. Smith, *The Legislative*

Way of Life (1940); L. Wilmerding, *The Spending Power: A History of the Efforts of Congress to Control Expenditures* (1943); H. J. Wilson, *Congress, Corruption and Compromise* (1951). Detailed data about Congress and its members can be found in the *Congressional Directory*, published by the Government Printing Office, each March.

The impact of political parties upon Congressional organization and action are treated variously in: P. D. Hasbrouck, *Party Government in the House of Representatives* (1927); G. Kammerer, *The Staffing of the Committees of Congress* (1949); D. B. Truman, *The Congressional Party* (1959); J. Turner, *Party and Constituency: Pressures on Congress* (1952). For the relationship to and impact of pressure groups upon the legislative process see the bibliographical section pertaining to interest groups.

The upper house of Congress has been made the subject of some special attention. The most authoritative work is G. H. Haynes, *The Senate of the United States*, 2 vols. (1938); but see also L. Rogers, *The American Senate* (1926), and W. S. White, *Citadel: The Story of the United States Senate* (1957). Of a more specialized nature are: F. Allen, *The Treaty As an Instrument of Legislation* (1952); F. L. Burdette, *Filibustering in the Senate* (1940); R. J. Dangerfield, *In Defense of the Senate: A Study in Treaty Making* (1933); J. P. Harris, *The Advice and Consent of the Senate* (1953).

THE EXECUTIVE BRANCH

General studies of the history and development of the office of the President are often also useful for obtaining information on particular aspects of the office. Among the more recent ones are J. Bell, *The Splendid Misery: The Story of the Presidency and Power Politics at Close Range* (1960); W. E. Binkley, *The Man in the White House* (1958); L. H. Chamberlain, *The President, Congress, and Legislation* (1946); E. S. Corwin, *The President: Office and Powers*, 4th ed. (1957); E. S. Corwin and L. W. Koenig, *The Presidency Today* (1956); D. C. Coyle, *The Ordeal of the Presidency* (1960); E. B. Fincher, *The President of the United States* (1955); H. Finer, *The Presidency: Crisis and Regeneration* (1960); N. D. Grundstein, *Presidential Delegation of Authority in Wartime* (1961); J. Hart, *The American Presidency in Action, 1789* (1948); F. Heller, *The Presidency: A Modern Perspective* (1960); L. L. Henry, *Presidential Transitions* (1960); E. P. Herring, *Presidential Leadership* (1940); G. F. Milton, *The Use of Presidential Power* (1944); R. E. Neustadt, *Presidential Power: The Politics of Leadership* (1960); R. S. Rankin, *The Presidency in Transition* (1949); C. Rossiter, *Functions of Presidents* (1956); G. A. Schubert, *The Presidency in the Courts* (1957); N. J. Small, *Some Presidential Interpretations of the Presidency* (1932); R. G. Tugwell, *The Enlargement of the Presidency* (1960); T. H. White, *The Making of the President 1960* (1961).

Studies of the choice of Presidents include R. D. Hupman and S. H.

Still, eds., *Nomination and Election of the President and Vice President of the United States*, House Document 332, 86th Congress, 1st session (1959); *Nomination and Election of the President and Vice President*, Senate Judiciary Committee, 83d Congress, 1st session (1953); R. L. MacBride, *The American Electoral College* (1953); *The Electoral College*, Senate Document 242, 78th Congress, 2nd session (1944); L. Wilmerding, *The Electoral College* (1958).

On the subject of Presidential succession see R. C. Silva, *Presidential Succession* (1951); *Presidential Inability*, House Committee on the Judiciary, 84th Congress, 2nd session (1956).

On the organization of the President's office see L. Brownlow, *The President and the Presidency* (1949); E. H. Hobbs, *Behind the President: A Study of the Executive Office Agencies* (1954); L. W. Koenig, *Invisible Presidents* (1960); F. M. Marx, *The President and His Staff Services* (1947), and *The Administrative State* (1957); Nash, *Staffing the Presidency* (1952); *Report of the President's Committee on Administrative Management* (1937); Reports of the first and second Commissions on Organization of the Executive Branch of the Government (1949) and (1955).

Powers of the President: Special studies of the President's powers and their use may be found in C. Berdahl, *The War Powers of the President* (1921); W. E. Binkley, *The Powers of the President* (1937); J. P. Harris, *The Advice and Consent of the Senate* (1953); W. H. Humbert, *The Pardoning Power of the President* (1941); S. P. Huntington, *The Soldier and the State: The Theory and Politics of Civil-Military Relations* (1957); M. Jones, *et al, Legislative-Executive Relationships in the Government of the United States* (1956); J. G. Kerwin, ed., *Civil-Military Relationships in American Life* (1948); W. M. McClure, *International Executive Agreements* (1941); C. F. Morganston, *The Appointing and Removal Power of the President of the United States*, Senate Document 172, 70th Congress, 2nd session (1929); C. P. Patterson, *Presidential Government in the United States: The Unwritten Constitution* (1949); B. M. Rich, *The Presidents and Civil Disorders* (1941); C. Rossiter, *Constitutional Dictatorships* (1948); and *The Supreme Court and the Commander-in-Chief* (1950); *Executive Powers Under National Emergency*, Senate Document 133, 76th Congress, 2nd session (1939); L. Smith, *American Democracy and Military Power* (1951); *The Powers of the President as Commander-in-Chief of the Army and Navy of the United States*, House Document 443, 84th Congress, 2nd session (1956).

Foreign Affairs: Four authoritative general accounts of American diplomatic history are T. A. Bailey, *A Diplomatic History of the American People* (1950); S. F. Bemis, *A Diplomatic History of the United States* (1955); J. W. Pratt, *History of United States Foreign Policy* (1955); and W. Reitzel, *et al, United States Foreign Policy* (1956). Concerning the conduct of foreign affairs and the making of foreign policy see: Brookings

Institution, *Governmental Mechanism for the Conduct of United States Foreign Relations* (1949); H. N. Carroll, *The House of Representatives and Foreign Affairs* (1958); D. S. Cheevers and H. F. Haviland, *Foreign Policy and the Separation of Powers* (1952); E. S. Corwin, *The President's Control of Foreign Relations* (1917), and *Total War and the Constitution* (1947); W. Y. Elliott, ed., *United States Foreign Policy* (1952); K. London, *How Foreign Policy is Made* (1950); J. L. McCamy, *The Administration of American Foreign Affairs* (1950); J. M. Mathews, *American Foreign Relations, Conduct and Policies* (1938); E. Plischke, *Control of American Diplomacy* (1950); G. H. Stuart, *The Department of State: A History of Its Organization, Procedure and Personnel* (1949), and *American Diplomatic and Consular Practice* (1952).

The Cabinet: In spite of its uniqueness the President's cabinet has been virtually neglected, but several studies of it are available: R. F. Fenno, Jr., *The President's Cabinet* (1959); H. B. Learned, *The President's Cabinet* (1912); and H. W. Smith, *History of the Cabinet of the United States* (1925).

The Vice Presidency: The Vice Presidency has also been neglected until recently, but see: L. C. Hatch, *A History of the Vice Presidency* (1934); E. W. Waugh, *The Second Consul: The Vice Presidency* (1956); I. G. Williams, *The American Vice Presidency: New Look* (1954), and *The Rise of the Vice Presidency* (1956).

The Budget: On the rather technical subject of governmental budgeting see J. Burkhead, *Governmental Budgeting* (1956); P. H. Douglas, *Economy in the National Government* (1952); L. H. Kimmel, *Federal Budget and Fiscal Policy, 1789-1958* (1959); A. Smithies, *The Budgetary Process in the United States* (1955); P. J. Strayer, *Fiscal Policy and Politics* (1958); and S. G. Tickton, *The Budget in Transition* (1955).

Administration: The administrative history of the national government during the early and middle years of our constitutional life is examined in the monumental work of L. D. White, *The Federalists* (1948), *The Jeffersonians* (1951), *The Jacksonians* (1954), and *The Republican Era* (1957).

General studies of administration by government include C. C. Charlesworth, *Governmental Administration* (1951); A. Lepawsky, *Administration: The Art and Science of Organization and Management* (1949); J. D. Millett, *Management in the Public Service* (1954); E. S. Redford, *Ideal and Practice in Public Administration* (1958); K. Seckler-Hudson, *Organization and Management: Theory and Practice* (1955). Less general in scope are: J. W. Fesler, *Area and Administration* (1949); E. Latham, *et al,* *The Federal Field Service* (1947); J. R. Pennock, *Administration and the Rule of Law* (1941); D. B. Truman, *Administrative Decentralization* (1940); D. Waldo, *Perspectives on Administration* (1957). Administration is examined in the light of political theory by M. Dalton, *Men Who Manage, Fusions of Feeling and Theory in Administration* (1959); D. Waldo,

The Administrative State (1948) and from a sociological point of view by P. Blau in *Dynamics of Bureaucracy* (1955). Also of note is S. Wallace, *Federal Departmentalization* (1941).

The role of bureaucracy is examined in J. A. Burnham, *The Managerial Revolution* (1941); M. E. Dimock, *Administrative Vitality, The Conflict With Bureaucracy* (1959); C. S. Hyneman, *Bureaucracy in a Democracy* (1950); and F. M. Marx, *The Administrative State: An Introduction to Bureaucracy* (1957).

Administration in relation to the separation of powers is considered in: M. H. Bernstein, *Regulating Business by Independent Commissions* (1955); R. E. Cushman, *The Independent Regulatory Commission* (1942); J. M. Landis, *The Administrative Process* (1938); J. R. Pennock, *Administration and the Rule of Law* (1941).

For the relationship of administration to policy-making see: P. Appleby, *Big Democracy* (1945), and *Policy and Administration* (1949); E. S. Redford, ed., *Public Administration and Policy Formation* (1956); H. A. Simon, *Administrative Behavior: A Study of Decision-Making Processes in Administrative Organization* (1957).

Of primary importance to the problems of administrative reorganization are the *Report with Special Studies of Administrative Management in the Federal Government* of the President's Committee on Administrative Management, 1937 (1937); and the reports of the first and second Commissions on Organization of the Executive Branch of the Government, 1949 and 1955, as well as the respective task force reports. Valuable also are: H. Emmerich, *Essays on Federal Reorganization* (1950); L. Meriam and L. K. Schmeckebier, *Reorganization of the National Government* (1939); O. Kraines, *Congress and the Challenge of Big Government* (1958); A. C. Millspaugh, *Toward Efficient Democracy: The Question of Governmental Organization* (1949); B. D. Nash and C. Lynde, *A Hook in Leviathan* (1950).

The subject of personnel administration is one not considered by this text. For the students interested in pursuing the inquiry several texts are available, including: O. G. Stahl, *Public Personnel Administration,* 4th ed. (1956); N. J. Powell, *Personnel Administration in Government* (1956); W. G. Torpey, *Public Personnel Management* (1953); F. A. Nigro, *Public Personnel Administration* (1959).

Various aspects of the federal personnel system are considered in P. H. Appleby, *Morality and Administration in Democratic Government* (1952). M. Bernstein considers the non-career political appointee in Washington in *The Job of the Federal Executive* (1958); J. J. Corson, *Executives for the Federal Service;* and P. T. David and R. Pollock analyze the need for and role of career and political top-management executives in government in *Executives for Government* (1957). J. Crider's *The Bureaucrat* (1944) is a popularized account of the government employee in his natural habitat,

Washington. P. P. Van Riper, *History of the United States Civil Service Commission* (1958) recounts the history of the establishment and growth of the merit system. An historical and critical account of the competitive system is set out in W. S. Sayre, ed., *The Federal Government Service: Its Character, Prestige and Problems* (1955); and S. Spiro considers the *Government as Employer* (1948).

The loyalty-security problem was mentioned above in relation to individual rights, but it is considered as an aspect of personnel administration in E. Bontecou, *The Federal Loyalty-Security Program* (1953); R. S. Brown, *Loyalty and Security: Employment Tests in the United States* (1958), and A. Yarmolinski, ed., *Case Studies in Personnel Security* (1955).

THE JUDICIARY

Several non-technical studies of law and the judicial process are available, including H. J. Abraham, *Courts and Judges* (1959); C. P. Curtis, *Its Your Law* (1954); K. N. Lewellyn, *The Bramble Bush,* rev. ed. (1951); M. Radin, *The Law and You* (1948).

The place of law and lawyers in society is implicit in any analysis of the judicial process, but among works directed more specifically toward that subject are H. J. Abraham, *The Judicial Process* (1962); A. P. Blaustein and C. O. Porter, *The American Lawyer* (1954); M. Berger, *Equality by Statute* (1952); E. Cahn, *The Sense of Injustice* (1951), and *The Moral Decision* (1955); I. P. Callison, *Courts of Injustice* (1956); B. N. Cardozo, *Law and Literature* (1931), and *The Nature of the Judicial Process* (1921); J. Frank, *Law and the Modern Mind* (1930); O. W. Holmes, *The Common Law* (1881); J. W. Hurst, *Growth of American Law: The Lawmakers* (1950); R. Pound, *The Spirit of the Common Law* (1931), and *Introduction to the Philosophy of Law* (1954); V. Rosenblum, *Law as a Political Instrument* (1955); A. E. Sutherland, *The Law and One Man Among Many* (1956); A. E. Westin, *The Anatomy of a Constitutional Law Case* (1958).

Among available analyses of the organization, structure, and operation of the judicial system may be listed F. R. Aumann, *The Instrumentalities of Justice, Their Forms, Functions, and Limitations* (1956); W. W. Barron and A. Holtzoff, *Federal Practice and Procedure* (1950); E. Botein, *Trial Judge* (1952); C. W. Bunn, *A Brief Survey of the Jurisdiction and Practice of the Courts of the United States* (1949); H. G. Finns, *Federal Jurisdiction and Procedure* (1960); J. Frank, *Courts on Trial* (1949); R. J. Harris, *The Judicial Power of the United States* (1940); H. M. Hart and H. Wechsler, *The Federal Courts and the Federal System* (1953); L. Mayers, *The American Legal System* (1958); J. W. Moore, *Judicial Code, Commentary* (1949); L. R. Orfield, *Criminal Procedure from Arrest to Appeal* (1947); J. W. Peltason, *Federal Courts in the Political Process* (1955); R.

Pound, *The Organization of Courts* (1940). Critical commentaries on the American legal system include: W. Segal, *The Quest for Law* (1942), and *Law: The Science of Inefficiency* (1952). Of obvious significance is M. Wendell, *Relations Between the Federal and State Courts* (1949).

Numerous titles relate to the work and role of the Supreme Court in society and in the judicial system. Some have been listed above in regard to judicial review and constitutional adaptability. Others include A. Bickel, *The Least Dangerous Branch* (1962); C. L. Black, Jr., *The People and the Court: Judicial Review in a Democracy* (1960); R. K. Carr, *Democracy and the Supreme Court* (1936), and *The Supreme Court and Judicial Review* (1942); E. S. Corwin, *The Higher Law Background of American Constitutional Law* (1955); F. Frankfurter and J. M. Landis, *The Business of the Supreme Court* (1927); P. A. Freund, *On Understanding the Supreme Court* (1949); C. E. Hughes, *The Supreme Court of the United States* (1928); R. H. Jackson, *The Supreme Court in the American System of Justice* (1955); A. T. Mason and W. M. Beaney, *The Supreme Court in a Free Society* (1960); R. G. McCloskey, *The American Supreme Court* (1961), and *Essays in Constitutional Law* (1957); C. H. Pritchett, *The American Constitution* (1959), and *Congress v. the Supreme Court, 1957-1960* (1961); F. Rodell, *Nine Men* (1955); J. Schmidhauser, *Constitutional Law in the Political Process* (1963); G. A. Schubert, *Constitutional Politics* (1960); R. L. Stern and E. Gressman, *Supreme Court Practice* (1950); C. B. Swisher, *The Supreme Court in Modern Roles* (1958); A. Westin, *The Supreme Court: Views from Inside* (1961).

Special studies of judicial power include A. P. Blaustein and C. C. Ferguson, *Desegregation and the Law* (1962); D. R. Manwaring, *Render unto Caesar: The Flag-Salute Controversy* (1962); J. P. Roche, *Courts and Rights* (1961); B. Taper, *Gomillion versus Lightfoot* (1962); J. Tussman, *The Supreme Court and Church and State* (1962); C. M. Ziegler, *The Supreme Court and American Economic Life* (1962).

Index

B C D E F G H I J   0 6 9 8 7 6 5